Pro Spring Integration

Dr. Mark Lui
Mario Gray
Andy Chan
Josh Long

Apress®

Pro Spring Integration

ISBN-13 (pbk): 978-1-4302-3345-9

ISBN-13 (electronic): 978-1-4302-3346-6

Printed and bound in the United States of America (POD)

President and Publisher: Paul Manning
Lead Editor: Steve Anglin
Development Editor: Matthew Moodie
Technical Reviewers: Manuel Jordan Elera, Ndjobo Armel Fabrice
Editorial Board: Steve Anglin, Mark Beckner, Ewan Buckingham, Gary Cornell, Jonathan Gennick, Jonathan Hassell, Michelle Lowman, Matthew Moodie, Jeff Olson, Jeffrey Pepper, Frank Pohlmann, Douglas Pundick, Ben Renow-Clarke, Dominic Shakeshaft, Matt Wade, Tom Welsh
Coordinating Editor: Corbin Collins
Copy Editors: Damon Larson, Tracy Brown
Compositor: MacPS, LLC
Indexer: BIM Indexing & Proofreading Services
Artist: April Milne
Cover Designer: Anna Ishchenko

Distributed to the book trade worldwide by Springer Science+Business Media, LLC., 233 Spring Street, 6th Floor, New York, NY 10013. Phone 1-800-SPRINGER, fax (201) 348-4505, e-mail `orders-ny@springer-sbm.com`, or visit `www.springeronline.com`.

For information on translations, please e-mail `rights@apress.com`, or visit `www.apress.com`.

Apress and friends of ED books may be purchased in bulk for academic, corporate, or promotional use. eBook versions and licenses are also available for most titles. For more information, reference our Special Bulk Sales–eBook Licensing web page at `www.apress.com/info/bulksales`.

The source code for this book is available to readers at www.apress.com. You will need to answer questions pertaining to this book in order to successfully download the code.

To my wife, Susan.

—Mark Lui

To my wife, Fumiko, and daughter, Makani. Thank you for being there when I need you most.

—Mario Gray

To my wife, Eva.

—Andy Chan

To the Spring community: The Spring projects would not continue to be the most powerful way to meet the demands of tomorrow's applications, today, without you.

—Josh Long

Contents at a Glance

Contents

About the Authors

Dr. Mark Lui received his doctorate in physics from the University of California, Santa Barbara, and worked as a research scientist in the semiconductor industry for 11 years. He transitioned into the software industry, consulting in the areas of enterprise application integration, business process monitoring, and enterprise information integration, as well as general enterprise Java development. Mark is currently a senior software engineer at Shopzilla. He has experience using commercial-based solutions, such as webMethods and WebLogic, in addition to open source projects such as the Spring Framework, Spring Integration, and ActiveMQ. Mark can be reached at his blog site, `http://drmarklui.wordpress.com`, or via Twitter(`@drmarklui`).

Mario Gray is an engineer with more than a decade of experience in systems integration, systems administration, game programming, and highly available enterprise architectures. He is ever vigilant of force-multiplying technologies to better enable businesses. He has developed countless systems, including CRMs, market data ticker plants, and highly available web applications, using leading open source enterprise Java frameworks and tools. Mario has a record of successfully leveraging open source frameworks to better serve businesses. He lives in the city of Chandler, Arizona, with his wife, Fumiko, and his daughter, Makani. Outside of his career, he enjoys recreational sports, exercise, and family activities. He maintains a blog at `http://www.sudoinit5.com`, and can be reached at `mario@sudioinit5.com`.

Andy Chan was born in Hong Kong and was first introduced to computer programming using Applesoft BASIC on the Apple II computer when he was five years old. After he graduated from the University of California, Irvine, in information and computer science, he started his early career as a Windows NT software/driver developer using C/C++. He switched to the Java platform in the late 1990s and has been using Java to develop complex business applications. With more than 15 years of professional experience developing large-scale enterprise software systems, he currently works at Shopzilla as a software architect. Andy's current interest is dealing with big data using Hadoop and HBase. He can be found in the Los Angeles Hadoop Users Group (LA-HUG) and the Santa Monica Java Users Group (SM-JUG). He can be also reached via Twitter (`@iceycake`) or his blog site, at `http://www.iceycake.com`.

Josh Long is the Spring developer advocate for SpringSource, an editor for InfoQ.com, and author/coauthor of many things (including *Spring Recipes: A Problem-Solution Approach, Second Edition*, published by Apress). Josh has spoken at numerous different industry conferences, including Geecon, TheServerSide Java Symposium, SpringOne, OSCON, JavaZone, Devoxx, JAX, and Java2Days. When he's not hacking on Spring Integration and other open source code (see `http://git.springsource.org`, `http://github.com/SpringSource`, and `http://github.com/joshlong`), he can be found at the local Java user group, a coffee shop, or the airport. Josh likes solutions that push the boundaries of the technologies that enable them. His interests include scalability, big data, BPM, grid processing, RIA, mobile computing, and so-called smart systems. He blogs at `http://blog.springsource.org` and `http://www.joshlong.com`, and can be reached at `josh@joshlong.com`.

About the Technical Reviewers

Manuel Jordan Elera is a freelance Java developer who designs and develops personal systems for his customers using powerful frameworks based in Java, such as Spring, Hibernate, and others. Manuel is now an autodidact developer and enjoys learning new frameworks to get better results in his projects.

Manuel earned his degree in systems engineering and won the 2010 Springy Award for Community Champion. In his little free time, he likes reading the Bible and composing music with his guitar. Manuel is a senior member in the Spring Community Forums, in which he is known as dr_pompeii.

Manuel was the technical reviewer for *Pro SpringSource dm Server, Spring Enterprise Recipes, Spring Recipes, Second Edition*, and *Pro Spring Batch*—all published by Apress. He can be contacted through his blog, at `http://manueljordan.wordpress.com`.

Ndjobo Armel Fabrice is a computer design engineer, and a graduate of the National Advanced School of Engineering, Cameroon. Over the past few years, he has worked with EJB/JEE to realize several systems, including a helpLine system. Presently, he is part of the Java team of Delta Group, where he works with EJBs, Spring, and ICEfaces solutions. He is preparing for the OCJP certifications, and can be reached at `ndjoboarmel@gmail.com`.

Acknowledgments

I would like to thank my coauthors, Andy Chan, Mario Gray, and especially Josh Long, who had the confidence in having me work on this book project. My thanks go to the editorial staff at Apress whose constant diligence kept this project going. And I want to thank all my colleagues at Shopzilla, in particular Alex Dallal and Rob Roland, who were open to having messaging become a more common part of the Shopzilla architecture. In addition, I would like to thank my former colleagues Lyn Hardy and Mark Thomsen, who introduced me to the world of enterprise integration. And finally I would like to thank my wife, Susan, and children, Emily and Alex, who put up with my long hours seeing this book to completion.

Mark Lui

Many thanks to my wife, Fumiko, and our daughter, Makani; their patience has been taken to heart. I was very fortunate to have received their support, motivation, delicious meals, and enduring love, which gave me the drive to come this far. I commend my coauthors, Dr. Mark Lui, Josh Long, and Andy Chan; their commitment to delivering both a precise and enjoyable work is excellent. Their passion for the work was a highly uplifting influence throughout its production. It was a pleasure and a treat to work with this team! I would like to thank the technical reviewers, Manuel Jordan Elera and Ndjobo Armel Fabrice, for their dedication to ensuring the accuracy of this book. These guys have blown me away on several occasions. Finally, thank you to the Spring Integration team for producing the useful, highly regarded Spring Integration framework. And finally, thanks to my coworkers at Edward Jones, whose camaraderie has made for some of my best days.

Mario Gray

This book would not have been possible without the editorial staff at Apress, who worked tirelessly with us for the past few months. I'd especially like to thank one of our technical reviewers, Manuel Jordan Elera, for his valuable input and friendship. I'd like to thank all my coauthors, especially Dr. Mark Lui and Josh Long, who gave me a chance to work with them on this book. I also would like to thank my parents and friends for giving me all the support. Finally, I'd like to thank my lovely wife, Eva, and our dog, Charco, who spent a lot of late nights and weekends with me.

Andy Chan

I want to thank my coauthors, Dr. Mark Lui, Andy Chan, and Mario Gray, for their tireless efforts. This book wouldn't have been possible without the Apress editorial staff, and in particular Manuel Jordan Elera, with whom I've now had the privilege to work three times. I'd also especially like to thank Gary Mak, who contributed some content for this book from our previous book, *Spring Recipes: A Problem-Solution Approach, Second Edition*, and who remains a valuable friend and source of inspiration. A tip of the hat goes to Mark Fisher, Oleg Zhurakousky, the many other engineers who've contributed to Spring Integration, and of course to SpringSource—thanks for giving us something worth writing about! I'd like to thank, as always, my friends and family, and in particular my wife, Richelle, who has indulged my late nights and weekends with smiles, warm dinners, and ample coffee.

Josh Long

Introduction

The majority of the open source Java frameworks have focused on supporting database-backed web sites. Developers have leveraged these frameworks to create highly scalable and performant vertical applications using projects such as Spring and Hibernate. Recently, a number of frameworks have been developed with the purpose of solving the horizontal problem of integrating data and services between disparate applications across the enterprise. Spring Integration is one of these solutions.

Enterprise integration is an architectural approach for integrating disparate services and data in software. Enterprise integration seeks to simplify and automate business processes without requiring comprehensive changes to the existing applications and data structures. Spring Integration is an extension of Spring's Plain Old Java Object (POJO) programming model to support the standard integration patterns while building on the Spring Framework's existing support for integration with systems and users.

The Spring Framework is the most widely used framework in organizations today. Spring Integration works in terms of the fundamental idioms of integration, including messages, channels, and endpoints. It enables messaging within Spring-based applications and integrates with external systems via Spring Integration's adapter framework. The adapter framework provides a higher level of abstraction over Spring's existing support for remote method invocation, messaging, scheduling, and much more. Developers already familiar with the Spring Framework will find Spring Integration easy to pick up, since it uses the same development model and idioms.

This book will cover the vast world of enterprise application integration, as well as the application of the Spring Integration framework toward solving integration problems. The book can be summed up as the following:

- An introduction to the concepts of enterprise application integration.
- A reference on building event-driven applications using Spring Integration.
- A guide to solving common integration problems using Spring Integration.

Who This Book Is For

This book is for any developer looking for a more natural way to build event-driven applications using familiar Spring idioms and techniques. The book is also for architects seeking to better their applications and increase productivity in their developers. You should have a basic understanding of the Java language. A familiarity with the Spring Framework and messaging are useful, but not required, as we provide an introduction to those concepts.

How This Book Is Structured

To give you a quick idea of what this book covers, here's a brief chapter-by-chapter overview:

- *Chapter 1* provides an introduction to enterprise application integration—an architectural approach for integrating disparate services and data in software.
- *Chapter 2* takes a look as some of the alternative open source technologies for enterprise integration.
- *Chapter 3* introduces the Spring Framework and provides a glance at some of the major modules leveraged by Spring Integration.
- *Chapter 4* introduces several of the enterprise APIs supported by the core Spring Framework, including those for JDBC, object-relationship management, transactions, and remoting.
- *Chapter 5* introduces the basic Spring Integration components and how they extend the Spring Framework into the world of messaging and event-driven architectures.
- *Chapter 6* introduces the concept of a message channel and how the Spring Integration framework simplifies the development of message channels in an integration implementation.
- *Chapter 7* covers transformations, which allow the message payload to be modified to the format and structure required by the downstream endpoint. It also covers enrichment, which allows for augmenting and modifying the message header values as required for supporting downstream message handling and endpoint requirements.
- *Chapter 8* covers the different components available for controlling message flow in Spring Integration, and how to use a workflow engine with Spring Integration.
- *Chapter 9* focuses on endpoints that connect to the message channels, application code, external applications, and services.
- *Chapter 10* introduces the support for management and monitoring provided by Spring Integration and other available open source systems.
- *Chapter 11* discusses the Spring Integration channel adapters used to communicate with files, sockets, streams, file servers, and databases.
- *Chapter 12* focuses on enterprise messaging using transports such as Java Message Service (JMS) and the Advanced Message Queuing Protocol (AMQP).
- *Chapter 13* discusses the Spring Integration adapters that support integrating with e-mail, XMPP (Jabber, GTalk, Facebook Chat, etc.), news feeds (RSS, ATOM, etc.), and Twitter.
- *Chapter 14* covers how Spring Integration provides both client and server support for web services and how to integrate web services with the Spring Integration messaging framework.
- *Chapter 15* explores the support offered in the core Spring Integration framework to help you build your own adapters.
- *Chapter 16* focuses on how to increase performance by scaling out the hardware and how Spring Integration applications can take advantage of concurrency.

- *Chapter 17* reviews the Spring Batch project and how it can be used with Spring Integration.
- *Chapter 18* shows how Spring Integration can be used to create a basic web interface with the HTTP inbound and outbound gateways. It also discusses the Spring Integration support for the server pushing data to the client browser.

Conventions

Sometimes when we want you to pay particular attention to a part within a code example, we will make the font bold. Please note that the bold does not necessarily reflect a code change from the last version. In cases when a code line is too long to fit the page's width, we break it with a code continuation character, which looks like this: ➥. Please note that when you type out the code, you have to concatenate the line by yourself without any spaces.

Prerequisites

Because the Java programming language is platform independent, you are free to choose any supported operating system. However, some of the examples in this book use platform-specific paths. Translate them as necessary to your operating system's format before typing out the examples. To make the most of this book, install JDK version 1.5 or higher. You should have a Java IDE installed to make development easier. For this book, the sample code is Maven based. If you're running Eclipse and you install the m2eclipse plug-in, you can open the same code in Eclipse, and the class path and dependencies will be filled in the by the Maven metadata. If you're using Eclipse, you might prefer SpringSource's free SpringSource Tool Suite (STS) (`www.springsource.com/developer/sts`), which comes preloaded with all the plug-ins you will need to be as efficient as possible with the Spring Framework.
If you use NetBeans or IntelliJ IDEA, there are no special configuration requirements: they already support Maven out of the box and also provide some support for Spring.
This book uses Maven (2.2.1 or higher). The recommended approach is to simply use a tool like Maven, Ant, Ivy, or Gradle to handle dependency management. The Maven dependency coordinates given in this book can also be used with Ivy, Gradle, and others.

Downloading the Code

The source code for this book is available from the Apress web site (`www.apress.com`), in the Source Code section. The source code is organized by chapters, each of which includes one or more independent examples. Note that there are four Spring Integration sandbox projects used in this book. Sandbox projects tend to be a moving target and we will do our best to keep the information up to date at the Apress web site for any changes required to build these projects. More information about build the sandbox project may be found in the readme.txt file within the source code.

Contacting the Authors

We always welcome your questions and feedback regarding the content of this book. You can reach Mark Lui via his blog at `http://drmarklui.wordpress.com`, or via e-mail at `dr.mark.lui@gmail.com`. Mario Gray can be contacted through his blog at `http://www.sudoinit5.com`, or by e-mail at `mario@sudioinit5.com`. Andy Chan can be reached via Twitter (`@iceycake`) or his blog site, `http://www.iceycake.com`. Josh Long can be reached at his blog at `http://www.joshlong.com`, by e-mail at `josh@joshlong.com`, or on Twitter (`@starbuxman`).

CHAPTER 1

Enterprise Application Integration Fundamentals

Enterprise Application Integration (EAI) grew out of the incompatibility between the many different ERP applications prevalent during the 1990s and the many in-house applications that needed to use them. ERP applications like SAP, PeopleSoft, and JD Edwards, and customer relationship management systems (CRMs) like Clarify and Siebel quickly became enterprise data silos, and it became increasingly important to reuse the data and functionality in those systems. EAI is an architectural approach for integrating disparate services and data in software. EAI seeks to simplify and automate business processes without requiring comprehensive changes to the existing applications and data structures.

As an organization grows in size, it creates different departments with particular areas of focus, interests, and expertise. Partitioning is required to keep team sizes down to a manageable level and to foster hires of the best people for a particular set of responsibilities while providing enough autonomy to get the work done. While the instinct to partition is natural, all departments must also work together, sharing business processes and data in service of an overall goal and vision. Business processes develop over time, organically; some focus on the entire enterprise as a whole and some are unique to a particular area. Software applications are developed or purchased to support business processes. Organizations can end up with a wide range of sometimes overlapping, conflicting, or incompatible applications and systems. These applications may be based on different operating systems, may use different supporting databases, or be written in different computer languages. It can be very difficult to bridge these disparate applications and services, owing in part to technical incompatibilities and to the prohibitive costs of cross-training personnel in the various systems.

Integration of Data and Services Between Disparate Systems

The main driver for EAI is the desire to share data and business processes across existing applications within an enterprise. In a typical scenario, a company purchases a new CRM system (see Figure 1–1). This system is a major upgrade from the old homegrown mainframe system that has served the company well for many years. It is a common requirement to simultaneously employ the new system while still keeping the old system in service, usually because certain of the old system's functions aren't yet available in the new one. In such a scenario, new customer information is entered into the CRM but the legacy system must be synchronized to reflect the data to support required enterprise business processes. In addition, the CRM might also need to invoke some of the legacy system's functions.

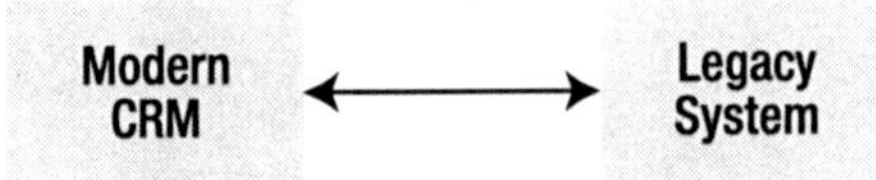

Figure 1-1. *Integration with Modern CRM and Legacy System*

Organizations often want to use the best of breed software solution. Although it is possible to purchase software applications from a single vendor to support a large enterprise's needs, organizations usually like to use what is considered the best software for each business function. This happens for several reasons: specialization sometimes yields better results, and it's always practical to avoid completely investing in one vendor. Support could be an issue if the vendor goes out of business. In addition, there is the possibility that only a custom application will fulfill the business needs. Even with modern systems there may not be a standard means of communication that would work with each vendor's software. Business applications can run on different operation systems such as Linux, Mac, Windows, Solaris, HP-UX, and IBM-AIX. These applications may be based on different databases, such as Oracle, DB2, SQL server, Sybase, RDB, and Informix. Applications are written in different languages such as Java, C, C++, .NET, Cobol, and ABAP. In addition the legacy mainframe systems (e.g., IBM and DEC) should not be forgotten.

Integration Between Information Silos

An information silo is defined as a management system that is incapable of reciprocal operation with other, related management systems. The focus of even internally built applications is inward, and the communication emphasis is vertical. Even with the current push toward open standards and the desire to exploit the power of the Internet, information silos are quite prevalent in most organizations. They are usually caused by the lack of communication and common goals between departments in an organization. Surveying the majority of the current open source framework, the focus is toward vertical database-backed web applications. There are fewer options for horizontal communication between these applications. This may be another driver, or just be symptomatic of the growth of information silos. Information silos limit the ability to achieve business process interoperability and prevent an organization from leveraging all the departments to work toward a common goal. In addition, it prevents the applications from using the full power of the internet. Integration between information silos is another problem that EAI attempts to resolve.

Integration Between Companies

With the power and promise of the Internet, an opportunity arose to improve communication between different companies. After the initial focus on business-to-consumer (B2C) applications, a movement took place to create business-to-business (B2B) systems. Electronic information exchange between different organizations has the potential to reduce cost, increase efficiency, and eliminate human error. The electronic data interchange (EDI) standard was created to support electronic commerce transactions between two computer systems or trading partners. EDI uses a series of electronic messages sent from one computer system to another without human intervention. The message must abide by strictly defined contracts. EDI's original intent was to create a common message standard for B2B communication. EDI is still heavily used, especially within the financial industry.

Although promising, EDI posed a number of issues stemming from a lack of a general purpose message format. EDI lacks obvious looping declarations. The separation of structure from the data increases the difficulty in extracting the proper information. EDI has no standard parsing API, and usually requires proprietary software.

Other industries also feature standards to facilitate partner communication. In the healthcare industry in the United States, for example, HL7 describes the secure exchange of patient health information and treatment.

In contrast, XML was created as a general-purpose data format that can be easily transmitted over the foundations of the Internet, including HTTP. XML has had a broad adoption and has become the de-facto standard for message exchange. Web services are a response to the need to expose business processes using HTTP communication. The growth of web services speaks to how important integration is.

Integration with Users

Today's applications aren't mainframe applications with amber-screen clients. They are web applications. Where "web application" might've described an application accessible from a web browser five years ago, today it describes an application that stores your information in one place and exposes its feature sets in many ways. Today's users increasingly rely on their tablet computers, their mobile devices, and their everyday tools—chat, e-mail, news feeds, and social networks, like Facebook or Twitter—to interact with these applications and with each other. Today's developer can no longer afford to expect the user to be at a desk, logged into a web page. She must go to where the user is and make it as easy as possible for those users to use the application. This is integration, and it's a key part of the most radical changes in application developments in the last five years.

Challenges

EAI implementations do not have the best reputation for success. There have been many reports that indicate the majority of EAI projects fail. And the failures are not usually due to software or technical issues, but to management challenges. Before getting into the management issues with EAI, a look the technical issues is appropriate.

Technology

EAI was originally dominated by the commercial vendors offering a number of proprietary solutions. Implementing an EAI solution required a strong knowledge of the vendor's software and tools. A number of the commercial products and approaches will be discussed later in this chapter. Until recently, viable open source frameworks did not exist. Although open source integration was possible, the results lacked the required management and monitoring capabilities for a production environment. In addition, these solutions required a great deal of custom coding of business logic and adapters to many of the existing enterprise applications. Spring Integration is one open source solution that has come of age and is ready to solve your integration requirements. Alternative open source solutions are discussed in Chapter 2.

Integration usually requires interfacing with a number of different technologies and business domains. SAP may be used for accounting, Siebel for customer relations, and PeopleSoft for human resources. All these applications have different technologies, configurations, and external communication protocols. It is usually very difficult to integrate with an application or system without knowledge of the underlying endpoint system. Adapter technology offsets some of these difficulties, but often there needs to be some configuration and software modifications to the applications to integrate. Different systems expose different integration options: SAP has business application programming interface (BAPI), Siebel has business components, and PeopleSoft has business objects. These systems are formidable, but usually require a system integrator to have some basic understanding of the applications with which to be connected, and the business domain with which they are part. Depending on the number of integration points, this can be quite a challenge.

Many times the target application cannot be changed or altered to enable the integration. The application may be a commercial product in which any changes would void the warranty and support process. Or the application could be legacy with which any change is difficult. Despite the widespread need for integration standards, only a few have emerged. XML and web services have received a great deal of hype, but these technologies are still marked with a large amount of fragmentation. Even with numerous standards organizations in the world today the specifications are becoming more and more inconsistent. Look at the number of Web Services (WS-*) standards and the number of corresponding Java specification requests (JSRs). The standards committees are typically dominated by the vendors with their own agenda. On a positive note, however, the open-source community more and more drives standards adoption.

Today's applications are often a myriad of many moving parts, separated by unknown networks and protocols. It is foolish to assume that both client and server will always be available. By using messaging to introduce asynchronous communication between two systems, you can not only decouple the producer from the uptime—after all the messages are buffered until both sides have capacity to handle it—you can also speed up the performance of individual components in the system since they no longer have to wait for each other before proceeding. Similarly, independent parts of a system may be scaled out to achieve capacity.

People

As with all business problems, solving the technical issues is the easy part. Dealing with the people issues is what's hard. It's no different with EAI. Implementing it may even be more difficult than implementing a vertical application, since it runs across the entire enterprise. EAI implementations often cross corporate boundaries, engage partners, and touch customers. This is where the real fun begins when internal corporate politics start entering into the mix causing simple questions to take months to resolve. One multinational company had a different set of software standards and practices dependent on which side of the Atlantic the division was located.

Integrations typically touch many parts of an organization with a different set of technologies as well as processes, management styles, and politics. The motivation for the integration implementation may be different for the various areas. Often one area may not want to share data with the other. A successful integration requires that there can be an agreement on what data will be shared, in what format, and how to map the different representations and interpretations between the areas. This in not always easy or achievable, and many times compromises must be reached.

The timing for implementing integration may be determined by different factors across an organization. One area might want the data made available as soon as possible where the other may be working on another project and have no motivation for the integration effort. This needs to be negotiated, because integration with an application usually requires access and support by the business owners.

Security is always an issue, because data may be proprietary because of privacy and/or business value. Integration requires access to this data and obtaining the appropriate authorization is not always easy. However, this access is vital to the success of the implementation where security requirement must be met.

A successful integration often requires both communication between computers systems as well as business units and information technology departments. Because of there wide scope, integration efforts have far reaching implications on the business. Failed integration processes can cost a business millions of dollars in lost orders, misrouted payments, and disgruntled customers. In the end however, working well with everyone from the business owners to the computer support staff is essential and often more important than the technical issues involving an integration. Integration frameworks such Spring Integration mitigate the technical barriers, but you must be sure to address business motivations as well.

Approaches

There have historically been four approaches to integration: file transfer, sharing a database, leveraging services, and asynchronous messaging. One way to look at these approaches is how they affect coupling in your architecture. Broadly, there are three types of coupling:

- **Spatial coupling** (communication): Spatial coupling describes the requirement of a producer to know how to communicate with another and how to overcome error scenarios in the communication. A server side fault in an RPC operation, for example, is an example of spatial coupling.
- **Temporal coupling** (buffering): Temporal coupling describes the requirement of a producer to be aware of, and available for, a consumer to share data. A decoupled system uses buffering so that a message may be sent, even if the consumer isn't available to receive it.
- **Logical coupling** (routing): Logical coupling describes the requirement of a producer to know how to connect with the consumer. One way to fix this is to introduce a central, shared location where both parties exchange data. Then, if a producer decides to move (change IP, put up a firewall, and so on) or decides to add extra steps before publishing messages, the client remains unaware as the client only concerns itself with the ultimate message payload.

File Transfer

Usually the first approach that comes to mind when sharing data is using a file (see Figure 1–2). If information is to be shared across two different applications, one system can produce a file containing the data of interest. The other system can poll for this file in a well-known, agreed upon directory or mount. Naturally, this directory might be anywhere—in an FTPS share, a SAN-based file system mount, an SFTP directory, a clustered file system like Hadoop's HDFS and VMware's VMFS. When it is available, the other system can process the file for the data. There must be an agreement when file transfer is employed as to which file format to use and how often to publish and consume the files. A major issue with using this approach is managing all the files and formats, and insuring that none of the files are missed. In addition, there is always a time lag based on the frequency of the file production and the consumption of the files. This may cause synchronization issues. File transfer integrations are temporally decoupled because neither the producer nor the consumer need be available for integration to occur. Additionally, the systems in file transfer integration only need to be aware of the shared mount, not each other, and thus they are logically decoupled, as well.

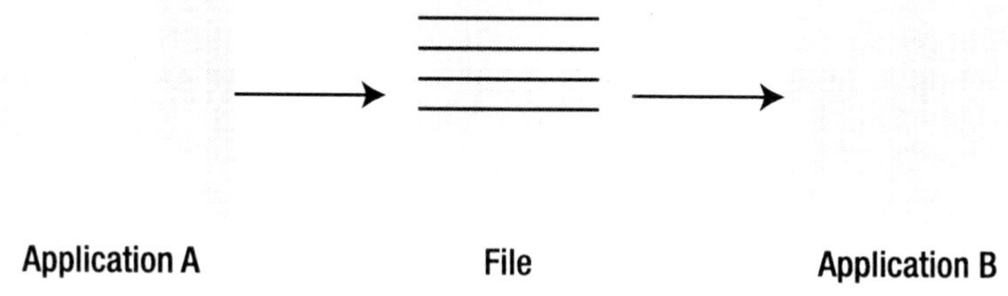

Figure 1–2. File Transfer Approach

Shared Database

What better way to share data than to used the same data source or shared database (see Figure 1–3). Integration between two systems is as simple as joining two tables. However, there are several issues that stem from using a shared database for integration. First, it is difficult to come up with a unified schema that will suit the needs of the different applications. Using a shared schema can potentially create interdependencies between two systems that may have different requirements and time schedules. Using a single dataset limits the potential to scale due to locking contention and network lag when distributing across multiple locations. Shared databases couple all systems involved to a well-known schema (the database table), though the various systems are temporally decoupled—one system does not need to be available for another system to communicate a change so long as the database is available. Because systems in a shared database don't need to be aware of each other, just the shared database, they are logically decoupled.

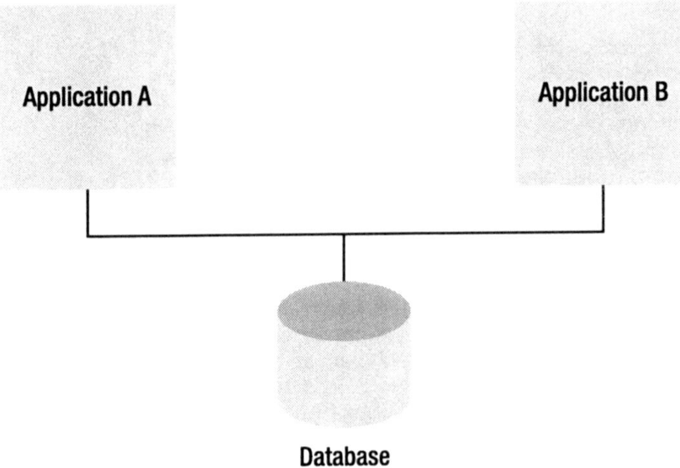

***Figure 1–3.** Shared Database Approach*

Remote Procedure Calls

If data or a process needs to be shared across an organization, one way to expose this functionality is through a remote service (see Figure 1–4). For example, an EJB service or a SOAP service allows functionality to be exposed to the rest of the enterprise. Using a service, the implementation is encapsulated, allowing the different applications to change the underlying implementation without affecting any integration solution as long as the service interface has not changed. The thing to remember about a service is that the integration is synchronous: both the client and the service must be available for integration to occur, and they must know about each other.

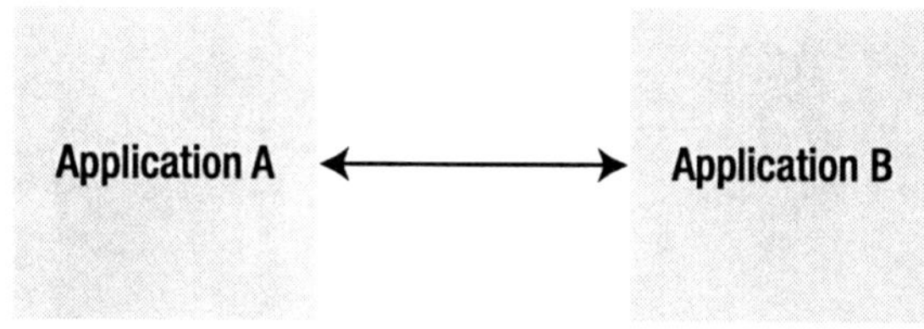

Figure 1–4. Remote Service Call Approach

Messaging

The challenge of integration is to enable applications to share functionality and data in real time without tightly coupling the systems together in a way that introduces reliability issues in terms of application execution and application development. File transfer works well for decoupling the different applications, but has inherent performance issues. Shared database insures that data access is timely, but ties all applications to a single database. In addition it does not allow for external applications to share their functional behavior. A remote service is a viable alternative; however, extending a single application model for integration brings up all sorts of issues. Working on a single application has the potential to become distributed development. Service calls seem like local calls, but must support all the functionality required when going across a network. They are slower and have the potential to fail. If one application goes down, it can bring down the entire enterprise. What is needed is something like file transfer, but without the performance issues.

Messaging is an approach to transfer packets of data frequently, immediately, reliably, and asynchronously using a customizable format. Two systems connect to a common messaging system and exchange data and invoke behavior using messages (see Figure 1–5). An example of this is the familiar hub-and-spoke Java messaging service (JMS) architecture. Sending a message does not require both systems to be up and running at the same time. In addition, using an asynchronous process forces the developers to think about the issues involved with working with a remote application. Messages can be transformed in transit without either the sender or receiver knowing about the modification. Both data and processes may be shared using messaging. Message may be broadcasted to multiple receivers or directed at one of many receivers. Messaging meets the needs for integration scalability and extensibility.

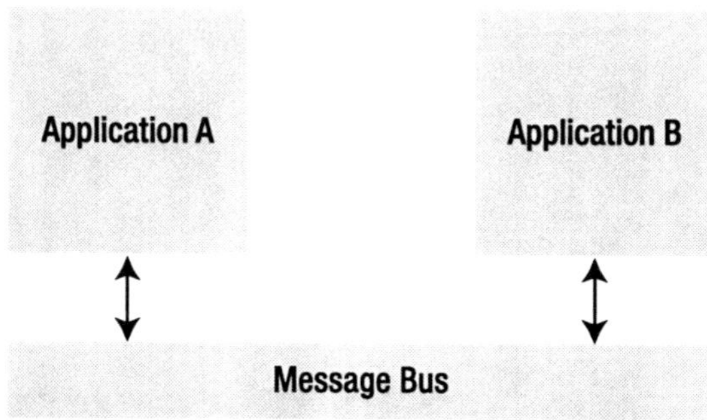

Figure 1–5. Messaging Approach

Event-Driven Architectures

Most systems are event-driven in nature. Systems react to changes and interesting events in the enterprise, not to some fixed routine. These events are conveyed as messages that contain information about the event and how to process it. Messaging decouples the producer and the consumer—they don't need to know about when the other is available, nor do the producer and the consumer need to be aware of the other's public interface or its speed. One publishes a message as quickly as possible and then leaves the consumer to process it at its own pace.

There are two approaches to communicating data across systems: the client needs to ask for the information (a pull system) or the remote system needs to send the data when something has changed (a push system).

The traditional approach for obtaining data is a pull system. Issuing a database query, a remote procedure call, or a web service call are all examples of pull-oriented communication. Integrations are often point-to-point, where any interested party needs to know how to speak to any other system directly to obtain a result. In architectures with many systems, maintaining these connections can become very tedious very quickly. Metcalfe's law (named for Robert Metcalf, co-inventor of Ethernet and founder of 3Com) describes the number of connections possible for compatible communicating devices. It can be used to calculate how much different connections are required for any number of partners in a system that need to communicate with each other using point-to-point communication. The formula–$n(n - 1)/2$ – where n is the number of connected nodes–can yield some very scary results! For two nodes or partners in an integration, one connection is required (2(2-1)/2 =1); for five nodes, ten connections are required (5(5-1)/2=10); and for ten nodes, 45 connection are required (10(10-1)/2 =45)!

Pull-based systems have synchronization gaps. A system may change but consumers of that event will only find out about the change on the next poll. Assuming a poll of ten seconds (for example), clients could possibly have data as far out of sync as 10 seconds. In some systems (social networking "status" updates, for example) this isn't a big deal. For other (stock market trading), this delay is intolerable.

Event Driven Architecture (EDA) is a software architecture pattern promoting the production, detection, and/or consumption of events as messages. In essence, EDA is an architecture where events are transmitted between loosely coupled software components and services. An event-driven system consists of event producers or publishers and event consumers or subscribers. Building applications and systems around an event-based architecture allows these applications and systems to be more responsive because event-driven systems are by design engineered to deal with unpredictable and asynchronous environments. A simple example of an event driven architecture is shown in Figure 1–6.

Figure 1–6. *Event-Driven Architecture (EDA)*

SEDA (Staged Event-Driven Architecture)

Staged event-driven architecture (SEDA) is an approach to build a system that can support massive concurrency without incurring many of the issues involved with using a traditional thread and event-based approach. The basic premise is to break the application logic into a series of stages connected by event queues. Each stage may be conditioned to handle increased load by increasing the number of threads for that stage (increasing concurrency). For more information on SEDA readers are advised to consult the paper *SEDA: An Architecture for Well-Conditioned, Scalable Internet Services*, by Matt Welsh, David Culler, and Eric Brewer. Interestingly, Eric Brewer also originated the CAP theorem.

EAI Architecture

EAI architectures have gone through various stages in development since their initial conception, which was with the purpose of dealing with sharing data and business processes across the enterprise. Older solutions used platform agnostic RPC like CORBA and Oracle (formerly BEA's) Tuxedo to integrate. In order to address the issues discussed previously regarding tight coupling and real-time access to data processes, EAI moved to message brokers. The connection to the disparate applications was done using an adapter to convert the application protocol to something the message broker would understand. The adapter software was usually run inside of some sort of container to provide basic application support such as configuration and lifecycle (see Figure 1–7).

Figure 1–7. Traditional EAI Adapter and Broker Architecture

At the same time the need for B2B integration drove the development of EDI and trading of documents via e-mail, FTPS/SFTP, and HTTP and others. Application server development followed to support these and other needs. Eventually, the application servers and adapter containers merged together (see Figure 1–8).

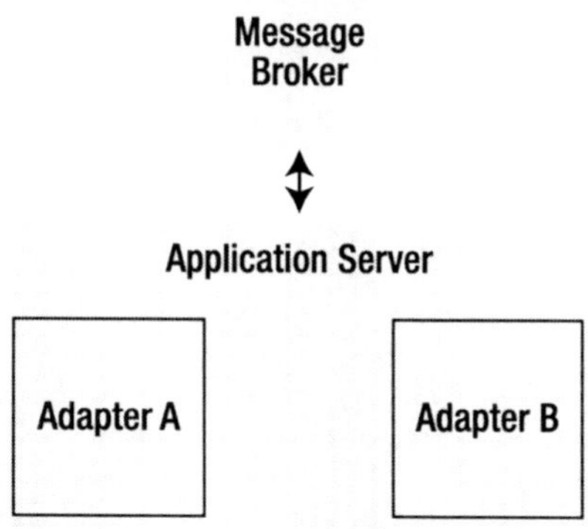

Figure 1–8. Application Server Architecture

After a slight diversion back to remote procedure calls with service-oriented architecture (SOA), it seems messaging technology has returned. Today's architectures demand common data exchange mechanisms (for which XML is ideal) and asynchronous, loosely coupled, stateless and horizontally scalable service tiers, for which messaging is ideally suited. The push toward open, standards-based integrations has given us the enterprise service bus (ESB). This is a lightweight adapter container with message routing capabilities based on open standards (see Figure 1–9).

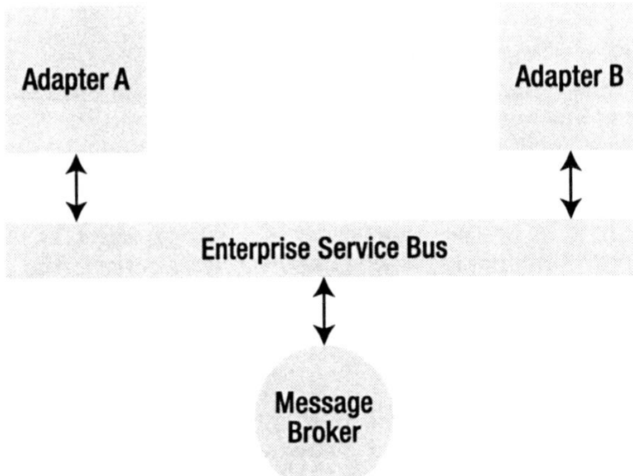

Figure 1–9. Enterprise Service Bus (ESB) Architecture

An ESB is still a server and still encourages isolated servers, but it provides ready-to-go routing and integration technologies. For many people, something lighter still is required–something that can be embedded or used standalone. To meet this call, integration frameworks like Apache Camel and Spring Integration have proven very successful. Even old-guard ESB vendors like MuleSoft are increasingly trying to enable use of their adapters independent of the broker through frameworks. Time will tell how this approach works.

Domination by Proprietary Solutions

EAI solutions have traditionally been dominated by costly proprietary solutions that required domain experts to implement. Until recently, these have been the best approach to solving integration problems. Some of the more popular integration products are discussed in the following sections.

webMethods (Active Software)

webMethods is an integration product suite now offered by Software AG. The main components of webMethods are the Integration Server and message broker. The Integration Server is the predecessor to the modern application server. Essentially an HTTP server on steroids, the Integration Server was developed to support B2B integration. With support for EDI and custom XML messages, and its own process flow language, Integration Server provides a platform to integration between companies over the Internet. With the acquisition of Active Software, webMethods added an enterprise integration platform to its offerings. Active Software products included an enterprise grade message broker and a suite of adapters supports integration with all the major ERP and legacy systems. Additional acquisitions added monitoring and business process support, and created a complete integration platform. Commercial products such as webMethods provide a suite of visual tools that simplify and accelerate the implementation of an integration solution.

Tibco

Tibco is another major player in the commercial enterprise integration platforms. Tibco has similar software offering to webMethods with messaging support from TIB/Rendezvous and an integration server package called ActiveIntegration. Tibco has been used in financial services, telecommunications, electronic commerce, transportation, manufacturing, and energy with an array of application adapters. Tibco enters the analytics and next-generation business intelligence markets by acquiring Spotfire, the grid computing and cloud computing markets by acquiring DataSynapse and enterprise data matching software product by acquiring Netrics.

Vitria

Vitria has the following two main software product lines.

- **BusinessWare:** This is Vitria's integration offering, which has a business process management (BPM) platform that allows its users to carry out general business process management, enterprise application integration, and B2B integration; it supports B2B standards such as EDI, ebXML, and AS2.
- **M3O:** This allows users to monitor and react to processes across a company's internal operations. It uses a combination of BPM, business activity monitoring (BAM), and web technologies.

IBM MQSeries

MQSeries is IBM's message-oriented middleware (MOM) offering. Combined with IBM WebSphere and supporting technologies, MQSeries offers a complete integration solution. This includes a suite of application adapters and visual tools for development and configuration.

SonicMQ

SonicMQ started life as a messaging broker implementing the JMS API. Later a Sonic ESB product was added, essentially a container supporting adapters and message routing configurations. Visual tool support called Sonic Workbench and a BPEL process engine server completed the offering, making it a full integration solution suite.

Axway Integrator

Axway also provides enterprise and business-to-business (B2B) integration applications. Axway's solutions feature a flexible integration and B2B framework, analytics, services and customized applications.

Oracle SOA Suite

Oracle ESB is largely composed of the message broker and application server from WebLogic and the message router from BEA AquaLogic. Together with some additional products from Oracle, this is an integration suite that includes visual tools.

Microsoft BizTalk

BizTalk is the Microsoft offering in the enterprise integration market. However, limitation in its product offering and its ability to run only on Windows has prevented larger market penetration.

EAI Patterns

In a broad sense, integration means connecting computer systems, companies, and people. There are three basic patterns that you see repeatedly when implementing integrations for enterprise customers: data synchronization, web portals, and workflow system. These three patterns cover the majority of integration implementation requests.

Data Synchronization

Data synchronization is the most requested type of integration for an organization, and is used when business processes in different parts of an organization require access to the same data. It's almost an anti-pattern, since this is usually a stop-gap approach where a façade pattern could be used instead. For example, a customer's address may be used in a customer relations management system, an accounting system to bill the customer, or a delivery system to ship a product to them. It is very typical for each system to have its own data store for customer information for a variety of reasons, including performance and unique domain models. If a customer makes a change, for example, to his address, each system must update its view of that customer information. This may be accomplished by implementing a data synchronization integration pattern (see Figure 1–10).

Data replication only works if each application uses the same database vendor and schema structure. This is usually not the case when each application has its own technology stack. Another approach is to export the data into files and re-import them into the other system. This approach can be slow, since it is difficult to determine what data has changed. Often all the data move between the systems. In addition, the timeliness of the data will be dependent on how often this synchronization process is run.

The standard integration approach to data synchronization is using a message-based system to move the data records inside the messages. A mechanism is needed to detect when a record is created or updated such as a database trigger or a hook or façade into the application to determine when to push the data to the other systems.

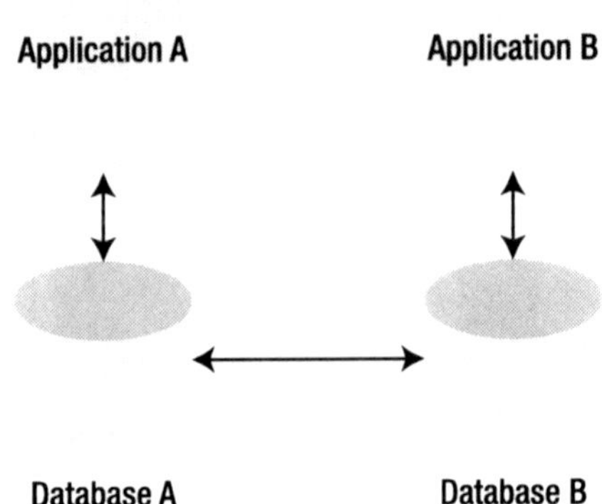

Figure 1–10. *Data Synchronization Pattern*

Web Portals

Often business owners and executives require information from different systems to answer specific questions or to get a general overview of the entire organization. It would be ideal to get this information from a single location rather that search across several different applications. For example, a customer agent needing to check the status of an order may need to access information from several sources, including the web application taking the order and the fulfillment system supported by a third-party application. Or maybe the business executive would like to monitor the activities of several different areas using a single web page instead of running several different applications. Web portals aggregate information from several different data sources into a single display without requiring the user to log in into the different applications supporting the various business areas.

Portal applications have become prevalent in recent years, allowing users to configure a web page consisting of different frames, or portlets, which allows a composite view (see Figure 1–11). In addition, most portal frameworks allow a certain amount of interaction between the different frames. Also, integration frameworks support combining multiple data sources into single model, including combining the information based on shared properties such as customer or order IDs.

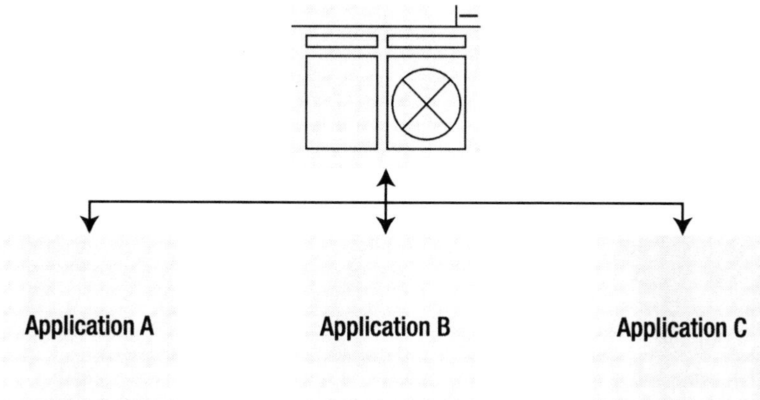

Figure 1–11. Web Portal Pattern

Workflow

A business process can span multiple business areas and systems within an organization, and may require both automatic agents and human actors to complete successfully. The canonical workflow example is that of a loan approval process, because it has multiple steps and enlists both human and system actors. The example goes like this: a customer requests a loan from a bank. The bank rep enters the request into the system where it will first pass basic validations–does the requester have good credit, does the requester have the required documents in order, and so on. If that checks out, and the loan is for an amount deemed to be low risk, the loan is approved. If the loan amount is high risk, it requires additional audits–somebody in the risk-assessment department needs to scrutinize the request manually and decide, on a case-by-case basis, whether the loan should be approved. Finally, a letter will be printed and sent to the requester to notify him of the status of the request (approved or not approved). In this example, the request moved through at least two different systems and required a worker of specific authority to examine the request for the process to terminate.

There are a number of workflow engines available using different methods of representing a process flow, such as BPEL and BPMN. The process flow can be designed at high level without concern for the actual implementation. Later the process can be implemented by integrating the workflow process with the different applications using an integration framework (see Figure 1–12).

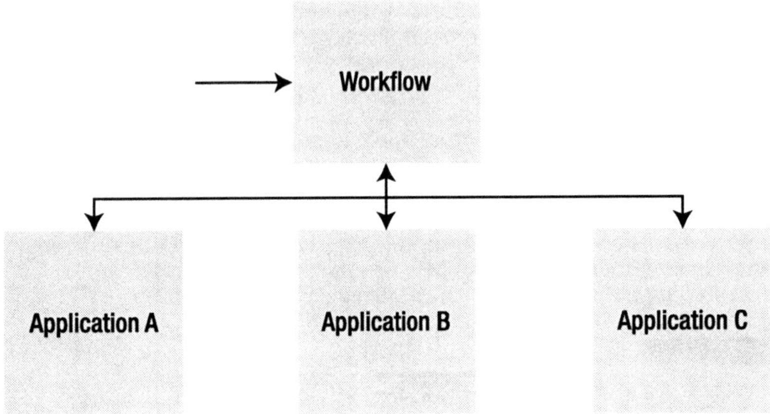

Figure 1–12. Workflow Pattern

Spring Integration Framework

The Spring Integration Framework is a response to the need for an open-source, straightforward integration framework that leverages the widely adopted Spring Framework. Spring Integration provides an extension of Spring's plain old Java object (POJO) programming model to support the standard integration patterns while building on the Spring Framework's existing support for enterprise integration. The Spring Framework is the most widely adapted framework used in organizations today. Spring Integration works in terms of the fundamental idioms of integration, including messages, channels, and endpoints. It enables messaging within Spring-based applications and integrates with external systems via Spring Integration's adapter framework. The adapter framework provides a higher-level of abstraction over Spring's existing support for remote method invocation, messaging, scheduling, and much more. Developers already familiar with the Spring Framework will find Spring Integration easy to pick up, since it uses the same development model and idioms.

Summary

This chapter has covered the basics of Enterprise Application Integration (EAI) and integration in general. It has addressed the motivations and challenges typical of an integration solution. We have covered the basic approaches to implementing integration: file transfer, database sharing, remote procedure calls, and messaging. The drive for real-time information has led to event-driven architectures where information is published as events (in messages) as soon as data is available.

We have looked at the historical evolution of the technology and discipline of integration. Application integration has been dominated by proprietary vendors for a long time. And finally, the three most commonly requested patterns for an integration solution were covered: data synchronization, web portal, and workflow.

CHAPTER 2

Exploring the Alternatives

The world of integration has a storied history and can be overwhelming to the newcomer. There are at least half a dozen viable open source solutions, and at least a dozen (*very*) expensive, proprietary integration solutions. Although the open source solutions can meet most integration challenges, there are some technologies that don't lend themselves to the open source ecosystem because they are of a proprietary nature, or represent a relatively niche concern that the community hasn't suitably addressed. For this reason, and because open source options hold the largest mindshare today, no proprietary options will be discussed in this book. The reader is encouraged as always to investigate alternative solutions.

While there is good guidance on the core language and idioms common to the discipline of *application integration*—such as *Enterprise Integration Patterns*[1], and *The Enterprise Service Bus*[2] —the various technologies are wildly divergent in architecture and development approach. Before diving headfirst into Spring Integration, we'll explore several of the available and popular open source integration frameworks. The two most popular projects are Mule ESB (`www.mulesoft.org`) and Apache ServiceMix (`http://servicemix.apache.org`). Each of these projects takes a different approach. This chapter will cover four different integration approaches:

- Mule provides a lightweight container and leverages a simple XML configuration file and Plain Old Java Objects (POJOs).
- ServiceMix is based on the Java Business Integration (JBI) standard and now supports OSGI.
- OpenESB is (`http://open-esb.dev.java.net`) the integration offering from Oracle based on the JBI and J2EE standards. OpenESB is designed to live in a J2EE application server like GlassFish.
- And there is always the do-it-yourself (DIY) approach. J2EE does provide the necessary support to implement integration, including the J2EE Connector Architecture (JCA). JCA is the J2EE framework for creating resource adapters (RAs) for connecting with external applications and systems.

The Spring Framework is the most widely used enterprise Java technology in the market today, and represents a natural avenue for integration because it provides a component model built on loosely coupled, clean POJO-centric code. The Spring Framework ships with simplifying libraries on top of that component model that simplify many enterprise concerns such as transaction management, data store access, messaging, and RPC or web services. The Spring Framework has been around for the better part

---

[1] Gregor Hohpe et. al.

[2] David A. Chappell

of the last decade, and is in use by countless governments and companies worldwide, including most of the Fortune 1000.

Camel, Mule, and ServiceMix all support the Spring Framework as a *component model*, in a fashion, but oddly ignore the support for core technologies that already come with Spring. Those familiar with the Spring Framework will find little to relate to when using these solutions beyond the component model. It is necessary to relearn core concepts such as transaction management, data access, and messaging.

A Basic Example of Integration

In order to survey the different open source integration offerings and to ensure an apples-to-apples comparison, a simple integration example will be implemented by each framework. The most basic example is to create an endpoint that publishes a message to a JMS queue. Then another endpoint will be created to receive the JMS message from the queue. This is the most basic example, with the endpoints representing one system sending a message to another system. The message may represent moving data or initiating a process between the two systems.

For simplicity, the endpoint in the example will be some sort of HTTP service that will allow starting a process using either a simple HTML page or a testing tool. The receiving endpoint will simply log a message to indicate that the message has been transferred. This is an event-driven architecture in its most simplistic form. In a real integration implementation, the endpoint would probably be an adapter that allows interfacing to a particular service or application.

Mule ESB

Probably one of the first widely accepted open source integration frameworks, Mule ESB was the result of Ross Mason's system integration consulting work looking for a method to increase productivity and maintainability of custom integration engagements.

Philosophy and Approach

Mule's approach was to create a lightweight container that can run standalone, without requiring the support of a J2EE application server where the integration component can be deployed. Although Mule can also be deployed within an application server, the standalone mode is the recommended approach, eliminating the overhead of a heavyweight container.

The service components are POJOs configured though an XML file for deployment in Mule. These components do not require any Mule-specific interfaces to implement or classes to extend from. Mule comes with a number of out-of-the-box service components, including those for message routing and data transformation. The messages within Mule may be in many formats from SOAP to binary. Mule also includes a suite of adapters (or *transports*, as they're called in Mule), supporting everything from JDBC to SMPP. One caveat is that some of the transports' functionality is limited unless if you don't purchase the enterprise edition of Mule.

Implementing the Integration Example

Mule ESB may be downloaded from `www.mulesoft.org`. This example uses Mule Community Edition 3.0.0. The installation is a simple as decompressing the TAR or ZIP file. Mule also requires that Java SE version 1.5 or greater be installed (version 1.6 is recommended). Maven 2.2.1 will be used as the build tool; it can be downloaded at `http://maven.apache.org`. In addition, the example will require downloading ActiveMQ to get the client JAR files. Mule no longer supplies these JAR files with its distribution. ActiveMQ 5.4.1 may be downloaded at `http://activemq.apache.org`. Copy the files in Listing 2–1 from the ActiveMQ `lib` directory and the file `activeio-core-3.1.2.jar` from the `lib\optional` directory to the Mule installation `lib/user` directory.

Listing 2–1. *ActiveMQ JAR Files Needed by Mule*

```
kahadb-5.4.1.jar
activemq-core-5.4.1.jar
activeio-core-3.1.2.jar
geronimo-j2ee-management_1.1_spec-1.0.1.jar
```

The basic project will be created using a Maven archetype provided by the Mule project. In order to use the archetype, the environmental properties `MULE_HOME` must be set to the Mule installation directory. In addition, the settings shown in Listing 2–2 must be added to the `settings.xml` file usually found in the Maven `.m2` repository directory.

Listing 2–2. *settings.xml File*

```
<settings>
  <pluginGroups>
    <pluginGroup>org.mule.tools</pluginGroup>
  </pluginGroups>
  ...
</settings>
```

Run the maven command:

```
mvn mule-project-archetype:create -DartifactId=mule-example -DmuleVersion=3.0.0
```

Maven will prompt with a number of questions. Enter `Mule Example` for the project description, enter `com/apress/prospringintegration/mule` for the Java package path, enter `http,jms,vm` for the Mule transports, and accept the defaults for the rest of the questions. The archetype will create a basic Mule project with the structure shown in Listing 2–3.

Listing 2–3. *mule-example Project Structure*

```
mule-example
--assembly.xml
--pom.xml
--MULE-README.txt
--src/main
  --app/mule-config.xml
  --java/com/apress/prospringintegration/mule/muleexample
  --org/mule (empty directory that can be deleted)
--src/test
  --resources/muleexample-functional-test-config.xml
  --java/com/apress/prospringintegration/mule/muleexample/MuleexampleTestCase.java
```

The `mule-config.xml` file shown in Listing 2–4 contains a skeleton Mule configuration. Due to a bug in the archetype, the last / in the default namespace `xmlns="http://www.mulesoft.org/schema/mule/core/"` must be removed. Listing 2–4 has the correction.

Listing 2–4. mule-config.xml

```
<?xml version="1.0" encoding="UTF-8"?>
<mule xmlns="http://www.mulesoft.org/schema/mule/core"
      xmlns:xsi="http://www.w3.org/2001/XMLSchema-instance"
      xmlns:spring="http://www.springframework.org/schema/beans"
      xmlns:http="http://www.mulesoft.org/schema/mule/http"
      xmlns:jms="http://www.mulesoft.org/schema/mule/jms"
      xmlns:vm="http://www.mulesoft.org/schema/mule/vm"
      xmlns:client="http://www.mulesoft.org/schema/mule/client"
      xmlns:cxf="http://www.mulesoft.org/schema/mule/cxf"
      xmlns:management="http://www.mulesoft.org/schema/mule/management"
      xmlns:scripting="http://www.mulesoft.org/schema/mule/scripting"
      xmlns:sxc="http://www.mulesoft.org/schema/mule/sxc"
      xmlns:mule-xml="http://www.mulesoft.org/schema/mule/xml"
      xsi:schemaLocation="
        http://www.mulesoft.org/schema/mule/core
        http://www.mulesoft.org/schema/mule/core/3.0/mule.xsd
        http://www.mulesoft.org/schema/mule/http
        http://www.mulesoft.org/schema/mule/http/3.0/mule-http.xsd
        http://www.mulesoft.org/schema/mule/jms
        http://www.mulesoft.org/schema/mule/jms/3.0/mule-jms.xsd
        http://www.mulesoft.org/schema/mule/vm
        http://www.mulesoft.org/schema/mule/vm/3.0/mule-vm.xsd
        http://www.mulesoft.org/schema/mule/client
        http://www.mulesoft.org/schema/mule/client/3.0/mule-client.xsd
        http://www.mulesoft.org/schema/mule/cxf
        http://www.mulesoft.org/schema/mule/cxf/3.0/mule-cxf.xsd
        http://www.mulesoft.org/schema/mule/management
        http://www.mulesoft.org/schema/mule/management/3.0/mule-management.xsd
        http://www.mulesoft.org/schema/mule/scripting
        http://www.mulesoft.org/schema/mule/scripting/3.0/mule-scripting.xsd
        http://www.mulesoft.org/schema/mule/sxc
        http://www.mulesoft.org/schema/mule/sxc/3.0/mule-sxc.xsd
        http://www.mulesoft.org/schema/mule/xml
        http://www.mulesoft.org/schema/mule/xml/3.0/mule-xml.xsd
        http://www.springframework.org/schema/beans
        http://www.springframework.org/schema/beans/spring-beans-3.0.xsd">

  <description>
    Mule Example
  </description>

  <flow name="main">
    <vm:inbound-endpoint path="in" exchange-pattern="request-response"/>

    <!-- TODO add your service component here.
     This can also be a Spring bean using <spring-object bean="name"/>
   -->
    <echo-component/>

    <vm:outbound-endpoint path="out"/>
  </flow>
</mule>
```

The first step is to configure ActiveMQ as the embedded JMS broker in Mule. Typically, the message broker is started as a separate external process to the Mule container. In this case, ActiveMQ will be started in the same JVM as Mule. This simplifies the example and also adds a JMS broker support to Mule. Add the element <jms:activemq-connector name="jmsConnector" specification="1.1" brokerURL="vm://localhost" /> within the mule element to the mule-config.xml file.

The next step is to configure a flow that sends a message to the JMS broker. The archetype creates a simple flow named main as a starting point. To allow this process to be started using an HTTP GET or POST, an HTTP transport needs to be added to the beginning of the flow. Then you can start the process by simply hitting the HTTP endpoint. Replace the element <vm:inbound-endpoint path="in" exchange-pattern="request-response"/> with the following:

```
<http:inbound-endpoint host="localhost" port="8192" path="example" keep-alive="true"/>
```

Note that the attribute keep-alive is set to true. This attribute controls if the socket connection is kept alive. Then the process may be started by using a browser with the address http://localhost:8192/example.

Note that the next line in the main flow is <echo-component>. This is a standard component that comes with Mule; it logs the inbound message and forwards it to the outbound endpoint. No transformer has been defined, so the message will simply be passed as is. This component may be replaced with a Spring bean for custom processing on the message. The final step for the main flow is to publish the message to the JMS broker. This is done using the JMS transport by replacing the element <vm:outbound-endpoint path="out"/> with <jms:outbound-endpoint queue="my.destination"/>. This will publish the message to the queue named my.destination. The configuration file is shown in Listing 2–5 with ActiveMQ and the main flow configured.

Listing 2–5. *mule-config.xml with ActiveMQ and Main Flow Configured*

```
...
  <jms:activemq-connector name="jmsConnector"
                          specification="1.1" brokerURL="vm://localhost"/>

  <flow name="main">
  <http:inbound-endpoint host="localhost"
                         port="8192" path="example" keep-alive="true"/>

  <!-- TODO add your service component here.
      This can also be a Spring bean using <spring-object bean="name"/>
    -->
  <echo-component/>

  <jms:outbound-endpoint queue="my.destination"/>
  </flow>
...
```

The last part of this example is to add a listener to the JMS queue my.destination to receive and log the message. A new flow element is added within the ulme element to support this functionality. Again, the JMS transport component is used as the inbound endpoint, and the VM component is used as the outbound endpoint to simply log the message. The address attribute is set to stdio://OUT to log to the console, and the exchange-pattern attribute is set to one-way so that no response input is expected. The complete Mule configuration file is shown in Listing 2–6.

Listing 2–6. *Complete mule-config.xml File*

```
<?xml version="1.0" encoding="UTF-8"?>
<mule xmlns="http://www.mulesoft.org/schema/mule/core"
      xmlns:xsi="http://www.w3.org/2001/XMLSchema-instance"
      xmlns:spring="http://www.springframework.org/schema/beans"
      xmlns:http="http://www.mulesoft.org/schema/mule/http"
      xmlns:jms="http://www.mulesoft.org/schema/mule/jms"
      xmlns:vm="http://www.mulesoft.org/schema/mule/vm"
      xmlns:client="http://www.mulesoft.org/schema/mule/client"
      xmlns:cxf="http://www.mulesoft.org/schema/mule/cxf"
      xmlns:management="http://www.mulesoft.org/schema/mule/management"
      xmlns:scripting="http://www.mulesoft.org/schema/mule/scripting"
      xmlns:sxc="http://www.mulesoft.org/schema/mule/sxc"
      xmlns:mule-xml="http://www.mulesoft.org/schema/mule/xml"
      xsi:schemaLocation="
          http://www.mulesoft.org/schema/mule/core
          http://www.mulesoft.org/schema/mule/core/3.0/mule.xsd
          http://www.mulesoft.org/schema/mule/http
          http://www.mulesoft.org/schema/mule/http/3.0/mule-http.xsd
          http://www.mulesoft.org/schema/mule/jms
          http://www.mulesoft.org/schema/mule/jms/3.0/mule-jms.xsd
          http://www.mulesoft.org/schema/mule/vm
          http://www.mulesoft.org/schema/mule/vm/3.0/mule-vm.xsd
          http://www.mulesoft.org/schema/mule/client
          http://www.mulesoft.org/schema/mule/client/3.0/mule-client.xsd
          http://www.mulesoft.org/schema/mule/cxf
          http://www.mulesoft.org/schema/mule/cxf/3.0/mule-cxf.xsd
          http://www.mulesoft.org/schema/mule/management
          http://www.mulesoft.org/schema/mule/management/3.0/mule-management.xsd
          http://www.mulesoft.org/schema/mule/scripting
          http://www.mulesoft.org/schema/mule/scripting/3.0/mule-scripting.xsd
          http://www.mulesoft.org/schema/mule/sxc
          http://www.mulesoft.org/schema/mule/sxc/3.0/mule-sxc.xsd
          http://www.mulesoft.org/schema/mule/xml
          http://www.mulesoft.org/schema/mule/xml/3.0/mule-xml.xsd
          http://www.springframework.org/schema/beans
          http://www.springframework.org/schema/beans/spring-beans-3.0.xsd">

  <description>
    Mule Example
  </description>

  <jms:activemq-connector name="jmsConnector"
                          specification="1.1" brokerURL="vm://localhost"/>

  <flow name="main">
    <http:inbound-endpoint host="localhost"
                           port="8192" path="example" keep-alive="true"/>

    <!-- TODO add your service component here.
     This can also be a Spring bean using <spring-object bean="name"/>
   -->
```

```
    <echo-component/>

    <jms:outbound-endpoint queue="my.destination"/>
  </flow>

  <flow name="jms-receive">
    <jms:inbound-endpoint queue="my.destination"/>

    <echo-component/>

    <outbound-endpoint address="stdio://OUT" exchange-pattern="one-way"/>
  </flow>
</mule>
```

One side note is that the Mule archetype also includes a sample unit test class. This allows sending messages to any custom-developed service components. Since no custom components have been used in this example, this test framework is not used.

With the configuration complete, the project may be built and deployed into Mule. Within the `mule-example` project directory, run the Maven command `mvn install`. This will build, test, and create a mule project archive, `muleexample-1.0-SNAPSHOT.zip`. Copy this archive file to the `apps` directory in the Mule installation. Start Mule ESB by issuing the command `bin/mule` in the Mule home directory, and the project will be deployed and started. You should now be able to test the example project by hitting the HTTP endpoint either through a browser or using a tool such as the Firefox plug-in Poster. The log files should show the message being published to and then received from the JMS broker.

ServiceMix

ServiceMix was one of the first and most popular integration frameworks to embrace the JBI standard. The ServiceMix 4 release adds OSGi support, allowing component deployment and life cycle management following the OSGi standard.

Philosophy and Approach

ServiceMix is a standalone JBI container. Although it can be deployed within an application server, it is optimized to run in standalone mode. ServiceMix comes with a wide range of adapters (or binding components, in JBI terms), from FTP to Extensible Messaging and Presense Protocol (XMPP). Internal logic within ServiceMix is contained in service engine components with support for scripting and Business Process Execution Language (BPEL).

One of the most interesting service engine components is for Camel support. Camel allows simple configuration of routing and mediation rules. All components deployed to ServiceMix must follow either the JBI or OSGi standard. In addition, the JBI standard requires that all messaging with ServiceMix be in XML format.

Implementing the Integration Example

ServiceMix may be downloaded at `http://servicemix.apache.org`. This example uses ServiceMix 4.2.0. All the components in this example will following the JBI standard, since the ServiceMix project has not ported all the binding components to OSGi at the time of writing this book. OSGi will, however, be leveraged to deploy the JBI components. ServiceMix has similar requirements for Java SE and Maven to

Mule, as discussed previously. ActiveMQ is included with ServiceMix to support remoting, clustering, reliability, and distributed failover. ActiveMQ will also be used as the message broker for this example.

To create the integration example, four service units will be needed. A JBI service unit (SU) is a JBI component packaged up with the necessary configuration files and dependencies so it may be deployed in a JBI container.

- An SU using a `servicemix-http` components will be used, allowing the process to be kicked off via an http endpoint.
- Two SUs using the `servicemix-jms` components will be needed: one for publishing the message to and one for receiving the message from the JMS broker.
- Finally a SU using the `servicemix-camel` component will be used to log the incoming JMS message.

In order to deploy the four SUs, you must wrap them up in a JBI Service Assembly (SA). A JBI SA is used to package up JBI SUs for deployment to a JBI compliant container. The concept is similar to a JEE EAR file.

First create the directory servicemix and change into that directory. Next create the SA and the four ServiceMix JBI SUs and the SA using the Maven archetypes by issuing the commands shown in Listing 2–7.

Listing 2–7. *Maven Archetype Creation Commands*

```
mvn archetype:create
  -DarchetypeGroupId=org.apache.servicemix.tooling
  -DarchetypeArtifactId=servicemix-jms-provider-service-unit
  -DarchetypeVersion=2010.02-SNAPSHOT
  -DremoteRepositories=https://repository.apache.org/content/groups/public
  -DgroupId=com.apress.prospringintegration.jms
  -DartifactId=jms-provider-su -Dversion=1.0-SNAPSHOT

mvn archetype:create
  -DarchetypeGroupId=org.apache.servicemix.tooling
  -DarchetypeArtifactId=servicemix-http-consumer-service-unit
  -DarchetypeVersion=2010.02-SNAPSHOT
  -DremoteRepositories=https://repository.apache.org/content/groups/public
  -DgroupId=com.apress.prospringintegration.jms
  -DartifactId=http-consumer-su
  -Dversion=1.0-SNAPSHOT

mvn archetype:create
  -DarchetypeGroupId=org.apache.servicemix.tooling
  -DarchetypeArtifactId=servicemix-service-assembly
  -DarchetypeVersion=2010.02-SNAPSHOT
  -DremoteRepositories=https://repository.apache.org/content/groups/public
  -DgroupId=com.apress.prospringintegration.jms
  -DartifactId=example-sa
  -Dversion=1.0-SNAPSHOT

mvn archetype:create
  -DarchetypeGroupId=org.apache.servicemix.tooling
  -DarchetypeArtifactId=servicemix-jms-consumer-service-unit
  -DarchetypeVersion=2010.02-SNAPSHOT
  -DremoteRepositories=https://repository.apache.org/content/groups/public
  -DgroupId=com.apress.prospringintegration.jms
```

```
  -DartifactId=jms-consumer-su
  -Dversion=1.0-SNAPSHOT

mvn archetype:create
  -DarchetypeGroupId=org.apache.servicemix.tooling
  -DarchetypeArtifactId=servicemix-camel-service-unit
  -DarchetypeVersion=2010.02-SNAPSHOT
  -DremoteRepositories=https://repository.apache.org/content/groups/public
  -DgroupId=com.apress.prospringintegration.jms
  -DartifactId=camel-su
  -Dversion=1.0-SNAPSHOT
```

The archetype will create boilerplate Maven modules with the following names for the four SUs and the SA:

- `http-consumer-su` for the http endpoint
- `jms-provider-su` for JMS publishing
- `jms-consumer-su` for JMS receiving
- `camel-su` to log the JMS message
- `example-sa` for the SA wrapper

In addition, a root Maven `pom.xml` file is needed. This will allow the entire project to be built with a single command. The root `pom.xml` to support this example is shown below in Listing 2–8.

Listing 2–8. Root pom.xml File

```
<?xml version="1.0" encoding="UTF-8"?>
<project xmlns="http://maven.apache.org/POM/4.0.0"
         xmlns:xsi="http://www.w3.org/2001/XMLSchema-instance"
         xsi:schemaLocation="http://maven.apache.org/POM/4.0.0
  http://maven.apache.org/maven-v4_0_0.xsd">

  <modelVersion>4.0.0</modelVersion>

  <groupId>com.apress.prospringintegration.servicemix</groupId>
  <artifactId>servicemix-example</artifactId>
  <packaging>pom</packaging>
  <version>1.0-SNAPSHOT</version>
  <name>ServiceMix Example</name>

  <modules>
    <module>http-consumer-su</module>
    <module>jms-provider-su</module>
    <module>jms-consumer-su</module>
    <module>camel-su</module>
    <module>example-sa</module>
  </modules>

</project>
```

Note that the SUs and SA are listed as Maven modules in the `pom.xml` file. The ServiceMix example project should now have the directory structure shown in Listing 2–9.

***Listing 2–9.** ServiceMix Example Project Directory Structure*

```
servicemix
--pom.xml
--camel-su
  --...
--http-consumer-su
  --...
--jms-consumer-su
  --...
--jms-provider-su
  --...
--example-sa
  --...
```

The example-sa SA must be configured to include the four SUs so that all the SU modules are compiled and packaged into a SA. This is done by adding each to the SUs as Maven dependencies to the example-sa pom.xml file. The additions to the pom.xml file are shown in Listing 2–10.

***Listing 2–10.** example-sa pom.xml Dependencies*

```
<dependencies>
  <dependency>
    <groupId>com.apress.prospringintegration.jms</groupId>
    <artifactId>http-consumer-su</artifactId>
    <version>1.0-SNAPSHOT</version>
  </dependency>
  <dependency>
    <groupId>com.apress.prospringintegration.jms</groupId>
    <artifactId>jms-provider-su</artifactId>
    <version>1.0-SNAPSHOT</version>
  </dependency>
  <dependency>
    <groupId>com.apress.prospringintegration.jms</groupId>
    <artifactId>jms-consumer-su</artifactId>
    <version>1.0-SNAPSHOT</version>
  </dependency>
  <dependency>
    <groupId>com.apress.prospringintegration.jms</groupId>
    <artifactId>camel-su</artifactId>
    <version>1.0-SNAPSHOT</version>
  </dependency>
</dependencies>
```

Next, the http-consumer-su SU needs to be configured. The SUs are configured through the xbean.xml file in the directory src/main/resources. The http:consumer element attributes need to be modified as listed in Table 2–1 to expose the http endpoint http://localhost:8192/example/ and send the message to the endpoint jms-provider.

Table 2–1. http-consumer Attributes

Attribute	Value
targetService	test:provider
targetEndpoint	jms-provider
locationURI	http://0.0.0.0:8192/example/
defaultMep	http://www.w3.org/2004/08/wsdl/in-only

At the writing of this book, the archetypes for ServiceMix 4.2.0 are still SNAPSHOT versions and require some modifications to work. Many of the namespaces are incorrect and some of the dependency versions have not been properly replaced. A working version of the xbean.xml file is shown in Listing 2–11.

Listing 2–11. http-consumer-su xbean.xml

```
<?xml version="1.0" encoding="UTF-8"?>
<beans xmlns:http="http://servicemix.apache.org/http/1.0"
       xmlns:test="http://servicemix.apache.org/test"
       xmlns="http://www.springframework.org/schema/beans"
       xmlns:xsi="http://www.w3.org/2001/XMLSchema-instance"
       xsi:schemaLocation="http://servicemix.apache.org/http/1.0
        http://servicemix.apache.org/schema/servicemix-http-2010.01.xsd
        http://www.springframework.org/schema/beans
        http://www.springframework.org/schema/beans/spring-beans-2.0.xsd">

  <http:consumer
      service="test:http"
      endpoint="http-endpoint"
      targetService="test:provider"
      targetEndpoint="jms-provider"
      locationURI="http://localhost:8192/example/"
      defaultMep="http://www.w3.org/2004/08/wsdl/in-only"/>

</beans>
```

Next, the jms-provider-su and jms-consumer-su SUs need to be configured. Again, the SUs are configured through the xbean.xml file in the src/main/resources directory of the SU project. The important attributes of the jms:provider element are shown in Table 2–2; they're configured to receive a message sent from the http-consumer-su component to the test:provider service. The jms-provider endpoint is configured to send a JMS message to the queue my.queue.

Table 2–2. jms-provider Attributes

Attribute	Value
service	test:provider
endpoint	jms-provider
destinationName	my.queue

The complete xbean.xml file for the jms-provider-su SU is shown in Listing 2–12. Note the amq:ConnectionFactory element that is configured to connect to the embedded ActiveMQ broker. Also note the use of the # symbol before the connectionFactory reference in the jms:provider element. This allows a reference to the ActiveMQ connection factory Spring bean.

***Listing 2–12.** jms-provider-su xbean.xml*

```
<?xml version="1.0" encoding="UTF-8"?>
<beans xmlns:jms="http://servicemix.apache.org/jms/1.0"
       xmlns:test="http://servicemix.apache.org/test"
       xmlns:amq="http://activemq.apache.org/schema/core"
       xmlns="http://www.springframework.org/schema/beans"
       xmlns:xsi="http://www.w3.org/2001/XMLSchema-instance"
       xsi:schemaLocation="http://servicemix.apache.org/jms/1.0
        http://servicemix.apache.org/schema/servicemix-jms-2010.01.xsd
        http://activemq.apache.org/schema/core
        http://activemq.apache.org/schema/core/activemq-core-5.3.0.xsd
        http://www.springframework.org/schema/beans
        http://www.springframework.org/schema/beans/spring-beans-2.0.xsd">

  <jms:provider service="test:provider"
                endpoint="jms-provider"
                destinationName="my.queue"
                connectionFactory="#connectionFactory"/>

  <amq:connectionFactory id="connectionFactory" brokerURL="tcp://localhost:61616"/>

</beans>
```

The jms-provider-su and jms-consumer-su SUs have the additional requirement of adding the ActiveMQ dependencies to the pom.xml file. The additional dependencies are shown in Listing 2–13.

***Listing 2–13.** jms-provider-su and jms-consumer-su pom.xml Additional Dependencies*

```
<dependency>
  <groupId>org.apache.activemq</groupId>
  <artifactId>activemq-core</artifactId>
  <version>5.3.0</version>
  <exclusions>
    <exclusion>
      <groupId>org.apache.activemq</groupId>
      <artifactId>activeio-core</artifactId>
```

```
        </exclusion>
        <exclusion>
          <groupId>org.apache.camel</groupId>
          <artifactId>camel-core</artifactId>
        </exclusion>
        <exclusion>
          <groupId>commons-logging</groupId>
          <artifactId>commons-logging</artifactId>
        </exclusion>
        <exclusion>
          <groupId>commons-logging</groupId>
          <artifactId>commons-logging-api</artifactId>
        </exclusion>
      </exclusions>
    </dependency>
        <!-- this is a dependency for ActiveMQ -->
    <dependency>
    <groupId>org.apache.geronimo.specs</groupId>
    <artifactId>geronimo-j2ee-management_1.1_spec</artifactId>
    <version>1.0.1</version>
    </dependency>
```

Then the `jms-consumer-su` SU needs to be configured to receive the JMS message from the destination queue `my.queue`. As with the other SU, the `xbean.xml` file in the `src/main/resources` directory needs to be modified. The attributes of the `jms:consumer` element need to be modified, with the `targetService` set to `test:consumer` and the `destinationName` set to `my.queue`. The attributes and their values are given in Table 2–3.

***Table 2–3.** jms-consumer Attributes*

Attribute	Value
service	test:consumer
endpoint	jms-consumer
targetService	test:consumer
destinationName	my.queue

The complete `xbean.xml` configuration file for the `jms-consumer-su` SU is given in Listing 2–14.

***Listing 2–14.** jms-consumer-su xbean.xml*

```
<?xml version="1.0" encoding="UTF-8"?>
<beans xmlns:jms="http://servicemix.apache.org/jms/1.0"
       xmlns:test="http://servicemix.apache.org/test"
       xmlns:amq="http://activemq.apache.org/schema/core"
       xmlns="http://www.springframework.org/schema/beans"
       xmlns:xsi="http://www.w3.org/2001/XMLSchema-instance"
       xsi:schemaLocation="http://servicemix.apache.org/jms/1.0
       http://servicemix.apache.org/schema/servicemix-jms-2010.01.xsd
```

```
       http://activemq.apache.org/schema/core
       http://activemq.apache.org/schema/core/activemq-core-5.3.0.xsd
       http://www.springframework.org/schema/beans
       http://www.springframework.org/schema/beans/spring-beans-2.0.xsd">

  <jms:consumer service="test:consumer"
                targetService="test:consumer"
                endpoint="jms-consumer"
                destinationName="my.queue"
                connectionFactory="#connectionFactory"
                concurrentConsumers="8"/>

  <amq:connectionFactory id="connectionFactory" brokerURL="tcp://localhost:61616"/>

</beans>
```

In addition, there is an issue with the `pom.xml` file generated by the `servicemix-jms-consumer-service-unit` artifact. The version element of one the plug-in dependencies is not correctly set. The `pom.xml` file with the correct version for the jbi-maven-plug-in element is shown in Listing 2–15.

Listing 2–15. *Corrected pom.xml for jms-consumer*

```
<?xml version="1.0" encoding="UTF-8"?>
<project xmlns="http://maven.apache.org/POM/4.0.0"
         xmlns:xsi="http://www.w3.org/2001/XMLSchema-instance"
         xsi:schemaLocation="http://maven.apache.org/POM/4.0.0
     http://maven.apache.org/xsd/maven-4.0.0.xsd">

  <modelVersion>4.0.0</modelVersion>

  <groupId>com.apress.prospringintegration.jms</groupId>
  <artifactId>jms-consumer-su</artifactId>
  <packaging>jbi-service-unit</packaging>
  <version>1.0-SNAPSHOT</version>
  <name>Apache ServiceMix :: JMS Consumer Service Unit</name>

  <dependencies>
    <dependency>
      <groupId>org.apache.servicemix</groupId>
      <artifactId>servicemix-jms</artifactId>
      <version>2010.01</version>
    </dependency>
  </dependencies>

  <build>
    <resources>
      <resource>
        <directory>src/main/resources</directory>
        <includes>
          <include>**/*</include>
        </includes>
      </resource>
    </resources>
    <plugins>
```

```
      <plugin>
        <groupId>org.apache.servicemix.tooling</groupId>
        <artifactId>jbi-maven-plugin</artifactId>
        <version>4.3</version>
        <extensions>true</extensions>
      </plugin>
    </plugins>
  </build>

</project>
```

The last SU to configure is camel-su. This SU is only used for logging the JMS message. But Camel has many more capabilities, including message routing and its own set of adapters. But this is beyond the scope of this book. Please refer to the Camel documentation for further information. In the case of Camel, the configurations are found in the file camel-context.xml in the src/main/resources directory. The configuration is straightforward, simply routing the JMS message from the jms-consumer endpoint to ServiceMix's built-in logging support. The camel-context.xml file is given in Listing 2–16.

Listing 2–16. *camel-su camel-context.xml*

```
<?xml version="1.0" encoding="UTF-8"?>
<beans xmlns="http://www.springframework.org/schema/beans"
       xmlns:xsi="http://www.w3.org/2001/XMLSchema-instance"
       xsi:schemaLocation="
       http://www.springframework.org/schema/beans
       http://www.springframework.org/schema/beans/spring-beans-2.0.xsd
       http://activemq.apache.org/camel/schema/spring
       http://activemq.apache.org/camel/schema/spring/camel-spring.xsd">

  <camelContext id="camel"
                xmlns="http://camel.apache.org/schema/spring">
    <route>
      <from uri="jbi:endpoint:http://servicemix.apache.org/test/consumer/jms-consumer" />
      <to uri="log:com.apress.prospringintegration.jms?level=INFO" />
    </route>
  </camelContext>

</beans>
```

This completes the configuration of the SU and SA for the integration example. The next step is to create the SA deployable by issuing the Maven command maven install. This will build all the SUs and SA, which will create the deployable ZIP file example-sa-1.0-SNAPSHOT.zip in the example-sa/target directory. This file may be deployed to ServiceMix using either Maven or the OSGi ServiceMix console. First, start ServiceMix by running the command bin/servicemix in the ServiceMix installation directory. This will bring up a console. Type the following command:

```
osgi:install -s mvn:com.apress.prospringintegration.jms/example-sa/1.0-SNAPSHOT/zip
```

Then type in log:display to list the logging file. If everything has gone well, there should not be any exceptions.

In order the test the endpoint, an XML message must be posted to the endpoint http://localhost:8192/example. Since ServiceMix messaging is limited to XML format, a simple text value will not work. Either use the client.html file provided by the ServiceMix installation in the directory examples/bridge-camel, or use the Firefox Poster plug-in to post an XML message. After the XML message is sent to ServiceMix, it should be published to the JMS broker, and then received and logged by ServiceMix. Either check the service log file or type in the command `log:display` in the console to see the message. Typical output is shown in Listing 2–17.

***Listing 2–17.** Sample Output for the ServiceMix Example*

```
21:19:35,233 | INFO  | x-camel-thread-3 | jms                                   | rg.
apache.camel.processor.Logger   88 | Exchange[BodyType:org.apache.servicemix.soa
p.util.stax.StaxSource, Body:<test>This is a test</test>]
```

OpenESB (GlassFish)

OpenESB is the integration solution from Sun (now Oracle) based on the JBI and J2EE standards.

Philosophy and Approach

OpenESB is designed to run in an application server such as GlassFish. It does not have any Maven support out of the box, and instead is tightly coupled to NetBeans IDE. OpenESB offered an alternative to the existing Oracle integration solutions, which include the Oracle SOA suite and BEA Aqualogic. Oracle recently reduced the funding to the OpenESB project, and OpenESB's future will heavily depend on community support if it is to survive. OpenESB is best used with a WSDL first approach, leveraging the NetBeans IDE and deploying to GlassFish. This is the approach that will be taken for the integration example.

Implementing the Integration Example

A SOAP endpoint will be created to kick off a BPEL process sending a JMS message. Another BPEL process will receive the JMS message and log the results. SOAP and BPEL are used to integrate easily with the OpenESB framework. OpenESB 2.2 may be downloaded from `https://open-esb.dev.java.net`. The full install package is used for this example.

1. Run the installation program to install NetBeans and GlassFish. (OpenESB requires Java SE 1.6.)
2. Start NetBeans by double-clicking the icon on Windows, or by typing the command `bin/netbeans` in the NetBeans installation home directory.
3. Once NetBeans has started, close the start page. Then you can start GlassFish from the IDE by going to the Services tab. Expand the Servers tab, right-click the GlassFish icon, and select Start from the menu. This will start the GlassFish application server, as shown in Figure 2–1.

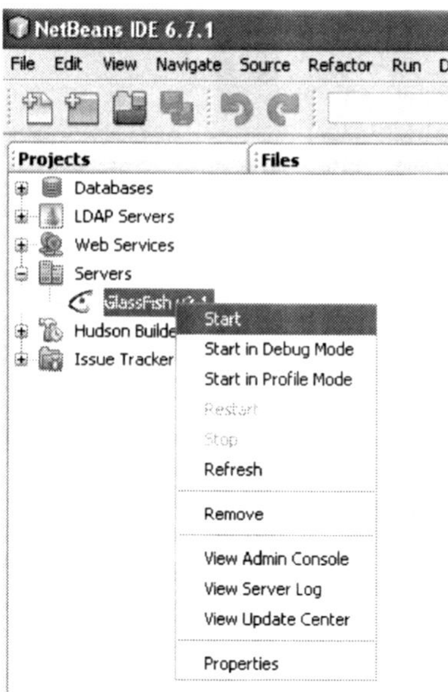

Figure 2–1. Starting the GlassFish application server

OpenESB is optimized to orchestrate the integration process using the BPEL process engine. The process engine will control the flow of the messages between the different components. The first step is to create the BPEL flow.

1. Start by creating a BPEL module by selecting File ➤ New Project from the main menu, which will bring up the New Project wizard.
2. Select the SOA category and the BPEL Module project, as shown in Figure 2–2.

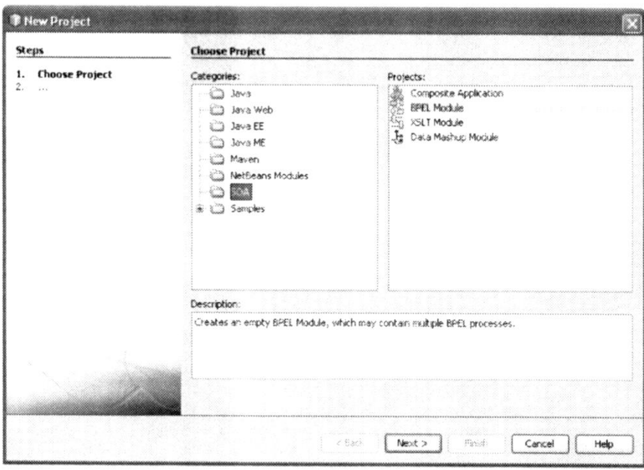

Figure 2–2. New Project wizard

3. Click the Next button, name the project JmsExample, and click the Finish button. This will create a BPEL project called JmsExample.

The next step is to create a WSDL file to represent the BPEL process interface. This allows the BPEL flow to be kicked off by a web service call. A SOAP RPC Literal WSDL file will be created, since it is the easiest to integrate with the testing framework in NetBeans.

1. Right-click the Process Files directory under the JmsExample BPEL module and select New ➤ WSDL Document. This should bring up the New WSDL Document wizard.

2. Name the WSDL document jmsProvider, select Concrete WSDL Document for the WSDL type, and accept the defaults, SOAP and RPC Literal, in the drop-down boxes below, as shown in Figure 2–3. Click the Next button, accept the defaults on the next two screens, and click Finish to create the WSDL document.

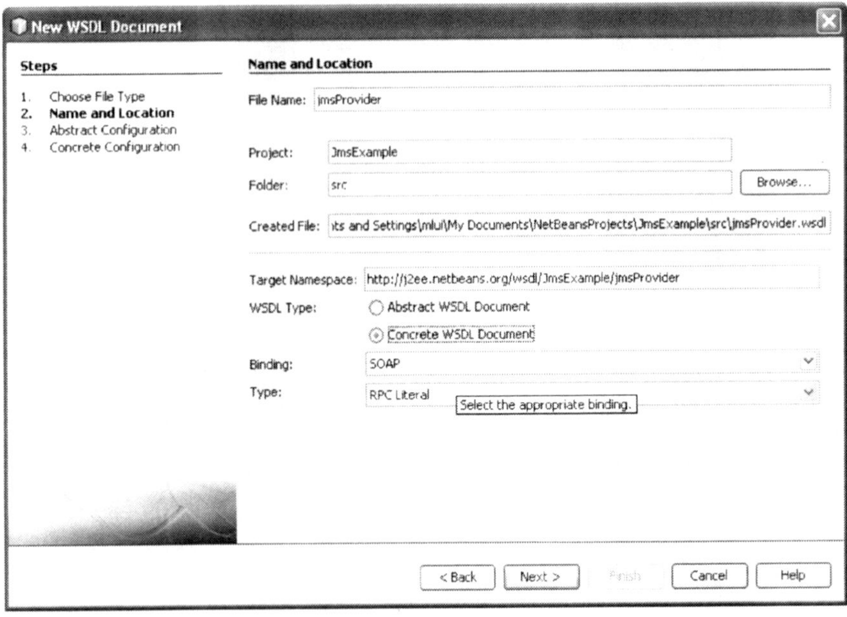

Figure 2–3. New WSDL Document wizard

3. Double-click `jmsExample.bpel` in project explorer on the left side of the IDE to bring up the BPEL design diagram. To add the WSDL document to the BPEL process, drag and drop the `jmsProvider.wsdl` file on the left side of the BPEL diagram. An orange dot will light up when the file is properly placed. The resulting BPEL diagram is shown in Figure 2–4.

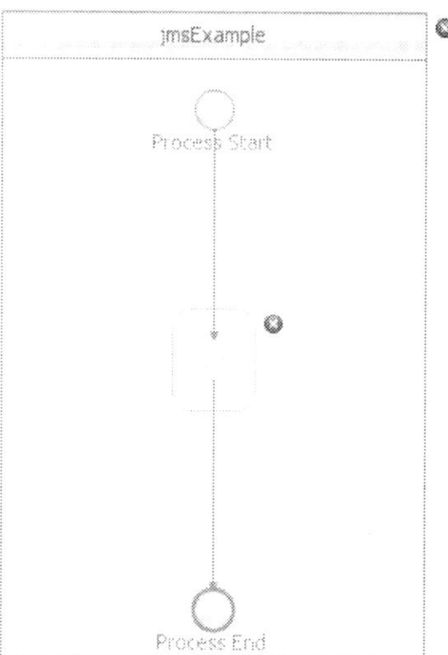

Figure 2–4. *jmsExample BPEL design diagram*

4. The next step will be to connect the SOAP WSDL to the BPEL process. The WSDL represents the SOAP binding component, which will be configured as an endpoint to the BPEL service engine. A Receive and Reply activity will be added to the BPEL process, and configured to receive the SOAP request and reply with a SOAP response. An Assign activity will be placed between the Receive and Reply activity so that the SOAP request message will be directly mapped to the response. Later, the same message payload will be sent to the JMS broker.
5. Drag and drop a Receive activity from the BPEL component palette on the left, as shown in Figure 2–5, to the center of the BPEL diagram. Again, an orange dot will appear when the activity is correctly placed.

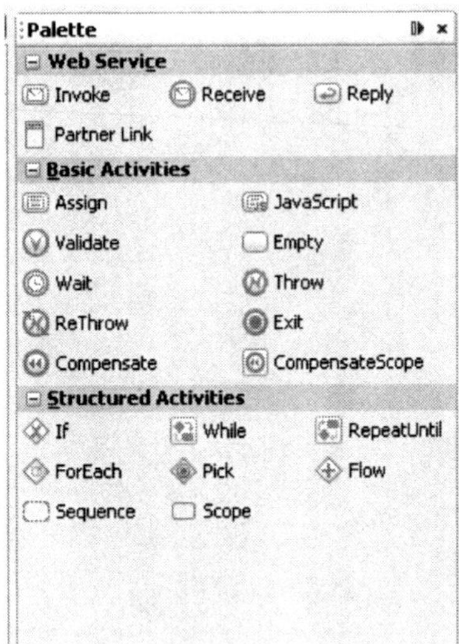

***Figure 2–5.** BPEL component palette*

6. Next, drag and drop the Assign activity right below the Receive activity. Similarly, drag and drop the Reply activity right below the Assign activity. The resultant BPEL diagram is shown in Figure 2–6.

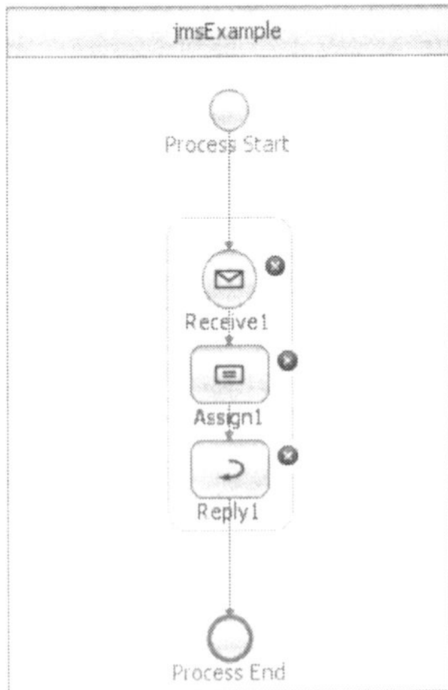

***Figure 2–6.** jmsExample BPEL diagram*

7. The BPEL activities are configured by double-clicking the icon in the jmsExample diagram, which will bring up the Property Editor.
8. Select PartnerLink1 and jmsProviderOperation from the Partner Link and Operation drop-downs, respectively, as shown in Figure 2–7. Then click OK. The BPEL process is now configured to start after receiving the SOAP request.

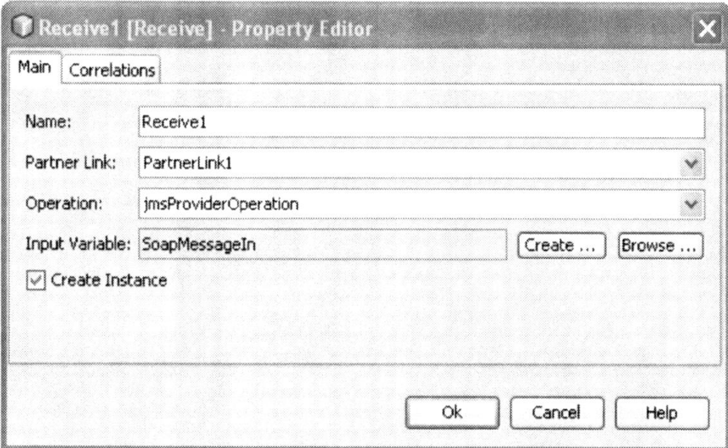

Figure 2–7. Configuring the Receive activity

9. Click the Create button to bring up the New Input Variable wizard, shown in Figure 2–8. Enter the name SoapMessageIn and click OK.

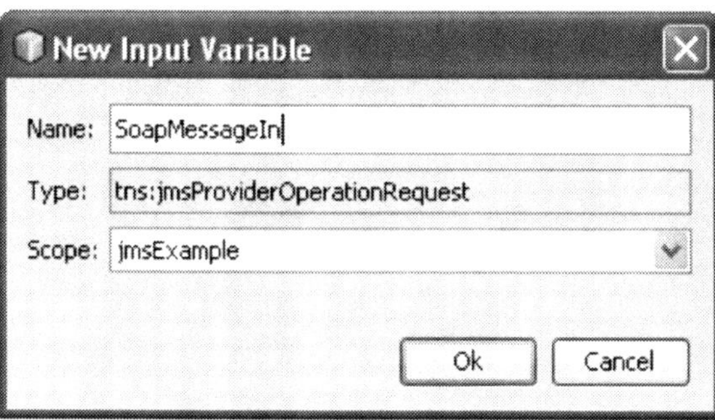

Figure 2–8. Configuring the Receive activity input variable

10. Next in the BPEL process is configured to Reply with a SOAP response. Double-click the Reply activity icon in the BPEL diagram to bring up the Property Editor.
11. Choose PartnerLink1 from the Partner Link drop-down and JmsProviderOperation from the Operation drop-down, as shown in Figure 2–9. The BPEL process with the configured SOAP endpoint is shown in Figure 2–10.

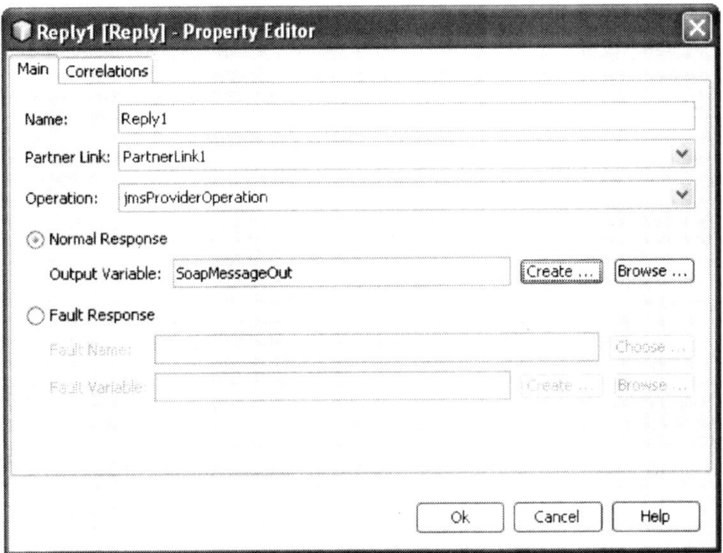

Figure 2–9. Configuring the Reply activity

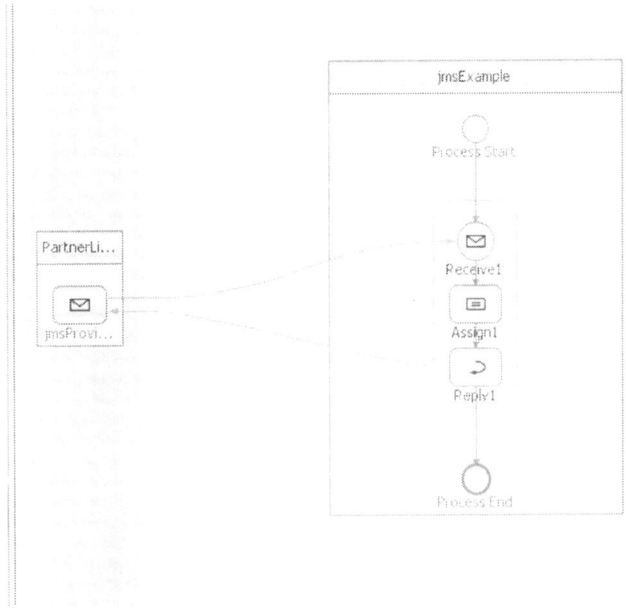

Figure 2–10. Complete jmsExample BPEL process

12. Again, click the Create button and specify a normal response output variable name of SoapMessageOut, as shown in Figure 2–11. Click the Ok button to return to the Property Editor. (To simplify the example, the fault response is not being used.)

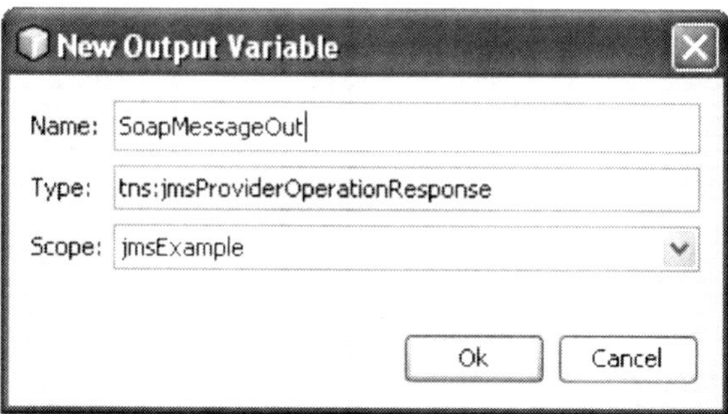

Figure 2–11. Configuring the Reply activity output variable

You configure the Assign activity by double-clicking its icon in the BPEL diagram, which brings up the data mapping tool. For simplicity, the input payload will be mapped to the output. The only purpose for exposing the BPEL process is to provide a hook to start it. The payload being passed is irrelevant to this example, and is directly mapped to ensure that the process is working. Drag the `part1` variable under `SoapMessageIn` on the right to the `part1` variable under `SoapMessageOut`, as shown in Figure 2–12.

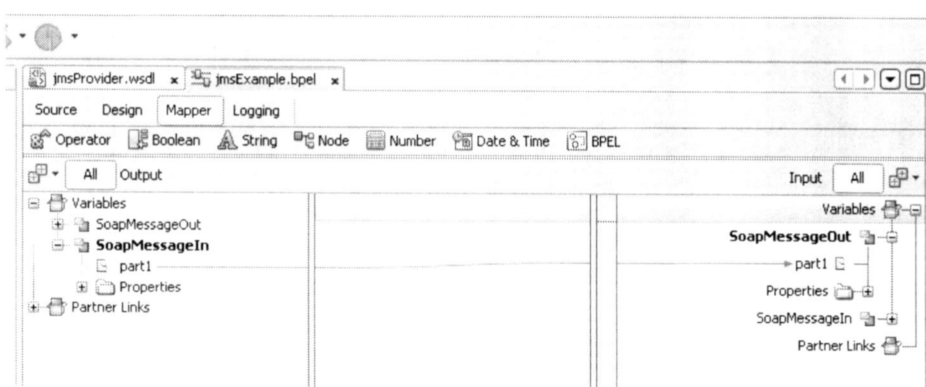

Figure 2–12. Configuring the Assign activity mapping

The JMS binding components now need to be configured for sending and receiving the JMS message. Again, the New WSDL Document wizard is used following the WSDL first approach used previously.

1. Right-click the Process Files directory under the jmsExample BPEL module in the project explorer, and select New ➤ WSDL Document.

2. Name the WSDL jmsPublish, select the Concrete WSDL Document radio button, and choose JMS from the Binding drop-down and Send from the Type drop-down, as shown in Figure 2–13. Click Next.

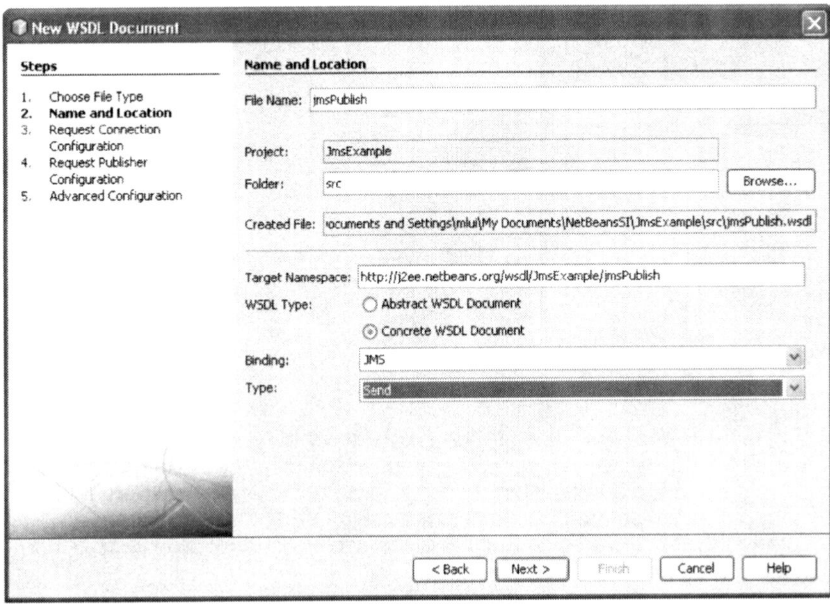

Figure 2–13. WSDL wizard for the Send JMS binding component

3. On the next screen, set the connection URL to `mq://localhost:7676`. This is the connection for the internal OpenESB JMS broker. Set the username and password to "guest," select the defaults for the embedded JMS broker, and click Next, as shown in Figure 2–14.

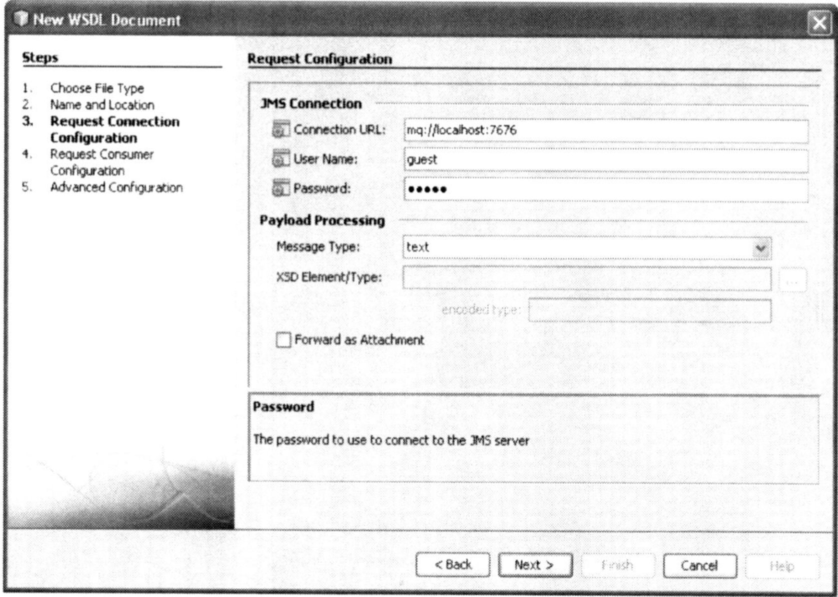

Figure 2–14. Setting the broker parameters

4. Click Finish to create the jmsPublish binding component. Repeat the same process to create the binding component to receive the JMS message.

5. Repeat the preceding steps to create the JMS component to receive the JMS message. Name the WSDL jmsReceive, select Concrete WSDL Document, and choose JMS and Receive from the drop-downs, as shown in Figure 2–15. The JMS configurations will be the same as those for jmsPublish, as shown in Figure 2–14.

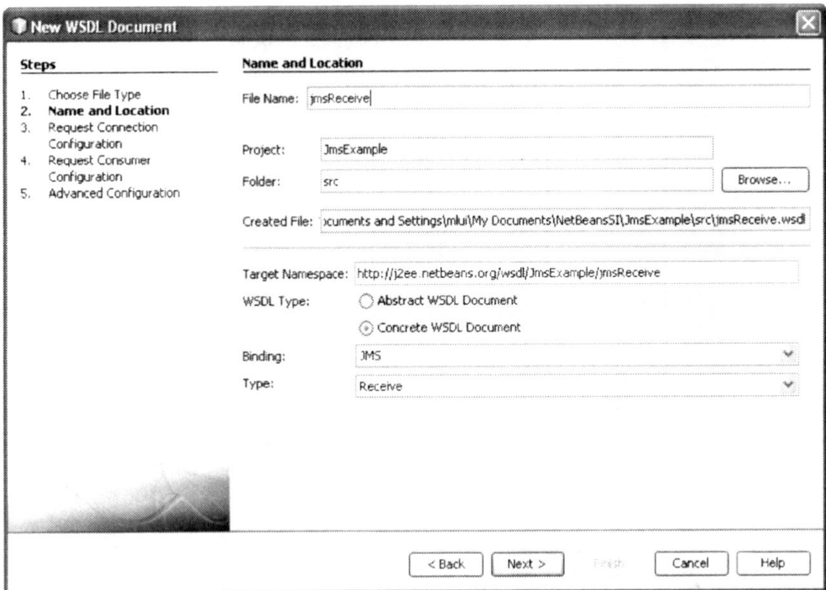

Figure 2–15. WSDL wizard for the Receive JMS binding component

6. Add the Invoke activity to the jmsExample BPEL process by dragging and dropping the icon from the BPEL component palette to right under the Receive activity.

7. Click the Ok button to return to the Property Editor. Choose PartnerLink2 from the Partner Link drop-down and JMSOutOperation from the Operation drop-down, as shown in Figure 2–16.

8. Double-click the Invoke icon to bring up the Property Editor. Click the Create button specify an input variable name of JMSMessageIn. Click the Ok button to complete the configuration.

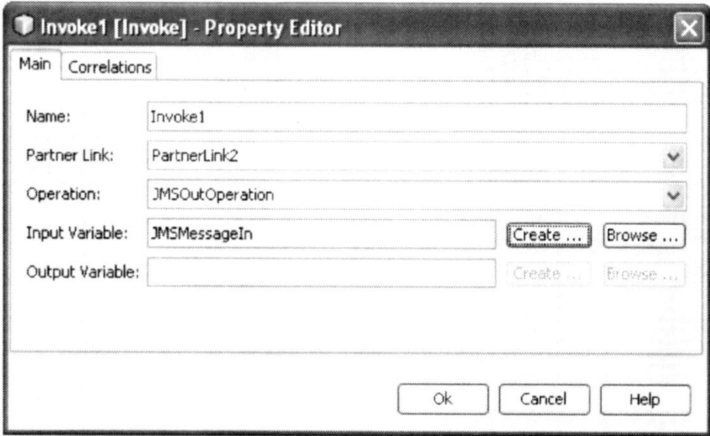

Figure 2–16. Configuring the Invoke activity for JMS Send

9. Place an Assign activity between the Receive and Invoke activities by dragging and dropping the Assign activity from the BPEL activity palette. Double-click the Assign activity to bring up the mapping tool. Expand and drag the `part1` variable under `SoapMessageIn` on the left side to the `part1` variable under `JMSMessageIn` on the right side to configure the SOAP payload to be sent to the JMS message broker, as shown in Figure 2–17. The final BPEL process is shown in Figure 2–18.

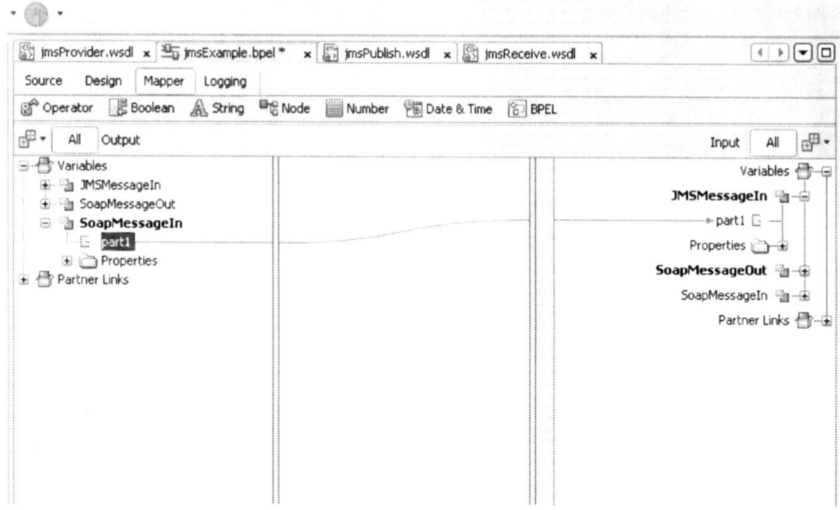

Figure 2–17. Configuring the Assign activity for JMS Send

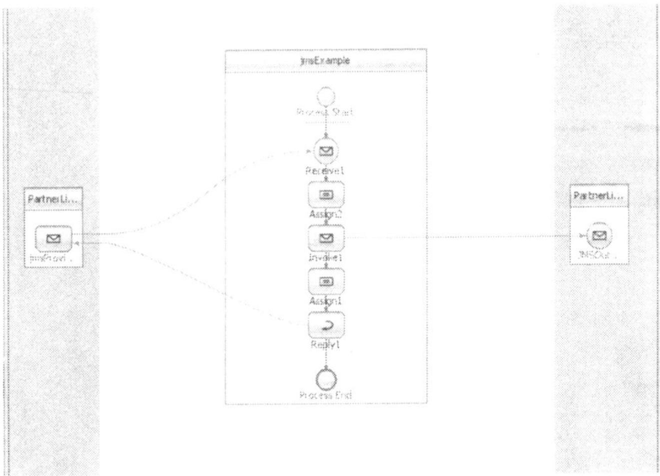

Figure 2–18. Complete jmsExample BPEL diagram which publishes a JMS message

10. Another BPEL process must be created to receive the JMS message from the broker. As with the jmsExample BPEL process, right-click the Process Files directory under the JmsExample BPEL module in the left-hand project explorer and select New ➤ BPEL Process. This will bring up the New BPEL Process wizard, as shown in Figure 2–19.

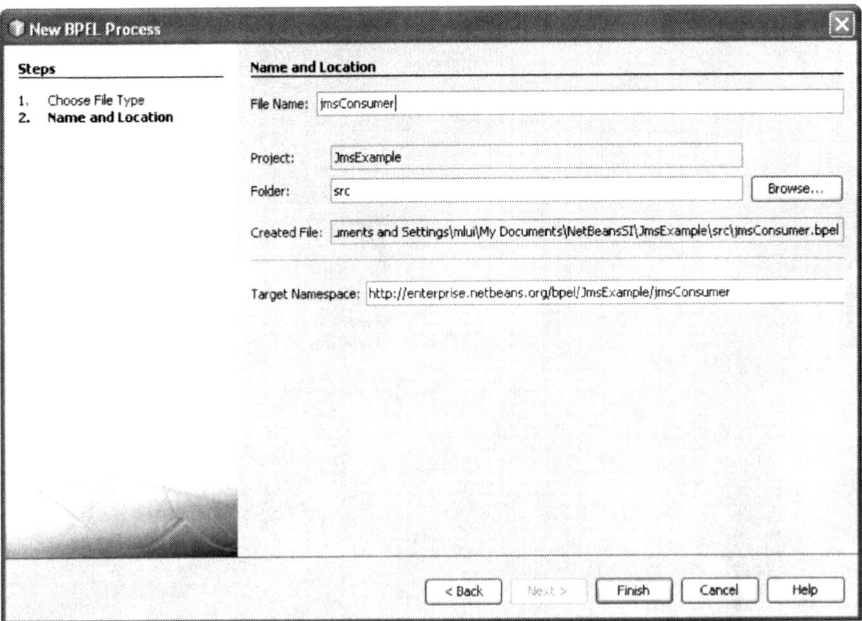

Figure 2–19. New BPEL Process wizard for the JMS Receive activity

11. Name the process jmsConsumer and click the Finish button.
12. Drag and drop the `jmsReceive.wsdl` binding component from the project explorer to the left side of the BPEL process diagram. As before, an orange dot will light up when the component is properly placed. Add a Receive activity from the component palette to the center of the BPEL design diagram.
13. Set Partner Link to PartnerLink1 and Operation to JMSInOperation, as shown in Figure 2–20.

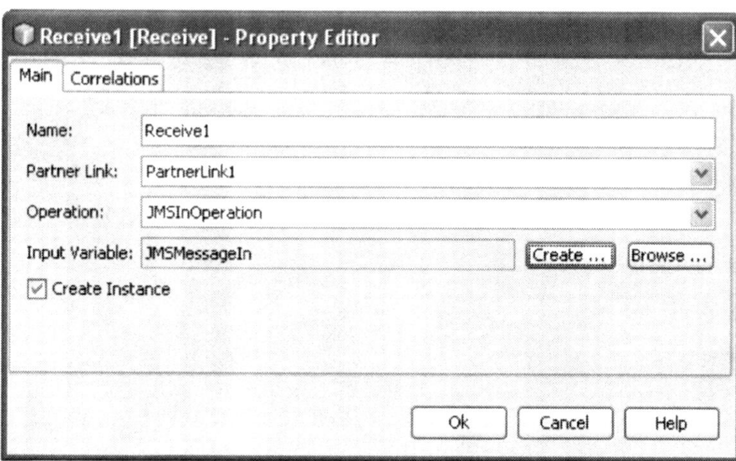

***Figure 2–20.** Property Editor for the JMS Receive activity*

14. Double-click the Receive activity to bring up the Property Editor. Click the Create button to specify an input variable name of JMSMessageIn. Click the Ok button to return to the Property Editor, and click Ok again to complete the configuration.

In order to show that the BPEL process does indeed receive the JMS message, logging will be added to the Receive activity.

1. Select the Receive activity in the BPEL process diagram and click the Logging button in the top menu. This will bring up the log mapping tool, as shown in Figure 2–21.

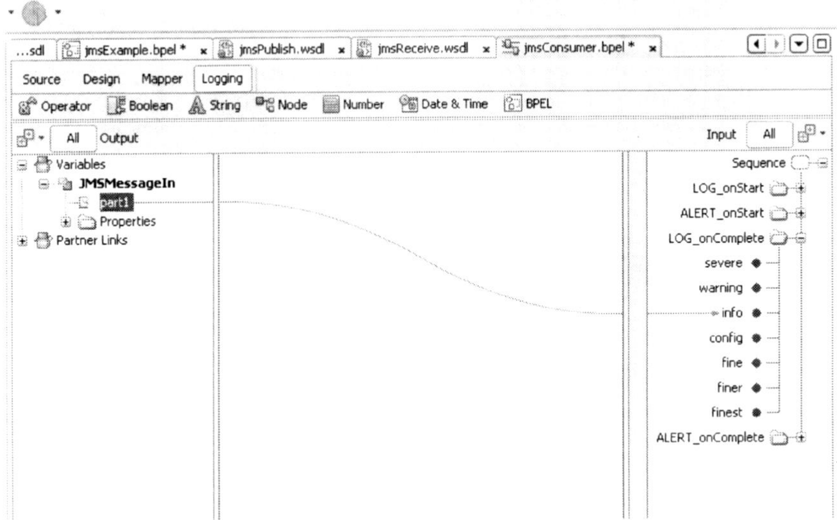

***Figure 2–21.** Log mapping for the incoming JMS message*

2. Expand and drag the `part1` variable under `JMSMessageIn` to the `info` logging variable under the `LOG_onComplete` directory. This will log the JMS message at the info level after the BPEL process receives the JMS message. The complete BPEL process is shown in Figure 2–22.

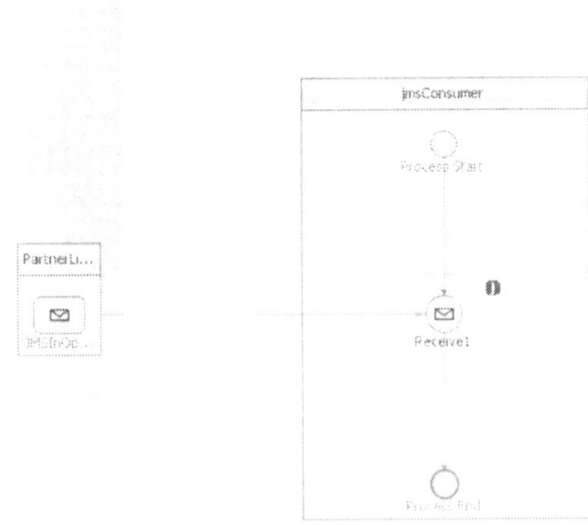

***Figure 2–22.** Complete jmsConsumer BPEL process*

3. Build the JmsExample BPEL module by right-clicking the JmsExample project in the left-hand project explorer and selecting Build. This will build the BPEL service unit.

In order to deploy the BPEL module service unit, you must wrap it in a composite application service assembly.

1. Select from NetBean's main menu File ➤ New Project to bring up the project wizard shown in Figure 2–23.

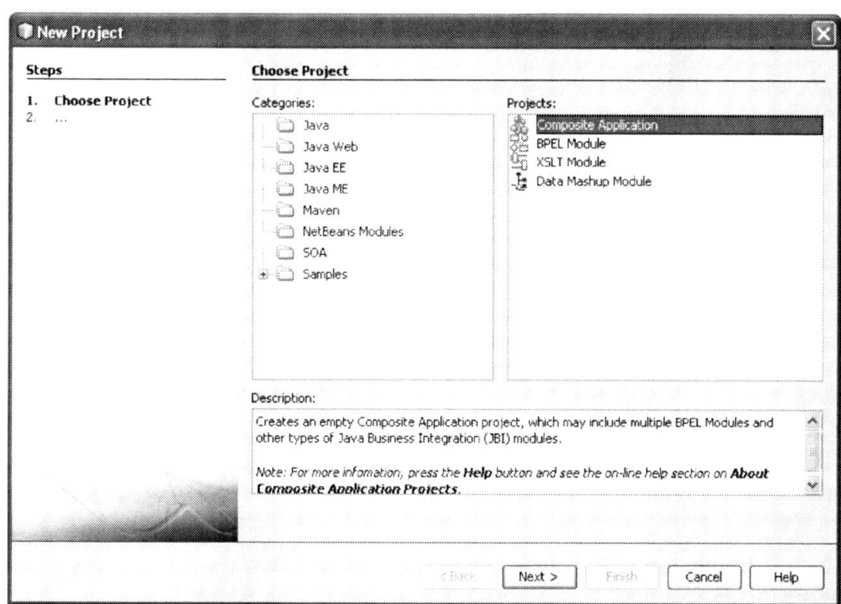

Figure 2–23. Creating the Composite Application project for the deployable service assembly

2. Select the SOA category and the Composite Application project.
3. Click the Next button and name the project JmsCAP (for JMS Composite Application project), and click the Finish button to create the project.
4. Drag and drop the JmsExample project onto the center of the JmsCAP composite application design diagram. Then build the JmsCAP composite application by right-clicking the JmsCAP project in the left-hand project explorer and selecting Build. This will build the composite application service assembly; the design diagram should look like Figure 2–24.

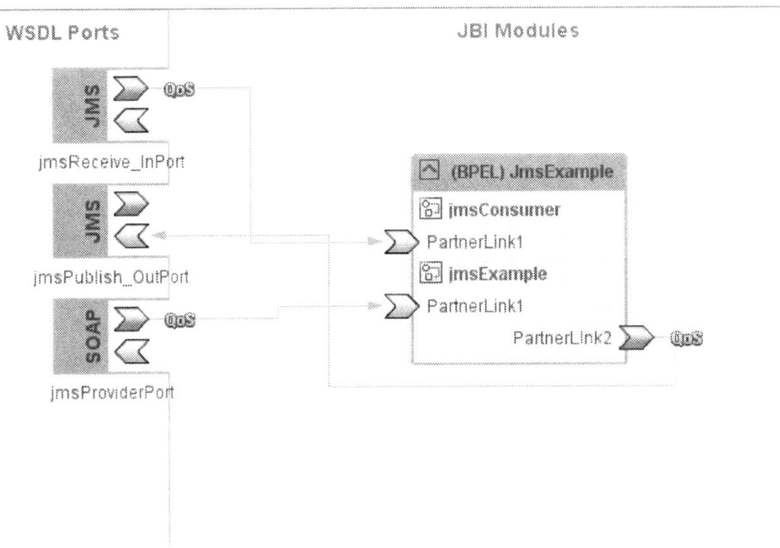

Figure 2–24. *Complete composite application service assembly*

5. You can now deploy the complete project to GlassFish by right-clicking the JmsCAP project and selecting Deploy. This completes creating the integration example using OpenESB.

The project may now be tested using NetBeans's built-in testing facility. A unit test may be created based on the jmsProvider WSDL, which drives the main BPEL process that publishes a JMS message.

1. Right-click the Test directory under the JmsCAP project and select New Test Case. This will bring up the Test Case wizard, as shown in Figure 2–25. Accept the defaults and click the Next button.

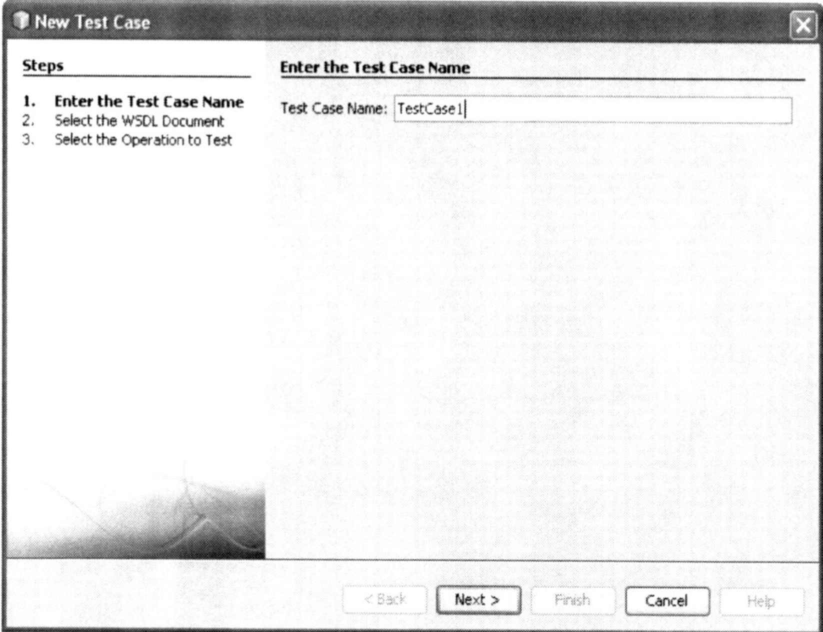

Figure 2–25. New Test Case wizard

2. Expand the JmsExample - Process File directory, select jmsProvider.wsdl, and click the Next button, as shown in Figure 2–26.

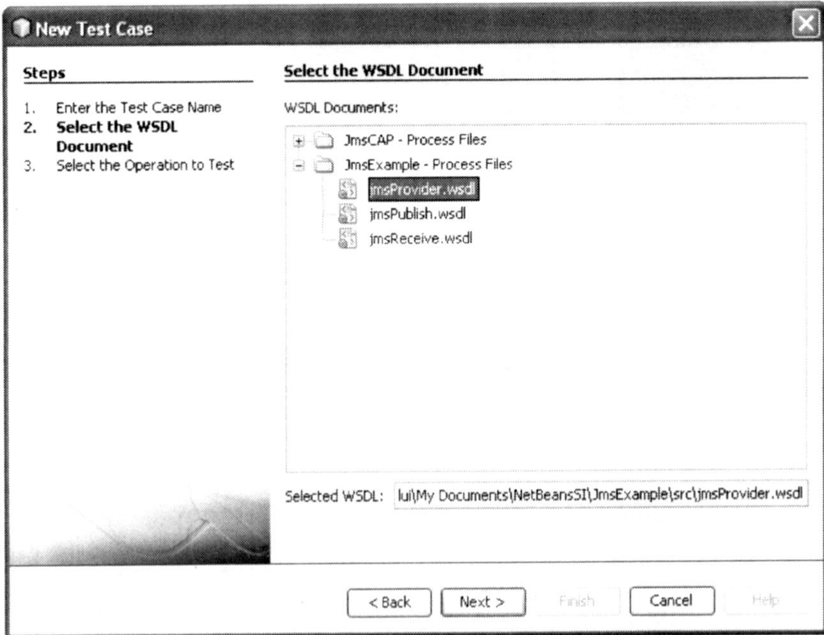

Figure 2–26. *Specifying the SOAP WSDL in the New Test Case wizard*

3. Select jmsProviderOperation and click Finish as shown in Figure 2–27. This creates a unit test for the SOAP endpoint. After creating the test case, the XML SOAP request will be displayed in NetBeans, as shown in Listing 2–18.

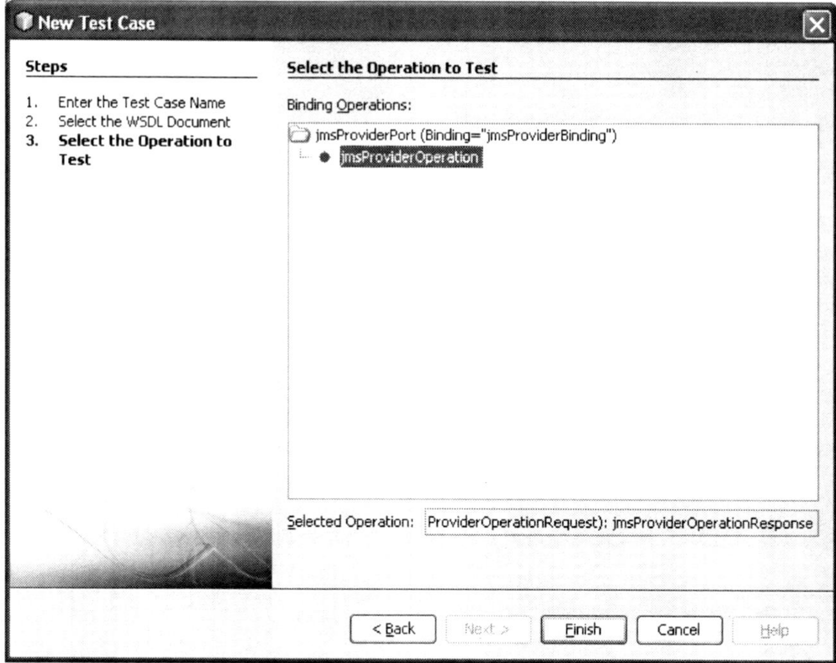

Figure 2–27. Specifying the WSDL operation in the Test Case wizard

Listing 2–18. Test Case SOAP XML Request Message

```
<soapenv:Envelope xsi:schemaLocation="http://schemas.xmlsoap.org/soap/envelope/➥
 http://schemas.xmlsoap.org/soap/envelope/" xmlns:xsi="http://www.w3.org/2001/➥
XMLSchema-instance" xmlns:xsd="http://www.w3.org/2001/XMLSchema"➥
 xmlns:soapenv="http://schemas.xmlsoap.org/soap/envelope/"➥
 xmlns:jms="http://j2ee.netbeans.org/wsdl/JmsExample/jmsProvider">
  <soapenv:Body>
    <jms:jmsProviderOperation>
      <part1>test</part1>
    </jms:jmsProviderOperation>
  </soapenv:Body>
</soapenv:Envelope>
```

4. Set the `part1` element to `test`. You can start the unit test by right-clicking TestCase1 under the Test directory and selecting Run. The unit test will fail since the results have not been properly set up.

5. On the dialog box, click Yes to the Overwrite Empty Output? button to save the SOAP response. Right-click the unit test results in the project explorer and select Use as Output to prevent future test failures. The SOAP response is shown in Listing 2–19.

Listing 2–19. Test Case SOAP XML Response Message

```
<?xml version="1.0" encoding="UTF-8" standalone="no"?>
<SOAP-ENV:Envelope xmlns:SOAP-ENV="http://schemas.xmlsoap.org/soap/envelope/"
    xmlns:xsi="http://www.w3.org/2001/XMLSchema-instance"
    xsi:schemaLocation="http://schemas.xmlsoap.org/soap/envelope/↩
 http://schemas.xmlsoap.org/soap/envelope/">
  <SOAP-ENV:Body>
    <m:jmsProviderOperationResponse xmlns:m=↩
"http://j2ee.netbeans.org/wsdl/JmsExample/jmsProvider">
      <part1>test</part1>
    </m:jmsProviderOperationResponse>
  </SOAP-ENV:Body>
</SOAP-ENV:Envelope>
```

6. Look at the GlassFish log output by selecting Output and GlassFish v2.1 in the bottom window. The JMS message received by the jmsConsumer BPEL process should be logged to the GlassFish console output.

DIY Architecture, or How Not to Do an Integration

The J2EE platform provides the necessary pieces to implement an integration without resorting to one of the integration frameworks. In this section, we'll go through it.

Philosophy and Approach

The JCA framework was developed to create a consistent method of connecting to external applications and systems—similar to JDBC for databases and JMS for messaging. However, creating a JCA RA or connection is still a complex process requiring the implementation of several interfaces and configuration files. Fortunately, RAs for the more common connectors are available either from open source projects or commercial vendors. Still, implementing an integration just using the J2EE platform requires a large amount of custom coding. The message routing and data transformation must all be written from scratch.

Implementing the Integration Example

The integration example may be implemented using the JBoss application server. The process may be kicked off by posting rom a web browser to a servlet. The servlet will publish the JMS message to the JMS broker embedded in JBoss. A message-driven EJB will receive the JMS message and log the message to the console. JBoss 4.2.3 may be downloaded from `http://jboss.org/jbossas/`. Installation just requires a simple decompression of the ZIP file. The integration example skeleton is created again using a Maven archetype. The project is created by issuing the Maven command in Listing 2–20.

Listing 2–20. Maven Command for Creating a Simple J2EE Project

```
mvn archetype:create
  -DgroupId=com.apress.prospringintegration.j2ee
  -DartifactId=j2ee-example
  -DarchetypeArtifactId=maven-archetype-j2ee-simple
```

The Maven command creates the project structure shown in Listing 2–21.

Listing 2–21. j2ee-example Project Structure

```
j2ee-example
--ear
  --pom.xml
--ejbs
  --src
    --main
      --resources
        --META-INF
          --ejb-jar.xml
  --pom.xml
--primary-source
  --pom.xml
--projects
  --logging
    --pom.xml
  --pom.xml
--servlets
  --servlet
    --src
      --main
        --webapp
          --WEB-INF
            --web.xml
          --index.jsp
    --pom.xml
  -- pom.xml
--src
  --main
    --resources
--pom.xml
```

Remove the element `<module>site</module>` from the `modules` element in the main `pom.xml` file in the `j2ee-example` directory. The `site` module is not being used for this example, and removing it will allow the project to be built. The first step is to create a servlet that will accept a form POST with the string parameter `message`. First, modify the servlet `pom.xml` file in the directory `servlets/servlet`. The dependencies for the servlet, MS client, and JBoss JARs are added. The modified `pom.xml` file is shown in Listing 2–22.

Listing 2–22. Servlet pom.xml

```
<project>
  <modelVersion>4.0.0</modelVersion>
  <groupId>root.project.servlets</groupId>
  <artifactId>servlet</artifactId>
  <packaging>war</packaging>
  <name>servlet</name>
  <parent>
    <groupId>root.project</groupId>
    <artifactId>servlets</artifactId>
    <version>1.0</version>
  </parent>
  <dependencies>
```

```
    <dependency>
      <groupId>root.project</groupId>
      <artifactId>primary-source</artifactId>
      <scope>provided</scope>
    </dependency>
    <dependency>
      <groupId>javax.servlet</groupId>
      <artifactId>servlet-api</artifactId>
      <version>2.4</version>
      <scope>provided</scope>
    </dependency>
    <dependency>
      <groupId>javax.jms</groupId>
      <artifactId>jms</artifactId>
      <version>1.1</version>
    </dependency>
    <dependency>
      <groupId>jboss</groupId>
      <artifactId>jbossmq-client</artifactId>
      <version>4.0.2</version>
    </dependency>
  </dependencies>
  <repositories>
    <repository>
      <id>jboss</id>
      <url>https://repository.jboss.org/nexus/content/groups/public</url>
      <releases>
      </releases>
      <snapshots>
        <enabled>false</enabled>
      </snapshots>
    </repository>
  </repositories>
</project>
```

The next step is to create the directory for the servlet. Under the directory `servlets/servlet/src/main`, add the directory structure `java/com/apress/prospringintegration/j2ee`. The servlet class is added to this directory, as shown in Listing 2–23.

Listing 2–23. *JmsServlet Class*

```
package com.apress.prospringintegration.j2ee.servlet;

import javax.jms.*;
import javax.naming.Context;
import javax.naming.InitialContext;
import javax.naming.NamingException;
import javax.servlet.RequestDispatcher;
import javax.servlet.ServletException;
import javax.servlet.http.HttpServlet;
import javax.servlet.http.HttpServletRequest;
import javax.servlet.http.HttpServletResponse;
import java.io.IOException;
```

```
public class JmsServlet extends HttpServlet {

    private static final String QUEUE_CONNECTION_FACTORY = "ConnectionFactory";
    private static final String EXAMPLE_QUEUE = "queue/examples/ExampleQueue";

    public void doGet(HttpServletRequest request, HttpServletResponse response)
            throws ServletException, IOException {
        doPost(request, response);
    }

    public void doPost(HttpServletRequest request, HttpServletResponse response)
            throws ServletException, IOException {
        System.out.println("Servlet JmsServlet");
        String message = request.getParameter("message");
        System.out.println("message: " + message);
        try {
            Connection connection = getConnectionFactory().createConnection();
            Session session = connection.createSession(false, Session.AUTO_ACKNOWLEDGE);
            MessageProducer messageProducer = session.createProducer(getDestination());
            Message jmsMessage = session.createTextMessage(message);
            messageProducer.send(jmsMessage);
            System.out.println("Message sent to " + EXAMPLE_QUEUE);
            messageProducer.close();
            session.close();
            connection.close();
        } catch (JMSException e) {
            e.printStackTrace();
        }
        request.setAttribute("started", "true");
        RequestDispatcher dispatcher =
                getServletContext().getRequestDispatcher("/index.jsp");
        dispatcher.forward(request, response);
    }

    private ConnectionFactory getConnectionFactory() {
        ConnectionFactory jmsConnectionFactory = null;
        try {
            Context ctx = new InitialContext();
            jmsConnectionFactory = (ConnectionFactory)➥
 ctx.lookup(QUEUE_CONNECTION_FACTORY);
        } catch (NamingException e) {
            e.printStackTrace();
        }
        return jmsConnectionFactory;
    }

    private Destination getDestination() {
        Destination jmsDestination = null;
        try {
            Context ctx = new InitialContext();
            jmsDestination = (Destination) ctx.lookup(EXAMPLE_QUEUE);
        } catch (NamingException e) {
            e.printStackTrace();
        }
```

```
        return jmsDestination;
    }
}
```

The servlet accepts a POST with the parameter message. Using the JMS API, the parameter is published to the JMS broker queue. Java Naming and Directory Interface (JNDI) is used to get the JMS connection factory and destination. The `web.xml` file will need to be modified to expose the servlet through the servlet container. The modified `web.xml` file is shown in Listing 2–24. Note that the servlet class is mapped to the path `/SendJmsMessage`.

***Listing 2–24.** web.xml File*

```
<?xml version="1.0" encoding="ISO-8859-1"?>
<web-app xmlns="http://java.sun.com/xml/ns/j2ee"
         xmlns:xsi="http://www.w3.org/2001/XMLSchema-instance"
         xsi:schemaLocation="http://java.sun.com/xml/ns/j2ee↵
 http://java.sun.com/xml/ns/j2ee/web-app_2_4.xsd"
         version="2.4">
  <display-name>jboss-jms example</display-name>

  <servlet>
    <servlet-name>JmsServlet</servlet-name>
    <servlet-class>com.apress.prospringintegration.j2ee.servlet.JmsServlet</servlet-class>
  </servlet>

  <servlet-mapping>
    <servlet-name>JmsServlet</servlet-name>
    <url-pattern>/SendJmsMessage</url-pattern>
  </servlet-mapping>

</web-app>
```

The final step for exposing the servlet is to create a form page to submit the parameter message. This JSP page is created by Maven, and may be modified as shown in Listing 2–25. This is a simple HTML form that posts the parameter message to the servlet. This completes the endpoint that publishes a JMS message to the broker.

***Listing 2–25.** index.jsp Page*

```
<html>
<body>
<h2>JMS Integration Example</h2>
<form name="jmsForm" action="SendJmsMessage">
    Message: <input type="text" name="message" size="40"><br/>
    <br/><br/>
    <input type="submit" value="Send"/>
</form>
</body>
</html>
```

A message-driven EJB will be needed to receive the JMS message and log to the console. EJB 3.0 will be used so that only a simple set of annotations will be needed to configure the bean. But first the `pom.xml` file in the `ejbs` directory will need to be modified to support the message-driven bean. Java SE 1.6.x is used, since version 1.5.x or higher is required to support an annotated EJB. In addition, all the required dependencies for EJB 3.0 and JMS will be added. The modified `pom.xml` file is shown in Listing 2–26.

Listing 2–26. *pom.xml for Message-Driven EJB*

```
<project>
  <modelVersion>4.0.0</modelVersion>
  <groupId>root.project</groupId>
  <artifactId>ejbs</artifactId>
  <packaging>ejb</packaging>
  <version>1.0</version>
  <name>enterprise java beans</name>
  <parent>
    <groupId>root</groupId>
    <artifactId>project</artifactId>
    <version>1.0</version>
  </parent>
  <dependencies>
    <dependency>
      <groupId>root.project</groupId>
      <artifactId>primary-source</artifactId>
    </dependency>
    <dependency>
      <groupId>root.project.projects</groupId>
      <artifactId>logging</artifactId>
    </dependency>
    <dependency>
      <groupId>jboss</groupId>
      <artifactId>jboss-ejb3x</artifactId>
      <version>4.2.3.GA</version>
    </dependency>
    <dependency>
      <groupId>jboss</groupId>
      <artifactId>jboss-j2ee</artifactId>
      <version>4.2.3.GA</version>
    </dependency>
    <dependency>
      <groupId>javax.jms</groupId>
      <artifactId>jms</artifactId>
      <version>1.1</version>
    </dependency>
    <dependency>
      <groupId>jboss</groupId>
      <artifactId>jbossmq-client</artifactId>
      <version>4.0.2</version>
    </dependency>
  </dependencies>
  <build>
    <plugins>
      <plugin>
        <artifactId>maven-compiler-plugin</artifactId>
        <configuration>
          <source>1.6</source>
          <target>1.6</target>
```

```
          </configuration>
        </plugin>
        <plugin>
          <groupId>org.apache.maven.plugins</groupId>
          <artifactId>maven-ejb-plugin</artifactId>
          <version>2.3</version>
          <configuration>
            <ejbVersion>3.0</ejbVersion>
          </configuration>
        </plugin>
      </plugins>
    </build>
    <repositories>
      <repository>
        <id>jboss</id>
        <url>https://repository.jboss.org/nexus/content/groups/public</url>
        <releases>
        </releases>
        <snapshots>
          <enabled>false</enabled>
        </snapshots>
      </repository>
    </repositories>
</project>
```

Delete the `ejb-jar.xml` in the directory `ejbs/src/main/resource/META-INF`. It is not required for an EJB 3.0 bean. In the directory `ejbs/src/main`, add the following directory structure: `java/com/apress/prospringintegration/ejb/`. Add the message-driven bean class `JmsMessageBean.java` shown in Listing 2–27.

Listing 2–27. *JmsMessageBean.java (Message-Driven Bean)*

```
package com.apress.prospringintegration.ejb;

import javax.annotation.Resource;
import javax.ejb.ActivationConfigProperty;
import javax.ejb.MessageDriven;
import javax.ejb.MessageDrivenContext;
import javax.jms.Message;
import javax.jms.MessageListener;
import javax.jms.TextMessage;

@MessageDriven(name = "JmsMessageBean", activationConfig = {
        @ActivationConfigProperty(propertyName = "destinationType",
                                  propertyValue = "javax.jms.Queue"),
        @ActivationConfigProperty(propertyName = "destination",
                                  propertyValue = "queue/examples/ExampleQueue")
})
public class JmsMessageBean implements MessageListener {

    @Resource
    private MessageDrivenContext context;

    @Override
```

```
    public void onMessage(Message message) {
        try {
            if (message instanceof TextMessage) {
                TextMessage objMessage = (TextMessage) message;
                String textMessage = objMessage.getText();
                System.out.println("**************************************************");
                System.out.println("Received JMS message. message: " + textMessage);
                System.out.println("**************************************************");
            } else {
                System.err.println("Expecting Text Message");
            }
        } catch (Throwable t) {
            t.printStackTrace();
            context.setRollbackOnly();
        }
    }
}
```

Note the MessageDriven annotation which sets the destination type to Queue and the queue name to queue/examples/ExampleQueue. The message driven bean will receive JMS messages from the queue when deployed in a J2EE application server. The bean class implements the MessageListener interface so that the message is sent to the onMessage method. The rest of the code extracts the test message and logs.

You can build the project by running the Maven command mvn clean install. The EAR file ear-1.0.ear will be created in the directory ear/target. To deploy the EAR file to JBoss, copy the file to the directory server/default/deploy in the JBoss installation home directory. Start the JBoss server by running the command bin/run.bat on Windows or bin/run.sh on Unix. You can run the integration example by entering http://localhost:8080/servlet/SendJmsMessage in a browser. The web page is shown in Figure 2–28. Enter a message into the form and click the Send button. The message will be published to the broker, received by the message-driven bean, and logged to the JBoss console.

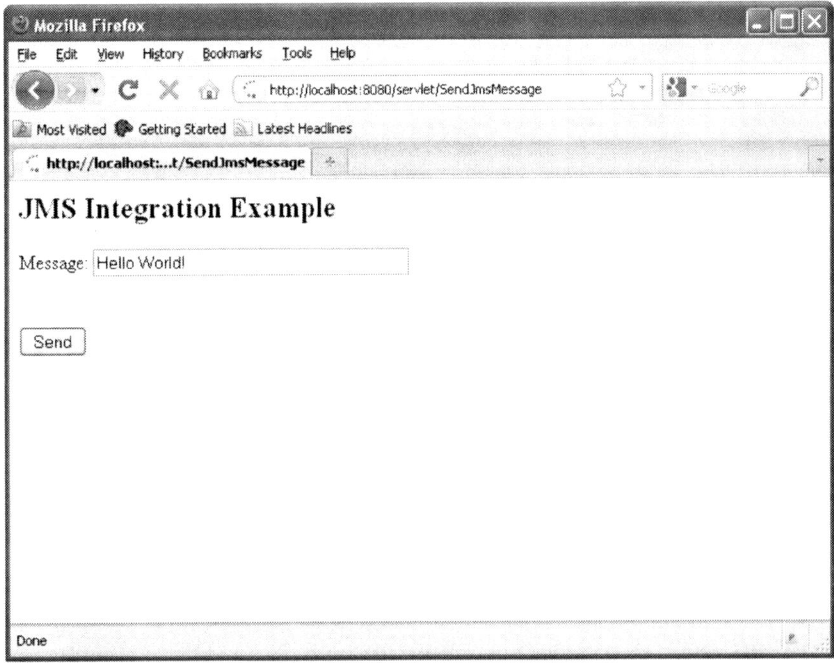

Figure 2–28. *j2ee-example Form Page*

How Do They Compare?

Four different frameworks have been used to handle an integration. They will now be compared on three criteria:

- Ease of use
- Maintainability
- Extensibility

Ease of Use

One of the most import aspects of a framework is how easy it is to use. A framework should reduce the amount of time for development, not create more complications.

- Mule is probably the easiest framework to use where the entire configuration takes place in a single XML file with custom logic in a Java POJO. The main limitation of Mule is the available transports or connections. Some of the important transports, such as JDBC, are limited in their functionality unless you purchase the enterprise edition.
- ServiceMix turned out to be quite complicated to configure with all its configuration and deployment files. The Maven archetypes simplified the development process, but were not always up to date with the latest version. Camel, which uses an approach similar to Mule, is an interesting addition to ServiceMix. It appears that Camel may even be used standalone with its own adapter support.
- OpenESB is definitely tightly coupled to the NetBeans IDE. OpenESB's reliance on the cryptic BPEL and WSDL languages, as well as its lack of Maven support, make the graphical design tool almost a requirement. Graphical tools always help with the visualization of the process flow, but issues with round-tripping between the design tool and code, along with issues with customization, usually offset the advantages. Even with the graphical tool, the number of steps required to create the simple integration examples was large.
- Implementing an integration strictly based on the J2EE platform is possible but difficult due to the large amount of interfaces to implement and configuration files to create.

Maintainability

One of the most important reasons for using a framework is maintainability. A framework typically forces the implementation to use a specific structure. This consistency and componentization allow future modifications to be made easily.

- Mule offers a consistent architecture but complete freedom in the process logic implementation. As long as this freedom is not violated, Mule should provide good maintainability.

- ServiceMix enforces a strict standard though the JBI specification and its component-based framework should produce a very maintainable code base.
- OpenESB is maintained through a graphical tool that has advantages and disadvantages. The tool enforces consistent implementation, but round-trip support with the actual code is always an issue. In addition, OpenESB's lack of Maven support causes difficulties with the current build processes.
- J2EE custom coding is probably not the way to go for maintainable code, since its lack of framework fails to enforce a consistent structure.

Extensibility

There are two major extensibility points for an integration framework. First, the adapter or connector framework allows integration with external applications and systems not currently supported by the particular framework. Second, extension of business logic, allowing for such things as custom message routing and data transformation, needs to be supported.

- Mule provides a framework and archetype to create custom transport components. In addition, all process flows can be sent through a simple POJO, providing an ideal extension point.
- ServiceMix also provides a framework for custom binding components and service engines. Interestingly, Camel, Mule and ServiceMix support the Spring component model.
- OpenESB also provides extension through JBI binding components and service engines. NetBeans provides wizards to create these custom extensions.
- J2EE extensions are done through EJBs and JCA RAs. RAs are complex to implement, as discussed previously.

Summary

This chapter covered a number of the alternatives to Spring Integration for an enterprise integration framework. Some of the possible alternatives not covered so far are Microsoft's BizTalk and the .NET framework. BizTalk's limitations—including its dependence on Windows—have prevented its market penetration.

All the different frameworks have their positives and negatives in terms of ease of use, maintainability, and extensibility; hopefully, this chapter has given a basis on which to compare them. The technologies discussed provide skin-deep support for the Spring component model, but fail to offer deep integration with the entire Spring portfolio. New, wayward developers must relearn the solution-specific way to solve problems already handily addressed by the Spring portfolio. Spring Integration, in contrast, is developed by the same people that made the Spring framework the most widely used Java technology today, and provides the most natural way to build lightweight, clean solutions to developers accustomed to Spring. The following chapters will focus on the strengths of Spring Integration and the reasons it is the integration solution of choice.

CHAPTER 3

Introduction to Core Spring Framework

Before diving into straight into Spring Integration, let's take a moment to review the basic Spring Framework on which Spring Integration is based. This chapter introduces the Spring Framework and provides a look at some of the major modules that support using Spring Integration. The Spring Framework provides a robust platform for developing complex enterprise solutions. Spring interfaces well with enterprise infrastructure such as JMS, JDBC, and JTA. Spring provides the best of both worlds: high-level abstractions when you want to apply features to your code with a minimal of changes, and accessible, low-level APIs that can be extended in an intuitive way.

Core Spring API Components

Spring is a container and component model. Everything else, including AOP, transactions, database access, web applications, and the like is built on top of this container and component model. Objects managed in the container do not have to know about Spring or the container because of Inversion of Control (IoC). This pattern specifies the involvement of the Spring container (which manages lifecycle), your object, and any other dependant objects – known as beans in Spring parlance. The container is able to inject any number or type of dependant beans together while specifying the relationship through configuration. Dependency injection is enabled by creating properties and matching setter methods of your target object for the types of objects that you expect to inject. Alternatively, objects may be injected during instantiation by providing a constructor with a signature that matches types you expect to inject. The core of Spring framework's functionality lies within this IoC container, which is discussed next.

The Inversion of Control Container

The Inversion of Control (IoC) container provides the dependency injection support to your applications that enables you to configure and integrate application and infrastructure components together (see Figure 3–1). Through IoC, your applications may achieve a low-level of coupling, because all of the bean configuration can be specified in terms of IoC idioms (such as property collaborators and constructors). Meanwhile, most if not all of your application's bean lifecycle (construction to destruction) may be managed from within the container. This enables you to declare *scope* – how and when a new object instance gets created, and when it gets destroyed. For example, the container may be instructed that a specific bean instance be created only once per thread, or that, upon destruction, a database bean may disconnect from any active connections. Through requests to the Spring IoC container, a new bean may either get constructed or a singleton bean may get passed back to the requesting bean. Either way, this is a transparent event that is configured along with the bean declaration.

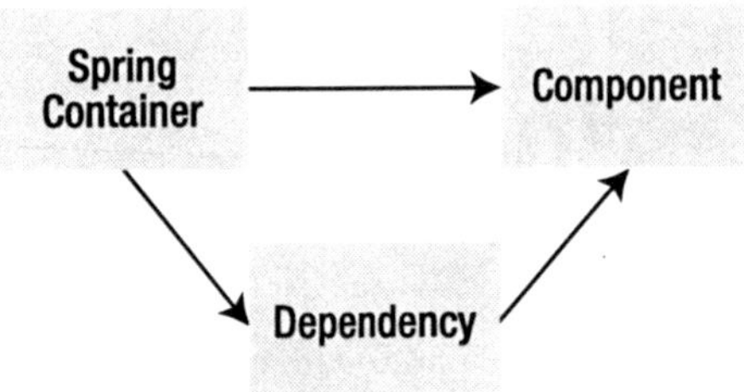

Figure 3–1. The IoC Process

Within the Spring framework are two packages: `org.springframework.beans` and `org.springframework.context` that expose the core functionality of the IoC container. The `org.springframework.beans.factory.BeanFactory` interface is designed to expose the basic functionality of any Spring container, and thus provides basic lifecycle methods for bean initialization and destruction. The `org.springframework.context.ApplicationContext` is a sub-interface of the `BeanFactory`, and offers more powerful features, such as Spring AOP integration, message resource handling, and further sub-interfaces, such as the `org.springframework.web.context.WebApplicationContext` used in web applications.

Spring Container Metadata Configuration

Spring provides several implementations of the `ApplicationContext` interface out of the box. In standalone applications using XML metadata (still commonplace today), it is common to create an instance of `org.springframework.context.support.ClassPathXmlApplicationContext` or `org.springframework.context.support.FileSystemXmlApplicationContext`. Configuration metadata consisting of bean definitions represented with XML or Java configuration is preferred for third-party APIs for which you do not have access to source code. In most other cases, configuration metadata – in addition to, or in place of XML – may be applied through Java annotations. To begin, we will illustrate XML configuration style as shown in Listing 3–1.

***Listing 3–1.** ioc_basics.xml – A Basic Spring Application Configuration File*

```
<?xml version="1.0" encoding="UTF-8"?>
<beans xmlns="http://www.springframework.org/schema/beans"
       xmlns:xsi="http://www.w3.org/2001/XMLSchema-instance"
       xsi:schemaLocation="http://www.springframework.org/schema/beans
    http://www.springframework.org/schema/beans/spring-beans-3.0.xsd">

 <bean class="com.apress.prospringintegration.corespring.iocbasics.BasicPOJO"/>

</beans>
```

This is a simple XML document that makes use of the Spring `beans` namespace – the basis for resolving your POJO within the Spring container. Let's take a look at the BasicPOJO object and expand on our metadata configuration further by populating the exposed properties with real values.

The properties that are wired directly by value using the `value` attribute must fit into one of the basic Java element types that are supported by locally available `PropertyEditors`. Spring provides a default set of `PropertyEditors` that encapsulate primitives such as `int`, `double`, and `String`, as well as more complex types such as `File`, `InputStream`, and URL. The range of `PropertyEditors` are discussed in depth later in this chapter when we explore defining a custom `PropertyEditor`.

Multiple Configuration Resources

As your application grows, it may become apparent that a large XML metadata file is cumbersome to evaluate and manage. To solve this, the XML file may be broken into multiple files, for example one file for JDBC and Hibernate configurations, another for JMX, and so on. Loading the files into your application can be done in a variety of ways. You may supply the relevant paths to ClassPathXmlApplicationContext or your ApplicationContext of choice. The more common approach is to supply resource paths to the import element within a *master* XML configuration file as shown in Listing 3–2.

***Listing 3–2.** Sample of Import Tag to Aid Configuration*

```
<beans>
  <import resource=”serviceDefinitions.xml” />
  <import resource=”serviceClients.xml” />
</beans>
```

Instantiating the IoC Container

To instantiate the IoC container and resolve a functional ApplicationContext instance, the relevant ApplicationContext implementation must be invoked with a specified configuration. With a standard Java application with XML metadata configuration, the ClassPathXmlApplicationContext will resolve any number of Spring XML configuration resources given a path relative to the base Java classpath. This constructor is overloaded with a variety of argument arrangements that provide ways to specify the resource locations. Spring also provides a number of other ApplicationContext implementations. For example, FileSystemXmlApplicationContext is used to load XML configuration from the file system (outside of the classpath), and AnnotationConfigApplicationContext supports loading annotated Java classes.

In Listing 3–3 the context constructor is given a single resolvable path of the Spring configuration XML file. If the XML resource were located outside of classpath, the absolute file system path would be provided to the FileSystemApplicationContext factory class to obtain the ApplicationContext.

***Listing 3–3.** BasicIoCMain.java – Single Line of Code to Startup you Application Context*

```
ApplicationContext ctx = new ClassPathXmlApplicationContext("ioc_basics.xml");
```

The next step is to obtain your configured beans. Simply calling ApplicationContext.getBean method (by passing it the class of the instance you want returned) will provide, by default, the singleton instance of the bean (see Listing 3–4). That is, every bean will be the same instance.

***Listing 3–4.** BasicIocMain.java - Obtaining a Bean Reference by Class.*

```
BasicPOJO basicPojo = ctx.getBean(BasicPOJO.class);
```

Alternatively, Spring can infer which bean definition your looking for by passing it the ID (or qualifier) of the bean instance instead of the bean class. This helps when dealing with multiple bean definitions of the same type. For instance, given a bean definition of the same BasicPojo class, Listing 3–5 illustrates the combined code effort in setting up and obtaining this bean resource.

***Listing 3–5.** BasicIocMain.java – Obtaining a Bean Reference by Name*

```
BasicPOJO basicPojo = (BasicPOJO)ctx.getBean("basic-pojo");
```

Bean Instantiation from the IoC Container

A basic operation in a Spring context is instantiating beans. This is done in a variety of ways; however, we will focus on the most common use cases. In this example, the `BasicPojo` bean provides both a no-arg and arguments-based constructor (see Listing 3–6). In addition, we have a POJO property named `color` with type `ColorEnum` (see Listing 3–7). We will use both `BasicPOJO` and `ColorEnum` objects to illustrate how you can define and populate your beans within Spring XML configuration.

***Listing 3–6.** Defining the BasicPOJO*

```
package com.apress.prospringintegration.corespring.iocbasics;

public class BasicPOJO {

    public String name;
    public ColorEnum color;
    public ColorRandomizer colorRandomizer;

    public BasicPOJO() {
    }

    public BasicPOJO(String name, ColorEnum color) {
        this.name = name;
        this.color = color;
    }

    public String getName() {
        return name;
    }

    public void setName(String name) {
        this.name = name;
    }

    public ColorEnum getColor() {
        return color;
    }

    public void setColor(ColorEnum color) {
        this.color = color;
    }

    public ColorRandomizer getColorRandomizer() {
        return colorRandomizer;
    }

    public void setColorRandomizer(ColorRandomizer colorRandomizer) {
        this.colorRandomizer = colorRandomizer;
    }
}
```

Listing 3–7. ColorEnum.java – Defining the ColorEnum

```
package com.apress.prospringintegration.corespring.iocbasics;

public enum ColorEnum {
    violet, blue, red, green, purple, orange, yellow
}
```

Constructor Injection

Constructor arguments may be set through XML configuration. This will enable you to inject dependencies through the constructor arguments. To do this, use the `constructor-arg` element within the bean definition, as shown in Listing 3–8.

Listing 3–8. ioc_basics.xml – XML Bean Construction using Parameterized Arguments

```
...
<bean id="constructor-setup"
      class="com.apress.prospringintegration.corespring.iocbasics.BasicPOJO">
  <constructor-arg name="name" value="red"/>
  <constructor-arg name="color" value="violet" />
</bean>
...
```

Bean References and Setter Injection

Bean properties may be injected into your target beans through references to other beans within the scope of your application context. This is known as bean collaboration. This requires defining the additional bean that you wish to refer to, also known as the collaborator. Using the `ref` attribute in the property tag enables us to tell Spring which bean we want to collaborate with, and thus have injected (see Listing 3–9).

Listing 3–9. ioc_basics.xml – XML Configuration for Bean Collaboration by Setting Injection

```
<bean id="no-args"
      class="com.apress.prospringintegration.corespring.iocbasics.BasicPOJO">
  <property name="color" ref="defaultColor"/>
  <property name="name" value="Mario"/>
</bean>

<bean id="defaultColor"
      class="com.apress.prospringintegration.corespring.iocbasics.ColorEnum"
      factory-method="valueOf">
  <constructor-arg value="blue"/>
</bean>
```

Static and Instance Factory Injection

Note the `factory-method` attribute on the defaultColor element. In this case the static factory method instantiation mechanism was used. Note also that the class attribute does not specify the type of object returned by a factory method, as it specifies only the type containing that factory method. For this simple example, a string was fed to the `enum` static factory method `valueOf`, which is the common approach to resolving `enum` constants from strings.

When static factory methods are not practical, use instance factory methods instead. These are methods that get invoked from existing beans on the container to provide new bean instances. The class in Listing 3–10 demonstrates instance factory methods to provide random ColorEnum instances.

Listing 3–10. *ColorRandomizer.java – Class Definition for the ColorRandomizer Factory Bean*

```
package com.apress.prospringintegration.corespring.iocbasics;

import java.util.Random;

public class ColorRandomizer {

    ColorEnum colorException;

    public ColorEnum randomColor() {
        ColorEnum[] allColors = ColorEnum.values();
        ColorEnum ret = null;
        do {
            ret = allColors[new Random().nextInt(allColors.length - 1)];
        }
        while (colorException != null && colorException == ret);

        return ret;
    }

    public ColorEnum exceptColor(ColorEnum ex) {
        ColorEnum ret = null;
        do {
            ret = randomColor();
        } while (ex != null && ex == ret);
        return ret;
    }

    public void setColorException(ColorEnum colorExceptions) {
        this.colorException = colorExceptions;
    }
}
```

To invoke the factory within our Spring context, ColorRandomizer will be defined as a bean, then one of its methods will be invoked in another bean definition as a way to vend an instance of ColorEnum. In Listing 3–11, we obtain two separate instances of ColorEnum using both ColorRandomizer factory methods to illustrate variances in factory method invocations.

Listing 3–11. *Obtaining Bean Instances from Factory Methods in Spring*

```
<!-- Factory bean for colors -->
<bean id="colorRandomizer"
      class="com.apress.prospringintegration.corespring.iocbasics.ColorRandomizer" />

<!-- gets a random color -->
<bean id="randomColor" factory-bean="colorRandomizer" factory-method="randomColor"/>

<!-- gets any color, except the random color defined above -->
<bean id="exclusiveColor" factory-bean="colorRandomizer" factory-method="exceptColor">
  <constructor-arg ref="randomColor"/>
</bean>
```

This example also shows a simple variation on `constructor-arg` element. When used with `factory-method`, it gets arranged as arguments to the factory method (instead of a constructor). This is the same as using a static factory-method where `factory-bean` is omitted.

An implementation class that utilizes the beans defined previously would look similar to Listing3–12.

Listing 3–12. *BasicIoCMain.java – Demonstrating Static and Factory Injection Client Code.*

```
ColorEnum colorEnum = (ColorEnum) app.getBean("randomColor");
System.out.println("randomColor: " + colorEnum);
colorEnum = (ColorEnum) app.getBean("exclusiveColor");
System.out.println("exclusiveColor: " + colorEnum);
```

Bean Scopes

Spring uses the notion of bean scopes to determine how beans defined in the IoC container get issued to the application upon request with `getBean` methods, or through bean references. A bean's scope is set with the `scope` attribute in the bean element, or by using the `@Bean` annotation in the class file. Spring defaults to the `singleton` scope, where a single instance of the bean gets shared throughout the entire container. Spring provides a total of six bean scopes out of the box for use in specific context implementations, although only `singleton`, `prototype`, and `thread` are available through all context implementation. The other scopes – `request`, `session`, and `globalSession` – are available only to application contexts that are web-friendly, such as `WebApplicationContext`.

Table 3–1. *Bean scopes available in Spring*

Singleton	Single bean instance per container, shared throughout the IoC container.
Prototype	New bean instance created per request.
Request	Web application contexts only: Creates a bean instance per HTTP request.
Session	Web application contexts only: Creates a bean instance per HTTP session.
GlobalSession	Web portlet only: Creates a bean instance per Global HTTP session.
Thread*	Creates a bean instance per thread. Similar to request scope.

** Thread scope is not registered by default, and requires registration with the CustomScopeConfigurer bean.*

To illustrate the behavior of prototype- and singleton-scoped beans, Listing 3–13 declares two beans of the same type, which differ only in scope. The value from the singleton-scoped bean should always return the same value, whereas the prototype-scoped bean will always return different values (since the factory returns random numbers). Listing 3–13 shows the Spring configuration file and Listing 3–14 shows the main class.

Listing 3–13. *ioc_basics.xml – Overriding Default Scope for Beans with XML Metadata*

```
<beans…>
<bean id="randomeverytime" factory-bean="colorRandomizer" factory-method="randomColor"
      scope="prototype"/>
```

```
<bean id="alwaysthesame" factory-bean="colorRandomizer factory-method="randomColor"
      scope="singleton"/>
</beans>
```

Listing 3–14. *BasicIocMain.java –Simple For-Loop*

```
public static void demonstrateScopes(ApplicationContext ctx) {
    for (int i = 0; i < 5; i++) {
        System.out.println("randomeverytime: " +
                ctx.getBean("randomeverytime", ColorEnum.class));
        System.out.println("alwaysthesame: " +
            ctx.getBean("alwaysthesame", ColorEnum.class));
    }
}
```

The output of this loop will emit text similar to Listing 3–15.

Listing 3–15. *Output of Bean Scope Induced Behavior*

```
randomeverytime: green
alwaysthesame: orange
randomeverytime: purple
alwaysthesame: orange
randomeverytime: violet
alwaysthesame: orange
randomeverytime: violet
alwaysthesame: orange
randomeverytime: green
alwaysthesame: orange
```

You register the `thread` scope, or any other custom scope, in XML by defining a `org.springframework.beans.factory.config.CustomScopeConfigurer` bean. Pass the scope implementation class to the map property scopes. The map property is evaluated with the key providing the scope name, and value having the scope's implementation class. Registering in this fashion is always compatible to `@Bean` annotated properties with the `@Scope` annotation. That is, a scope definition once enabled for any given scope is activated throughout the container and for all manners of configuration (see Listing3–16).

Listing 3–16. *Ioc_basics.xml – Registering Custom Scopes in XML*

```
<beans…>

<bean class="org.springframework.beans.factory.config.CustomScopeConfigurer">
  <property name="scopes">
    <map>
      <entry key="thread">
        <bean class="org.springframework.context.support.SimpleThreadScope"/>
      </entry>
    </map>
  </property>
</bean>

<bean id="threadColor" factory-bean="colorRandomizer" factory-method="randomColor"
      scope="thread"/>

</beans…>
```

Or, you may register the custom scope in Java by invoking registerScope method on a ConfigurableBeanFactory implementation such as XmlBeanFactory. This is useful where Java configuration is used.

Listing 3–17 will create a Spring context, request the thread-scoped threadColor bean, and display its value on the parent thread. When the same bean is requested from the child thread, org.springframework.context.support.SimpleThreadScope evaluates a java.lang.ThreadLocal variable that determines how the application should handle the bean request. In this case, a new instance of threadColor is factoried, and its value displayed.

Listing 3–17. *BasicThreadColorRunnable.java –Thread-Scoped Beans*

```
package com.apress.prospringintegration.corespring.iocbasics;

import org.springframework.context.ApplicationContext;
import org.springframework.context.support.ClassPathXmlApplicationContext;

public class BasicThreadColorRunnable implements Runnable {
    ApplicationContext ctx;

    public BasicThreadColorRunnable(ApplicationContext ctx) {
        this.ctx = ctx;
    }

    public final void run() {
        try {
            ColorEnum color = ctx.getBean("threadColor", ColorEnum.class);
            System.out.println("Child Thread color: " + color);
        } finally {
            // do nothing
        }
    }

    public static void main(String[] args) throws Exception {
        ApplicationContext app = new ClassPathXmlApplicationContext("ioc_basics.xml");
        ColorEnum threadColor = app.getBean("threadColor", ColorEnum.class);
        System.out.println("Parent thread color: " + threadColor);

        BasicThreadColorRunnable dcr = new BasicThreadColorRunnable(app);
        new Thread(dcr).start();
    }
}
```

■ **Note** Use ThreadScope with care! As of Spring 3.0, the ThreadScope does not support the destructive callback methods, meaning special resources associated with beans of this scope may never get closed, Garbage-Collected, and so on!

Customizing Bean Initialization and Disposal

Spring enables you to interact with the post-initialization and pre-destruction lifecycles of your beans so they can perform certain actions at those lifecycle endpoints. Such tasks may include connecting to a remote database server, or performing initialization tests upon startup, and disconnecting network connections, or cleaning up memory upon disposal. To gain better awareness of Spring lifecycle management, the following list shows each step of the process in which the IoC container engages your beans.

1. Create the bean instance via constructor or factory method.
2. Set the values and bean references to bean properties.
3. Call initialization callback methods.
4. Bean is ready for use.
5. Upon container shutdown, call destruction callback methods.

There are a few ways to take advantage of callbacks for initialization and destruction. First, Spring offered the `org.springframework.beans.factory.InitializingBean` and `org.springframework.beans.factory.DisposableBean` lifecycle interfaces. Overriding these interfaces exposed two methods – `afterPropertiesSet` and `destroy` (the notion of constructors and destructors will be familiar to C++ users) for post-initialization and pre-destruction, respectively. The same functionality may also be obtained by specifying an arbitrary method name to the `init-method` and `destroy-method` bean attributes within (XML or `@Bean` annotation) metadata configuration. Additionally, you can specify the JSR-250 (Common Annotations for Java Platform) annotations `@PostConstruct` and `@PreDestroy`. To leverage JSR-250 lifecycle annotations within Spring, you must register a org.springframework.context.annotation.CommonAnnotationBeanPostProcessor instance in the IoC container. An example of using the initialization and destruction callbacks is shown in Listing3–18 and 3–19.

Listing 3–18. *ioc_basics.xml –initialization and Destruction Callbacks*

```
<beans>
…
  <bean id="loggingColors"
        class="com.apress.prospringintegration.corespring.iocbasics.LoggingColorRandomizer"
        destroy-method="complete" init-method="init">
    <property name="logFile" value="colorLog.txt"/>
  </bean>
</beans>
```

Listing 3–19. *LoggingColorRandomizer.java – Initialization and Destructive Callbacks to POJO*

```
package com.apress.prospringintegration.corespring.iocbasics;

import java.io.File;
import java.io.FileWriter;
import java.io.IOException;

public class LoggingColorRandomizer extends ColorRandomizer {
    File logFile;
    FileWriter writer;

    public void setLogFile(File f) {
        this.logFile = f;
    }
```

```
void writeFileLine(String str) {
    try {
        writer.write(str + "\n");
        writer.flush();
    } catch (Exception e) {
        e.printStackTrace();
    }
}

public void init() throws IOException {
    writer = new FileWriter(logFile, true);
    writeFileLine("initialized.");
}

@Override
public ColorEnum randomColor() {
    ColorEnum col = super.randomColor();
    writeFileLine("randomColor: " + col);
    return col;
}

@Override
public ColorEnum exceptColor(ColorEnum ex) {
    ColorEnum col = super.exceptColor(ex);
    writeFileLine(" exceptColor:" + col);
    return col;
}

public void complete() throws IOException {
    writeFileLine("closed.\n");
    writer.close();
}
```

Simplifying Configuration with Bean Autowiring

In addition to explicit XML dependency definitions, Spring enables informal dependency resolution through the `autowired` mechanism. Whereas you would use the `ref` attribute to direct Spring at a particular bean collaborator, you use the `autowired` attribute to enable Spring to automatically choose a bean based off one of several strategies shown in Table 3–2.

Table 3–2. Spring Bean Autowiring Strategies

Strategy Name	Description
No	Autowiring is not performed. This is the default behavior.
byname	Autowire by property name. Spring will match a bean name in your context with the name of a property on the bean to be autowired. This only works if there is a setter for the property to be wired; for example, a bean named `colorTable` can be used to autowire a property of the same name given setter `setColorTable`.
byType	Autowires property by type, given that the bean instance within the context is unique to the type. When more than one bean exists of the same type, an exception is thrown. If no bean exists of such type, nothing happens.
Constructor	Applies the behavior of `byType` to constructor arguments.

** The default mode no can be changed by setting the default-autowire attribute of the <beans> root element. A bean may have its own mode specified that overrides this default-autowire mode.*

The deprecated (since 3.0) `Autowire` strategy `autodetect` was removed, because it does not convey a clear usage when providing `@Autowired` in Java code. Autowiring `byName` is accomplished by simply defining the target properties with a name that ensures a matching bean with the same id will be found. This is illustrated in listing 3–20.

Listing 3–20. *Ioc_basics.xml – Spring configuration for Autowire by Name*

```
<!-- autowiring by name -->
<bean id="autowire-named"
      class="com.apress.prospringintegration.corespring.iocbasics.BasicPOJO"
      autowire="byName"/>
<!-- autowires to color property on demo bean -->
<bean factory-bean="colorRandomizer" factory-method="randomColor" id="color" />
```

To enable autowiring on BasicPOJO, the `autowire` attribute is set to the `byName` strategy. This will ensure that `BasicPOJO.colorRandomizer` gets injected with the bean defined earlier called `colorRandomizer`. In addition, `BasicPOJO.color` will be injected with the bean named `color`.

Autowiring Beans byType

Similarly, `byType` autowire can be used, but first we need to ensure there is a unique bean instance of the type we want autowired. The problem with autowiring by type is that there is sometimes more than one bean that is eligible by type alone. Therefore, Spring will not be able to decide which bean is most suitable for the property, and hence cannot perform autowiring. In this case, Spring will throw an `UnsatisfiedDependencyException` if more than one bean is found for autowiring. We recommend limiting the use of byType autowiring, because it will reduce the readability of your Spring configuration. Use it where component dependencies are not complicated. An example of byType autowiring is shown in Listing 3–21 and 3–22.

Listing 3–21. ColorPicker.java – byType Autowiring

```
package com.apress.prospringintegration.corespring.iocbasics;

public class ColorPicker {

    ColorRandomizer colorRandomizer;

    public ColorRandomizer getColorRandomizer() {
        return colorRandomizer;
    }

    public void setColorRandomizer(ColorRandomizer colorRandomizer) {
        this.colorRandomizer = colorRandomizer;
    }
}
```

Listing 3–22. ioc_basics.xml – Bean Definition for ColorPicker using byType Autowiring

```
<!-- Autowiring by type -->
<bean id="colorPicker"
      class="com.apress.prospringintegration.corespring.iocbasics.ColorPicker"
      autowire="byType"/>
```

Autowiring Beans by Annotation

In addition to using XML constructs, bean dependencies may be configured through annotations. Spring comes with support for JSR-250 annotations such as @Resource, @PostConstruct, and @PreDestroy and JSR330 – Dependency Injection for Java – including annotations such as @Inject, @Qualifier, @Named, and @Provider.

Spring annotations are presented in your context by placing the annotation-config tag from the namespace context within your XML-based Spring configuration file. When using XML and annotations together, the key is to remember that the behavior of Spring IoC is to wire up beans in the order of the elements in the XML configuration file. Thus, if there are overlapping dependencies between annotations and XML, the bean instances will come from the elements that come after the annotation-config tag.

Listing 3–23 shows the addition of the context namespace and the annotation-config element.

Listing 3–23. ioc_annotations.xml – Spring Configuration File using Annotation Driven Configuration

```
<?xml version="1.0" encoding="UTF-8"?>
<beans xmlns="http://www.springframework.org/schema/beans"
       xmlns:xsi="http://www.w3.org/2001/XMLSchema-instance"
       xmlns:context="http://www.springframework.org/schema/context"
       xsi:schemaLocation="http://www.springframework.org/schema/beans
    http://www.springframework.org/schema/beans/spring-beans-3.0.xsd
    http://www.springframework.org/schema/context
    http://www.springframework.org/schema/context/spring-context-3.0.xsd">

  <context:annotation-config/>

  <bean name="colorPicker"
        class="com.apress.prospringintegration.corespring.config.annotation.ColorPicker"
```

```
            primary="true"/>

    <bean
        name="colorRandomizer"
        class="com.apress.prospringintegration.corespring.config.annotation.ColorRandomizer"/>

    <!-- Qualifier can be used to obtain this by name -->
    <bean
        name="noRedColors"
        class="com.apress.prospringintegration.corespring.config.annotation.ColorRandomizer">
      <property name="colorException" value="red"/>
    </bean>

    <!-- Bean demonstrates qualifier for XML elements -->
    <bean
        class="com.apress.prospringintegration.corespring.config.annotation.ColorRandomizer">
      <qualifier
          type="com.apress.prospringintegration.corespring.config.annotation.Randomizer"
          value="noOrange"/>
      <property name="colorException" value="orange"/>
    </bean>

    <!-- A bunch of colors to populate a Collection -->
    <bean id="primaryColor" factory-bean="colorRandomizer" factory-method="randomColor"
          primary="true"/>
    <bean id="anotherColor" factory-bean="colorRandomizer" factory-method="randomColor"/>
    <bean id="extraColor" factory-bean="colorRandomizer" factory-method="randomColor"/>

</beans>
```

We can now embellish our POJO with Spring annotations to define the standard bean definition behavior that was previously specified through Spring XML (see Listing 3–24).

Listing 3–24. *ColorPicker.java – Class with Annotations*

```
package com.apress.prospringintegration.corespring.config.annotation;
import org.springframework.beans.factory.annotation.Autowired;

public class ColorPicker {

    @Autowired(required = true)
    ColorRandomizer colorRandomizer;

    public ColorRandomizer getColorRandomizer() {
        return colorRandomizer;
    }
    public void setColorRandomizer(ColorRandomizer colorRandomizer) {
        this.colorRandomizer = colorRandomizer;
    }
}
```

Add the `@Autowired` annotation to a field or setter method of a field that you want autowire. This annotation can be applied to any property that has a bean instance resolvable in the container. The required attribute indicates that our `colorRandomizer` property must be configured at initialization time, by explicit definition or through autowiring. If Spring does not find any property of the given type/name, a NullPointerException will be thrown during initialization.

In a similar way, the @Autowired annotation may be added to a type-safe collection. By specifying the type information of the collection, all beans of compatible type will be picked up by the autowire. Listing 3–25 will result with both ColorRandomizer instances being added to the list.

Listing 3–25. *ColorPicker.java – A Type-Safe Collection Auto-Wiring Example*

```
package com.apress.prospringintegration.corespring.config.annotation;

import org.springframework.beans.factory.annotation.Autowired;
import java.util.List;

public class ColorPicker {

    @Autowired
    List<ColorRandomizer> colorRandomizers;

    @Autowired
    Map<String, ColorEnum>  colors;
    // …
}
```

In addition, when applying @Autowired to a type-safe java.util.Map with string as the key, Spring will add all the beans of the compatible type using the bean name as the key to the target map.

Differentiating Auto-Wired Beans

Beans' autowired by name will only resolve instances by the name of the corresponding property. Furthermore, byType autowiring can only work when a single instance of a type exists in the context. ApplicationContext will throw UnsatisfiedDependencyException if you request an auto-wired bean of a type defined more than once in the container. To solve this problem, Spring enables you to define a bean with one or more characteristic attributes that allow your application to make the right bean selection choice. Use the @Primary annotation or primary element when declaring a bean to denote preference when using byType auto-wire, as shown in Listing 3–26.

Listing 3–26. *ioc_annotations.xml – Bean Declaration Specified as Primary*

```
<beans>
…
  <bean name="colorPicker"
        class="com.apress.prospringintegration.corespring.config.annotation.ColorPicker"
        primary="true"/>
…
</beans>
```

Spring also provides the @Qualifier annotation so you can specify a candidate bean by providing its name as the value, as shown in Listing 3–27.

Listing 3–27. *ColorPicker.java – Using @Qualifier to Narrow @Autowired Selection*

```
package com.apress.prospringintegration.corespring.config.annotation;

import org.springframework.beans.factory.annotation.Autowired;
```

```
import org.springframework.beans.factory.annotation.Qualifier;

public class ColorPicker {
    //...
    @Autowired
    @Qualifier("noRedColors")
     ColorRandomizer noRedRandomColors;
    //...
}
```

If @Qualifier does not specify uniqueness in value, an auto-wired typed collection property may be declare in your POJO, and by using @Qualifier, filter beans based on a qualifier element specified in the bean definitions. Additionally, @Qualifier can be chained with custom annotations to provide a specific type of bean configuration (see Listing 3–28). This is useful if you want a specific type of bean and configuration injected wherever an annotation decorates a field or setter method.

Listing 3–28. *Randomizer.java – Reusable Custom Bean Configuration using Qualifier*

```
package com.apress.prospringintegration.corespring.config.annotation;

import org.springframework.beans.factory.annotation.Qualifier;

import java.lang.annotation.ElementType;
import java.lang.annotation.Retention;
import java.lang.annotation.RetentionPolicy;
import java.lang.annotation.Target;

@Retention(RetentionPolicy.RUNTIME)
@Target({ElementType.FIELD, ElementType.PARAMETER})
@Qualifier
public @interface Randomizer {
    String value();
}
```

This annotation may then be applied to an @Autowired bean property, as shown in Listing 3–29.

Listing 3–29. *ColorPicker.java – Consuming Custom Qualifier Configuration*

```
package com.apress.prospringintegration.corespring.config.annotation;
public class ColorPicker {
    @Autowired
    @Randomizer("noOrange")
    public ColorRandomizer noRedRandomColors;
    //...
}
```

This qualifier needs to be provided to the target bean that wants to be auto-wired to the preceding property. The qualifier is added by the using the qualifier element with the type set to the annotation interface. The qualifier value is specified in the value attribute (see Listing 3–30). The value attribute is then mapped to the String value attribute of the annotation.

Listing 3–30. *ioc_annotation.xml – Specifying the Qualifier Element*

```
<bean class="com.apress.prospringintegration.corespring.config.annotation.ColorRandomizer">
  <qualifier type="com.apress.prospringintegration.corespring.config.annotation.Randomizer"
          value="noOrange"/>
```

```
  <property name="colorException" value="orange"/>
</bean>
```

Autowiring by Name

To auto-wire a bean property by name, a setter method, a constructor, or a field can be annotated with the JSR-250 @Resource annotation. By default, Spring will attempt to find a bean with the same name as this property. In addition, the bean name may be explicitly defined in its name attribute. To use JSR-250 annotations, you have to include the JSR 250 dependency as shown in Listing 3–31. See Listing 3–32 for an example using the @Resource annotation.

***Listing 3–31.** pom.xml – Maven Dependency for Adding JSR 250*

```
<dependency>
  <groupId>javax.annotation</groupId>
  <artifactId>jsr250-api</artifactId>
  <version>1.0</version>
</dependency>
```

***Listing 3–32.** ColorPicker.java – Autowiring a Bean with the JSR-250 @Resource Annotation*

```
public class ColorPicker {
    @Resource(name= "colorRandomizer")
    ColorRandomizer namedColorRandomizer;
    //...
}
```

Automatically Discovering Beans on the Classpath

To further simplify configuration, enable component scanning that removes the need for XML bean tags in most cases. Component scanning may be enabled by importing the context schema into your application configuration. Then configure the component-scan element by specifying a single or comma-delimited list of base-packages to scan with the base-package attribute as shown in Listing 3–33.

Classes annotated as component stereotypes including (but not limited to) @Configuration, @Component, @Repository, @Service, @Controller, or JSR-330 annotations, such as @Named are inclusive to the auto-scan default filter. Once auto-detected, components become Spring beans and are placed at the root of the application context.

***Listing 3–33.** ioc_component_scan.xml – Enabling Component Scanning*

```
<?xml version="1.0" encoding="UTF-8"?>
<beans xmlns="http://www.springframework.org/schema/beans"
       xmlns:xsi="http://www.w3.org/2001/XMLSchema-instance"
       xmlns:context="http://www.springframework.org/schema/context"
       xsi:schemaLocation="http://www.springframework.org/schema/beans
    http://www.springframework.org/schema/beans/spring-beans-3.0.xsd
    http://www.springframework.org/schema/context
    http://www.springframework.org/schema/context/spring-context-3.0.xsd">

  <context:component-scan
     base-package="com.apress.prospringintegration.corespring.config.componentscan"/>
```

```
</beans>
```

To migrate an application to component scanning, simply remove the bean definitions that were provided earlier, decorate your application objects with the `@Component` annotation, and provide the value as the bean name. If a value is not specified, the bean name will default to the class name where the first letter is lower case. Two examples are given in Listing 3–34 and 3–35 with bean names `colorRandomizer` and `colorPicker`, respectively. Both classes will be available as Spring beans without required the bean element in the Spring configuration XML.

Listing 3–34. *ColorRandomizer.java – Using Component Scanning*

```
package com.apress.prospringintegration.corespring.config.componentscan;

import org.springframework.stereotype.Component;

import java.util.Random;

@Component
public class ColorRandomizer {
    ColorEnum colorException;

    public ColorEnum randomColor() {
        ColorEnum[] allColors = ColorEnum.values();
        ColorEnum ret = null;
        do {
            ret = allColors[new Random().nextInt(allColors.length - 1)];
        }
        while (colorException != null && colorException == ret);

        return ret;
    }

    public ColorEnum exceptColor(ColorEnum ex) {
        ColorEnum ret = null;
        do {
            ret = randomColor();
        } while (ex != null && ex == ret);
        return ret;
    }

    public void setColorException(ColorEnum colorExceptions) {
        this.colorException = colorExceptions;
    }
}
```

Listing 3–35. *ColorPicker.java – Using Component Scanning*

```
package com.apress.prospringintegration.corespring.config.componentscan;

import org.springframework.beans.factory.annotation.Autowired;
import org.springframework.stereotype.Component;

@Component
public class ColorPicker {
```

```
    @Autowired(required = true)
    ColorRandomizer colorRandomizer;

    public ColorRandomizer getColorRandomizer() {
        return colorRandomizer;
    }

    public void setColorRandomizer(ColorRandomizer colorRandomizer) {
        this.colorRandomizer = colorRandomizer;
    }
}
```

Further Reducing XML with Java Configuration

The Java configuration project started as a standalone project at SpringSource and developed over the years. It was ultimately integrated into the core Spring framework with version 3.0. With this integration, you gain a powerful `ApplicationContext` configuration abstraction that retains the same level of isolation as its XML cousin; that is, it will not bother any of your code to use it! Your application may include APIs for which classes you cannot or may not want to modify with annotation decorations. Thus it has become customary to configure these types of components with bean declarations, property editors, or custom schema definitions.

Java configuration leverages CGLIB to provide a proxy of your `@Configuration` annotated classes that enables the cached singleton behavior intrinsic to the Spring IoC. Because of this, the CGLIB dependency must be included with your project. The maven dependency is shown in Listing 3–36.

Listing 3–36. *CGLIB maven dependency*

```
<dependency>
    <groupId>cglib</groupId>
    <artifactId>cglib</artifactId>
    <version>2.2</version>
</dependency>
```

The simplest way to configure an application is to use a hybrid Spring XML and Java onfiguration. Simply create a vanilla XML configuration file enabled with `component-scan` from the `context` namespace and let Spring do the rest of the work (see Listing 3–37). This way, you retain the ability, for example, to continue using custom/bundled namespace elements or to include any unmanaged XML configuration metadata.

Listing 3–37. *ioc_java_config.xml – Enable Component Scan to Support JavaConfiguration*

```
<?xml version="1.0" encoding="UTF-8"?>
<beans xmlns="http://www.springframework.org/schema/beans"
       xmlns:xsi="http://www.w3.org/2001/XMLSchema-instance"
       xmlns:context="http://www.springframework.org/schema/context"
       xsi:schemaLocation="http://www.springframework.org/schema/beans
    http://www.springframework.org/schema/beans/spring-beans-3.0.xsd
    http://www.springframework.org/schema/context
    http://www.springframework.org/schema/context/spring-context-3.0.xsd">

  <context:component-scan
      base-package=
          "com.apress.prospringintegration.corespring.config.componentscan.javaconfig"/>

</beans>
```

@Configuration classes are just like regular @Components classes, except that methods annotated with @Bean are used to factory beans. Note that a @Component with @Bean annotated methods works the same way, except that scopes are not respected and the @Bean methods are re-invoked (no caching in play), so @Configuration is preferred, even though it requires CGLIB. A basic Java configuration is shown in Listing 3–38.

Listing 3–38. *Configuration.java – Basic Java Configuration*

```
package com.apress.prospringintegration.corespring.config.componentscan.javaconfig;

import com.apress.prospringintegration.corespring.config.componentscan.ColorEnum;
import com.apress.prospringintegration.corespring.config.componentscan.ColorRandomizer;
import org.springframework.context.annotation.Bean;
import org.springframework.context.annotation.DependsOn;
import org.springframework.context.annotation.Lazy;
import org.springframework.context.annotation.Scope;
import org.springframework.stereotype.Component;

@Component
public class Configuration {
    @Bean(name = "theOnlyColorRandomizer")
    @Lazy
    public ColorRandomizer colorRandomizer() {
        return new ColorRandomizer();
    }

    @Bean(name = "randomColor")
    @Scope("prototype")
    @DependsOn({"theOnlyColorRandomizer"})
    public ColorEnum randomColor() {
        return colorRandomizer().randomColor();
    }
}
```

The bean configuration options available with Spring XML are also available through Java configuration. In the previous example we were able to specify a bean scope, through the @Scope annotation. The dependent bean's lifecycle is specified through the @Lazy attribute, which specifies the delaying of bean construction until it is required to satisfy a dependency or it is explicitly accessed from the context. Finally, we specified the @DependsOn annotation that specifies that the creation of a bean must come after the creation of some other bean, whose existence might be crucial to the correct creation of the bean.

With the Spring beans in hand using Java configuration, let's use them in an example. Listing 3–39 creates the Spring context and then obtains a reference to the theOnlyColorRandomizer bean create with Java configuration. Java configuration provides the same functionality of Spring XML with the ease and ability to refactor in Java.

Listing 3–39. *MainJavaConfig – Using Spring XML and Java Configuration*

```
package com.apress.prospringintegration.corespring.config.componentscan.javaconfig;

import com.apress.prospringintegration.corespring.config.componentscan.ColorEnum;
import com.apress.prospringintegration.corespring.config.componentscan.ColorRandomizer;
import org.springframework.context.ApplicationContext;
import org.springframework.context.support.ClassPathXmlApplicationContext;
```

```
public class MainJavaConfig {
    public static void main(String[] args) throws Exception {
        ApplicationContext context =
                new ClassPathXmlApplicationContext("ioc_java_config.xml");
        ColorRandomizer cr =
                context.getBean("theOnlyColorRandomizer", ColorRandomizer.class);
        System.out.println(cr.randomColor());

        for (int i = 0; i < 5; i++)
            System.out.println("randomcolor: " +
                    context.getBean("randomColor", ColorEnum.class));
    }
}
```

Importing additional Java configuration `@Configuration` classes is as simple as annotating the `@Configuration` class with `@Import` annotations. You can import any number of configurations and the Spring container will add the bean definitions to the current context. If there is a need to import an XML configuration within a Java configuration, then load them with the `@ImportResource` annotation and pass an XML resource path as the value.

Making Beans Aware of the Container

Usually your objects are indifferent to the container. However, to gain access to low-level IoC functionality, you may implement a specific `Aware` interface on the bean classes. In general, you should be cautious of this type of container access, because it can add Spring specifics that may not make for a thoroughly decoupled IoC integration. To establish specific context awareness, you should follow the convention of least access is best. For example, rather than harnessing the `ApplicationContext` to obtain `MessageSources`, you should implement the MessageSourceAware interface to obtain that functionality. Table 3–3 lists various types of resource access Aware interfaces.

Table 3–3. *Aware interfaces*

Aware Interface	Target Resource
Org.springframework.beans.factory.BeanNameAware	The bean of its instances configured in the IoC container.
Org.springframework.beans.factory.BeanFactoryAware	The current bean factory, through which you can invoke the container's services.
Org.springframework.context.ApplicationContextAware	The current application context, through which you can invoke the container's services.
Org.springframework.context.MessageSourceAware	A message source, through which you can resolve text messages.
Org.springframework.context.ApplicationEventPublisherAware	An application event publisher, through which you can publish application events.
Org.springframework.context.ResourceLoaderAware	A resource loader, through which you can load external resources.

In order to take advantage of any Aware interfaces, simply implement the interface and stored the resource passed in through the interface methods. Additionally, some of the Aware interfaces – notably the ones that provide infrastructure resources such as the ApplicationContext descendants – are byType autowire-able through @Autowired annotation of constructor arguments, setter-method, or field. Again, always keep in mind that best practice is to choose an Aware interface with the least IoC container coverage exposed to satisfy your own requirements.

Autowired constructor or setter method injects the Aware interface property after the bean properties have been set, but before the initialization callback methods are called, as illustrated in the following list:

1. Create bean instance, through constructor or factory method.
2. Populate collaborators and references.
3. Call setter method of the Aware interface, or inject through @Autowired.
4. Call initialization callback methods.
5. The bean is configured and ready for use.
6. Upon container shutdown, destruction callback methods are invoked.

The example shown in Listing 3–40 illustrates implementing the Aware interface. You only need to override the setBeanName method to accomplish this.

Listing 3–40. *Aware Interface Example*

```
package com.apress.prospringintegration.corespring.awareinterface;

import org.springframework.beans.factory.BeanNameAware;
public class MyBeanAware implements BeanNameAware {
    String beanName;

    public void setBeanName(String name) {
        this.beanName = name;
    }
}
```

Externalizing Bean Property Values

Your application will likely be filled with a variety of bean configuration details, such as host names, web service URLs, file paths, id's, and the like, which you probably already externalize to *.property files. Many enterprise application developers take this approach to resourcing in bean properties as a matter of good practice to keep configuration data separate from implementation details. Thus, it is no question that you should do the same with any Spring-based application.

Spring provides the org.springframework.beans.factory.config.PropertyPlaceholderConfigurer for you to externalize part of a bean configuration into a property file. To resolve a property, you can use variables in the form of ${var} in your configuration file and PropertyPlaceholderConfigurer will match your property key names with that of the variable name.

You can register PropertyPlaceholderConfigurer within your application context by using the <context:property-placeholder> element, and specifying the (classpath resolvable) path of a .properties file to the location attribute. See Listing 3–41.

Listing 3–41. Using PropertyPlaceholderConfigurer for External Properties File

```
<?xml version="1.0" encoding="UTF-8"?>
<beans xmlns="http://www.springframework.org/schema/beans"
       xmlns:xsi="http://www.w3.org/2001/XMLSchema-instance"
       xmlns:context="http://www.springframework.org/schema/context"
       xsi:schemaLocation="http://www.springframework.org/schema/beans
    http://www.springframework.org/schema/beans/spring-beans-3.0.xsd
    http://www.springframework.org/schema/context
    http://www.springframework.org/schema/context/spring-context-3.0.xsd">

  <context:property-placeholder location="logging-paths.properties"/>

  <bean id="logPath" class="java.lang.String">
    <constructor-arg value="${log.path}"/>
  </bean>

</beans>
```

Internationalization (i18n) Using MessageSource

For your application to support internationalization (i18n), it must be able to resolve text messages for different locales. The solution to this is actually baked into J2SE as something we have all come to know and love – the ResourceBundle. These are property files that contain a key/message pair and follow a special naming convention for the file name. For non-default resource bundles that are specific to a locale such as the US or the UK, the file is simply named according to the Locale string representation of that localization. For further information about the ResourceBundle see the Java SDK documentation.

The component typically used to extract messages is the MessageSource interface, which defines several methods for this task. Actually, ApplicationContext already extends the interface org.springframework.context.MessageSource, so all application contexts are able to resolve text messages. The Spring container delegates the message resolution to a bean with the exact name messageSource. org.springframework.context.ResourceBundleMessageSource is a common MessageSource implementation that may be simply defined with the id messageSource, and populate it's basename(s) property with the names of the resource bundles from which you want to extract messages (see Listing 3–42).

Listing 3–42. ioc_resource_bundles.xml – Spring Configuration for MessageSource Resolution

```
<?xml version="1.0" encoding="UTF-8"?>
<beans xmlns="http://www.springframework.org/schema/beans"
       xmlns:xsi="http://www.w3.org/2001/XMLSchema-instance"
       xsi:schemaLocation="http://www.springframework.org/schema/beans
    http://www.springframework.org/schema/beans/spring-beans-3.0.xsd">

  <bean id="messageSource"
        class="org.springframework.context.support.ResourceBundleMessageSource">
    <property name="basenames">
      <list>
        <value>resource_bundle_confirmation</value>
        <value>resource_bundle_postprocess</value>
      </list>
    </property>
  </bean>
</beans>
```

The example default properties contents for resource_bundle_confirmation.properties must be put in the default classpath resolvable resources directory when using Maven.

```
queued = Your data file has been queued for processing.
```

A British translation of the properties contents is in resource_bundle_confirmation_en_GB.properties.

```
queued = By George! Your data is queued.
```

MessageSource implements the three common methods for accessing messages in a resource bundle. These methods all accept the key, the locale, and a MessageFormat style arguments array. Optionally, a default value may be specified that gets used a message even if the message key was not found. Table 3–4 provides more detail on the three methods.

Table 3–4. *MessageSource Methods Common for Message Resolution*

getMessage(String key, Object[] msgArgs, String defaultMessage,Locale locale)
getMessage(String key, Object[]msgArgs, Locale locale)
getMessage(MessageSourceResolvable resolvable, Locale locale)

The support interface, org.springframework.context.MesageSourceResolvable, allows keeping all of the necessary details to resolve a default message in a single location. Maintaining message parameters may take some effort, thus by using the org.springframework.context.support.DefaultMessageSourceResolvable implementation class as a factory for message resolution, you are enabled to programmatically or declaratively manage message keys. In its constructor, specify a search list of message keys (that will use the first key it can resolve), a list of message replacement values, and a default message.

An example is shown in Listing 3–43. First the example class will retrieve the message for the key queued in the US, then the message for the UK will be retrieve next. Finally, the message will be retrieve for the key complete and include an additional input as part of the message returned.

Listing 3–43. *Example using Resources Bundle*

```
package com.apress.prospringintegration.corespring.i18n;

import org.springframework.context.ApplicationContext;
import org.springframework.context.MessageSourceAware;
import org.springframework.context.MessageSourceResolvable;
import org.springframework.context.support.ClassPathXmlApplicationContext;
import org.springframework.context.support.DefaultMessageSourceResolvable;

import java.util.Locale;

public class MainI18n {

    public static void main(String[] args) {
        ApplicationContext ctx =
                new ClassPathXmlApplicationContext("ioc_resource_bundles.xml");

        String qMessage = ctx.getMessage("queued", null, Locale.US);
        System.out.println(qMessage);

        qMessage = ctx.getMessage("queued", null, Locale.UK);
```

```
        System.out.println(qMessage);

        String filename = "ProSpringIntegration.xml";
        MessageSourceResolvable processed =
                new DefaultMessageSourceResolvable(new String[]{"complete"},
                        new String[]{filename}, " Your data has been processed!");
        String msrQmessage = ctx.getMessage(processed, Locale.FRANCE);
        System.out.println(msrQmessage);

    }
}
```

Aspect-Oriented Framework

Aspect-Oriented Programming (AOP) lets you apply cross-cutting concerns to your object-oriented code in a clean way. For example, you might use AOP to time all method execution times in your beans. Generally speaking, aspects get applied as one or more execution blocks known as *advices*, by specifying the locations they may execute, through an expression known as a *pointcut*. Within Spring AOP, advices can get executed before, after and around methods. Spring AOP supports the method advices only to the beans declared in the IoC container.

Spring enables AOP programming implements in two ways: through its internal framework – Spring AOP – which is a consistent implementation across versions of the dynamic proxy pattern that lets you create advices, pointcuts, and auto-proxies. And Spring supports the use of Aspects written with AspectJ annotations in its AOP framework. Since AspectJ annotations are supported by a growing number of AOP frameworks, your AspectJ-style aspects will likely remain intact across other AOP frameworks that support AspectJ.

However, keep in mind that since Spring AOP is leveraging AspectJ within its own framework, that is not the same as using the AspectJ Framework directly. To repeat, Spring AOP only allows the aspects to apply to beans declared in the IoC container. To enable similar AOP usage elsewhere, you must engage the AspectJ Framework directly.

Aspect-Oriented Programming with AspectJ

To Enable AOP aspect in your context, simply include the relevant AOP namespace into your context and define an empty XML element `<aop:aspectj-autoproxy/>` in your Spring configuration file. Proxies will be created automatically for any beans that are matched by your pointcuts. The Spring configuration file for the AOP example is shown in Listing 3–44. It includes both the `aspectj-autoproxy` element to support AOP and the `component-scan` element to support component scanning and Java configuration.

***Listing 3–44.** ioc_aop.xml – This Configuration Enables AspectJ*

```
<?xml version="1.0" encoding="UTF-8"?>
<beans xmlns="http://www.springframework.org/schema/beans"
       xmlns:xsi="http://www.w3.org/2001/XMLSchema-instance"
       xmlns:aop="http://www.springframework.org/schema/aop"
       xmlns:context="http://www.springframework.org/schema/context"
       xsi:schemaLocation="http://www.springframework.org/schema/beans
    http://www.springframework.org/schema/beans/spring-beans-3.0.xsd
    http://www.springframework.org/schema/aop
    http://www.springframework.org/schema/aop/spring-aop-3.0.xsd
    http://www.springframework.org/schema/context
    http://www.springframework.org/schema/context/spring-context-3.0.xsd">
```

```
    <context:component-scan base-package="com.apress.prospringintegration.corespring.aop"/>
    <aop:aspectj-autoproxy/>

</beans>
```

Additionally a domain object will be defined for our example. The class shown in Listing 3–45 describes a simple sales order processing data.

***Listing 3–45.** PurchaseOrder Domain Object*

```
package com.apress.prospringintegration.corespring.aop;

import java.util.Date;

public class PurchaseOrder {
    float itemCost;
    float discountAmt;
    Date processedTime;

    public Date getProcessedTime() {
        return processedTime;
    }

    public void setProcessedTime(Date processedTime) {
        this.processedTime = processedTime;
    }

    public float getDiscountAmount() {
        return discountAmt;
    }

    public void setDiscountAmount(float discountedAmount) {
        this.discountAmt = discountedAmount;
    }

    public float getItemCost() {
        return itemCost;
    }

    public void setItemCost(float itemCost) {
        this.itemCost = itemCost;
    }
}
```

Next, an interface is defined to represent processing a PurchaseOrder and returning a Receipt. The interface is shown in Listing 3–46.

***Listing 3–46.** Purchase Order Processing Interface Definition*

```
package com.apress.prospringintegration.corespring.aop;

public interface PurchaseOrderProcessor {
    public Receipt processPurchaseOrder(PurchaseOrder order);
}
```

Finally, the purchase order processing implement is created as shown in Listing 3–47. It will generate a Receipt based on the purchase amount, set the current date, and provide a random authorization code. Note the @Component annotation so that the bean does not need to be defined in the Spring configuration XML.

***Listing 3–47.** Purchase Order Processing Implementation*

```
package com.apress.prospringintegration.corespring.aop;

import org.springframework.stereotype.Component;

import java.util.Calendar;

@Component
public class PurchaseOrderProcessorImpl implements PurchaseOrderProcessor {

    public Receipt processPurchaseOrder(PurchaseOrder order) {
        order.setProcessedTime(Calendar.getInstance().getTime());
        Receipt receipt = new Receipt();
        receipt.setPurchaseAmt(order.getItemCost());
        receipt.setAuthcode(Math.round(Math.random() * 2000000));

        return receipt;
    }
}
```

Declaring Aspects with AspectJ Annotations

A hypothetical situation will be created in order to exercise the functionality of each of the aspect types. The annotated aspect class is shown in Listing 3–48. Again, note the use of the @Component annotation so that the bean does not need to be defined in the Spring configuration XML. The @Aspect annotation declares that this class will have aspects. The first case is a need to output a log for every processPurchaseOrder invocation. This is easily achieved with a Before aspect where a pointcut that executes advise code before the method PurchaseOrderProcessor.processPurchaseOrder. This results in a single log line denoting that processPurchaseOrder is about to execute.

***Listing 3–48.** Declaring Aspects with AspectJ Annotations*

```
package com.apress.prospringintegration.corespring.aop;

import org.apache.commons.logging.Log;
import org.apache.commons.logging.LogFactory;
import org.aspectj.lang.JoinPoint;
import org.aspectj.lang.ProceedingJoinPoint;
import org.aspectj.lang.annotation.*;
import org.springframework.stereotype.Component;

@Aspect
@Component
public class PurchaseOrderProcessorAspect {

    private Log log = LogFactory.getLog(this.getClass());

    @Before("execution(*➥
com.apress.prospringintegration.corespring.aop.PurchaseOrderProcessor.processPurchaseOrder(➥
..))")
```

```
    public void logBefore() {
        log.info("The PurchaseOrder is being processed");
    }

    @After("execution(*➥
com.apress.prospringintegration.corespring.aop.PurchaseOrderProcessor.processPurchaseOrder(➥
..))")
    public void logAfter(JoinPoint joinPoint) {

        PurchaseOrder purchaseOrder = (PurchaseOrder) joinPoint.getArgs()[0];
        log.info("The PurchaseOrder was processed at: " + purchaseOrder.getProcessedTime());
    }

    @AfterReturning(
            pointcut = "execution(*➥
com.apress.prospringintegration.corespring.aop.PurchaseOrderProcessor.processPurchaseOrder(➥
..))",
            returning = "result")
    public void adviceAfterReturning(JoinPoint joinPoint, Object result) {

        Receipt receipt = (Receipt) result;
        log.info("The receipt value is:" + receipt.getAuthcode());
    }

    @AfterThrowing(throwing = "e",
            pointcut = "execution(* *.process*(..))")
    public void afterThrowingAdvice(JoinPoint joinPoint, Throwable e) {
        String methodName = joinPoint.getSignature().getName();
        log.error("An error " + e + " was thrown in " + methodName);
    }

    @Around("execution(*➥
com.apress.prospringintegration.corespring.aop.PurchaseOrderProcessor.processPurchaseOrder(➥
..))")
    public Object logAround(ProceedingJoinPoint joinPoint) throws Throwable {
        String methodName = joinPoint.getSignature().getName();
        log.info(" Method: " + methodName);
        try {
            Object result = joinPoint.proceed();
            log.info(" Method: " + methodName + "returns " + result);
            return result;
        } catch (IllegalArgumentException e) {
            log.error(e);
            throw e;
        }
    }
}
```

It often makes sense to have additional data about the method invocation, such as the arguments passed and the return type. Access may be gained to a method's details by declaring the `JoinPoint` type as an argument to your advice method. In next aspect, the `After` advice is used and a JoinPoint argument declared to interrogate some order details. The After advice will execute immediately after the join point is complete, when a result is returned or when an abnormal Exception is thrown.

After returning advices allow you to perform logic only when a join point returns. After returning advices also let you explore the return value of a join point. This is done through adding more detail to your @AfterReturning annotation. This extra detail is needed to define explicitly both the pointcut and the returning value at the same time (usually, our annotations just expect the pointcut expression). By defining a value for the returning parameter in the annotation, an argument of the same name must also be defined within the advice method signature.

Continuing on with AOP advice types, an advice that is executed when an exception gets thrown is desired. This can be achieved by defining an after throwing advice whose defined behavior is to get executed only when an Exception is thrown by a join point. The @AfterThrowing annotation exposes its 'throwing' parameter similar to the @AfterReturning annotation. Our advice method receives a reference to the type thrown by the join point. In this case, we operate by capturing the type java.lang.Throwable – the super class of all errors and exceptions – that gives our advice compatibility to all Throwable types thrown by the join points.

When just one side of a join point is not enough, we can declare the most powerful of all advices – the around advice. This advice envelops the join point's execution, in effect providing all aspect functionalities in one single advice. Control of the original join point execution is enabled through the PreceedingJoinPoint Object, a subclass of JoinPoint. The proceed method will carry on with the original join point execution and return its return value. Alternately, you can shortcut the original join point, and provide your own behavior. It is advised to use this advice very sparingly, as it is easy to lose track of join point intersections.

To demonstrate, an order object is processed – generated by RandomPurchaseOrderGenerator – and send it through our PurchaseOrderProcessor bean using the main class shown in Listing 3–49.

Listing 3–49. *Advise Example main Class*

```
package com.apress.prospringintegration.corespring.aop;

import org.springframework.context.ApplicationContext;
import org.springframework.context.support.ClassPathXmlApplicationContext;

public class MainAOP {
    public static void main(String[] args) throws Exception {

        ApplicationContext app = new ClassPathXmlApplicationContext("ioc_aop.xml");
        PurchaseOrderProcessor orderProcessor = app.getBean(PurchaseOrderProcessor.class);

        PurchaseOrder order = new PurchaseOrder();
        order.setItemCost(1000.00f);
        Receipt receipt = orderProcessor.processPurchaseOrder(order);

    }
}
```

Defining Advice Order

When two or more advices intersect at the same join point, which one takes precedence? Spring AOP simply follows an undefined order, unless it is specified explicitly. This can be solved by using the @Order annotation, or by implementing the org.springframework.core.Ordered interface in you aspect class. A single property expected by both declarations is the order value; a high value indicates low priority, a low value gives it higher precedence.

To demonstrate, we will define a new aspect – the PurchaseOrderProcessorStatsAspect – to log execution time as shown in Listing 3–50. Since its measuring execution time, this logic will lend itself well to Around advice. It will need to be first in precedence as well, which is accomplished by implementing the Ordered interface, then assigning it's order to 0 by implementing the `Ordered.getOrder` method.

Listing 3–50. *Aspect with Defined Order*

```
package com.apress.prospringintegration.corespring.aop;

import org.apache.commons.logging.Log;
import org.apache.commons.logging.LogFactory;
import org.aspectj.lang.ProceedingJoinPoint;
import org.aspectj.lang.annotation.Around;
import org.aspectj.lang.annotation.Aspect;
import org.springframework.core.Ordered;
import org.springframework.stereotype.Component;

import java.util.Calendar;

@Aspect
@Component
public class PurchaseOrderProcessorStatsAspect implements Ordered {
    public int getOrder() {
        return 0;
    }

    private Log log = LogFactory.getLog(this.getClass());

    @Around("execution(*
com.apress.prospringintegration.corespring.aop.PurchaseOrderProcessor.processPurchaseOrder(..)
)")
    public Object aroundStatsAdvice(ProceedingJoinPoint joinPoint) throws Throwable {
        String methodName = joinPoint.getSignature().getName();
        String classPackage = joinPoint.getSignature().getClass().getPackage().getName();

        String fullCall = classPackage + "." + methodName;
        try {
            long tStart = Calendar.getInstance().getTimeInMillis();
            Object result = joinPoint.proceed();
            long tEnd = Calendar.getInstance().getTimeInMillis();

            log.info(" Method: " + fullCall + " took " + (tEnd - tStart) + " miliseconds");
            return result;
        } catch (IllegalArgumentException e) {
            log.error(e);
            throw e;
        }
    }
}
```

However, to guarantee it has precedence, we will need to specify order to the other aspect, which takes place at the same join point. The aspect precedence will be defined in this aspect by using the `@Order` annotation. See Listing 3–51.

Listing 3–51. Specify Order using @Order

```
package com.apress.prospringintegration.corespring.aop;

@Aspect
@org.springframework.core.annotation.Order(1)
@Component
public class PurchaseOrderProcessorAspect {
...
}
```

Introducing Behaviors to Your Beans

In AOP parlance, an *introduction* is a special type of advice that enables your objects to implement an interface dynamically, by providing the implementation class for that interface. This can be multiplied which, in effect gives the impression of multiple inheritance to your beans. To define introduction, use the `@DeclareParents` annotation, which gives matching types a new parent.

Invoking an introduced interface is simply a matter of casting the appropriate interface on the matched parent type. For example, we would like to provide order discounts for special sales. In order to do so, we will need to provide a new processor for handling discounts. We expand our retail domain with the necessary logic for processing specific types of discounts. First an `enum` is defined for the different discounts available as shown in Listing 3–52.

Listing 3–52. Defining the Order Discount Domain

```
package com.apress.prospringintegration.corespring.aop;

public enum DiscountStrategy {
    NO(0.0f),
    HALF_OFF_ENTIRE(0.5f),
    QUARTER_OFF_ENTIRE(0.25f);

    float discountRate;

    DiscountStrategy(float rate) {
        discountRate = rate;
    }
}
```

Next the process order discount interface needs to be defined. As shown in Listing 3–53, it will take a `PurchaseOrder` and a `DiscountStrategy` defined previously and return a `Receipt` back.

Listing 3–53. Purchase Order Discount Interface Definition

```
package com.apress.prospringintegration.corespring.aop;

public interface PurchaseOrderDiscountProcessor {

    public Receipt processDiscountOrder(PurchaseOrder order,
                                        DiscountStrategy discountStrategy)
            throws Exception;
}
```

Finally the purchase order discount processing implementation needs to be defined. The class is shown in Listing 3–54. This class has a similar function to previous purchase order processing class but with the addition of the discount calculation.

Listing 3–54. *Purchase Order Discount Class Implementation*

```
package com.apress.prospringintegration.corespring.aop;

import java.util.Calendar;

public class PurchaseOrderDiscountProcessorImpl
        implements PurchaseOrderDiscountProcessor {

    public Receipt processDiscountOrder(PurchaseOrder order,
                                        DiscountStrategy discountStrategy)
            throws Exception {

        order.setProcessedTime(Calendar.getInstance().getTime());
        float cost = order.getItemCost();
        float discountAmt = cost * discountStrategy.discountRate;
        order.setDiscountAmount(discountAmt);

        Receipt receipt = new Receipt();

        receipt.setPurchaseAmt(cost);
        receipt.setDiscountedAmount(discountAmt);
        receipt.setAuthcode(Math.round(Math.random() * 2000000));

        return receipt;
    }
}
```

Now, our objective is to have discount order processing performed within the PurchaseOrderProcessor. With introduction, you can enable PurchaseOrderProcessor to dynamically implement the PurchaseOrderDiscountProcessor. This is done with the @DeclareParents annotation as shown in Listing 3–55. This aspect can switch out the implementation.

Listing 3–55. *Defining an Introduction*

```
package com.apress.prospringintegration.corespring.aop;

import org.aspectj.lang.annotation.Aspect;
import org.aspectj.lang.annotation.DeclareParents;
import org.springframework.stereotype.Component;

@Aspect
@Component
public class DiscountedOrderIntroduction {
    @DeclareParents(
        value = "com.apress.prospringintegration.corespring.aop.PurchaseOrderProcessorImpl",
        defaultImpl = PurchaseOrderDiscountProcessorImpl.class
    )
    public PurchaseOrderDiscountProcessor discountOrderProcessor;
}
```

We can now obtain and invoke the `PurchaseOrderDiscountProcessor` methods on `PurchaseOrderProcessor` through type casting as shown in Listing 3–56.

Listing 3–56. *Introduction Example main Class*

```
package com.apress.prospringintegration.corespring.aop;

import org.springframework.context.ApplicationContext;
import org.springframework.context.support.ClassPathXmlApplicationContext;

public class MainAOP {
    public static void main(String[] args) throws Exception {

        ApplicationContext app = new ClassPathXmlApplicationContext("ioc_aop.xml");
        PurchaseOrderProcessor orderProcessor =
                app.getBean(PurchaseOrderProcessor.class);

        PurchaseOrder order = new PurchaseOrder();
        order.setItemCost(1000.00f);
        Receipt receipt = orderProcessor.processPurchaseOrder(order);

        PurchaseOrderDiscountProcessor orderDiscountProcessor =
                (PurchaseOrderDiscountProcessor) orderProcessor;
        Receipt discountedReceipt =
                orderDiscountProcessor.processDiscountOrder(order,
                        DiscountStrategy.HALF_OFF_ENTIRE);

        System.out.println(
                String.format("Total discounted purchase amount (given %s discount): %f ",
                        DiscountStrategy.HALF_OFF_ENTIRE,
                        (discountedReceipt.getPurchaseAmt() -
                                discountedReceipt.getDiscountedAmount())));
    }
}
```

Writing Custom Spring Namespaces

Applications may use common components that enable specific functionality required by business needs. Typically, components are either wired into their collaborators or instantiated outright on the class itself – for example, a date parser object. In addition, developers may be bound to specific initialization or use-case logic in each instance – things such as connection orientation and factory instantiation. While it makes plenty of sense to do so in normal coding fashion, there could be side effects, such as constrained API coupling. When configuring with XML metadata, wiring these types of components may not be the easiest thing to do in case there are many properties to set. The IDE is not aware of each optional/mandated property a bean exposes, and thus the developer must have complete documentation to properly configure the beans.

The concept of XML namespaces has been around since Spring 2.0, which itself exposes a number of schemas designed represent each major component of the framework. The current best practice is to use XML only when needed, however it may be of benefit to use a custom XML schema to bring order to an un-orderly component configuration. Thus, Spring offers custom XML extensions as a way to define and configure your critical or oft-used components, thus giving downstream developers the option to wire beans using XML components specifically designed for your use cases. This extension can greatly simplify application development by housing all API specific code within the NamespaceHandler, and by aiding the developer through schema-aware XML editors within the IDE.

An XML configuration starts with the schema contract that is required to use in order to bring the necessary functionality to an application. Listing 3–57 shows a typical XML Schema Definition (XSD) file that will include standard XSD namespace definitions, and optionally, any Spring schema you may want to use within your extension.

Listing 3–57. *strnorm.xsd – Used for Creating Custom Bean Definitions*

```
<?xml version="1.0" encoding="UTF-8"?>
<xsd:schema xmlns="http://www.mycompany.com/schema/strnorm"
            xmlns:xsd="http://www.w3.org/2001/XMLSchema"
            xmlns:beans="http://www.springframework.org/schema/beans"
            targetNamespace="http://www.mycompany.com/schema/strnorm"
            elementFormDefault="qualified"
            attributeFormDefault="unqualified">
  <xsd:import namespace="http://www.springframework.org/schema/beans"/>
  <xsd:element name="normalize">
    <xsd:complexType>
      <xsd:complexContent>
        <xsd:extension base="beans:identifiedType">
          <xsd:attribute name="strategy" type="normalizeStrategy" use="required"/>
        </xsd:extension>
      </xsd:complexContent>
    </xsd:complexType>
  </xsd:element>
  <xsd:simpleType name="normalizeStrategy">
    <xsd:restriction base="xsd:string">
      <xsd:enumeration value="UPPER"/>
      <xsd:enumeration value="LOWER"/>
    </xsd:restriction>
  </xsd:simpleType>
</xsd:schema>
```

This schema definition utilizes Spring's beans namespace for the identifiedType complex type that enables the Spring container to identify this custom bean definition type through a unique value you specify in the id attribute. Spring will also generate its own id value when you do not specify one. Thus we may also utilize other namespace elements made available by the beans schema. See the reference manual for more information about beans schema usage. In order to provide this schema to our XML configuration, we follow with the typical schemas declaration with the addition of the strnorm setup. The resulting Spring container configuration, with strnorm:normalize declaration that yields an instance of StringNormalizer, may look something like the example in Listing 3–58.

Listing 3–58. *Example for Setup and Usage of Custom Scheme ioc_namespace.xml*

```
<?xml version="1.0" encoding="UTF-8"?>
<beans xmlns="http://www.springframework.org/schema/beans"
       xmlns:xsi="http://www.w3.org/2001/XMLSchema-instance"
       xmlns:strnorm="http://www.mycompany.com/schema/strnorm"
       xsi:schemaLocation="http://www.mycompany.com/schema/strnorm
    http://www.mycompany.com/schema/strnorm/strnorm.xsd
    http://www.springframework.org/schema/beans
    http://www.springframework.org/schema/beans/spring-beans-3.0.xsd">
```

```
  <strnorm:normalize id="stringnormalizer" strategy="UPPER"/>
</beans>
```

In order to make use of your new schema, there must be some way to interpret the XML and instantiate a bean of the type that your definition represents. This is done by implementing `org.springframework.beans.factory.support.BeanDefinitionParser`, or in this case, (implementing) `org.springframework.beans.factory.xml.AbstractSingleBeanDefinitionParser`. This class does much of the boilerplate of creating a `BeanDefinition`. It exposes the doParse method that allows your implementation to parse a provided `org.w3c.dom.Element`, and build a `BeanDefinition` with a provided `BeanDefinitionBuilder` instance. Your implementation of `AbstractSingleBeanDefinitionParser` will also specify a `getClassName` method that tells `BeanDefinition` what type of class the element represents. Listing 3–59 is an example of implementing a `BeanDefinitionParser`.

Listing 3–59. *Implementing an AbstractSingleBeanDefinitionParser*

```
package com.apress.prospringintegration.corespring.namespaces;

import org.springframework.beans.factory.support.BeanDefinitionBuilder;
import org.springframework.beans.factory.xml.AbstractSingleBeanDefinitionParser;
import org.w3c.dom.Element;

public class StringNormalizerBeanDefinitionParser
        extends AbstractSingleBeanDefinitionParser {
    protected Class getBeanClass(Element element) {
        return StringNormalizer.class;
    }

    protected void doParse(Element element, BeanDefinitionBuilder bean) {
        // this will never be null since the schema explicitly
        // requires that a value be supplied
        String strategy = element.getAttribute("strategy");
        bean.addConstructorArgValue(StringNormalizationStrategies.valueOf(strategy));
    }
}
```

The Spring XML infrastructure employs a number of `org.springframework.beans.factory.xml.NamespaceHandler` implementations to parse elements it encounters such as those supported in the `jdbc`, `jmx`, and `util` namespaces. Thus, you will need to define a Namespace Handler to take care of parsing your own custom elements. However, Spring provides a convenience class for most of the use cases of wiring a `BeanDefinition` from your custom namespace elements.

Writing the Namespace Handler

The `NamespaceHandlerSupport` class is used to delegate element parsing to your `BeanDefinitionParser`, or `BeanDefinitionDecorator` implementations. Parsing delegation is made possible through registration of a parser implementation to a target element name. To illustrate custom namespace handling, which covers the top-level elements in the schema defined earlier, we will register the `StringNormalizerBeanDefinitionParser` subclass as shown in Listing 3–60.

Listing 3–60. *Using the NamespaceHandlerSupport class*

```
package com.apress.prospringintegration.corespring.namespaces;

import org.springframework.beans.factory.xml.NamespaceHandlerSupport;

public class NSNormalizerHandler extends NamespaceHandlerSupport {
    public void init() {
        registerBeanDefinitionParser("normalize",
                new StringNormalizerBeanDefinitionParser());
    }
}
```

The NamespaceHandlerSupport convenience class also provides methods that enable processing elements in two other scenarios. Override the registerBeanDefinitionDecoratorForAttribute method for attributes on existing namespaces, such as bean, util or other custom namespaces. Additionally, you can override the registerBeanDefinitionDecorator method to process child elements within other existing namespaces. Both methods expect a BeanDefinitionDecorator, which provides the necessary abstractions to decorate – by supplying additional bean configuration information – the BeanDefinition you are working on by implementing the decorate method.

Table 3–5. *NamespaceHandlerSupport Parsing Use-Cases Supported in Spring 3.0*

Parser Registration Method	Parsing Use Case	Parser Super-Class
registerBeanDefinitionParser	Top-level Elements under 'beans'	BeanDefinitionParser
registerBeanDefinitionDecorator	Nested Elements under 'bean'	BeanDefinitionDecorator
registerBeandefinitionDecoratorForAttribute	Attributes under 'bean'	BeanDefinitionDecorator

To enable your custom schema and handler under Spring XML parsing apparatus, you will create two files. First is the spring.handlers file, which defines NamespaceHandler class to XML Schema URI resolution. Second is the spring.schema file, which defines the relationship between XML Schema URI and the schema definition file resolvable in classpath. By placing the two files in META-INF of your .JAR file or exploded directory layout, Spring's XML apparatus will detect them upon context initialization. The two files are shown in Listing 3–61 and 3–62.

Listing 3–61. *spring.handlers File*

```
http\://www.mycompany.com/schema/strnorm=com.apress.prospringintegration.corespring.namespaces
.NSNormalizerHandler
```

Listing 3–62. *spring.schema File*

```
http\://www.mycompany.com/schema/strnorm/strnorm.xsd=/strnorm.xsd
```

The Namespace Handler can be tested with the following main program. This will cause the namespace handler to invoke, thus making the text all uppercase in output. See Listing 3–63.

Listing 3–63. Custom Namespace Nxample main Class

```
package com.apress.prospringintegration.corespring.namespaces;

import org.springframework.context.ApplicationContext;
import org.springframework.context.support.ClassPathXmlApplicationContext;

public class MainNS {

    public static void main(String[] args) {
        ApplicationContext context =
                new ClassPathXmlApplicationContext("ioc_namespace.xml");

        StringNormalizer stringNormalizer = context.getBean(StringNormalizer.class);
        String myStr = "Welcome to The WoRLD OF SpRiNG!";
        System.out.println("The context String normalizer says: " +
                stringNormalizer.normalize(myStr));
    }
}
```

The Spring Expression Language

Spring 3.0 saw the introduction of the Spring Expression Language (SpEL), which provides functionality similar to the Unified EL from JSF and JSP, or Object Graph Navigation Language (OGNL). SpEL provides easy-to-use infrastructure that can be leveraged outside of the Spring container. Within the container, it can be used to make configuration much easier in a lot of cases.

Today, there are many different types of expression languages in the enterprise space. If you use WebWork/Struts 2 or Tapestry 4, you've no doubt used OGNL. If you have used JSP or JSF in recent years, you have used one or both of the expression languages that are available in those environments. If you have used JBoss Seam, you have used the expression language made available there, which is a superset of the standard expression language shipped with JSF (Unified EL).

The expression language draws its heritage from many places. Certainly, it is a superset of what is available via the Unified EL. Spring.NET has had a similar expression language for a while, and the feedback has been very favorable. The need to evaluate certain expressions at arbitrary points in a life cycle, such as during a scoped beans initialization, contributed to some of the qualities of this expression language.

Some of these expression languages are very powerful, bordering on being scripting languages in their own right. The SpEL is no different. It is available almost everywhere you can imagine needing it—from annotations to XML configuration. The SpringSource Tool Suite also provides robust support for the expression language in the way of auto-completion and lookup.

Features of the Language Syntax

The expression language supports a long list of features. Table 3–6 outlines the various constructs and demonstrates their usage.

Table 3–6. Expression Language Features

Type	Use	Example
Literal expression	The simplest thing you can do in the expression language, essentially the same as if you were writing Java code. The language supports `String` literals as well as all sorts of numbers.	`2342` `'Hello Pro Spring Integration'`
Boolean and relational operator	The expression language enables evaluating conditionals using standard idioms from Java.	`T(java.lang.Math).random()➥` `> .5`
Standard expression	You can iterate and return the properties on beans in the same way you might with Unified EL, separating each de-referenced property with a period and using JavaBean-style naming conventions. In the example to the right, the expression would be equivalent to `getCat().getMate().getName()`.	`cat.mate.name`
Class expression	`T()`tells the expression language to act on the type of the class, not an instance. In the examples on the right, the first would yield the `Class` instance for `java.lang.Math` -- equivalent to calling `java.lang.Math.class`. The second example calls a static method on a given type. Thus, `T(java.lang.Math).random()`is equivalent to calling `java.lang.Math.random()`.	`T(java.lang.Math)` `T(java.lang.Math).random()`

Accessing arrays, lists, maps	You can index lists, arrays, and maps using brackets and the key, which for arrays or lists is the index number, and for maps is an object. In the examples, you see a `java.util.List` with four `chars` being indexed at index 1, which returns '`b.`' The second example demonstrates accessing a map by the index `'OR'`, yielding the value associated with that key.	`T(java.util.Arrays).asList( ➥`
		`'a','b','c','d')[1]`
		`T(SpelExamplesDemo)➥`
		`.MapOfStatesAndCapitals['OR']`

Relational operators	You can compare or equate values, and the returned value will be a boolean.	`23 == person.age` `'fala' < 'fido'`

Calling constructor	You can create objects and invoke their constructors. Here, you create simple `String` and `Cat` objects.	`new String('Hello Pro Spring➥`
		`Integration,!')`
		`new Cat('Felix')`

Ternary operator	Ternary expressions work as you'd expect, yielding the value in the true case.	`T(java.lang.Math).random() >➥`
		`.5 ? 'She loves me' : 'She➥`
		`loves me not'`

Type	Use	Example
Variable	The SpEL lets you set and evaluate variables. The variables can be installed by the context of the expression parser, and there are some implicit variables, such as `#this`, which always refer to the root object of the context.	`#this.firstName` `#customer.email`
Collection projection	A very powerful feature inside of SpEL is the capability to perform very sophisticated manipulations of maps and collections. Here, you create a projection for the list `cats`. In this example, the returned value is a collection of as many elements being iterated that has the value for the name property on each cat in the collection. In this case, `cats` is a collection of `Cat` objects. The returned value is a collection of `String` objects.	`cats.![name]`

Collection selection	Selection lets you dynamically filter objects from a collection or map by evaluating a predicate on each item in the collection and keeping only those elements for which the predicate is true. In this case, you evaluate the `java.util.Map.Entry.value` property for each `Entry` in the `Map` and if the value (in this case a `String`), lowercased, starts with "s," then it is kept. Everything else is discarded.	`mapOfStatesAndCapitals.?➥`
		`[value.toLowerCase().➥`
		`startsWith('s')]`

Templated expression	You can use the expression language to evaluate expressions inside of string expressions. The result is returned. In this case, the result is dynamically created by evaluating the ternary expression and including `'good'` or `'bad'` based on the result.	`Your fortune is ${T(java➥`
		`.lang.Math).random()> .5 ?➥`
		`'good' : 'bad'}`

Method invocation	Methods may be invoked in instances just as you would in Java. This is a marked improvement over the basic JSF or JSP expression languages.	`'Hello, World'.toLowerCase()`

Uses of the Language in Your Configurations

The expression language is available via XML or annotations. The expressions are evaluated at creation time for the bean, not at the initialization of the context. This has the effect that beans created in a custom scope are not configured until the bean is in the appropriate scope. You can use them in the same way via XML or annotations.

The first example is the injection of a named expression language variable, `systemProperties`, which is just a special variable for the `java.util.Properties` instance that's available from `System.getProperties`. Listing 3–64 shows the injection of a system property itself directly into a String variable.

Listing 3–64. *Example of SpEL for Locating SystemProperty*

```
@Value("#{systemProperties}")
private Properties systemProperties;

@Value("#{systemProperties['user.region'] }")
private String userRegion;
```

You can also inject the result of computations or method invocations. Here, you are injecting the value of a computation directly into a variable, as in Listing 3–65.

Listing 3–65. *SpEL for Value Injection into a Variable*

```
@Value("#{  T(java.lang.Math).random() * 100.0 }")
private double randomNumber;
```

Listing 3–66 assumes that another bean is configured in the context with the name `emailUtilities`. In return, the bean has JavaBean-style properties that are injected into the following fields;

Listing 3–66. *Evaluating JavaBean Property Expression*

```
package com.apress.prospringintegration.corespring.spel;

import org.springframework.beans.factory.annotation.Value;
import org.springframework.stereotype.Component;

import java.util.Properties;

@Component
public class SpELPOJO {

    @Value("#{emailUtilities.email}")
    private String email;

    @Value("#{emailUtilities.password}")
    private String password;

    @Value("#{emailUtilities.host}")
    private String host;

}
```

You can also use the expression language to inject references to other named beans in the same context, as shown in Listing 3–67.

Listing 3–67. *Using @Value to Inject Reference into Other Object*

```
@Value("#{emailUtilities}")
            private EmailUtilities emailUtilities;
```

In this case, because there is only one bean in the context with the interface `EmailUtilities`, you could also do the following shown in Listing 3–68.

Listing 3–68. *Without using SpEL*

```
@Autowired
private EmailUtilities emailUtilities;
```

Although there are other mechanisms for discriminating against beans of the same interface, the expression language becomes very handy here, because it lets you simply discriminate by bean `id`. You can use the expression language in your XML configurations in exactly the same way as with the annotation support. Even the prefix #{ and the suffix } are the same (see Listing 3–69).

Listing 3–69. *Using SpEL in Spring XML*

```
<bean class="...SomeObject"
      p:randomNumber="#{ T(java.lang.Math).random() * 10.0 }"/>
```

Finally, it is important to note that, as always, you may use a property placeholder in your Spring configuration in tandem with your SpEL statements. Additionally, property placeholders are supported in `@Value` annotations, as well as shown in Listing 3–70.

Listing 3–70. *Evaluationg Property Placeholders*

```
@Value("${user.home}")
private String userHome;
```

Summary

This chapter has covered the core architecture of the Spring framework. We discussed how to initialize the Spring container with XML metadata or a Java class using an implementation of `ApplicationContext` that supports your application or component configuration style. The traditional XML metadata file suffices for any basic use case; however, the Java configuration supports a more readable and imminently modifiable configuration style. This way, downstream edits of your components may be seen more as Java-based component editing rather than often cryptic XML metadata configuration changes.

Complexity takes the place of simple and elegant configuration; however, the custom namespace helps to bridge API knowledge gap. It is optimal when boiling down intricate and/or terse configuration details, simplifying them to within a fraction of their original code or XML complexity.

Spring's support for AOP may be utilized to implement functionality across disparate components. Five types of advices were covered in this chapter: `before`, `after`, `after returning`, `after throwing`, and `around`. In addition, the introduction advice was introduced – a special AOP advice that allows objects to implement an interface dynamically by providing an implementation class. Introduction advices are useful when additional behaviors and states to a pre-existing group of objects is required.

Other advanced IoC container features have been covered, such as externalizing bean configuration into properties files, accessing resource bundles, and wiring external name/value pairs into your beans. Injecting application components is further simplified with Spring `Aware` interfaces, annotations, and through the powerful Spring Expression Language. All these features come in handy when developing Spring Integration components.

CHAPTER 4

Introduction to Enterprise Spring

This chapter introduces several of the APIs supported by the core Spring Framework, including Java Database Connectivity (JDBC), object-relationship management, transactions, and remoting. Many of the interfaces from this support will appear in the corresponding components in Spring Integration and other frameworks that build on them.

Data Access Framework

Access to a relational database is a common requirement for most enterprise applications. JDBC is a part of Java SE that defines a set of standard APIs for access to relational databases in a vendor-independent fashion. The purpose of JDBC is to provide an API through which SQL statements may be executed against a relational database. However, when using JDBC, database-related resources and database exceptions must be handled explicitly outside of the API. To simply using JDBC, Spring provides an abstraction framework for interfacing with JDBC. At the heart of the Spring JDBC framework, the `JdbcTemplate`, is designed to provide convenient callback methods for different type of operations. Many of the template methods are convenience methods that reduce operations to one-liners; however there are also methods that take callbacks. These callbacks are lower level and surface the most interesting parts of the raw JDBC API.

If raw JDBC will not satisfy your requirements or if your application would benefit from higher-level abstraction, then Spring's support for Object Relational Mapping (ORM) solutions will interest you. In this section, you will also learn how to integrate ORM frameworks into your Spring applications. Spring supports most of the popular ORM and data mapping frameworks, including Hibernate, JDO, and Java Persistence API (JPA). Classic TopLink is not supported starting from Spring 3.0, but because TopLink shifted focus from internal native (classic) to JPA via EclipseLink. Spring's JPA support may be used for TopLink. The focus of this section will be on JDBC, Hibernate ORM, and JPA. Spring's support for these ORM frameworks is consistent, so it can be easily applied to other ORM frameworks as well.

ORM lets developers map objects to database tables. Usually, the mapping is of object properties to database table columns. Once a database schema is correctly mapped, a developer may query and update the database using plain old objects, evading most of the low-level SQL that is being generated by the ORM framework. Hibernate, one of the most popular open source ORM frameworks community, and supports most JDBC-compliant databases. Beyond the basic ORM features, Hibernate supports more advanced features such as collection mapping, bi-directional associations, filters, and componentized mappings. Hibernate supports the variations between SQL vendors through SQL dialects. Hibernate provides a powerful querying language called Hibernate Query Language (HQL) that provides the ability to write simple but powerful object queries.

JPA defines a set of standard annotations and APIs for object persistence in both the Java SE and Java EE platforms. JPA is defined as part of the EJB 3.0 specification in JSR-220. You can compare JPA with the JDBC API and a JPA engine with a JDBC driver. Hibernate can be configured as a JPA-compliant engine through an extension module called Hibernate Entity Manager. This section will mainly demonstrate JPA with Hibernate as the underlying engine.

Selecting a Relational Model

We are going to define a simple model and application for stock inventory and order processing whose major functions are the basic Create, Read, Update, and Delete (CRUD) operations on an inventory of stocks and a collection of orders. The entities will be stored in a relational database and accessed by JDBC using Spring's `JdbcTemplate`.

Before diving into the stock inventory order application, we must select a database. To minimize memory consumption and simplify configuration, we will used the embedded H2 database. H2 is a full-featured, open source relational database engine implemented in pure Java. This lends itself towards ease-of-deployment, and configurability. However, any JDBC-compliant database may be used with these examples.

H2 can run in either the embedded mode or the client/server mode. For our purposes, the embedded mode is appropriate because it allows the example code to quickly setup, and teardown entire table schemas and datasets. The following Maven dependencies shown in Listing 4–1 are required for the following examples.

Listing 4–1. *Enabling H2 for your Application - pom.xml*

```
<dependency>
   <groupId>cglib</groupId>
   <artifactId>cglib-nodep</artifactId>
   <version>2.2</version>
</dependency>
<dependency>
  <groupId>com.h2database</groupId>
  <artifactId>h2</artifactId>
  <version>1.2.144</version>
</dependency>
```

This example will take an approach of designing table a schema that has a close match between domain object properties and relational model columns. In other words, we simply create a near one to one relationship between table and domain model. H2 provides plenty of options for creating and defining tables complete with primitive types, constraints, indexes, and more. The SQL script for creating the STOCK table is shown in Listing 4–2.

Listing 4–2. *STOCKS Table Definition Script stocks.ddl.sql*

```
drop table STOCKS;

create table STOCKS (
  ID SERIAL,
  INVENTORY_CODE VARCHAR(25) NOT NULL,
  SYMBOL VARCHAR(4),
  EXCHANGE_ID VARCHAR(10),
  PRICE_PER_SHARE DECIMAL (6,2) NOT NULL,
  QUANTITY_AVAILABLE INTEGER NOT NULL,
  PURCHASE_DATE DATE NOT NULL,
  CONSTRAINT PK_STOCKID PRIMARY KEY (ID),
  CONSTRAINT INV_CODE UNIQUE(INVENTORY_CODE)
);
```

The Stock domain object is shown in Listing 4–3.

Listing 4–3. *Stock Domain Object*

```
package com.apress.prospringintegration.springenterprise.stocks.model.;

import java.util.Date;

public class Stock {
    int id;
    String inventoryCode;
    String symbol;
    String exchangeId;
    float sharePrice;
    int quantityAvailable;
    Date purchaseDate;

    // Getters and Setters removed for brevity

}
```

Configuring an Embedded Data Source

Configuring the Spring context for an embedded database is simple: use the `jdbc` namespace to enable the `embedded-database` namespace elements. The `embedded-database` element enables application context bootstrapping and creates the `javax.sql.DataSource`. The type of database may be specified with the type attribute; it supports H2, HSQL, and DERBY. The script element lets you select a SQL script that will run when the data source is constructed. This gives you a chance to initialize database schemas. This is very useful in a testing environment. For more flexible initialization, use the `initialize-database` element to specify the specific SQL/DDL scripts and the type of failures to ignore. The Spring configuration file for configuring the embedded data source is shown in Listing 4–4.

Listing 4–4. *Spring Configuration for Connecting to Embedded database data-access.xml*

```
<?xml version="1.0" encoding="UTF-8"?>
<beans xmlns="http://www.springframework.org/schema/beans"
       xmlns:xsi="http://www.w3.org/2001/XMLSchema-instance"
       xmlns:jdbc="http://www.springframework.org/schema/jdbc"
       xmlns:context="http://www.springframework.org/schema/context"
       xmlns:tx="http://www.springframework.org/schema/tx"
       xsi:schemaLocation="http://www.springframework.org/schema/beans
    http://www.springframework.org/schema/beans/spring-beans-3.0.xsd
    http://www.springframework.org/schema/tx
    http://www.springframework.org/schema/tx/spring-tx-3.0.xsd
    http://www.springframework.org/schema/context
    http://www.springframework.org/schema/context/spring-context-3.0.xsd
    http://www.springframework.org/schema/beans
    http://www.springframework.org/schema/beans/spring-beans-3.0.xsd
    http://www.springframework.org/schema/jdbc
    http://www.springframework.org/schema/jdbc/spring-jdbc-3.0.xsd">

  <context:property-placeholder location="StocksJDBC.properties"/>
  <context:component-scan
      base-package="com.apress.prospringintegration.springenterprise.stocks.dao.jdbc"/>
```

```
  <jdbc:embedded-database type="H2" id="h2DataSource"/>

  <jdbc:initialize-database data-source="h2DataSource" ignore-failures="DROPS">
    <jdbc:script location="/STOCKS.DDL.SQL"/>
  </jdbc:initialize-database>

</beans>
```

Configuring a Remote Data Source

The `javax.sql.DataSource` is a standard interface defined by the JDBC specification that factories `java.sql.Connection` instances. There are many `DataSource` connection pool implementations provided by different vendors and projects: C3PO and Apache Commons DBCP are popular open-source options, and most applications servers will provide their own implementation. It is very easy to switch between different data source implementations, because of the common `DataSource` interface. Spring also provides several convenient but less powerful data source implementations. The simplest one is `org.springframework.jdbc.datasource.DriverManagerDataSource`, which opens a new connection every time it is requested. The database properties and Java configuration are shown in Listings 4–5 and 4–6, respectively.

Listing 4–5. *Configuration of a JDBC DataSource Properties StockJDBC.properties*

```
jdbc.url=jdbc:h2:tcp://localhost/~/test
jdbc.username=sa
jdbc.password=
jdbc.driver=org.h2.Driver
```

Listing 4–6. *Java Configuration for Data Source*

```
package com.apress.prospringintegration.springenterprise.stocks.config;

import org.springframework.beans.factory.annotation.Value;
import org.springframework.context.annotation.Bean;
import org.springframework.context.annotation.Configuration;
import org.springframework.jdbc.datasource.DriverManagerDataSource;

import javax.sql.DataSource;

@Configuration
public class StocksBaseConfig {

    @Value("${jdbc.url}")
    String jdbcUrl;

    @Value("${jdbc.username}")
    String username;

    @Value("${jdbc.password}")
    String password;

    @Value("#{h2DataSource}")
    DataSource embeddedDataSource;
```

```
    @Bean
    public DataSource dataSource() {
        return embeddedDataSource;
    }

    // Remote Data Source ( just for illustrating remote connection )
    @Bean
    public DataSource remoteDataSource() {
        return new DriverManagerDataSource(jdbcUrl, username, password);
    }
}
```

DriverManagerDataSource is not an efficient data source implementation, because it opens a new connection for the client every time it is requested. Another data source implementation provided by Spring is the org.springframework.jdbc.datasource.SingleConnectionDataSource (a DriverManagerDataSource subclass). As its name indicates, this maintains only a single connection that is reused all the time and never closed. Obviously, it is not suitable in a multithreaded environment.

Spring's own data source implementations are mainly used for testing purposes. However, many production data source implementations support connection pooling. For example, the Database Connection Pooling Services (DBCP) module of the Apache Commons Library has several data source implementations that support connection pooling. Of these, BasicDataSource accepts the same connection properties as DriverManagerDataSource and allows you to specify the initial connection size and maximum active connections for the connection pool.

Basic JdbcTemplate Usages

The org.springframework.jdbc.core.JdbcTemplate class declares a number of overloaded update, query, and execute methods that enable control of the overall query and update task. For example, different varieties of the update method allow you to choose how ResultSets are interpreted into application-specific objects, and thus manipulated. JdbcTemplate is threadsafe, which implies that it can be injected into your service and DAO objects, which must sustain concurrent access from clients. To use the JdbcTemplate, create an instance of it and pass in the data source for this template as a constructor argument. The JdbcTemplate configuration is shown in Listing 4–7.

Listing 4–7. *Configuration of JdbcTemplate as an IoC dependency*

```
package com.apress.prospringintegration.springenterprise.stocks.dao.jdbc;

import com.apress.prospringintegration.springenterprise.stocks.config.StocksBaseConfig;
import org.springframework.context.annotation.Bean;
import org.springframework.context.annotation.Configuration;
import org.springframework.context.annotation.ImportResource;
import org.springframework.jdbc.core.JdbcTemplate;

@Configuration
@ImportResource("classpath:data-access.xml")
public class StocksJdbcConfig extends StocksBaseConfig {

    // JDBC Template
    @Bean
    public JdbcTemplate jdbcTemplate() {
        return new JdbcTemplate(dataSource());
    }
}
```

There are two options to provide the `JdbcTemplate` dependency to a DAO or other data repository: simply use a setter method or extend `JdbcDaoSupport`. Extending `JdbcDaoSupport` provides the advantage of not having to determine whether the template has been initialized, in addition to other sanity checks. The super class `org.springframework.jdbc.core.support.JdbcDaoSupport` exposes the `getJdbcTemplate` method for your subclass to retrieve the template instance. In this example, we will define a very simple data model, Data Access Object (DAO) interface (see Listing 4–8) and implementation (see Listing 4–9), and a few key `JdbcTemplate` callback implementations that illustrate its usage.

Listing 4–8. *The DAO Interface for the Stock Mode.*

```
package com.apress.prospringintegration.springenterprise.stocks.dao;

import com.apress.prospringintegration.springenterprise.stocks.model.Stock;

import java.util.List;

public interface StockDao {

    public void insert(Stock stock);

    public void update(Stock stock);

    public void delete(Stock product);

    public Stock findByInventoryCode(String iCode);

    public List<Stock> findAvailableStockBySymbol(String symbol);

    public List<Stock> get();
}
```

Listing 4–9. *The JdbcTemplateStockDAO featuring JdbcTemplate*

```
package com.apress.prospringintegration.springenterprise.stocks.dao.jdbc;

import com.apress.prospringintegration.springenterprise.stocks.dao.StockDao;
import com.apress.prospringintegration.springenterprise.stocks.model.Stock;
import org.springframework.beans.factory.annotation.Autowired;
import org.springframework.jdbc.core.JdbcTemplate;
import org.springframework.jdbc.core.PreparedStatementCreator;
import org.springframework.jdbc.core.RowMapper;
import org.springframework.jdbc.support.GeneratedKeyHolder;
import org.springframework.jdbc.support.KeyHolder;
import org.springframework.stereotype.Component;

import java.sql.Connection;
import java.sql.PreparedStatement;
import java.sql.ResultSet;
import java.sql.SQLException;
import java.util.List;

@Component
public class JdbcTemplateStockDao implements StockDao {
```

```
private JdbcTemplate jdbcTemplate;

@Autowired
public void setJdbcTemplate(JdbcTemplate t){
    this.jdbcTemplate = t;
}

public void insert(Stock stock) {
    KeyHolder keyHolder = new GeneratedKeyHolder();
    this.jdbcTemplate.update(new PSStockCreater(stock), keyHolder);

    stock.setId(keyHolder.getKey().intValue());
}

@Override
public void update(final Stock stock) {
    jdbcTemplate.update(new PreparedStatementCreator() {
        public PreparedStatement createPreparedStatement(Connection connection)
                throws SQLException {
            String sql = "UPDATE STOCKS SET SYMBOL = ?, INVENTORY_CODE = ?, " +
                    "PRICE_PER_SHARE = ?, QUANTITY_AVAILABLE = ?, " +
                    "EXCHANGE_ID = ?, PURCHASE_DATE = ? where ID = ?";
            PreparedStatement ps = connection.prepareStatement(sql);
            ps.setString(1, stock.getSymbol());
            ps.setString(2, stock.getInventoryCode());
            ps.setFloat(3, stock.getSharePrice());
            ps.setFloat(4, stock.getQuantityAvailable());
            ps.setString(5, stock.getExchangeId());
            ps.setDate(6, new java.sql.Date(stock.getPurchaseDate().getTime()));
            ps.setInt(7, stock.getId());
            return ps;
        }
    });
}

@Override
public void delete(Stock stock) {
    jdbcTemplate.update("delete from STOCKS where id = ?", stock.getId());
}

@Override
public List<Stock> findAvailableStockBySymbol(String symbol) {
    String sql = " SELECT * from STOCKS" +
            " WHERE SYMBOL = ? order by PRICE_PER_SHARE";
    List<Stock> ret = jdbcTemplate.query(
            sql,
            new Object[]{symbol},
            new RowMapper<Stock>() {
                public Stock mapRow(ResultSet rs, int rowNum) throws SQLException {
                    Stock s = new Stock(
                            rs.getString("SYMBOL"),
                            rs.getString("INVENTORY_CODE"),
                            rs.getString("EXCHANGE_ID"),
                            rs.getFloat("PRICE_PER_SHARE"),
```

```
                                rs.getInt("QUANTITY_AVAILABLE"),
                                rs.getDate("PURCHASE_DATE")
                        );
                        return s;
                    }
                });

        return ret;
    }

    @Override
    public List<Stock> get() {
        List<Stock> ret = jdbcTemplate.query("select * from STOCKS", new StockMapper());
        return ret;
    }

    @Override
    public Stock findByInventoryCode(String iCode) {
        String sql = " SELECT * from STOCKS" +
                " WHERE INVENTORY_CODE = ?";
        return jdbcTemplate.queryForObject(sql,
                new Object[]{iCode},
                new StockMapper());
    }
}
```

JdbcTemplate Callback Interfaces

The `org.springframework.jdbc.core` package defines two callback interfaces – `PreparedStatementCreator` and `RowCallbackHandler` – that let you tailor how `PreparedStatements` are created and specify how rows (`javax.sql.ResultSets`) should be mapped to objects, respectively. You can implement any of these callback interfaces and pass its instance to the corresponding `update` method on `JDBCTemplate` to complete the selected task. In this example, we define a `PSStockCreater` class that has the task of inserting data into the `STOCKS` table, as shown in Listing 4–10.

Listing 4–10. *A PreparedStatementCreater Implementation*

```
package com.apress.prospringintegration.springenterprise.stocks.dao.jdbc;

import com.apress.prospringintegration.springenterprise.stocks.model.Stock;
import org.springframework.jdbc.core.PreparedStatementCreator;

import java.sql.Connection;
import java.sql.PreparedStatement;
import java.sql.SQLException;
import java.sql.Statement;

public class PSStockCreater implements PreparedStatementCreator {
    private Stock stock;

    public PSStockCreater(Stock stock) {
        this.stock = stock;
    }
```

```
    public PreparedStatement createPreparedStatement(Connection connection)
            throws SQLException {
        String sql =
                "INSERT INTO" +
                        "STOCKS (SYMBOL, INVENTORY_CODE, PRICE_PER_SHARE," +
                        "QUANTITY_AVAILABLE, EXCHANGE_ID, PURCHASE_DATE) " +
                        " VALUES (?, ?, ?, ?, ?, ?)";
        PreparedStatement ps =
                connection.prepareStatement(sql, Statement.RETURN_GENERATED_KEYS);

        ps.setString(1, stock.getSymbol());
        ps.setString(2, stock.getInventoryCode());
        ps.setFloat(3, stock.getSharePrice());
        ps.setFloat(4, stock.getQuantityAvailable());
        ps.setString(5, stock.getExchangeId());
        ps.setDate(6, new java.sql.Date(stock.getPurchaseDate().getTime()));
        return ps;
    }
}
```

Since the STOCKS table makes use of an auto-generated column, the generated value must be maintained for subsequent updates. The `Connection.prepareStatement` method exposes a second argument to specify how to obtain any auto-generated keys. The simplest option is passing the constant `java.sql.Statement.RETURN_GENERATED_KEYS`. Or, an array of strings may be passed specifying the column names that possess auto-generation, for example, ID. In this case a `KeyHolder` class implementation must be supplied to hold these auto-generated values. In Listing 4–11, an instance of `GeneratedKeyHolder` is provided as the second argument to the method `jdbcTemplate.update`, then `GeneratedKeyHolder` instance is interrogated for key values upon successful SQL operation completion.

Listing 4–11. *Invoking the JdbcTemplateand with a Callback*

```
package com.apress.prospringintegration.springenterprise.stocks.dao.jdbc;

import com.apress.prospringintegration.springenterprise.stocks.dao.jdbc.PSStockCreater;
...
@Component
public class JdbcTemplateStockDao implements StockDao {
//...
    @Override
    public void insert(Stock stock) {
        KeyHolder keyHolder = new GeneratedKeyHolder();
        jdbcTemplate.update(new PSStockCreater(stock), keyHolder);
        stock.setId(keyHolder.getKey().intValue());
    }
//...
}
```

Standard updates look almost nothing like regular JDBC code, in that the update query text include the argument replacement values. Spring will go an extra step and determine the SQL types for the arguments you pass in. In this regard, simple update and query operations can fit into one line. Listing 4–12 uses `JdbcTemplate.update` method to simply delete rows.

Listing 4–12. Using JdbcTemplate to update a table

```
@Override
public void delete(Stock stock) {
    jdbcTemplate.update("delete from STOCKS where id = ?", stock.getId());
}
```

Using JdbcTemplate to Query

As with updates, Spring provides a way to execute queries using a number of overloaded query methods to streamline query execution and result generation. A best practice is to use the org.springframework.jdbc.core.RowMapper<T> interface in JdbcTemplate code to yield the most compact code. Like PreparedStatementCreator, it is best to decide how your code uses a ResultSet, and extract that recipe out accordingly; either inline or in a separate (and re-usable) implementation class. The RowMapper<T> interface has a single method, mapRow, which you're expected to implement to construct an object. Depending on the query function, a single object or multiple objects may be returned as the method's return value. When using queryForObject method to return single domain objects, as shown in Listing 4–13, you need to ensure that your query will always return only one single row of data, otherwise a IncorrectResultSizeDataAccessException is thrown.

Listing 4–13. Method using RowMapper<T> Inline to Obtain a Single Object Instance

```
@Override
public Stock findByInventoryCode(String iCode) {
    String sql = " SELECT * from STOCKS" +
            " WHERE INVENTORY_CODE = ?";
    return jdbcTemplate.queryForObject(sql, new StockMapper(), iCode );
    // the last argument is a varargs array
}
```

The RowMapper<Stock> implementation as an external class is shown in Listing 4–14.

Listing 4–14. RowMapper<Stock> Implementation

```
package com.apress.prospringintegration.springenterprise.stocks.dao.jdbc;

import com.apress.prospringintegration.springenterprise.stocks.model.Stock;
import org.springframework.jdbc.core.RowMapper;
import java.sql.ResultSet;
import java.sql.SQLException;

public class StockMapper implements RowMapper<Stock> {
    public Stock mapRow(ResultSet rs, int rowNum) throws SQLException {
         Stock stock = new Stock(
                             rs.getString("SYMBOL"),
                             rs.getString("INVENTORY_CODE"),
                             rs.getString("EXCHANGE_ID"),
                             rs.getFloat("PRICE_PER_SHARE"),
                             rs.getInt("QUANTITY_AVAILABLE"),
                             rs.getDate("PURCHASE_DATE")
                      );
        stock.setId(rs.getInt("ID"));
                      return stock;
```

```
    }
}
```

An implementation of RowMapper<T> as an inline class is shown in Listing 4–15. The query method returns a List of Stock objects.

Listing 4–15. *Method using RowMapper<T> to Return a List of Objects*

```
    @Override
    public List<Stock> findAvailableStockBySymbol(String symbol) {
        String sql = " SELECT * from STOCKS" +
                " WHERE SYMBOL = ? order by PRICE_PER_SHARE";
        List<Stock> ret = jdbcTemplate.query(
                sql,
                new Object[]{symbol},
                new RowMapper<Stock>() {
                    public Stock mapRow(ResultSet rs, int rowNum) throws SQLException {
                        return new Stock(
                                rs.getString("SYMBOL"),
                                rs.getString("INVENTORY_CODE"),
                                rs.getString("EXCHANGE_ID"),
                                rs.getFloat("PRICE_PER_SHARE"),
                                rs.getInt("QUANTITY_AVAILABLE"),
                                rs.getDate("PURCHASE_DATE")
                        );
                    }
                });

        return ret;
    }
```

The JdbcTemplateStockDao may be exercised by using the main class shown in Listing 4–16. The Spring context is created and a reference to the JdbcTemplateStockDao is obtained. Two Stock instances are inserted into the database and the first instance is retrieved using the findByInventoryCode method.

Listing 4–16. *Example main Class for JdbcTemplate*

```
package com.apress.prospringintegration.springenterprise.stocks.runner;

import com.apress.prospringintegration.springenterprise.stocks.dao.StockDao;
import com.apress.prospringintegration.springenterprise.stocks.model.Stock;
import org.springframework.context.ApplicationContext;
import org.springframework.context.support.ClassPathXmlApplicationContext;

import java.util.Calendar;

public class MainJdbcTemplate {
    public static void main(String[] args) {
        GenericApplicationContext context =
                new AnnotationConfigApplicationContext(
                        "com.apress.prospringintegration.springenterprise.stocks.dao.jdbc");
        StockDao stockDao =
                context.getBean("jdbcTemplateStockDao", StockDao.class);
        Stock stock = new Stock("ORAC", "JDBCTPL0001", "QQQQ", 120.0f, 1100,
                Calendar.getInstance().getTime());
```

```
        stockDao.insert(stock);

        stock = new Stock("APRS", "JDBCTPL0002", "QQQQ", 150.00F, 1500,
                Calendar.getInstance().getTime());
        stockDao.insert(stock);

        stock = stockDao.findByInventoryCode("JDBCTPL0001");

        if (stock != null) {
            System.out.println("Template Version");
            System.out.println("Stock Symbol :" + stock.getSymbol());
            System.out.println("Inventory Code :" + stock.getInventoryCode());
            System.out.println("purchased price:" + stock.getSharePrice());
            System.out.println("Exchange ID:" + stock.getExchangeId());
            System.out.println("Quantity Available :" + stock.getQuantityAvailable());
        }
    }
}
```

As noted, this style of DAO implementation uses JDBC directly, and even with templates it employs redundant boilerplate code. Eventually, your application will become burdened with this infrastructure code, and DAO methods will get much larger and less maintainable. In addition to boilerplate code, JDBC does not make handling relationships easy; associated entities must be handled on a per-use basis by creating and persisting the object in the DAO. Executing another query through the same or separate DAO solves this, or as will be shown next, by using an ORM framework.

Integrating Hibernate 3 and Spring

To use Hibernate, your applications will need the following library dependencies. The required dependencies are shown in Listing 4–17.

Listing 4–17. *Maven Dependency Setup to Use Hibernate pom.xml*

```
<dependency>
  <groupId>org.hibernate</groupId>
  <artifactId>hibernate-core</artifactId>
  <version>3.3.2.GA</version>
</dependency>
<dependency>
  <groupId>org.hibernate</groupId>
  <artifactId>hibernate-annotations</artifactId>
  <version>3.4.0.GA</version>
</dependency>
<dependency>
  <groupId>org.hibernate</groupId>
  <artifactId>hibernate-commons-annotations</artifactId>
  <version>3.3.0.ga</version>
</dependency>
<dependency>
  <groupId>org.hibernate</groupId>
  <artifactId>hibernate-entitymanager</artifactId>
  <version>3.4.0.GA</version>
</dependency>
<dependency>
```

```
    <groupId>org.slf4j</groupId>
    <artifactId>slf4j-log4j12</artifactId>
    <version>1.5.6</version>
  </dependency>
```

To map entity classes using Hibernate XML mappings, a single mapping file may be used for each class or a large file supporting several classes. In practice, one mapping file for each class should be used following the naming convention of appending the class name with `.hbm.xml` for ease of maintenance. Based on this convention, the mapping file for the `Stock` class will be named `stocks.hbm.xml`.

Listing 4–18. *Defining the Hibernate Mapping XML Configuration stocks.hbm.xml*

```
<!DOCTYPE hibernate-mapping
    PUBLIC "-//Hibernate/Hibernate Mapping DTED 3.0//EN"
    "http://hibernate.sourceforge.net/hibernate-mapping-3.0.dtd">
<hibernate-mapping package="com.apress.prospringintegration.springenterprise.stocks.model">
  <class name="Stock" table="STOCKS">
    <id name="id" type="int" column="ID">
      <generator class="identity"/>
    </id>
    <property name="symbol" type="string">
      <column name="SYMBOL" length="5" not-null="true"/>
    </property>
    <property name="exchangeId" type="string" column="EXCHANGE_ID"/>
    <property name="quantityAvailable" type="int" column="QUANTITY_AVAILABLE"/>
    <property name="sharePrice" type="float" column="PRICE_PER_SHARE"/>
    <property name="purchaseDate" type="date" column="PURCHASE_DATE"/>
    <property name="inventoryCode" type="string" column="INVENTORY_CODE"/>
  </class>
</hibernate-mapping>
```

In the mapping file, the table name will be specified for the entity class and a table column for each property. In addition, column details such as column length, not-null constraints, and unique constraints may be specified. Also, each entity must have an identifier defined, which can be generated automatically or assigned manually. In this example, the identifier will be generated using a table identity column.

Each application that uses Hibernate requires a global configuration file to configure properties such as the database settings (either JDBC connection properties or the data source's JNDI name), the database dialect, the mapping metadata's locations, and so on. When using XML mapping files to define mapping metadata, the locations of the XML files must be specified. By default, Hibernate will read `hibernate.cfg.xml` from the root of the classpath. If there is a hibernate.properties file on the classpath, that file will be consulted first with the XML file taking precedence. The Hibernate configuration file is shown in Listing 4–19.

Listing 4–19. *Hibernate Configuration File hibernate.cfg.xml*

```
<!DOCTYPE hibernate-configuration PUBLIC
    "-//Hibernate/Hibernate Configuration DTD 3.0//EN"
    "http://hibernate.sourceforge.net/hibernate-configuration-3.0.dtd">
<hibernate-configuration>
  <session-factory>
    <property name="hibernate.dialect">org.hibernate.dialect.H2Dialect</property>
    <property name="hiberante.show_sql">true</property>
    <property name="hibernate.format_sql">true</property>
    <mapping resource="stocks.hbm.xml"/>
```

```
  </session-factory>
</hibernate-configuration>
```

Configuring a Hibernate SessionFactory

The Hibernate `org.hibernate.SessionFactory` is used for all access to the database through the domain objects. The Java configuration for the `SessionFactory` is shown in Listing 4–20.

***Listing 4–20. Java** configuration Defining a Hibernate SessionFactory*

```
package com.apress.prospringintegration.springenterprise.stocks.dao.hibernate;

import com.apress.prospringintegration.springenterprise.stocks.config.StocksBaseConfig;
import org.springframework.beans.factory.annotation.Value;
import org.springframework.context.annotation.Bean;
import org.springframework.context.annotation.Configuration;
import org.springframework.context.annotation.ImportResource;
import org.springframework.core.io.Resource;
import org.springframework.orm.hibernate3.HibernateTemplate;
import org.springframework.orm.hibernate3.LocalSessionFactoryBean;

@Configuration
@ImportResource("classpath:hibernate-data-access.xml")
public class StocksHibernateConfig extends StocksBaseConfig {

    @Value("hibernate.cfg.xml")
    private Resource hibernateConfigResource;

    Resource hibernateConfigResource() {
        return hibernateConfigResource;
    }

    // Local Session Factory for getting hibernate connections
    @Bean
    LocalSessionFactoryBean sessionFactory() {
        LocalSessionFactoryBean sb = new LocalSessionFactoryBean();
        sb.setDataSource(dataSource());
        sb.setConfigLocation(hibernateConfigResource());
        return sb;
    }

    // Hibernate Template
    @Bean
    public HibernateTemplate hibernateTemplate() {
        return new HibernateTemplate(sessionFactory().getObject());
    }
}
```

Before you can persist your records, the tables will need to be created in a database schema to store the object data. When using an ORM framework like Hibernate, you are not required to design the tables by yourself. If the `hbm2ddl.auto` property is set to `update`, Hibernate will update the database schema and create the tables when necessary. Naturally, this option should not be enabled in production, but it can be a great speed boost for development.

The Hibernate Template

Although you can access Hibernate using the SessionFactory directly, an easier method is to use the provided org.springframework.orm.hibernate3.HibernateTemplate. Similar to the JdbcTemplate, Spring's HibernateTemplate abstracts away much of boilerplate code, and enables quicker development. Another advantage of using the HibernateTemplate is that it will translate native Hibernate exceptions into exceptions in Spring's org.springframework.dao.DataAccessException hierarchy. This allows consistent exception handling for all the data access strategies in Spring. For example, if a database constraint is violated when persisting an object, Hibernate usually throws an org.hibernate.exception.ConstraintViolationException. This Exception will be translated by the HibernateTemplate into org.springframework.dao.DataIntegrityViolationException, which is a subclass of org.springframework.dao.DataAccessException.

Using the HibernateTemplate, the StockDao may be implemented, as shown in Listing 4–21.

Listing 4–21. *StockDao Implementation using HibernateTemplate*

```
package com.apress.prospringintegration.springenterprise.stocks.dao.hibernate;

import com.apress.prospringintegration.springenterprise.stocks.dao.StockDao;
import com.apress.prospringintegration.springenterprise.stocks.model.Stock;
import org.springframework.beans.factory.annotation.Autowired;
import org.springframework.orm.hibernate3.HibernateTemplate;
import org.springframework.stereotype.Component;

import java.util.List;

@Component
public class HibernateStockDao implements StockDao {

    @Autowired
    HibernateTemplate hibernateTemplate;

    @Override
    public void insert(Stock stock) {
        hibernateTemplate.persist(stock);
    }

    @Override
    public void update(Stock stock) {
        hibernateTemplate.merge(stock);
    }

    @Override
    public void delete(Stock stock) {
        hibernateTemplate.delete(stock);
    }

    @Override
    public List<Stock> get() {
        return hibernateTemplate.find("from Stock s");
    }

    @Override
    public Stock findByInventoryCode(String iCode) {
```

```
        Stock found = null;
        String query = "from Stock s where s.inventoryCode =?";
        List ret = hibernateTemplate.find(query, iCode);
        if (ret != null && ret.size() > 0) {
            found = (Stock) ret.get(0);
        }

        return found;
    }

    @Override
    public List<Stock> findAvailableStockBySymbol(String symbol) {
        String query = "from Stock s where s.symbol =? and s.quantityAvailable>0";
        return hibernateTemplate.find(query, symbol);
    }
}
```

The following main class shown in Listing 4–22 may be used to test some of the DAO methods. It also demonstrates an entity's typical life cycle.

Listing 4–22. Main class for Executing HibernateTemplate DAO Methods

```
package com.apress.prospringintegration.springenterprise.stocks.runner;

import com.apress.prospringintegration.springenterprise.stocks.dao.StockDao;
import
com.apress.prospringintegration.springenterprise.stocks.dao.hibernate.HibernateStockDao;
import com.apress.prospringintegration.springenterprise.stocks.model.Stock;
import org.springframework.context.annotation.AnnotationConfigApplicationContext;
import org.springframework.context.support.GenericApplicationContext;

import java.util.Calendar;

public class MainHibernate {
    public static void main(String[] args) {
        GenericApplicationContext context =
            new AnnotationConfigApplicationContext(
                "com.apress.prospringintegration.springenterprise.stocks.dao.hibernate");

        StockDao stockDao =
                context.getBean("hibernateStockDao", HibernateStockDao.class);
        Stock stock =
                new Stock("ORAC", "HIBERNATEMAIN0001", "QQQQ", 120.0f, 1100,
                        Calendar.getInstance().getTime());
        stockDao.insert(stock);

        stock = stockDao.findByInventoryCode("HIBERNATEMAIN0001");

        if (stock != null) {
            System.out.println("Stock Symbol :" + stock.getSymbol());
            System.out.println("Inventory Code :" + stock.getInventoryCode());
            System.out.println("purchased price:" + stock.getSharePrice());
            System.out.println("Exchange ID:" + stock.getExchangeId());
```

```
            System.out.println("Quantity Available :" + stock.getQuantityAvailable());
        }
    }
}
```

The example main class demonstrates the ability to persist and retrieve the Stock domain object. The Spring context is created and used to obtain a reference to the HiberateStockDao instance. A Stock object is created, persisted, and retrieved based on the inventoryCode property.

Persistence with Hibernate in a JPA Context

JPA annotations are standardized in the JSR-220 specification so all JPA-compliant ORM frameworks, including Hibernate, support them. Moreover, the use of annotations are often more convenient providing the ability to edit the mapping metadata within the domain object source code.

The Stock class shown in Listing 4–23 illustrates the use of JPA annotations to define mapping metadata. The Stock entity object is embellished using javax.persistence annotation.

Listing 4–23. *JPA Annotated Entity Class*

```
package com.apress.prospringintegration.springenterprise.stocks.model;

import javax.persistence.*;
import java.util.Calendar;
import java.util.Date;

// Represents stocks in an inventory
@Entity
@Table(name = "STOCKS")
public class Stock {

    @Id
    @Column(name = "ID")
    @GeneratedValue(strategy = GenerationType.IDENTITY)
    int id;

    @Column(name = "INVENTORY_CODE", nullable = false)
    String inventoryCode;

    @Column(name = "SYMBOL")
    String symbol;

    @Column(name = "EXCHANGE_ID")
    String exchangeId;

    @Column(name = "PRICE_PER_SHARE")
    float sharePrice;

    @Column(name = "QUANTITY_AVAILABLE")
    int quantityAvailable;

    @Column(name = "PURCHASE_DATE")
    Date purchaseDate;
```

```
    public Stock() {
    }

    public Stock(String symbol, String inventoryCode, String exchange,
                float purchasedPrice, int quantityAvailable, Date purchaseDate) {
        this.symbol = symbol;
        this.inventoryCode = inventoryCode;
        this.exchangeId = exchange;
        this.sharePrice = purchasedPrice;
        this.quantityAvailable = quantityAvailable;
        this.purchaseDate =
                purchaseDate != null ? purchaseDate : Calendar.getInstance().getTime();
    }

    // Getters and Setters removed for brevity

}
```

Each entity class must be annotated with the @javax.persistence.Entity annotation. The table name for an entity class specified using the @javax.persistence.Table annotation.

For each property, you can specify a column name and column details using the @javax.persistence.Column annotation. Each entity class must have an identifier defined by @javax.persistence.Id annotation. You can choose a strategy for identifier generation using the @javax.persistence.GeneratedValue annotation. Here, a table identity column will generate the identifier value.

Hibernate supports both native XML mapping files and JPA annotations as means of defining mapping metadata. It is optional to specify mapped classes through a configuration element in the Hibernate configuration or persistence.xml file. Hibernate will automatically detect them at runtime. The Hibernate configuration for JPA is shown in Listing 4–24.

Listing 4–24. *Hibernate Configuration for JPA Annotations hibernate-jpa-cfg.xml*

```
<!DOCTYPE hibernate-configuration PUBLIC
    "-//Hibernate/Hibernate Configuration DTD 3.0//EN"
    "http://hibernate.sourceforge.net/hibernate-configuration-3.0.dtd">
<hibernate-configuration>
  <session-factory/>
</hibernate-configuration>
```

In the JPA context, your Hibernate configuration items can be consolidated with the entity manager configuration inside of META-INF/persistence.xml. This will help ensure maintainability; besides, Hibernate observes the same set of configuration properties here too. For this example, the empty Hibernate configuration is specified to prevent Hibernate from auto detecting the hibernate.cfg.xml file already present on the classpath. Hibernate is also configured so that entity definitions are drawn from class metadata only, because otherwise the hibernate.hbm.xml file would get automatically detected. This also means that that explicit mapping elements are not required, as all valid @Entity mapped classes will get auto detected by Hibernate.

Listing 4–25. *Entity Manager Configurationwith Hibernate META-INF/persistence.xml*

```
<?xml version="1.0" encoding="UTF-8" standalone="no"?>
<persistence xmlns="http://java.sun.com/xml/ns/persistence"
             xmlns:xsi="http://www.w3.org/2001/XMLSchema-instance" version="1.0"
             xsi:schemaLocation="http://java.sun.com/xml/ns/persistence
        http://java.sun.com/xml/ns/persistence/persistence_1_0.xsd">
```

```
  <persistence-unit name="persistenceUnit"
                    transaction-type="RESOURCE_LOCAL">
    <provider>org.hibernate.ejb.HibernatePersistence</provider>
    <properties>
      <property name="hibernate.dialect" value="org.hibernate.dialect.H2Dialect"/>
      <!--value='create' to build a new database on each run; value='update'
          to modify an existing database; value='create-drop' means the same as 'create'
          but also drops tables when Hibernate closes; value='validate' makes no changes
          to the database -->
      <!-- <property name="hibernate.hbm2ddl.auto" value="true"/> -->
      <property name="hibernate.ejb.cfgfile" value="hibernate-jpa-cfg.xml"/>
      <property name="hiberante.show_sql" value="true"/>
      <property name="hibernate.archive.autodetection" value="class"/>

    </properties>
  </persistence-unit>
</persistence>
```

Configuration and Usage of JpaTemplate

These examples will not make direct use of the EntityManager, but instead provide a JPA context to your Spring-based application. The LocalContainerEntityManagerFactoryBean instance will be created which is responsible for creating the entity manager factory by loading the persistence.xml. This class also provides convenience for overriding some configurations in the JPA configuration file, such as the data source and database dialect. The Java configuration for creating the JpaTemplate is shown in Listing 4–26.

Listing 4–26. *Java Configuration for Hibernate-based JPA Support*

```
package com.apress.prospringintegration.springenterprise.stocks.dao.jpa;

import com.apress.prospringintegration.springenterprise.stocks.config.StocksBaseConfig;
import org.hibernate.SessionFactory;
import org.hibernate.ejb.HibernateEntityManagerFactory;
import org.springframework.context.annotation.Bean;
import org.springframework.context.annotation.Configuration;
import org.springframework.context.annotation.ImportResource;
import org.springframework.orm.hibernate3.HibernateTemplate;
import org.springframework.orm.jpa.JpaTemplate;
import org.springframework.orm.jpa.JpaTransactionManager;
import org.springframework.orm.jpa.LocalContainerEntityManagerFactoryBean;

@Configuration
@ImportResource("classpath:jpa-data-access.xml")
public class StocksJpaConfig extends StocksBaseConfig {

    // Entity Manger for JPA
    @Bean
    public LocalContainerEntityManagerFactoryBean entityManagerFactory() {
        LocalContainerEntityManagerFactoryBean entityManagerFactory =
                new LocalContainerEntityManagerFactoryBean();
        entityManagerFactory.setDataSource(dataSource());
        return entityManagerFactory;
    }
```

```
    // JPA Template
    @Bean
    public JpaTemplate jpaTemplate() {
        return new JpaTemplate(entityManagerFactory().getObject());
    }

    // Transaction Manager for JPA
    @Bean
    public JpaTransactionManager transactionManager() {
        return new JpaTransactionManager(entityManagerFactory().getObject());
    }

    // Local Session Factory for getting hibernate connections
    @Bean
    SessionFactory sessionFactory() {
        return ((HibernateEntityManagerFactory)
                 entityManagerFactory().getObject()).getSessionFactory();
    }

    // Hibernate Template
    @Bean
    public HibernateTemplate hibernateTemplate() {
        return new HibernateTemplate(sessionFactory());
    }
}
```

Because Hibernate is configured through JPA persistence, obtaining a Hibernate SessionFactory is a little less straightforward, but it's also less cumbersome. The glue is the HibernateEntityManagerFactory, which extends the EntityManagerFactory interface, which contains a method to obtain a reference to the Hibernate SessionFactory instance. Thus, obtaining a SessionFactory is made through the casting the EntityManagerFactory to the HibernateEntityManager as seen in the configuration class for this example.

Spring provides the HibernateTemplate and JpaTemplate classes that enable the same simplified programming style enjoyed with JdbcTemplate. Like their JdbcTemplate counterpart, these template classes also enforce resource creation and disposal to ensure that Hibernate session and JPA entity managers are properly managed. The StockDao implementation using the JpaTemplate is shown in Listing 4–27.

Listing 4–27. *Implementation of StockDao using JpaTemplate*

```
package com.apress.prospringintegration.springenterprise.stocks.dao.jpa;

import com.apress.prospringintegration.springenterprise.stocks.dao.StockDao;
import com.apress.prospringintegration.springenterprise.stocks.model.Stock;
import org.springframework.beans.factory.annotation.Autowired;
import org.springframework.orm.jpa.JpaTemplate;
import org.springframework.stereotype.Component;
import org.springframework.stereotype.Repository;
import org.springframework.test.context.transaction.TransactionConfiguration;
import org.springframework.transaction.annotation.Transactional;

import java.util.List;

@TransactionConfiguration(transactionManager = "transactionManager")
```

```
@Component
public class JpaStockDao implements StockDao {
    @Autowired
    private JpaTemplate jpaTemplate;

    @Override
    @Transactional
    public void insert(Stock stock) {
        jpaTemplate.persist(stock);
    }

    @Override
    @Transactional
    public void update(Stock stock) {
        jpaTemplate.merge(stock);
    }

    @Override
    @Transactional
    public void delete(Stock stock) {
        jpaTemplate.refresh(stock);
    }

    @Override
    @SuppressWarnings("unchecked")
    @Transactional(readOnly = true)
    public List<Stock> findAvailableStockBySymbol(String symbol) {
        return (List<Stock>) jpaTemplate.find("from Stock s where s.symbol=?", symbol);
    }

    @Override
    @Transactional(readOnly = true)
    public Stock findByInventoryCode(String iCode) {
        return jpaTemplate.find(Stock.class, iCode);
    }

    @Override
    @Transactional(readOnly = true)
    public List<Stock> get() {
        return jpaTemplate.find("from Stock s");
    }
}
```

These DAO implementation methods are all declared to be transactional with the `@Transactional` annotation. The `@Transactional` method turns on transaction demarcation for all method invocations in a given thread: thus, if a method is invoked and it turn invokes another method, they will both participate in the same transaction. The transaction will commit all the changes by the outermost method invocation in a given thread. To gain this functionality, you must enable the Spring `tx` schema element `<tx:annotation-driven>` in the Spring configuration file as shown in Listing 4–28.

Listing 4–28. *Declarative Transaction Management jpa-data-access.xml*

```
<?xml version="1.0" encoding="UTF-8"?>
<beans xmlns="http://www.springframework.org/schema/beans"
       xmlns:xsi="http://www.w3.org/2001/XMLSchema-instance"
       xmlns:jdbc="http://www.springframework.org/schema/jdbc"
       xmlns:context="http://www.springframework.org/schema/context"
       xmlns:tx="http://www.springframework.org/schema/tx"
       xsi:schemaLocation="http://www.springframework.org/schema/beans
    http://www.springframework.org/schema/beans/spring-beans-3.0.xsd
    http://www.springframework.org/schema/tx
    http://www.springframework.org/schema/tx/spring-tx-3.0.xsd
    http://www.springframework.org/schema/context
    http://www.springframework.org/schema/context/spring-context-3.0.xsd
    http://www.springframework.org/schema/beans
    http://www.springframework.org/schema/beans/spring-beans-3.0.xsd
    http://www.springframework.org/schema/jdbc
    http://www.springframework.org/schema/jdbc/spring-jdbc-3.0.xsd">

  <context:property-placeholder location="StocksJDBC.properties"/>
  <context:component-scan
     base-package="com.apress.prospringintegration.springenterprise.stocks.dao.jpa"/>

  <jdbc:embedded-database type="H2" id="h2DataSource"/>

  <jdbc:initialize-database data-source="h2DataSource" ignore-failures="DROPS">
    <jdbc:script location="/STOCKS.DDL.SQL"/>
  </jdbc:initialize-database>

  <!--proxy-target-class set to true because CGLIB hides our bean when usingTransactional-->
  <tx:annotation-driven proxy-target-class="true"/>

</beans>
```

By default, this element looks for an `org.springframework.transaction.PlatformTransactionManager` manager bean instance by the name of `transactionManager`, so a `PlatformTransactionManager` must be declared based on the persistence API that is being used. In this case, the Spring provided `org.springframework.orm.jpa.JPATransactionManager` is used which requires the `EntityManagerFactory` property to be set as shown in Listing 4–26. Transaction management will be discussed in more detail following.

The `StockDao` implementation using `JpaTemplate` may be tested using the main class shown in Listing 4–29. The main class creates the Spring context and obtains a reference to the `JpaStockDao` instance. A Stock object is created and persisted using the JpaStockDao instance and then retrieved using the `findAvailableStockBySymbol` method.

Listing 4–29. *Main class Demonstrating JpaStockDao*

```
package com.apress.prospringintegration.springenterprise.stocks.runner;

import com.apress.prospringintegration.springenterprise.stocks.dao.StockDao;
import com.apress.prospringintegration.springenterprise.stocks.model.Stock;
```

```
import org.springframework.context.annotation.AnnotationConfigApplicationContext;
import org.springframework.context.support.GenericApplicationContext;

import java.util.Calendar;
import java.util.List;

public class MainHibernateJPA {
    public static void main(String[] args) {
        GenericApplicationContext context =
                new AnnotationConfigApplicationContext(
                        "com.apress.prospringintegration.springenterprise.stocks.dao.jpa");

        StockDao stockDao = context.getBean("jpaStockDao", StockDao.class);
        Stock stock =
                new Stock("ORAC", "JPAMAIN0001", "QQQQ", 120.0f, 1100,
                        Calendar.getInstance().getTime());
        stockDao.insert(stock);

        List<Stock> stocks = stockDao.findAvailableStockBySymbol("ORAC");

        if (stocks != null && stocks.size() > 0) {
            stock = stocks.get(0);
            System.out.println("Stock Symbol :" + stock.getSymbol());
            System.out.println("Inventory Code :" + stock.getInventoryCode());
            System.out.println("purchased price:" + stock.getSharePrice());
            System.out.println("Exchange ID:" + stock.getExchangeId());
            System.out.println("Quantity Available :" + stock.getQuantityAvailable());
        }
    }
}
```

Using JPA EntityManagers Directly

The JpaTemplate provides a clean way to work with JPA, just as the HibernateTemplate provides a convenient way to work with Hibernate's Sessions. However, we can do better. In EJB 3.0, applications can inject a JPA EntityManager instance and use that to work with the backend datastore. This, of course, doesn't work in Java SE, but it is a compelling programming model, so Spring brings it to you in any environment. EJB 3.0 beans are stateful by default. EJB beans are passivated and activated for each request. EJB beans are not shared across requests, and EJB beans are pooled. When a method is invoked on an EJB, the invocation can manipulate class state and work with values in a thread-safe way with no extra care. Spring beans, on the other hand, are stateless, so it is up to you to ensure that any state is also thread safe. A JPA EntityManager is *not* thread safe, however. So, injecting a regular EntityManager is a recipe for disaster in a shared, concurrently accessed DAO. Spring provides a way around this and lets you inject an EntityManager proxy. The proxy is simply a wrapper that delegates to a thread-local EntityManager. Clients can have their cake and eat it too: EntityManager access is now threadsafe, *and* your Spring beans retain the advantages of being stateless.

Let's look at the previous example, slightly reworked to support this style of programming. First, let's look at the revised configuration as shown in Listing 4–30.

Listing 4–30. Java Configuration for using EntityManager Directly

```
package com.apress.prospringintegration.springenterprise.stocks.dao.jpaandentitymanagers;


import com.apress.prospringintegration.springenterprise.stocks.config.StocksBaseConfig;
import org.hibernate.SessionFactory;
import org.hibernate.ejb.HibernateEntityManagerFactory;
import org.springframework.context.annotation.Bean;
import org.springframework.context.annotation.Configuration;
import org.springframework.context.annotation.ImportResource;
import org.springframework.dao.annotation.PersistenceExceptionTranslationPostProcessor;
import org.springframework.orm.hibernate3.HibernateTemplate;
import org.springframework.orm.jpa.JpaTemplate;
import org.springframework.orm.jpa.JpaTransactionManager;
import org.springframework.orm.jpa.LocalContainerEntityManagerFactoryBean;

@Configuration
@ImportResource("classpath:jpa-entity-manager.xml")
public class StocksJpaConfig extends StocksBaseConfig {

    // Entity Manger for JPA
    @Bean
    public LocalContainerEntityManagerFactoryBean entityManagerFactory() {
        LocalContainerEntityManagerFactoryBean entityManagerFactory =
                new LocalContainerEntityManagerFactoryBean();
        entityManagerFactory.setDataSource(dataSource());
        return entityManagerFactory;
    }

    // JPA Template
    @Bean
    public JpaTemplate jpaTemplate() {
        return new JpaTemplate(entityManagerFactory().getObject());
    }

    // Transaction Manager for JPA
    @Bean
    public JpaTransactionManager transactionManager() {
        return new JpaTransactionManager(entityManagerFactory().getObject());
    }

    // Since we're no longer using the JpaTemplate, we don't benefit from the exception
translation
    // so we need to turn this on explicitly
    @Bean
    public PersistenceExceptionTranslationPostProcessor
persistenceExceptionTranslationPostProcessor() { ➥
        PersistenceExceptionTranslationPostProcessor
persistenceExceptionTranslationPostProcessor = ➥
                new PersistenceExceptionTranslationPostProcessor();
        return persistenceExceptionTranslationPostProcessor;
    }
}
```

You can see we've omitted the `JpaTemplate` (naturally) and included something that would appear to have almost no relation to JPA at all – a `PersistenceExceptionTranslationPostProcessor`. The `PersistenceExceptionTranslationPostProcessor` is something that normally lives in the background – you rarely need to deal with it directly since all the persistence technologies already provide equivalent support. As you know, the various persistence technologies in the Spring framework provide consistent exception translation. Spring provides a consistent exception hierarchy and then translates various JDBC, JPA and Hibernate (among others) exceptions into this hierarchy so that you can deal with exceptions in a consistent way across all persistence technologies. As we are foregoing the `JpaTemplate`, we need to reinstate this behavior manually by registering the bean with the context manually.

Now we can rework our DAOs to use this support. Let's look at our `StockJpaDao`, as shown in Listing 4–31.

Listing 4–31. *DAO using EntityManager Directly*

```
package com.apress.prospringintegration.springenterprise.stocks.dao.jpaandentitymanagers;


import com.apress.prospringintegration.springenterprise.stocks.dao.StockDao;
import com.apress.prospringintegration.springenterprise.stocks.model.Stock;
import org.springframework.stereotype.Component;
import org.springframework.test.context.transaction.TransactionConfiguration;
import org.springframework.transaction.annotation.Transactional;

import javax.persistence.EntityManager;
import javax.persistence.PersistenceContext;
import javax.persistence.Query;
import java.util.List;

@TransactionConfiguration(transactionManager = "transactionManager")
@Component
public class JpaStockDao implements StockDao {

    @PersistenceContext
    private EntityManager entityManager;

    @Override
    @Transactional
    public void insert(Stock stock) {
        this.entityManager.persist(stock);
    }

    @Override
    @Transactional
    public void update(Stock stock) {
        this.entityManager.merge(stock);
    }


    @Override
    @Transactional
    public void delete(Stock stock) {
        entityManager.remove(stock);
    }
```

```
    @Override
    @SuppressWarnings("unchecked")
    @Transactional(readOnly = true)
    public List<Stock> findAvailableStockBySymbol(String symbol) {
        Query qu = entityManager.createQuery(
                " from Stock s where s.symbol = :stock ");
        qu.setParameter("stock", symbol);
        return (List<Stock>) qu.getResultList();
    }

    @Override
    @Transactional(readOnly = true)
    public Stock findByInventoryCode(String iCode) {
        return entityManager.find(Stock.class, iCode);
    }

    @Override
    @Transactional(readOnly = true)
    public List<Stock> get() {
        return (List<Stock>) entityManager.createQuery("from Stock").getResultList();
    }
}
```

Not bad! The code is now almost as brief as the original `JpaTemplate`-based example, and is very apparent in function. There is equivalent support for Hibernate `Sessions`, as well.

Transaction Management Framework

Transactions enable controllable concurrent access of data by multiple business operations, thus safeguarding integrity. In the event of sudden system outages, transactions ensure that data remains in a consistent state. Transactions also define business units of work – usually several data commits and reads taken as a whole. To do this, a per-thread transaction context is defined which encapsulates all operations bound to it under a given unit of work that will either entirely complete with a commit, or roll back as a whole - undoing all operations if any single part fails. This may be illustrated with discrete steps using the following pseudo code as shown in Listing 4–32.

***Listing 4–32.** Pseudocode Illustrating Typical Business Logic Within a Transaction*

```
Begin transaction
        Deduct inventory (sql write)
        Debit client bank account (sql write)
        Credit business funds (sql write)
        Update history log (sql write)
Commit transaction
```

The four individual steps behave as an indivisible unit of work, thus the final outcome is determined by each one of the steps. When one step fails, the unit fails – any state changes are unwound, and the transaction rolls back. Conversely, when they all succeed, the transaction is committed and the final state is saved. When designing your application, you determine the individual units of work. The concepts of transactions can be stated as a group of four well defined properties known as ACID: Atomicity, Consistency, Isolation, and Durability. This is explained in Table 4–1.

Table 4–1. Fundamental Transaction Concepts

Atomicity	A transaction is an atomic operation that consists of a series of actions. The atomicity of a transaction ensures that the actions either complete entirely, or take no effect at all.
Consistency	Once all actions of a transaction have completed, the transaction is committed. Then your data and resources will be in a consistent state that conforms to business rules.
Isolation	Because there may be many transactions processing with the same data set at the same time, each transaction should be isolated from others to prevent data corruption.
Durability	Once a transaction has completed, its result should be durable to survive any system failure such as power failure to a critical database system. Usually, the result of a transaction is written to persistent storage.

Most resources that you interact with provide a notion of a transaction: database commits may be aggregated and committed, JMS messages may be acknowledged or not, and so on. Many different APIs provide a concept that basically feels like a transaction, even if it's not exposed as such. These transactions are generally referred to as *local transactions.*

A process might conduct operations in multiple contexts spanning disparate internal/external departments, business partners, and/or vendors. These operations enlist multiple resources – a local transaction will not suffice. Global transactions – in contrast to local transactions, which are resource-specific – span multiple transactional resources and are managed by a third-party transaction monitor. The transaction monitor coordinates all the enlisted transactions to create a transaction. The API typically used to describe the interaction between transactional resources and a third party monitor is called the Java Transaction API (JTA). Most global transaction monitors work through an implementation of two-phase commit (2PC). 2PC works by enlisting a resource in a coordinated transaction, preparing that transaction, and then – when all enlisted resources are prepared – committing all of the resources. Java EE application servers provide JTA implementations, and there are also open-source or commercial JTA implementations that can be embedded in your application if your server doesn't have one already built in.

Spring Transaction Management

Clearly, you have choices to make: whether to use local transactions or global transactions and, if you're using global transactions, which should you use? Spring provides both programmatic and declarative transaction management. The programmatic approach exposes the underlying JTA or non-JTA implementation by the `org.springframework.transaction.PlatformTransactionManager` interface and related sub-classes. This provides a consistent API to deal with all transactions in a similar way, indifferent to how the underlying API exposes the transaction. Declarative transactions are applied using Aspect Oriented Programming (AOP) to define transaction boundaries. This approach allows for much less invasive transaction control, in that it departs from coding directly to the underlying API.

The basic transactional unit of work in a Spring transaction is exposed through the `org.springframework.transaction.TransactionDefinition` interface, which controls basic properties of a transaction.

Table 4–2. TransactionDefinition Transactional Concepts

Isolation	Like the ACID Isolation principle, this defines degree of isolation of the given transaction (for example, visibility of results from another uncommitted transaction).
Propagation	Determines controlling scope of the transaction that is it supports a set of properties, similar to EJB CMT's `javax.ejb.TransactionAttributeType` constants.
Timeout	Governs the duration a transaction should execute before timing out and automatically being rolling back.
Read-Only	Defines a read-only transaction that cannot make any writes to transactional resources.

Let your business case justify the level of isolation you need in any given transaction. However, do note that the choice you make can greatly have impact on performance. Spring supports five levels of isolation that are given as static properties on the `TransactionDefinition` interface as shown in Table 4–3.

Table 4–3. Transactional Isolation Levels

`DEFAULT`	Default level for the PlatformTransactionManager. For example, most databases use `READ_COMMITTED` by default.
`READ_UNCOMMITTED`	Lowest isolation, highest concurrency; allows this transaction to see changes from other uncommitted transactions.
`READ_COMMITTED`	Less concurrency; ensures that other transactions cannot see uncommitted data, however you can see inserts and updates from other transactions.
`REPEATABLE_READ`	More isolated than read_commited; that is you can guarantee that data selects will always contain the same dataset until the transaction completes.
`SERIALIZABLE`	Lowest concurrency; all transactions are repeatable_read, and are serialized in execution order. No concurrency is guaranteed.

In addition to isolation levels, Spring provides a finer grained `org.springframework.transaction.interceptor.TransactionAttribute` interface that enables you to declaratively specify a strategy that determines which specific subclasses of `java.lang.Throwable` cause rollback. By default, if no exceptions are specified, any Throwable thrown will cause a rollback.

Controlling Transaction Propagation with the TransactionStatus Interface

To provide fine-grained transaction monitoring, Spring provides the `org.springframework.transaction.TransactionStatus` interface that allows your application to check the status of the running transaction, whether it is new, read-only, or rollback only. This simple interface exposes the `setRollbackOnly` method, which causes the current transaction to rollback and end as opposed to having a transaction abnormally terminate through an exception. The propagation behavior is similar to the `org.springframework.transaction.TransactionDefinition` interface. This interface will seem familiar to EJB CMT transaction attributes (see Table 4–4).

Table 4–4. *Propagation Strategy Properties as Defined in TransactionDefinition*

`REQUIRED`	Transaction either exists, or a new one is started.
`SUPPORTS`	Transaction either exists, or execution is done non-transactional. This still enables participation in greater transactional contexts by providing a transaction scope to operate resources in.
`MANDATORY`	Transaction must be active, or `RemoteException` is thrown.
`REQUIRES_NEW`	Active transactions are suspended, and a new one started. Otherwise, a new transaction is started in the absence of an active transaction.
`NOT_SUPPORTED`	Doesn't support execution within an active transaction. Will suspend any active transaction.
`NEVER`	If a transaction exists, then `RemoteException` is thrown. Otherwise, execution is non-transactional.
`NESTED`	If a transaction is active, then propagation mode switches to REQUIRED. Otherwise, it runs in a new, nested transaction. You can rollback nested transactions, or the containing transactions with the support through JDBC 3.0 Savepoint API.

Introduction to PlatformTransactionManager and Implementations

The `org.springframework.transaction.PlatformTransactionManager` interface uses `TransactionDefinition` and `TransactionStatus` to create and manage transactions. This is a Service Provider Interface (SPI) that can also be mocked and stubbed to provide programmatic transaction management. Any given implementation of this interface contains the salient details of the underling transaction manager. For example, the `DataSourceTransactionManager` manages transactions performed within a JDBC `DataSource`, `JdoTransactionManager` controls transactions performed in a JDO session, `HibernateTransactionManager` does the same in a Hibernate session, and `JpaTransactionManager` supports transaction for JPA.

Setting Up Transaction Control with TransactionTemplate

Spring offers a convenient approach to wrapping execution logic inside of a transaction by providing the `TransactionTemplate`. This class, similar to `JdbcTemplate`, allows you to enforce your transaction logic through the callback class that implements the `TransactionCallback<T>` interface. By passing your `TransactionCallback<T>` implementation to the `TransactionTemplate.execute` method, you gain the triple advantage of more concise and readable code, and not having to manage boilerplate transaction management code for the affected operations. As with a JdbcTemplate, configuring and injecting a TransactionTemplate is simply a matter of injecting the TransactionTemplate with a TransactionManager, then injecting the template into your bean of preference.

The Java configuration remains similar to earlier StockConfig configurations with the presence of a dataSource, jdbcTemplate, and other common data resources. Here, a TransactionTemplate is configured with the corresponding PlatformTransactionManager instance. The TransactionTemplate instance will get injected into dependent DAO repositories. The Java Configuration is shown in Listing 4–33.

Listing 4–33. *Configuring Spring Container with TransactionManager*

```
package com.apress.prospringintegration.springenterprise.stocks.transactions.template;

import org.springframework.beans.factory.annotation.Autowired;
import org.springframework.context.annotation.Bean;
import org.springframework.context.annotation.Configuration;
import org.springframework.context.annotation.ImportResource;
import org.springframework.jdbc.datasource.DataSourceTransactionManager;
import org.springframework.transaction.PlatformTransactionManager;
import org.springframework.transaction.support.TransactionTemplate;

import javax.sql.DataSource;

@Configuration
@ImportResource("tx_template.xml")
public class TransactionalConfig {
    @Autowired
    private DataSource dataSource;

    @Bean
    public PlatformTransactionManager transactionManager() throws Exception {
        DataSourceTransactionManager dtm = new DataSourceTransactionManager();
        dtm.setDataSource(dataSource);
        dtm.setDefaultTimeout(30);
        return dtm;
    }

    @Bean
    public TransactionTemplate transactionTemplate() throws Exception {
        return new TransactionTemplate(transactionManager());
    }
}
```

This example will utilize an unreliable stock data insertion technique to provide the transactional logic illustration. It will begin to insert several stocks and upon (randomly manufactured) coincidence, generate a constraint violation, which produces an exception that interrupts the process. The objective in this is to demonstrate the rollback phase. The preFillStocks method shown in Listing 4–34 will perform a series of insert/updates where the inventoryCode property will be set to the same value for two different rows creating a constraint violation. This will cause all of the insert/updates to rollback.

***Listing 4–34.** Transaction-based Insert/Update that will Create Random Constraint Violation*

```
package com.apress.prospringintegration.springenterprise.stocks.transactions.template;

import com.apress.prospringintegration.springenterprise.stocks.dao.StockBrokerService;
import com.apress.prospringintegration.springenterprise.stocks.dao.StockDao;
import com.apress.prospringintegration.springenterprise.stocks.model.Stock;
import org.springframework.beans.factory.annotation.Autowired;
import org.springframework.beans.factory.annotation.Qualifier;
import org.springframework.stereotype.Component;
import org.springframework.transaction.TransactionStatus;
import org.springframework.transaction.support.TransactionCallbackWithoutResult;
import org.springframework.transaction.support.TransactionTemplate;

import java.util.Calendar;
import java.util.Random;

@Component
public class TransactionalStockBrokerService implements StockBrokerService {
    @Autowired
    @Qualifier("transactionTemplate")
    private TransactionTemplate transactionTemplate;

    @Autowired
    @Qualifier("jdbcTemplateStockDao")
    private StockDao stockDao;

    // inserts at least 25% duplicate inventory code.
    public void preFillStocks(final String exchangeId, final String... symbols) {
        final Random random = new Random();

        transactionTemplate.execute(new TransactionCallbackWithoutResult() {
            protected void doInTransactionWithoutResult(TransactionStatus status) {
                int i = 0;
                for (String sym : symbols) {
                    float pp = (float) Math.random() * 100.0f;
                    int qq = (int) Math.random() * 250;
                    Stock s = new Stock(sym, "INV00" + i, exchangeId, pp, qq, Calendar
                            .getInstance().getTime());
                    stockDao.insert(s);
                    System.out.println("ORIG INVENTORY: " + s.getInventoryCode() + " ");
                    int randomized = (random.nextInt(100) % 4) == 0 ? 0 : i;
                    s.setInventoryCode("INV00" + randomized);
                    System.out.println("NEW RANDOMIZED INVENTORY:"
                            + s.getInventoryCode() + " " + randomized);
                    stockDao.update(s);
                    i++;
                }
            }
        });
    }
}
```

The main class for the TransactionTemplate example is shown in Listing 4–35. The main class creates a Spring context and obtains a reference to the transactionalStockBrokerService instance. Calling the preFillStocks method will attempt to insert six new stocks resulting in a constraint violation causing the transaction to rollback. The main class will log that no rows have been added to the database.

Listing 4–35. *Main Class for Demostrating the TransactionTemplate*

```
package com.apress.prospringintegration.springenterprise.stocks.runner;

import com.apress.prospringintegration.springenterprise.stocks.dao.StockDao;
import com.apress.prospringintegration.springenterprise.stocks.dao.jdbc.JdbcTemplateStockDao;
import com.apress.prospringintegration.springenterprise.stocks.model.Stock;
import
com.apress.prospringintegration.springenterprise.stocks.transactions.template.TransactionalSto
ckBrokerService;
import org.springframework.context.annotation.AnnotationConfigApplicationContext;
import org.springframework.context.support.GenericApplicationContext;

public class MainTxJdbc {
    public static void main(String[] args) {
        GenericApplicationContext context = new AnnotationConfigApplicationContext(
            "com.apress.prospringintegration.springenterprise.stocks.transactions.template",
            "com.apress.prospringintegration.springenterprise.stocks.dao.jdbc");

        TransactionalStockBrokerService uStockDao =
                context.getBean("transactionalStockBrokerService",
                        TransactionalStockBrokerService.class);
        try {
            uStockDao.preFillStocks("TEST", "IBM", "INTC", "MSFT", "ORAC", "C");
        } catch (Exception ex) {
            System.out.println("Exception: " + ex.getMessage());
        }

        StockDao stockDao = context.getBean(JdbcTemplateStockDao.class);
        System.out.println("Total rows inserted: " + stockDao.get().size());
        for (Stock s : stockDao.get()) {
            System.out.println("Stock added: " + s.getSymbol());
        }
    }
}
```

Declaring Transactions with Transaction Advices

Spring offers AOP-based support for declarative transactions. This advice can be enabled with AOP configuration facilities defined in the aop schema. AOP support requires the addition Maven dependency:

```
<dependency>
  <groupId>org.aspectj</groupId>
  <artifactId>aspectjweaver</artifactId>
  <version>1.6.8</version>
</dependency>
```

To enable declarative transaction management, add the <tx:advice> element to the Spring configuration file shown in Listing 4–36. This advice will need to be associated with a pointcut. Because a transaction advice is declared outside the <aop:config> element, it cannot link with a pointcut directly. An advisor must be declared in the <aop:config> element to associate an advice with a pointcut.

Listing 4–36. *Defining a Transaction Advice and Pointcut with Spring XML tx_aop.xml*

```
<?xml version="1.0" encoding="UTF-8"?>
<beans xmlns="http://www.springframework.org/schema/beans"
       xmlns:xsi="http://www.w3.org/2001/XMLSchema-instance"
       xmlns:aop="http://www.springframework.org/schema/aop"
       xmlns:tx="http://www.springframework.org/schema/tx"
       xmlns:context="http://www.springframework.org/schema/context"
       xsi:schemaLocation="http://www.springframework.org/schema/beans
    http://www.springframework.org/schema/beans/spring-beans-3.0.xsd
    http://www.springframework.org/schema/tx
    http://www.springframework.org/schema/tx/spring-tx-3.0.xsd
    http://www.springframework.org/schema/aop
    http://www.springframework.org/schema/aop/spring-aop-3.0.xsd
    http://www.springframework.org/schema/context
    http://www.springframework.org/schema/context/spring-context-3.0.xsd">

  <context:component-scan base-➥
package="com.apress.prospringintegration.springenterprise.stocks.transactions.aopdeclarative"➥
/>

  <tx:advice id="txAdvice" transaction-manager="transactionManager">
    <tx:attributes>
      <tx:method name="find*" read-only="true"/>
      <tx:method name="*"/>
    </tx:attributes>
  </tx:advice>

  <aop:config>
    <aop:pointcut id="stockBrokerOperation"
                  expression="execution(* ➥
com.apress.prospringintegration.springenterprise.stocks.dao.StockBrokerService.*(..))"/>
    <aop:advisor advice-ref="txAdvice" pointcut-ref="stockBrokerOperation"/>
  </aop:config>

</beans>
```

The preceding AspectJ pointcut expression matches all the methods declared in the StockBrokerService interface. However, because Spring AOP is based on proxies, it can apply only to public methods. Thus only public methods can be made transactional with Spring AOP.

Each transaction advice requires an identifier and a reference to a transaction manager in the IoC container. If you do not specify a transaction manager explicitly, Spring will search the application context for a PlatformTransactionManager with a bean name of transactionManager. The methods that require transaction management are specified with multiple <tx:method> elements inside the <tx:attributes> element. The method name supports wildcards for you to match a group of many methods. Transaction attributes may also be defined for each group of methods. The default attributes are listed in Table 4–5 .

Table 4–5. Attribues Used with tx:attributes with Their Defaults

Attribute	Required	Default
name	Yes	n/a
propagation	No	REQUIRED
isolation	No	DEFAULT
timeout	No	-1
read-only	No	False
rollback-for	No	N/A
no-rollback-for	No	N/A

Obtaining the AOPStockBrokerService bean is simply a matter of retrieving it from the IoC container. This is because this bean's methods are matched by the pointcut and that causes Spring to return a proxy that has transaction management enabled for this bean.

The StockBrokerService implementation will be modified to remove the TransactionalTemplate since we are no longer coding with the transaction system directly. This proxied version will perform all transactional duties enabled by the <aop:config> element in the Spring configuration file. The modified AopStockBrokerService implementation is shown in Listing 4–37.

Listing 4–37. StockBrokerService Implementation using Transaction Advice

```
package com.apress.prospringintegration.springenterprise.stocks.transactions.aopdeclarative;

import com.apress.prospringintegration.springenterprise.stocks.dao.StockBrokerService;
import com.apress.prospringintegration.springenterprise.stocks.dao.StockDao;
import com.apress.prospringintegration.springenterprise.stocks.model.Stock;
import org.springframework.beans.factory.annotation.Autowired;
import org.springframework.beans.factory.annotation.Qualifier;
import org.springframework.stereotype.Component;

import java.util.Calendar;
import java.util.Random;

@Component
public class AopStockBrokerService implements StockBrokerService {

    @Autowired
    @Qualifier("hibernateStockDao")
    private StockDao stockDao;

    private Random random = new Random();

    // inserts at least 25% duplicate inventory code.
    public void preFillStocks(final String exchangeId, final String... symbols) {
```

```
        int i = 0;
        for (String sym : symbols) {
            float pp = (float) Math.random() * 100.0f;
            int qq = (int) Math.random() * 250;
            Stock s = new Stock(sym, "INV00" + i, exchangeId, pp, qq, Calendar
                    .getInstance().getTime());
            stockDao.insert(s);
            System.out.println("ORIG INVENTORY: " + s.getInventoryCode() + " ");
            int randomized = (random.nextInt(100) % 4) == 0 ? 0 : i;
            s.setInventoryCode("INV00" + randomized);
            System.out.println("NEW RANDOMIZED INVENTORY:"
                    + s.getInventoryCode() + " " + randomized);
            stockDao.update(s);
            i++;
        }
    }
}
```

To demonstrate that Spring transaction support can be used with any of the Spring DAO templates, this example has also been modified to use Hibernate instead of JDBC. Note that the `StockDao` is using the `HibernateStockDao` implementation. In addition, the `PlatformTransactionManager` implementation is `HibernateTransactionManager`, as shown in Listing 4–38. Note that the Hibernate `sessionFactory` is now required.

Listing 4–38. *Java Configuration for AOP transaction using Hibernate*

```
package com.apress.prospringintegration.springenterprise.stocks.transactions.aopdeclarative;

import org.hibernate.SessionFactory;
import org.springframework.beans.factory.annotation.Autowired;
import org.springframework.context.annotation.Bean;
import org.springframework.context.annotation.Configuration;
import org.springframework.context.annotation.ImportResource;
import org.springframework.orm.hibernate3.HibernateTransactionManager;
import org.springframework.transaction.PlatformTransactionManager;

@Configuration
@ImportResource("tx_aop.xml")
public class TxAOPConfig {
    @Autowired
    private SessionFactory sessionFactory;

    @Bean
    public PlatformTransactionManager transactionManager() throws Exception {
        HibernateTransactionManager dtm = new HibernateTransactionManager();
        dtm.setSessionFactory(sessionFactory);
        dtm.setDefaultTimeout(30);
        return dtm;
    }
}
```

The main class to run the AOP transaction example with Hibernate as shown in Listing 4–39 will be similar to the previous example. The main class creates a Spring context and obtains a reference to the `aopStockBrokerService` instance. Calling the `preFillStocks` method will attempt to insert six new stocks resulting in a constraint violation causing the transaction to rollback. The main class will log that no rows have been added to the database.

Listing 4–39. Transaction Advise Main Class

```
package com.apress.prospringintegration.springenterprise.stocks.runner;

import com.apress.prospringintegration.springenterprise.stocks.dao.StockBrokerService;
import com.apress.prospringintegration.springenterprise.stocks.dao.StockDao;
import
com.apress.prospringintegration.springenterprise.stocks.dao.hibernate.HibernateStockDao;
import com.apress.prospringintegration.springenterprise.stocks.model.Stock;
import org.springframework.context.annotation.AnnotationConfigApplicationContext;
import org.springframework.context.support.GenericApplicationContext;

public class MainTxAop {
    public static void main(String[] args) throws Exception {
        GenericApplicationContext context = new AnnotationConfigApplicationContext(
      "com.apress.prospringintegration.springenterprise.stocks.transactions.aopdeclarative",
      "com.apress.prospringintegration.springenterprise.stocks.dao.hibernate");

        StockBrokerService broker =
                context.getBean("aopStockBrokerService", StockBrokerService.class);
        try {
            broker.preFillStocks("QQQQ", "INTC", "IBM", "XLA", "MGM", "C");
        } catch (Exception ex) {
            System.out.println("Exception: " + ex.getMessage());
        }

        StockDao stockDao = context.getBean(HibernateStockDao.class);
        System.out.println("Total rows inserted: " + stockDao.get().size());
        for (Stock s : stockDao.get()) {
            System.out.println("Stock added: " + s.getSymbol());
        }
    }
}
```

Declarative Transaction Managing with the @Transactional Annotation

Declaring transactions in the bean configuration file requires knowledge of AOP concepts such as pointcuts, advices, and advisors. While the solution is advantageous in eliminating complex transaction API code, it does not come without its price. Developers who do not or cannot engage in the nitty-gritty of aspects declaration may find it hard to enable declarative transaction management. That is why in addition to declaring transactions in the bean configuration file with pointcut, advices, and advisors, Spring allows you to declare transactions by annotating your transactional methods with `@Transactional` enabled by the `<tx:annotation-driven>` element in the XML metadata configuration. Thus, to define a method as transactional, you annotate with `@Transactional` and provide any one of the arguments that define the transactional behavior. Note that you should only annotate public methods due to the proxy-base limitations of Spring AOP. The `StockBrokerService` implementation using the `@Transactional` annotation is shown in Listing 4–40.

Listing 4–40. Declaring methods with @Transactional

```
package com.apress.prospringintegration.springenterprise.stocks.transactions.annotation;

import com.apress.prospringintegration.springenterprise.stocks.dao.StockBrokerService;
import com.apress.prospringintegration.springenterprise.stocks.dao.StockDao;
import com.apress.prospringintegration.springenterprise.stocks.model.Stock;
import org.springframework.beans.factory.annotation.Autowired;
import org.springframework.beans.factory.annotation.Qualifier;
import org.springframework.orm.hibernate3.HibernateTemplate;
import org.springframework.stereotype.Component;
import org.springframework.transaction.annotation.Transactional;

import java.util.Calendar;
import java.util.Random;

@Component
public class AnnotationTxStockBrokerService implements StockBrokerService {

    @Autowired
    private HibernateTemplate hibernateTemplate;

    @Autowired
    @Qualifier("hibernateStockDao")
    private StockDao stockDao;

    Random random = new Random();

    @Transactional
    public void preFillStocks(final String exchangeId, final String... symbols) {
        int i = 0;
        for (String sym : symbols) {
            float pp = (float) Math.random() * 100.0f;
            int qq = (int) Math.random() * 250;
            Stock s = new Stock(sym, "INV00" + i, exchangeId, pp, qq, Calendar
                    .getInstance().getTime());
            stockDao.insert(s);
            System.out.println("ORIG INVENTORY: " + s.getInventoryCode() + " ");
            int randomized = (random.nextInt(100) % 4) == 0 ? 0 : i;
            s.setInventoryCode("INV00" + randomized);
            System.out.println("NEW RANDOMIZED INVENTORY:"
                    + s.getInventoryCode() + " " + randomized);
            stockDao.update(s);
            i++;
        }
    }

}
```

The `@Transactional` annotation may be applied at the method level or the class level. When applying this annotation to a class, all of the public methods within this class will be defined as transactional. Although you can apply `@Transactional` to interfaces or method declarations in an interface, it is not recommended because there may be conflicts with class-based proxies (CGLIB proxies).

In the bean configuration file, you only need to enable the `<tx:annotation-driven>` element and specify a transaction manager for it as shown in Listing 4–41. That way, Spring will advise methods on classes defined with `@Transactional`, and individual methods with `@Transactional`, for beans that are declared in the IoC container.

***Listing 4–41.** Declaring tx:annotation-driven tx_annotation.xml*

```
<?xml version="1.0" encoding="UTF-8"?>
<beans xmlns="http://www.springframework.org/schema/beans"
       xmlns:xsi="http://www.w3.org/2001/XMLSchema-instance"
       xmlns:tx="http://www.springframework.org/schema/tx"
       xmlns:context="http://www.springframework.org/schema/context"
       xsi:schemaLocation="http://www.springframework.org/schema/beans
    http://www.springframework.org/schema/beans/spring-beans-3.0.xsd
    http://www.springframework.org/schema/tx
    http://www.springframework.org/schema/tx/spring-tx-3.0.xsd
    http://www.springframework.org/schema/context
    http://www.springframework.org/schema/context/spring-context.xsd">

  <context:component-scan
      base-
package="com.apress.prospringintegration.springenterprise.stocks.transactions.annotation"/>

  <tx:annotation-driven transaction-manager="transactionManager"/>

</beans>
```

Again, this example is using Hibernate, which requires the `HibernateTransactionManager` and the dependent Hibernate `sessionFactory` as shown in Listing 4–42.

***Listing 4–42.** Demonstration of Transactional Property Attributes*

```
package com.apress.prospringintegration.springenterprise.stocks.transactions.annotation;

import org.hibernate.SessionFactory;
import org.springframework.beans.factory.annotation.Autowired;
import org.springframework.context.annotation.Bean;
import org.springframework.context.annotation.Configuration;
import org.springframework.context.annotation.ImportResource;
import org.springframework.orm.hibernate3.HibernateTransactionManager;
import org.springframework.transaction.PlatformTransactionManager;

@Configuration
@ImportResource("tx_annotation.xml")
public class TxAnnotationConfig {
    @Autowired
    private SessionFactory sessionFactory;

    @Bean
    public PlatformTransactionManager transactionManager() throws Exception {
        HibernateTransactionManager dtm = new HibernateTransactionManager ();
        dtm.setSessionFactory(sessionFactory);
        dtm.setDefaultTimeout(30);
        return dtm;
    }
}
```

The main class to run the AOP transaction example with Hibernate as shown in Listing 4–43 will be similar to the previous examples. The main class creates a Spring context and obtains a reference to the annotationTxStockBrokerService instance. Calling the preFillStocks method will attempt to insert six new stocks resulting in a constraint violation causing the transaction to rollback. The main class will log that no rows have been added to the database.

Listing 4–43. Executing Class for @Transaction Methods

```
package com.apress.prospringintegration.springenterprise.stocks.runner;

import com.apress.prospringintegration.springenterprise.stocks.dao.StockBrokerService;
import com.apress.prospringintegration.springenterprise.stocks.dao.StockDao;
import
com.apress.prospringintegration.springenterprise.stocks.dao.hibernate.HibernateStockDao;
import com.apress.prospringintegration.springenterprise.stocks.model.Stock;
import
com.apress.prospringintegration.springenterprise.stocks.transactions.annotation.AnnotationTxSt
ockBrokerService;
import org.springframework.context.annotation.AnnotationConfigApplicationContext;
import org.springframework.context.support.GenericApplicationContext;

public class MainTxAnnotation {
    public static void main(String[] args) throws Exception {
        GenericApplicationContext context = new AnnotationConfigApplicationContext(
            "com.apress.prospringintegration.springenterprise.stocks.transactions.annotation",
            "com.apress.prospringintegration.springenterprise.stocks.dao.hibernate");

        StockBrokerService broker =
                context.getBean("annotationTxStockBrokerService", StockBrokerService.class);
        try {
            broker.preFillStocks("QQQQ", "INTC", "IBM", "XLA", "MGM", "C");
        } catch(Exception ex) {
            System.out.println("Exception: " + ex.getMessage());
        }

        StockDao stockDao = context.getBean(HibernateStockDao.class);
        System.out.println("Total rows inserted: " + stockDao.get().size());
        for (Stock s : stockDao.get()) {
            System.out.println("Stock added: " + s.getSymbol());
        }
    }
}
```

Because Spring auto-detects a PlatformTransactionManager named transactionManager in the container, you can further reduce configuration by naming your local transaction manager transactionManager, that way you will not need to specify the transaction-manager attribute in <tx:annotation-driven>.

In addition to declaring a method transactional with the @Transactional behavior, you may specify any of the TransactionDefinition properties as described at the beginning of this section. You simply describe a transactional behavior as an attribute to the @Transactional annotation.

For example, given a stock ordering system, we may want to find a stock that meets our criteria for price, quantity, and symbol. Because a transaction (or other transaction running) may acquire locks on rows and tables, a long transaction will tie up resources and have an impact on overall performance. If a transaction only reads, rather than update data, the database engine could optimize this transaction. In this case you can tailor the behavior of the transaction management by marking the transaction as readOnly (see Listing 4–44).

Listing 4–44. Demonstration of @Transactional Property Attributes

```
@Transactional(isolation = Isolation.REPEATABLE_READ,
        timeout = 30,
        readOnly = true)
public BestAsk findBestPrice(Order o) throws Exception {
    BestAsk bestAsk = new BestAsk();
    List<Stock> rets = hibernateTemplate.find("from Stock s where " +
            "s.pricePerShare <= ? and " +
            "s.quantityAvailable >= ? and s.symbol = ?",
            new Object[]{o.getBid(), o.getQuantity(), o.getSymbol()}, String.class);
    if (!rets.isEmpty()) {
        Stock stock = stockDao.findByInventoryCode(rets.get(0).getInventoryCode());
        bestAsk.setStock(stock);
    }

    return bestAsk;
}
```

The timeout transaction attribute indicates how long your transaction can survive before it is forced to roll back. This can prevent a long transaction from tying up resources. The read-only attribute indicates that this transaction will only read, but not update, data. The read-only flag is just a hint to enable a resource to optimize the transaction, and a resource might not necessarily cause a failure if a write is attempted.

Additionally, Spring's DataSourceTransactionManager may be setup with a default timeout value. This comes in handy when setup is done via Java configuration as are most of the examples as shown in Listing 4–45.

Listing 4–45. Setting the Default Timeout Property

```
@Bean
public PlatformTransactionManager transactionManager() throws Exception {
    DataSourceTransactionManager dtm = new DataSourceTransactionManager();
    dtm.setDataSource(dataSource);
    dtm.setDefaultTimeout(30);
    return dtm;
}
```

Spring Remoting

It is standard organizational strategy to compartmentalize data based on requirements such as human resource management, or product inventory tracking. The source of such data can often be confined to storage that is not accessible through conventional means, such as a database, or file. This is the motivation for remote computing services to provide a link to data across business tiers.

In this section, we are going to discuss how you can leverage Spring remoting. Spring supports a variety of remoting technologies in a consistent manner. On the server side, Spring allows exposing an arbitrary bean as a remote service through a service exporter. On the client side, Spring provides many proxy factory beans for you to create a local proxy for a remote service so that you can use the same remote service interface as if it were a local bean.

The Spring Framework features integration classes for remoting using the technologies shown in Table 4–6.

Table 4–6. Spring Remoting Technology Support

RMI	Traditional Java to Java Remote Method Invocation protocol.
HTTP INVOKER	Initiative by the Spring developers to enable Java serialization via HTTP.
HESSIAN	A lightweight binary HTTP based protocol developed by Caucho.
Burlap	Caucho's XML variety of Hessian. The two APIs are entirely interchangeable.
JAX-RPC	J2EE 1.4's web service API that features WSDL 1.1, SOAP 1.1 using HTTP 1.1 as the transport.
JAX-WS	Successor to JAX-RPC introduced in Java EE 5 featuring SOAP 1.2, JAXB data mapping, MTOM, and more.
JMS	Java Message Service for integrating a wide ranges of messaging products, such a MQueue series.

In order to gain insight on the bigger picture of Spring remoting integration, we will take a look at RMI service exposition, and RMI client usage. The other technologies are configured in virtually the same way. Remote Method Invocation (RMI) is the Java-based remoting technology that allows multiple Java applications running in different JVMs to communicate with each other. RMI utilizes Java serialization to marshal and un-marshal method arguments and return values. It uses direct TCP/IP sockets for transport, and the RMI Registry that defines service endpoints. A simple service implementation using RMI gives you a setup that mirrors EJB remoting only it does not provide hooks for security contexts, or remote transaction propagation. However, Spring enables you to propagate contexts such as Spring security context by wiring one to the `org.springframework.remoting.rmi.RmiServiceExporter` bean instance.
Spring exposes support for RMI through either the traditional `java.rmi.Remote` interface, or transparently through RMI invokers. Choose RMI invokers using `org.springframework.remoting.rmi.RmiServiceExporter` if you have existing Spring applications deployed or wish to begin with a fresh start using RMI. If you already have traditional RMI service endpoints deployed and need to inter-operate, then you must use the `Remote` and `java.rmi.RemoteException` classes.

■ **Note** As of Java SE 6, you no longer have to execute rmic to generate RMI stub and skeletons, as this is done completely inline by the Runtime.

Exposing and Invoking Services with RMI

Spring provides the `org.springframework.remoting.rmi` package that contains remoting facilitates that reduce complexity in exposing RMI services. You can leverage this on the server side by wiring `RmiServiceExporter` to export a Spring bean as an RMI service, enabling remote method invocation. On the client side, you simply wire RmiProxyFactoryBean with connectivity details to your service interface and that will create a proxy to your remote service.

Let us begin with a simple stock quoting scenario: we have a stock quoting service that delivers stock quotes, and a client that requests quotes for individual companies. But first, we need to setup the model. Note that all RMI transferrable objects must implement the java.io.Serializable interface; otherwise you will get a java.rmi.UnmarshalException. The Quote domain class is shown in Listing 4–46.

Listing 4–46. *Quote Domain Object*

```
package com.apress.prospringintegration.springenterprise.stocks.model;

import java.io.Serializable;

public class Quote implements Serializable {

    private String symbol;
    private float price;
    private String exchangeId;

    public Quote(String symbol, float price, String exchangeId) {
        this.symbol = symbol;
        this.price = price;
        this.exchangeId = exchangeId;
    }

    public Quote() {
    }

    public String getSymbol() {
        return symbol;
    }

    public void setSymbol(String symbol) {
        this.symbol = symbol;
    }

    public float getPrice() {
        return price;
    }

    public void setPrice(float price) {
        this.price = price;
    }

    public String getExchangeId() {
        return exchangeId;
    }

    public void setExchangeId(String exchangeId) {
        this.exchangeId = exchangeId;
    }
}
```

Let us define the Quote service interface that includes the method getQuote(String symbol), which returns a Quote with randomized price. The method getAllSymbols will simply return a list of symbols for which you have requested (see Listing 4–47).

Listing 4–47. *QuoteService Interface*

```
package com.apress.prospringintegration.springenterprise.stocks.service;

import com.apress.prospringintegration.springenterprise.stocks.model.Quote;

import java.util.List;

public interface QuoteService {

    public Quote getQuote(String symbol);

    public List<String> getAllSymbols();
}
```

In addition to the interface, it is necessary to provide a full implementation as shown in Listing 4–48. In production applications, you will want this service to query some message oriented stock ticker system. Here, we are going to randomize stock symbols, and quote values.

Listing 4–48. *QuoteService Business Implementation*

```
package com.apress.prospringintegration.springenterprise.stocks.service;

import com.apress.prospringintegration.springenterprise.stocks.model.Quote;
import java.util.ArrayList;
import java.util.HashMap;
import java.util.List;
import java.util.Map;

public class QuoteServiceImpl implements QuoteService {

    Map<String, Quote> quoteUniverse = new HashMap<String, Quote>();
    public Quote getQuote(String symbol) {
        if(quoteUniverse.containsKey(symbol))
            return quoteUniverse.get(symbol);
        Quote q = new Quote(symbol,(float)Math.random()*100,"NYSE");
        quoteUniverse.put(symbol, q);
        return q;
    }

    public List<String> getAllSymbols() {
        List<String> keyList = new ArrayList();
            keyList.addAll(quoteUniverse.keySet());
        return keyList;
    }
}
```

At this point, we have enough application detail that will enable us to expose our QuoteService remotely. We will use Spring's remoting facilities here to configure a bean for the StockQuote service implementation and expose it as an RMI service by using RmiServiceExporter. The Java configuration is shown in Listing 4–49.

***Listing 4–49.** Java Configuration for Exposing RMI services*

```
package com.apress.prospringintegration.springenterprise.stocks.service;

import org.springframework.context.annotation.Bean;
import org.springframework.context.annotation.Configuration;
import org.springframework.remoting.rmi.RmiServiceExporter;

@Configuration
public class RmiServiceConfig {

    @Bean
    public QuoteService quoteService() {
        return new QuoteServiceImpl();
    }

    @Bean
    public RmiServiceExporter serviceExporter() throws Exception {
        RmiServiceExporter se = new RmiServiceExporter();
        se.setServiceName("QuoteService");
        se.setService(quoteService());
        se.setServiceInterface(QuoteService.class);
        //se.setRegistryHost("localhost");
        //se.setRegistryPort(1399);
        se.afterPropertiesSet();
        return se;
    }
}
```

The salient configuration bits here are defined in the `RmiServiceExporter` bean. The `serviceName` property specifies the endpoint name that will be defined in the RMI registry. We also specify `serviceInterface` and `service` to define our service interface and concrete implementation respectively. The configuration properties `registryPort` and `registryHost` allow you to bind to an existing registry. In the absence of registry configuration properties, a new registry would get started which defaults to localhost at port 1099.

Bootstrapping the RMI service is straightforward. You simply create an application context for the Spring configuration or Java configuration containing your service configuration as shown in Listing 4–50.

***Listing 4–50.** Bootstrapping RMI Services in J2SE*

```
package com.apress.prospringintegration.springenterprise.stocks.runner;

import com.apress.prospringintegration.springenterprise.stocks.service.RmiServiceConfig;
import org.springframework.context.annotation.AnnotationConfigApplicationContext;

public class MainRmiService {
    public static void main(String[] args) {
        new AnnotationConfigApplicationContext(RmiServiceConfig.class);
    }
}
```

Running this program causes remote services to begin listening in the background on port 1099. Now we are going to illustrate remote service invocation through a Spring generated proxy. The RMI proxy generator class, `RmiProxyFactoryBean` enables declarative proxy generation that is injectable as a dependency in your client class. The example below shows how this is simply accomplished. We create our client class that will get injected with a proxy of our service interface, and it additionally serves as the execution bootstrap (see Listing 4–51).

Listing 4–51. *A Simple QuoteService Client Implementation*

```
package com.apress.prospringintegration.springenterprise.stocks.runner;

import com.apress.prospringintegration.springenterprise.stocks.client.QuoteServiceClient;
import com.apress.prospringintegration.springenterprise.stocks.model.Quote;
import org.springframework.context.annotation.AnnotationConfigApplicationContext;
import org.springframework.context.support.GenericApplicationContext;

import java.util.ArrayList;
import java.util.List;

public class MainRmiClient {
    public static void main(String[] args) {
        GenericApplicationContext context =
                new AnnotationConfigApplicationContext(
                        "com.apress.prospringintegration.springenterprise.stocks.client");

        QuoteServiceClient client =
                context.getBean("client", QuoteServiceClient.class);

        List<Quote> myQuotes = new ArrayList<Quote>();
        myQuotes.add(client.getMyQuote("APRESS"));
        myQuotes.add(client.getMyQuote("SPRNG"));
        myQuotes.add(client.getMyQuote("INTGRN"));

        for (Quote myQuote : myQuotes) {
            System.out.println("Symbol : " + myQuote.getSymbol());
            System.out.println("Price  :" + myQuote.getPrice());
            System.out.println("Exchange: " + myQuote.getExchangeId());
        }
    }
}
```

We are ready to wire a client using the proxy factory. The generated proxy contains all of the necessary RMI boilerplate, so we only need to concentrate on our particular business implementation. The following configuration does the client-side wiring. In configuring any `InitializingBean` instance such as the `RmiProxyFactoryBean`, it is important to call the `afterPropertiesSet()` method to invoke special bean initialization logic (see Listing 4–52).

Listing 4–52. *Java Configuration for a (QuoteClient) RMI client*

```
package com.apress.prospringintegration.springenterprise.stocks.client;

import com.apress.prospringintegration.springenterprise.stocks.service.QuoteService;
import org.springframework.context.annotation.Bean;
import org.springframework.context.annotation.Configuration;
import org.springframework.remoting.rmi.RmiProxyFactoryBean;

@Configuration
public class RMIClientConfig {
```

```
    @Bean
    public QuoteService quoteServiceBean() {
        RmiProxyFactoryBean factory = new RmiProxyFactoryBean();
        factory.setServiceUrl("rmi://localhost:1099/QuoteService");
        factory.setServiceInterface(QuoteService.class);
        factory.afterPropertiesSet();
        return (QuoteService) factory.getObject();
    }

    @Bean
    public QuoteServiceClient client() {
        QuoteServiceClient qc = new QuoteServiceClient();
        qc.setMyQuoteService(quoteServiceBean());
        return qc;
    }
}
```

Run the main class `MainRmiService` to start the RMI service then run the client main class `MainRmiClient`. The client will connect to the remote RMI service return three quotes, as shown in Listing 4–53.

***Listing 4–53.** Results of Running the RMI Exmple Client*

```
Symbol : APRESS
Price  :51.866577
Exchange: NYSE
Symbol : SPRNG
Price  :63.999958
Exchange: NYSE
Symbol : INTGRN
Price  :94.239365
Exchange: NYSE
```

Summary

This chapter has covered some of the building blocks in Spring's enterprise support. We have covered how to use Spring's database support to enable querying and updating relational databases. We demonstrated the benefits of Spring's template support for ORM-support and standard JDBC technologies simplifying demanding query tasks. In addition, we have learned about Spring's support for transaction management, as well as motivation for their use. A database may be setup and with minimal configuration, transactions may be used to enforce a high degree of integrity in the database. Finally, we demonstrated how to setup an RMI endpoint and consume one with minimal configuration and coding.

CHAPTER 5

Introduction to Spring Integration

Spring Integration is an extension to the Spring Framework. It provides support for the standard patterns typically used in enterprise integration. Spring Integration adds lightweight messaging and support for integrating with external systems and services using an adapter framework. Adapters enable a higher-level abstraction for communication with external systems and for Spring's support for data and remote access as well as scheduling. Spring Integration continues Spring's component model approach to creating maintainable and testable code.

This chapter will introduce the basic Spring Integration components and how they extend the Spring Framework into the world of messaging and event-driven architectures. Maven will be leveraged as the build and project management tool. The basic of how to use Maven with Spring Integration will be covered. Maven allows for easy integration with most Java IDEs. We will walk through building your first Spring Integration example. The basic integration example used to compare the alternative technologies in Chapter 2 will be used to demonstrate Spring Integration's ease of use. We will also address how Spring Integration plays with other Spring technologies. Spring Integration can enhance other projects with messaging and integration support.

Spring Integration Basics

A little bit of history and a review of the Spring approach is a good way to get started with Spring Integration. Spring Integration adds essentially three components to the core Spring Framework: messages, message channels, and endpoints. These three components and how they can be leveraged to support messaging and an event-driven architecture will be discussed.

History

Spring has become one of the most widely used frameworks for building vertical, database-backed web applications. The developers of the Spring Framework recognized the similarities between the common patterns used in Spring and those used for enterprise integration. By introducing messaging though component support for a pipes-and-filters model, Spring Integration began providing support for application integration across an enterprise. Most organizations have many different applications for different business domains, potentially using different technologies. Spring Integration facilitates horizontal interoperability across the enterprise.

Conceptually, a *filter* is any component that can consume or produce messages. A *pipe* describes how the messages move between the filters (in Spring Integration, these pipes are called *channels*). This model lets Spring Integration solutions leverage the advantages of messaging, loose coupling, performance, scalability, flexibility, and filtering.

Familiar Spring Idioms

Spring provides an Inversion of Control (IoC) container. IoC is used to free components in the container from the particulars of dependant resource creation and acquisition. Spring uses aspect-oriented programming support to move cross-cutting concerns such as transaction support to the container, and frees the developer from having to address these concerns in code.

Spring Integration takes the theme even further by freeing the integration code from having to know when and where data comes from, and how it does so. The framework handles where the business logic should be executed; it directs the message to the appropriate component and where the response should be sent—providing support for message routing and filtering. In addition, Spring Integration provides message transformation support so that the resultant application will be agnostic to the underlying message format and transport.

Spring Integration follows the same configuration scenarios as the Spring Framework, providing options for configuration through annotations, Java configuration, XML with namespace support, XML with the "standard" `bean` element, and direct access to the underlying API.

Low Coupling, High Productivity

Spring Integration makes it easy to compose single-focused POJO Spring beans in complex integrations. There is rarely any need to couple your code to the Spring Integration API.

Messages

A message is a generic wrapper for any Java object combined with metadata used by Spring Integration to handle the object. As shown in the `Message` interface in Listing 5–1, the Java object is the payload property, and the metadata is stored as a collection of message headers, which is in essence a `Map` with a `String` key and an `Object` value.

Listing 5–1. *Spring Integration Message Interface*

```
public interface org.springframework.integration.Message<T> {

        MessageHeaders getHeaders();

        T getPayload();

}
```

Headers

The `org.springframework.integration.MessageHeaders` object is a `String/Object Map` that typically maintains values for message housekeeping chores. `MessageHeaders` are immutable and are usually created using the `MessageBuilder` API. There are a number of predefined entries (headers), including `id`, `timestamp`, `correlation id`, and `priority`. In addition, the headers can maintain values required by the adapter endpoints (e.g., the file name for the file adapter or the email address for the mail adapter). Headers may be used any key/value pair required by the developer.

Payloads

The message payload can be any POJO. Spring Integration does not require message payloads to be in some sort of canonical payload or self-describing format. You can avail yourself of transformers to implement a canonical data model, as appropriate, but your hands aren't tied if this isn't appropriate for your application. Transformation support allows converting any payload into any type of format required by the message endpoint. This is in keeping with the noninvasive nature of Spring Integration.

Message Channels

A message channel is the component through which messages are moved. Message publishers send messages to the channel, and message consumers receive messages from the channel. The channel effectively decouples the producer and consumer. There are two types of messaging scenarios: *point-to-point*, in which a message is received only once, by a single consumer; and *publish/subscribe*, in which one or more consumers can attempt to receive a single message.

There are different ways to use a message channel, but generally your configuration will change according to whether you want messages on the channel to be published to you, or whether you want them queued.

Message Endpoints

A message endpoint is the abstraction layer between the application code and the messaging framework. An endpoint broadly defines all the types of components used in Spring Integration. It handles such tasks as producing and consuming messages, as well as interfacing with application code, external services, and applications. When data travels through a Spring Integration solution, it moves along channels from one endpoint to another. Data can come into the framework from external systems using a specific type of endpoint called an adapter. Spring Integration provides a number of adapters that interface with external applications and services; handling the interaction with the messaging infrastructure often only requires declarative configuration. Spring Integration provides a framework to build custom adapter endpoints in the (hopefully rare) event that the out-of-the-box adapters do not suffice.

The main endpoint types supported by Spring Integration are as follows:

- *Transformer*: Converts the message content or structure.
- *Filter*: Determines if the message should be passed to the message channel.
- *Router*: Can determine which channel to send a particular message based on its content.
- *Splitter*: Can break an incoming message into multiple messages and send them to the appropriate channel.
- *Aggregator*: Can combine multiple messages into one. An aggregator is more complex than a splitter often required to maintain state.
- *Service activator*: Is the interface between the message channel and a service instance, many times containing the application code for business logic.
- *Channel adapter*: Is used to connect the message channel to another system or transport.

All of these message endpoints will be discussed in more detail in a Chapters 7, 8 and 9.

Event-Driven Architecture

What is an event? In formal terms, an event is a significant change in state In an event-driven architecture, this event get sent or published to all interested parties. The subscribing parties can look at the event and choose to respond or ignore it. The response may include invoking a service, running a business process, or publishing another event.

Event-driven architecture is loosely coupled, meaning that the publisher of the event has no knowledge of what the consumers do downstream after the event has been processed. Spring Integration is well suited for this type of architecture, as it captures events as messages.

Event-driven architecture usually refers to simple event processing in which a published event leads to some downstream action. This type of processing is well suited to performing a real-time flow of work. By contrast, complex event processing (CEP) usually involves evaluating an aggregation of events, typically coming from all levels of a business. This may require analysis, correlation, and pattern matching to determine the appropriate action to be taken. Business process management (BPM) is a typical use case for CEP. There can be a number of different events that occur and only a certain combination of events will require a response. Spring Integration has the basic building blocks for CEP, including routers and aggregators (which will be discussed in Chapter 8).

First Steps for Spring Integration

Getting started with Spring Integration is straightforward, and only requires some basic steps. We will start with creating a Maven project and show how to add the necessary library support. The simplest method to create a Maven project is to use an archetype, as follows:

1. For a command window, enter `mvn archetype:generate`.
2. Choose `maven-archetype-quickstart` from the list of options, which provides a sample Maven project.
3. Select the latest version of the archetype and enter `com.apress.prospringintegration` for the `groupId`, `firstproject` for the `artifactId`, and the defaults for `version` and `package` . Then enter Return to create the project.

The Maven dependencies shown in Listing 5–2 will be needed for the examples in this chapter.

***Listing 5–2.** Maven Dependencies for Spring Integration*

```
<dependency>
  <groupId>org.springframework.integration</groupId>
  <artifactId>spring-integration-core</artifactId>
  <version>2.0.1.RELEASE</version>
</dependency>
<dependency>
  <groupId>org.springframework.integration</groupId>
  <artifactId>spring-integration-jms</artifactId>
  <version>2.0.1.RELEASE</version>
</dependency>
```

In addition, the Spring repositories shown in Listing 5–3 may be needed, especially when using the milestone and snapshot releases required throughout this book.

Listing 5–3. *Spring Maven Repositories*

```
<repositories>
  <repository>
    <id>repository.springframework.maven.release</id>
    <name>Spring Framework Maven Release Repository</name>
    <url>http://maven.springframework.org/release</url>
  </repository>
  <repository>
    <id>org.springframework.maven.milestone</id>
    <name>Maven Central Compatible Spring Milestone Repository</name>
    <url>http://maven.springframework.org/milestone</url>
  </repository>
  <repository>
    <id>org.springframework.maven.snapshot</id>
    <name>Maven Central Compatible Spring Snapshot Repository</name>
    <url>http://maven.springframework.org/snapshot</url>
  </repository>
</repositories>
```

The following configuration must be added to ensure that the code compiles against Java SE 6, and that the resources directory isn't filtered.

Listing 5–4. *pom.xml Build Element for Java SE 6*

```
<build>
  <resources>
    <resource>
      <directory>src/main/resources</directory>
      <filtering>false</filtering>
    </resource>
  </resources>
  <plugins>
    <plugin>
      <groupId>org.apache.maven.plugins</groupId>
      <artifactId>maven-compiler-plugin</artifactId>
      <configuration>
        <source>1.6</source>
        <target>1.6</target>
      </configuration>
    </plugin>
  </plugins>
</build>
```

How to Set Up Your IDE

Most IDEs can automatically import the Maven project just created. Once imported, there is nothing else in particular you need to start with Spring Integration. Eclipse (and the Maven plug-in, called the m2eclipse plug-in), STS (which will be described below), and IntelliJ IDEA all come with support for importing a Maven project.

Starting Your First Spring Integration Project

Each Spring Integration application is completely embedded, and needs no server infrastructure. In fact, a Spring Integration application can be deployed inside another application—for example, in your web application endpoint. Spring Integration flips the deployment paradigms of most integration frameworks on their heads. That is, Spring Integration is deployed into your application; your application is not deployed into Spring Integration, as you might expect. There are no start and stop scripts and no ports to guard.

The simplest possible working Spring Integration application is a simple Java `public static void main` method to bootstrap a Spring context, as shown in Listing 5–5.

***Listing 5–5.** Class to Start Spring Integration Application*

```
package com.apress.prospringintegration;

import org.springframework.context.support.ClassPathXmlApplicationContext;

public class App {
    public static void main(String[] args) {
        ClassPathXmlApplicationContext context =
                new ClassPathXmlApplicationContext("classpath:spring-context.xml");
        context.start();
    }
}
```

A standard Spring application context has been created and started. The contents of the Spring application context will be discussed shortly, but this example is shown to demonstrate the simplicity of starting a Spring Integration application. Next, the configuration file will be created for creating a simple input channel, a service activator to respond to a message published to the channel, and an output channel where the service activator sends it return value. This is shown in Listing 5–6.

***Listing 5–6.** Spring Configuration File spring-context.xml*

```
<?xml version="1.0" encoding="UTF-8"?>
<beans xmlns="http://www.springframework.org/schema/beans"
       xmlns:xsi="http://www.w3.org/2001/XMLSchema-instance"
       xmlns:si="http://www.springframework.org/schema/integration"
       xmlns:context="http://www.springframework.org/schema/context"
       xsi:schemaLocation="
    http://www.springframework.org/schema/beans
    http://www.springframework.org/schema/beans/spring-beans-3.0.xsd
    http://www.springframework.org/schema/integration
    http://www.springframework.org/schema/integration/spring-integration-2.0.xsd
    http://www.springframework.org/schema/context
    http://www.springframework.org/schema/context/spring-context-3.0.xsd">

  <context:component-scan base-package="com.apress.prospringintegration"/>

  <int:channel id="input"/>

  <int:channel id="output">
    <int:queue capacity="10"/>
  </int:channel>
```

```
    <int:service-activator input-channel="input"
                           output-channel="output"
                           ref="messageHandler"/>

</beans>
```

A point-to-point direct channel input is created using the channel element, and a queue channel output is created by adding the queue element. In addition, a service activator messageHandler is created using the service-activator element. As discussed, Spring Integration supports annotations for configuring Spring bean components. By adding the component-scan element of the context library, any Java class in the package com.apress.prospringintegration with the annotation @Component will be configured as a Spring bean. By convention, the bean named messageHandler will refer to the class MessageHandler, resolved by capitalizing the first letter of the bean name. Thus, if a message is sent the channel input, it will be forwarded to the service activator class MessageHandler. Since no method has been configured in the Spring configuration class, the message will be directed to the method annotated with @ServiceActivator. The MessageHandler class is shown in Listing 5–7.

Listing 5–7. *Service Activator Class MessageHandler*

```
package com.apress.prospringintegration;

import org.springframework.integration.annotation.ServiceActivator;
import org.springframework.stereotype.Component;

@Component
public class MessageHandler {

    @ServiceActivator
    public String handleMessage(String message) {
        System.out.println("Received message: " + message);
        return "MESSAGE:" + message;
    }
}
```

Note that the MessageHandler class has the required annotations for component scanning and the service activator annotation that directs the input message to the handleMessage method. This is a good time to describe the convention for mapping the Message object to the method signature. Typically, the method signature will either map to the Message payload or the Message object itself. (Other mapping scenarios will be discussed in Chapter 7) In the case of this example, the method signature maps to the String payload. The message payload will be logged and forwarded to the output channel, and prefixed with MESSAGE:.

To test this example, the main method just shown will be augmented to send a message to the input channel and poll the output channel for the resultant message. The modified App class is shown in Listing 5–8.

Listing 5–8. *Example Spring Integration Test Class App*

```
package com.apress.prospringintegration;

import org.springframework.context.support.ClassPathXmlApplicationContext;
import org.springframework.integration.Message;
import org.springframework.integration.MessageChannel;
```

```
import org.springframework.integration.core.PollableChannel;
import org.springframework.integration.support.MessageBuilder;

public class App {
    public static void main(String[] args) {
        ClassPathXmlApplicationContext context =
                new ClassPathXmlApplicationContext("classpath:spring-context.xml");
        context.start();

        MessageChannel input =
                (MessageChannel) context.getBean("input", MessageChannel.class );
        PollableChannel output =
                (PollableChannel) context.getBean("output", PollableChannel.class );
        input.send(MessageBuilder.withPayload("Pro Spring Integration Example").build());
        Message<?> reply = output.receive();
        System.out.println("received: " + reply);

    }
}
```

The result of running the example code is shown in Listing 5–9.

***Listing 5–9.** Results of Running the Example Code*

```
Received message: Pro Spring Integration Example
received: [Payload=MESSAGE:Pro Spring Integration Example][Headers={timestamp=1296618370609,↵
 id=d4c9fac6-655b-45f3-aa4e-e02c1167eb74}]
```

The main method accesses the input and output channel beans through the Spring context. A message is sent to the input channel with the string value Pro Spring Integration Example. Then the resultant Message is polled from the output channel. Of special note is the MessageBuilder utility class. This class provides support for creating a Spring Integration Message object with methods for specifying the payload and header values. In addition, there are other methods supporting enrichment of the header values (e.g., setHeader, setPriority, and setCorrelationId). With this, you've completed your first working Spring Integration program!

To extend this example and to provide a comparison to the example used in exploring alternative integration frameworks in Chapter 2, the example will be modified to send and receive the message to and from a JMS broker. This example will use the ActiveMQ JMS message broker, as described in Chapter 2. To support the ActiveMQ broker and JMS, the following Maven dependencies must be added to the pom.xml file shown in Listing 5–10.

***Listing 5–10.** Maven Dependencies to Support ActiveMQ and JMS*

```
<dependency>
  <groupId>org.apache.activemq</groupId>
  <artifactId>activemq-core</artifactId>
  <version>5.4.1</version>
</dependency>
  <dependency>
    <groupId>javax.jms</groupId>
    <artifactId>jms</artifactId>
    <version>1.1</version>
  </dependency>
```

To simplify the example, an embedded ActiveMQ JMS broker is created using context scanning and Java configuration. The `@Bean` annotation creates the `connectionFactory` bean using a `CachingConnectionFactory`, and creates an embedded broker using the broker URL `vm://localhost`. This will create the required connection factory for the message-driven and outbound JMS channel adapters. The Java configuration file is shown in Listing 5–11.

Listing 5–11. *Configuring the JMS Connection Using the JmsConfiguration Class*

```
package com.apress.prospringintegration;

import org.apache.activemq.ActiveMQConnectionFactory;
import org.springframework.context.annotation.Bean;
import org.springframework.jms.connection.CachingConnectionFactory;
import org.springframework.stereotype.Component;

import javax.jms.ConnectionFactory;

@Component
public class JmsConfiguration {

    @Bean(name = "connectionFactory")
    public ConnectionFactory getConnectionFactory() {
        ActiveMQConnectionFactory targetConnectionFactory = new ActiveMQConnectionFactory();
        targetConnectionFactory.setBrokerURL("vm://localhost");

        CachingConnectionFactory connectionFactory =
                new CachingConnectionFactory(targetConnectionFactory);
        connectionFactory.setSessionCacheSize(10);
        connectionFactory.setCacheProducers(false);

        return connectionFactory;
    }
}
```

The first requirement for interacting with a JMS broker from Spring Integration is to add the namespace support, as shown in Listing 5–12. Note the addition of the `jms` namespace. By default, the message-driven and outbound JMS channel adapters use the connection factory with the default name `connectionFactory`, so it does not need to be declared in the adapter configuration. The `message-driven-channel-adapter` element is used instead of the `inbound-channel-adapter` element since it does not require polling, and will forward the JMS message as soon as it is received. Based on the configuration file, when a message is send to the `input` channel, it will be converted to a JMS message and sent to the `requestQueue` destination. By convention, a JMS text message is used since the input `Message` payload is a `String`. (Further information about JMS message mapping will be discussed in Chapter 12) The JMS message is then received by the message-driven adapter and forwarded to the `output` `Message` channel. The text message is converted to a `String` and sent as the `Message` payload.

Listing 5–12. *Spring Configuration File for Sending and Receiving a JMS Message*

```
<?xml version="1.0" encoding="UTF-8"?>
<beans xmlns="http://www.springframework.org/schema/beans"
       xmlns:xsi="http://www.w3.org/2001/XMLSchema-instance"
       xmlns:int ="http://www.springframework.org/schema/integration"
       xmlns:jms="http://www.springframework.org/schema/integration/jms"
       xmlns:context="http://www.springframework.org/schema/context"
```

```
        xsi:schemaLocation="
     http://www.springframework.org/schema/beans
     http://www.springframework.org/schema/beans/spring-beans-3.0.xsd
     http://www.springframework.org/schema/integration
     http://www.springframework.org/schema/integration/spring-integration-2.0.xsd
     http://www.springframework.org/schema/integration/jms
     http://www.springframework.org/schema/integration/jms/spring-integration-jms-2.0.xsd
     http://www.springframework.org/schema/context
     http://www.springframework.org/schema/context/spring-context-3.0.xsd">

  <context:component-scan base-package="com.apress.prospringintegration"/>

  <int:channel id="input"/>

  <jms:outbound-channel-adapter channel="input" destination-name="requestQueue"/>

  <jms:message-driven-channel-adapter channel="output" destination-name="requestQueue"/>

  <int:channel id="output">
    <int:queue capacity="10"/>
  </int:channel>

</beans>
```

To test the JmsApp class, run the JMS Spring Integration example application, as shown in Listing 5–13. It should look familiar, since it is almost identical to the first integration project example shown previously. The only change is the reference to the Spring configuration file jms-spring-context.xml. This demonstrates the power of Spring Integration, in which the underlying transport mechanism is irrelevant to the application code. Only a simple configuration change was required to move from the internal message transport to a JMS broker.

Listing 5–13. *Example JMS Spring Integration Test Class*

```
package com.apress.prospringintegration;

import org.springframework.context.support.ClassPathXmlApplicationContext;
import org.springframework.integration.Message;
import org.springframework.integration.MessageChannel;
import org.springframework.integration.core.PollableChannel;
import org.springframework.integration.support.MessageBuilder;

public class JmsApp {
        public static void main(String[] args) {
        ClassPathXmlApplicationContext context =
                new ClassPathXmlApplicationContext("classpath:jms-spring-context.xml");
        context.start();

        MessageChannel input = (MessageChannel) context.getBean("input");
        PollableChannel output = (PollableChannel) context.getBean("output");
        input.send(MessageBuilder.withPayload("Pro Spring Integration Example").build());
        Message<?> reply = output.receive();
        System.out.println("received: " + reply);

    }
}
```

Using Spring Roo to Bootstrap Your Project

Spring Roo is a tool for rapidly developing database-backed web sites using convention over configuration, similar to Ruby on Rails. It creates a Spring-based Java application and supports the entire life cycle, from development to deployment to production. Spring Roo provides a shell interface that creates a web application from the back-end persistence to the front-end CRUD interface, requiring only a domain model definition. The supporting framework uses AOP so that it's noninvasive and easily removable. There is currently an add-on in development for adding Spring Integration to the Spring Roo project, which will bring rapid convention-over-configuration development to enterprise integration. This Spring Roo add-on is still in early development at the time of this writing, so an example will not be provided, but we recommend keeping an eye out for its release.

Using SpringSource Tool Suite's Visual Support

SpringSource Tool Suite (STS) is an Eclipse IDE bundled with a set of plug-ins specifically designed for developing Spring-powered enterprise applications. The most important addition for Spring Integration is the graphical Spring configuration design editor. This is an excellent tool for visualizing how your Spring Integration application is wired together between endpoints and channels. You can download STS from `www.springsource.com/developer/sts`.

For proper Maven integration a Java Development Kit (JDK), not Java Runtime Environment (JRE) must be specified as a runtime parameter using the `-vm` option in the `STS.ini` file. The line shown in Listing 5–14 should be added to the `STS.ini` file located in the STS installation directory.

Listing 5–14. *STS.ini File with –vm Option Pointing to the JDK*

```
-vm /path/to/javaw
```

Starting STS displays the familiar Eclipse application's welcome screen. Close the welcome page and STS will appear, as shown in Figure 5–1.

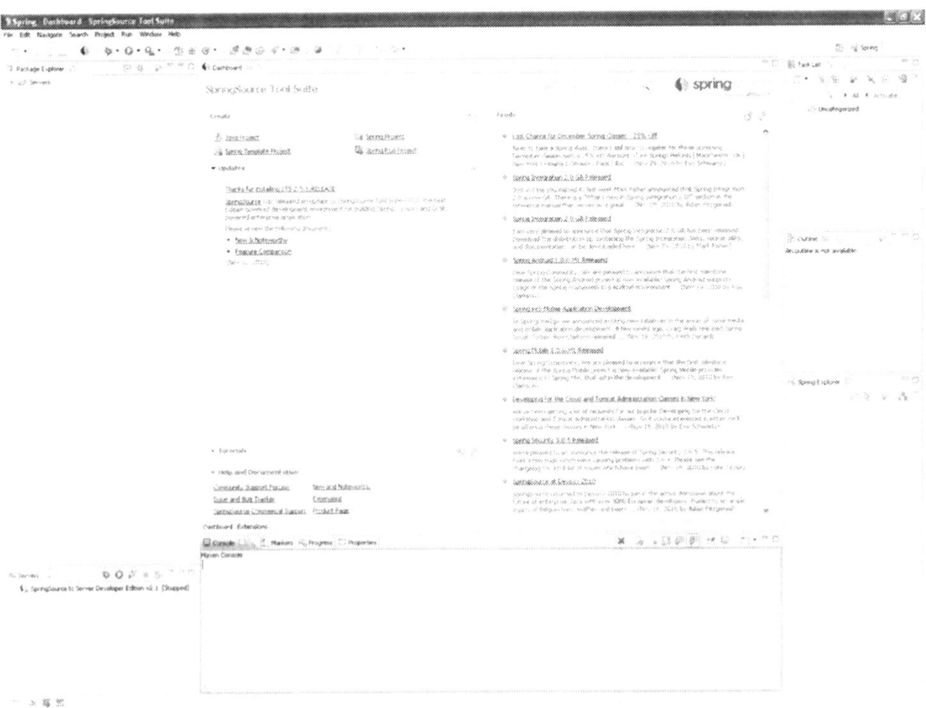

Figure 5–1. STS IDE

Creating a Spring Integration Application Using STS

STS has a number of starting templates for creating a Spring application. The templates create a Maven-based application that includes unit test support. To create a Spring project, select New ➤ Spring Template Project from the File menu, as shown in Figure 5–2.

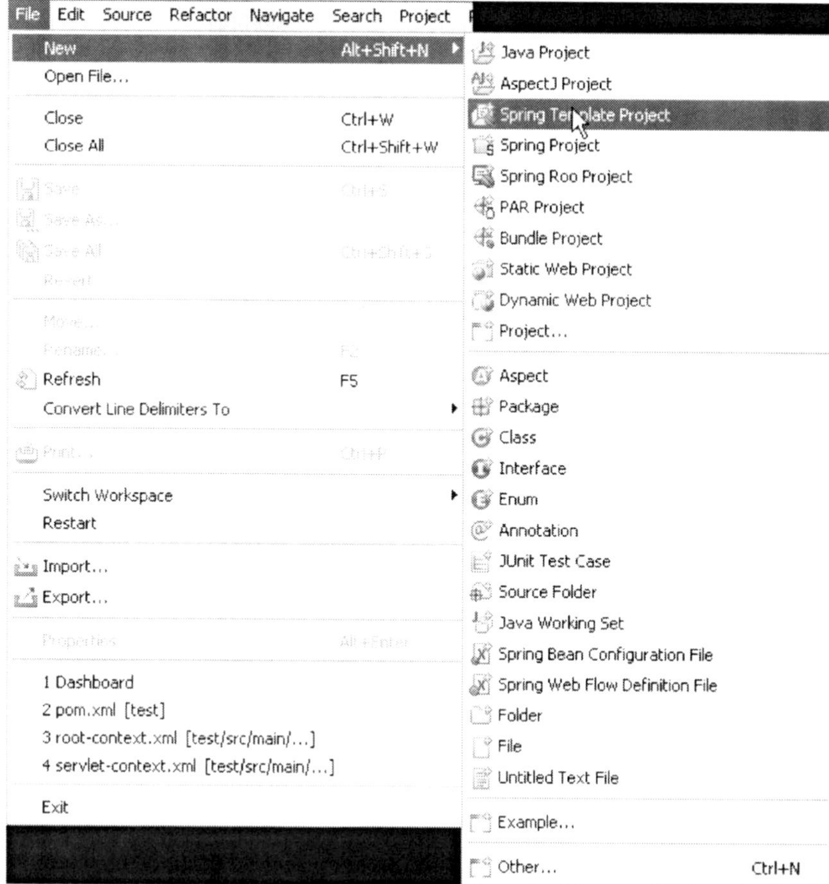

Figure 5–2. Creating a Spring project in STS

This will bring up the New Template Project wizard. STS comes with a number of templates for supporting projects ranging from web applications using Hibernate and JPA to Spring Batch. For this example, select the Simple Spring Utility Project, as shown in Figure 5–3, which will create a basic Spring project including an integration test to load the Spring context.

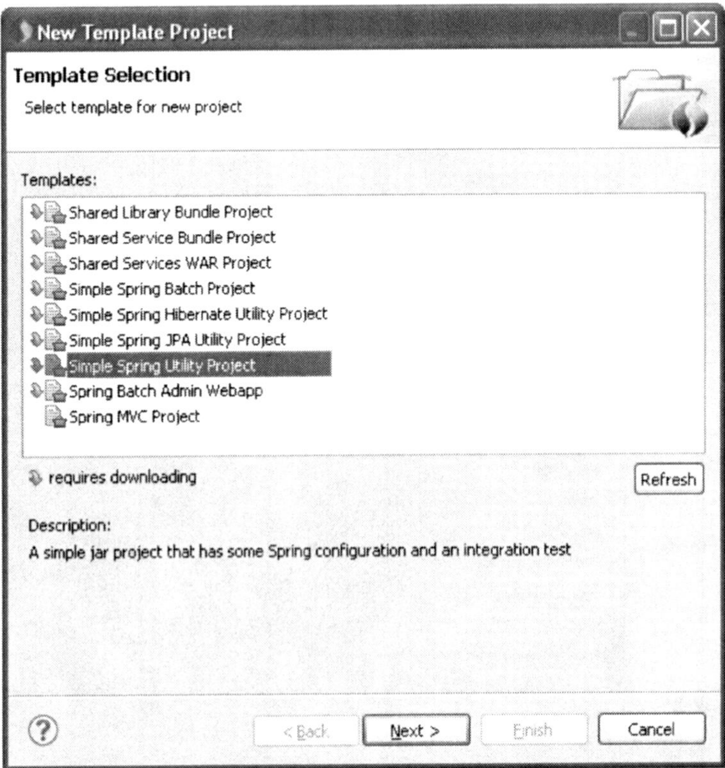

Figure 5–3. *STS Project wizard*

Next, specify `sts-project` as the project name and `com.apress.prospringintegration` as the package name. This will build a Maven project called `sts-project` with the base package `com.apress.prospringintegration`, as shown in Figure 5–4.

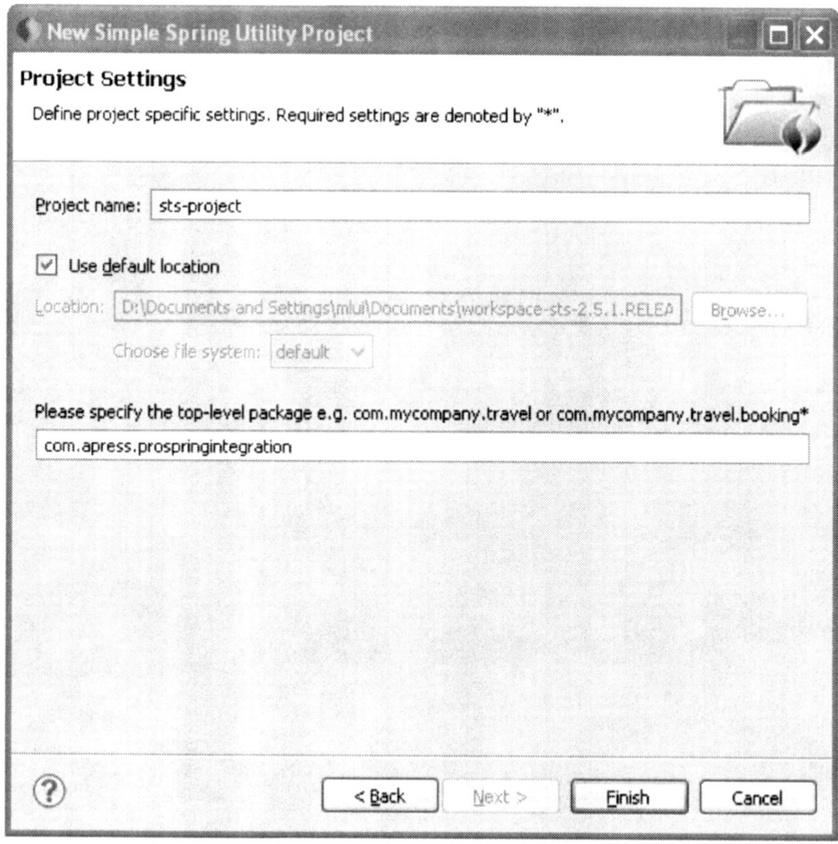

Figure 5–4. Specifying the project and package names

A basic Maven project will be created with the project structure shown in Figure 5–5. All of the basic classes and configuration files will be created, including the root Maven `pom.xml` file, the Spring configuration file `app-context.xml`, and the integration unit test file `ExampleConfigurationTests.java`, which leverages the Spring testing harness that loads the Spring context.

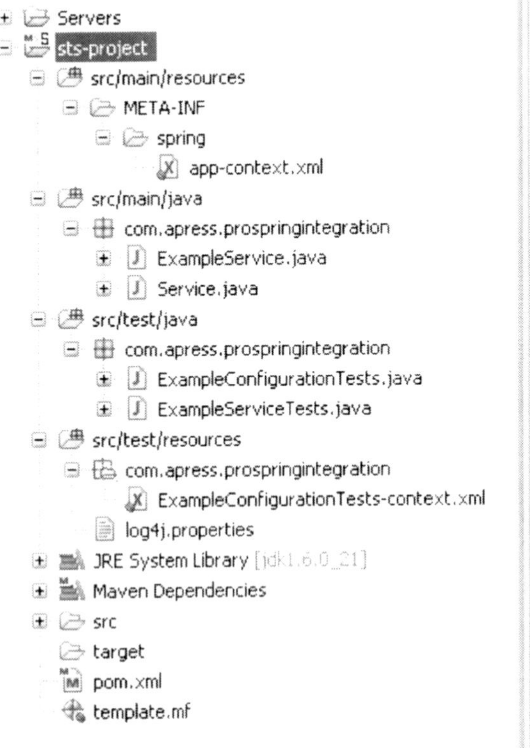

Figure 5–5. *STS Spring project*

Next, we will create an example similar to the first Spring project using STS, in which a message will published to a channel. An outbound JMS adapter will forward the message to the ActiveMQ JMS broker. A message-driven JMS channel adapter will receive the message and forward it to a service activator, which will log the message.

The first step is to add the Maven dependencies to the `pom.xml` file, as shown in Listing 5–12. Add the Spring Integration core and JMS dependencies to support our example. Also, add the ActiveMQ client and the CGLIB library to support context scanning to simplify the XML configuration. The `spring-context` dependency is removed, since it has already been brought in as a Spring Integration dependency, and to prevent version conflicts (see Listing 5–15). Also, a number of files may be removed from the project since they will not be used. These include `ExampleService.java`, `Service.java`, and `ExampleServiceTests.java`.

Listing 5–15. *STS pom.xml Maven Confiuration File*

```
<dependency>
  <groupId>org.springframework.integration</groupId>
  <artifactId>spring-integration-core</artifactId>
  <version>2.0.1.RELEASE</version>
</dependency>
<dependency>
```

```
    <groupId>org.springframework.integration</groupId>
    <artifactId>spring-integration-jms</artifactId>
    <version>2.0.1.RELEASE</version>
  </dependency>
  <dependency>
    <groupId>org.apache.activemq</groupId>
    <artifactId>activemq-core</artifactId>
    <version>5.4.1</version>
  </dependency>
  <dependency>
    <groupId>cglib</groupId>
    <artifactId>cglib-nodep</artifactId>
    <version>2.2</version>
  </dependency>
```

Creating the Integration

One of the best features of using STS with Spring Integration is the design editor for wiring up the channels and endpoints used in the application. The design editor supports two-way round-tripping between the XML source file and the graphic design editor. Any changes in either the design or Spring XML configuration file will be synchronized with the other representation. The design editor also supports importing Spring configuration files created by other editors or IDEs. In order to use the STS integration design editor, the required Spring Integration namespaces must be added. You can do this by first double-clicking the `app-context.xml` Spring configuration file in the Project Explorer. Then select the Namespaces tab, as shown in Figure 5–6. For our example, select the `int` and `int-jms` Spring Integration namespaces, as well as the Spring `context`, in order to support context scanning. This will result in some additional tabs appearing in the design editor, including integration-graph, which is the Spring Integration design editor.

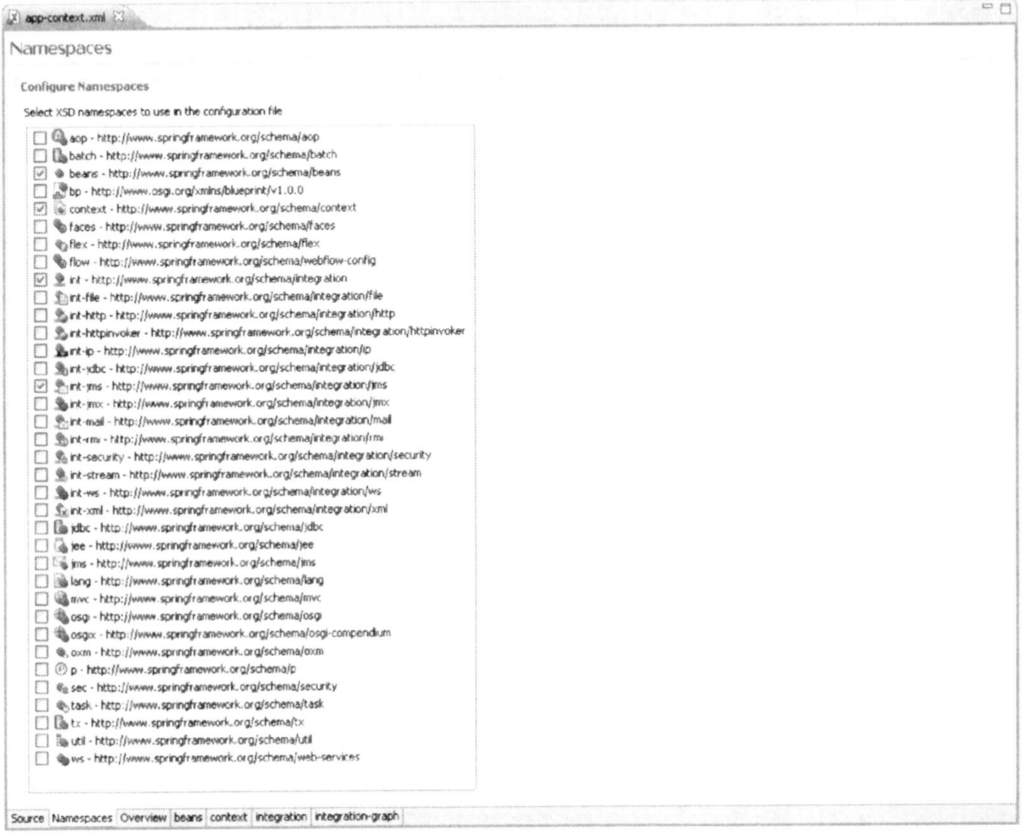

***Figure 5–6.** Namespace Selection for the Spring Configuration Design Editor*

You can configure the previous integration example by dragging and dropping components onto the design pane. First select the Channels tab on the left side, and drag and drop two channel components to represent the input and output channels. You can name a component by double-clicking it, which will bring up the Properties pane in the lower window. Name one of the channels `input` and the other `output`. The resulting design will look something like Figure 5–7.

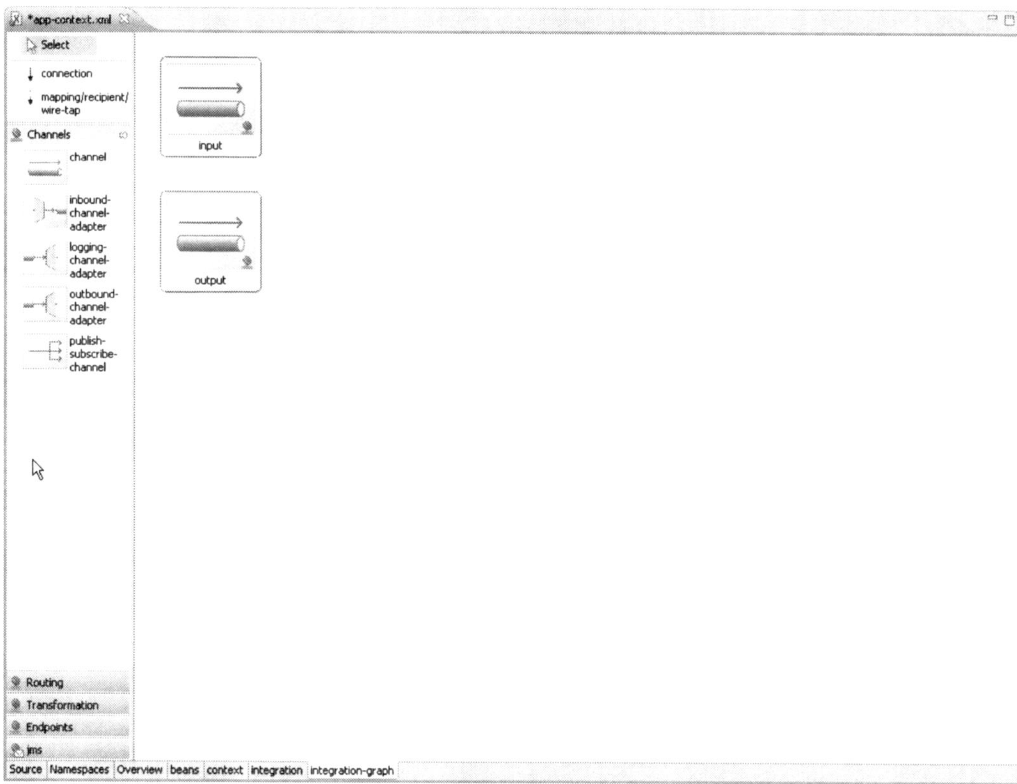

Figure 5–7. *STS Spring Integration Design Editor*

The next step is to add the JMS outbound channel adapter and the JMS message-driven channel adapter. Select the jms tab on the left side to bring up the JMS components. Drag and drop the outbound and message-driven JMS channel adapters onto the design pane. Name the outbound adapter `jmsOut` and the message-driven adapter `jmsIn`. In addition, set the `destination-name` properties to `test.queue` for both of the components so they will use the same JMS queue. The result should look similar to Figure 5–8.

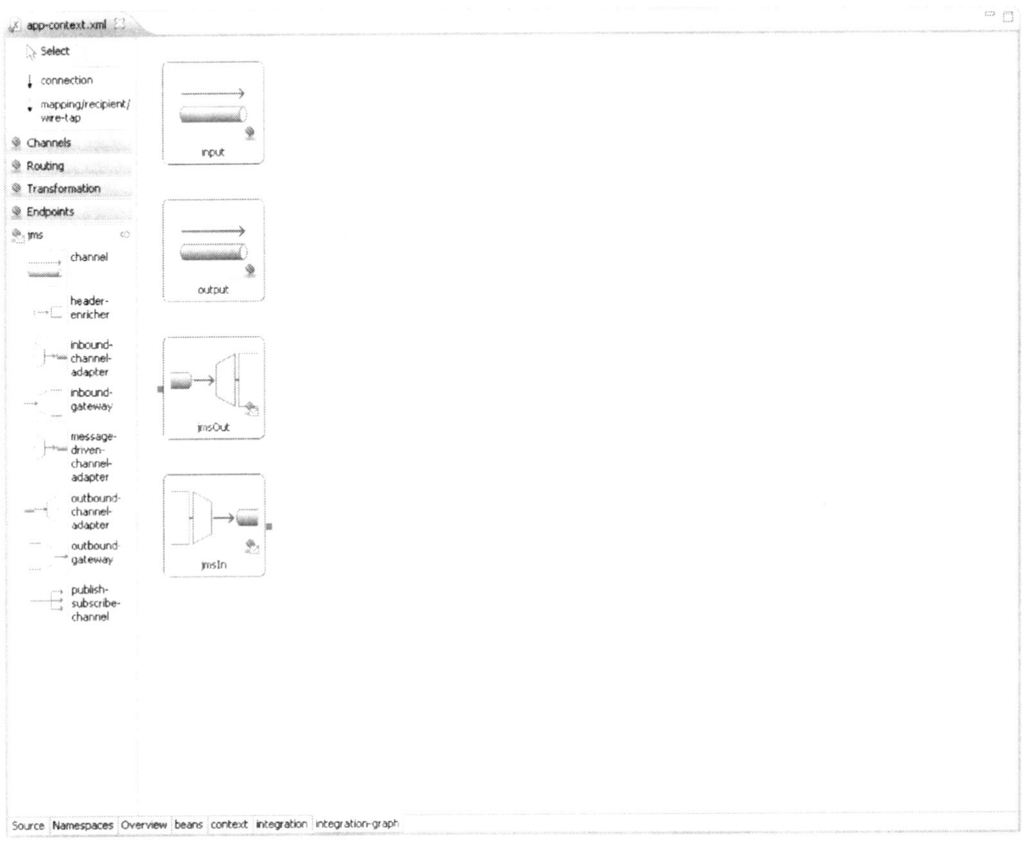

Figure 5–8. *Adding Adapters using the Design Editor*

The last component to add for this example is the service activator used to receive the incoming JMS message and log it. Select the Endpoints tab on the left, and drag and drop the `service-activator` endpoint to the design pane. Name the `service-activator` endpoint `messageHandler`. In addition, set the `ref` property to `jmsHandler` to reference the Spring service activator, which we will created shortly. The resultant diagram should look like Figure 5–9. The Spring Integration example is now ready for wiring up.

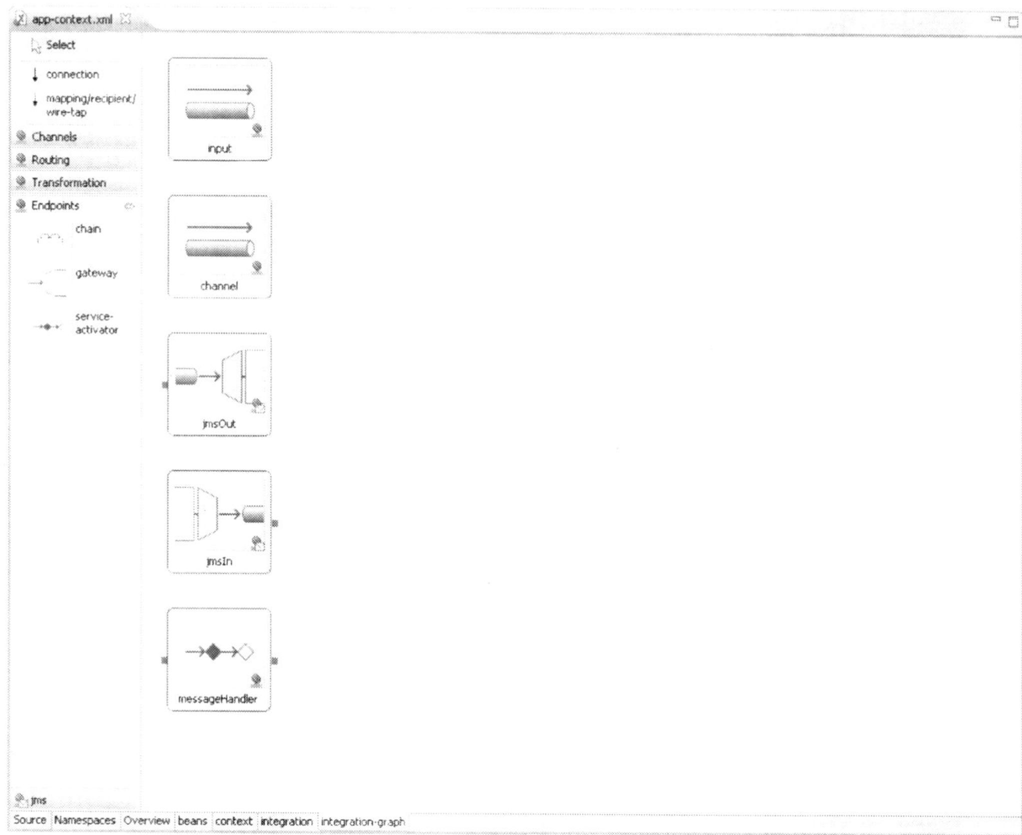

***Figure 5–9.** Adding Service Activator with Design Editor*

The last step is to wire up the channels to the endpoints. Select the connection icon on the left side. This will allow creating connections between the channels and endpoints. Drag a connection between the input channel and the `jmsOut` outbound channel adapter. Then drag a connection between the `jmsIn` message-driven adapter and the output channel. Finally, drag a connection between the output channel and the `messageHandler` service activator. The final design should look like Figure 5–10. This completes the initial design. The next step is to review the `app-context.xml` file.

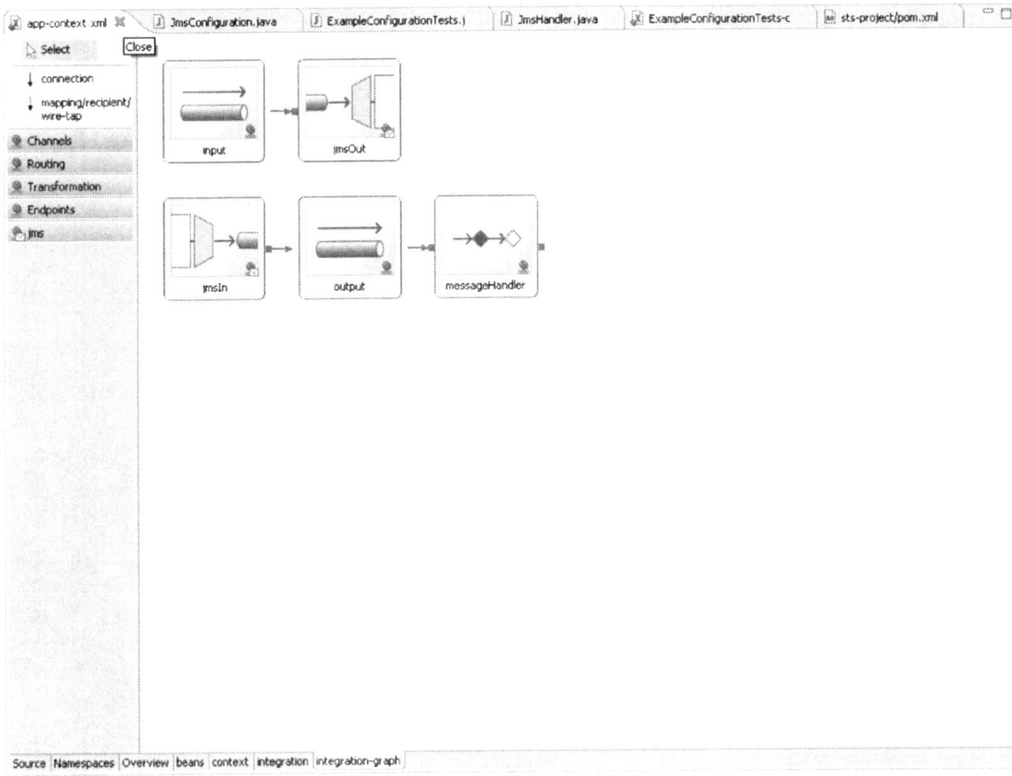

Figure 5–10. Wiring Components with Design Editor

You will need to make some modifications to the app-context.xml file. First, remove the service bean since it is not being used. Then add component scanning to support annotations for the service activator class by setting the base package to com.apress.prospringintegration. This will allow any class in this package to be scanned for annotation support. Component scanning will be used for the service activator and the JMS connection factory. The final app-context.xml file is shown in Listing 5–16.

Listing 5–16. Spring Integration Configuration file app-context.xml

```
<?xml version="1.0" encoding="UTF-8"?>
<beans xmlns="http://www.springframework.org/schema/beans"
       xmlns:xsi="http://www.w3.org/2001/XMLSchema-instance"
       xmlns:int="http://www.springframework.org/schema/integration"
       xmlns:int-jms="http://www.springframework.org/schema/integration/jms"
       xmlns:context="http://www.springframework.org/schema/context"
       xsi:schemaLocation="http://www.springframework.org/schema/integration
    http://www.springframework.org/schema/integration/spring-integration-2.0.xsd
    http://www.springframework.org/schema/integration/jms
    http://www.springframework.org/schema/integration/jms/spring-integration-jms-2.0.xsd
    http://www.springframework.org/schema/beans
    http://www.springframework.org/schema/beans/spring-beans-3.0.xsd
```

```
    http://www.springframework.org/schema/context
    http://www.springframework.org/schema/context/spring-context-3.0.xsd">

  <description>Example configuration to get you started.</description>

  <context:component-scan
      base-package="com.apress.prospringintegration"></context:component-scan>

  <int:channel id="input"></int:channel>

  <int:channel id="output"></int:channel>

  <int-jms:outbound-channel-adapter id="jmsOut" channel="input"
                                    destination-name="test.queue">
  </int-jms:outbound-channel-adapter>

  <int-jms:message-driven-channel-adapter id="jmsIn" channel="output"
                                          destination-name="test.queue"/>

  <int:service-activator id="messageHandler" input-channel="output"
                         ref="jmsHandler">
  </int:service-activator>

</beans>
```

The ActiveMQ configuration will be done using the Spring Java configuration support. Using a Java class, annotations, and component scanning, you can configure the ActiveMQ connection factory as shown in Listing 5–17. The Spring bean is named `connectionFactory`, which is the default connection factory bean name for the JMS channel adapters. The broker URL is set to `vm://localhost` to enable the embedded ActiveMQ JMS broker. This is done to simplify the example.

***Listing 5–17.** ActiveMQ Connection Factory Configuration*

```
package com.apress.prospringintegration;

import org.apache.activemq.ActiveMQConnectionFactory;
import org.springframework.context.annotation.Bean;
import org.springframework.jms.connection.CachingConnectionFactory;
import org.springframework.stereotype.Component;

import javax.jms.ConnectionFactory;

@Component
public class JmsConfiguration {

    @Bean(name = "connectionFactory")
    public ConnectionFactory getConnectionFactory() {
        ActiveMQConnectionFactory targetConnectionFactory = new ActiveMQConnectionFactory();
        targetConnectionFactory.setBrokerURL("vm://localhost");

        CachingConnectionFactory connectionFactory =
                new CachingConnectionFactory(targetConnectionFactory);
        connectionFactory.setSessionCacheSize(10);
        connectionFactory.setCacheProducers(false);
```

```
        return connectionFactory;
    }
}
```

The final piece of the message chain is to create the service activator class. This class will receive the message from the output channel and log it to the console. Again, component scanning and annotations are used to identify the Spring bean and service activator method. The class is shown in Listing 5–18.

Listing 5–18. *Service Activator Class*

```
package com.apress.prospringintegration;

import org.springframework.integration.annotation.ServiceActivator;
import org.springframework.stereotype.Component;

@Component
public class JmsHandler {
    @ServiceActivator
    public void handleMessage(String message) {
        System.out.println("Received message: " + message);
    }
}
```

Testing the Integration

In order to test the Spring Integration example, the Spring test harness created by the STS Spring template will be used (see Listing 5–19). The input channel is autowired and the `MessageBuilder` utility class is used to send a message to the input channel. The test harness loads the Spring context, runs the test cases, and then exits. A delay is added to ensure that the JMS message is received by the message-driven adapter.

Listing 5–19. *Spring Integration Test Class*

```
package com.apress.prospringintegration;

import org.junit.Test;
import org.junit.runner.RunWith;
import org.springframework.beans.factory.annotation.Autowired;
import org.springframework.integration.MessageChannel;
import org.springframework.integration.support.MessageBuilder;
import org.springframework.test.context.ContextConfiguration;
import org.springframework.test.context.junit4.SpringJUnit4ClassRunner;

@ContextConfiguration
@RunWith(SpringJUnit4ClassRunner.class)
public class ExampleConfigurationTests {

        @Autowired
        private MessageChannel input;

        @Test
```

```
        public void testSendingMessage() throws Exception {
                input.send(MessageBuilder.withPayload("Pro Spring Integration Example")
                                .build());

                Thread.sleep(5000);
        }
}
```

You can execute the text code by right-clicking the `ExampleConfigurationTest` class in the Package Explorer window and selecting Run As ➤ JUnit Test. The unit test will run and the message payload "Pro Spring Integration Example" will be logged in the console window.

Playing Well With Others

Since Spring Integration uses the underlying model and abstraction of Spring, it can work well with the other Spring projects. Some of the different possibilities in this regard will be discussed in more detail in later chapters.

Spring Batch

Despite all the movement toward services and message-based architectures, we often still need to process large sets of data using batch processes. Spring Batch is optimized for these types of needs (e.g., reading-in large flat files containing millions of rows of data and processing on some sort of calendar bases). Spring Integration interfaces easily with Spring Batch, using messaging to start jobs and publish events for processing "done" notifications and error handling. Many of the administrative requirements can be fulfilled using both of the projects. Using Spring Integration with Spring Batch will be discussed in detail in a Chapter 17.

Spring BlazeDS

BlazeDS is a server-side Java remoting and messaging technology for interfacing with the Adobe Flex and Adobe AIR rich web clients. It allows bidirectional messaging between the web client and server. Spring BlazeDS Integration is Spring project to support interfacing a Spring web application with Adobe Flex, a rich front end client. The messaging technology can be further enhanced by leveraging Spring Integration. This technology will be discussed in more detail in Chapter 18.

Summary

This chapter introduced the basic Spring Integration components and how they extend the Spring Framework into the world of messaging and event-driven architecture. We covered how Maven can be leveraged as the build and project management tool, and we discussed how to use Maven with Spring Integration. In addition, we showed how Maven can be integrated with most Java IDEs. We also demonstrated how to build a Spring Integration application. The example was extended to create the same application used in Chapter 2. Finally, we discussed how Spring Integration can be used with other Spring projects. Spring Integration can enhance other projects with messaging and integration support.

CHAPTER 6

Channels

According to Enterprise Integration Patterns,[1] a *message channel* is a virtual data pipe that connects a sender to one or more receivers. The message channel decouples the sender and the receivers so the sender does not necessary know who will receive the messages.

There are two major types of message channels: *point-to-point* channels and *publisher-subscriber* channels. By selecting the different type of message channel, the application can control the behavior of how the receivers get messages. The Spring Integration framework simplifies the development of message channels in an integration implementation.

EAI Message Channel Patterns

Spring Integration supports the design patterns that are defined in *Enterprise Integration Patterns.* Since this is not a book on patterns, it will help to be already be familiar with basic integration design patterns. However, for general context, the basic message channel design patterns are reviewed following.

The message channel design pattern is very simple. The message contains a piece of information that needs to be passed between different components, which can either be in a process or across different applications in different servers. For example, a chain retail store inventory system can send a message with the string "Inventory is running low with Item #12345" to the corporate warehouse so it can send more inventory back to the store. Besides strings, a message can contain any data type that the applications can understand.

The message endpoints are the components that interact with the messages. The endpoint that sends messages to the message channel is called the *sender* or *producer*. The endpoint that receives message from the message channel is called the *receiver* or *consumer*. The sender puts the data into a message and the receiver takes the data out from the message. As a result, the sender and receiver need to understand the data that they are exchanging. Besides sender and receiver, the message endpoint can filter messages within a channel or route the messages to the other channel. Some message endpoints can even split a message into multiple messages and route them into different channels.

The message channel connects multiple endpoints together. Messages can be produced and sent from multiple senders and received by one or more receivers depending on the type of message channel. The channel ensures that the messages can be sent and received between endpoints safely. Since the application data is encapsulated within the message, the message channel does not need to understand the message payload. In other words, the message channel design pattern decouples the message sender and receiver.

In order to make the endpoints easily interact with the message channels, each message channel has a unique name, so each of the channels can be seen as a logical address. There are also different types of message channels that behave differently with regard to how to handle messages.

---

[1] Gregor Hohpe, op. cit.

Point-to-Point Channel

The point-to-point channel (see Figure 6–1) guarantees that there is only one receiver that receives the same message from the sender at any given time. Spring Integration provides several types of point-to-point channel implementations: `QueueChannel`, `PriorityChannel`, `RendezvousChannel`, `DirectChannel`, `ExecutorChannel`, and `NullChannel`.

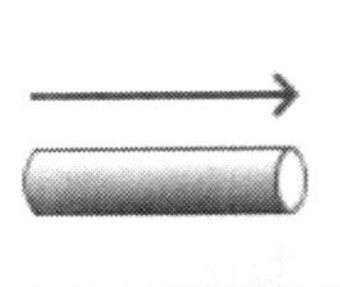

Figure 6–1. *Point-to-point Channel*

Publish-Subscribe Channel

The publish-subscribe channel (see Figurre 6–2) allows one-to-many relationship between the producer and consumer, such that multiple consumers may receive the same message. The message is marked as "received" and removed from the channel when all the subscribed receivers have consumed the message. Spring Integration currently provides a publish-subscribe–style message channel implementation, which is `PublishSubscribeChannel`.

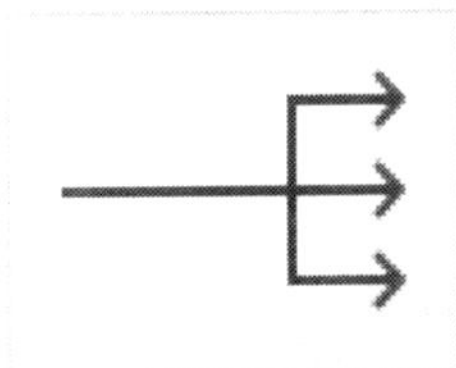

Figure 6–2. *Publish-subscribe Channel*

Data-Typed Channel

Applications can use the message channel to transfer different types of data between the message sender and receiver. In order to process the message correctly, the receivers need to have knowledge about the message data type. For example, the sender can send object A and object B into the same message channel. The receiver needs to determine the object type in order to apply different business logic to handle the message. Usually, the determination is made by including a format indicator as part of the message or in the message header.

However, if there are two different channels, each can only have single data type, one for the object A and one for the object B, and the receiver will know data type of messages without using a format indicator. A message channel that only contains single type of object or message is called a *data-typed* channel. An example of a channel that can handle different types of data and a *data-type* channel is shown in Figure 6–3.

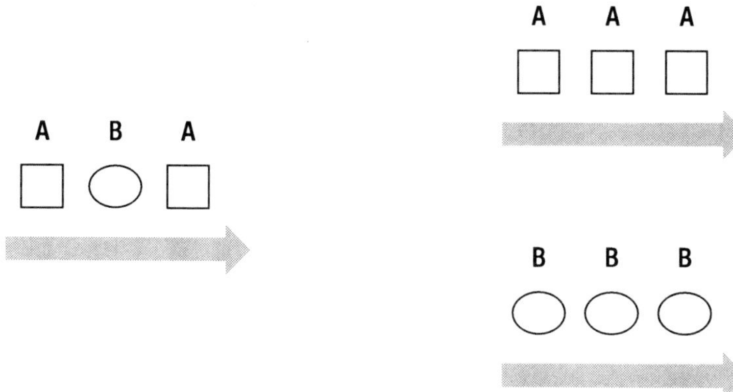

Figure 6–3. Message Channel with Multiple Data Types vs. Data-Typed Channels

Spring Integration message channels can be configured to constrain to handle messages of one or more specified payload types. For instance:

```
<channel id="messageChannel" />
```

This Spring Integration message channel can receive any kind of data type. However, the following message channel can only receive objects of class `a.A`:

```
<channel id="queueChannel" datatype="a.A" />
```

We will discuss data-typed channels in more detail later in this chapter.

Invalid Message Channel

When the application receives a message from the channel, the application may decide not to process the incoming message because the data within the message may not pass validation or the application may not support the incoming message data type. The message will be routed into the invalid message channel (see Figure 6–4), allowing further handling by the other process/application. In Spring Integration, the validation would be done by a message filter, which will be discussed in more depth in Chapter 8.

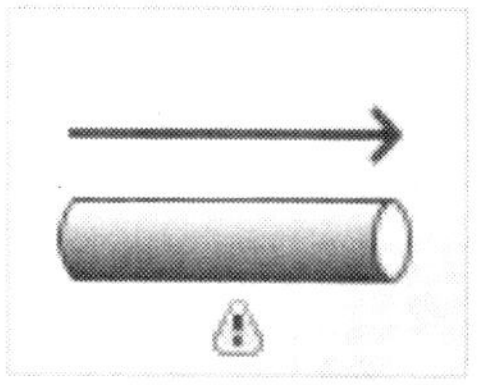

Figure 6–4. Invalid Message Channel

Dead Letter Channel

When an application fails to deliver a message to the message channel after all the retry attempts, the message will be sent to the dead letter channel and will be handled further by the another process or application listening for messages on that channel (see Figure 6–5).

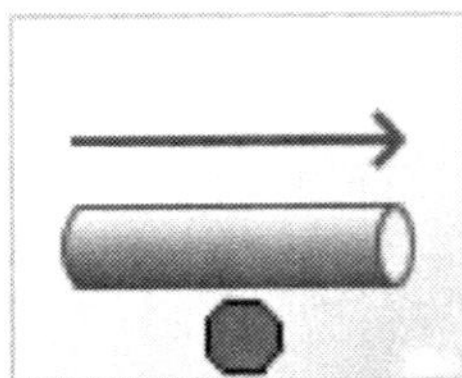

Figure 6–5. *Dead Letter Channel*

Channel Adapter

The channel adapter (see Figure 6–6) allows an application to connect to the messaging system. Most applications are not designed to communicate with a messaging system in the first place. By using a common interface or application programming interface (API), applications can be easily integrated with different messaging system implementations.

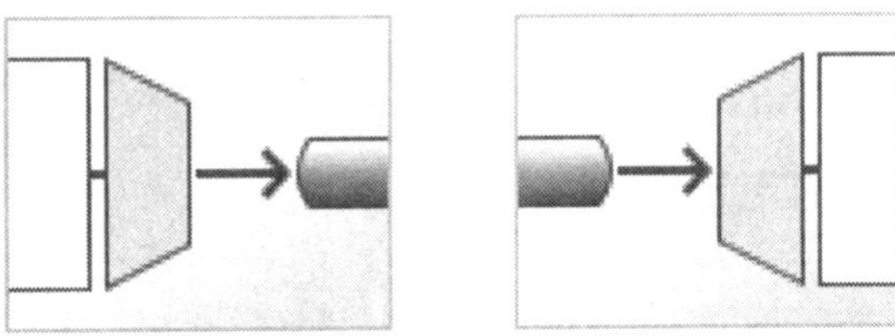

Figure 6–6. *Channel Adapter*

Messaging Bridge

A messaging bridge is a relatively trivial endpoint that simply connects two message channels or channel adapters (see Figure 6–7). For example, the developer may want to connect a `PollableChannel` to a `SubscribableChannel` so that the subscribing endpoints don't have to worry about any polling configuration. Instead, the messaging bridge provides the polling support. Messaging bridges will be discussed in depth in Chapter 8.

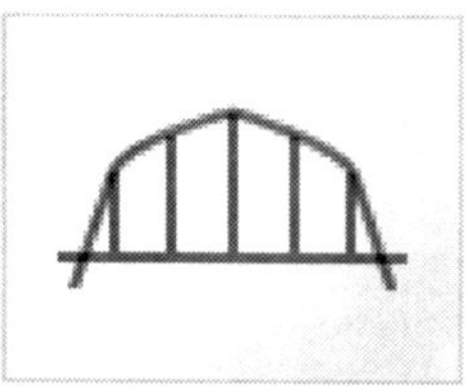

Figure 6–7. Messaging Bridge

Message Bus

According to *Enterprise Integration Patterns*[2], a message bus is a combination of a canonical data model, a common command set, and a messaging infrastructure that allows different systems to communicate through a shared set of interfaces. By leveraging Spring Integration adapters and transformers, message channels can be connected and used to create a message bus allowing communication between different systems.

Guaranteed Delivery

Messages are normally stored in memory and wait for delivery by the messaging system. If the message system crashes, all the messages will be lost. In order to guarantee the delivery, the messaging system can use a data store to persist the messages. By default, all the Spring Integration channels store messages in memory. In Spring Integration 2.0, message channels can now be backed by the JMS broker. In other words, messages are stored in an external JMS broker instead of in application memory. Message channels are just another strategy interface and can be tailored to your specific needs as required; implementations can be built that delegate to any data store mechanism conceivable using the MessageStore interface or - for more control – by implementing the MessageChannel interface itself.

Choosing a Channel Instance

It is very easy to apply the message channel design patterns using Spring Integration. All the Spring Integration channels implement the `org.springframework.integration.MessageChannel` interface shown in Listing 6–1. This interface defines how a sender sends a message to the channel. This is required since different types of message channels can receive messages in different ways. Depending on the type of message channel implementations, the send operation can be blocked indefinitely or for a given timeout until the message is received.

***Listing 6–1.** MessageChannel.java*

```
package org.springframework.integration;

public interface MessageChannel {

    boolean send(Message<?> message);
```

[2] Gregor Hohpe op. cit.

```
    boolean send(Message<?> message, long timeout);

}
```

There are two different implementations for receiving messages from the channel in Spring Integration: `org.springframework.integration.core.PollableChannel` and `org.springframework.integration.core.SubscribableChannel`. Both of the implementations are unique subinterfaces of the `MessageChannel` interface.

`PollableChannel` (see Listing 6–2) allows the receiver to poll message from the message channel periodically. The receiver can choose to wait indefinitely or for a given timeout until a message arrives This gives for the receiver the flexibility to decide when to get the message from the channel.

Listing 6–2. *PollableChannel.java*

```
package org.springframework.integration.core;

import org.springframework.integration.Message;
import org.springframework.integration.MessageChannel;

public interface PollableChannel extends MessageChannel {

    Message<?> receive();

    Message<?> receive(long timeout);

}
```

The alternative way to receive messages is by using the `SubscribableChannel` (see Listing 6–3), which allows the sender to push the message to the subscribed receiver(s). When the sender sends a message, the subscribed receiver(s) will receive the message and process the message by the provided `org.springframework.integration.core.MessageHandler` using the Gang-of-Four (GoF) Observer pattern.[3] Once a message has been sent to the channel, all the subscribed message handlers will be involved.

Listing 6–3. *SubscribableChannel.java*

```
package org.springframework.integration.core;

import org.springframework.integration.MessageChannel;

public interface SubscribableChannel extends MessageChannel {

    boolean subscribe(MessageHandler handler);

    boolean unsubscribe(MessageHandler handler);

}
```

The `MessageHandler` interface (see Listing 6–4) contains only one method, which will handle the pushed message from the `SubscribableChannel` channel. The interface also throws `org.springframework.integration.MessageException`. Depending on the message channel implementation, each exception may be handled differently (one such possibility is failover). As a result,

---

[3] Erich Gamma, Richard Helm, Ralph Johnson, John M. Vlissides

it is always a good idea to throw the appropriate exception. Table 6–1 gives some message handler–related exceptions.

Listing 6–4. *MessageHandler.java*

```
package org.springframework.integration.core;

import org.springframework.integration.Message;
import org.springframework.integration.MessagingException;

public interface MessageHandler {

    void handleMessage(Message<?> message) throws MessageException;

}
```

Table 6–1. *Message Exceptions*

`MessageRejectedException`	A message has been rejected by a selector.
`MessageHandlingException`	An error occurred during message handling.
`MessageDeliveryException`	An error occurred during message delivery (e.g., a network connectivity issue, a JMS broker error, a storage issue, etc.).
`MessageTimeoutException`	A timeout elapsed prior to successful message delivery.

Once you have decided how the application will receive messages, you can choose the type of message channel implementation (point-to-point or publish-subscribe).

Point-to-Point Channel

Spring Integration provides several different implementations of the point-to-point channel pattern. Let's look at the different point-to-point channel options.

QueueChannel

The `org.springframework.integration.channel.QueueChannel` class (see Figure 6–8) is the simplest implementation of the `MessageChannel` interface. `QueueChannel` has point-to-point semantics. In other words, even if the channel has multiple consumers, only one of them should receive any message sent to that channel. `QueueChannel` also provides mechanisms to filter and purge messages that satisfy certain criteria. In addition, `QueueChannel` stores all the messages in memory. By default, `QueueChannel` can use all the available memory to store messages. To avoid running out of memory, it's always better to initiate the `QueueChannel` instance with a channel capacity limiting the number of messages maintained in the queue.

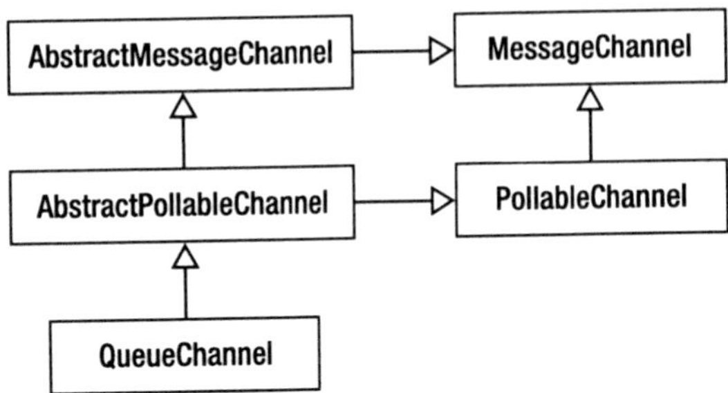

Figure 6–8. Queue Channel Class Diagram

Assuming we are building a problem-reporting system, each problem can be described using a Ticket. The problem will be reported by using a Problem reporter application. The Ticket will be packaged into a message and submitted to a QueueChannel. Next, the TicketReceiver will receive the Ticket message from the submitted order and the problem will be resolved. Let's look at the definitions for the various classes involved. First the class defining the Ticket message is shown in Listing 6–5.

Listing 6–5. *Ticket.java*

```
package com.apress.prospringintegration.channels.core;

import java.util.Calendar;

public class Ticket {

  public enum Priority {
    low,
    medium,
    high,
    emergency
  }

  private long ticketId;
  private Calendar issueDateTime;
  private String description;
  private Priority priority;

  public Ticket() {
  }

  public long getTicketId() {
    return ticketId;
  }

  public void setTicketId(long ticketId) {
    this.ticketId = ticketId;
  }

  public Calendar getIssueDateTime() {
    return issueDateTime;
  }
```

```
  public void setIssueDateTime(Calendar issueDateTime) {
    this.issueDateTime = issueDateTime;
  }

  public String getDescription() {
    return description;
  }

  public void setDescription(String description) {
    this.description = description;
  }

  public Priority getPriority() {
    return priority;
  }

  public void setPriority(Priority priority) {
    this.priority = priority;
  }

  public String toString() {
    return String.format("Ticket# %d: [%s] %s", ticketId, priority, description);
  }
}
```

The ProblemReporter class, shown in Listing 6–6, is a component which sends the Ticket message to the message channel ticketChannel when the openTicket method is invoked.

Listing 6–6. *ProblemReporter.java*

```
package com.apress.prospringintegration.channels.directchannel;

import com.apress.prospringintegration.channels.core.Ticket;
import org.springframework.beans.factory.annotation.Value;
import org.springframework.integration.channel.DirectChannel;
import org.springframework.integration.support.MessageBuilder;
import org.springframework.stereotype.Component;

@Component
public class ProblemReporter {

  private DirectChannel channel;

  @Value("#{ticketChannel}")
  public void setChannel(DirectChannel channel) {
    this.channel = channel;
  }

  void openTicket(Ticket ticket) {
    channel.send(MessageBuilder.withPayload( ticket).build() );
    System.out.println("Ticket Sent - " + ticket.toString());
  }
}
```

The TicketReceiver class shown in Listing 6–7 receives the Ticket message sent to the message channel ticketChannel.

***Listing 6–7.** TicketReceiver.java*

```
package com.apress.prospringintegration.channels.queuechannel;

import com.apress.prospringintegration.channels.core.Ticket;
import org.springframework.beans.factory.annotation.Value;
import org.springframework.integration.Message;
import org.springframework.integration.channel.QueueChannel;
import org.springframework.stereotype.Component;

@Component
public class TicketReceiver implements Runnable {

  final static int RECEIVE_TIMEOUT = 1000;

  protected QueueChannel channel;

  @Value("#{ticketChannel}")
  public void setChannel(QueueChannel channel) {
    this.channel = channel;
  }

  public void handleTicketMessage() {
    Message<?> ticketMessage;

    while (true) {
      ticketMessage = channel.receive(RECEIVE_TIMEOUT);
      if (ticketMessage != null) {
        handleTicket( (Ticket) ticketMessage.getPayload() );
      } else {
        try {
          /** Handle some other tasks **/
          Thread.sleep(1000);
        } catch (InterruptedException ex) {
          ex.printStackTrace();
        }
      }
    }
  }

  void handleTicket(Ticket ticket) {
    System.out.println("Received ticket - " + ticket.toString());
  }

  @Override
  public void run() {
    handleTicketMessage();
  }
}
```

The TicketGenerator class shown in Listing 6–8 creates the Ticket messages with different priority levels.

Listing 6–8. TicketGenerator.java

```
package com.apress.prospringintegration.channels.core;

import com.apress.prospringintegration.channels.core.Ticket.Priority;
import org.springframework.stereotype.Component;

import java.util.ArrayList;
import java.util.GregorianCalendar;
import java.util.List;

@Component
public class TicketGenerator {
    private long nextTicketId;

    public TicketGenerator() {
        this.nextTicketId = 1000l;
    }

    public List<Ticket> createTickets() {
        List<Ticket> tickets = new ArrayList<Ticket>();

        tickets.add(createLowPriorityTicket());
        tickets.add(createLowPriorityTicket());
        tickets.add(createLowPriorityTicket());
        tickets.add(createLowPriorityTicket());
        tickets.add(createLowPriorityTicket());
        tickets.add(createMediumPriorityTicket());
        tickets.add(createMediumPriorityTicket());
        tickets.add(createMediumPriorityTicket());
        tickets.add(createMediumPriorityTicket());
        tickets.add(createMediumPriorityTicket());
        tickets.add(createHighPriorityTicket());
        tickets.add(createHighPriorityTicket());
        tickets.add(createHighPriorityTicket());
        tickets.add(createHighPriorityTicket());
        tickets.add(createHighPriorityTicket());
        tickets.add(createEmergencyTicket());
        tickets.add(createEmergencyTicket());
        tickets.add(createEmergencyTicket());
        tickets.add(createEmergencyTicket());
        tickets.add(createEmergencyTicket());

        return tickets;
    }

    Ticket createEmergencyTicket() {
        return createTicket(Priority.emergency,
                "Urgent problem. Fix immediately or revenue will be lost!");
    }
```

```
    Ticket createHighPriorityTicket() {
        return createTicket(Priority.high,
                "Serious issue. Fix immediately.");
    }

    Ticket createMediumPriorityTicket() {
        return createTicket(Priority.medium,
                "There is an issue; take a look whenever you have time.");
    }

    Ticket createLowPriorityTicket() {
        return createTicket(Priority.low,
                "Some minor problems have been found.");
    }

    Ticket createTicket(Priority priority, String description) {
        Ticket ticket = new Ticket();
        ticket.setTicketId(nextTicketId++);
        ticket.setPriority(priority);
        ticket.setIssueDateTime(GregorianCalendar.getInstance());
        ticket.setDescription(description);

        return ticket;
    }
}
```

The main class TicketMain shown in Listing 6–9 creates the Spring context and initialize the various components described above.

Listing 6–9. TicketMain.java

```
package com.apress.prospringintegration.channels.queuechannel;

import com.apress.prospringintegration.channels.core.Ticket;
import com.apress.prospringintegration.channels.core.TicketGenerator;
import org.springframework.context.support.ClassPathXmlApplicationContext;

import java.util.List;

public class TicketMain {

    public static void main(String[] args) {
        String contextName = "queue-channel.xml";

        ClassPathXmlApplicationContext applicationContext =
                new ClassPathXmlApplicationContext(contextName);
        applicationContext.start();

        ProblemReporter problemReporter =
                applicationContext.getBean(ProblemReporter.class);
        TicketReceiver ticketReceiver =
                applicationContext.getBean("ticketReceiver", TicketReceiver.class);
        TicketGenerator ticketGenerator =
                applicationContext.getBean(TicketGenerator.class);
```

```
        List<Ticket> tickets = ticketGenerator.createTickets();
        for (Ticket ticket : tickets) {
            problemReporter.openTicket(ticket);
        }

        Thread consumerThread = new Thread(ticketReceiver);
        consumerThread.start();
    }
}
```

The Spring configuration for the Ticket reporter example is shown in Listing 6–10.

Listing 6–10. *queue-channel.xml*

```
<?xml version="1.0" encoding="UTF-8"?>
<beans xmlns="http://www.springframework.org/schema/beans"
       xmlns:xsi="http://www.w3.org/2001/XMLSchema-instance"
       xmlns:context="http://www.springframework.org/schema/context"
       xmlns:int="http://www.springframework.org/schema/integration"
       xsi:schemaLocation="http://www.springframework.org/schema/integration
    http://www.springframework.org/schema/integration/spring-integration-2.0.xsd
    http://www.springframework.org/schema/beans
    http://www.springframework.org/schema/beans/spring-beans-3.0.xsd
    http://www.springframework.org/schema/context
    http://www.springframework.org/schema/context/spring-context-3.0.xsd">

  <context:component-scan
      base-package="com.apress.prospringintegration.channels.queuechannel"/>
  <context:component-scan
      base-package="com.apress.prospringintegration.channels.core"/>

  <int:channel id="ticketChannel"
               datatype="com.apress.prospringintegration.channels.core.Ticket">
    <int:queue capacity="50"/>
  </int:channel>

</beans>
```

QueueChannel is defined using the Spring Integration namespace in the Spring bean configuration file. Most of the beans used in the example were annotated with @Component, which means we don't need to explicitly register them with the Spring application context because they will be picked up the context:component-scan element. The Spring Integration namespace will be discussed later in this chapter. TicketMain's main method calls the TicketGenerator class to create a list of Ticket instances with different ticket priority values. The list of Ticket objects will be sent to a QueueChannel. TicketReceiver runs in a separate worker thread and polls the same QueueChannel to receive messages. Figure 6–9 shows the output of the preceding code:

```
Ticket Sent - Ticket# 1000: [low] Some minor problems have been found.
Ticket Sent - Ticket# 1001: [low] Some minor problems have been found.
Ticket Sent - Ticket# 1002: [low] Some minor problems have been found.
Ticket Sent - Ticket# 1003: [low] Some minor problems have been found.
Ticket Sent - Ticket# 1004: [low] Some minor problems have been found.
Ticket Sent - Ticket# 1005: [medium] There is an issue; take a look whenever you have time.
Ticket Sent - Ticket# 1006: [medium] There is an issue; take a look whenever you have time.
Ticket Sent - Ticket# 1007: [medium] There is an issue; take a look whenever you have time.
Ticket Sent - Ticket# 1008: [medium] There is an issue; take a look whenever you have time.
Ticket Sent - Ticket# 1009: [medium] There is an issue; take a look whenever you have time.
Ticket Sent - Ticket# 1010: [high] Serious issue. Fix immediately.
Ticket Sent - Ticket# 1011: [high] Serious issue. Fix immediately.
Ticket Sent - Ticket# 1012: [high] Serious issue. Fix immediately.
Ticket Sent - Ticket# 1013: [high] Serious issue. Fix immediately.
Ticket Sent - Ticket# 1014: [high] Serious issue. Fix immediately.
Ticket Sent - Ticket# 1015: [emergency] Urgent problem. Fix immediately or revenue will be lost!
Ticket Sent - Ticket# 1016: [emergency] Urgent problem. Fix immediately or revenue will be lost!
Ticket Sent - Ticket# 1017: [emergency] Urgent problem. Fix immediately or revenue will be lost!
Ticket Sent - Ticket# 1018: [emergency] Urgent problem. Fix immediately or revenue will be lost!
Ticket Sent - Ticket# 1019: [emergency] Urgent problem. Fix immediately or revenue will be lost!
Received ticket - Ticket# 1000: [low] Some minor problems have been found.
Received ticket - Ticket# 1001: [low] Some minor problems have been found.
Received ticket - Ticket# 1002: [low] Some minor problems have been found.
Received ticket - Ticket# 1003: [low] Some minor problems have been found.
Received ticket - Ticket# 1004: [low] Some minor problems have been found.
Received ticket - Ticket# 1005: [medium] There is an issue; take a look whenever you have time.
Received ticket - Ticket# 1006: [medium] There is an issue; take a look whenever you have time.
Received ticket - Ticket# 1007: [medium] There is an issue; take a look whenever you have time.
Received ticket - Ticket# 1008: [medium] There is an issue; take a look whenever you have time.
Received ticket - Ticket# 1009: [medium] There is an issue; take a look whenever you have time.
Received ticket - Ticket# 1010: [high] Serious issue. Fix immediately.
Received ticket - Ticket# 1011: [high] Serious issue. Fix immediately.
Received ticket - Ticket# 1012: [high] Serious issue. Fix immediately.
Received ticket - Ticket# 1013: [high] Serious issue. Fix immediately.
Received ticket - Ticket# 1014: [high] Serious issue. Fix immediately.
Received ticket - Ticket# 1015: [emergency] Urgent problem. Fix immediately or revenue will be lost!
Received ticket - Ticket# 1016: [emergency] Urgent problem. Fix immediately or revenue will be lost!
Received ticket - Ticket# 1017: [emergency] Urgent problem. Fix immediately or revenue will be lost!
Received ticket - Ticket# 1018: [emergency] Urgent problem. Fix immediately or revenue will be lost!
Received ticket - Ticket# 1019: [emergency] Urgent problem. Fix immediately or revenue will be lost!
```

Figure 6–9. *TicketMain Output*

`QueueChannel` works exactly like a queue, which handles the message First In First Out (FIFO). In the preceding example, `ProblemReporter` wraps the `Ticket` into a `Message` and puts into the `QueueChannel`.

```
queueChannel.send(new GenericMessage<Ticket>(ticket));
```

`org.springframework.integration.message.GenericMessage` implements the `org.springframework.integration.Message` interface shown in Listing 6–11, which only contains two methods: `getHeaders` and `getPayload`.

Listing 6–11. *Message.java*

```
package org.springframework.integration;

public interface Message<T> {

        MessageHeaders getHeaders();

        T getPayload();

}
```

The `Message` interface is simple: a message contains a message header and a payload. The message header is a map collection that consists of the key / value pairs shown in Table 6–2.

Table 6–2. Message Header

Header Name	Header Data Type
ID	java.util.UUID
TIMESTAMP	java.lang.Long
CORRELATION_ID	java.lang.Object
REPLY_CHANNEL	java.lang.Object
ERROR_CHANNEL	java.lang.Object
SEQUENCE_NUMBER	java.lang.Integer
SEQUENCE_SIZE	java.lang.Integer
EXPIRATION_DATE	java.lang.Long
PRIORITY	java.lang.Integer

QueueChannel's send method does not block as long as the channel is not full. By default, QueueChannel is unbounded. In order to avoid the application running out of memory, it is always a good idea to specify the capacity value for a bounded QueueChannel.

```
// channel.receive will be blocked until a message arrives
ticketMessage = channel.receive();

// channel.receive will be blocked for 1000ms
// or until a message arrives within the timeout period
ticketMessage = channel.receive(1000);
```

The TicketReceiver will poll from QueueChannel. If there is no message, TicketReceiver will wait and block until a message can be received. However, in some situations, the application may want to handle something while waiting for the next message.

```
public void handleTicketMessage() {
    Message<?> ticketMessage = null;

    while (true) {
        ticketMessage = channel.receive(RECEIVE_TIMEOUT);
        if (ticketMessage != null) {
            handleTicket( (Ticket) ticketMessage.getPayload());
        } else {
            try {
                /** Handle some other tasks **/
                Thread.sleep(1000);
            }
            catch (InterruptedException ex) {
                ex.printStackTrace();
            }
        }
    }
}
```

In this case, TicketReceiver will wait for about 1 second for the next message. If there is nothing in QueueChannel, the block will be released so TicketReceiver can handle something else and try to poll the message from the channel once again.

In reality, however, the emergency priority ticket should be handled first because the problem may be urgent. However, QueueChannel is operating as a FIFO queue. As a result, QueueChannel provides a feature that can drain specific messages out from the channel by using org.springframework.integration.core.MessageSelector. The MessageSelector interface looks like Listing 6–12.

Listing 6–12. *MessageSelector.java*

```
package org.springframework.integration.core;

import org.springframework.integration.Message;

public interface MessageSelector {

    boolean accept(Message<?> message);

}
```

The MessageSelector interface only contains the accept method, which takes a Message object. If the object can be accepted, the method will return a true value. The ticket handling example is modified take the tickets with emergency priority first using the MessageSelector as shown in Listing 6–13. This MessageSelector returns true for non-emergency tickets.

Listing 6–13. *EmergencyTicketSelector.java*

```
package com.apress.prospringintegration.channels.queuechannel;

import com.apress.prospringintegration.channels.core.Ticket;
import com.apress.prospringintegration.channels.core.Ticket.Priority;
import org.springframework.integration.Message;
import org.springframework.integration.core.MessageSelector;
import org.springframework.stereotype.Component;

@Component
public class EmergencyTicketSelector implements MessageSelector {
  @Override
  public boolean accept(Message<?> message) {
    return ((Ticket) message.getPayload()).getPriority() != Priority.emergency;
  }
}
```

The EmergencyTicketReceiver class shown in Listing 6–14 first pull any emergency ticket by purging all emergency tickets using the MessageSelector described above. The purge method removes and returns any message not accepted by the MessageSelector. The emergency tickets are then processed first.

Listing 6–14. *EmergencyTicketReceiver.java*

```
package com.apress.prospringintegration.channels.queuechannel;

import com.apress.prospringintegration.channels.core.Ticket;
import org.springframework.beans.factory.annotation.Autowired;
```

```
import org.springframework.beans.factory.annotation.Required;
import org.springframework.beans.factory.annotation.Value;
import org.springframework.integration.Message;
import org.springframework.integration.core.MessageSelector;
import org.springframework.stereotype.Component;
import org.springframework.util.Assert;

import java.util.List;

@Component
public class EmergencyTicketReceiver extends TicketReceiver {

  private MessageSelector emergencyTicketSelector;

  @Autowired
  public void setEmergencyTicketSelector(MessageSelector emergencyTicketSelector) {
    this.emergencyTicketSelector = emergencyTicketSelector;
  }

  @Override
  public void handleTicketMessage() {
    Message<?> ticketMessage = null;

    while (true) {
      List<Message<?>> emergencyTicketMessages = channel.purge(emergencyTicketSelector);
      handleEmergencyTickets(emergencyTicketMessages);

      ticketMessage = channel.receive(RECEIVE_TIMEOUT);
      if (ticketMessage != null) {
        handleTicket((Ticket) ticketMessage.getPayload());
      } else {
        try {
          /** Handle some other tasks **/
          Thread.sleep(1000);
        } catch (InterruptedException ex) {
          ex.printStackTrace();
        }
      }
    }
  }

  void handleEmergencyTickets(List<Message<?>> highPriorityTicketMessages) {
    Assert.notNull(highPriorityTicketMessages);
    for (Message<?> ticketMessage : highPriorityTicketMessages) {
      handleTicket((Ticket) ticketMessage.getPayload());
    }
  }
}
```

The output looks like Figure 6–10. Pay attention to the tickets that have emergency priority. Instead of appearing at the very end of the list, all the tickets with emergency priority are received at the very top.

```
Ticket Sent - Ticket# 1000: [low] Some minor problems have been found.
Ticket Sent - Ticket# 1001: [low] Some minor problems have been found.
Ticket Sent - Ticket# 1002: [low] Some minor problems have been found.
Ticket Sent - Ticket# 1003: [low] Some minor problems have been found.
Ticket Sent - Ticket# 1004: [low] Some minor problems have been found.
Ticket Sent - Ticket# 1005: [medium] There is an issue; take a look whenever you have time.
Ticket Sent - Ticket# 1006: [medium] There is an issue; take a look whenever you have time.
Ticket Sent - Ticket# 1007: [medium] There is an issue; take a look whenever you have time.
Ticket Sent - Ticket# 1008: [medium] There is an issue; take a look whenever you have time.
Ticket Sent - Ticket# 1009: [medium] There is an issue; take a look whenever you have time.
Ticket Sent - Ticket# 1010: [high] Serious issue. Fix immediately.
Ticket Sent - Ticket# 1011: [high] Serious issue. Fix immediately.
Ticket Sent - Ticket# 1012: [high] Serious issue. Fix immediately.
Ticket Sent - Ticket# 1013: [high] Serious issue. Fix immediately.
Ticket Sent - Ticket# 1014: [high] Serious issue. Fix immediately.
Ticket Sent - Ticket# 1015: [emergency] Urgent problem. Fix immediately or revenue will be lost!
Ticket Sent - Ticket# 1016: [emergency] Urgent problem. Fix immediately or revenue will be lost!
Ticket Sent - Ticket# 1017: [emergency] Urgent problem. Fix immediately or revenue will be lost!
Ticket Sent - Ticket# 1018: [emergency] Urgent problem. Fix immediately or revenue will be lost!
Ticket Sent - Ticket# 1019: [emergency] Urgent problem. Fix immediately or revenue will be lost!
Received ticket - Ticket# 1015: [emergency] Urgent problem. Fix immediately or revenue will be lost!
Received ticket - Ticket# 1016: [emergency] Urgent problem. Fix immediately or revenue will be lost!
Received ticket - Ticket# 1017: [emergency] Urgent problem. Fix immediately or revenue will be lost!
Received ticket - Ticket# 1018: [emergency] Urgent problem. Fix immediately or revenue will be lost!
Received ticket - Ticket# 1019: [emergency] Urgent problem. Fix immediately or revenue will be lost!
Received ticket - Ticket# 1000: [low] Some minor problems have been found.
Received ticket - Ticket# 1001: [low] Some minor problems have been found.
Received ticket - Ticket# 1002: [low] Some minor problems have been found.
Received ticket - Ticket# 1003: [low] Some minor problems have been found.
Received ticket - Ticket# 1004: [low] Some minor problems have been found.
Received ticket - Ticket# 1005: [medium] There is an issue; take a look whenever you have time.
Received ticket - Ticket# 1006: [medium] There is an issue; take a look whenever you have time.
Received ticket - Ticket# 1007: [medium] There is an issue; take a look whenever you have time.
Received ticket - Ticket# 1008: [medium] There is an issue; take a look whenever you have time.
Received ticket - Ticket# 1009: [medium] There is an issue; take a look whenever you have time.
Received ticket - Ticket# 1010: [high] Serious issue. Fix immediately.
Received ticket - Ticket# 1011: [high] Serious issue. Fix immediately.
Received ticket - Ticket# 1012: [high] Serious issue. Fix immediately.
Received ticket - Ticket# 1013: [high] Serious issue. Fix immediately.
Received ticket - Ticket# 1014: [high] Serious issue. Fix immediately.
```

***Figure 6–10.** EmergencyTicketMain Output*

In the preceding example, the purge method is used to select and remove the messages that contain the emergency priority ticket. All the emergency tickets must be handled first, and then QueueChannel can be polled as usual. This solution is quite complicated; however, Spring Integration provides a better solution to handle this use case.

PriorityChannel

`org.springframework.integration.channel.PriorityChannel` is a subclass of `QueueChannel` as shown in Figure 6–11. It works exactly like `QueueChannel`, except that it allows the endpoint to receive messages in a specified priority based on a comparator similar to how a Java `Collection` is sorted. By default, `PriorityChannel` uses a default comparator based on the value in the message header `PRIORITY` field. By using `PriorityChannel`, the way the emergency tickets are handled in the previous example can be greatly simplified.

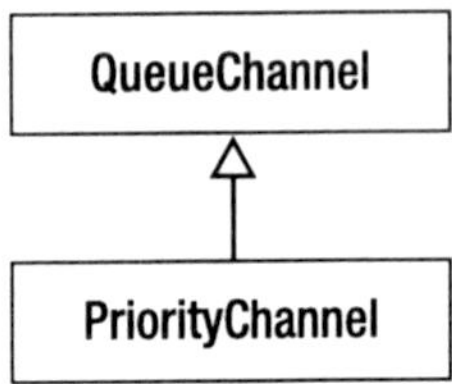

***Figure 6–11.** PriorityChannel Class Diagram*

The preceding example is modified to leverage the `PriorityChannel`. First the ticket receiver code is modified to use the `PriorityChannel` as shown in Listing 6–15.

Listing 6–15. *PriorityTicketReceiver.java*

```
package com.apress.prospringintegration.channels.prioritychannel;

import com.apress.prospringintegration.channels.core.Ticket;
import org.springframework.beans.factory.annotation.Autowired;
import org.springframework.beans.factory.annotation.Required;
import org.springframework.beans.factory.annotation.Value;
import org.springframework.integration.Message;
import org.springframework.integration.channel.PriorityChannel;
import org.springframework.stereotype.Component;

@Component
public class PriorityTicketReceiver implements Runnable {
  private final static int RECEIVE_TIMEOUT = 1000;

  private PriorityChannel channel;

  @Value("#{ticketChannel}")
  public void setChannel(PriorityChannel channel) {
    this.channel = channel;
  }

  public void handleTicketMessage() {
    Message<?> ticketMessage = null;

    while (true) {
      ticketMessage = channel.receive(RECEIVE_TIMEOUT);
      if (ticketMessage != null) {
        handleTicket((Ticket) ticketMessage.getPayload());
      } else {
        try {
          /** Handle some other tasks **/

          Thread.sleep(1000);
        } catch (InterruptedException ex) {
          ex.printStackTrace();
        }
      }
    }
  }

  void handleTicket(Ticket ticket) {
    System.out.println("Received ticket - " + ticket.toString());
  }

  @Override
  public void run() {
    handleTicketMessage();
  }
}
```

Next the ProblemReporter class is modified to use the PriorityChannel as shown in Listing 6–16.

Listing 6–16. *ProblemReporter.java*

```
package com.apress.prospringintegration.channels.prioritychannel;

import com.apress.prospringintegration.channels.core.Ticket;
import org.springframework.beans.factory.annotation.Required;
import org.springframework.beans.factory.annotation.Value;
import org.springframework.integration.channel.PriorityChannel;
import org.springframework.integration.message.GenericMessage;
import org.springframework.stereotype.Component;

@Component
public class ProblemReporter {
  protected PriorityChannel channel;

  @Value("#{ticketChannel}")
  public void setChannel(PriorityChannel channel) {
    this.channel = channel;
  }

  void openTicket(Ticket ticket) {
    channel.send(new GenericMessage<Ticket>(ticket));
    System.out.println("Ticket Sent - " + ticket.toString());
  }
}
```

The PriorityTicketReceiver code looks very similar to the original TicketReceiver implementation using QueueChannel. How can PriorityChannel know which message has higher priority? By default, PriorityChannel inspects the message org.springframework.integration.MessageHeaders's PRIORITY field. The larger the value, the higher priority the message has. In order to take advantage the default behavior of PriorityChannel, a priority needs to be assigned to the message header when the message is created. This is done in the PriorityProblemReporter class as shown in Listing 6–17.

Listing 6–17. *PriorityProblemReporter.java*

```
package com.apress.prospringintegration.channels.prioritychannel;

import com.apress.prospringintegration.channels.core.Ticket;
import org.springframework.integration.MessageHeaders;
import org.springframework.integration.message.GenericMessage;
import org.springframework.stereotype.Component;

import java.util.HashMap;
import java.util.Map;

@Component
public class PriorityProblemReporter extends ProblemReporter {

  void openTicket(Ticket ticket) {
    Map<String, Object> messageHeader = new HashMap<String, Object>();
    messageHeader.put(MessageHeaders.PRIORITY, ticket.getPriority().ordinal());
```

```
    channel.send(new GenericMessage<Ticket>(ticket, messageHeader));
    System.out.println("Ticket Sent - " + ticket.toString());
  }
}
```

By default, the `PriorityChannel` comparator compares the `PRIORITY` field in the message header to determine the priority. The default comparator can be customized by replacing it with a custom comparator. The code in Listing 6–18 shows a custom comparator which compares the priority values stored in the `Ticket` object instead of using the `PRIORITY` field in the message header.

Listing 6–18. *TicketMessagePriorityComparator.java*

```
package com.apress.prospringintegration.channels.prioritychannel;

import com.apress.prospringintegration.channels.core.Ticket;
import org.springframework.integration.Message;
import org.springframework.stereotype.Component;

import java.util.Comparator;

@Component
public class TicketMessagePriorityComparator
    implements Comparator<Message<Ticket>> {

  @Override
  public int compare(Message<Ticket> message1, Message<Ticket> message2) {
    Integer priority1 = message1.getPayload().getPriority().ordinal();
    Integer priority2 = message2.getPayload().getPriority().ordinal();

    priority1 = priority1 != null ? priority1 : 0;
    priority2 = priority2 != null ? priority2 : 0;

    return priority2.compareTo(priority1);
  }
}
```

Instead of comparing the message header's `PRIORITY` field, `TicketMessagePriorityComparator` compares the `Ticket`'s `priority` value instead. Once the new comparator is implemented, it needs to be assigned to the `PriorityChannel` instance. The following file shown in Listing 6–19 configures the requisite Spring Integration channel, and assigns it a reference to the `TicketMessagePriorityComparator`, which is picked up and registered because it has the `@Component` annotation on it.

Listing 6–19. *priority-channel.xml*

```
<?xml version="1.0" encoding="UTF-8"?>
<beans xmlns="http://www.springframework.org/schema/beans"
       xmlns:xsi="http://www.w3.org/2001/XMLSchema-instance"
       xmlns:int="http://www.springframework.org/schema/integration"
       xmlns:context="http://www.springframework.org/schema/context"
       xsi:schemaLocation="http://www.springframework.org/schema/integration
    http://www.springframework.org/schema/integration/spring-integration-2.0.xsd
    http://www.springframework.org/schema/beans
    http://www.springframework.org/schema/beans/spring-beans-3.0.xsd
    http://www.springframework.org/schema/context
    http://www.springframework.org/schema/context/spring-context-3.0.xsd">
```

```
  <context:component-scan
      base-package="com.apress.prospringintegration.channels.prioritychannel"/>
  <context:component-scan
      base-package="com.apress.prospringintegration.channels.core"/>

  <int:channel id="ticketChannel"
               datatype="com.apress.prospringintegration.channels.core.Ticket">
    <int:priority-queue capacity="50"
                        comparator="ticketMessagePriorityComparator"/>
  </int:channel>


</beans>
```

Once again, PriorityChannel is defined in the Spring bean configuration file and the comparator can be overridden in the configuration file.

```
<int:channel id="ticketChannel" datatype="com.apress.prospringintegration.channels.Ticket">
    <int:priority-queue capacity="50" comparator="ticketMessagePriorityComparator" />
</int:channel>
```

The output looks like Figure 6–12, and it looks the same as the output for EmergencyTicketMain earlier in the chapter, in the "QueueChannel" section.

```
Ticket Sent - Ticket# 1000: [low] Some minor problems have been found.
Ticket Sent - Ticket# 1001: [low] Some minor problems have been found.
Ticket Sent - Ticket# 1002: [low] Some minor problems have been found.
Ticket Sent - Ticket# 1003: [low] Some minor problems have been found.
Ticket Sent - Ticket# 1004: [low] Some minor problems have been found.
Ticket Sent - Ticket# 1005: [medium] There is an issue; take a look whenever you have time.
Ticket Sent - Ticket# 1006: [medium] There is an issue; take a look whenever you have time.
Ticket Sent - Ticket# 1007: [medium] There is an issue; take a look whenever you have time.
Ticket Sent - Ticket# 1008: [medium] There is an issue; take a look whenever you have time.
Ticket Sent - Ticket# 1009: [medium] There is an issue; take a look whenever you have time.
Ticket Sent - Ticket# 1010: [high] Serious issue. Fix immediately.
Ticket Sent - Ticket# 1011: [high] Serious issue. Fix immediately.
Ticket Sent - Ticket# 1012: [high] Serious issue. Fix immediately.
Ticket Sent - Ticket# 1013: [high] Serious issue. Fix immediately.
Ticket Sent - Ticket# 1014: [high] Serious issue. Fix immediately.
Ticket Sent - Ticket# 1015: [emergency] Urgent problem. Fix immediately or revenue will be lost!
Ticket Sent - Ticket# 1016: [emergency] Urgent problem. Fix immediately or revenue will be lost!
Ticket Sent - Ticket# 1017: [emergency] Urgent problem. Fix immediately or revenue will be lost!
Ticket Sent - Ticket# 1018: [emergency] Urgent problem. Fix immediately or revenue will be lost!
Ticket Sent - Ticket# 1019: [emergency] Urgent problem. Fix immediately or revenue will be lost!
Received ticket - Ticket# 1015: [emergency] Urgent problem. Fix immediately or revenue will be lost!
Received ticket - Ticket# 1016: [emergency] Urgent problem. Fix immediately or revenue will be lost!
Received ticket - Ticket# 1017: [emergency] Urgent problem. Fix immediately or revenue will be lost!
Received ticket - Ticket# 1018: [emergency] Urgent problem. Fix immediately or revenue will be lost!
Received ticket - Ticket# 1019: [emergency] Urgent problem. Fix immediately or revenue will be lost!
Received ticket - Ticket# 1010: [high] Serious issue. Fix immediately.
Received ticket - Ticket# 1014: [high] Serious issue. Fix immediately.
Received ticket - Ticket# 1011: [high] Serious issue. Fix immediately.
Received ticket - Ticket# 1012: [high] Serious issue. Fix immediately.
Received ticket - Ticket# 1013: [high] Serious issue. Fix immediately.
Received ticket - Ticket# 1009: [medium] There is an issue; take a look whenever you have time.
Received ticket - Ticket# 1008: [medium] There is an issue; take a look whenever you have time.
Received ticket - Ticket# 1005: [medium] There is an issue; take a look whenever you have time.
Received ticket - Ticket# 1007: [medium] There is an issue; take a look whenever you have time.
Received ticket - Ticket# 1006: [medium] There is an issue; take a look whenever you have time.
Received ticket - Ticket# 1002: [low] Some minor problems have been found.
Received ticket - Ticket# 1004: [low] Some minor problems have been found.
Received ticket - Ticket# 1001: [low] Some minor problems have been found.
Received ticket - Ticket# 1000: [low] Some minor problems have been found.
Received ticket - Ticket# 1003: [low] Some minor problems have been found.
```

Figure 6–12. *EmergencyTicketMain Output*

RendezvousChannel

`org.springframework.integration.channel.RendezvousChannel` is a synchronized version of `QueueChannel` as shown in Figure 6–13. It uses a zero-capacity `SynchronousQueue` instead of `BlockingQueue` internally. The sender will be blocked until the receiver receives the message from the channel. In other words, the sender cannot send the second message until the receiver retrieves the message from the channel; or, the receiver will block until the sender sends a message to `RendezvousChannel`. The behavior is similar to a semaphore running in multiple threads; as a result, it is very useful to use `RendezvousChannel` to synchronize multiple threads when semaphores are not an option.

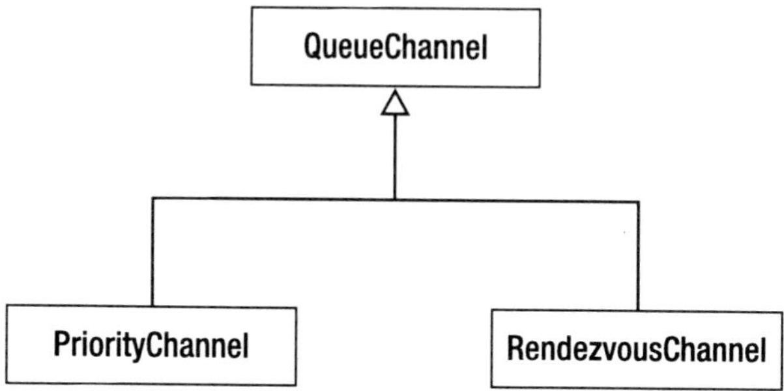

Figure 6–13. *RendezvousChannel Class Diagram*

The ticket handling example is modified to use a `RendezvousChannel`. The sender cannot send the next message until the previous one is received. The `ProblemReporter` class is modified to use the `RendezvousChannel` as shown in Listing 6–20.

Listing 6–20. *ProblemReporter.java*

```
package com.apress.prospringintegration.channels.rendezvouschannel;

import com.apress.prospringintegration.channels.core.Ticket;
import org.springframework.beans.factory.annotation.Value;
import org.springframework.integration.channel.RendezvousChannel;
import org.springframework.integration.support.MessageBuilder;
import org.springframework.stereotype.Component;

@Component
public class ProblemReporter {
  private RendezvousChannel channel;

  public ProblemReporter() {
  }

  @Value("#{ticketChannel}")
  public void setChannel(RendezvousChannel channel) {
    this.channel = channel;
  }

  void openTicket(Ticket ticket) {
    channel.send(MessageBuilder.withPayload(ticket).build());
    System.out.println("Ticket Sent - " + ticket.toString());
```

```
  }
}
```

Next the TicketReceiver class is modified to use the RendezvousChannel as shown in Listing 6–21.

Listing 6–21. *TicketReceiver.java*

```
package com.apress.prospringintegration.channels.rendezvouschannel;

import com.apress.prospringintegration.channels.core.Ticket;
import org.springframework.beans.factory.annotation.Value;
import org.springframework.integration.Message;
import org.springframework.integration.channel.RendezvousChannel;
import org.springframework.stereotype.Component;

@Component
public class TicketReceiver implements Runnable {

  private final static int RECEIVE_TIMEOUT = 1000;

  private RendezvousChannel channel;

  @Value("#{ticketChannel}")
  public void setChannel(RendezvousChannel channel) {
    this.channel = channel;
  }

  void handleTicket(Ticket ticket) {
    System.out.println("Received ticket - " + ticket.toString());
  }

  @Override
  public void run() {
    Message<?> ticketMessage ;

    while (true) {
      ticketMessage = channel.receive(RECEIVE_TIMEOUT);
      if (ticketMessage != null) {
        handleTicket((Ticket) ticketMessage.getPayload());
      } else {
        try {
          /** Handle some other tasks **/

          Thread.sleep(1000);
        } catch (InterruptedException ex) {
          ex.printStackTrace();
        }
      }
    }
  }
}
```

Finally the Main class is modified, as shown in Listing 6–22, so that the message consumer thread starts up first. Otherwise, the thread will be blocked by RendezvousChannel after sending the first message.

Listing 6–22. Main.java

```
package com.apress.prospringintegration.channels.rendezvouschannel;

import com.apress.prospringintegration.channels.core.Ticket;
import com.apress.prospringintegration.channels.core.TicketGenerator;
import org.springframework.context.support.ClassPathXmlApplicationContext;

import java.util.List;

public class Main {
  public static void main(String[] args) throws Throwable {
    String contextName = "rendezvous-channel.xml";

    ClassPathXmlApplicationContext applicationContext =
         new ClassPathXmlApplicationContext(contextName);
    applicationContext.start();

    ProblemReporter problemReporter = applicationContext.getBean(ProblemReporter.class);
    TicketReceiver ticketReceiver = applicationContext.getBean(TicketReceiver.class);
    TicketGenerator ticketGenerator = applicationContext.getBean(TicketGenerator.class);

    // start *before* message publication because it'll block on put
    Thread consumerThread = new Thread(ticketReceiver);
    consumerThread.start();

    List<Ticket> tickets = ticketGenerator.createTickets();
    for (Ticket ticket : tickets) {
      problemReporter.openTicket(ticket);
    }
  }
}
```

The output for the RenezvousChannel example looks like Figure 6–14.

```
Ticket Sent - Ticket# 1000: [low] Some minor problems have been found.
Received ticket - Ticket# 1000: [low] Some minor problems have been found.
Ticket Sent - Ticket# 1001: [low] Some minor problems have been found.
Received ticket - Ticket# 1001: [low] Some minor problems have been found.
Ticket Sent - Ticket# 1002: [low] Some minor problems have been found.
Received ticket - Ticket# 1002: [low] Some minor problems have been found.
Ticket Sent - Ticket# 1003: [low] Some minor problems have been found.
Received ticket - Ticket# 1003: [low] Some minor problems have been found.
Ticket Sent - Ticket# 1004: [low] Some minor problems have been found.
Received ticket - Ticket# 1004: [low] Some minor problems have been found.
Ticket Sent - Ticket# 1005: [medium] There is an issue; take a look whenever you have time.
Received ticket - Ticket# 1005: [medium] There is an issue; take a look whenever you have time.
Ticket Sent - Ticket# 1006: [medium] There is an issue; take a look whenever you have time.
Received ticket - Ticket# 1006: [medium] There is an issue; take a look whenever you have time.
Ticket Sent - Ticket# 1007: [medium] There is an issue; take a look whenever you have time.
Received ticket - Ticket# 1007: [medium] There is an issue; take a look whenever you have time.
Received ticket - Ticket# 1008: [medium] There is an issue; take a look whenever you have time.
Ticket Sent - Ticket# 1008: [medium] There is an issue; take a look whenever you have time.
Ticket Sent - Ticket# 1009: [medium] There is an issue; take a look whenever you have time.
Received ticket - Ticket# 1009: [medium] There is an issue; take a look whenever you have time.
Ticket Sent - Ticket# 1010: [high] Serious issue. Fix immediately.
Received ticket - Ticket# 1010: [high] Serious issue. Fix immediately.
Ticket Sent - Ticket# 1011: [high] Serious issue. Fix immediately.
Received ticket - Ticket# 1011: [high] Serious issue. Fix immediately.
Ticket Sent - Ticket# 1012: [high] Serious issue. Fix immediately.
Received ticket - Ticket# 1012: [high] Serious issue. Fix immediately.
Ticket Sent - Ticket# 1013: [high] Serious issue. Fix immediately.
Received ticket - Ticket# 1013: [high] Serious issue. Fix immediately.
Received ticket - Ticket# 1014: [high] Serious issue. Fix immediately.
Ticket Sent - Ticket# 1014: [high] Serious issue. Fix immediately.
Ticket Sent - Ticket# 1015: [emergency] Urgent problem. Fix immediately or revenue will be lost!
Received ticket - Ticket# 1015: [emergency] Urgent problem. Fix immediately or revenue will be lost!
Received ticket - Ticket# 1016: [emergency] Urgent problem. Fix immediately or revenue will be lost!
Ticket Sent - Ticket# 1016: [emergency] Urgent problem. Fix immediately or revenue will be lost!
Ticket Sent - Ticket# 1017: [emergency] Urgent problem. Fix immediately or revenue will be lost!
Received ticket - Ticket# 1017: [emergency] Urgent problem. Fix immediately or revenue will be lost!
Received ticket - Ticket# 1018: [emergency] Urgent problem. Fix immediately or revenue will be lost!
Ticket Sent - Ticket# 1018: [emergency] Urgent problem. Fix immediately or revenue will be lost!
Ticket Sent - Ticket# 1019: [emergency] Urgent problem. Fix immediately or revenue will be lost!
Received ticket - Ticket# 1019: [emergency] Urgent problem. Fix immediately or revenue will be lost!
```

Figure 6–14. RendezvousChannel Main Output

DirectChannel

`org.springframework.integration.channel.DirectChannel` is a mixture of the point-to-point and publish-subscribe channels as shown in Figure 6–15. It uses the publish-subscribe pattern so the message will be pushed to the receiver, but only one of the receivers can receive the same message at any given time. As a result, `DirectChannel` is actually a point-to-point channel. Since `DirectChannel` does not add any overhead, it is the default channel type within Spring Integration.

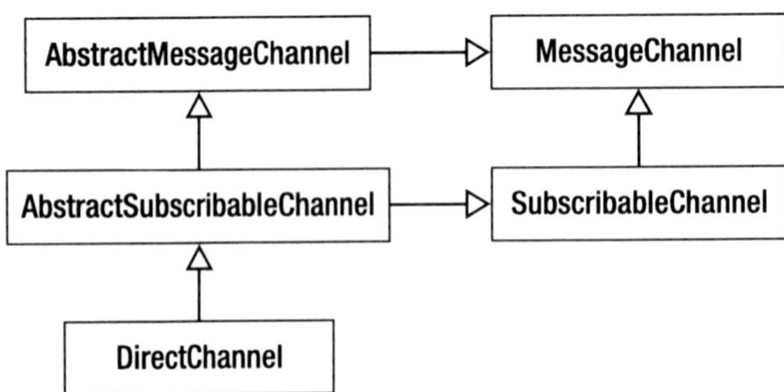

Figure 6–15. DirectChannel Class Diagram

The ticket handling example is modified to use a DirectChannel. The DirectChannel is point-to-point where only one receiver can receive each message. A TicketMessageHandler class is created to receive the incoming Ticket message as shown in Listing 6–23.

Listing 6–23. *TicketMessageHandler.java*

```
package com.apress.prospringintegration.channels.directchannel;

import com.apress.prospringintegration.channels.core.Ticket;
import org.springframework.integration.Message;
import org.springframework.integration.MessageRejectedException;
import org.springframework.integration.MessagingException;
import org.springframework.integration.core.MessageHandler;
import org.springframework.stereotype.Component;

@Component
public class TicketMessageHandler implements MessageHandler {

  @Override
  public void handleMessage(Message<?> message)
      throws MessagingException {
    Object payload = message.getPayload();

    if (payload instanceof Ticket) {
      handleTicket((Ticket) payload);
    } else {
      throw new MessageRejectedException(message, "Unknown data type has been received.");
    }
  }

  void handleTicket(Ticket ticket) {
    System.out.println("Received ticket - " + ticket.toString());
  }
}
```

Next the ProblemReport class is modified to use a DirectChannel as shown in Listing 6–24.

Listing 6–24. *ProblemReporter.java*

```
package com.apress.prospringintegration.channels.directchannel;

import com.apress.prospringintegration.channels.core.Ticket;
import org.springframework.beans.factory.annotation.Value;
import org.springframework.integration.channel.DirectChannel;
import org.springframework.integration.support.MessageBuilder;
import org.springframework.stereotype.Component;

@Component
public class ProblemReporter {

  private DirectChannel channel;

  @Value("#{ticketChannel}")
  public void setChannel(DirectChannel channel) {
    this.channel = channel;
```

```
  }

  void openTicket(Ticket ticket) {
    channel.send(MessageBuilder.withPayload( ticket).build() );
    System.out.println("Ticket Sent - " + ticket.toString());
  }
}
```

The Main class, as shown in Listing 6–25, is modified to subscribe the `TicketMessageHandler` to the `DirectChannel` `ticketChannel`.

Listing 6–25. Main.java

```
package com.apress.prospringintegration.channels.directchannel;

import com.apress.prospringintegration.channels.core.Ticket;
import com.apress.prospringintegration.channels.core.TicketGenerator;
import org.springframework.context.support.ClassPathXmlApplicationContext;
import org.springframework.integration.channel.DirectChannel;

import java.util.List;

public class Main {

    public static void main(String[] args) throws Exception {

        String contextName = "direct-channel.xml";

        ClassPathXmlApplicationContext applicationContext =
                new ClassPathXmlApplicationContext(contextName);
        applicationContext.start();

        ProblemReporter problemReporter =
                applicationContext.getBean(ProblemReporter.class);
        TicketGenerator ticketGenerator =
                applicationContext.getBean(TicketGenerator.class);
        TicketMessageHandler ticketMessageHandler =
                applicationContext.getBean(TicketMessageHandler.class);

        DirectChannel channel =
                applicationContext.getBean("ticketChannel", DirectChannel.class);
        channel.subscribe(ticketMessageHandler);

        List<Ticket> tickets = ticketGenerator.createTickets();
        for (Ticket ticket : tickets) {
            problemReporter.openTicket(ticket);
        }
    }
}
```

The Spring configuration is shown in Listing 6–26 again leveraging component scanning to simplify and reduce the amount of XML configuration.

Listing 6–26. direct-channel.xml

```
<?xml version="1.0" encoding="UTF-8"?>
<beans xmlns="http://www.springframework.org/schema/beans"
       xmlns:xsi="http://www.w3.org/2001/XMLSchema-instance"
       xmlns:int="http://www.springframework.org/schema/integration"
       xmlns:context="http://www.springframework.org/schema/context"
       xsi:schemaLocation="http://www.springframework.org/schema/integration
    http://www.springframework.org/schema/integration/spring-integration-2.0.xsd
    http://www.springframework.org/schema/beans
    http://www.springframework.org/schema/beans/spring-beans-3.0.xsd
    http://www.springframework.org/schema/context
    http://www.springframework.org/schema/context/spring-context.xsd">

  <context:component-scan
      base-package="com.apress.prospringintegration.channels.directchannel"/>
  <context:component-scan
      base-package="com.apress.prospringintegration.channels.core"/>

  <int:channel id="ticketChannel"/>


</beans>
```

Although DirectChannel acts like a point-to-point channel, it allows multiple receivers to subscribe to the channel just like the other publish-subscribe channels. By default, DirectChannel sends unique messages to each of the subscribed receivers in round-robin fashion, and it is the only strategy out of the box for now. Additional strategies will be added in future versions of Spring Integration. However, developers can create their own strategies by providing a custom load-balancing algorithm by implementing the org.springframework.integration.dispatcher.LoadBalancingStrategy interface.

```
public interface LoadBalancingStrategy {

    public Iterator<MessageHandler> getHandlerIterator(
          Message<?> message, List<MessageHandler> handlers);

}
```

DirectChannel will perform the handleMessage method within the sender's thread before the send() method returns. It is very useful for supporting transactions for both send and receive operations. For example, if the handleTicket method writes to the database and JDBCException has been thrown from the database-related operation, the handleMessage method will cascade the error and throw a MessageException. The DirectChannel dispatchers will fail back all the subsequent handlers. By default, DirectChannel has failover turned on, which means an exception will be thrown only if all the handlers have tried to handle the message.

ExecutorChannel

org.springframework.integration.channel.ExecutorChannel is a point-to-point message channel that's very similar to the DirectChannel as shown in Figure 6–16. However, it allows the dispatching to happen in an instance of org.springframework.core.task.TaskExecutor in a thread separate from the sender thread. In other words, the send method of ExecutorChannel will not be blocked. As a result, ExecutorChannel does not support transactions across the sender and receiver, as does DirectChannel.

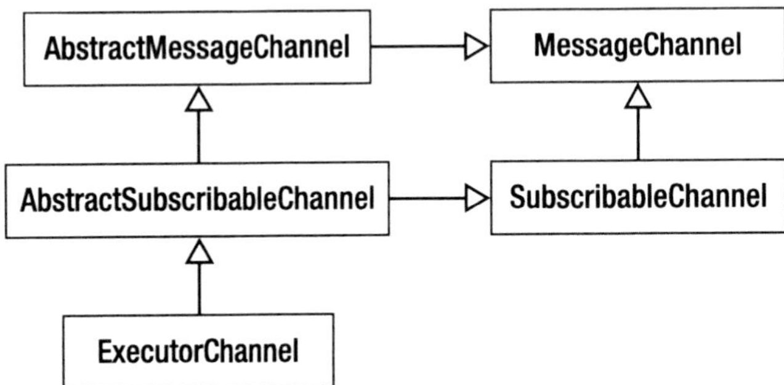

Figure 6–16. *ExecutorChannel Class Diagram*

NullChannel

The org.springframework.integration.channel.NullChannel implementation as shown in Figure 6–17 is very interesting. NullChannel is a dummy message channel that does nothing. It does not pass any messages from the sender to the receiver. NullChannel's send method always returns true, while its receive() method always returns a null value. In other words, NullChannel always returns success when attempting to send, while the channel always appears to contain nothing during receiving. Due to the special behavior of NullChannel, it is mainly used for unit testing, integration testing, and debugging.

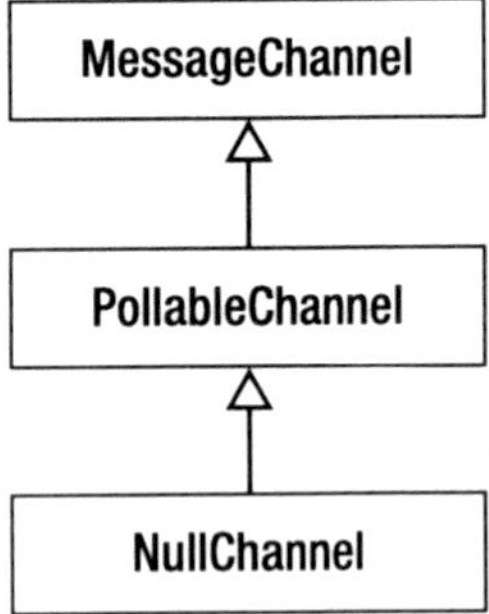

Figure 6–17. *NullChannel Class Diagram*

Scoped Channel

In Spring Integration 1.0, developers can use ThreadLocalChannel to restrict the scope of the message channel within the same thread. In Spring Integration 2.0, ThreadLocalChannel is replaced by a more general scope support. By simply defining the channel scope attribute, no other thread will be able to access a message within the thread-scoped message channel.

Publish-Subscribe Channel

The `org.springframework.integration.channel.PublishSubscribeChannel` implementation is the basic publish-subscribe channel implementation of the pattern as shown in Figure 6–18. The message channel broadcasts any sent messages to all of the channel subscribers. In addition, the messages are pushed to the consumers instead of the consumers polling for the messages.

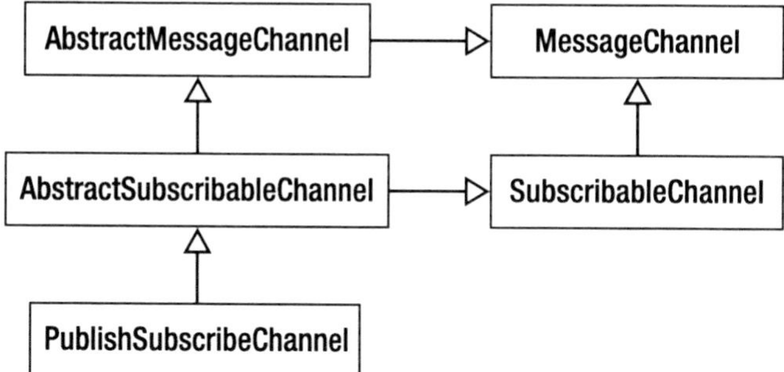

Figure 6–18. *PublishSubscribeChannel Class Diagram*

Channel Interceptors

One of the important features of enterprise integration is the ability to capture information when the messages passing through the system. This is very useful when you want to intercept messages within the channel and inspect them before they reach their destinations. Spring Integration provides the opportunity to intercept the messages during the send and receive operations. This is where the `ChannelInterceptor` interface comes into play as shown in Listing 6–27.

Listing 6–27. *ChannelInterceptor.java*

```
package org.springframework.integration.channel;

import org.springframework.integration.Message;
import org.springframework.integration.MessageChannel;

public interface ChannelInterceptor {

    Message<?> preSend(Message<?> message, MessageChannel channel);

    void postSend(Message<?> message, MessageChannel channel, boolean sent);

    boolean preReceive(MessageChannel channel);

    Message<?> postReceive(Message<?> message, MessageChannel channel);

}
```

`ChannelInterceptor` allows the message to be intercepted before it's sent, after it's sent, before it's received, and after received. There are many methods to prevent a message from being processed in the channel downstream. For example, `preSend` can return `null` to prevent the message from being sent to the message channel. postReceived can return null to prevent the message from passing from the message channel into the consumer.

Since only the PollableChannel interface has the receive operation, preReceive and postReceive will be invoked only for PollableChannel implementations. The different available interceptor methods for the various message channels are shown in Table 6–3.

Table 6–3. Message Channels and Interceptors

Message Channels	preSend()	preReceive()	postSend()	postReceive()
QueueChannel	Yes	Yes	Yes	Yes
PriorityChannel	Yes	Yes	Yes	Yes
RendezvousChannel	Yes	Yes	Yes	Yes
DirectChannel	Yes	No	Yes	No
ExecutorChannel	Yes	No	Yes	No
NullChannel	Yes	Yes	Yes	Yes
PublishSubscribeChannel	Yes	No	Yes	No

Once we have implemented a ChannelInterceptor, we need to add it into the channel. We can add one or more interceptors into a channel. The interceptors will be invoked in order within the list.

```
messageChannel.addInterceptor(channelInterceptor);
```

```
messageChannel.setInterceptors(channelInterceptorList);
```

MessagingTemplate

Spring Integration provides MessagingTemplate as a very easy way to integrate a messaging system into applications. It supports many common message channel operations, such as send and receive. MessagingTemplate also supports transactions by providing a PlatformTransactionManager. Let's rewrite our problem-reporting system example from earlier in the chapter using MessagingTemplate. The ProblemReporter code is modified to use the MessagingTemplate as shown in Listing 6–28. The MessagingTemplate can also build the Spring Integration Message instance.

Listing 6–28. ProblemReporter.java

```
package com.apress.prospringintegration.channels.messagingtemplate;

import com.apress.prospringintegration.channels.core.Ticket;
import org.springframework.beans.factory.annotation.Autowired;
import org.springframework.beans.factory.annotation.Required;
import org.springframework.integration.core.MessagingTemplate;
import org.springframework.integration.message.GenericMessage;
import org.springframework.integration.support.MessageBuilder;
```

```
import org.springframework.stereotype.Component;

@Component
public class ProblemReporter {

  private MessagingTemplate messagingTemplate;

  @Autowired
  public void setMessagingTemplate(MessagingTemplate messagingTemplate) {
    this.messagingTemplate = messagingTemplate;
  }

  public void openTicket(Ticket ticket) {
    messagingTemplate.convertAndSend(ticket);
    System.out.println("Ticket Sent - " + ticket.toString());
  }

}
```

The MessagingTemplate can also be used to receive messages as shown in Listing 6–29.

Listing 6–29. *TicketReceiver.java*

```
package com.apress.prospringintegration.channels.messagingtemplate;

import com.apress.prospringintegration.channels.core.Ticket;
import org.springframework.beans.factory.annotation.Autowired;
import org.springframework.beans.factory.annotation.Required;
import org.springframework.integration.Message;
import org.springframework.integration.core.MessagingTemplate;
import org.springframework.stereotype.Component;

@Component
public class TicketReceiver implements Runnable {

  private final static int RECEIVE_TIMEOUT = 1000;

  private MessagingTemplate messagingTemplate;

  @Autowired
  public void setMessagingTemplate(MessagingTemplate messagingTemplate) {
    this.messagingTemplate = messagingTemplate;
    this.messagingTemplate.setReceiveTimeout(RECEIVE_TIMEOUT);
  }

  public void handleTicketMessage() {
    Message<?> ticketMessage;

    while (true) {
      ticketMessage = messagingTemplate.receive();
      if (ticketMessage != null) {
        handleTicket((Ticket) ticketMessage.getPayload());
      } else {
        /* Perform Some Other Tasks Here */
      }
```

```
    }
  }

  void handleTicket(Ticket ticket) {
    System.out.println("Received ticket - " + ticket.toString());
  }

  @Override
  public void run() {
    handleTicketMessage();
  }
}
```

The `Main` class stays the same as shown in Listing 6–30.

Listing 6–30. *Main.java*

```
package com.apress.prospringintegration.channels.messagingtemplate;

import com.apress.prospringintegration.channels.core.Ticket;
import com.apress.prospringintegration.channels.core.TicketGenerator;
import org.springframework.context.support.ClassPathXmlApplicationContext;

import java.util.List;

public class Main {

    public static void main(String[] args) {
        String contextName = "messaging-template.xml";

        ClassPathXmlApplicationContext applicationContext =
                new ClassPathXmlApplicationContext(contextName);
        applicationContext.start();


        ProblemReporter problemReporter =
                applicationContext.getBean(ProblemReporter.class);
        TicketReceiver ticketReceiver =
                applicationContext.getBean(TicketReceiver.class);
        TicketGenerator ticketGenerator =
                applicationContext.getBean(TicketGenerator.class);


        List<Ticket> tickets = ticketGenerator.createTickets();
        for (Ticket ticket : tickets) {
            problemReporter.openTicket(ticket);
        }

        Thread consumerThread = new Thread(ticketReceiver);
        consumerThread.start();
    }
}
```

The Spring configuration file when using the `MessageTemplate` also stays the same as shown in Listing 6–31.

Listing 6–31. messaging-template.xml

```
<?xml version="1.0" encoding="UTF-8"?>
<beans xmlns="http://www.springframework.org/schema/beans"
xmlns:xsi="http://www.w3.org/2001/XMLSchema-instance"
       xmlns:context="http://www.springframework.org/schema/context"
       xmlns:int="http://www.springframework.org/schema/integration"
       xsi:schemaLocation="http://www.springframework.org/schema/integration
    http://www.springframework.org/schema/integration/spring-integration-2.0.xsd
    http://www.springframework.org/schema/beans
    http://www.springframework.org/schema/beans/spring-beans-3.0.xsd
    http://www.springframework.org/schema/context
    http://www.springframework.org/schema/context/spring-context-3.0.xsd">

  <context:component-scan
      base-package="com.apress.prospringintegration.channels.messagingtemplate"/>
  <context:component-scan
      base-package="com.apress.prospringintegration.channels.core"/>

  <int:channel id="ticketChannel"
               datatype="com.apress.prospringintegration.channels.core.Ticket">
    <int:priority-queue capacity="50"/>
  </int:channel>
</beans>
```

This is simialar to previous iterations of the file. It relies on the definitions established by component scannning the package and picking up the beans defined with @Component. Additionally, it relies on definitions established when the Java configuration class is scanned and bean definitions loaded:

```
package com.apress.prospringintegration.channels.messagingtemplate;

import org.springframework.beans.factory.annotation.Value;
import org.springframework.context.annotation.Bean;
import org.springframework.context.annotation.Configuration;
import org.springframework.integration.MessageChannel;
import org.springframework.integration.core.MessagingTemplate;

@Configuration
public class MessagingTemplateConfiguration {

  @Value("#{ticketChannel}")
  private MessageChannel messageChannel;

  @Bean
  public MessagingTemplate messagingTemplate() {
    MessagingTemplate messagingTemplate = new MessagingTemplate();
    messagingTemplate.setDefaultChannel(this.messageChannel);
    messagingTemplate.setReceiveTimeout(1000);
    return messagingTemplate;
  }
}
```

Configuring a Message Channel

In this section, we'll look at how to configure the different kinds of message channels using the Spring Integration XML namespace in the Spring bean configuration file. Make sure the Spring bean configuration file includes the Spring Integration namespace, like this:

```
<?xml version="1.0" encoding="UTF-8"?>
<beans xmlns="http://www.springframework.org/schema/beans"
       xmlns:xsi="http://www.w3.org/2001/XMLSchema-instance"
       xmlns:context="http://www.springframework.org/schema/context"
       xmlns:int="http://www.springframework.org/schema/integration"
       xsi:schemaLocation="http://www.springframework.org/schema/integration
    http://www.springframework.org/schema/integration/spring-integration-2.0.xsd
    http://www.springframework.org/schema/beans
    http://www.springframework.org/schema/beans/spring-beans-3.0.xsd
    http://www.springframework.org/schema/context
    http://www.springframework.org/schema/context/spring-context-3.0.xsd">
</beans>
```

QueueChannel

In order to create a channel instance, you can use the channel element in the Spring configuration file.

```
<int:channel id="queueChannel" />
```

The preceding example creates a QueueChannel using all default configurations. In order words, the channel is unbound on capacity. This is very dangerous, since the JVM may run out of memory. It is always a good idea to limit the number of messages in the channel.

```
<int:channel id="queueChannel">
    <int:queue capacity="50" />
</int:channel>
```

The preceding example limits the channel capacity to 50 messages. Once the channel reaches maximum capacity, all the send operations will be blocked until the channel capacity frees up.

Spring Integration also supports the data type channel design pattern by setting the datatypes element to a specific class. By default, all the Spring Integration message channels accept any type of message payload.

```
<int:channel id="queueChannel"
        datatype="com.apress.prospringintegration.channels.Ticket">
    <int:queue capacity="50" />
</int:channel>
```

PriorityChannel

Very similar to QueueChannel, PriorityChannel can also specify the queue capacity and data type. It is also a good idea to specify the queue capacity to avoid running out of memory.

```
<int:channel id="priorityChannel"
        datatype="com.apress.prospringintegration.channels.Ticket">
    <int:priority-queue capacity="50"/>
</int:channel>
```

By default, PriorityChannel uses the PRIORITY message header to determine the priority of the incoming messages.

```
package com.apress.prospringintegration.channels.prioritychannel;

import com.apress.prospringintegration.channels.core.Ticket;
import org.springframework.integration.Message;
import org.springframework.stereotype.Component;

import java.util.Comparator;

@SuppressWarnings("unused")
@Component
public class TicketMessagePriorityComparator
    implements Comparator<Message<Ticket>> {

  @Override
  public int compare(Message<Ticket> message1, Message<Ticket> message2) {
    Integer priority1 = message1.getPayload().getPriority().ordinal();
    Integer priority2 = message2.getPayload().getPriority().ordinal();

    priority1 = priority1 != null ? priority1 : 0;
    priority2 = priority2 != null ? priority2 : 0;

    return priority2.compareTo(priority1);
  }
}
```

However, we can provide a custom comparator to change the behavior of PriorityChannel:

```
<int:channel id="priorityChannel"
        datatype="com.apress.prospringintegration.channels.Ticket">
    <int:priority-queue capacity="50" comparator="ticketPriorityComparator" />
</int:channel>
```

RendezvousChannel

RendezvousChannel does not provide any additional configuration options other than setting the data type. Since it is a zero-capacity channel, the capacity cannot be changed. As a result, only one message can pass through the channel at any given time.

```
<int:channel id="rendezvousChannel"
        datatype="com.apress.prospringintegration.channels.Ticket">
        <rendezvous-queue/>
</int:channel>
```

DirectChannel

DirectChannel is the default type of Spring Integration channel. As a result, it requires nothing to specify the channel instance.

```
<int:channel id="directChannel"/>
```

Similar to the rest of the Spring Integration message channels, DirectChannel allows users to specify the payload data type. It also allows developers to enable/disable failover and specify the load-balancing strategy. The default configuration for the DirectChannel is failover enabled and round-robin load-balancing.

```
<int:channel id="directChannel"
        datatype="com.apress.prospringintegration.channels.Ticket">
        <int:dispatcher failover="true" load-balancer="none"/>
</int:channel>
```

ExecutorChannel

In order to use ExecutorChannel, we need to assign an executor to the channel dispatcher. In addition, ExecutorChannel supports the failover and load-balancing options.

```
<int:channel id="executorChannel"
        datatype="com.apress.prospringintegration.channels.Ticket">
        <int:dispatcher task-executor="performTicketExecutor"/>
</int:channel>
```

The task-executor attribute supports any Spring TaskExecutor implementation.

PublishSubscribeChannel

Similar to ExecutorChannel, the PublishSubscribeChannel supports any TaskExecutor implementation for the task-executor attribute. By default, Spring Integration will not assign a correlation ID to the outgoing messages. This may be overridden by using the apply-sequence attribute.

```
<int:publish-subscribe-channel id="publishSubscribeChannel"
        task-executor="performTicketExecutor" apply-sequence="true"/>
```

ChannelInterceptor

In order to assign interceptors to a channel, we can use the interceptor's subelement within the Spring configuration file.

```
<int:channel id="messageChannel">
  <int:interceptors>
    <ref bean="interceptor1"/>
    <ref bean="interceptor2"/>
    <ref bean="interceptor3"/>
  </int:interceptors>
</int:channel>
```

Sometimes, we may want to assign the same interceptor to all the message channels. We can use the following configuration:

```
<int:channel-interceptor ref="interceptor1"/>
```

The preceding example will assign interceptor1 to all the message channels. However, sometimes we may just want the interceptor to be assigned to certain channels.

```
<int:channel-interceptor ref="interceptor1" pattern="ticketChannel, emergencyChannel"/>
```

We can use the wildcard in the pattern attribute and also specify the position to insert the interceptor into the list.

```
<int:channel-interceptor ref="interceptor1" pattern="ticketChannel, emergency*,↵
 lowPriority*" order="2"/>
```

Backing Up a Channel

By default, Spring Integration message channels store messages in memory. This is because memory is fast and easy to implement. However, the number of messages that can be stored will be bounded by the available server memory. In addition, the channel may run out of memory very easily in a high-throughput integrated system. Even worse, all the messages will be gone if the system crashes. It is very unscalable and unreliable to use only memory to back up a message channel.

A pair of inbound and outbound channel adapters (endpoints and adapters will be discussed in more depth in Chapter 9) may be used to integrate the channels into a file system or JDBC data store. However, this approach is complicated because it still involves two channel adapters even though we are only dealing with a single channel.

Here is where Spring Integration 2.0 comes to the rescue; a message channel can be backed by JMS as an alternative to memory as shown in Figure 6–19. The JMS-backed message channel decouples the message producer and consumer by making messaging asynchronously. Instead of messages being stored in memory, they are stored in the JMS messaging system which can in turn store the messages however it see fits, be it to disk, or in memory, or any other configuration supported by the JMS broker. In addition, depending on the JMS configuration, the message endpoints can now scale out and run within different processes or servers.

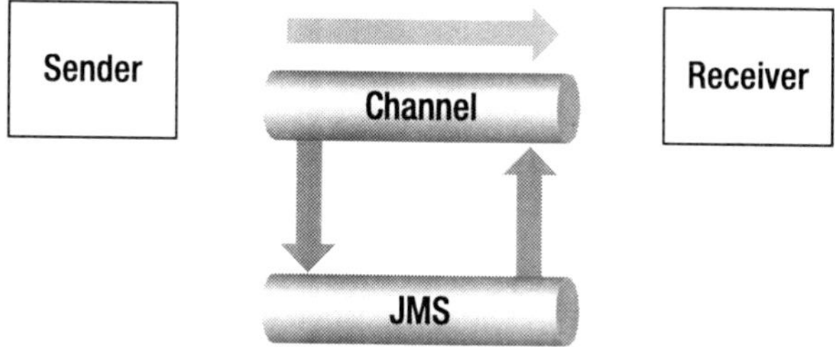

Figure 6–19. JMS-backed Message Channel

The preceding example defines a point-to-point message channel. In order to use JMS to back this channel, we will use the jms namespace and provide the JMS queue destination name. Make sure to include the Spring Integration JMS namespace. The resulting configuration is in many ways very comparable to the default, in-memory channel configuration, just from a different namespace.

```
<?xml version="1.0" encoding="UTF-8"?>
<beans xmlns="http://www.springframework.org/schema/beans"
       xmlns:xsi="http://www.w3.org/2001/XMLSchema-instance"
       xmlns:context="http://www.springframework.org/schema/context"
       xmlns:int="http://www.springframework.org/schema/integration"
       xmlns:int-jms="http://www.springframework.org/schema/integration/jms"
       xsi:schemaLocation="http://www.springframework.org/schema/integration
    http://www.springframework.org/schema/integration/spring-integration-2.0.xsd
    http://www.springframework.org/schema/integration/jms
```

```
    http://www.springframework.org/schema/integration/jms/spring-integration-jms.xsd
    http://www.springframework.org/schema/beans
    http://www.springframework.org/schema/beans/spring-beans-3.0.xsd
    http://www.springframework.org/schema/context
    http://www.springframework.org/schema/context/spring-context-3.0.xsd">
  <int-jms:channel id=”channel” queue-name=”jmsQueue” />

</beans>
```

By default, Spring Integration uses org.springframework.jms.support.destination.DynamicDestinationResolver to resolve the JMS queue name into the actual JMS destination. It also looks for a ConnectionFactory reference with the bean name connectionFactory. In order to make the preceding example work, we need to provide the connection factory reference.

```
// org.springframework.jms.connection.CachingConnectionFactory
// is a convenient way to work with JMS connection factories
@Bean
public CachingConnectionFactory connectionFactory(){
  CachingConnectionFactory ccf = new CachingConnectionFactory();
  ActiveMQConnectionFactory cf = new ActiveMQConnectionFactory();
  cf.setBrokerURL("vm://localhost");
  ccf.setTargetConnectionFactory(cf);
  return ccf;
}

<int-jms:channel id="channel" queue-name="jmsQueue" />
```

We can provide a custom connection factory bean with a name other than connectionFactory.

```
@Bean
public CachingConnectionFactory jmsConnectionFactory(){
  CachingConnectionFactory ccf = new CachingConnectionFactory();
  ActiveMQConnectionFactory cf = new ActiveMQConnectionFactory();
  cf.setBrokerURL("vm://localhost");
  ccf.setTargetConnectionFactory(cf);
  return ccf ;
}

<int-jms:channel id="channel" queue-name="jmsQueue" connection-factory=➥
"jmsConnectionFactory" />
```

We can provide the queue reference instead of using the JMS queue destination name.

```
<int-jms:channel id="channel" queue="jmsQueue" />
```

In order to back a publish-subscribe message channel using JMS, we will provide the JMS topic name.

```
<int-jms:publish-subscribe-channel id="channel" topic-name="jmsTopic"
        connection-factory="jmsConnectionFactory" />
```

We also can use a topic reference instead of the JMS topic destination name.

```
<int-jms:publish-subscribe-channel id="channel" topic="jmsTopic" />
```

Now we have JMS-backed message channels, which are scalable and reliable. Spring Integration 2.0 makes it very easy.

Summary

Spring Integration is inspired by *Enterprise Integration Patterns*.[4] This chapter has specifically looked at how Spring Integration has implemented the message channel pattern. By providing various implementations of the point-to-point message channel and the publish-subscribe message channel, applications can communicate by sending messages with each other via the channels. The message operations can be shared in multiple threads or only exists in local thread.

By using the XML namespace in the Spring bean configuration file, developers can easily switch between different channel implementations. Sometimes it is necessary to invoke the messaging system within the application code. Spring Integration provides a messaging template, which supports a variety of operations for sending messages to the channels.

Since Spring Integration message channels store messages in memory, the channels are unbounded by default. To avoid running out of memory, it is always a good idea to bind the message channels by specifying the capacity. However, memory-based message channels will lose all the messages if the application crashes or the server shuts down. In order to make the message channel durable, Spring Integration 2.0 introduces JMS-backed message channels so the messages are stored within a JMS broker instead of in memory.

In the next couple chapters, we will discuss how to connect message channels with internal or external systems by using endpoints, adapters, transformers, and routers.

[4] Gregor Hohpe, op. cit.

CHAPTER 7

Transformations and Enrichment

One approaches integration so that two or more applications may share services and data. One of the key challenges of integration is that the underlying data models of any two given applications are likely different, or incompatible. The various properties of, say, a customer record, can vary for a simple field such as an address. Some applications define the complete address as a single property, and others break down the address into the street number, street, city, state, zip code, and so on. In addition, the exchange format of the record itself may be incompatible: system A might expect a serialized Java object, and system B might expect an XML-encoded record or some other serialization. An integration platform should be able to adapt messages as required by consumers. Care should be taken that data is of as high fidelity as possible when moving from system to system. To support an extensible framework for data transformation, integration platforms support transformation.

A message used to support communication between the integration endpoints typically consists of two parts: the *payload*, which is the actual data being sent, and the *header*, which is used for information supporting the housekeeping tasks or service support required for the messaging service. In addition to providing support for transforming the message payload, there is often a need to add header data—to *enrich* it with—metadata required to support processing by downstream components.

Transformation is ideal when adapting data from one system to another, usually when the interchange is conceptually common, but different with regard to implementations among the multiple systems. On a small scale, this approach works fine: two transformations are required for a single, bidirectional connection. Things quickly become untenable as more systems are added, however; in the worst case, for every new system added, a connection (and transformation) between it and every other system is required. This quickly becomes nightmarishly tedious! Metcalfe's Law states that the value of a network is proportional to the square of the number of connected users in the system, and describes quadratic growth. A common way to reduce this complexity is to have a central node mediate communication on behalf of all the other nodes; all nodes need only to be adapted to send messages to, and receive messages from, this central node. The central node in turn routes to all other nodes. This is where the canonical data model pattern is most effective.

For those coming to Spring Integration from other products, the fact that Spring Integration itself doesn't mandate a canonical data model might be surprising. Spring Integration makes no assumptions about how messages travel inside the framework. A message might not ever leave the JVM, so there is no need for their payload be serialized in some form. Messages might not even live outside of a transaction, so there's no requirement that they even be marshalled, necessarily. Inbound adapters will often deliver messages with payloads specific to the inbound adapter; the inbound channel adapter in the file namespace, for example, delivers messages of type `java.io.File`, and must be transformed as required to something else. Outbound adapters, in the same way, will expect inbound message payloads to be of a known type, and will fail to work if this expectation isn't met. The framework provides several built-in transformers, and the ability to write your own, to meet these requirements.

The Canonical Data Model Concept

The canonical, or universal, data model is a concept that was developed to support the varying data representations of the same conceptual object. For example, customer relationship management (CRM) systems need to define an object representing a customer. However, the data model used for the different applications may be quite different. A canonical data model is a data structure that is agreed upon or contracted to be used for passing an object such as a customer across the enterprise or within an industry. For example, a new CRM system is purchased and must be integrated with a legacy mainframe system. The CRM system needs to obtain customer information from the legacy system. In addition, there are other systems within the organization that also will need access to the customer information. In order to integrate the various applications, a canonical data model is created for a customer object.

In the integration shown in Figure 7–1, the various data representations of a customer are transformed into the canonical data model. Thus, all interested parties will be able to communicate, since all are using the same canonical data model. In addition, the various endpoints will not need to know about the other internal data structures, since everything is being converted to the canonical.

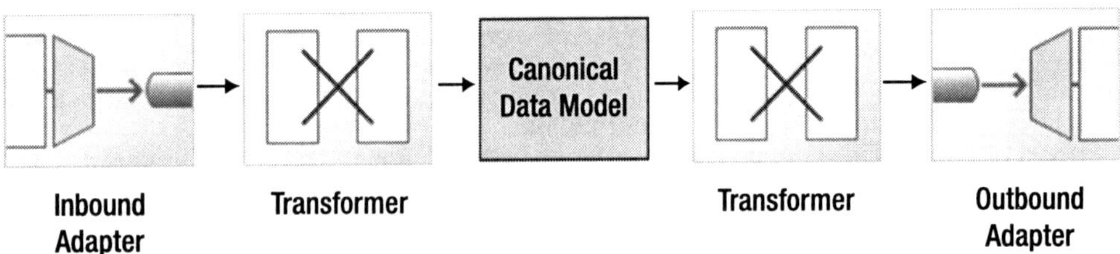

Figure 7–1. The Canonical Data Model

An example of a canonical data model is shown in Listing 7–1. An agreement was reached to use a Java bean representation for a customer object. All endpoints will be required to transform to this representation when communicating across the integration platform. Note the annotation `@Component` in the canonical data model class. This is used to support *component scanning*, in which the bean is brought into the Spring context using just a simple annotation without requiring any additional XML configuration information. A `toString` method is added to support logging in the following examples.

Listing 7–1. Canonical Data Model Representation of a Customer

```
package com.apress.prospringintegration.transform;

import org.springframework.stereotype.Component;

@Component
public class Customer {
    private String firstName;
    private String lastName;
    private String address;
    private String city;
    private String state;
    private String zip;

    public String getFirstName() {
        return firstName;
```

```
    }

    public void setFirstName(String firstName) {
        this.firstName = firstName;
    }

    public String getLastName() {
        return lastName;
    }

    public void setLastName(String lastName) {
        this.lastName = lastName;
    }

    public String getAddress() {
        return address;
    }

    public void setAddress(String address) {
        this.address = address;
    }

    public String getCity() {
        return city;
    }

    public void setCity(String city) {
        this.city = city;
    }

    public String getState() {
        return state;
    }

    public void setState(String state) {
        this.state = state;
    }

    public String getZip() {
        return zip;
    }

    public void setZip(String zip) {
        this.zip = zip;
    }

    @Override
    public String toString() {
        return "Customer{" +
                "firstName='" + firstName + '\'' +
                ", lastName='" + lastName + '\'' +
                ", address='" + address + '\'' +
                ", city='" + city + '\'' +
                ", state='" + state + '\'' +
```

```
                    ", zip='" + zip + '\'' +
                    '}';
    }
}
```

Spring Integration Transformer

To support message conversion or transformations, Spring Integration has the concept of a *message transformer*. This allows the message payload to be modified using a Spring bean. A transformer, like most Spring Integration components, accepts an input channel for the incoming message and an output channel for the modified message.

Transforming a Message

The `transformer` element is part of the Spring Integration namespace, and is used as shown in Listing 7–2.

Listing 7–2. *Spring Configuration File transformer.xml Demostrating the transformer Element*

```
<?xml version="1.0" encoding="UTF-8"?>
<beans xmlns="http://www.springframework.org/schema/beans"
       xmlns:xsi="http://www.w3.org/2001/XMLSchema-instance"
       xmlns:int="http://www.springframework.org/schema/integration"
       xmlns:context="http://www.springframework.org/schema/context"
       xsi:schemaLocation="http://www.springframework.org/schema/beans
    http://www.springframework.org/schema/beans/spring-beans.xsd
    http://www.springframework.org/schema/integration
    http://www.springframework.org/schema/integration/spring-integration-2.0.xsd
    http://www.springframework.org/schema/context
    http://www.springframework.org/schema/context/spring-context-3.0.xsd">

  <context:component-scan base-package="com.apress.prospringintegration.transform"/>

  <int:transformer input-channel="input"
                   output-channel="output"
                   ref="mapper"/>

  <int:channel id="input"/>

  <int:channel id="output">
    <int:queue capacity="10"/>
  </int:channel>

</beans>
```

The `ref` attribute points to the Spring bean with the transformation method defined either through the `method` attribute, as is done in Listing 7–2, or using the `@Transformer` attribute, as shown in Listing 7–3. A bean with only one method is valid, and Spring Integration will attempt to use that one method. It is a better practice to stipulate which method should be used with the `@Transformer` annotation, or through the `method` attribute in the XML schema. The transformer class may also be defined using an inner bean definition (in Spring XML), but the `ref` attribute must not be defined, as it will create an ambiguous condition and cause an exception to be thrown. In this example, component scanning is used, and eliminates the need for a bean element definition. The customer information is passed through the input channel as a Map. The map method coverts the customer data into the Customer canonical object described previously.

Listing 7–3. The Mapper Transformation Class

```
package com.apress.prospringintegration.transform;

import org.springframework.integration.annotation.Transformer;
import org.springframework.stereotype.Component;

import java.util.Map;

@Component
public class Mapper {

    @Transformer
    public Customer map(Map<String, String> message) {
        Customer customer = new Customer();

        customer.setFirstName(message.get("firstName"));
        customer.setLastName(message.get("lastName"));
        customer.setAddress(message.get("address"));
        customer.setCity(message.get("city"));
        customer.setState(message.get("state"));
        customer.setZip(message.get("zip"));
        return customer;
    }
}
```

To test the example transformer code, a simple main class Transformer, as shown in Listing 7–4, is created to push a Map object to the input channel and poll for the output channel Customer object. A Map object is created and populated with the customer data, and then sent to the input channel. The output channel is then polled for the resultant Customer object. The result of running the Transformer class is shown in Listing 7.5.

Listing 7–4. Transformer.java Class Used to Test a Basic Transformation

```
package com.apress.prospringintegration.transform;

import org.springframework.context.support.ClassPathXmlApplicationContext;
import org.springframework.integration.Message;
import org.springframework.integration.MessageChannel;
import org.springframework.integration.core.PollableChannel;
import org.springframework.integration.support.MessageBuilder;

import java.util.HashMap;
import java.util.Map;

public class Transformer {
    public static void main(String[] args) {
        ClassPathXmlApplicationContext context =
                new ClassPathXmlApplicationContext("classpath:transformer.xml");

        MessageChannel input = context.getBean("input", MessageChannel.class);
```

```
        PollableChannel output = context.getBean("output", PollableChannel.class);

        Map<String, String> customerMap = new HashMap<String, String>();
        customerMap.put("firstName", "John");
        customerMap.put("lastName", "Smith");
        customerMap.put("address", "100 State Street");
        customerMap.put("city", "Los Angeles");
        customerMap.put("state", "CA");
        customerMap.put("zip", "90064");

        Message<Map<String, String>> message =
                MessageBuilder.withPayload(customerMap).build();
        input.send(message);

        Message<?> reply = output.receive();
        System.out.println("received: " + reply.getPayload());
    }
}
```

Listing 7–5. *Result of Running the Simple Spring Integration Transfomration*

```
received: Customer{firstName='John', lastName='Smith', address='100 State Street', city='Los
Angeles', state='CA', zip='90064'}
```

There are several options for the transformer method input parameter type and the return value type. The method argument may be

- `org.springframework.integration.Message`
- The payload type of the incoming `Message`, which is used in the preceding example.
- The header values separately, or the entire header `Map` using the `@Header` or `@Headers` annotation, respectively. Augmenting and using the message headers values will be discussed more following.

The return value may be any type, and will be sent to the output channel as the payload of the message, with the following exceptions:

- If the return type is `Message`, it will be sent to the output channel as the `Message` type.
- If the return type is a `Map` and the input payload was not a `Map`, then the `Map` entries will be added to the incoming message header `Map using String key values.`
- The transformer handles `null` return values by not sending any message to the output channel.

If the return type is `void`, then Spring Integration will consult the reply channel header in the inbound `message` and try to forward the message on that.

Built-In Transformers

Spring Integration comes with several out-of-the-box transformer implementations in the core. There are many more not encompassed in the following list that come as appropriate with specific namespaces; for example, the `file` namespace ships with support for transforming `java.io.File` objects to various target types:

- `object-to-string-transformer`
- `payload-serializing-transformer`
- `payload-deserializing-transformer`
- `object-to-map-transformer`
- `map-to-object-transformer`
- `json-to-object-transformer`
- `object-to-json-transformer`
- `payload-type-converting-transformer`

Using the object-to-string Transformer

The first transformation supports the standard operation of converting an object to a string. This is a very common scenario (e.g., sending a message to a file adapter). An example of using the `object-to-string` transformer is shown in Listing 7–6.

Listing 7–6. Example of the object-to-string Transformer

```
<?xml version="1.0" encoding="UTF-8"?>
<beans xmlns="http://www.springframework.org/schema/beans"
       xmlns:xsi="http://www.w3.org/2001/XMLSchema-instance"
       xmlns:int="http://www.springframework.org/schema/integration"
       xsi:schemaLocation="http://www.springframework.org/schema/beans
    http://www.springframework.org/schema/beans/spring-beans.xsd
    http://www.springframework.org/schema/integration
    http://www.springframework.org/schema/integration/spring-integration-2.0.xsd">

  <int:object-to-string-transformer input-channel="input" output-channel="output"/>

  <int:channel id="input"/>

  <int:channel id="output">
    <int:queue capacity="10"/>
  </int:channel>

</beans>
```

The message payload coming in on the channel input is converted to a string using the `toString()` method of the incoming object and send as the payload to the channel output. This transformer works fine as long as the toString() method has the desired behavior; otherwise, a custom transformer will need to be used, as discussed previously.

Using the payload-serializing and payload-deserializing Transformers

The next two transformers, payload-serializing-transformer and payload-deserializing-transformer, perform the symmetric operation of serializing an object to a byte array and deserializing the byte array back into an object. This transformer is useful since many adapters and JMS work well with this format. An example of using this transformer is shown in Listing 7–7.

Listing 7–7. *Example of payload-serializing-transformer and payload deserializing-transformer*

```
<?xml version="1.0" encoding="UTF-8"?>
<beans xmlns="http://www.springframework.org/schema/beans"
       xmlns:xsi="http://www.w3.org/2001/XMLSchema-instance"
       xmlns:int="http://www.springframework.org/schema/integration"
       xsi:schemaLocation="http://www.springframework.org/schema/beans
    http://www.springframework.org/schema/beans/spring-beans.xsd
    http://www.springframework.org/schema/integration
    http://www.springframework.org/schema/integration/spring-integration-2.0.xsd">

  <int:payload-serializing-transformer input-channel="input"
                                       output-channel="byte-array"/>

  <int:payload-deserializing-transformer input-channel="byte-array"
                                         output-channel="output"/>

  <int:logging-channel-adapter id="logger"
                               log-full-message="true"
                               level="INFO"/>

  <int:channel id="input"/>

  <int:channel id="byte-array">
    <int:interceptors>
      <int:wire-tap channel="logger"/>
    </int:interceptors>
  </int:channel>

  <int:channel id="output">
    <int:queue capacity="10"/>
  </int:channel>

</beans>
```

In this example, the payload of the incoming message on channel input is transformed into a byte array. The logging adapter is used to see the transformed byte array. Then the byte array is transformed back into the original object. A Wire Tap interceptor is used to log the message as it goes through the byte-array channel. This is a useful tool for debugging; it allows the message to be logged any time it goes through the intercepted channel. To test the example, a simple main class SerializerTransformer is created (as shown in Listing 7–8), much like the previous example. The message is logged before it's sent to the input channel, after it's transformed to a byte array, and after it's transformed back to a Map object.

Listing 7–8. *Main Class SerializerTransformer Used for Testing the Serializing Transformer*

```
package com.apress.prospringintegration.transform;

import org.springframework.context.support.ClassPathXmlApplicationContext;
import org.springframework.integration.Message;
import org.springframework.integration.MessageChannel;
import org.springframework.integration.core.PollableChannel;
import org.springframework.integration.support.MessageBuilder;

import java.util.HashMap;
import java.util.Map;

public class SerializerTransformer {
    public static void main(String[] args) {
        ClassPathXmlApplicationContext context =
                new ClassPathXmlApplicationContext("classpath:serializer-transformer.xml");

        MessageChannel input = context.getBean("input", MessageChannel.class);
        PollableChannel output = context.getBean("output", PollableChannel.class);

        Map<String, String> customerMap = new HashMap<String, String>();
        customerMap.put("firstName", "John");
        customerMap.put("lastName", "Smith");
        customerMap.put("address", "100 State Street");
        customerMap.put("city", "Los Angeles");
        customerMap.put("state", "CA");
        customerMap.put("zip", "90064");

        System.out.println("toString(): " + customerMap.toString());

        Message<Map<String, String>> message =
                MessageBuilder.withPayload(customerMap).build();
        input.send(message);

        Message<?> reply = output.receive();
        System.out.println("received: " + reply.getPayload());
    }
}
```

The results of running the class SerializerTransformer is shown in Listing 7–9.The initial message is a Map object. After transformation, the message is now a byte array. Finally, the message is transformed back into a Map object.

Listing 7–9. *Results of Running the Serializing Transformer*

```
toString(): {zip=90064, lastName=Smith, address=100 State Street, state=CA, firstName=John,
city=Los Angeles}

INFO : org.springframework.integration.handler.LoggingHandler -
[Payload=[B@97d01f][Headers={timestamp=1293421055587, id=97270abd-f449-410e-a99b-
edb85b0f88df}]
```

```
received: {lastName=Smith, zip=90064, address=100 State Street, state=CA, firstName=John,
city=Los Angeles}
```

Using the object-to-map and a map-to-object Transformers

It is very common to convert an object into a `Map` representation. This eliminates the need to serialize the object when sending it as a JMS message or to simplify the mapping process when transforming it into a different object required for another endpoint. Spring Integration provides an `object-to-map` transformer and a `map-to-object` transformer to support this need. The `Map` key is based on the Spring Expression Language. An example of this transformer is shown in Listing 7–10.

Listing 7–10. *Example of object-to-map-transformer and map-to-object-transformer*

```
<?xml version="1.0" encoding="UTF-8"?>
<beans xmlns="http://www.springframework.org/schema/beans"
       xmlns:xsi="http://www.w3.org/2001/XMLSchema-instance"
       xmlns:int="http://www.springframework.org/schema/integration"
       xsi:schemaLocation="http://www.springframework.org/schema/beans
    http://www.springframework.org/schema/beans/spring-beans.xsd
    http://www.springframework.org/schema/integration
    http://www.springframework.org/schema/integration/spring-integration-2.0.xsd">

  <int:object-to-map-transformer input-channel="input"
                                 output-channel="map"/>

  <int:map-to-object-transformer input-channel="map"
                                 output-channel="output"
                                 type="com.apress.prospringintegration.transform.Customer"/>

  <int:logging-channel-adapter id="logger"
                               log-full-message="true"
                               level="INFO"/>

  <int:channel id="input"/>

  <int:channel id="map">
    <int:interceptors>
      <int:wire-tap channel="logger"/>
    </int:interceptors>
  </int:channel>

  <int:channel id="output">
    <int:queue capacity="10"/>
  </int:channel>

</beans>
```

The incoming message object payload from the `input` channel is transformed into a `Map` object and sent to the `map` channel. The logging adapter is used to log the `Map` object. Then the `Map` object is transformed back into the original object and sent as the payload to the `output` channel. Note that the object class must be specified through the `type` attribute. The `main` class to test this example is again similar to the previous example, as shown in Listing 7–11. A `Customer` object is created and populated, and sent to the `input` channel. The object is converted to a `Map` representation and logged by the Wire

Tap interceptor. The `Map` is then transformed back to a `Customer` object and polled and logged by the `MapTransformer` class. The results are shown in Listing 7–12.

Listing 7–11. MapTransformer main Class Used to Test object-to-map-transformer

```
package com.apress.prospringintegration.transform;

import org.springframework.context.support.ClassPathXmlApplicationContext;
import org.springframework.integration.Message;
import org.springframework.integration.MessageChannel;
import org.springframework.integration.core.PollableChannel;
import org.springframework.integration.support.MessageBuilder;

public class MapTransformer {
    public static void main(String[] args) {
        ClassPathXmlApplicationContext context =
                new ClassPathXmlApplicationContext("classpath:map-transformer.xml");

        MessageChannel input = context.getBean("input", MessageChannel.class);
        PollableChannel output = context.getBean("output", PollableChannel.class);

        Customer customer = new Customer();
        customer.setFirstName("John");
        customer.setLastName("Smith");
        customer.setAddress("100 State Street");
        customer.setCity("Los Angeles");
        customer.setState("CA");
        customer.setZip("90064");

        System.out.println("toString(): " + customer.toString());

        Message<Customer> message = MessageBuilder.withPayload(customer).build();
        input.send(message);

        Message<?> reply = output.receive();
        System.out.println("received: " + reply.getPayload());
    }
}
```

Listing 7–12. Output of Running the Map Transformer Example

```
toString(): Customer{firstName='John', lastName='Smith', address='100 State Street', city='Los
Angeles', state='CA', zip='90064'}

INFO : org.springframework.integration.handler.LoggingHandler - [Payload={zip=90064,
lastName=Smith, address=100 State Street, state=CA, firstName=John, city=Los
Angeles}][Headers={timestamp=1293423769790, id=81efb6d4-2d1f-44f0-b0ea-a2b8208ce7e9}]

received: Customer{firstName='John', lastName='Smith', address='100 State Street', city='Los
Angeles', state='CA', zip='90064'}
```

Using the object-to-json and json-to-object Transformers

JSON is a very common data format, especially for communicating with the browser's JavaScript engine. Spring Integration has two transformers, `object-to-json-transformer` and `json-to-object-transformer`, which convert an object to a JSON representation and back from JSON to the object, respectively. An example of these transformers is shown in Listing 7–13.

***Listing 7–13.** Example of object-to-json-transformer and json-to-object-transformer*

```
<?xml version="1.0" encoding="UTF-8"?>
<beans xmlns="http://www.springframework.org/schema/beans"
       xmlns:xsi="http://www.w3.org/2001/XMLSchema-instance"
       xmlns:int="http://www.springframework.org/schema/integration"
       xmlns:context="http://www.springframework.org/schema/context"
       xsi:schemaLocation="http://www.springframework.org/schema/beans
    http://www.springframework.org/schema/beans/spring-beans.xsd
    http://www.springframework.org/schema/integration
    http://www.springframework.org/schema/integration/spring-integration-2.0.xsd
    http://www.springframework.org/schema/context
    http://www.springframework.org/schema/context/spring-context-3.0.xsd">

  <context:component-scan base-package="com.apress.prospringintegration.transform"/>

  <int:object-to-json-transformer input-channel="input"
                                  output-channel="json"/>

  <int:json-to-object-transformer input-channel="json"
                                  output-channel="output"
                                  type="com.apress.prospringintegration.transform.Customer"/>

  <int:logging-channel-adapter id="logger" log-full-message="true" level="INFO"/>

  <int:channel id="input"/>

  <int:channel id="json">
    <int:interceptors>
      <int:wire-tap channel="logger"/>
    </int:interceptors>
  </int:channel>

  <int:channel id="output">
    <int:queue capacity="10"/>
  </int:channel>

</beans>
```

The payload on the incoming message on the input channel is transformed into JSON and converted back into the object as the payload of the message on the output channel. The logging adapter is used to log the intermediate JSON representation. Again, a simple `main` class, `JsonTransformer`, is created to run the example, as shown in Listing 7–14.

Listing 7–14. *JsonTranformer main Class to Run the JSON Transformer Example*

```
package com.apress.prospringintegration.transform;

import org.springframework.context.support.ClassPathXmlApplicationContext;
import org.springframework.integration.Message;
import org.springframework.integration.MessageChannel;
import org.springframework.integration.core.PollableChannel;
import org.springframework.integration.support.MessageBuilder;

public class JsonTransformer {
        public static void main(String[] args) {
        ClassPathXmlApplicationContext context =
                new ClassPathXmlApplicationContext("classpath:json-transformer.xml");

        MessageChannel input = context.getBean("input", MessageChannel.class);
        PollableChannel output = context.getBean("output", PollableChannel.class);

        Customer customer = new Customer();
        customer.setFirstName("John");
        customer.setLastName("Smith");
        customer.setAddress("100 State Street");
        customer.setCity("Los Angeles");
        customer.setState("CA");
        customer.setZip("90064");

        System.out.println("toString(): " + customer.toString());

        Message<Customer> message = MessageBuilder.withPayload(customer).build();
        input.send(message);

        Message<?> reply = output.receive();
        System.out.println("received: " + reply.getPayload());
    }
}
```

Running the JSON example will produce the results shown in Listing 7–15. As can be seen by the Wire Tap interceptor logging, the customer information is in JSON format.

Listing 7–15. *JSON Transformer Example Results*

```
toString(): Customer{firstName='John', lastName='Smith', address='100 State Street', city='Los
Angeles', state='CA', zip='90064'}

INFO : org.springframework.integration.handler.LoggingHandler -
[Payload={"firstName":"John","lastName":"Smith","city":"Los
Angeles","zip":"90064","address":"100 State
Street","state":"CA"}][Headers={timestamp=1293423966087, id=7f54c01e-f3bd-4661-b24e-
0285bba5ff7c}]

received: Customer{firstName='John', lastName='Smith', address='100 State Street', city='Los
Angeles', state='CA', zip='90064'}
```

Using XML Transformers

Unlike the Java Business Integration (JBI) specification, or many of the other integration servers, Spring Integration does not require the message payload to be XML based. However, Spring Integration does provide convenience transformers for XML payloads if this is required. Spring Integration provides two transformers based on the Spring OXM (Object-to-XML Mapping) framework's `org.springframework.oxm.Marshaller` and `org.springframework.oxm.Unmarshaller` classes, which support serializing an object to XML, and an XML stream to an object, respectively. There are implementations for JAXB, Castor, XMLBeans, JiBX, and XStream at the moment. Castor will be used to demonstrate the XML transformers, since it requires minimal configuration to work. The other implementations work in a similar fashion.

To support the XML transformers and Castor, the dependencies shown in Listing 7–16 must be added.

Listing 7–16. *Additional Maven Dependencies Required for the XML Transformers*

```
<dependency>
  <groupId>org.springframework.integration</groupId>
  <artifactId>spring-integration-xml</artifactId>
  <version>2.0.1.RELEASE</version>
</dependency>
<dependency>
  <groupId>org.codehaus.castor</groupId>
  <artifactId>castor</artifactId>
  <version>1.2</version>
</dependency>
<dependency>
  <groupId>xerces</groupId>
  <artifactId>xercesImpl</artifactId>
  <version>2.9.1</version>
</dependency>
```

Castor version 1.2 is used for this example since, at the time of writing, Spring has not been updated to work with version 1.3. A separate Spring Integration XML namespace is required to use the XML transformers. A simple example that converts the `Customer` canonical object into XML and back into the object is shown in Listing 7–17.

Listing 7–17. *XML Transformer Example*

```
<?xml version="1.0" encoding="UTF-8"?>
<beans xmlns="http://www.springframework.org/schema/beans"
       xmlns:xsi="http://www.w3.org/2001/XMLSchema-instance"
       xmlns:int="http://www.springframework.org/schema/integration"
       xmlns:int-xml="http://www.springframework.org/schema/integration/xml"
       xmlns:context="http://www.springframework.org/schema/context"
       xsi:schemaLocation="http://www.springframework.org/schema/beans
    http://www.springframework.org/schema/beans/spring-beans.xsd
    http://www.springframework.org/schema/integration
    http://www.springframework.org/schema/integration/spring-integration-2.0.xsd
    http://www.springframework.org/schema/integration/xml
    http://www.springframework.org/schema/integration/xml/spring-integration-xml.xsd
    http://www.springframework.org/schema/context
    http://www.springframework.org/schema/context/spring-context-3.0.xsd">
```

```
  <context:component-scan base-package="com.apress.prospringintegration.transform"/>

  <int-xml:marshalling-transformer input-channel="input"
                                   output-channel="xml"
                                   marshaller="marshaller"
                                   result-type="StringResult"/>

  <int-xml:unmarshalling-transformer id="defaultUnmarshaller"
                                     input-channel="xml-string"
                                     output-channel="output"
                                     unmarshaller="marshaller"/>

  <int:object-to-string-transformer input-channel="xml" output-channel="xml-string"/>

  <int:logging-channel-adapter id="logger" log-full-message="true" level="INFO"/>

  <int:channel id="input"/>

  <int:channel id="xml-string"/>

  <int:channel id="xml">
    <int:interceptors>
      <int:wire-tap channel="logger"/>
    </int:interceptors>
  </int:channel>

  <int:channel id="output">
    <int:queue capacity="10"/>
  </int:channel>
</beans>
```

Note the addition of the Spring Integration XML namespace. marshalling-transformer is used to convert an input channel payload object into XML using the org.springframework.oxm.castor.CastorMashaller configured using the Java configuration XmlConfiguration, as shown in Listing 7–18.

Listing 7–18. *Java Configuration XmlConfiguration*

```
package com.apress.prospringintegration.transform;

import org.springframework.context.annotation.Bean;
import org.springframework.context.annotation.Configuration;
import org.springframework.oxm.castor.CastorMarshaller;

@Configuration
public class XmlConfiguration {

    @Bean
    public CastorMarshaller marshaller() {
        return new CastorMarshaller();
    }
}
```

The output payload of the xml channel may either be a string that uses the result-type attribute of StringResult or an XML Document that uses DomResult. You can configure additional Result type outputs by setting the org.springframework.integration.xml.result.ResultFactory interface using the optional result-transformer attribute. For this example, the XML is returned in the payload as a javax.xml.transform.Result-wrapped string value. The XML is logged using the logging adapter, and then converted to a pure string using the object-to-string-transformer to allow it to be sent to the unmarshalling-transformer. The CastorMashaller supports both marshalling and unmarshalling, and is used in conjunction with the unmarshalling-transformer to convert the XML back into the Customer object. The other Marshaller and Unmarshaller implementations work in a similar fashion.

The XML transformation example may be run using the main class XmlTransformer shown in Listing 7–19.

Listing 7–19. *XMLTranformer main Class for Running the XML Transformer Example*

```
package com.apress.prospringintegration.transform;

import org.springframework.context.support.ClassPathXmlApplicationContext;
import org.springframework.integration.Message;
import org.springframework.integration.MessageChannel;
import org.springframework.integration.core.PollableChannel;
import org.springframework.integration.support.MessageBuilder;

public class XmlTransformer {
    public static void main(String[] args) {
        ClassPathXmlApplicationContext context =
                new ClassPathXmlApplicationContext("classpath:xml-transformer.xml");

        MessageChannel input = context.getBean("input", MessageChannel.class);
        PollableChannel output = context.getBean("output", PollableChannel.class);

        Customer customer = new Customer();
        customer.setFirstName("John");
        customer.setLastName("Smith");
        customer.setAddress("100 State Street");
        customer.setCity("Los Angeles");
        customer.setState("CA");
        customer.setZip("90064");

        System.out.println("toString(): " + customer.toString());

        Message<Customer> message = MessageBuilder.withPayload(customer).build();
        input.send(message);

        Message<?> reply = output.receive();
        System.out.println("received: " + reply.getPayload());
    }
}
```

Again, the same pattern is used to demonstrate the XML transformer. A Customer object is created and passed to the XML transformer through the input channel. The object is transformed into an XML representation and logged using the Wire Tap interceptor. Then the XML payload is converted back to the Customer object. The results of running the example are shown in Listing 7–20. As can be seen in the results, the Customer object is converted into an XML message.

Listing 7–20. The Results of Running the XML Transformer Example

```
toString(): Customer{firstName='John', lastName='Smith', address='100 State Street', city='Los
Angeles', state='CA', zip='90064'}

INFO : org.springframework.integration.handler.LoggingHandler - [Payload=<?xml version="1.0"
encoding="UTF-8"?>
<customer><address>100 State Street</address><last-name>Smith</last-
name><zip>90064</zip><first-name>John</first-name><state>CA</state><city>Los
Angeles</city></customer>][Headers={timestamp=1293427154837, id=9e3c590f-8312-4812-9d6e-
ccee89bd5db9}]

received: Customer{firstName='John', lastName='Smith', address='100 State Street', city='Los
Angeles', state='CA', zip='90064'}
```

Leveraging Transformations in Integration

Transformers are a required component for any integration framework. A Spring Integration implementation will be created that receives a JMS `Map` message. A `Map` message is used to eliminate the requirement to serialize the object, which would affect performance in a production scenario. The `Map` message will be transformed into the canonical `Customer` object. Spring Integration does not require the message payload to be XML, eliminating the expensive XML parsing requirements. The canonical `Customer` object is then transformed into JSON to meet the needs of the final endpoint.

Implementing this integration is straightforward. ActiveMQ will be used as the message broker; it can be downloaded from `http://activemq.apache.org`. Installation of ActiveMQ is straightforward. Simply decompress the installation archive and start by running the command `bin/activemq.sh` for Linux (Unix), or `bin/activemq.bat` for Windows. Alternatively, an embedded ActiveMQ broker may be used with the URL `vm://localhost`, which is leveraged by this example. An ActiveMQ broker will be initialized with the loading of the Spring context. The initial JMS message will be sent, leveraging the Spring `org.springframework.jms.core.JmsTemplate`. The Maven dependencies shown in Listing 7–21 must be added to support JMS and ActiveMQ.

Listing 7–21. Maven Dependencies for JMS and ActiveMQ

```
    <dependency>
      <groupId>org.springframework</groupId>
      <artifactId>spring-jms</artifactId>
      <version>2.0.1.RELEASE</version>
    </dependency>
    <dependency>
      <groupId>org.springframework.integration</groupId>
      <artifactId>spring-integration-jms</artifactId>
      <version>2.0.1.RELEASE</version>
    </dependency>
    <dependency>
      <groupId>org.apache.activemq</groupId>
     <artifactId>activemq-core</artifactId>
      <version>5.4.0</version>
    </dependency>
    <dependency>
      <groupId>javax.jms</groupId>
      <artifactId>jms</artifactId>
```

```
    <version>1.1</version>
  </dependency>
```

The JMS Map message is published, leveraging the Spring JmsTemplate. As shown in Listing 7–22, the customer information is placed in a JMS Map message and sent using the JmsTemplate. The final message in the output channel is logged to show the result.

***Listing 7–22.** Integration Example Using Transformers*

```
package com.apress.prospringintegration.transform;

import org.springframework.context.support.ClassPathXmlApplicationContext;
import org.springframework.integration.Message;
import org.springframework.integration.core.PollableChannel;
import org.springframework.jms.core.JmsTemplate;
import org.springframework.jms.core.MessageCreator;

import javax.jms.JMSException;
import javax.jms.MapMessage;
import javax.jms.Session;

public class IntegrationTransformer {
    public static void main(String[] args) {
        ClassPathXmlApplicationContext context =
                new ClassPathXmlApplicationContext("classpath:integration-transformer.xml");

        JmsTemplate jmsTemplate = context.getBean("jmsTemplate", JmsTemplate.class);

        jmsTemplate.send(new MessageCreator() {

            @Override
            public javax.jms.Message createMessage(Session session) throws JMSException {
                MapMessage message = session.createMapMessage();
                message.setString("firstName", "John");
                message.setString("lastName", "Smith");
                message.setString("address", "100 State Street");
                message.setString("city", "Los Angeles");
                message.setString("state", "CA");
                message.setString("zip", "90064");
                System.out.println("Sending message: " + message);
                return message;
            }
        });

        PollableChannel output = (PollableChannel) context.getBean("output");
        Message<?> reply = output.receive();
        System.out.println("received: " + reply.getPayload());
    }
}
```

The Spring configuration file for the integration example is shown in Listing 7–23. Note the additional namespace definitions to support JMS.

Listing 7–23. *Spring Configuration File for the Integration Example*

```
<?xml version="1.0" encoding="UTF-8"?>
<beans xmlns="http://www.springframework.org/schema/beans"
       xmlns:xsi="http://www.w3.org/2001/XMLSchema-instance"
       xmlns:int="http://www.springframework.org/schema/integration"
       xmlns:jms="http://www.springframework.org/schema/integration/jms"
       xmlns:context="http://www.springframework.org/schema/context"
       xsi:schemaLocation="http://www.springframework.org/schema/beans
      http://www.springframework.org/schema/beans/spring-beans-3.0.xsd
      http://www.springframework.org/schema/integration
      http://www.springframework.org/schema/integration/spring-integration-2.0.xsd
      http://www.springframework.org/schema/integration/jms
      http://www.springframework.org/schema/integration/jms/spring-integration-jms-2.0.xsd
      http://www.springframework.org/schema/context
      http://www.springframework.org/schema/context/spring-context-3.0.xsd">

  <context:component-scan base-package="com.apress.prospringintegration.transform"/>

  <jms:message-driven-channel-adapter
      channel="map"
      extract-payload="true"
      connection-factory="cachingConnectionFactory"
      destination-name="transformation.example.queue"/>

  <int:map-to-object-transformer input-channel="map"
                                 output-channel="json"
                                 type="com.apress.prospringintegration.transform.Customer"/>

  <int:transformer input-channel="json"
                   output-channel="output"
                   ref="objectToJsonTransformer"/>

  <int:logging-channel-adapter id="logger"
                               log-full-message="true"
                               level="INFO"/>

  <int:channel id="json">
    <int:interceptors>
      <int:wire-tap channel="logger"/>
    </int:interceptors>
  </int:channel>

  <int:channel id="map">
    <int:interceptors>
      <int:wire-tap channel="logger"/>
    </int:interceptors>
  </int:channel>

  <int:channel id="output">
    <int:queue capacity="10"/>
  </int:channel>

</beans>
```

Spring Java configuration is used to create the JMS factory and JMS template, as shown in Listing 7–24. As discussed previously, the embedded broker is created by setting the URL to vm://localhost.

***Listing 7–24.** Java Configuration for JMS*

```
package com.apress.prospringintegration.transform;

import org.apache.activemq.ActiveMQConnectionFactory;
import org.springframework.context.annotation.Bean;
import org.springframework.context.annotation.Configuration;
import org.springframework.jms.connection.CachingConnectionFactory;
import org.springframework.jms.core.JmsTemplate;

@Configuration
public class IntegrationConfiguration {

    @Bean
    public JmsTemplate jmsTemplate() {
        JmsTemplate jmsTemplate = new JmsTemplate();
        jmsTemplate.setConnectionFactory(cachingConnectionFactory());
        jmsTemplate.setDefaultDestinationName("transformation.example.queue");
        return jmsTemplate;
    }

    @Bean
    public CachingConnectionFactory cachingConnectionFactory() {
        CachingConnectionFactory cachingConnectionFactory =
                new CachingConnectionFactory();
        cachingConnectionFactory.setTargetConnectionFactory(activeMQConnectionFactory());
        cachingConnectionFactory.setSessionCacheSize(10);
        cachingConnectionFactory.setCacheProducers(false);
        return cachingConnectionFactory;
    }

    @Bean
    public ActiveMQConnectionFactory activeMQConnectionFactory() {
        ActiveMQConnectionFactory activeMQConnectionFactory =
                new ActiveMQConnectionFactory();
        activeMQConnectionFactory.setBrokerURL("vm://localhost");
        return activeMQConnectionFactory;
    }

}
```

The JmsTemplate is configured to send a message to the JMS queue transformation.example.queue. A message-driven-channel-adapter is used to receive the message from the same queue. The Map message is converted to the canonical Customer object using the map-to-object-transformer. The Customer object is then converted to a JSON representation using the object-to-json transformer for delivery to the final endpoint. The logger adapter is used to see how the message appears at each of the intermediate channels. As demonstrated by this example, Spring Integration can easily be configured to address a real integration scenario.

The results of this example are shown in Listing 7–25. As can be seen from the results, a JMS message is sent as a MapMessage. The MapMessage is then received from the JMS queue and converted to a Customer object, and then to a JSON representation.

Listing 7–25. *Results of the Integration Transformation Example*

```
Sending message: ActiveMQMapMessage {commandId = 0, responseRequired = false, messageId =
null, originalDestination = null, originalTransactionId = null, producerId = null, destination
= null, transactionId = null, expiration = 0, timestamp = 0, arrival = 0, brokerInTime = 0,
brokerOutTime = 0, correlationId = null, replyTo = null, persistent = false, type = null,
priority = 0, groupID = null, groupSequence = 0, targetConsumerId = null, compressed = false,
userID = null, content = null, marshalledProperties = null, dataStructure = null,
redeliveryCounter = 0, size = 0, properties = null, readOnlyProperties = false, readOnlyBody =
false, droppable = false} ActiveMQMapMessage{ theTable = {zip=90064, lastName=Smith,
address=100 State Street, state=CA, firstName=John, city=Los Angeles} }

INFO : org.springframework.integration.handler.LoggingHandler - [Payload={zip=90064,
lastName=Smith, address=100 State Street, state=CA, firstName=John, city=Los
Angeles}][Headers={timestamp=1293430883884, id=abc20ed2-b970-4f2c-8fe0-cb3dcfbe78d1,
JMSXDeliveryCount=1, JMSExpiration=0, JMSRedelivered=false, jms_redelivered=false,
JMSDeliveryMode=2, JMSPriority=4, JMSXGroupSeq=0, JMSTimestamp=1293430883821,
jms_messageId=ID:susan-3870-1293430883321-3:0:2:1:1}]

INFO : org.springframework.integration.handler.LoggingHandler -
[Payload=Customer{firstName='John', lastName='Smith', address='100 State Street', city='Los
Angeles', state='CA', zip='90064'}][Headers={timestamp=1293430883946, id=9bd5d8d2-b2a1-4a22-
999b-f8ad3785c262, JMSXDeliveryCount=1, JMSExpiration=0, jms_redelivered=false,
JMSRedelivered=false, JMSDeliveryMode=2, JMSPriority=4, JMSXGroupSeq=0,
jms_messageId=ID:susan-3870-1293430883321-3:0:2:1:1, JMSTimestamp=1293430883821}]

received: {"firstName":"John","lastName":"Smith","city":"Los
Angeles","zip":"90064","address":"100 State Street","state":"CA"}
```

Header Enrichers

A Spring Integration Message consists of two parts:

- The message payload object itself.
- The header, which is an instance of Spring Integration's MessageHeaders class, which in turn extends Map<String,?>. The headers are key/value pairs that provide metadata to components in Spring Integration or to other business components in an integration flow.

Spring Integration can augment or enrich header information. The header-enricher element provides a simple means to add additional header entries to a message. For example, the value 12 may be added to the key count, and an instance of the Customer object may be added to the key headerBean within the header Map using the header-enricher, as shown in Listing 7–26. The count might be used as an index of the message for removing duplicate messages, or for potentially correlating more than one message.

Listing 7–26. *Header Enricher Configuration Example*

```
<?xml version="1.0" encoding="UTF-8"?>
<beans xmlns="http://www.springframework.org/schema/beans"
       xmlns:xsi="http://www.w3.org/2001/XMLSchema-instance"
       xmlns:int="http://www.springframework.org/schema/integration"
```

```
       xmlns:context="http://www.springframework.org/schema/context"
       xsi:schemaLocation="http://www.springframework.org/schema/beans
    http://www.springframework.org/schema/beans/spring-beans.xsd
    http://www.springframework.org/schema/integration
    http://www.springframework.org/schema/integration/spring-integration-2.0.xsd
    http://www.springframework.org/schema/context
    http://www.springframework.org/schema/context/spring-context-3.0.xsd">

  <context:component-scan base-package="com.apress.prospringintegration.transform"/>

  <int:header-enricher input-channel="input" output-channel="interceptor">
    <int:header name="count" value="12"/>
    <int:header name="headerBean" ref="customer"/>
  </int:header-enricher>

  <int:transformer input-channel="interceptor"
                   output-channel="output"
                   ref="headerInterceptor"/>

  <int:channel id="input"/>

  <int:channel id="interceptor"/>

  <int:channel id="output">
    <int:queue capacity="10"/>
  </int:channel>

</beans>
```

Spring Integration also provides the annotations @Header and @Headers to access individual header values and the complete header Map as parameters to a method used for transformation. For example, to retrieve the header value key to the count parameter, use the @Header annotation, as shown in Listing 7–27. Alternatively, the entire Map of headers can be injected using the @Headers annotation, as shown in the example following.

Listing 7–27. *@Header and @Headers Annotation Example*

```
package com.apress.prospringintegration.transform;

import org.springframework.integration.*;
import org.springframework.integration.annotation.Header;
import org.springframework.integration.annotation.Headers;
import org.springframework.integration.annotation.Transformer;
import org.springframework.stereotype.Component;

import java.util.Map;

@Component
public class HeaderInterceptor {

    @Transformer
    public Customer map( Message<Map<String, String>> messageObj,
        @Header("count") int count, @Headers Map<String, Object> headerMap) {
```

```
        Customer customer = new Customer();

        Map<String,String> message=messageObj.getPayload();

        customer.setFirstName(message.get("firstName"));
        customer.setLastName(message.get("lastName"));
        customer.setAddress(message.get("address"));
        customer.setCity(message.get("city"));
        customer.setState(message.get("state"));
        customer.setZip(message.get("zip"));

        System.out.println("Count:" + count);

        for (String key : headerMap.keySet()) {
            System.out.println("Key: " + key + "  Value: " + headerMap.get(key));
        }
        return customer;
    }
}
```

In the preceding example, the first parameter is assumed to be a reference to the payload, even though it is not so-annotated. The second parameter is annotated with the `@Header` annotation, which has a value of `count`. This string is the key of the header. If the code is compiled with debug symbols, then Spring Integration can *see* the name of the parameter in the method definition and can map that to a header, negating the need to explicitly specify the key. Thus, `@Header int count` is the same as `@Header("count") int count`. While this is *possible*, it's not encouraged: it is easy to forget to include debug symbols, and failure to do so can introduce some very nasty bugs. Debug symbols are typically turned off in production-bound builds, which is the last place one hopes to find bugs in their code. *Always* specify a header key. Header keys don't have to be literal strings, and can be the result of any constant expression, including static variables. Many modules provide adapters and specific support for those adapters. They also publish well-known headers that might be of use to users of the module. While there are no hard-and-fast rules, look for a `*Headers` class (e.g., `FileHeaders`) that contains public static final Strings that can be used to key into a header `Map` to avoid hard-coding header keys in code. For example:

```
public void doSomethingWithFile(@Header(FileHeaders.FILENAME) String fileName) {
  ...
}
```

Finally, a header may be influenced programmatically using the `MessageBuilder` class. The example in Listing 7–28 shows another method for adding the header value `12` to the key `count`. This technique is completely customizable.

Listing 7–28. *Modifying the Header Using the Spring Integration API*

```
package com.apress.prospringintegration.transform;

import org.springframework.integration.Message;
import org.springframework.integration.annotation.Transformer;
import org.springframework.integration.support.MessageBuilder;
import org.springframework.stereotype.Component;

import java.util.Map;
```

```
@Component
public class HeaderMapper {

    @Transformer
    public Message<Customer> map(Message<Map<String, String>> message) {

        Map<String, String> mapMessage = message.getPayload();
        Customer customer = new Customer();

        customer.setFirstName(mapMessage.get("firstName"));
        customer.setLastName(mapMessage.get("lastName"));
        customer.setAddress(mapMessage.get("address"));
        customer.setCity(mapMessage.get("city"));
        customer.setState(mapMessage.get("state"));
        customer.setZip(mapMessage.get("zip"));


        return MessageBuilder.withPayload(customer)
                .copyHeadersIfAbsent(message.getHeaders())
                .setHeaderIfAbsent("count", 12).build();
    }
}
```

Bear in mind that Spring Integration Messages and MessageHeaders are immutable, so it's not possible to modify headers in a message, only to create a new message that's cloned from existing headers and use a new value for the new header. Even though MessageHeaders advertises the contract of java.util.Map, it doesn't fully support it.

Message Mappers: Moving Transformation into the Framework

Method-Mapping Transformation

Spring Integration uses a set of default rules and conventions to map the channel Message object to the target methods. This allows for adapting to most situations without resorting to addition configuration settings. The different scenarios will be described following.

The Spring Integration Message consists of two main parts, as discussed previously: the payload, and the header Map, which is a key/value pair where the key is a string and the value is an object. Spring Integration follows the basic premise that the mapping of the payload takes precedence over all other possibilities. Since a method can only return a single object or primitive, the complication occurs with how the input parameters are mapped. Starting with the return value, there are basically three possibilities for the return type:

- Object/primitive: This is mapped to the payload of the outgoing Message.
- Message: This will be the outgoing Message.
- void: This outputs no message.

The mapping for the methods' arguments is much more involved:

- The simplest case is no argument, in which no data from the Message is passed to the outbound channel, and the method acts as an event or trigger to invoke the method.
- The next case is a single argument in which there can be three situations:
  - First, an object/primitive argument type which is not a Map will pass as the message payload. If the message payload is not the same type as the argument, an attempt will be made to convert the payload to the argument type.
  - The second possibility is that the argument type will be a Message in which the Message object will be passed as is.
  - The last possibility is that the argument type is a Map. If the message payload is of type Map, the payload will be passed, since the payload always takes priority. However, if the payload is not a Map type, the Message header will be passed.
- If there is more than one argument, the situation is even more complicated. For this, Spring Integration provides annotations to solve the problem.

Some examples of the different mapping situations are given in Listing 7–29.

Listing 7–29. *Simple Mapping Examples*

```
public String example(Object object);

public Message example(Object object);

public Message example(Message message);

public Message example(Map map);
```

In the first case, the input object is the Message payload and the String is returned in the Message payload. In the second case, the input object is passed as the Message payload and the return value is the Message. In the third case, the input is a Message and the output is a newly created Message. In the last case, if the input Message payload is not a Map type, the Message header will be passed as a Message header with a returned Message output.

Spring Integration provides several annotations to support the most complex case, when more than one argument exists in the method signature. A Message payload is denoted by @Payload, and, as discussed previously, a header value is noted by @Header and the entire header Map by @Headers. This prevents ambiguity when more than one object could be mapped to the payload or header (e.g., if the payload is a string object, and in addition, one of the header elements needs to be passed). The string payload is designated by the @Payload annotation and the header element count is designated by the @Header annotation, as shown in Listing 7–30.

Listing 7–30. *Mappping Annotation Example*

```
public String example(@Payload String message, @Header("count") int count);
```

Finally, Spring Integration supports multiple methods within a transformer where the payload type can be used to determine which method is to be called. The different method signatures within the same class must be unambiguous in mapping to the payload type; otherwise, an exception will be thrown. Alternatively, the method attribute must be used in the transformer element. Examples of method signatures that may be mapped are shown in Listing 7–31 It is clear which method to choose when the payload is either a `String` or `Long` type.

Listing 7–31. Method Mapping Example

```
public interface Example {

    public Message method(String message);

    public Message method(Long message);
}
```

However, if the method signatures are ambiguous in determining how to map the payload type, an exception will be thrown, as in the example in Listing 7–32.

Listing 7–32. Method Mapping Example That Will Throw an Exception

```
public interface Example {

    public Message method(Long message, Map header);

    public Message method(Long message);
}
```

ConversionService

Spring 3 debuted support for the `ConversionService`, a framework-wide registry of known `Converter` objects that many satellite frameworks—including Spring MVC and Spring Integration—consume for common conversion tasks. One use of the `ConversionService` is when the default method-mapping rules fail: if your configuration really does expect an object of type `F` to be passed into an endpoint method with a parameter of type `Y`, and `Y` is not assignable to `F`, then it has to be converted.

Spring Integration already employs a few `Converter` instances out of the box with its own instance of the `ConversionService`, which has the bean name `integrationConversionService`. Spring Integration consults this instance for any applicable converters, looking for a converter that can help it convert the instance of type `Y` into an instance of type `F`. If the default resolution and conversion rules don't meet the requirement, or there's a conversion that's likely to be common enough that the rules should be available framework-wide, then register the converter with Spring Integration. Inject an instance of the `ConversionService` and register the instance through code or, more straightforwardly, use the simple Spring Integration namespace support's `converter` element:

```
<int:converter ref = "aConverterInstance" />
```

This will register the converter with the Spring Integration `ConversionService` instance.

Summary

This chapter covered how Spring Integration supports transformations, allowing the message payload to be modified to the format and structure required by the downstream endpoint. A number of examples were given, showing the built-in transformation support for `Map`, JSON, and XML messages, as well as object serialization. A simple integration example was given, demonstrating how easy it is to transform the message payloads as required for the different endpoints that may be encountered in real situations. In addition, Spring Integration supports augmenting and modifying the message header values as required for supporting downstream message handling and endpoint requirements. Several examples were shown demonstrating Spring Integration support for modifying the message header. Finally, the default rules and conventions were discussed on how Spring Integration maps the `Message` object to the method arguments and return values.

CHAPTER 8

Message Flow: Routing and Filtering

Messages *usually* move in a system in a straight line, moving from one endpoint to the next. On occasion, however, a little bit of flexibility is required; a message might need to visit two different endpoints at the same time, or it might need to be conditionally sent to one and not another. The progression of messages through a system is like the progression of a steady stream; it takes skill and ingenuity (and care!) to safely route the flow.

In Spring Integration, a message *router* decides what channel or channels should receive the message next. This decision is based on the message's content and/or metadata contained in the message header. A message *filter* determines if the message should be passed to the output channel at all, again based on the message's content and/or metadata. A message *splitter* partitions an inbound message into several parts and sends the resultant messages out. An *aggregator* is the counterpart to the splitter; it combines multiple messages into a single message. A *resequencer* works like a splitter, but does not process the messages in any way; it simply releases the messages to downstream components in a particular order. These are the different components available for controlling message flows in Spring Integration. They will all be discussed in this chapter. This chapter will also discuss simplifying the configuration using a message handler chain.

Messaging is inherently stateless. Spring Integration lets you work with the allusion of state by propagating headers from endpoint to endpoint. This lets you make local decisions, to act in the integration flow with the knowledge of the state of any given message at any given time, but it does not afford you the big-picture view of a directed process. This is where a workflow steps in. Workflow and how to use a workflow engine with Spring Integration is the last topic in this chapter.

Message Flow Patterns

Message routing is simple: specific data will only go to particular endpoints based on the payload or metadata. For example, a stock market data feed system will typically handle a few dozen types of market instruments whose routes are negotiated in terms of market sector, equity type, and region. This is where a message router can be leveraged. Filtering provides a way to gate the flow of messages based on some condition, which can be very useful as well. This is similar to TCP/IP where firewalls can provide deep-packet inspection to selectively meter traffic.

Enterprise applications with many discrete datasets may need to process a large amount of information where sending an entire set of data to one location for processing is inefficient. Partitionable data can be efficiently processed by splitting it and processing the pieces.

Let's look at some of the common types of routing.

Router

Routing is one of the most common patterns in data processing today. Data at every level—protocol suites all the way up to full blown APIs—all provide a way to move data in different ways based on conditions. In Spring Integration, a router can do things like forward messages to multiple endpoints or determine which from among many is to receive a message.

Filter

A message filter complements a router in determining whether an incoming message is to be forwarded to a channel or not. The logic is simply stated as "forward, or don't forward" based on evaluative logic declared in configuration or custom code. Traditionally, filters are put between channels with a high message flow where the need to reduce the number of messages is necessary.

Splitter

A splitter is a component that takes a single message and breaks it into multiple individual messages. An example of where this might be useful is an order processing system where a single order contains many line items that describe products made by different companies. Identifying the line item and the corresponding vendor will allow the splitter to create an individual message for each company. Thus, using a splitter enables a seamless way to direct the orders to a specific vendor.

Aggregator

An aggregator component accepts multiple related messages and then assembles them into a single message. Its job is the inverse of the splitter, as it is common to find an aggregator downstream of a splitter. The aggregator uses a construct known as correlation strategy to determine related messages within a group. The process that gives indication of a complete group is known as the completion strategy. For example, through a common property (e.g. order ID), a completion condition may be identified that causes an aggregator to compile a new message. In this case, a delivery-ready message for a product order may only be created once all collaborating vendors have produced order-procurement messages in response to an order-request. The message sent by the aggregator may further the order down the pipeline. Spring Integration provides a number of strategies to achieve this efficiently and simply. In addition, you may also define your own.

Resequencer

A resequencer consumes many correlated messages and reassigns the order in which they are delivered. It is similar to the aggregator in that the messages consumed belong to some correlation group; however, it differs where message delivery is taken into consideration. While an aggregator combines messages to form a single message, a resequencer simply reorders messages to allow consistent consumption on the downstream message endpoint.

Message Flows Using Spring Integration

Let's look at how Spring Integration implements the common message flow patterns. Examples will be provided for each of the patterns. A known list of channels may be specified for a router where the incoming `Message<T>` may be passed. This means that the process flow may be changed conditionally, and it also means that a message may be forwarded to as many (or as few) channels as desired. The `org.springframework.integration.router` package provides several convenient router implementations, such as payload type–based routing `PayloadTypeRouter` and routing to a list of channels `RecipientListRouter`.

For example, imagine a processing pipeline in which investment instruments are routed depending on their type, such as stocks or bonds. When each instrument is finally processed, specific fields may get added that are relevant to that instrument type. The domain object that represents each investment is shown in Listing 8–1.

***Listing 8–1.** Investment Domain Object*

```
package com.apress.prospringintegration.messageflow.domain;

public class MarketItem {

    String type;
    String symbol;
    String description;
    String price;
    String openPrice;

    public MarketItem() {
    }

    // setters and getters removed for brevity
}
```

For testing purposes, a utility class is created to generate a `list` of `MarketItems` that may be sent to the message channel. The class is shown in Listing 8–2.

***Listing 8–2.** Utility Class for Generating MarketItem Instances*

```
package com.apress.prospringintegration.messageflow.domain;

import org.springframework.stereotype.Component;

import java.util.ArrayList;
import java.util.List;

@Component
public class MarketItemCreator {

    public List<MarketItem> getMarketItems() {
        List<MarketItem> marketItems = new ArrayList<MarketItem>();

        MarketItem marketItem = new MarketItem();
        marketItem.setSymbol("IBM");
        marketItem.setDescription("International Business Machines");
        marketItem.setOpenPrice("130.00");
        marketItem.setPrice("135.00");
        marketItem.setType("stock");
        marketItems.add(marketItem);
```

```
        marketItem = new MarketItem();
        marketItem.setSymbol("PBNDXX");
        marketItem.setDescription("A Par Bond");
        marketItem.setOpenPrice("50.00");
        marketItem.setPrice("55.00");
        marketItem.setType("bond");
        marketItems.add(marketItem);

        marketItem = new MarketItem();
        marketItem.setSymbol("MUFX");
        marketItem.setDescription("Mutual Bonds");
        marketItem.setOpenPrice("50.00");
        marketItem.setPrice("55.00");
        marketItem.setType("bond");
        marketItems.add(marketItem);

        marketItem = new MarketItem();
        marketItem.setSymbol("stock");
        marketItem.setDescription("Intel Corp.");
        marketItem.setOpenPrice("130.00");
        marketItem.setPrice("135.00");
        marketItem.setType("stock");
        marketItems.add(marketItem);

        return marketItems;
    }
}
```

The router element makes defining a router as simple as specifying an input channel and a router implementation bean. As with other Spring Integration components, routing can be implemented directly using Spring Integration's annotation support with a `@Router` annotated method on any plain old Java object (POJO). This annotation expects the evaluation result of either a string for the channel name, a `collection` of names of `MessageChannels`, or a single `MessageChannel`. An example of a custom router component is shown in Listing 8–3. The message will be passed to the message channel with the name matching the `MarketItem` property type.

Listing 8–3. *Implementing a Router using @Router*

```
package com.apress.prospringintegration.messageflow.router;

import com.apress.prospringintegration.messageflow.domain.MarketItem;
import org.springframework.integration.annotation.Router;
import org.springframework.stereotype.Component;

@Component
public class MarketItemTypeRouter {

    @Router
    public String route(MarketItem item) {

        String channelId = item.getType();
        return channelId;
    }
}
```

The Spring configuration for the router example is shown in Listing 8–4. The router determines the outbound message destination based on the router component `marketItemTypeRouter`.

***Listing 8–4.** Spring Configuration for router-item-type.xml*

```
<?xml version="1.0" encoding="UTF-8"?>
<beans xmlns="http://www.springframework.org/schema/beans"
       xmlns:xsi="http://www.w3.org/2001/XMLSchema-instance"
       xmlns:int="http://www.springframework.org/schema/integration"
       xmlns:context="http://www.springframework.org/schema/context"
       xsi:schemaLocation="http://www.springframework.org/schema/beans
          http://www.springframework.org/schema/beans/spring-beans-3.0.xsd
    http://www.springframework.org/schema/integration
    http://www.springframework.org/schema/integration/spring-integration-2.0.xsd
    http://www.springframework.org/schema/context
    http://www.springframework.org/schema/context/spring-context-3.0.xsd">

  <context:component-scan
      base-package="com.apress.prospringintegration.messageflow.router"/>
  <context:component-scan
      base-package="com.apress.prospringintegration.messageflow.domain"/>

  <int:channel id="marketItemChannel"/>

  <int:channel id="stock"/>
  <int:channel id="bond"/>

  <int:router input-channel="marketItemChannel" ref="marketItemTypeRouter"/>

  <int:service-activator input-channel="stock" ref="stockRegistrar"/>

  <int:service-activator input-channel="bond" ref="bondRegistrar"/>

</beans>
```

`MarketItem` message payloads with type `stock` will be sent to the service activator `stockRegistrar` and message payloads with the type `bond` will be sent to the service activator `bondRegistrar`. The two service activators shown in Listings 8–5 and 8–6 simply log the `MarketItem` description.

***Listing 8–5.** Service Activator for Type Stock*

```
package com.apress.prospringintegration.messageflow.domain;

import com.apress.prospringintegration.messageflow.domain.MarketItem;
import org.springframework.integration.annotation.ServiceActivator;
import org.springframework.stereotype.Component;

@Component
public class StockRegistrar {

    @ServiceActivator
    public void registerStock(MarketItem item) {
        System.out.println("Registering stock: " + item.getDescription());
    }
}
```

Listing 8–6. Service Activator for Type Bond

```
package com.apress.prospringintegration.messageflow.domain;

import com.apress.prospringintegration.messageflow.domain.MarketItem;
import org.springframework.integration.annotation.ServiceActivator;
import org.springframework.stereotype.Component;

@Component
public class BondRegistrar {

    @ServiceActivator
    public void registerBond(MarketItem item) {
        System.out.println("Registering bond: " + item.getDescription());
    }
}
```

This example router may be run with the main class shown in Listing 8–7. The main class creates the Spring context and obtains a reference to the message channel `marketItemChannel` and the `MarketItemCreator` utility class used for creating a sample set of `MarketItems`. The messages are sent to the channel and routed based on the type property.

Listing 8–7. Main Class for Router Example

```
package com.apress.prospringintegration.messageflow.router;

import com.apress.prospringintegration.messageflow.domain.MarketItem;
import com.apress.prospringintegration.messageflow.domain.MarketItemCreator;
import org.springframework.context.ApplicationContext;
import org.springframework.context.support.ClassPathXmlApplicationContext;
import org.springframework.integration.MessageChannel;
import org.springframework.integration.support.MessageBuilder;

public class MainItemTypeRouter {
    public static void main(String[] args) throws Exception {
        ApplicationContext context =
                new ClassPathXmlApplicationContext("router-item-type.xml");

        MessageChannel channel =
                context.getBean("marketItemChannel", MessageChannel.class);
        MarketItemCreator marketItemCreator =
                context.getBean("marketItemCreator", MarketItemCreator.class);

        for (MarketItem marketItem : marketItemCreator.getMarketItems()) {
            channel.send(MessageBuilder.withPayload(marketItem).build());
        }
    }
}
```

A router may also be defined through a SpEL expression that will evaluate to either a collection of channel names or a single one, like so:

```
<router input-channel="marketItemChannel" expression="payload.getType()"/>
```

These samples present two possibilities for providing content-based routing. Both methods are very powerful ways to expose routing to your application because they keep routing logic to a minimum. The first example uses a @Router annotated method on an ordinary POJO that expects a MarketItem instance. The MarketItem.type property value is used to determine the destination channel name, thus stock or bond.

The second router exposes an expression-based router, which utilizes a SpEL evaluation to compute the destination channel name. In this way, you need not provide code for simple references that can be evaluated with SpEL for the next step, whether it is a message channel or endpoint.

Dynamic Expression–Based Routing

Instead of standard routing using a @Router annotation or any one of the common implementations defined in the org.springframework.integration.router package, you may optionally specify a resource bundle–based router expression through the expression element. This enables dynamic routing that can be configured simply by modifying a property value in the resource bundle or properties file. Expression routing requires defining a bean of the type org.springframework.integration.expression.ReloadableResourceBundleExpressionSource. This bean exposes a resource bundle to your component for property extraction and requires two properties to be set: the basename that will hold reference to the expression, and cacheSeconds that defines how often to reload the resource for updates so that expressions can be modified. The ReloadableResourceBundleExpressionSource instance is define using Java configuration, as shown in Listing 8–8.

***Listing 8–8.** Java Configuration for Dynamic Router*

```
package com.apress.prospringintegration.messageflow.router;

import org.springframework.context.annotation.Bean;
import org.springframework.context.annotation.Configuration;
import org.springframework.integration.expression.ReloadableResourceBundleExpressionSource;

@Configuration
public class RouterConfiguration {

    @Bean
    public ReloadableResourceBundleExpressionSource reloadableRouteExpressions() {
        ReloadableResourceBundleExpressionSource reloadableRouteExpressions =
                new ReloadableResourceBundleExpressionSource();
        reloadableRouteExpressions.setBasename("router-expressions");
        reloadableRouteExpressions.setCacheSeconds(10);
        return reloadableRouteExpressions;
    }
}
```

The Spring configuration for using a dynamic expression–based router is shown in Listing 8–9. This configuration is identical to the previous example in Listing 8–4 except for the additional expression element.

***Listing 8–9.** Spring Configuration for Router Using Resources-Based Expression (router-dynamic.xml)*

```
<?xml version="1.0" encoding="UTF-8"?>
<beans xmlns="http://www.springframework.org/schema/beans"
       xmlns:xsi="http://www.w3.org/2001/XMLSchema-instance"
```

```
        xmlns:int="http://www.springframework.org/schema/integration"
        xmlns:context="http://www.springframework.org/schema/context"
        xsi:schemaLocation="http://www.springframework.org/schema/beans
           http://www.springframework.org/schema/beans/spring-beans-3.0.xsd
    http://www.springframework.org/schema/context
    http://www.springframework.org/schema/context/spring-context-3.0.xsd
    http://www.springframework.org/schema/integration
    http://www.springframework.org/schema/integration/spring-integration-2.0.xsd">

  <context:component-scan
      base-package="com.apress.prospringintegration.messageflow.router"/>
  <context:component-scan
      base-package="com.apress.prospringintegration.messageflow.domain"/>

  <int:channel id="marketItemChannel"/>

  <int:channel id="stock"/>
  <int:channel id="bond"/>

  <int:router input-channel="marketItemChannel">
    <int:expression key="route-list" source="reloadableRouteExpressions"/>
  </int:router>

  <int:service-activator input-channel="stock" ref="stockRegistrar"/>

  <int:service-activator input-channel="bond" ref="bondRegistrar"/>

</beans>
```

■ **Note** The `expression` subelement is defined as an element decorator and can be applied to any `router`, `aggregator`, `filter`, or `splitter` elements.

When defining a router for use with resource bundles, the actual property key must be specified through the key attribute of the `expression` element. This will be used to identify the expression that will get evaluated to produce a channel name. To define the resource bundle, one or more name/value pairs are needed that identify the desired expressions. Since you declared property `basename` called `router-expressions`, you will need to create a file called `router-expressions.properties`, as shown in Listing 8–10, and place it on the `classpath`.

***Listing 8–10.** Expression Indicating Destination Channel Based on ITEM_TYPE Header Attribute router-expresions.properties*

```
route-list=headers.ITEM_TYPE
```

The example in Listing 8–10 will route the message based on the header `ITEM_TYPE`. The main class for this example is shown in Listing 8–11. This main class is similar to the previous example in Listing 8–7 except that `MarketItem` type is copied to the header `ITEM_TYPE` to properly route the message. What is significant about this example is that the routing rule may be changed dynamically by simple modifying the properties file.

Listing 8–11. *Main Class for Dynamic Expression–Based Routing*

```
package com.apress.prospringintegration.messageflow.router;

import com.apress.prospringintegration.messageflow.domain.MarketItem;
import com.apress.prospringintegration.messageflow.domain.MarketItemCreator;
import org.springframework.context.ApplicationContext;
import org.springframework.context.support.ClassPathXmlApplicationContext;
import org.springframework.integration.MessageChannel;
import org.springframework.integration.support.MessageBuilder;

public class MainDynamicRouter {
    public static void main(String[] args) throws Exception {
        ApplicationContext context =
                new ClassPathXmlApplicationContext("router-dynamic.xml");

        MessageChannel channel =
                context.getBean("marketItemChannel", MessageChannel.class);
        MarketItemCreator marketItemCreator =
                context.getBean("marketItemCreator", MarketItemCreator.class);

        for (MarketItem marketItem : marketItemCreator.getMarketItems()) {
            channel.send(MessageBuilder.withPayload(marketItem)
                    .setHeader("ITEM_TYPE", marketItem.getType()).build());
        }
    }

}
```

Recipient-List Router

The recipient-list router forwards messages to a known or inferred collection of recipient channels. The recipient-list router may be configured using the `recipient-list-router` namespace element supported by Spring Integration. For example, you may want a recipient-list router that forwards `MarketItems` to one channel for database persistence, and another to the stock channel for dissemination to downstream clients listening for market data updates of a particular kind. In the Spring configuration shown in Listing 8–12, all messages will go to the `bondRegistrar` service activator representing a persistence endpoint, but only the messages with the type `stock` will go to the `stockRegistrar` service activator.

Listing 8–12. *Spring Configuration for Recipient-List Router (router-recipientlist.xml)*

```
<?xml version="1.0" encoding="UTF-8"?>
<beans xmlns="http://www.springframework.org/schema/beans"
       xmlns:xsi="http://www.w3.org/2001/XMLSchema-instance"
       xmlns:int="http://www.springframework.org/schema/integration"
       xmlns:context="http://www.springframework.org/schema/context"
       xsi:schemaLocation="http://www.springframework.org/schema/beans
    http://www.springframework.org/schema/beans/spring-beans-3.0.xsd
    http://www.springframework.org/schema/integration
    http://www.springframework.org/schema/integration/spring-integration-2.0.xsd
    http://www.springframework.org/schema/context
    http://www.springframework.org/schema/context/spring-context.xsd">
```

```
  <context:component-scan
      base-package="com.apress.prospringintegration.messageflow.router"/>
  <context:component-scan
      base-package="com.apress.prospringintegration.messageflow.domain"/>

  <int:channel id="marketItemChannel"/>

  <int:channel id="stockChannel"/>
  <int:channel id="persist"/>

  <int:recipient-list-router input-channel="marketItemChannel">
    <int:recipient channel="stockChannel"
                   selector-expression="payload.type.equals('stock')"/>
    <int:recipient channel="persist"/>
  </int:recipient-list-router>

  <int:service-activator input-channel="stockChannel" ref="stockRegistrar"/>

  <int:service-activator input-channel="persist" ref="bondRegistrar"/>


</beans>
```

Note that the selector-expression will default to `true` should the expression be un-evaluable or undefined. That is, if `payload.type` does not exist in the message being evaluated, then the expression will default to `true`. Messages will always get sent to a declared outbound channel.

The recipient-list router may be run using the same main class as the dynamic router. Change the referenced Spring configuration file to `router-recipientlist.xml`. Only the `MarketItem` with the type `stock` will go to the `stockRegistrar`. All `MarketItems` will go to the `bondRegistrar`.he `bondRegistrar`.

Filters

Filters are used to regulate the type of message traffic going to downstream components and have such benefits as limiting bandwidth consumption. Spring Integration enables filtering using the `org.springframework.integration.core.MessageSelector` interface that exposes a single method called `accept`. This method evaluates to a `boolean` based on the implementation code. Returning `true` will forward the message to the output channel. Returning `false` will cause the message to be dropped. In the example shown in Listing 8–13, a simple `MarketItemFilter` filter is defined to only accept stock type of `MarketItem` with the type `stock`.

Listing 8–13. *Implementation of the Filter Using MessageSelector*

```
package com.apress.prospringintegration.messageflow.filter;

import com.apress.prospringintegration.messageflow.domain.MarketItem;
import org.springframework.integration.Message;
import org.springframework.integration.core.MessageSelector;
import org.springframework.stereotype.Component;

@Component
public class MessageSelectorStockItemFilter implements MessageSelector {
```

```
    @Override
    public boolean accept(Message<?> message) {
        MarketItem item = (MarketItem) message.getPayload();
        return (item != null && item.getType().equals("stock"));
    }
}
```

The Spring configuration for the `MessageSelector` example is shown in Listing 8–14. This filter may be used to allow only the `MarketItem` message with the type `stock` to be forwarded to the `stockRegistrar` service activator.

Listing 8–14. *Spring Configuration for a MessageSelector Type Filter (filter-selector.xml)*

```
<?xml version="1.0" encoding="UTF-8"?>
<beans xmlns="http://www.springframework.org/schema/beans"
       xmlns:xsi="http://www.w3.org/2001/XMLSchema-instance"
       xmlns:int="http://www.springframework.org/schema/integration"
       xmlns:context="http://www.springframework.org/schema/context"
       xsi:schemaLocation="http://www.springframework.org/schema/beans
    http://www.springframework.org/schema/beans/spring-beans-3.0.xsd
    http://www.springframework.org/schema/integration
    http://www.springframework.org/schema/integration/spring-integration-2.0.xsd
    http://www.springframework.org/schema/context
    http://www.springframework.org/schema/context/spring-context-3.0.xsd">

  <context:component-scan
      base-package="com.apress.prospringintegration.messageflow.filter"/>
  <context:component-scan
      base-package="com.apress.prospringintegration.messageflow.domain"/>

  <int:filter ref="messageSelectorStockItemFilter"
              input-channel="marketItemChannel"
              output-channel="filteredItemsChannel"/>

  <int:channel id="filteredItemsChannel"/>

  <int:service-activator input-channel="filteredItemsChannel" ref="stockRegistrar"/>

</beans>
```

The message selector filter example may be run with the main class shown in Listing 8–15. The main class creates the Spring context and obtains a reference to the message channel `marketItemChannel` and the `MarketItemCreator` utility class used to create a sample set of `MarketItems`. The messages are sent to the channel and filtered based on the type property. Only `MarketItems` with the type `stock` will be allowed through.

Listing 8–15. *Main Class for MessageSelector Filter*

```
package com.apress.prospringintegration.messageflow.filter;

import com.apress.prospringintegration.messageflow.domain.MarketItem;
import com.apress.prospringintegration.messageflow.domain.MarketItemCreator;
import org.springframework.context.ApplicationContext;
import org.springframework.context.support.ClassPathXmlApplicationContext;
import org.springframework.integration.MessageChannel;
```

```
import org.springframework.integration.support.MessageBuilder;

public class MainMessageSelectorItemFilter {
    public static void main(String[] args) throws Exception {
        ApplicationContext context =
                new ClassPathXmlApplicationContext("filter-selector.xml");

        MessageChannel channel =
                context.getBean("marketItemChannel", MessageChannel.class);
        MarketItemCreator marketItemCreator =
                context.getBean("marketItemCreator", MarketItemCreator.class);

        for (MarketItem marketItem : marketItemCreator.getMarketItems()) {
            channel.send(MessageBuilder.withPayload(marketItem).build());
        }
    }
}
```

Spring Integration also supports a @Filter annotation to support message filters. The @Filter annotation expects a method that evaluates a boolean return type and accepts one of the following, similar to the other Spring Integration strategic interfaces:

- An argument type of parameterized message.
- The type expected within the payload.
- Some parameterized header variant, as shown in Listing 8–16.

The example POJO shown in Listing 8–16 exposes the @Filter annotated filtering method. When using both a MessageSelector and @Filter annotated method in the same class, the MessageSelector accept method will take precedence. It is recommended that @Filter method exist within a separate class.

Listing 8–16. *Implementing a Filter Using @Filter Annotation*

```
package com.apress.prospringintegration.messageflow.filter;

import com.apress.prospringintegration.messageflow.domain.MarketItem;
import org.springframework.integration.annotation.Filter;
import org.springframework.integration.annotation.Header;
import org.springframework.stereotype.Component;

@Component
public class MarketItemFilter {

    @Filter
    public boolean acceptViaHeader(@Header("ITEM_TYPE") String itemType) {
        return itemType.equals("stock");
    }
}
```

The Spring configuration file using the annotated filter is shown in Listing 8–17. The header ITEM_TYPE must be set to stock for the message to be forwarded through the filter.

Listing 8–17. Alternate Filter Declaration Using the Annotated Filter Class (filter-item.xml)

```
<?xml version="1.0" encoding="UTF-8"?>
<beans xmlns="http://www.springframework.org/schema/beans"
       xmlns:xsi="http://www.w3.org/2001/XMLSchema-instance"
       xmlns:int="http://www.springframework.org/schema/integration"
       xmlns:context="http://www.springframework.org/schema/context"
       xsi:schemaLocation="http://www.springframework.org/schema/beans
          http://www.springframework.org/schema/beans/spring-beans-3.0.xsd
    http://www.springframework.org/schema/integration
    http://www.springframework.org/schema/integration/spring-integration-2.0.xsd
    http://www.springframework.org/schema/context
    http://www.springframework.org/schema/context/spring-context-3.0.xsd">

  <context:component-scan
      base-package="com.apress.prospringintegration.messageflow.filter"/>
  <context:component-scan
      base-package="com.apress.prospringintegration.messageflow.domain"/>

  <int:filter ref="marketItemFilter"
              input-channel="marketItemChannel"
              output-channel="filteredItemsChannel"/>

  <int:channel id="filteredItemsChannel"/>

  <int:service-activator ref="stockRegistrar" input-channel="filteredItemsChannel"/>

</beans>
```

The main class for this example is shown in Listing 8–18. This main class is similar to the previous example in Listing 8–15 except that `MarketItem` type is copied to the header `ITEM_TYPE` to properly route the message. Again, only `MarketItems` with the type `stock` will be allowed through.

Listing 8–18. Main Class for Annotated Filter Class

```
package com.apress.prospringintegration.messageflow.filter;

import com.apress.prospringintegration.messageflow.domain.MarketItem;
import com.apress.prospringintegration.messageflow.domain.MarketItemCreator;
import org.springframework.context.ApplicationContext;
import org.springframework.context.support.ClassPathXmlApplicationContext;
import org.springframework.integration.MessageChannel;
import org.springframework.integration.support.MessageBuilder;

public class MainItemFilter {
    public static void main(String[] args) throws Exception {
        ApplicationContext context = new ClassPathXmlApplicationContext("filter-item.xml");

        MessageChannel channel =
                context.getBean("marketItemChannel", MessageChannel.class);
        MarketItemCreator marketItemCreator =
                context.getBean("marketItemCreator", MarketItemCreator.class);

        for (MarketItem marketItem : marketItemCreator.getMarketItems()) {
```

```
                channel.send(MessageBuilder.withPayload(marketItem)
                        .setHeader("ITEM_TYPE", marketItem.getType()).build());
            }
        }
    }
```

Filtering logic containing complex lookups often lend themselves to Java implementations. However, in the case of simple evaluations as in the examples thus far, you may opt for a more streamlined approach of using SpEL expressions to define the evaluation logic. By using the `expression` attribute of the `filter` element, you can control through SpEL expressions how payloads and/or headers are interpreted to produce a `Boolean` result that filters your messages. An example using SpEL is shown in Listing 8–19.

***Listing 8–19.** Message Filtering Using Spring Expressions (filter-expression.xml)*

```
<?xml version="1.0" encoding="UTF-8"?>
<beans xmlns="http://www.springframework.org/schema/beans"
       xmlns:xsi="http://www.w3.org/2001/XMLSchema-instance"
       xmlns:int="http://www.springframework.org/schema/integration"
       xmlns:context="http://www.springframework.org/schema/context"
       xsi:schemaLocation="http://www.springframework.org/schema/beans
    http://www.springframework.org/schema/beans/spring-beans-3.0.xsd
    http://www.springframework.org/schema/integration
    http://www.springframework.org/schema/integration/spring-integration-2.0.xsd
    http://www.springframework.org/schema/context
    http://www.springframework.org/schema/context/spring-context-3.0.xsd">

  <context:component-scan
      base-package="com.apress.prospringintegration.messageflow.filter"/>
  <context:component-scan
      base-package="com.apress.prospringintegration.messageflow.domain"/>

  <int:channel id="filteredItemsChannel"/>

  <int:filter input-channel="marketItemChannel"
              output-channel="filteredItemsChannel"
              expression="headers.containsKey('ITEM_TYPE') and↵
 headers.ITEM_TYPE.equals('stock')"
              throw-exception-on-rejection="false" />


  <int:service-activator input-channel="filteredItemsChannel" ref="stockRegistrar" />

</beans>
```

Listing 8–19 evaluates the header `ITEM_TYPE` by first checking that the `ITEM_TYPE` header is available. If the check was not performed and the `ITEM_TYPE` header was absent, then SpEL would have thrown an unsightly exception message in the middle of operation. This makes it important for SpEL expressions to be verified for their effectiveness. Limit ambiguity by restricting expressions to only the simplest terms possible—header evaluation and/or simple POJO or String payload evaluation.

The Spring expression filter example may be run using the same main class as the annotated filter example. Change the reference Spring configuration file to `filter-expression.xml`. Again, only `MarketItems` with the type `stock` will be allowed through.

Dynamic Filtering

In addition to being easier to manage, Spring Integration enables the `expression` element within `filter` that enables using filtering expressions to dynamically control filtering through resource bundles. Also, this allows configuration of filter logic to be defined in a properties file. An administrator may change the filtering logic without taking down the whole system.

As with the router, dynamic filtering uses an instance of `ReloadableResourceBundleExpressionSource`. This example will be configured in the exact same way as the router example. Thus, the filtering decision logic is configured using properties files or other resource bundle implementations. The Spring configuration for a dynamic filter is shown in Listing 8–20.

Listing 8–20. *Spring Configuration for Reloadable Resource (Expression)-Based Filter (filter-dynamic.xml)*

```
<?xml version="1.0" encoding="UTF-8"?>
<beans xmlns="http://www.springframework.org/schema/beans"
       xmlns:xsi="http://www.w3.org/2001/XMLSchema-instance"
       xmlns:int="http://www.springframework.org/schema/integration"
       xmlns:context="http://www.springframework.org/schema/context"
       xsi:schemaLocation="http://www.springframework.org/schema/beans
          http://www.springframework.org/schema/beans/spring-beans-3.0.xsd
    http://www.springframework.org/schema/context
    http://www.springframework.org/schema/context/spring-context-3.0.xsd
    http://www.springframework.org/schema/integration
    http://www.springframework.org/schema/integration/spring-integration-2.0.xsd">

  <context:component-scan
      base-package="com.apress.prospringintegration.messageflow.filter"/>
  <context:component-scan
      base-package="com.apress.prospringintegration.messageflow.domain"/>

  <!--  Spel resource defined filtering (Dynamic Filtering)-->
  <int:filter input-channel="marketItemChannel"
              output-channel="filteredItemsChannel">
    <int:expression key="filter.byType" source="filterRules"/>
  </int:filter>

  <int:channel id="filteredItemsChannel"/>
  <int:service-activator ref="stockRegistrar"
                         input-channel="filteredItemsChannel"/>

</beans>
```

The properties file using the dynamic filter is shown in Listing 8–21. The filter will only allow a message with the header `ITEM_TYPE` set to `stock` to be forwarded.

Listing 8–21. *Expression-Based Filtration via Resource Bundle filter-rules.properties*

```
filter.byType= headers.containsKey('ITEM_TYPE') and headers.ITEM_TYPE.equals('stock')
```

The Spring dynamic filter example may be run using the same main class as the annotated filter example. Change the reference Spring configuration file to `filter-dynamic.xml`. Again, only `MarketItems` with the type `stock` will be allowed through.

Splitter

It is often useful to divide large payloads into separate messages with separate processing flows. In Spring Integration, this is accomplished by using a splitter component. A splitter takes an input message and splits the message into multiple messages based on custom implementation code. The resultant messages are forwarded to the output channel of the splitter component. For some common cases, Spring Integration comes with splitters that require no customization. One example is a splitter that allows splitting a message based on a SpEL expression, thus enabling a very powerful expression-based splitter.

An application of a splitter could be to handle an incoming message with multiple properties where each of the properties needs to be processed by different downstream components. The configuration of this example is shown in Listing 8–22.

Listing 8–22. *Configuration of Message Splitter (splitter.xml)*

```
<?xml version="1.0" encoding="UTF-8"?>
<beans xmlns="http://www.springframework.org/schema/beans"
       xmlns:xsi="http://www.w3.org/2001/XMLSchema-instance"
       xmlns:int="http://www.springframework.org/schema/integration"
       xmlns:context="http://www.springframework.org/schema/context"
       xsi:schemaLocation="http://www.springframework.org/schema/beans
    http://www.springframework.org/schema/beans/spring-beans-3.0.xsd
    http://www.springframework.org/schema/context
    http://www.springframework.org/schema/context/spring-context-3.0.xsd
    http://www.springframework.org/schema/integration
    http://www.springframework.org/schema/integration/spring-integration-2.0.xsd">

  <context:component-scan
     base-package="com.apress.prospringintegration.messageflow.splitter"/>
  <context:component-scan
     base-package="com.apress.prospringintegration.messageflow.domain"/>

  <int:channel id="marketDataInputChannel"/>

  <int:channel id="marketDataSplitterChannel"/>

  <int:splitter input-channel="marketDataInputChannel"
                ref="marketDataSplitter"
                output-channel="marketDataSplitterChannel"/>

  <int:service-activator input-channel="marketDataSplitterChannel"
                         ref="marketDataServiceActivator"/>

</beans>
```

The configuration file is similar to previous examples except for the addition of the `splitter` element. The splitter leverages the base class `org.springframework.integration.splitter.AbstractMessageSplitter` and handles the housekeeping tasks of generating appropriate message header values for `CORRELATION_ID`, `SEQUENCE_SIZE`, and `SEQUENCE_NUMBER`. The `CORRELATION_ID` is a unique ID for all downstream messages that originated from the same message before the splitter. The `SEQUENCE_SIZE` is the total number of messages after the splitter and the `SEQUENCE_NUMBER` is the index of the individual messages after the splitter. These header values are essential when attempting to recompose or aggregate the original message; this will be discussed in more detail later in this chapter.

The Java code is similar to the routers and filters, except that the return type of the method annotated by the `@Splitter` annotation is of type `java.util.Collection<Field>`. The incoming message with MarketItem as a payload will be split into a collection of messages with the individual `Field` instances as the payload. An example of a splitter implementation is shown in Listing 8–23.

Listing 8–23. *Implementing a Splitter by the @Splitter Method Annotation*

```
package com.apress.prospringintegration.messageflow.splitter;

import com.apress.prospringintegration.messageflow.domain.Field;
import com.apress.prospringintegration.messageflow.domain.FieldDescriptor;
import com.apress.prospringintegration.messageflow.domain.MarketItem;
import org.springframework.integration.annotation.Splitter;
import org.springframework.stereotype.Component;

import java.util.ArrayList;
import java.util.Collection;
import java.util.List;

@Component
public class MarketDataSplitter {
    /* Splitter that produces individual fields for aggregation */
    @Splitter
    public Collection<Field> splitItem(MarketItem marketItem) {
        List<Field> messages = new ArrayList<Field>();

        Field field = new Field(FieldDescriptor.SYMBOL, marketItem.getSymbol());
        messages.add(field);

        field = new Field(FieldDescriptor.DESC, marketItem.getDescription());
        messages.add(field);

        field = new Field(FieldDescriptor.PRICE, marketItem.getPrice());
        messages.add(field);

        field = new Field(FieldDescriptor.OPEN_PRICE, marketItem.getOpenPrice());
        messages.add(field);

        field = new Field(FieldDescriptor.TYPE, marketItem.getType());
        messages.add(field);

        return messages;
    }
}
```

The `MarketDataSplitter` implementation breaks the incoming `MarketItem` object into individual `Field` instances based on the `MarketItem` properties. The `Field` domain class is shown in Listing 8–24. The `Field` class maintains a `FieldDescriptor`, shown in Listing 8–25, which is an `enum` representing each of the `MarketItem` properties. The `Field` class also contains the actual property value. The `MarketDataSplitter.split` method creates a collection of individual messages for each of the `MarketItem` properties.

***Listing 8–24.** Example Data Model for Demonstrating Splitter*

```
package com.apress.prospringintegration.messageflow.domain;

public class Field implements Serializable {
    private static final long serialVersionUID = 1L;

    FieldDescriptor fieldDescriptor;
    String value;

    public Field() {
    }

    public Field(FieldDescriptor fd, String value) {
        this.fieldDescriptor = fd;
        this.value = value;
    }

    // setters and getters removed for brevity

}
```

***Listing 8–25.** Example Data Model Enum for Demonstrating Splitter*

```
package com.apress.prospringintegration.messageflow.domain;

public enum FieldDescriptor {

    TYPE(1),
    SYMBOL(2),
    DESC(4),
    OPEN_PRICE(8),
    PRICE(16),
    ALL(1 + 2 + 4 + 8 + 16);

    private final int fieldId;

    FieldDescriptor(int id) {
        this.fieldId = id;
    }

    public int fieldId() {
        return fieldId;
    }

}
```

To demonstrate how the splitter works, a service activator is created that logs the individual `Field` instance and header values, as shown in Listing 8–26. This service activator is wired to consume the outbound messages from the splitter.

***Listing 8–26.** Produces Text Feedback Upon Successful Message Splitting*

```
package com.apress.prospringintegration.messageflow.splitter;

import com.apress.prospringintegration.messageflow.domain.Field;
import org.springframework.integration.annotation.Headers;
import org.springframework.integration.annotation.ServiceActivator;
import org.springframework.stereotype.Component;

import java.text.MessageFormat;
import java.util.Map;

@Component
public class MarketDataServiceActivator {
    @ServiceActivator
    public void handleField(Field dataField, @Headers Map<String, Object> headerMap) {

        System.out.println(MessageFormat
                .format("{0}:{1}", dataField.getFieldDescriptor().toString(),
                        dataField.getValue()));

        for (String key : headerMap.keySet()) {
            Object value = headerMap.get(key);
            System.out.println(MessageFormat
                    .format("header {0}:{1}", key, value));
        }
    }

}
```

In order to run the example splitter, a main class is created, as shown in Listing 8–27. The main class creates the Spring context and obtains a reference to the message channel `marketDataInputChannel` and the utility class `MarketItemCreator`. The `MarketItemCreator` creates a collection of `MarketItem` instances and sends them as a message payload to the channel `marketDataInputChannel`.

***Listing 8–27.** Running the Splitter Workflow*

```
package com.apress.prospringintegration.messageflow.splitter;

import com.apress.prospringintegration.messageflow.domain.MarketItem;
import com.apress.prospringintegration.messageflow.domain.MarketItemCreator;
import org.springframework.context.ApplicationContext;
import org.springframework.context.support.ClassPathXmlApplicationContext;
import org.springframework.integration.MessageChannel;
import org.springframework.integration.support.MessageBuilder;

public class MainMarketDataSplitter {
    public static void main(String[] args) throws Exception {
        ApplicationContext context =
                new ClassPathXmlApplicationContext("splitter.xml");

        MessageChannel channel =
                context.getBean("marketDataInputChannel", MessageChannel.class);
        MarketItemCreator marketItemCreator =
```

```
                context.getBean("marketItemCreator", MarketItemCreator.class);

        for (MarketItem marketItem : marketItemCreator.getMarketItems()) {
            channel.send(MessageBuilder.withPayload(marketItem).build());
        }
    }
}
```

A message payload is passed in as a MarketItem to the method splitItem. The method must return a collection, an array of type T or a Message<T>; in this case, Collection<Field> is returned. Spring Integration sends each Field instance in the collection as message payload to the output channel marketDataSplitterChannel. Often, messages are split so that the individual pieces can be forwarded to processing that is more focused. Because the individual messages are more manageable, the processing requirements are lowered. This is true in many architectures. For example, map/reduce solution tasks are split, processed in parallel, and then combined or reduced. The fork/join constructs in a BPM system allows control flow to proceed in parallel so that the total work product can be achieved in less time.

In this case, you are breaking a MarketItem into individual properties. The next step will be to reconstruct the complete MarketItem from the Field messages being sent. A separate component is required to help construct this final object: an aggregator that will gather (or aggregate) messages into a single message.

Aggregator

An aggregator is the inverse of a splitter: it combines any number of messages into one and sends it to the output channel. An aggregator collects a series of messages (based on a specified correlation between the messages) and publishes a single message to the components downstream.

Suppose that you are about to receive a series of messages with different information about a product, but you do not know the order in which the messages will come and when they will come. In addition, some of the message data is volatile (such as price). This is similar to a market feed system where the data of known products is always changing, thus maintaining an up-to-date snapshot for use in purchasing is of utmost importance. The purchaser can't bid until she's satisfied with a price. An aggregator facilitates this scenario by enabling the piecemeal construction of the datasets.

A common aggregation strategy concern is how to determine when all aggregates are received and when to commence the aggregation process. Spring Integration provides a few common methods to determine how many messages to read before aggregating the results. By default, the Spring Integration aggregator uses the class org.springframework.integration.aggregator.SequenceSizeReleaseStrategy that simply determines completion based on the total number of message received with the same CORRELATION_ID and unique SEQUENCE_NUMBER versus the SEQUENCE_SIZE message header. The default header value is provided by the splitter, although there is nothing preventing you from creating the header values yourself to determine how many messages the aggregator should look for and the index of the message relative to the expected total count (e.g., 3 of 22).

The next concern is how message groups are identified. There are many techniques available for Spring Integration to use to correlate incoming messages. Spring Integration provides a default correlation strategy using org.springframework.integration.aggregator.HeaderAttributeCorrelationStrategy. This correlation strategy uses the value of the header CORRELATION_ID to determine if the messages are part of the same group.

In the splitter example, the MarketItem object was split into the individual properties represented by the Field object. You would now like to take the individual Field messages and reunite them back into the MarketItem object. In this example, you will use the default release strategy and the default correlation strategy. The only custom logic is a POJO with an @Aggregator annotated method expecting a collection of Message<Field> objects. The aggregator method needs to combine the individual Field objects and return a MarketItem instance for further processing downstream. The Spring configuration for the aggregation example is shown in Listing 8–28. It is the same as the splitter example with the additional downstream aggregator.

Listing 8–28. *Configuration of an Aggregator Downstream from a Splitter (aggregator.xml)*

```
<?xml version="1.0" encoding="UTF-8"?>
<beans xmlns="http://www.springframework.org/schema/beans"
       xmlns:xsi="http://www.w3.org/2001/XMLSchema-instance"
       xmlns:int="http://www.springframework.org/schema/integration"
       xmlns:context="http://www.springframework.org/schema/context"
       xsi:schemaLocation="http://www.springframework.org/schema/beans
    http://www.springframework.org/schema/beans/spring-beans-3.0.xsd
    http://www.springframework.org/schema/context
    http://www.springframework.org/schema/context/spring-context-3.0.xsd
    http://www.springframework.org/schema/integration
    http://www.springframework.org/schema/integration/spring-integration-2.0.xsd">

  <context:component-scan
      base-package="com.apress.prospringintegration.messageflow.splitter"/>
  <context:component-scan
      base-package="com.apress.prospringintegration.messageflow.aggregator"/>
  <context:component-scan
      base-package="com.apress.prospringintegration.messageflow.domain"/>

  <int:channel id="marketDataInputChannel"/>

  <int:channel id="marketDataSplitterChannel"/>

  <int:channel id="marketDataAggregatorChannel"/>

  <int:splitter input-channel="marketDataInputChannel" ref="marketDataSplitter"
                output-channel="marketDataSplitterChannel"/>

  <int:service-activator input-channel="marketDataSplitterChannel"
                         output-channel="marketDataAggregatorChannel"
                         ref="marketFieldServiceActivator"/>

  <int:aggregator input-channel="marketDataAggregatorChannel"
                  output-channel="marketDataOutputChannel"
                  ref="marketDataAggregator"/>

  <int:service-activator input-channel="marketDataOutputChannel"
                         ref="marketItemServiceActivator"/>

</beans>
```

The service activator used in the splitter example is modified to return a Field object for the downstream aggregation. The modified service activator is shown in Listing 8–29.

Listing 8–29. *Service Activator Modified to Return Field Object*

```
package com.apress.prospringintegration.messageflow.aggregator;

import com.apress.prospringintegration.messageflow.domain.Field;
```

```
import org.springframework.integration.annotation.Headers;
import org.springframework.integration.annotation.ServiceActivator;
import org.springframework.stereotype.Component;

import java.text.MessageFormat;
import java.util.Map;

@Component
public class MarketFieldServiceActivator {
    @ServiceActivator
    public Field handleField(Field dataField, @Headers Map<String, Object> headerMap) {

        System.out.println(MessageFormat
                .format("{0}:{1}", dataField.getFieldDescriptor().toString(),
                        dataField.getValue()));

        for (String key : headerMap.keySet()) {
            Object value = headerMap.get(key);
            System.out.println(MessageFormat
                    .format("header {0}:{1}", key, value));
        }

        return dataField;
    }
}
```

The implementation for `MarketItemFieldsAggregator` is shown in Listing 8–30. The `handleFieldData` method takes the collection of `Field` objects that are used to set the properties of a new `MarketItem` instance. The `MarketItem` instance with the properties from the aggregated messages is returned by the `handleFieldData` method and sent to the output channel.

Listing 8–30. *Implementing an Aggregator using @Aggregator*

```
package com.apress.prospringintegration.messageflow.aggregator;

import com.apress.prospringintegration.messageflow.domain.Field;
import com.apress.prospringintegration.messageflow.domain.FieldDescriptor;
import com.apress.prospringintegration.messageflow.domain.MarketItem;
import org.springframework.integration.annotation.Aggregator;
import org.springframework.stereotype.Component;

import java.util.List;

@Component
public class MarketDataAggregator {

    @Aggregator
    public MarketItem handleFieldData(List<Field> fields) {
        MarketItem marketItem = new MarketItem();

        for (Field field : fields) {
            if (field.getFieldDescriptor().equals(FieldDescriptor.TYPE)) {
                marketItem.setType(field.getValue());
            } else if (field.getFieldDescriptor().equals(FieldDescriptor.SYMBOL)) {
```

```
                marketItem.setSymbol(field.getValue());
            } else if (field.getFieldDescriptor().equals(FieldDescriptor.PRICE)) {
                marketItem.setPrice(field.getValue());
            } else if (field.getFieldDescriptor().equals(FieldDescriptor.OPEN_PRICE)) {
                marketItem.setOpenPrice(field.getValue());
            } else if (field.getFieldDescriptor().equals(FieldDescriptor.DESC)) {
                marketItem.setDescription(field.getValue());
            }
        }

        return marketItem;
    }
}
```

The service activator MarketItemServiceActivator (shown in Listing 8–31) is place at the end of the message flow to see that the MarketItem instance contains all of the aggregated Field messages. The publishItem method simply logs all of the property values.

Listing 8–31. *Allows Visualization of Aggregation Products*

```
package com.apress.prospringintegration.messageflow.aggregator;

import com.apress.prospringintegration.messageflow.domain.MarketItem;
import org.springframework.integration.annotation.ServiceActivator;
import org.springframework.stereotype.Component;

import java.text.MessageFormat;

@Component
public class MarketItemServiceActivator {

    @ServiceActivator
    public void publishItem(MarketItem m) {
        System.out.println(MessageFormat.format("Aggregated on:\n" +
                "Symbol: {0}\n" +
                "Type: {1}\n" +
                "Desc: {2}\n" +
                "Price: {3}\n",
                m.getSymbol(), m.getType(), m.getDescription(), m.getPrice()));
    }

}
```

The main class for running the aggregator example is shown in Listing 8–32. The main class is identical to the splitter example except for referring to the aggregator.xml Spring configuration file. The Spring configuration file has the addition aggregator element wired to the MarketItemServiceActivator service activator to see the aggregated MarketItem instance.

Listing 8–32. *Executing the Aggregator Example*

```
package com.apress.prospringintegration.messageflow.aggregator;

import com.apress.prospringintegration.messageflow.domain.MarketItem;
import com.apress.prospringintegration.messageflow.domain.MarketItemCreator;
import org.springframework.context.ApplicationContext;
```

```
import org.springframework.context.support.ClassPathXmlApplicationContext;
import org.springframework.integration.MessageChannel;
import org.springframework.integration.support.MessageBuilder;

public class MainMarketDataAggregator {
    public static void main(String[] args) throws Exception {
        ApplicationContext context =
                new ClassPathXmlApplicationContext("aggregator.xml");

        MessageChannel channel =
                context.getBean("marketDataInputChannel", MessageChannel.class);
        MarketItemCreator marketItemCreator =
                context.getBean("marketItemCreator", MarketItemCreator.class);

        for (MarketItem marketItem : marketItemCreator.getMarketItems()) {
            channel.send(MessageBuilder.withPayload(marketItem).build());
        }
    }
}
```

Maintaining MessageGroup State

Aggregators bear the responsibility for holding a reference to every un-released message within a message group in memory. This is the behavior when using the default `org.springframework.integration.store.MessageGroupStore` implementation `org.springframework.integration.store.SimpleMessageStore`. `SimpleMessageStore` uses a `java.util.Map` implementation to store messages. Spring Integration also provides the `org.springframework.integration.jdbc.JdbcMessageStore` that allows persisting message data in relational databases. Since the messages are maintain in a database, they are not lost if, for whatever reason, the Spring Integration application were to go down. In addition, the integration process could be spread across several instances since the state is maintained in an external database. This will be discussed in more detail in Chapter 16.

Note All message payloads using the `JdbcMessageStore` must implement the interface `Serializable`.

The aggregator example may be modified to use the `JdbcMessageStore`, as shown in Listing 8–33.

Listing 8–33. Enabling Enhanced MessageGroup for Persistence Aggregator (jdbc.xml)

```
<?xml version="1.0" encoding="UTF-8"?>
<beans xmlns="http://www.springframework.org/schema/beans"
       xmlns:xsi="http://www.w3.org/2001/XMLSchema-instance"
       xmlns:int="http://www.springframework.org/schema/integration"
       xmlns:context="http://www.springframework.org/schema/context"
       xmlns:jdbc="http://www.springframework.org/schema/jdbc"
       xsi:schemaLocation="http://www.springframework.org/schema/beans
          http://www.springframework.org/schema/beans/spring-beans-3.0.xsd
    http://www.springframework.org/schema/context
```

```
    http://www.springframework.org/schema/context/spring-context-3.0.xsd
    http://www.springframework.org/schema/integration
    http://www.springframework.org/schema/integration/spring-integration-2.0.xsd
    http://www.springframework.org/schema/jdbc
    http://www.springframework.org/schema/jdbc/spring-jdbc-3.0.xsd">

  <context:component-scan
      base-package="com.apress.prospringintegration.messageflow.splitter"/>
  <context:component-scan
      base-package="com.apress.prospringintegration.messageflow.aggregator"/>
  <context:component-scan
      base-package="com.apress.prospringintegration.messageflow.domain"/>
  <context:component-scan
      base-package="com.apress.prospringintegration.messageflow.messagegroup"/>

  <int:channel id="marketDataInputChannel"/>

  <int:channel id="marketDataSplitterChannel"/>

  <int:channel id="marketDataAggregatorChannel"/>

  <int:splitter input-channel="marketDataInputChannel" ref="marketDataSplitter"
                output-channel="marketDataSplitterChannel"/>

  <int:service-activator input-channel="marketDataSplitterChannel"
                         output-channel="marketDataAggregatorChannel"
                         ref="marketFieldServiceActivator"/>

  <int:aggregator input-channel="marketDataAggregatorChannel"
                  output-channel="marketDataOutputChannel"
                  ref="marketDataAggregator"
                  message-store="jdbcMessageGroupStore"/>

  <int:service-activator input-channel="marketDataOutputChannel"
                         ref="marketItemServiceActivator"/>

  <jdbc:embedded-database id="dataSource" type="H2">
    <jdbc:script
        location="classpath:org/springframework/integration/jdbc/schema-h2.sql"/>
  </jdbc:embedded-database>


</beans>
```

The database is initialized by providing a schema setup script to jdbc:script element for the data source. In this example, the H2 database is used in the embedded mode for simplicity. The setup scripts are available in the org.springframework.integration.jdbc package. There are a number of schemas available for most database vendors including MySql, Oracle, Sybase, and Postgres. The message group store is configured using Java configuration, as shown in Listing 8–34. The main class for the previous aggregator example may be used to run this example; simply change the Spring configuration file to aggregator-jdbc.xml.

Listing 8–34. *Java Configuration for Messsage Group Store*

```
package com.apress.prospringintegration.messageflow.messagegroup;

import org.springframework.beans.factory.annotation.Autowired;
import org.springframework.context.annotation.Bean;
import org.springframework.context.annotation.Configuration;
import org.springframework.integration.jdbc.JdbcMessageStore;

import javax.sql.DataSource;

@Configuration
public class MessageGroupStoreConfiguration {

    @Autowired
    private DataSource dataSource;

    @Bean
    public JdbcMessageStore jdbcMessageGroupStore() {
        JdbcMessageStore jdbcMessageGroupStore = new JdbcMessageStore(dataSource);
        return jdbcMessageGroupStore;
    }
}
```

Customizing Aggregation Release Strategy

Aggregation algorithms compute the condition when all the messages are present; in other words, if the all the attributes of a product such as current price, producer, and name are available, this signals that the message group is ready for aggregation. Spring Integration exposes this functionality through the `org.springframework.integration.ReleaseStrategy` interface that contains the `canRelease` method. It is used to determine when the aggregation process code can proceed. In most use cases, when defining a custom release strategy, it is not necessary to override the `canRelease` method directly. Instead, you can implement a @ReleaseStrategy annotated method in any POJO to return `true` when the aggregation can take place.

An example of a custom release strategy is shown in Listing 8–35. The release strategy method takes a collection of `Field` instances and checks if all properties are present. When this condition is met, the method returns `true`. The custom logic uses a bitmask approach.

Listing 8–35. *Implementing a Release Strategy using @Release*

```
package com.apress.prospringintegration.messageflow.aggregator;

import com.apress.prospringintegration.messageflow.domain.Field;
import com.apress.prospringintegration.messageflow.domain.FieldDescriptor;
import org.springframework.integration.annotation.ReleaseStrategy;
import org.springframework.stereotype.Component;

import java.util.List;

/**
 * Completion Strategy Bean for determining whether all fields are present
 */
@Component
```

```
public class MarketItemFieldCompletion {
    /**
     * Determines whether all fields are present.
     */
    @ReleaseStrategy
    public boolean isFieldComplete(List<Field> fields) {
        int fieldComplete = 0;
        for (Field f : fields) {
            fieldComplete = fieldComplete + f.getFieldDescriptor().fieldId();
        }
        return fieldComplete == (FieldDescriptor.ALL.fieldId());
    }
}
```

The Spring configuration file for the custom release strategy is identical to the first aggregator example with the addition of the release-strategy element being set to the marketItemFieldCompletion component, as shown in Listing 8–36. Again, this example may be run using the aggregator main class and pointing to the aggregator-release.xml Spring configuration file.

***Listing 8–36.** Adding a Release-Strategy Element to an Aggregator (aggregator-release.xml)*

```
<?xml version="1.0" encoding="UTF-8"?>
<beans xmlns="http://www.springframework.org/schema/beans"
       xmlns:xsi="http://www.w3.org/2001/XMLSchema-instance"
       xmlns:int="http://www.springframework.org/schema/integration"
       xmlns:context="http://www.springframework.org/schema/context"
       xsi:schemaLocation="http://www.springframework.org/schema/beans
          http://www.springframework.org/schema/beans/spring-beans-3.0.xsd
    http://www.springframework.org/schema/context
    http://www.springframework.org/schema/context/spring-context-3.0.xsd
    http://www.springframework.org/schema/integration
    http://www.springframework.org/schema/integration/spring-integration-2.0.xsd">

  <context:component-scan
      base-package="com.apress.prospringintegration.messageflow.splitter"/>
  <context:component-scan
      base-package="com.apress.prospringintegration.messageflow.aggregator"/>
  <context:component-scan
      base-package="com.apress.prospringintegration.messageflow.domain"/>

  <int:channel id="marketDataInputChannel"/>

  <int:channel id="marketDataSplitterChannel"/>

  <int:channel id="marketDataAggregatorChannel"/>

  <int:splitter input-channel="marketDataInputChannel" ref="marketDataSplitter"
                output-channel="marketDataSplitterChannel"/>

  <int:service-activator input-channel="marketDataSplitterChannel"
                         output-channel="marketDataAggregatorChannel"
                         ref="marketFieldServiceActivator"/>

  <int:aggregator input-channel="marketDataAggregatorChannel"
```

```
                    output-channel="marketDataOutputChannel"
                    ref="marketDataAggregator"
                    release-strategy="marketItemFieldCompletion"/>

    <int:service-activator input-channel="marketDataOutputChannel"
                           ref="marketItemServiceActivator"/>

</beans>
```

Resequencer

Sometimes part of a process chain will take an inordinate amount of time to complete message delivery while other related messages moving through a different part of the process will finish quickly. In order to guarantee that delivery of messages is in a particular order, perhaps because of some business rule such as in an auction house or stock-market bid system where message order is important, a resequencer may be used to insure that messages order is preserved.

A resequencer provides a way to insure that messages remain in sequence as determined by the value of the message header `SEQUENCE_NUMBER`. When out-of-sequence messages are encountered, they are held in a `MessageGroupStore` until a message is received that fulfills the sequence. A resequencer may go a step further and hold all messages until the entire sequence is fulfilled. Either way, Spring Integration exposes resequencing strategies in one simple configuration element, the `resequencer`. In addition, a release strategy may be specified through the `release-partial-sequence` attribute that, when set to true, will send the messages as soon as they are available. The default value is false, which means that the messages are sent only after all have arrived. In addition, messages that linger too long may be dropped thanks to the `discard-channel` attribute.

Here's a simple example that sends an out-of-sequence set of messages with the payload `Bid`. `Bid` is a simple domain object shown in Listing 8–37. This class has two properties: a `date` and `int` value for the sequence order.

Listing 8–37. *Bid Domain Class*

```
package com.apress.prospringintegration.messageflow.resequencer;

import java.util.Date;

public class Bid {
    Date time;
    int order;

    public Bid() {
    }

    public Bid(Date time, int order) {
        this.time = time;
        this.order = order;
    }

    public Date getTime() {
        return time;
    }

    public void setTime(Date time) {
        this.time = time;
```

```
    }

    public int getOrder() {
        return order;
    }

    public void setOrder(int order) {
        this.order = order;
    }
}
```

A component class shown in Listing 8–38 is created to generate the Bid instance and publish to the message channel inboundChannel. The Bid instances are created with a descending order value. Messages are then sent to the message channel inboundChannel setting the message header SEQUENCE_NUMBER to the order value and the SEQUENCE_SIZE to the total number of Bid instances. The date property is set before the message is sent and a one second delay is added after each message is sent.

Listing 8–38. *Component Class that Generates Out-of-Sequence Bid Instances*

```
package com.apress.prospringintegration.messageflow.resequencer;

import org.springframework.beans.factory.annotation.Autowired;
import org.springframework.beans.factory.annotation.Qualifier;
import org.springframework.beans.factory.annotation.Value;
import org.springframework.integration.Message;
import org.springframework.integration.MessageChannel;
import org.springframework.integration.core.MessagingTemplate;
import org.springframework.integration.support.MessageBuilder;
import org.springframework.stereotype.Component;

import java.util.ArrayList;
import java.util.Calendar;
import java.util.Date;
import java.util.List;

@Component
public class SimpleSendingClient {

    @Autowired
    @Qualifier("inboundChannel")
    private MessageChannel channel;

    public void kickOff() {
        List<Bid> bids = getBids();
        for (Bid b : bids) {
            b.setTime(new Date());
            Message<Bid> message = MessageBuilder.withPayload(b)
                    .setCorrelationId("BID").setSequenceNumber(b.getOrder())
                    .setSequenceSize(bids.size()).build();
            channel.send(message);
            try {
                Thread.sleep(1000);
            } catch (InterruptedException e) {
```

```
                // do nothing
            }
        }
    }

    /**
     * Generate a list of bids with some time inbetween bids
     */
    public List<Bid> getBids() {
        List<Bid> bids = new ArrayList<Bid>();
        for(int order = 5; order > 0; order--) {
            Bid bid = new Bid();
            bid.setOrder(order);
            bids.add(bid);
        }
        return bids;
    }
}
```

The Spring configuration for the resequencer example is shown in Listing 8–39. The resequencer is using a default setting where all messages must arrive before being sent to the output channel in the correct order.

***Listing 8–39.** Configuring a Resequencer (resequencer.xml)*

```
<?xml version="1.0" encoding="UTF-8"?>
<beans xmlns="http://www.springframework.org/schema/beans"
       xmlns:xsi="http://www.w3.org/2001/XMLSchema-instance"
       xmlns:int="http://www.springframework.org/schema/integration"
       xmlns:context="http://www.springframework.org/schema/context"
       xsi:schemaLocation="http://www.springframework.org/schema/beans
    http://www.springframework.org/schema/beans/spring-beans-3.0.xsd
    http://www.springframework.org/schema/context
    http://www.springframework.org/schema/context/spring-context-3.0.xsd
    http://www.springframework.org/schema/integration
    http://www.springframework.org/schema/integration/spring-integration-2.0.xsd">

  <context:component-scan
      base-package="com.apress.prospringintegration.messageflow.resequencer"/>

  <int:channel id="inboundChannel"/>

  <int:resequencer input-channel="inboundChannel" output-channel="outboundChannel"/>

  <int:channel id="outboundChannel"/>

  <int:service-activator input-channel="outboundChannel" ref="bidListener"/>


</beans>
```

The main class for the resequencer example is shown in Listing 8–40. The main class will create the Spring context and obtain a reference for the `simpleSendingClient`. The method `kickOff` will be called, causing the out-of-sequence messages to be sent with a one-second delay between each send. The resequencer will wait for all messages to arrive, and then send them out in the correct order.

***Listing 8–40.** Main Class for Resequencer Example*

```
package com.apress.prospringintegration.messageflow.resequencer;

import org.springframework.context.ApplicationContext;
import org.springframework.context.support.ClassPathXmlApplicationContext;

public class MainResequencer {
    public static void main(String[] args) throws Exception {

        ApplicationContext context =
                new ClassPathXmlApplicationContext("resequencer.xml");

        SimpleSendingClient simple =
                context.getBean("simpleSendingClient", SimpleSendingClient.class);
        simple.kickOff();
    }
}
```

Message Handler Chain

A `org.springframework.integration.handler.MesssageHandlerChain` is an implementation of `MessageHandler` that can be configured as a single endpoint while delegating a chain of other handlers such as filters, transformers, etc. This can simplify configuration when a set of handlers needs to be connected in a linear fashion. The `MessageHandlerChain` is configured through in Spring XML using the `chain` element.

The aggregator example may be rewritten using the `MessageHandlerChain`, as shown in Listing 8–41. The Spring configuration file will work identically to the one in Listing 8–28. There is no need to create the intermediate message channel since Spring Integration will create anonymous channel for you.

***Listing 8–41.** Aggregator Example using MessageHandlerChain (aggregator-chain.xml)*

```
<?xml version="1.0" encoding="UTF-8"?>
<beans xmlns="http://www.springframework.org/schema/beans"
       xmlns:xsi="http://www.w3.org/2001/XMLSchema-instance"
       xmlns:int="http://www.springframework.org/schema/integration"
       xmlns:context="http://www.springframework.org/schema/context"
       xsi:schemaLocation="http://www.springframework.org/schema/beans
          http://www.springframework.org/schema/beans/spring-beans-3.0.xsd
    http://www.springframework.org/schema/context
    http://www.springframework.org/schema/context/spring-context-3.0.xsd
    http://www.springframework.org/schema/integration
    http://www.springframework.org/schema/integration/spring-integration-2.0.xsd">

  <context:component-scan
      base-package="com.apress.prospringintegration.messageflow.splitter"/>
  <context:component-scan
      base-package="com.apress.prospringintegration.messageflow.aggregator"/>
  <context:component-scan
      base-package="com.apress.prospringintegration.messageflow.domain"/>

  <int:channel id="marketDataInputChannel"/>
```

```
  <int:chain input-channel="marketDataInputChannel">
    <int:splitter ref="marketDataSplitter"/>
    <int:service-activator ref="marketFieldServiceActivator"/>
    <int:aggregator ref="marketDataAggregator"/>
    <int:service-activator ref="marketItemServiceActivator"/>
  </int:chain>

</beans>
```

Message Bridge

A message bridge is simply an endpoint that connects two message channels or two channel adapters together. For a `PollableChannel` or a `SubscribableChannel` adapter, the message bridge provides a polling configuration.

For example, the previous example in Listing 8–41 for the aggregator using the `MessageHandlerChain` may be rewritten as shown in Listing 8–42. An intermediate message channel `bridgeChannel` is added between the message channel `marketDataInputChannel` and the `MessageHandlerChain`. The message bridge connects the message channels `marketDataInputChannel` and `bridgeChannel`.

Listing 8–42. *Aggregator Example Using Message Bridge*

```
<?xml version="1.0" encoding="UTF-8"?>
<beans xmlns="http://www.springframework.org/schema/beans"
       xmlns:xsi="http://www.w3.org/2001/XMLSchema-instance"
       xmlns:int="http://www.springframework.org/schema/integration"
       xmlns:context="http://www.springframework.org/schema/context"
       xsi:schemaLocation="http://www.springframework.org/schema/beans
          http://www.springframework.org/schema/beans/spring-beans-3.0.xsd
    http://www.springframework.org/schema/context
    http://www.springframework.org/schema/context/spring-context-3.0.xsd
    http://www.springframework.org/schema/integration
    http://www.springframework.org/schema/integration/spring-integration-2.0.xsd">

  <context:component-scan
      base-package="com.apress.prospringintegration.messageflow.splitter"/>
  <context:component-scan
      base-package="com.apress.prospringintegration.messageflow.aggregator"/>
  <context:component-scan
      base-package="com.apress.prospringintegration.messageflow.domain"/>

  <int:channel id="marketDataInputChannel"/>

  <int:channel id="bridgeChannel"/>

  <int:bridge input-channel="marketDataInputChannel" output-channel="bridgeChannel"/>

  <int:chain input-channel="bridgeChannel">
    <int:splitter ref="marketDataSplitter"/>
    <int:service-activator ref="marketFieldServiceActivator"/>
    <int:aggregator ref="marketDataAggregator"/>
    <int:service-activator ref="marketItemServiceActivator"/>
  </int:chain>

</beans>
```

Workflow

Messaging is inherently stateless. Messages pass through endpoints and Spring Integration needs to *infer* where to send the message next. Spring Integration can provide the appearance of state because it has a bird's eye view of the entire integration; from that vantage point, it's easy to manipulate the various exchanges to propagate state, be it message payloads or headers. However, in truth, there is no real state. As soon as a message has left an endpoint, the endpoint will *forget* that the message ever passed through it. Similarly, while it is clear to you, the implementer, that the series of steps that a message must negotiate to achieve a larger goal make up a larger process, each endpoint is oblivious to this larger process—to any *process state*.

Messaging is a very quick, easy way to describe processes without any intrinsic state. However, sometimes an architecture requires process state. One scenario that begs for workflow is if you want to enlist multiple system actors over possibly long periods of time. Coordinating system *and* human actors can be daunting; without a proper workflow system, it would fall on you, the developer, to build out these state machines. Another common motivation behind workflow adaptation is ability to audit; a workflow guards system and process state. You can query it for information on workflow processes both in-flight and completed. You can ask it questions like "How many of our customer fulfillment processes have been 100 percent completed?" or "How many users have been converted from leads into two year subscriptions in our marketing campaigns?" These answers can't be obtained from stateless messaging processes.

A business is only as good as its processes. Often, businesses will thread together the contributions of multiple resources (people, automated computer processes, and so forth) to achieve a greater result. These individual contributions by people and automatic services are most efficient when single-focused and, ideally, reused. The simplest example of this might be a conveyor belt in a car factory. A product enters the line at the beginning of the conveyer belt and is worked on by any number of individuals or machines until finally the output of the work reaches the end of the line, at which point the job is done. One machine paints the chassis; another machine lowers the engine into the car. A person attaches the chairs and another person installs the radio. These people and machines do their work without worrying about what is going to happen to the car next.

Another process—to take the car example even further—is that of a car dealership. It takes a number of people to get you into a new car! It starts when you enter the car dealership. A sales representative walks with you, showing off models and answering questions. Finally, your eye catches the glimmer of a silver Porsche. This is it! No need to carry on searching. The next part of the process begins.

You enter an office where somebody starts prompting you for information to purchase the vehicle. There are three conditions: you have cash on hand, you require a loan, or you already have a loan from another bank. If you have cash on hand, you give it to them and wait an hour for them to count it (because Porsches are not cheap). Perhaps you have a check from the bank, in which case you give them that. Alternatively, you begin the process of applying for a loan with the dealership. Eventually, the pecuniary details are sorted, credit scores checked, driver's license and insurance verified, and you begin signing paperwork, lots of paperwork. If you have already paid for the car, the dealership draws up the paperwork to ensure proper title and registration. If you are establishing a loan with the dealership, you fill out that paperwork, work on registration, and so on.

Eventually, someone gives you the keys and the relevant paperwork and you are done. Or so you think. You make a break for the door, itching to see how fast you can get the car to 65 (the maximum speed limit on your area freeway, conditions permitting, of course). At the door, you are all but assaulted with one last packet of brochures and business cards and a branded pen and the good wishes of the grinning sales representatives. You shrug them off and break for the car, jumping into the sporty convertible's driver's seat. As you leave, you turn the music up and speed off into the horizon.

Eventually you will remember that you left your wife at the dealership, but for now, the fruit of all that bureaucracy is too sweet to ignore.

The process of buying a car may seem like it takes forever, and indeed, it does take a long time. However, the process is efficient in that all actions that *could* be completed at the same time *are* being completed at the same time—by multiple workers. Further, because each actor in the process knows her part, each individual step is as efficient as possible. No need for every worker to wear many poorly fitted hats, as they say. Instead, resources can focus on optimizing their specific functions. It is crucial to be able to orchestrate a process like this in the enterprise.

You can extrapolate here, too. These examples are relatively small, though, and perhaps the inefficiencies of the worst-case scenario for the process are tolerable. The inefficiencies are overwhelmingly untenable in even slightly larger business processes, though! For example, imagine the new-hire process at a large company. Beyond the initial process of interviewing and a background security check, there is the provisioning that is required to get the new employee installed. The IT department needs to repurpose a laptop, image it, and install an operating system. Somebody needs to create a user account for that employee and ensure that LDAP and e-mail are accessible. Somebody needs to ready a security card so that the employee can use the elevator or enter the building. Somebody needs to make sure the employee's desk station or office is clean and that remnants from the previous occupant are gone. Somebody needs to get forms for the health insurance or benefits, and somebody needs to give the new employee a walk around the office and introduce the staff.

Imagine having only one person to do all of that for each employee. In a bigger company, this process would soon become overwhelming! Indeed, many of the tasks mentioned themselves require several steps to achieve the goal. Thus, the main process—integrating a new employee in the company—has multiple subprocesses. If many people perform all the tasks concurrently, however, the process becomes manageable. Additionally, not all people are suited to doing all of those tasks. A little specialization makes for a lot of efficiency.

Thus, processes, and the understanding of those processes, are *crucial* to a business. It is from this revelation that the study of business management emerged. Business Process Management (BPM) originally described how to best orchestrate technology and people to the betterment of the business, but it was a business person's preoccupation, not a technologist's. As it became apparent that businesses were already leveraging technology, the next hurdle was to codify the notion of a business process. How could software systems know—and react to—what the immovable enterprises and unbending market forces demanded? BPM provides the answer. It describes, in higher-level diagrams, the flow a given process takes from start to finish. These diagrams are useful both to the business analyst and to the programmer because they describe two sides of the same coin: to the business analyst, a functioning strategy, and to the programmer, a way of tracking all the details of an otherwise complex process that enlists much of the company's technologies. Once a process is codified, it can be reused and reapplied in the same way a programmer reuses a class in Java.

Software Processes

Thus, the unit of work—that which is required to achieve a quantifiable goal—for a business is rarely a single request/response. Even the simplest of processes in a business requires at least a few steps. This is true not only in business but in your users' use cases. Short of simple read-only scenarios such as looking at a web page for the news, most meaningful processes require multiple steps. Think through the sign-up process of your typical web application. It begins with a user visiting a site and filling out a form. The user completes the form and submits the finalized data, after satisfying validation. If you think about it, however, this is just the beginning of the work for this very simple process. Typically, to avoid spam, a verification e-mail is sent to the user. When the user reads the e-mail, she clicks on the verification link, confirming both her intentions as a registrant and that she is not a robot. This tells the server that the user is a valid user, so it sends a welcome e-mail. That's four steps with two different roles! This involved process, when translated into an activity diagram, is shown in Figure 8-1. The two roles (user and system) are shown as swim lanes. Rounded shapes inside the swim lanes are states. Process flows from one state to another, following the path of the connecting lines.

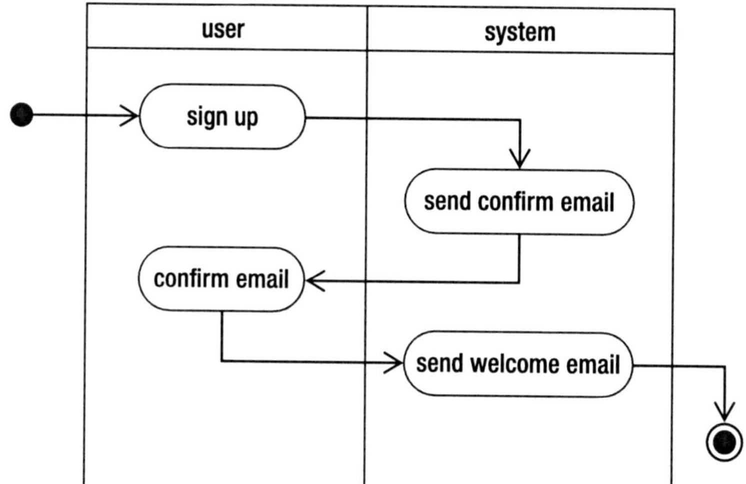

***Figure 8–1.** Activity Diagram for Sign-up Process*

For such a simple process, it might be tempting to keep track of the state of the process in the domain model. After all, some of the state, such as the sign-up date, can certainly be regarded as business data belonging to model entities. Such a date is valuable for revenue recognition. The date when the welcome e-mail was sent is probably not very important, though. The situation will escalate if you send out more e-mail. If you build other kinds of processes involving the user, management of the user's state within those processes will become a burden on your system and will complicate the schema.

A workflow system extricates that process state from the domain and into a separate layer called a *business process*. A workflow system also typically models which agents in the system do what work, providing work lists for different agents in the system.

A workflow engine lets you model the process in a higher-level form, roughly corresponding in code to what a UML activity diagram can describe. Because a workflow is high-level, specifying how a business process is leveraged as an executable component of a system is a dizzyingly vast task. In industry, there are standards for the language used to model a business process as well as the model of the engine that is used to run the business process. Additionally, there are standards specifying interoperability, how endpoints are mapped to the agents being orchestrated by the process, and much more. All this can quickly become overwhelming.

Let's look at some of these standards in Table 8–1.

Table 8–1. Some of the Myriad, Significant Standards Surrounding BPM

Standard Name	Standards Group	Description
WS-BPEL (BPEL)	OASIS	A language that, when deployed to a BPEL container, describes the execution of a process. It interfaces with the outside world via the invocation of external web services. This language describes the runtime behavior of a process. It has several flaws, not the least of which is the reliance on web service technology and the lack of work list support.
WS-BPEL (BPEL 2.0)	OASIS	This is largely an upgrade to its predecessor, clarifying the behavior at runtime of certain elements and adding more expressive elements to the language.
WS-BPEL for People (BPEL4People)	OASIS	The main feature common to traditional workflow systems is the ability to support work lists for actors in a process. BPEL had no such support, as it did not support human tasks (that is, wait states for people). This specification addresses that exact shortcoming.
Business Process Modeling Notation (BPMN)	Originally BPMI, then OMG, as the two organizations merged	This provides a set of diagramming notations that describe a business process. This notation is akin to UML's activity diagram, though the specification also describes (informally) how the notations relate to runtime languages such as BPEL. The notation is sometimes ambiguous, however, and one of the formidable challenges facing BPM vendors is creating a drawing tool that can take a round-trip to BPEL and back, providing seamless authoring.
XML Process Definition Language	Workflow Management Coalition (WfMC)	This one describes the interchange of diagrams between modeling tools, especially how elements are displayed and the semantics of those elements to the target notation.
Business Process Modeling Notation 2 (BPMN 2)	OMG	BPMN 2 rectifies the discrepancies between BPEL and BPMN 1.0: that BPMN 1.0 could only be used to draw—and not execute—business processes, and that BPMN could be used to create process definitions that BPEL could not execute. BPMN 2 specifies both the diagramming notations as well as the runtime execution semantics. The specification went final January 2011.

As you can see, there are some problems. Some of these standards are ill suited to real business needs, even once the busywork is surmounted. Some of the workflow engines lack adequate support for work lists, essentially making the processes useless for anything that models human interaction—a typical requirement.

Introducing Activiti, an Apache 2 Licensed BPMN 2 Engine

A few viable implementations offer compelling alternatives. One is Alfresco's Activiti (`www.activiti.org`) project, a popular open source (Apache 2 licensed) BPMN 2 implementation. There are alternative open source workflow engines (e.g., Enhydra Shark or OpenWFE) and proprietary engines from Tibco, IBM, Oracle, WebMethods, and so forth. In our opinion, Activiti is powerful enough for easily 80 percent of the situations you are likely to encounter and can at least facilitate solutions for another 10 percent.

Activiti enjoys the best integration with Spring of any workflow engine because SpringSource engineers contribute to the project and because the Spring Integration and Activiti teams have worked to build solid integration. The Activiti/Spring integration story has many facets. The SpringSource and the Activiti teams ensure that Activiti BPMN 2 processes could reference Spring beans (as opposed to classes configured using the Activiti configuration XML). The Activiti Process Engine can be configured entirely in Spring's IoC container: there is a Spring bean factory to configure the engine, transactions can be handled using Spring's `PlatformTransactionManager` hierarchy, etc. The Spring Integration support is currently in the Spring Integration sandbox and is tentatively scheduled for the Spring Integration 2.1 release. The adapters are working and complete, but there is no namespace support yet. The basic setup is not likely to change even if the classes do in the final release. Thus, upgrading should just be a matter of updating the configuration to reflect the new code.

Exploring the nuances of BPMN 2 is out of the scope of this chapter (indeed, you could fill a whole book with it!). Let's take a look at a simple "Hello, World!" process definition in Activiti's BPMN 2 implementation in Listing 8–43 to understand some of BPMN's finer points.

***Listing 8–43.** Activiti "Hello, World!" Example (hello.bpmn20.xml)*

```
<?xml version="1.0" encoding="UTF-8"?>
<definitions id="definitions"
             xmlns="http://www.omg.org/spec/BPMN/20100524/MODEL"
             xmlns:xsi="http://www.w3.org/2001/XMLSchema-instance"
             xmlns:activiti="http://activiti.org/bpmn"
             typeLanguage="http://www.w3.org/2001/XMLSchema"
             expressionLanguage="http://www.w3.org/1999/XPath"
             targetNamespace="http://www.activiti.org/bpmn2.0">

  <process id="hello">

    <startEvent id="start"/>

    <sequenceFlow id="sf1" sourceRef="start" targetRef="helloScriptTask"/>

    <scriptTask id="helloScriptTask" name="Execute script" scriptFormat="groovy">
      <script>
        println 'hello ' + customerId + '!'
      </script>
    </scriptTask>

    <sequenceFlow id="sf2" sourceRef="helloScriptTask" targetRef="end"/>

    <endEvent id="end"/>

  </process>

</definitions>
```

There's a lot going on here, but don't be alarmed. Let's dissect it element by element. Right off the bat, you will notice that the file is XML, and that the large swath of text at the top merely serves to import other XML definitions. The next element is the `process` element, which wraps a single process definition. You will see that the `sequenceFlow` elements inside the process definition seem to serve only to string together the other elements in the XML file, very much like `channel` elements do in Spring Integration. This leaves only three real elements of substance left: `startEvent`, `scriptTask`, and `endEvent`. The `startEvent` and `endEvent` elements are perfunctory; they provide a way to reference the beginning and end of the process. They are little more than waypoints on your journey and can be reused as-is for most process definitions. The last element is the `scriptTask`. The `scriptTask` element lets developers embed scripts and run them. In this case, you use the Groovy scripting language to print a message to standard out, "hello," followed by the process variable `customerId`, followed by an exclamation mark.

When you start a business process, you may pass in process variables. These process variables may be accessed from the process definition. This is very similar to accessing message headers from within Spring Integration. The process variables provide a way to differentiate one process instance from another. A process instance then has variables local to its execution and can start and stop execution, but it always follows the sample's general steps laid out by its definition. In a way, this relationship is very similar to that of a method invocation and the definition of that method in the class. As you can see here, process variables are available inside the process definition as well as from Java code that interacts with the `org.activiti.engine.runtime.ProcessInstance` classes.

With the analysis complete, let's look at it again from afar. The file essentially defines three elements:

- `startEvent`
- `scriptTask`
- `endEvent`

Each element corresponds to the notion of a state or an execution in workflow. At runtime, the states are executed one after another according to the sequence established by the `sequenceFlow` element. Many different elements are used in this fashion. They provide many different behaviors including complex routing (conditionals, switch, for-each), concurrency, forking, joining, and sequences. In many ways, this will seem familiar to users of Spring Integration.

The XML definition above is a process definition. When Activiti reads the process definition, it will store the process definition as rows in database tables. When starting a new business process, you are, in essence, patterning a new object graph from the template definition. This new object graph is a runtime reflection of the steps in the process definition that tracks the data and state specific to a single use of a business process. The XML definition is the *process definition*, and the same series of steps defined in the XML, when executed at runtime, is the *process instance*. A process definition is like a template of the process, and the instance is an object graph created with that template as its basis but with instance-specific data.

Configuring Activiti with Spring

Activiti ships with fantastic Spring support. Let's configure a working Activiti process engine first. This step is not Spring Integration-specific but is helpful in understanding how the Spring Integration support actually works. The central class in Activiti is the `org.activiti.engine.ProcessEngine`. You can obtain references to all the other services you will need to work with Activiti from this central interface. The `ProcessEngine` may be configured in a number of different ways, but you will use the Spring-specific factory bean. To obtain Activiti and the corresponding Spring support, add the following Maven dependencies to your `pom.xml` file, as shown in Listing 8–44.

Listing 8–44. *Activiti Maven Dependencies*

```
<dependency>
  <groupId>org.activiti</groupId>
  <artifactId>activiti-engine</artifactId>
  <version>5.2</version>
</dependency>
<dependency>
  <groupId>org.activiti</groupId>
  <artifactId>activiti-spring</artifactId>
  <version>5.2</version>
</dependency>
```

These declarations bring in the core engine as well as the Spring-specific support. To configure Activiti, you need to configure a data source and transaction management. Activiti stores its process state in a database and uses the Apache MyBatis project to handle persistence. Most of the following configuration is old hat, so it will not be covered here. For your configuration, you are using one of Activiti's supported databases, H2, because it's easy to configure. The MySQL and PostgreSQL databases are also supported, with more support on its way. The Java configuration is shown in Listing 8–45.

Listing 8–45. *Java Configuration for Activiti*

```
package com.apress.prospringintegration.messageflow.workflow;

import org.activiti.spring.ProcessEngineFactoryBean;
import org.activiti.spring.SpringProcessEngineConfiguration;
import org.apache.commons.logging.Log;
import org.apache.commons.logging.LogFactory;
import org.springframework.beans.factory.annotation.Value;
import org.springframework.context.annotation.Bean;
import org.springframework.jdbc.datasource.DataSourceTransactionManager;
import org.springframework.jdbc.datasource.TransactionAwareDataSourceProxy;

import javax.annotation.PostConstruct;
import javax.sql.DataSource;

/**
 * configuration that is common to all of your workflow examples
 */
public class ActivitiProcessEngineConfiguration {

    private Log log = LogFactory.getLog(getClass());

    @Value("#{dataSource}")
    private DataSource dataSource;

    @PostConstruct
    public void setup() {
        log.debug("starting up " + getClass().getName());
    }

    private String getDatabaseSchemaUpdate() {
        return SpringProcessEngineConfiguration.DB_SCHEMA_UPDATE_TRUE;
    }
```

```
    @Bean
    public ProcessEngineFactoryBean processEngine() {
        ProcessEngineFactoryBean processEngineFactoryBean =
                new ProcessEngineFactoryBean();

        SpringProcessEngineConfiguration configuration =
                new SpringProcessEngineConfiguration();
        configuration.setTransactionManager(dataSourceTransactionManager());
        configuration.setDatabaseType("h2");
        configuration.setJobExecutorActivate(false);
        configuration.setDataSource(targetDataSource());
        configuration.setDatabaseSchemaUpdate(getDatabaseSchemaUpdate());
        processEngineFactoryBean.setProcessEngineConfiguration(configuration);
        return processEngineFactoryBean;
    }

    @Bean
    public DataSource targetDataSource() {
        TransactionAwareDataSourceProxy transactionAwareDataSourceProxy =
                new TransactionAwareDataSourceProxy();
        transactionAwareDataSourceProxy.setTargetDataSource(dataSource);
        return transactionAwareDataSourceProxy;
    }

    @Bean
    public DataSourceTransactionManager dataSourceTransactionManager() {
        DataSourceTransactionManager dataSourceTransactionManager =
                new DataSourceTransactionManager();
        dataSourceTransactionManager.setDataSource(this.targetDataSource());
        return dataSourceTransactionManager;
    }
}
```

The only interesting object is the ProcessEngineFactoryBean, which is highlighted. The majority of the configuration options, such as dataSource and transactionManagement, are obvious. The getDatabaseSchemaUpdate property tells Activiti if it should attempt to install the various tables on startup if the database doesn't already have them. Naturally, this is something you should consider varying based on your environment—leave it on in development, off in production, etc.

The configuration is enough to be able to run the BPMN 2 process that you declared earlier. Let's build a simple example, as shown in Listing 8–46.

Listing 8–46. *Simple Activiti Example*

```
package com.apress.prospringintegration.messageflow.workflow;

import org.activiti.engine.ProcessEngine;
import org.activiti.engine.RepositoryService;
import org.activiti.engine.repository.DeploymentBuilder;
import org.activiti.engine.runtime.ProcessInstance;
import org.apache.commons.logging.Log;
import org.apache.commons.logging.LogFactory;
import org.springframework.context.support.ClassPathXmlApplicationContext;
```

```
import java.util.HashMap;
import java.util.Map;

/**
 * Simple client to exercise your
 */
public class WorkflowMainClient {

    static private Log log = LogFactory.getLog(WorkflowMainClient.class);

    static void deployProcessDefinitions(ProcessEngine processEngine,
                                         String... processDefinitionNames)
            throws Exception {
        RepositoryService repositoryService = processEngine.getRepositoryService();
        for (String processDefinitionName : processDefinitionNames) {
            DeploymentBuilder deployment = repositoryService.createDeployment()
                    .addClasspathResource(processDefinitionName);
            deployment.deploy();
        }
    }

    public static void main(String[] ars) throws Exception {
        ClassPathXmlApplicationContext classPathXmlApplicationContext =
                new ClassPathXmlApplicationContext("workflow-gateway.xml");
        classPathXmlApplicationContext.start();

        ProcessEngine processEngine =
                classPathXmlApplicationContext.getBean(ProcessEngine.class);

        deployProcessDefinitions(processEngine,
                "processes/hello.bpmn20.xml", "processes/gateway.bpmn20.xml");

        Map<String, Object> processVariables = new HashMap<String, Object>();
        processVariables.put("customerId", 2);

        ProcessInstance pi = processEngine.getRuntimeService()
                .startProcessInstanceByKey("sigateway", processVariables);

        log.debug("the process instance has been started: PI ID # " + pi.getId());

        Thread.sleep(1000 * 20);
        log.debug("waited 20s");
    }
}
```

The code instantiates the XML file that in turn picks up the Java configuration defined previously. In the configuration, you could have specified one property on the `ProcessEngineFactoryBean–configuration.setDeploymentResources`. This property expects an array of Spring `org.springframework.io.Resource` instances that reference the process definition XML files. Each time Activiti starts up, it parses the definitions and then attempts to install the definitions into the database as a new version if the files conflict with existing versions or the definitions don't already exist in the database. If nothing has changed, Activiti simply leaves the definitions alone. This feature is powerful; it implies that you can deploy a process definition, run it a few times, stop the code, update the definition, and redeploy—and all the existing process definitions will still continue to work until they have completed. The latest version of the definition is used by default unless you explicitly specify the older version. There is no need to worry too much about process migration or long lived processes in flight that need to be updated. If you do not specify the `deploymentResources` property in the `ProcessEngineFactoryBean`, then you need to deploy the process definition manually, as you have here in the `deployProcessDefinitions` method where you use the `ProcessEngine's RepositoryService` reference to create a `deployment` object and then deploy that object.

In the client, you create a `Map` with `String` keys and `Object` values to specify the process variables. The process variables are available in the process definition by the key. Remember, process variables are serialized in the database, and while there are some intelligent strategies in play to serialize all the basic primitive Java types as well as serializable objects, you should stick with primitive values. This means that instead of storing a whole object, you might consider simply storing its ID. This strategy has the same benefits in Activiti as it does in Spring Integration where it is called the *claim-check pattern*: it is faster to run, messages are lighter, and you don't face the brittleness of transporting and deserializing objects across different environments and clients.

Next, you use the `ProcessEngine` to get a reference to the `RuntimeService`, and then use that to start the process instance, using the ID value you specified in the `process` element in the process definition XML, "hello." This spawns a process instance and makes those process variables available to the steps inside the `ProcessInstance`. The `startProcessInstanceByKey` method blocks as it executes the steps in the process, one by one, until it completes. This is true, with one exception: wait-states.

Wait-states are exactly what their name implies: breaks in the action or pauses. There are a few particularly important uses for wait-states. One is to model human interactions when a process reaches a point when a person has to do the work. Another is to model automatic system process that might take a while or whose duration is unknown and whose eventual conclusion is the signal that the process can continue. It is in this last case—long running, automatic processes of indeterminate duration—that the Spring Integration gateway lives.

The Spring Integration Inbound Activiti Gateway

The Spring Integration gateway is declared in Spring as a regular bean but implements the Activiti machinery required so that it can be used in Activiti as a wait-state. This lets it enjoy all the properties as any other built-in wait-state in Activiti. Once the process enters Spring Integration Activiti gateway, the enclosing transaction is committed and the process stops. In the previous Activiti example, the call to `startProcessInstanceByKey` would return at this point. The process is not finished, however. It's simply sleeping. To move it forward, it has to be *signaled*. Signaling an Activiti process instance causes it to wake up and proceed executing. Once the process instance is executing again, it will keep executing until it reaches another wait-state or until the process is finished. The Spring Integration gateway takes advantage of this setup and sends a message *to* Spring Integration when the wait-state is entered. As this is a gateway, Spring Integration sends a response.

From the Spring Integration perspective, the request *from* Activiti is an *inbound* message. The inbound message has a header (`ActivitiConstants.WELL_KNOWN_EXECUTION_ID_HEADER_KEY`) that carries the execution ID (the ID that Activiti needs in order to know which process instance to signal). Implementers are free to do with the inbound message what they like—use adapters, hook into all the various Spring Integration endpoints, etc. The only requirement is that a reply message carrying the execution ID be sent on the reply channel configured on the gateway. It doesn't matter when or by whom the reply is sent, so long as that reply message has the execution ID header. From the Spring Integration perspective, the reply is an *outbound* message.

Let's update the Spring configuration to use the Activiti gateway. First, add something like the configuration class shown in Listing 8–47.

Listing 8–47. *Java Configuration for Activiti Gateway*

```
package com.apress.prospringintegration.messageflow.workflow;

import org.activiti.engine.ProcessEngine;
import org.springframework.beans.factory.annotation.Value;
import org.springframework.context.annotation.Bean;
import org.springframework.context.annotation.Configuration;
import org.springframework.integration.MessageChannel;
import org.springframework.integration.activiti.gateway.AsyncActivityBehaviorMessagingGateway;

/**
 * Activiti gateway configuration
 */
@Configuration
@SuppressWarnings("unused")
public class ActivitiGatewayConfiguration extends ActivitiProcessEngineConfiguration {

    // inbound: from Activiti TO Spring Integration
    @Value("#{request}")
    private MessageChannel request;

    // outbound: from Spring Integration TO Activiti
    @Value("#{response}")
    private MessageChannel response;

    @Bean
    public AsyncActivityBehaviorMessagingGateway gateway() throws Exception {

        ProcessEngine engine = processEngine().getObject();

        AsyncActivityBehaviorMessagingGateway gateway =
                new AsyncActivityBehaviorMessagingGateway();
        gateway.setForwardProcessVariablesAsMessageHeaders(true);
        gateway.setProcessEngine(engine);
        gateway.setUpdateProcessVariablesFromReplyMessageHeaders(true);
        gateway.setRequestChannel(request);
        gateway.setReplyChannel(response);
        return gateway;

    }

}
```

In the configuration, you inject two channels—request and response–declared in the XML and then use them to set up an instance of AsyncActivityBehaviorMessagingGateway. The gateway requires a reference to the ProcessEngine you configured previously. The gateway also has one more feature you will see reflected here: it can conveniently propagate process variables as message headers on the request message and propagate messages as process variables on the reply message. To enable both of these behaviors, set the updateProcessVariablesFromReplyMessageHeaders and forwardProcessVariablesAsMessageHeaders headers to true.

Next, you need to configure the Spring Integration channels and have Spring Integration do something with the data. In this example, you will simply have the request come into Spring Integration, visit a simple service-activator endpoint, and send a reply on the response channel. There's no need to even show the service activator here; assume it's a class with a method annotated with `@ServiceActivator` that takes a message with a header under the key `ActivitiConstants.WELL_KNOWN_EXECUTION_ID_HEADER_KEY` and returns a message with that same header and value. The Spring configuration is shown in Listing 8–48.

***Listing 8–48.** Spring Configuration for Activiti Gateway (workflow-gateway.xml)*

```
<?xml version="1.0" encoding="UTF-8"?>
<beans xmlns="http://www.springframework.org/schema/beans"
       xmlns:xsi="http://www.w3.org/2001/XMLSchema-instance"
       xmlns:int="http://www.springframework.org/schema/integration"
       xmlns:context="http://www.springframework.org/schema/context"
       xmlns:jdbc="http://www.springframework.org/schema/jdbc"
       xsi:schemaLocation="http://www.springframework.org/schema/beans
    http://www.springframework.org/schema/beans/spring-beans-3.0.xsd
    http://www.springframework.org/schema/integration
    http://www.springframework.org/schema/integration/spring-integration.xsd
    http://www.springframework.org/schema/context
    http://www.springframework.org/schema/context/spring-context-3.0.xsd
    http://www.springframework.org/schema/jdbc
    http://www.springframework.org/schema/jdbc/spring-jdbc.xsd">

  <context:component-scan
     base-package="com.apress.prospringintegration.messageflow.workflow"/>

  <context:property-placeholder location="workflow.properties"/>

  <int:channel id="request">
    <int:queue capacity="10"/>
  </int:channel>

  <int:service-activator input-channel="request"
                         output-channel="response"
                         ref="loggingServiceActivator">
    <int:poller fixed-rate="1000"/>
  </int:service-activator>

  <int:channel id="response"/>

  <jdbc:embedded-database id="dataSource" type="H2"/>

</beans>
```

The final piece of the puzzle is the BPMN process definition that employs this gateway, as shown in Listing 8–49.

***Listing 8–49.** BPMN Process Definition for Activiti Gateway (gateway.bpmn20.xml)*

```
<?xml version="1.0" encoding="UTF-8"?>
<definitions id="definitions"
             xmlns="http://www.omg.org/spec/BPMN/20100524/MODEL"
             xmlns:xsi="http://www.w3.org/2001/XMLSchema-instance"
             xmlns:activiti="http://activiti.org/bpmn"
             typeLanguage="http://www.w3.org/2001/XMLSchema"
```

```
             expressionLanguage="http://www.w3.org/1999/XPath"
             targetNamespace="http://www.activiti.org/bpmn2.0">

  <process id="sigateway">

    <startEvent id="start"/>

    <sequenceFlow id="sf1" sourceRef="start" targetRef="gw"/>

    <serviceTask id="gw" name="Spring Integration Gateway"
                 activiti:delegateExpression="#{gateway}"/>

    <sequenceFlow id="sf2" sourceRef="gw" targetRef="script"/>

    <scriptTask id="script" name="Execute script" scriptFormat="groovy">
      <script>
        println '...finishing the script task.'
      </script>
    </scriptTask>

    <sequenceFlow id="sf3" sourceRef="script" targetRef="end"/>

    <endEvent id="end"/>

  </process>

</definitions>
```

Did you catch the change? A bit underwhelming, right? The only real difference between this and the first example is that you employ a generic BPMN `serviceTask` element and use the Activiti specific attribute (`activity:delegateExpression`) to employ the gateway bean from Spring. That's it! You can run this in exactly the same way as you did before. Therefore, the sequence of events is as follows:

- The process starts.
- The process enters the `startEvent`.
- The process moves immediately to the `serviceTask` where Activiti invokes your gateway, sending a request message with an `executionID` in it. After the request message is sent, the process stops. From the invoker's perspective, `startProcessInstanceByKey` returns.
- In Spring Integration, the request message enters through the Activiti gateway, travels on the request channel, passes through the `service-activator` and then travels on the `response` channel back to the Activiti gateway.
- In Activiti, the `serviceTask` starts up again, and execution proceeds.
- The `scriptTask` is executed.
- Then, the `endEvent` is reached and the process ultimately terminates.

The result is service orchestration and a clean decoupling of concerns: Activiti takes care of making sure that things happen when they are supposed to, Spring Integration does the heavy lifting, and Activiti guards the process state. You have no doubt already put your business logic in Spring and in Spring Integration, and Spring Integration is a great vehicle to connect Activiti to other systems. Suppose you have a business process that requires notifications (you could use Spring Integration to send e-mail or ping people on Google Talk chat with almost effortless ease!), or communication with another system (you could use Spring Integration to invoke web services).

Summary

In this chapter, you learned that there are several components available for controlling message flows in Spring Integration: message routers determine which downstream channel or channels should receive the message next or at all; message filters decide if the message should be passed to the output channel or not; message splitters break a message into several messages to be processed independently; the message aggregator combines several messages into a single message; and resequencers release messages in a specific order. You have looked at message chain handlers that simplify configuration for a linear sequence of endpoints and message bridges that connect two message channels or adapters. Finally, you've contemplated the times when state must be maintained in an integration, potentially requiring a workflow, and you have explored how Spring Integration may be used with a workflow engine.

CHAPTER 9

Endpoints and Adapters

An endpoint describes how application code communicates with the messaging framework. An endpoint also hides the complexity of interacting with the messaging system, allowing the developer to focus on the business logic instead of the details of how to send and receive messages. In previous chapters, we discussed the many endpoints that connect with directly with the Spring Integration Framework. These endpoints include transformers (discussed in Chapter 7), and routers, splitters, aggregators, and messaging bridges (discussed in Chapter 8). In this chapter we will focus on the endpoints that connect to the message channels, application code, external applications, and services. These include channel adapters, services activators, and messaging gateways. Finally, the topic of how secure and send messages to a secure message channel will be covered.

Messaging Endpoint API

Spring Integration provides a general API that supports sending and consuming messages to and from a message channel. Sending messages is very straightforward, but receiving them can be more complicated. There are two types of message consumers: *polling consumers* and *event-driven consumers*. which will be discussed in this chapter.

Polling and Event-Driven Consumers

A Spring Integration consumer can either pull messages from a channel periodically (using polling), or simply process messages when messages are given to it by the channel. Using polling, the application can control when to receive the messages from the message channel. When an application is busy, it has the option of slowing down the message consumption. However, there is the issue of latency since the messages are polled at a specified rate. The other option is an event-driven consumer, where the application handles the messages as soon as they arrive. Event-driven consumers will have no latency, and a fixed set of concurrent consumers can be used to throttle the load.

Message Assignment vs. Message Grab

When the message consumer is much slower than the message sender, there is a potential for large numbers of messages to queue up in the message channel. One approach to offset this problem is to add additional message consumers to handle the load. A better approach is to use the message dispatcher pattern, which allows a message consumer to receive messages, and delegates the messages to multiple message handlers. By using this pattern, the application can throttle the speed of message consumption. In Spring Integration, both polling and event-driven consumers accept a task executor that can dispatch the messages to separate worker threads to handle messages concurrently (see Figure 9–1). This is known as an executor channel, and was discussed in Chapter 6. More detailed discussion about the task executor can be found in Chapter 16.

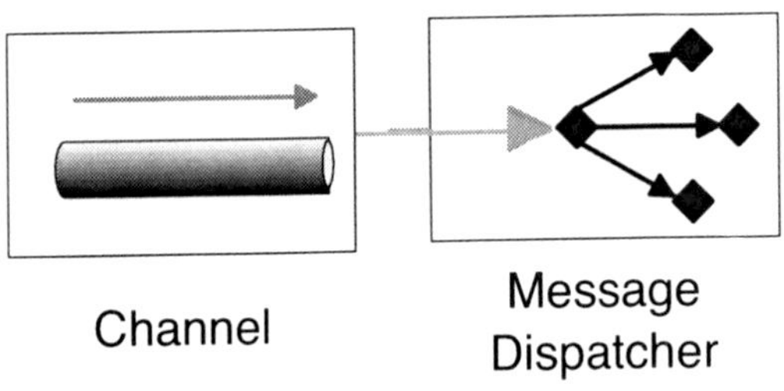

***Figure 9–1.** The Message Dispatcher Dispatches Messages Received from the Message Channel.*

Synchronous and Asynchronous Services

A synchronous endpoint does not return until the downstream processing is finished. On the other hand, a asynchronous endpoint returns immediately, allowing the downstream process to run in another execution thread. It is often difficult to decide if a service endpoint should be exposed synchronously or asynchronously, since different clients may have different requirements. As a result, we would like to support both types of service endpoints. Using service activator, which will be discussed in more detail following, a synchronous service endpoint can be exposed as an asynchronous service endpoint as well. A service activator can be used to connect a message channel to the synchronous service endpoint. As a result, the synchronous client can invoke the application directly, while the asynchronous client can invoke the asynchronous endpoint by sending a message to the message channel.

Enterprise Integration Patterns[1] defines a number of patterns on how to consume a message, but only a few patterns on how to send a message. This is because sending a message from an application to a messaging system is very simple. The application only needs to package the data into a message and send to the message to the channel. However, receiving messages is another story. There are many factors that need to be considered when an application receives a message.

First, in order to receive a message, the application needs to understand how to retrieve a message from the message channel. The application may need to poll the message channel for messages. If the message channel is empty, the application may be blocked until a message arrives, or if the polling times out until the application can process some other business logic. Once the message arrives, the application can handle the message within the same thread or hand it off to a separate thread. To make things more complicated, the application may not poll the message channel, but will instead delegate the message to a dispatcher once it arrives in the message channel.

As discussed in Chapter 8, an endpoint that sends messages is called the message sender or producer, and the endpoint that receives messages is called the message receiver or consumer. Message endpoints can be defined similarly. A message endpoint that receives messages from a message channel is called the *inbound message endpoint*. A message endpoint that sends messages to a message channel is called the *outbound message endpoint*. Both the inbound and outbound message endpoints can be polling or event-driven.

---

[1] Gregor Hohpe op. cit.

The polling endpoint will send messages to the message channel periodically or receive messages from the message channel by polling. Alternatively, the event-driven endpoint will send messages to the message channel when it needs to, or receive messages from the message channel once a message has been sent.

Polling Consumers

Spring Integration enables two applications to communicate with each other via a message channel. This decoupling also allows the two applications processes to happen at different speeds (see Figure 9–2).

Figure 9–2. *Application Decoupling via a Message Channel*

For example, assume application B is a very busy system and has limited resources. If application A processes and produces messages faster than application B can handle, application B will be overloaded. In order to avoid this, application B needs to stop consuming messages when it is too busy. Depending on the type and capacity of the message channel queue, application A may fill up the message channel queue and block until the queue is freed up by application B.

Polling can be used as a throttling mechanism because the receiving application has control over when to consume messages from the messaging system. When the application is busy or short of resources, it has the option to stop consuming messages. Spring Integration implements polling by using the class `org.springframework.integration.endpoint.PollingConsumer`. The `PollingConsumer` interface defines an endpoint that interacts a message channel; this channel implements the `org.springframework.integration.core.PollableChannel` interface.

In Chapter 6, messages were received from `QueueChannel` by directly calling the `PollableChannel`'s `receive` method. Let's modify the example used in Chapter 6 to use a `PollingConsumer`. Listing 9–1 is the `Ticket` model class, and Listing 9–2 shows the generator class that produces a list of `Ticket` objects.

Listing 9–1. *Ticket.java*

```
package com.apress.prospringintegration.endpoints.core;

import java.util.Calendar;

public class Ticket
{
    public enum Priority
    {
        low,
        medium,
        high,
        emergency
    }

    private long ticketId;
    private Calendar issueDateTime;
    private String description;
    private Priority priority;
```

```
    public Ticket()
    {
    }

    public long getTicketId()
    {
        return ticketId;
    }

    public void setTicketId(long ticketId)
    {
        this.ticketId = ticketId;
    }

    public Calendar getIssueDateTime()
    {
        return issueDateTime;
    }

    public void setIssueDateTime(Calendar issueDateTime)
    {
        this.issueDateTime = issueDateTime;
    }

    public String getDescription()
    {
        return description;
    }

    public void setDescription(String description)
    {
        this.description = description;
    }

    public Priority getPriority()
    {
        return priority;
    }

    public void setPriority(Priority priority)
    {
        this.priority = priority;
    }

    public String toString()
    {
        return String.format("Ticket# %d: [%s] %s", ticketId, priority, description);
    }
}
```

Listing 9–2. *TicketGenerator.java*

```
package com.apress.prospringintegration.endpoints.core;

import com.apress.prospringintegration.endpoints.core.Ticket.Priority;
import org.springframework.stereotype.Component;

import java.util.ArrayList;
import java.util.GregorianCalendar;
import java.util.List;

@Component
public class TicketGenerator {
    private long nextTicketId;

    public TicketGenerator() {
        this.nextTicketId = 1000L;
    }

    public List<Ticket> createTickets() {
        List<Ticket> tickets = new ArrayList<Ticket>();

        tickets.add(createLowPriorityTicket());
        tickets.add(createLowPriorityTicket());
        tickets.add(createLowPriorityTicket());
        tickets.add(createLowPriorityTicket());
        tickets.add(createLowPriorityTicket());
        tickets.add(createMediumPriorityTicket());
        tickets.add(createMediumPriorityTicket());
        tickets.add(createMediumPriorityTicket());
        tickets.add(createMediumPriorityTicket());
        tickets.add(createMediumPriorityTicket());
        tickets.add(createHighPriorityTicket());
        tickets.add(createHighPriorityTicket());
        tickets.add(createHighPriorityTicket());
        tickets.add(createHighPriorityTicket());
        tickets.add(createHighPriorityTicket());
        tickets.add(createEmergencyTicket());
        tickets.add(createEmergencyTicket());
        tickets.add(createEmergencyTicket());
        tickets.add(createEmergencyTicket());
        tickets.add(createEmergencyTicket());

        return tickets;
    }

    Ticket createEmergencyTicket() {
        return createTicket(Priority.emergency,
                "Urgent problem. Fix immediately or revenue will be lost!");
    }

    Ticket createHighPriorityTicket() {
        return createTicket(Priority.high,
                "Serious issue. Fix immediately.");
```

```
    }

    Ticket createMediumPriorityTicket() {
        return createTicket(Priority.medium,
                "There is an issue; take a look whenever you have time.");
    }

    Ticket createLowPriorityTicket() {
        return createTicket(Priority.low,
                "Some minor problems have been found.");
    }


    Ticket createTicket(Priority priority, String description) {
        Ticket ticket = new Ticket();
        ticket.setTicketId(nextTicketId++);
        ticket.setPriority(priority);
        ticket.setIssueDateTime(GregorianCalendar.getInstance());
        ticket.setDescription(description);

        return ticket;
    }
}
```

Listing 9–3 shows the `TicketMessageHandler` that implements the `org.springframework.integration.core.MessageHandler` interface. For every received message from the message channel, the `handleMessage` method will be invoked. In the current implementation, the `Ticket` object will be extracted from the message, and the content of the `Ticket` will be displayed to the console.

Listing 9–3. *TicketMessageHandler.java*

```
package com.apress.prospringintegration.endpoints.eventdrivenconsumer;

import com.apress.prospringintegration.endpoints.core.Ticket;
import org.springframework.integration.Message;
import org.springframework.integration.MessageDeliveryException;
import org.springframework.integration.MessageHandlingException;
import org.springframework.integration.MessageRejectedException;
import org.springframework.integration.core.MessageHandler;
import org.springframework.stereotype.Component;

@Component
public class TicketMessageHandler implements MessageHandler {

    @Override
    public void handleMessage(Message<?> message)
            throws MessageHandlingException, MessageDeliveryException {
        Object payload = message.getPayload();

        if (payload instanceof Ticket) {
            handleTicket((Ticket) payload);
        } else {
            throw new MessageRejectedException(message,
                    "Unknown data type has been received.");
```

```
        }
    }

    void handleTicket(Ticket ticket) {
        System.out.println("Received ticket - " + ticket.toString());
    }
}
```

The ProblemReporter class creates a message with the payload Ticket and sends the message to the message channel, as shown in Listing 9–4.

Listing 9–4. *ProblemReporter.java*

```
package com.apress.prospringintegration.endpoints.pollingconsumer;

import com.apress.prospringintegration.endpoints.core.Ticket;
import org.springframework.beans.factory.annotation.Value;
import org.springframework.integration.channel.QueueChannel;
import org.springframework.integration.support.MessageBuilder;
import org.springframework.stereotype.Component;

@Component
public class ProblemReporter {

    private QueueChannel channel;

    public ProblemReporter() {
    }

    @Value("#{ticketChannel}")
    public void setChannel(QueueChannel channel) {
        this.channel = channel;
    }

    void openTicket(Ticket ticket) {
        channel.send(MessageBuilder.withPayload(ticket).build());
        System.out.println("Ticket Sent - " + ticket.toString());
    }
}
```

The Spring configuration file is shown in Listing 9–5. Component scanning is used for the ticket generator and message handling classes. A queue channel named ticketChannel is configured with a queue size of 50 messages.

Listing 9–5. *polling-consumer.xml*

```
<?xml version="1.0" encoding="UTF-8"?>
<beans xmlns="http://www.springframework.org/schema/beans"
       xmlns:xsi="http://www.w3.org/2001/XMLSchema-instance"
       xmlns:int="http://www.springframework.org/schema/integration"
       xmlns:context="http://www.springframework.org/schema/context"
       xsi:schemaLocation="http://www.springframework.org/schema/integration
    http://www.springframework.org/schema/integration/spring-integration-2.0.xsd
    http://www.springframework.org/schema/beans
    http://www.springframework.org/schema/beans/spring-beans-3.0.xsd
```

```
    http://www.springframework.org/schema/context
    http://www.springframework.org/schema/context/spring-context-3.0.xsd">

  <context:component-scan
     base-package="com.apress.prospringintegration.endpoints.core"/>

  <context:component-scan
     base-package="com.apress.prospringintegration.endpoints.pollingconsumer"/>

  <int:channel id="ticketChannel">
    <int:queue capacity="50"/>
  </int:channel>

</beans>
```

The main class using the PollingConsumer is shown in Listing 9–6. The PollingConsumer will poll the incoming message channel. Once a message has been polled from the message channel, the message will be delegated to the TicketMessageHandler instance. The PollingConsumer requires a trigger in order to poll messages defined by the org.springframework.scheduling.Trigger interface. There are two Trigger implementations: org.springframework.scheduling.support.PeriodicTrigger and org.springframework.scheduling.support.CronTrigger.

In this example, the PeriodicTrigger implementation is used. The first trigger will happen after 5000 ms, and each of following triggers will wait 1,000 ms between each poll. The time actually starts after the first completion of message handling if setFixedRate is false; otherwise, the time will be measured exactly between each scheduled polling.

Listing 9–6. *Main.java for Polling Consumer*

```
package com.apress.prospringintegration.endpoints.pollingconsumer;

import com.apress.prospringintegration.endpoints.core.Ticket;
import com.apress.prospringintegration.endpoints.core.TicketGenerator;
import org.springframework.context.support.ClassPathXmlApplicationContext;
import org.springframework.integration.channel.QueueChannel;
import org.springframework.integration.endpoint.PollingConsumer;
import org.springframework.integration.scheduling.PollerMetadata;
import org.springframework.scheduling.support.PeriodicTrigger;

import java.util.List;

public class Main {
    private final static int RECEIVE_TIMEOUT = 1000;

    public static void main(String[] args) {
        String contextName = "polling-consumer.xml";

        ClassPathXmlApplicationContext applicationContext =
                new ClassPathXmlApplicationContext(contextName);
        applicationContext.start();

        ProblemReporter problemReporter =
                applicationContext.getBean(ProblemReporter.class);
        TicketMessageHandler ticketMessageHandler =
                applicationContext.getBean(TicketMessageHandler.class);
```

```
        TicketGenerator ticketGenerator =
                applicationContext.getBean(TicketGenerator.class);

        QueueChannel channel =
                applicationContext.getBean("ticketChannel", QueueChannel.class);

        // Define the polling consumer
        PollingConsumer ticketConsumer =
                new PollingConsumer(channel, ticketMessageHandler);
        ticketConsumer.setReceiveTimeout(RECEIVE_TIMEOUT);
        ticketConsumer.setBeanFactory(applicationContext);

        // Set up the poller using periodic trigger
        PeriodicTrigger periodicTrigger = new PeriodicTrigger(1000);
        periodicTrigger.setInitialDelay(5000);
        periodicTrigger.setFixedRate(false);

        PollerMetadata pollerMetadata = new PollerMetadata();
        pollerMetadata.setTrigger(periodicTrigger);
        pollerMetadata.setMaxMessagesPerPoll(3);

        ticketConsumer.setPollerMetadata(pollerMetadata);

        // Starts the polling consumer in the other thread
        ticketConsumer.start();

        // Generates messages and sends to the channel
        List<Ticket> tickets = ticketGenerator.createTickets();
        while (true) {
            for (Ticket ticket : tickets) {
                problemReporter.openTicket(ticket);
            }
        }

    }

}
```

The PollingConsumer also can be polled based on a more complex schedule by using CronTrigger. The CronTrigger implementation supports cron expressions. In the following example, ticketConsumer will poll every minute.

```
CronTrigger cronTrigger = new CronTrigger("0 * * * * *");
```

The cron expression contains six space-separated fields: Second, Minute, Hour, Day of Month, Month, and Day of Week.

```
/* Trigger every hour after business hour (after 6:00pm) */
new CronTrigger("* 0 19-00 * * *");

/* Trigger between 09:00am to 05:00pm 15 minutes past every hour only on Monday to Friday */
new CronTrigger("* 15 9-17 * * MON-FRI");
```

The PollingConsumer also supports batch polling. By using the setMaxMessagesPerPoll method, PollingConsumer will keep polling the message channel until reaching the specific value or a null value.

By combining the setMaxMessagesPerPoll method with the setReceiveTimeout method, there will be some interesting behavior. Considering the following code examples:

```
// Example 1
PollerMetadata pollerMetadata = new PollerMetadata();
pollerMetadata.setTrigger(periodicTrigger);
pollerMetadata.setMaxMessagesPerPoll(10);
ticketConsumer.setPollerMetadata(pollerMetadata);
ticketConsumer.setReceiveTimeout(100);

// Example 2
PollerMetadata pollerMetadata = new PollerMetadata();
pollerMetadata.setTrigger(periodicTrigger);
pollerMetadata.setMaxMessagesPerPoll(100);
ticketConsumer.setPollerMetadata(pollerMetadata);
ticketConsumer.setReceiveTimeout(10);
```

Assume that there are 1,000 messages in the message channel and it is waiting for polling. The first example has a 100-ms receive timeout and maximum ten messages per poll. This means that the endpoint will receive ten messages per second; in other words, it will take 1 second to drain the message channel. In the second example, the PollingConsumer has a 10-ms receive timeout and maximum 100 messages per poll. This means that the endpoint will take 100 ms to drain the message channel.

The PollingConsumer needs at least a single thread to perform message polling and handling. However, the PollingConsumer can delegate the message to the message handler in the separated threads by using the setTaskExecutor method with the Spring org.springframework.core.task.TaskExecutor interface. It also supports Spring managed transactions by calling the setTransactionManager method.

Event-Driven Consumers

Although a polling consumer is good for throttling when the receiving application is too busy, it involves active polling, so resources are wasted if there is no message to consume from the message channel. Event-driven consumers are very different from polling consumers. Event-driven consumers will handle a message as soon as the message has been delivered from the message channel. Instead of actively polling, an event-driven consumer does nothing but wait for the messages coming from the message channel. The org.springframework.integration.endpoint.EventDrivenConsumer only supports channels that implement the org.springframework.integration.core.SubscribableChannel interface, such as DirectChannel, ExecutorChannel, PublishSubscribeChannel, and SubscribableJmsChannel. In Chapter 6, the message receiver was implemented by calling SubscribableChannel's subscribe method.

The problem reporter example will be modified to use an event-driven consumer. The ProblemReporter class shown in Listing 9–7 is modified to use DirectChannel.

Listing 9–7. *ProblemReporter.java for Event-Driven Consumer*

```
package com.apress.prospringintegration.endpoints.eventdrivenconsumer;

import com.apress.prospringintegration.endpoints.core.Ticket;
import org.springframework.beans.factory.annotation.Value;
import org.springframework.integration.channel.DirectChannel;
import org.springframework.integration.message.GenericMessage;
import org.springframework.stereotype.Component;

@Component
```

```
public class ProblemReporter {
    private DirectChannel channel;

    public ProblemReporter() {
    }

    @Value("#{ticketChannel}")
    public void setChannel(DirectChannel channel) {
        this.channel = channel;
    }

    void openTicket(Ticket ticket) {
        channel.send(new GenericMessage<Ticket>(ticket));
        System.out.println("Ticket Sent - " + ticket.toString());
    }
}
```

The Spring configuration file is shown in Listing 9–8. Again, component scanning is used to configure the required classes.

Listing 9–8. *Spring Configuration for Event-Driven Consumer event-driven-consumer.xml*

```
<?xml version="1.0" encoding="UTF-8"?>
<beans xmlns="http://www.springframework.org/schema/beans"
       xmlns:xsi="http://www.w3.org/2001/XMLSchema-instance"
       xmlns:int="http://www.springframework.org/schema/integration"
       xmlns:context="http://www.springframework.org/schema/context"
       xsi:schemaLocation="http://www.springframework.org/schema/integration
    http://www.springframework.org/schema/integration/spring-integration-2.0.xsd
    http://www.springframework.org/schema/beans
    http://www.springframework.org/schema/beans/spring-beans-3.0.xsd
    http://www.springframework.org/schema/context
    http://www.springframework.org/schema/context/spring-context-3.0.xsd">

  <context:component-scan
      base-package="com.apress.prospringintegration.endpoints.core"/>

  <context:component-scan
      base-package="com.apress.prospringintegration.endpoints.eventdrivenconsumer"/>

  <int:channel id="ticketChannel">
    <int:dispatcher failover="true" load-balancer="none"/>
  </int:channel>

</beans>
```

The event-driven consumer `main` class is shown in Listing 9–9. A reference to the direct channel `ticketChannel` and to the message handler `TicketMessageHandler` class is passed to the `EventDrivenConsumer`. Once a message has arrived from the message channel, the message will be dispatched to the provided message handler. There is no need to define a trigger since the message is pushed to the message consumer instead of polled.

Listing 9–9. Main.java for Event-Driven Consumer

```
package com.apress.prospringintegration.endpoints.eventdrivenconsumer;

import com.apress.prospringintegration.endpoints.core.Ticket;
import com.apress.prospringintegration.endpoints.core.TicketGenerator;
import org.springframework.context.support.ClassPathXmlApplicationContext;
import org.springframework.integration.channel.DirectChannel;
import org.springframework.integration.endpoint.EventDrivenConsumer;

import java.util.List;

public class Main {

    public static void main(String[] args) {
        String contextName = "event-driven-consumer.xml";

        ClassPathXmlApplicationContext applicationContext =
                new ClassPathXmlApplicationContext(contextName);
        applicationContext.start();

        ProblemReporter problemReporter =
                applicationContext.getBean(ProblemReporter.class);
        TicketGenerator ticketGenerator =
                applicationContext.getBean(TicketGenerator.class);
        TicketMessageHandler ticketMessageHandler =
                applicationContext.getBean(TicketMessageHandler.class);

        DirectChannel channel =
                applicationContext.getBean("ticketChannel", DirectChannel.class);

        EventDrivenConsumer eventDrivenConsumer =
                new EventDrivenConsumer(channel, ticketMessageHandler);
        eventDrivenConsumer.start();

        List<Ticket> tickets = ticketGenerator.createTickets();

        int count = 0;
        while (count++ < 5) {
            for (Ticket ticket : tickets) {
                problemReporter.openTicket(ticket);
            }
        }
    }
}
```

ConsumerEndpointFactoryBean

So far, the examples have required knowing of the type of messaging channel in order to decide which type of consumer to use. Spring Integration also provides an endpoint factory `org.springframework.integration.config.ConsumerEndpointFactoryBean` that works for any kind of message channel. Simply provide a MessageChannel, MessageHandler, and (if polling is required) PollerMetatdata reference, and this factory class will do the rest.

To demonstrate the power of the ConsumerEndpointFactoryBean factory, the previous event-driven consumer example will be modified to use the factory class. Minimal changes are required to the event-driven consumer example to use the factory. Java configuration provides a simple means of creating the endpoint, as shown in Listing 9–10. ConsumerEndpointFactoryBean is instantiated, and a reference is passed to the MessageChannel ticketChannel and the MessageHandler ticketMessageHandler. The PollerMetadata reference is not required since this is an event-driven endpoint.

Listing 9–10. *ConsumerEndpointFactoryBean Example Java Configuration*

```
package com.apress.prospringintegration.endpoints.consumerendpointfactory;

import org.springframework.beans.factory.annotation.Value;
import org.springframework.context.annotation.Bean;
import org.springframework.context.annotation.Configuration;
import org.springframework.integration.MessageChannel;
import org.springframework.integration.config.ConsumerEndpointFactoryBean;
import org.springframework.integration.core.MessageHandler;

@Configuration
public class ConsumerEndpointConfiguration {

    @Value("#{ticketChannel}")
    private MessageChannel inputChannel;

    @Value("#{ticketMessageHandler}")
    private MessageHandler handler;

    @Bean
    public ConsumerEndpointFactoryBean consumerEndpoint() {
        ConsumerEndpointFactoryBean factoryBean = new ConsumerEndpointFactoryBean();
        factoryBean.setInputChannel(inputChannel);
        factoryBean.setHandler(handler);
        // Need to set pollerMetadata for polling consumer
        //factoryBean.setPollerMetadata(pollerMetadata);
        return factoryBean;
    }
}
```

Using Java configuration only requires adding the configuration class to the component-scanning package path, as shown in Listing 9–11. The only other elements in the Spring configuration file are component scanning for the message-sending components and the message channel itself.

Listing 9–11. *ConsumerEndpointFactoryBean Spring Configuration consumer-endpoint-factory.xml*

```
<?xml version="1.0" encoding="UTF-8"?>
<beans xmlns="http://www.springframework.org/schema/beans"
       xmlns:xsi="http://www.w3.org/2001/XMLSchema-instance"
       xmlns:int="http://www.springframework.org/schema/integration"
       xmlns:context="http://www.springframework.org/schema/context"
       xsi:schemaLocation="http://www.springframework.org/schema/integration
    http://www.springframework.org/schema/integration/spring-integration-2.0.xsd
    http://www.springframework.org/schema/beans
```

```
    http://www.springframework.org/schema/beans/spring-beans-3.0.xsd
    http://www.springframework.org/schema/context
    http://www.springframework.org/schema/context/spring-context-3.0.xsd">

  <context:component-scan
      base-package="com.apress.prospringintegration.endpoints.core"/>

  <context:component-scan
      base-package="com.apress.prospringintegration.endpoints.consumerendpointfactory"/>

  <int:channel id="ticketChannel"/>

</beans>
```

The ConsumerEndpointFactoryBean example main class is shown in Listing 9–12. The only code required for creating the endpoint are the calls to create and start the Spring context. The rest of the code is for supporting sending the message. The most important feature of the ConsumerEndpointFactoryBean factory is that it works for any type of message channel implementation.

Listing 9–12. *ConsumerEndpointFactoryBean Example main Class*

```
package com.apress.prospringintegration.endpoints.consumerendpointfactory;

import com.apress.prospringintegration.endpoints.core.Ticket;
import com.apress.prospringintegration.endpoints.core.TicketGenerator;
import org.springframework.context.support.ClassPathXmlApplicationContext;
import org.springframework.integration.channel.DirectChannel;
import org.springframework.integration.endpoint.EventDrivenConsumer;

import java.util.List;

public class Main {

    public static void main(String[] args) {
        ClassPathXmlApplicationContext applicationContext =
                new ClassPathXmlApplicationContext("consumer-endpoint-factory.xml");
        applicationContext.start();

        ProblemReporter problemReporter =
                applicationContext.getBean(ProblemReporter.class);
        TicketGenerator ticketGenerator =
                applicationContext.getBean(TicketGenerator.class);

        List<Ticket> tickets = ticketGenerator.createTickets();

        int count = 0;
        while (count++ < 5) {
            for (Ticket ticket : tickets) {
                problemReporter.openTicket(ticket);
            }
        }
    }
}
```

Service Activator

A service activator is a Spring Integration generic endpoint that handles incoming messages (see Figure 9–3). A service activator could be a method within a regular Java object; it does not have to implement the message handler using the MessageHandler interface.

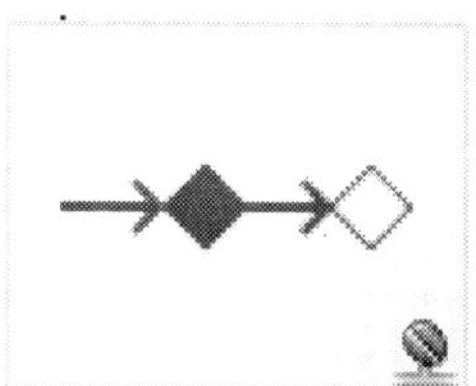

Figure 9–3. *Service Activator*

Consider the same ticketing system example just discussed. Ticket objects are created by the TicketGenerator class, and the Ticket objects will be packaged into messages and sent to the message channel ticketChannel by the ProblemReporter class. Instead of using a PollingConsumer or EventDrivenConsumer, a service activator will be used to receive messages from the ticketChannel. In addition, an internal ticket counter will be added, which will be incremented for each received Ticket message. The ticket counter value will be sent to the counterChannel message channel and will be handled by the another service activator (see Figure 9–4).

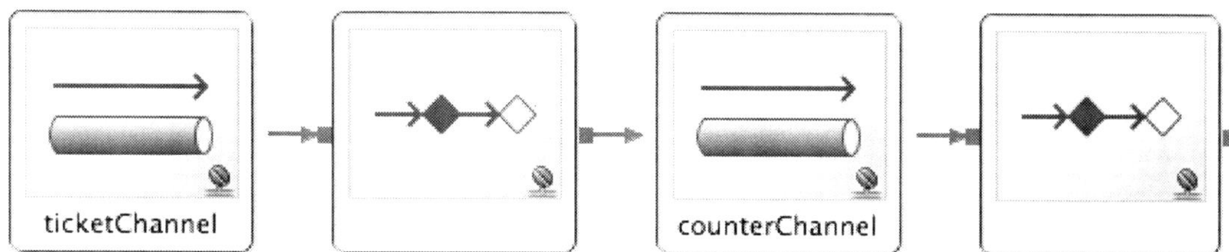

Figure 9–4. *Ticket Counter Service Activator*

The Ticket, TicketGenerator, and ProblemReporter classes are the same as the previous examples. The TicketReceiver instance, however, is modified to become a service activator, as shown in Listing 9–13. A service activator can be any method, which is annotated by @ServiceActivator or specified by the service activator configuration. The method handleTicket will handle any message directed at this service activator.

Listing 9–13. *Service Activator Class TicketReceiver.java*

```
package com.apress.prospringintegration.serviceactivator;

import org.springframework.beans.factory.annotation.Value;
import org.springframework.integration.MessageChannel;
import org.springframework.integration.annotation.ServiceActivator;
import org.springframework.integration.support.MessageBuilder;
```

```
import org.springframework.stereotype.Component;

@Component
public class TicketReceiver {

    private MessageChannel counterChannel;
    private long counter;

    @Value("#{counterChannel}")
    public void setCounterChannel(MessageChannel counterChannel) {
        this.counterChannel = counterChannel;
    }

    @ServiceActivator
    public void handleTicket(Ticket ticket) {
        System.out.println("Received ticket - " + ticket.toString());
        counterChannel.send(MessageBuilder.withPayload(new Long(counter++)).build());
    }
}
```

In the same manner, a service activator class, Counter, is created using the @ServiceActivator annotation, as shown in Listing 9–14. The method handleCounter will handle any message directed at this service activator.

Listing 9–14. *Service Activator Class Counter.java*

```
package com.apress.prospringintegration.serviceactivator;

import org.springframework.integration.annotation.ServiceActivator;
import org.springframework.stereotype.Component;

@Component
public class Counter {
    @ServiceActivator
    public void handleCounter(Long count) {
        System.out.println(count.toString());
    }
}
```

The service activator is defined in the Spring configuration file, as shown as Listing 9–15. The service activator requires an input message channel and an optional output message channel. If the method is annotated by using the @ServiceActivator annotation, a ref value to the service activator object is needed; otherwise, a method value needs to be provided to specify the service activator method.

Listing 9–15. *service-activator.xml*

```
<?xml version="1.0" encoding="UTF-8"?>
<beans xmlns="http://www.springframework.org/schema/beans"
       xmlns:xsi="http://www.w3.org/2001/XMLSchema-instance"
       xmlns:context="http://www.springframework.org/schema/context"
       xmlns:int="http://www.springframework.org/schema/integration"
       xsi:schemaLocation="http://www.springframework.org/schema/integration
    http://www.springframework.org/schema/integration/spring-integration-2.0.xsd
    http://www.springframework.org/schema/beans
```

```
    http://www.springframework.org/schema/beans/spring-beans-3.0.xsd
    http://www.springframework.org/schema/context
    http://www.springframework.org/schema/context/spring-context-3.0.xsd">

  <context:component-scan base-package="com.apress.prospringintegration.serviceactivator"/>

  <int:channel id="ticketChannel"/>
  <int:channel id="counterChannel"/>

  <int:service-activator input-channel="ticketChannel"
                         output-channel="counterChannel"
                         ref="ticketReceiver"/>

  <int:service-activator input-channel="counterChannel"
                         ref="counter"/>

</beans>
```

The main class for the service activator example is shown in Listing 9–16. The Spring context will be created, and messages with the Ticket payload will be published to the ticketChannel message channel. From there, the message will hit the ticketReceiver service activator, where the Ticket payload details will be logged to the console. Then the total number of tickets handled so far will be publish to the counterChannel message channel. The counter service activator will then log the total count.

Listing 9–16. *Service Activator Example main Class*

```
package com.apress.prospringintegration.serviceactivator;

import org.springframework.context.support.ClassPathXmlApplicationContext;

import java.util.List;

public class Main {

    public static void main(String[] args)
            throws Exception {
        String contextName = "service-activator.xml";

        ClassPathXmlApplicationContext applicationContext =
                new ClassPathXmlApplicationContext(contextName);
        applicationContext.start();

        ProblemReporter problemReporter =
                applicationContext.getBean(ProblemReporter.class);
        TicketGenerator ticketGenerator =
                applicationContext.getBean(TicketGenerator.class);

        while (true) {
            List<Ticket> tickets = ticketGenerator.createTickets();
            for (Ticket ticket : tickets) {
                problemReporter.openTicket(ticket);
            }
```

```
                Thread.sleep(500);
            }
        }
}
```

Spring Integration Adapters

The adapter is the most important component for enterprise system integration. As discussed in Chapter 1, most corporations contain a variety of applications, technologies, and processes across the enterprise. An integration must be able to connect with disparate applications and services potentially using different communication protocols and underlying technologies. Adapters provide the bridge between integration framework and the external systems and services. Adapters can either be inbound or outbound as shown in Figure 9–5.

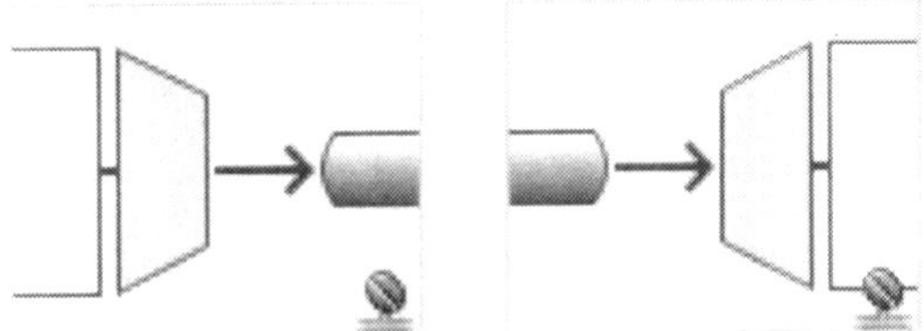

Figure 9–5. *Inbound and Outbond Channel Adapters*

Spring Integration contains several out-of-the-box adapters to support different kinds of protocols and technologies, including file, JDBC, JMD, web services, and mail adapters. In addition, Spring Integration provides an adapter framework to support adding additional endpoints not supported by current version.

File System Adapters

Other than TCP/IP, the file system provides one of the easiest ways to share data across multiple applications. The applications create files in a shared file system and share the data by consuming the files. Chapter 11 will discussed file adapters in detail.

Database (JDBC) Adapters

Many applications share information by storing the data in a database. Almost every organization has a database server; as a result, this is an important adapter for implementing an enterprise integration, and will be discussed in Chapter 11.

JMS Adapters

JMS is currently the most common messaging protocol for Java applications. The applications connect to a message broker and exchange data/events using messages. Due to the nature of messaging system, JMS allows applications to communicate asynchronously. Spring Integration provides a JMS adapter as well as native support for backing the message channels with a JMS message broker. The JMS adapter will be discussed in Chapter 12.

Web Services Adapters

Web services are the basis of service-oriented architecture (SOA). Web services support includes HTTP-RPC, SOAP, or REST. The applications exchange information by calling a web services endpoint. The web services adapter will be discussed in Chapter 14.

Custom Adapters

Spring Integration provides adapters for the most common communication protocols and systems, but there will come a time when the out-of-the-box adapters do not meet your present integration needs. For this, Spring Integration provides a framework for creating your own custom adapter. Custom adapters will be discussed in detail in Chapter 15.

Configuring an Adapter Through the XML Namespace

Let's modify the ticketing system example to use channel adapters as shown in Figure 9–6.

Figure 9–6. Inbound and Outbound Channel Adapters Connecting ticketChannel

There are no changes required for the `Ticket`, `TicketGenerator`, or `TicketMessageHandler` classes. However, the `ProblemReporter` class must be modified as shown in Listing 9–17. The `openTickets` method is modified to return a `Ticket` instead of a `Message` instance.

Listing 9–17. ProblemReporter.java

```
package com.apress.prospringintegration.adapters;

import org.springframework.beans.factory.annotation.Autowired;
import org.springframework.stereotype.Component;

import java.util.List;

@Component
public class ProblemReporter {

    @Autowired
    private TicketGenerator ticketGenerator;
    private List<Ticket> tickets;

    public Ticket openTickets() {
        if (tickets == null) {
```

```
            tickets = ticketGenerator.createTickets();
        }

        Ticket ticket = tickets.remove(0);
        System.out.println("Ticket Sent - " + ticket.toString());

        return ticket;
    }
}
```

Instead of sending the ticket messages into the message channel directly, the modified version only creates the Ticket bean by using the openTickets method. In order to integrate the ProblemReporter class into the messaging framework, an inbound channel adapter is used, as shown in the Spring configuration file in Listing 9–18.

Listing 9–18. *Spring Configuration for Channel Adapter Example adapters.xml*

```
<?xml version="1.0" encoding="UTF-8"?>
<beans xmlns="http://www.springframework.org/schema/beans"
       xmlns:xsi="http://www.w3.org/2001/XMLSchema-instance"
       xmlns:int="http://www.springframework.org/schema/integration"
       xmlns:context="http://www.springframework.org/schema/context"
       xsi:schemaLocation="http://www.springframework.org/schema/integration
    http://www.springframework.org/schema/integration/spring-integration-2.0.xsd
    http://www.springframework.org/schema/beans
    http://www.springframework.org/schema/beans/spring-beans-3.0.xsd
    http://www.springframework.org/schema/context
    http://www.springframework.org/schema/context/spring-context-3.0.xsd">

  <context:component-scan base-package="com.apress.prospringintegration.adapters"/>

  <int:channel id="ticketChannel">
    <int:queue capacity="50"/>
  </int:channel>

  <int:inbound-channel-adapter channel="ticketChannel"
                               ref="problemReporter"
                               method="openTickets">
    <int:poller>
      <int:interval-trigger interval="500"/>
    </int:poller>
  </int:inbound-channel-adapter>

  <int:outbound-channel-adapter channel="ticketChannel"
                                ref="ticketMessageHandler"
                                method="handleMessage">
    <int:poller>
      <int:interval-trigger interval="1000"/>
    </int:poller>
  </int:outbound-channel-adapter>

</beans>
```

The inbound message endpoint will invoke the `openTickets` method on the `problemReporter` bean every 1,000 ms, and send the returned `Ticket` instance as a message payload to the `ticketChannel` channel. Similar to the `PollingConsumer`, the `poller` within the inbound channel adapter can be replaced by a `CronTrigger` for more complex polling schedules.

```
<inbound-channel-adapter ref="problemReporter" method="openTickets" channel="ticketChannel">
    <poller cron="* 1 * * * MON-FRI"/>
</inbound-channel-adapter>
```

The outbound message endpoint is very similar to the inbound message endpoint. If the channel type is `PollableChannel`, `PollingConsumer` will be used as the outbound endpoint; if the channel type is `SubscribableChannel`, `EventDrivenConsumer` will be used, and a `poller` will not be required. In this example, `ticketChannel` is configured as a `PollableChannel`, requiring the additional `poller` element.

The channel adapter `main` class is shown in Listing 9–19. This class simply loads the Spring context to start up the channel adapters. The inbound channel adapter will publish a message to the `ticketChannel` message channel. In turn, the outbound adapter will receive the message from `ticketChannel` and log the `Ticket` payload to the console using the message handler class `TicketMessageHandler`.

Listing 9–19. *Main.java for the Channel Adapter*

```
package com.apress.prospringintegration.adapters;

import org.springframework.context.support.ClassPathXmlApplicationContext;

public class Main {

    public static void main(String[] args) {
        ClassPathXmlApplicationContext applicationContext =
                new ClassPathXmlApplicationContext("adapters.xml");
        applicationContext.start();
    }
}
```

Configuring Adapters with STS

Instead of hand-coding the Spring configuration file, we can use SpringSource Tool Suite (STS) 2.5.2 to define channel adapters via its graphical interface. For this example, STS must be installed on your computer. STS can be downloaded from `www.springsource.com/products/springsource-tool-suite-download`. More information about STS can be found in Chapter 5.

1. From the STS menu, select File ➤ New ➤ Spring Template Project. Select Simple Spring Utility Project, and then click the Next button. Enter a project name, such as `sts-example`, and a package name of `com.apress.prospringintegration`, and then click Finish. This will create a simple Spring project and the Spring configuration file `app-context.xml` in the directory `src/main/resources`.

2. Next, open the Spring configuration file `app-context.xml` by double-clicking in the Package Explorer. Click the Namespaces tab and add the Spring Integration namespace, as shown in Figure 9–7.

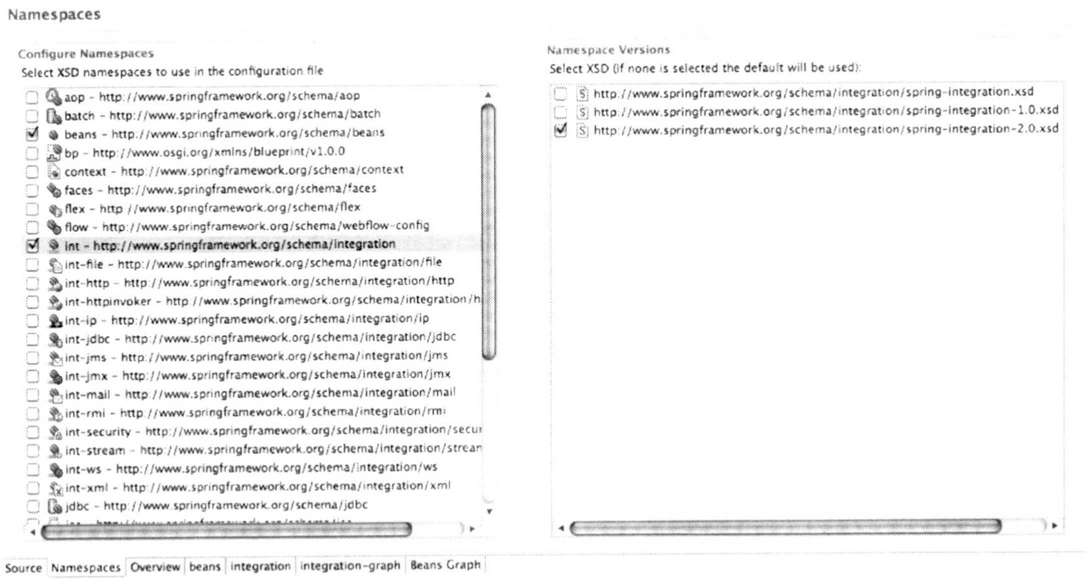

Figure 9–7. Adding the Spring Integration 2.0 Namespace

3. After adding the Spring Integration namespace, the integration and integration-graph tabs will appear, as shown in Figure 9–8. Next, switch to the integration-graph tab and create a channel by dragging the channel icon to the workspace.

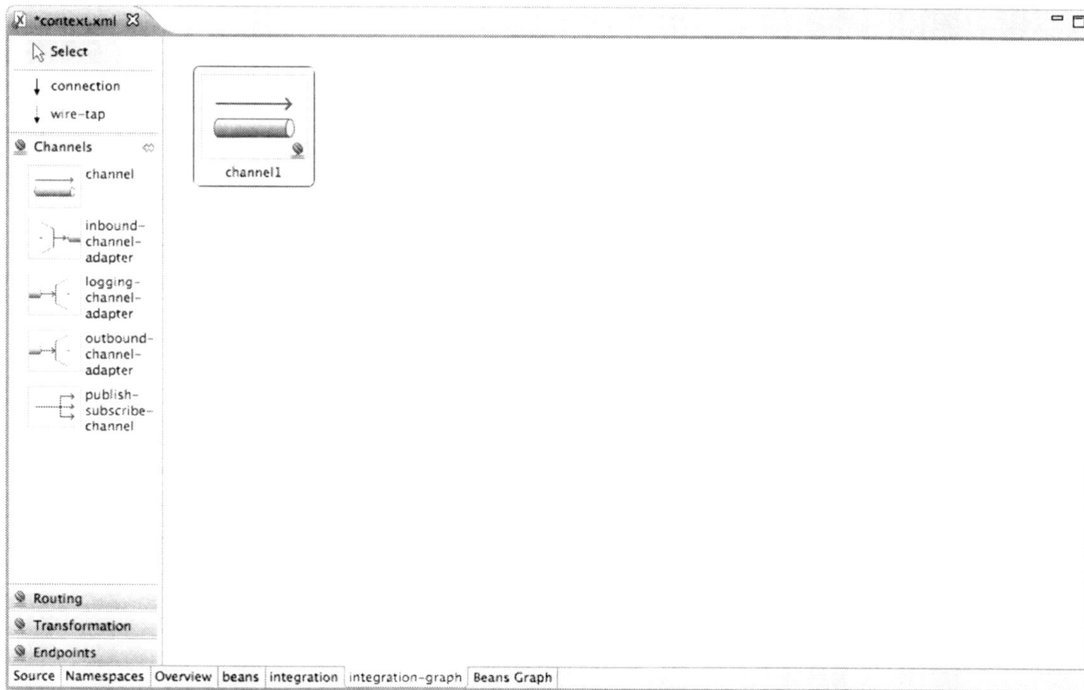

Figure 9–8. Adding a Channel using STS

4. Double-click the channel icon in the workspace to bring up the Properties pane, and modify the properties to assign the ID `ticketChannel`, as shown in Figure 9–9.

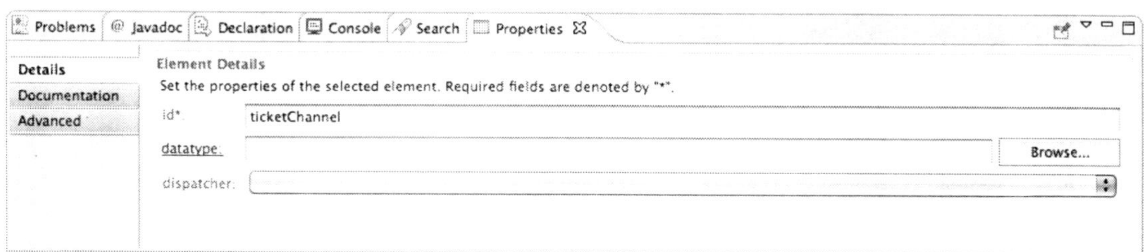

Figure 9–9. Channel Properties

5. Next drag the inbound-channel-adapter icon from the left side toolbar to the workspace. In order to connect the inbound channel adapter to the channel, select connection from the toolbar and drag a line from the inbound channel adapter to the channel, as shown in Figure 9–10.

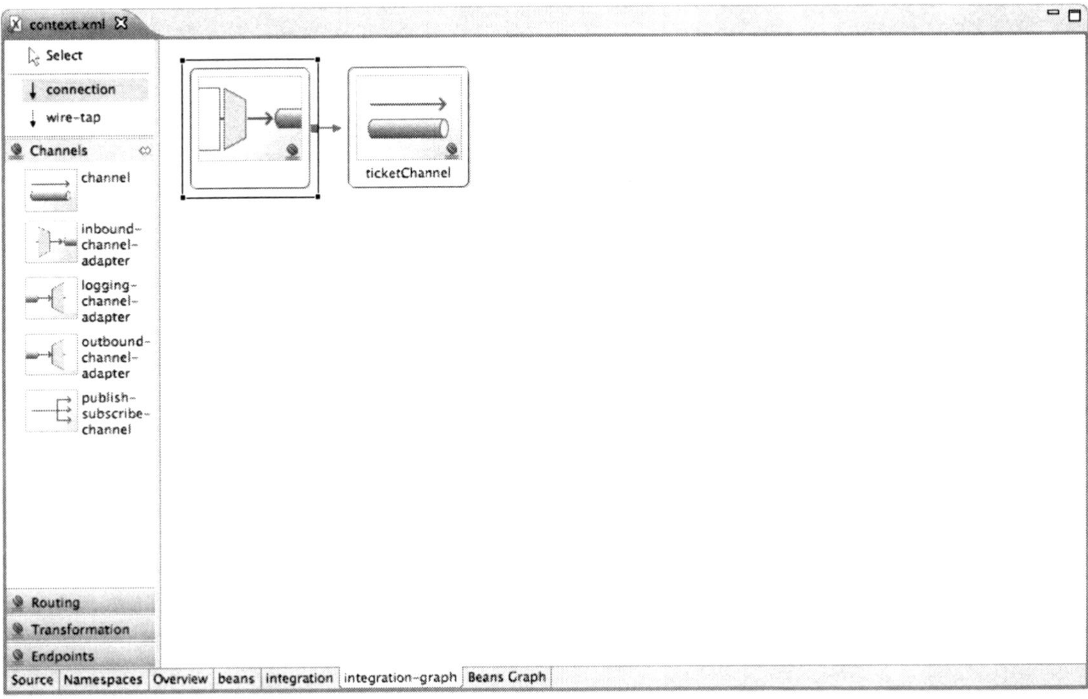

Figure 9–10. Connecting the Inbound Channel Adapter to the Channel

6. Select the inbound-channel-adapter icon to bring up the Properties pane, and modify the adapter properties as shown in Figure 9–11.

Figure 9–11. Inbound Channel Adapter Properties

7. Create the outbound channel adapter by following the same process as for the inbound channel adapter. The main difference is that the connection needs to be drawn from the channel to the outbound-channel-adapter icon, as shown in Figure 9–12.

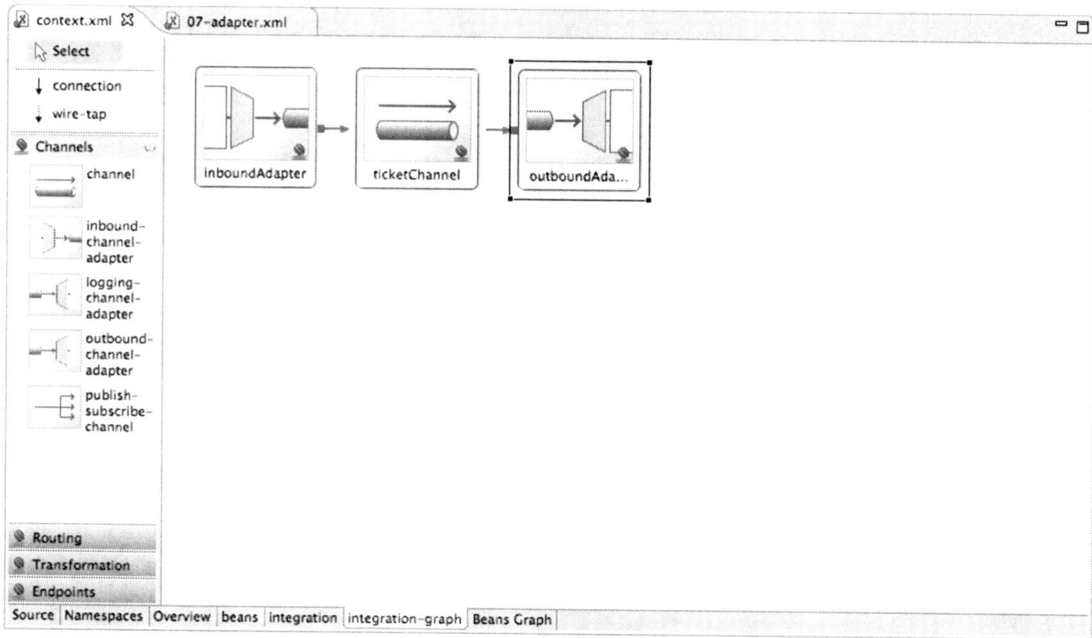

Figure 9–12. Adding an Outbound Channel Adapter to the Channel

8. Select the outbound channel adapter to bring up the Properties pane, and enter the values shown in Figure 9–13.

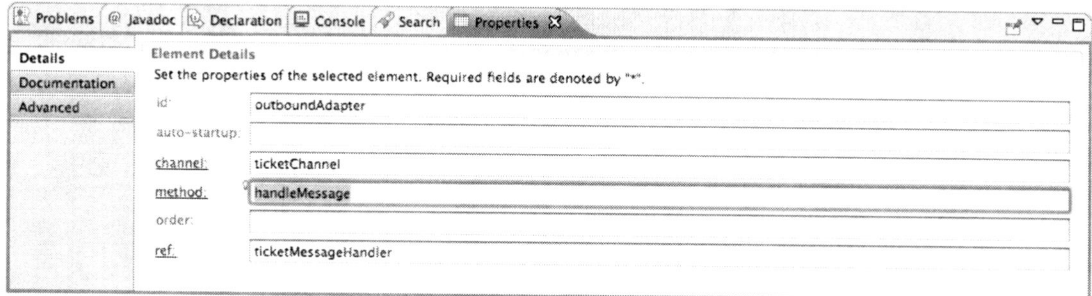

Figure 9–13. Outbound Channel Adapter Properties

9. Now click the Source tab and examine the Spring configuration file, as shown in Figure 9–14.

context.xml

```xml
<?xml version="1.0" encoding="UTF-8"?>
<beans xmlns="http://www.springframework.org/schema/beans"
  xmlns:xsi="http://www.w3.org/2001/XMLSchema-instance"
  xmlns:int="http://www.springframework.org/schema/integration"
  xsi:schemaLocation="http://www.springframework.org/schema/integration http://www.springframework.org/schema/integration/spring-integration-2.0.xsd
        http://www.springframework.org/schema/beans http://www.springframework.org/schema/beans/spring-beans.xsd">

  <int:channel id="ticketChannel"></int:channel>

  <int:inbound-channel-adapter channel="ticketChannel"
    id="inboundAdapter" ref="problemReporter" method="openTickets">
  </int:inbound-channel-adapter>
  <int:outbound-channel-adapter channel="ticketChannel"
    id="outboundAdapter" ref="ticketMessageHandler"
    method="handleMessage">
  </int:outbound-channel-adapter>
</beans>
```

Source | Namespaces | Overview | beans | integration | integration-graph | Beans Graph

Figure 9–14. *Spring Configuration for the Channel and Adapters*

STS has created the entire Spring configuration file. The only thing left is defining the Spring beans, as with other Spring applications. Using STS, we can visually create and connect Spring Integration components without typing a single line of XML.

Messaging Gateways

A messaging gateway is essentially a façade that allows the interface to a messaging system to be represented as a method or service call (see Figure 9–15). Typically, integrating an application with a messaging framework requires composing messages and moving them through message channels using inbound and outbound channel adapters, as discussed previously. This approach typically achieves the objective of integration, although it requires that application have knowledge of the messaging system. This tightly couples the application to the messaging framework. A gateway can be used to eliminate this coupling by creating a façade layer that abstracts away the functionality of the messaging system into a discrete interface. Thus, the application will only see a simple method or service interface, and will not be directly dependent on JMS or Spring Integration.

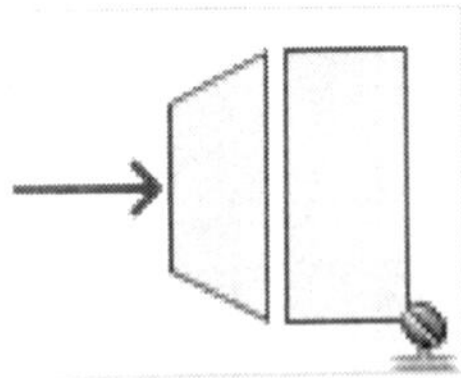

Figure 9–15. *Gateway*

A messaging gateway is a pattern designed to hide the underlying communication details from the application using it. It places an interface between the application and the target messaging infrastructure by providing a proxy, similar to what is seen in a remote façade. When a gateway is exposed with a simple method call that return values, it implies that for each request message generated when the method is called, there is a reply message generated when the method returns. Since messaging is by nature asynchronous, there is no guarantee that for each request there will be a reply. Spring Integration introduces support for an asynchronous gateway by providing a convenient method of starting a flow when a reply message cannot be assured to return in a timely fashion (or at all). Asynchronous gateways will be discussed in more detail following.

Spring Integration Support for Gateways

Let's get started with a simple example that illustrates an inbound messaging gateway. Spring Integration provides a `org.springframework.integration.gateway.GatewayProxyFactoryBean` that generates a proxy for the service interface; this proxy can safely interact with the Spring Integration framework. A messaging gateway can be created using the gateway namespace shown in Listing 9–20.

Listing 9–20. *Gateway Example Spring Configuration gateway-simple.xml*

```
<?xml version="1.0" encoding="UTF-8"?>
<beans xmlns="http://www.springframework.org/schema/beans"
       xmlns:xsi="http://www.w3.org/2001/XMLSchema-instance"
       xmlns:int="http://www.springframework.org/schema/integration"
       xmlns:context="http://www.springframework.org/schema/context"
       xsi:schemaLocation="http://www.springframework.org/schema/beans
    http://www.springframework.org/schema/beans/spring-beans-3.0.xsd
    http://www.springframework.org/schema/context
    http://www.springframework.org/schema/context/spring-context-3.0.xsd
    http://www.springframework.org/schema/integration
    http://www.springframework.org/schema/integration/spring-integration-2.0.xsd">

  <context:component-scan base-package="com.apress.prospringintegration.gateways"/>

  <int:channel id="ticketRequests">
    <int:interceptors>
      <int:wire-tap channel="logger"/>
    </int:interceptors>
  </int:channel>

  <int:channel id="ticketReplies">
    <int:queue capacity="10"/>
    <int:interceptors>
      <int:wire-tap channel="logger"/>
    </int:interceptors>
  </int:channel>

  <int:channel id="request"/>
  <int:channel id="reply"/>

  <int:logging-channel-adapter id="logger" level="INFO"/>

  <int:gateway id="ticketIssueGateway"
               default-request-channel="request"
               default-reply-channel="reply"
```

```
            service-interface=
                "com.apress.prospringintegration.gateways.client.TicketIssuer"/>

    <int:service-activator input-channel="ticketRequests"
                           output-channel="ticketReplies"
                           ref="ticketIssuerService"/>

</beans>
```

A ticketIssueGateway messaging gateway is configured based on the interface com.apress.prospringintegration.gateway.client.TicketIssuer shown in Listing 9–21. The default request and reply channels are set to the channels request and reply, respectively. A reply channel is not required when configuring a gateway, since the gateway will create a temporary point-to-point reply channel; this channel is anonymous, and is added to the message header with the name replyChannel. If a publish-subscribe-channel is required, for example because there are other interested listeners, the reply channel needs to be explicitly defined.

There is always the possibility that the gateway invocation may result in errors. By default, any downstream error will result in an org.springframework.integration.MessagingException being thrown back to the gateway. You can also capture errors by defining an error channel using the gateway attribute error-channel.

The reason the request and reply channels are prefixed with default is because there is a mechanism to specify these channels on a per-method basis using the @Gateway annotation. In the TicketIssuer interface shown in Listing 9–21, the request and reply channels are overwritten with the ticketRequests and ticketReplies channels, respectively.

Listing 9–21. *Gateway Example Service Interface TicketIssuer.java*

```
package com.apress.prospringintegration.gateways.client;

import com.apress.prospringintegration.gateways.model.Ticket;
import org.springframework.integration.annotation.Gateway;

public interface TicketIssuer {

    @Gateway(replyChannel = "ticketReplies", requestChannel = "ticketRequests")
    public Ticket issueTicket(long ticketId);
}
```

A service activator is used to receive the request message from the gateway, as shown in Listing 9–22. The TicketIssuerService will take in incoming ticketId, create a Ticket instance, and send it to the reply channel.

Listing 9–22. *Gateway Example Service Activator TicketIssuerService.java*

```
package com.apress.prospringintegration.gateways.service;

import com.apress.prospringintegration.gateways.client.TicketIssuer;
import com.apress.prospringintegration.gateways.model.Ticket;
import org.springframework.integration.annotation.ServiceActivator;
import org.springframework.stereotype.Component;

import java.util.Date;

@Component
public class TicketIssuerService implements TicketIssuer {
```

```
    @ServiceActivator
    public Ticket issueTicket(long ticketId) {
        Ticket t = new Ticket();
        t.setIssueDateTime(new Date());
        t.setDescription("New Ticket");
        t.setPriority(Ticket.Priority.medium);
        t.setTicketId(ticketId);

        System.out.println("Issuing a Ticket: " + t.getIssueDateTime());

        return t;
    }
}
```

The Spring Integration configuration message flows are illustrated in Figure 9–16.

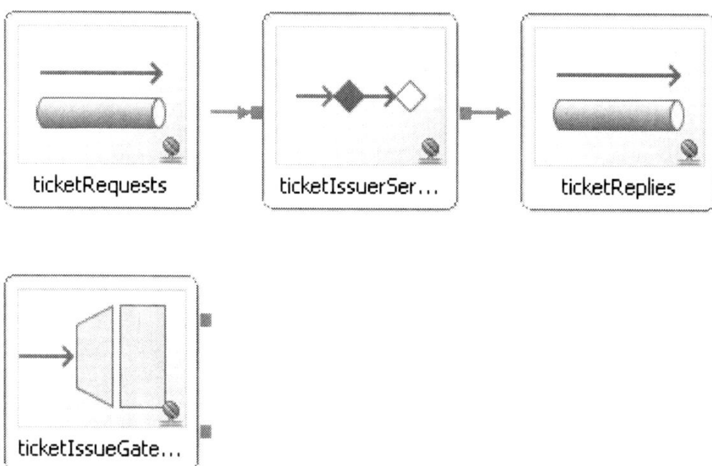

Figure 9–16. Simple Gateway Example

The gateway example can be tested using the simple `main` class shown in Listing 9–23. The `main` class creates the Spring context and obtains a reference to the `ticketIssueGateway` gateway. The `ticketIssueGateway` method `issueTicket` is called, resulting in a message sent to the `ticketRequestChannel`. The `ticketIssuerService` service activator receives the incoming message, creates the `Ticket` instance, and sends it to the `ticketReplies` channel. The `ticketIssuerGateway` receives an incoming `Ticket` message and logs its information. This represents a full integration with Spring Integration using only a simple method invocation.

Listing 9–23. Gateway Example main Class MainSimpleGateway.java

```
package com.apress.prospringintegration.gateways.client;

import com.apress.prospringintegration.gateways.model.Ticket;
import org.springframework.context.support.ClassPathXmlApplicationContext;
```

```
public class MainSimpleGateway {

    public static void main(String[] args) throws Exception {
        ClassPathXmlApplicationContext context =
                new ClassPathXmlApplicationContext("ioc-gateway-simple.xml");

        TicketIssuer ticketIssuer =
                context.getBean("ticketIssueGateway", TicketIssuer.class);

        Ticket ticket = ticketIssuer.issueTicket(100L);
        System.out.println("Ticket: " + ticket + " was issued on: " +
                ticket.getIssueDateTime() + " with ticket id: " +
                ticket.getTicketId());
    }
}
```

Asynchronous Gateways

The previous example showed a synchronous gateway, where there the method invocation will not return until the gateway receives the reply message. As discussed previously, messaging is asynchronous by nature, and there may be no way to know if or when a reply message will be returned. Spring Integration supports asynchronous gateways for this reason.

The only change required to create an asynchronous gateway is to modify the return type of the service interface to `java.util.concurrent.Future`, as shown in Listing 9–24. When the Spring Integration gateway detects that the return type is `Future`, it will immediate switch to the asynchronous mode using the `org.springframework.core.task.AsychTaskExectutor`. The method call will immediately return a `Future` instance. Then the `Future` instance can be handle as desired.

***Listing 9–24.** Asynchronous Gateway Service Interface*

```
package com.apress.prospringintegration.gateways.client;

import com.apress.prospringintegration.gateways.model.Ticket;
import org.springframework.integration.annotation.Gateway;

import java.util.concurrent.Future;

public interface TicketIssuerAsync {
    @Gateway(replyChannel = "ticketReplies", requestChannel = "ticketRequests")
    public Future<Ticket> issueTicket(long ticketId);
}
```

The Spring configuration file and `main` class are modified to use the asynchronous service interface. The `main` class is shown in Listing 9–25. In this version, a timeout is set in which the code will wait for no longer than 1,000 seconds for the reply to return.

***Listing 9–25.** Asynchronous Gateway Example main Class*

```
package com.apress.prospringintegration.gateways.client;

import com.apress.prospringintegration.gateways.model.Ticket;
import org.springframework.context.support.ClassPathXmlApplicationContext;
```

```
import java.util.concurrent.Future;
import java.util.concurrent.TimeUnit;

public class MainAsyncGateway {
    public static void main(String[] args) throws Exception {
        ClassPathXmlApplicationContext context =
                new ClassPathXmlApplicationContext("gateway-async.xml");

        TicketIssuerAsync ticketIssuerAsync =
                context.getBean("ticketIssueGatewayAsync", TicketIssuerAsync.class);

        Future<Ticket> result = ticketIssuerAsync.issueTicket(100L);

        Ticket ticket = result.get(1000, TimeUnit.SECONDS);
        System.out.println("Ticket: " + ticket + " was issued on: " +
                ticket.getIssueDateTime() + " with ticket id: " +
                ticket.getTicketId());
    }
}
```

Gateways Receiving No Response

A gateway maps a method invocation to a messaging system. However, a typical method invocation generally expects the method to always return, or at least throw an exception. This is not the case for a messaging system in which the reply message may be delayed or never arrive. Therefore, it is important to understand the behavior of a synchronous gateway when there is no response.

One of the attributes that make the gateway more predictable is `reply-timeout`. We will cover how the synchronous gateway behaves in relation to this attribute for both single-threaded scenarios (in which all downstream components are connected via a direct channel) and multithreaded scenarios (in which there may be a pollable or executor channel that breaks the thread boundary downstream).

For long-running downstream processes in the single-threaded case, the `reply-timeout` setting will have no effect. For the multithread case, the method will return once the timeout has been reached or the reply message has returned. In the case of a timeout, the returned value may be `null` or the reply message could come at a later time.

For downstream components returning a `null` reply in both the single-threaded and multithread cases, the gateway method will hang indefinitely unless the `reply-timeout` setting has be configured, or the `requires-reply` value has been set on the downstream components. If either of these have been set, an exception will be thrown back to the gateway for a `null` reply.

In the situation where the downstream component return signature is void while the gateway is nonvoid, the gateway method call will hang indefinitely in both the single-threaded and multithreaded cases. The `reply-timeout` attribute will have no effect.

If a downstream component throws a `RuntimeException`, it will be sent back to the gateway as an error message and rethrown by the gateway method.

It is important to realize that there are several scenarios where a gateway method invocation can hang indefinitely, even if the `reply-timeout` attribute for the gateway and `requires-reply` attribute for the down stream components have been set. Even more importantly, there are cases where the `reply-timeout` attribute will not help. Therefore, it is important to analyze your message flow, consider using these attribute settings, and consider using an asynchronous gateway when appropriate.

In addition, when using a router, remember that setting `resolution-required` to `true` will cause an exception only if the router is unable to resolve a particular channel. Similar to a filter, the `throw-exception-on-reject` will throw an exception if the filter if the message is rejected.

Inbound/Outbound Gateways via JMS

Many of the Spring Integration adapters (including HTTP and JMS) support inbound and outbound gateways. The next example will take a look at the inbound and outbound JMS gateways. The previous example for the synchronous gateway will be modified to use a JMS broker between the inbound message gateway `TicketIssuer` and the service activator `TicketIssuerService`. The inbound gateway will use the outbound JMS gateway to communicate with the JMS broker (client), and the service activator will use the inbound JMS gateway to communicate with the JMS broker (server).

Since Spring Integration will need to connect to a JMS broker, a connection factory is required. A Java configuration file will be used to create the connection factory, as shown in Listing 9–26. For simplicity, an embedded ActiveMQ broker will be configured using the URL `vm://localhost`.

***Listing 9–26.** Java Configuration for the JMS Connection Factory*

```
package com.apress.prospringintegration.gateways.service;

import org.apache.activemq.ActiveMQConnectionFactory;
import org.springframework.context.annotation.Bean;
import org.springframework.context.annotation.Configuration;

@Configuration
public class JmsConfiguration {

    @Bean
    public ActiveMQConnectionFactory connectionFactory() {
        ActiveMQConnectionFactory connectionFactory =
                new ActiveMQConnectionFactory("vm://localhost");
        return connectionFactory;
    }
}
```

The Spring configuration for the client side of the JMS gateway example is shown in Listing 9–27. This configuration is the same as the previous example, except the service activator has been replaced with a JMS `outbound-gateway` using the `jms` namespace. The JMS outbound gateway is configured for a request/reply using the destination queue `issue.request`.

***Listing 9–27.** JMS Gateway Example Client Spring Configuration gateway-jms-client.xml*

```
<?xml version="1.0" encoding="UTF-8"?>
<beans xmlns="http://www.springframework.org/schema/beans"
       xmlns:xsi="http://www.w3.org/2001/XMLSchema-instance"
       xmlns:int="http://www.springframework.org/schema/integration"
       xmlns:context="http://www.springframework.org/schema/context"
       xmlns:jms="http://www.springframework.org/schema/integration/jms"
       xsi:schemaLocation="http://www.springframework.org/schema/beans
    http://www.springframework.org/schema/beans/spring-beans-3.0.xsd
    http://www.springframework.org/schema/context
    http://www.springframework.org/schema/context/spring-context-3.0.xsd
    http://www.springframework.org/schema/integration
    http://www.springframework.org/schema/integration/spring-integration-2.0.xsd
    http://www.springframework.org/schema/integration/jms
    http://www.springframework.org/schema/integration/jms/spring-integration-jms-2.0.xsd">

  <context:component-scan base-package="com.apress.prospringintegration.gateways.service"/>
```

```
  <int:logging-channel-adapter id="logger" level="INFO" log-full-message="true"/>

  <int:channel id="ticketRequests">
    <int:interceptors>
      <int:wire-tap channel="logger"/>
    </int:interceptors>
  </int:channel>

  <int:channel id="ticketReplies">
    <int:queue capacity="10"/>
    <int:interceptors>
      <int:wire-tap channel="logger"/>
    </int:interceptors>
  </int:channel>

  <int:gateway id="ticketIssueGateway"
               service-interface=
                   "com.apress.prospringintegration.gateways.client.TicketIssuer"/>

  <jms:outbound-gateway
      request-destination-name="issue.request"
      request-channel="ticketRequests"
      reply-channel="ticketReplies"
      connection-factory="connectionFactory"/>

</beans>
```

The server-side Spring configuration is shown in Listing 9–28. Again, the Spring configuration file is the same as the previous example, except now the inbound gateway is replaced with a JMS inbound-gateway. The JMS inbound-gateway is configured for a request/reply using the destination queue issue.request. What is interesting in this example is that there is no mention of a response channel for either the service activator or the inbound JMS gateway. The service activator will look for a reply channel and fail to find one. Instead, it will use the reply channel created by the inbound JMS gateway, which was created based on the header metadata of the inbound JMS message. Thus, everything just works without additional specification.

Listing 9–28. *JMS Gateway Example Server Spring Configuration gateway-jms-server.xml*

```
<?xml version="1.0" encoding="UTF-8"?>
<beans xmlns="http://www.springframework.org/schema/beans"
       xmlns:xsi="http://www.w3.org/2001/XMLSchema-instance"
       xmlns:int="http://www.springframework.org/schema/integration"
       xmlns:context="http://www.springframework.org/schema/context"
       xmlns:jms="http://www.springframework.org/schema/integration/jms"
       xsi:schemaLocation="http://www.springframework.org/schema/beans
    http://www.springframework.org/schema/beans/spring-beans-3.0.xsd
    http://www.springframework.org/schema/context
    http://www.springframework.org/schema/context/spring-context-3.0.xsd
    http://www.springframework.org/schema/integration
    http://www.springframework.org/schema/integration/spring-integration-2.0.xsd
    http://www.springframework.org/schema/integration/jms
    http://www.springframework.org/schema/integration/jms/spring-integration-jms-2.0.xsd">
```

```
    <context:component-scan base-package="com.apress.prospringintegration.gateways.service"/>

    <int:logging-channel-adapter id="logger" level="INFO" log-full-message="true"/>

    <int:channel id="inboundTicketRequests">
      <int:interceptors>
        <int:wire-tap channel="logger"/>
      </int:interceptors>
    </int:channel>

    <jms:inbound-gateway request-channel="inboundTicketRequests"
                         request-destination-name="issue.request"
                         connection-factory="connectionFactory"/>

    <int:service-activator id="ticketIssuer"
                           input-channel="inboundTicketRequests"
                           ref="ticketIssuerService"/>

</beans>
```

The main class to run the JMS gateway example is shown in Listing 9–29. The main class creates the Spring context based on the two Spring configuration files. The main class obtains a reference to the ticketIssueGateway gateway. The ticketIssueGateway method issueTicket is called, resulting in a message being sent to the ticketRequestChannel. This message is sent to the JMS broker via the JMS outbound gateway. The message is received by the JMS inbound gateway and sent to the inboundTicketRequests channel. The ticketIssuerService service activator creates the Ticket instance and sends it to the ticketReplies channel. The message is sent to the JMS broker via the inbound JMS gateway. The message is received by the JMS outbound gateway and sent to the ticketReplies channel. The ticketIssuerGateway receives in incoming Ticket and logs its information. The complex message processing is well hidden by the simple gateway configuration. This demonstrates the power of the gateway pattern.

Listing 9–29. *MainJMSGateway.java*

```
package com.apress.prospringintegration.gateways.client;

import com.apress.prospringintegration.gateways.model.Ticket;
import org.springframework.context.support.ClassPathXmlApplicationContext;

public class MainJMSGateway {
    public static void main(String[] args) throws Exception {
        ClassPathXmlApplicationContext ctx =
                new ClassPathXmlApplicationContext("gateway-jms-service.xml");

        ClassPathXmlApplicationContext ctx1 =
                new ClassPathXmlApplicationContext("gateway-jms-client.xml");

        TicketIssuer ticketIssuer = ctx1.getBean("ticketIssueGateway",
                TicketIssuer.class);

        Ticket ticket = ticketIssuer.issueTicket(1);
```

```
        System.out.println("Ticket " + ticket + " was issued on:" +
                ticket.getIssueDateTime() + " with ticket id: " +
                ticket.getTicketId());
    }
}
```

Secure Channels

As a last topic in this chapter, the subject of security will be touched on—specifically how to secure a message channel. Spring Integration uses the Spring Security project (`http://static.springsource.org/spring-security/site`) to provide role-based security for sending to a message channel and receiving invocations.

Spring Integration provides the interceptor `org.springframework.integration.security.channel.ChannelSecurityInterceptor`, which extends `org.springframework.security.access.intercept.AbstractSecurityInterceptor` for intercepting send and receive calls on message channels. Access decisions are based on the access policies for specific channels, based on the metadata obtained from `org.springframework.integration.security.channel.ChannelSecurityMetadataSource`. The interceptor requires that a valid `org.springframework.security.core.context.SecurityContext` has been established by authenticating with Spring Security.

The `si-security` namespace is provided to configure security constraints. This namespace allows defining one or more channel name patterns in relation to the security constraints for sending and receiving messages via a message channel. The pattern is a regular expression (regex).

In the Spring configuration file shown in Listing 9–30, the `secure-channels` element establishes that any channel with an ID prefix of secure will have access limited to the roles `ROLE_ADMIN` and `ROLE_PRESIDENT` for sending, and `ROLE_USER`, `ROLE_ADMIN`, and `ROLE_PRESIDENT` for receiving. The `secure-channels` element requires an `org.springframework.security.authentication.AuthenticationManager` configured in this example using the Spring security namespace. In this example, the username secureuser has the roles `ROLE_USER` and `ROLE_ADMIN`, and the username `unsecureuser` has the role `ROLE_USER`. Thus, based on the current configuration, only the username `secureuser` can send and receive messages via channels prefixed with secure.

Listing 9–30. *Secure Channel Example Spring Configuration secure-channel.xml*

```
<?xml version="1.0" encoding="UTF-8"?>
<beans xmlns="http://www.springframework.org/schema/beans"
       xmlns:int="http://www.springframework.org/schema/integration"
       xmlns:xsi="http://www.w3.org/2001/XMLSchema-instance"
       xmlns:security="http://www.springframework.org/schema/security"
       xmlns:context="http://www.springframework.org/schema/context"
       xmlns:si-security="http://www.springframework.org/schema/integration/security"
       xsi:schemaLocation="http://www.springframework.org/schema/beans
    http://www.springframework.org/schema/beans/spring-beans.xsd
    http://www.springframework.org/schema/integration
    http://www.springframework.org/schema/integration/spring-integration-2.0.xsd
    http://www.springframework.org/schema/security
    http://www.springframework.org/schema/security/spring-security-3.0.xsd
    http://www.springframework.org/schema/context
    http://www.springframework.org/schema/context/spring-context.xsd
    http://www.springframework.org/schema/integration/security
    http://www.springframework.org/schema/integration/security/spring-integration-security-➥
2.0.xsd">
```

```
  <context:component-scan base-package="com.apress.prospringintegration.security"/>

  <security:authentication-manager alias="authenticationManager">
    <security:authentication-provider user-service-ref="userDetailsService"/>
  </security:authentication-manager>

  <security:user-service id="userDetailsService">
    <security:user name="secureuser" password="password"
                   authorities="ROLE_USER, ROLE_ADMIN"/>
    <security:user name="unsecureuser" password="password"
                   authorities="ROLE_USER"/>
  </security:user-service>

  <si-security:secured-channels>
    <si-security:access-policy pattern="secure.*"
                               send-access="ROLE_ADMIN, ROLE_PRESIDENT"
                               receive-access="ROLE_USER, ROLE_ADMIN, ROLE_PRESIDENT"/>
  </si-security:secured-channels>

  <int:logging-channel-adapter channel="secureCustomerData"
                               log-full-message="true"/>

  <int:channel id="secureCustomerData"/>

</beans>
```

The `secure-channels` namespace element also requires an `org.springframework.security.access.AccessDecisionManager`, which is created using the Java configuration file shown in Listing 9–31.

***Listing 9–31.** Java Configuration File accessDecisionManager*

```
package com.apress.prospringintegration.security;

import org.springframework.context.annotation.Bean;
import org.springframework.context.annotation.Configuration;
import org.springframework.security.access.AccessDecisionVoter;
import org.springframework.security.access.vote.AffirmativeBased;
import org.springframework.security.access.vote.RoleVoter;

import java.util.Arrays;

@Configuration
public class SecurityConfiguration {

    @Bean
    public AffirmativeBased accessDecisionManager() {
        AffirmativeBased affirmativeBased = new AffirmativeBased();
        affirmativeBased.setAllowIfAllAbstainDecisions(true);
        affirmativeBased.setDecisionVoters(
                Arrays.asList((AccessDecisionVoter) new RoleVoter()));

        return affirmativeBased;
    }
}
```

In a typical application, the SecurityContext is established via authentication through Spring Security. For this example, a simple token-based approach will be taken. The example main class for the secure channel example is shown in Listing 9–32. The main class first creates a SecurityContext with the username secureuser and tries to publish a message to the channel secureCustomerData. Since secureuser has the role ROLE_ADMIN, this username is able to send the message. Next, a SecurityContext is created with the username unsecureuser, and the main class tries to publish a message to the channel secureCustomerData. Since this username has the role ROLE_USER, this user is unable to send the message to the channel, and receives an exception.

Listing 9–32. *Secure Channel Example main Class*

```
package com.apress.prospringintegration.security;

import org.springframework.context.support.ClassPathXmlApplicationContext;
import org.springframework.integration.MessageChannel;
import org.springframework.integration.support.MessageBuilder;
import org.springframework.security.authentication.UsernamePasswordAuthenticationToken;
import org.springframework.security.core.GrantedAuthority;
import org.springframework.security.core.authority.GrantedAuthorityImpl;
import org.springframework.security.core.context.SecurityContext;
import org.springframework.security.core.context.SecurityContextHolder;
import org.springframework.security.core.context.SecurityContextImpl;
import org.springframework.util.CollectionUtils;

public class SecurityMain {

    public static void main(String[] args) throws Exception {

        ClassPathXmlApplicationContext context =
                new ClassPathXmlApplicationContext("classpath:secure-channel.xml");
        context.start();

        MessageChannel channel =
                context.getBean("secureCustomerData", MessageChannel.class);

        //Secure user with privileges
        login("secureuser", "password", "ROLE_ADMIN");
        try {
            send(channel, "hello secure world!");
        } catch (Exception ex) {
            System.out.println("Unable to send message for secureuser");
        }

        // Secure user with privileges
        login("unsecureuser", "password", "ROLE_USER");
        try {
            send(channel, "hello secure world!");
        } catch (Exception ex) {
            System.out.println("Unable to send message for unsecureuser");
            ex.printStackTrace();
        }

    }
```

```
    public static void login(String username, String password, String... roles) {
        SecurityContext context = createContext(username, password, roles);
        SecurityContextHolder.setContext(context);
    }

    public static void send(MessageChannel channel, String message) {
        channel.send(MessageBuilder.withPayload(message).build());
    }

    // Utility method taken from the Spring Integration tests to set up a context
    @SuppressWarnings("unchecked")
    public static SecurityContext createContext(String username,
                                                String password,
                                                String... roles) {
        SecurityContextImpl ctxImpl = new SecurityContextImpl();
        UsernamePasswordAuthenticationToken authToken;
        if (roles != null && roles.length > 0) {
            GrantedAuthority[] authorities = new GrantedAuthority[roles.length];
            for (int i = 0; i < roles.length; i++) {
                authorities[i] = new GrantedAuthorityImpl(roles[i]);
            }
            authToken = new UsernamePasswordAuthenticationToken(username, password,
                    CollectionUtils.arrayToList(authorities));
        } else {
            authToken = new UsernamePasswordAuthenticationToken(username, password);
        }
        ctxImpl.setAuthentication(authToken);
        return ctxImpl;
    }
}
```

Summary

An endpoint describes how application code communicates with the messaging framework. In this chapter, we covered the endpoints that connect to the message channel, application code, external applications, and services. These include messaging endpoints, channel adapters, service activators, and messaging gateways. Both polling and event-driven endpoints were discussed, as well as synchronous and asynchronous gateways. We used STS to show how a visual tool can be used to assist in configuring endpoints and message flows. Endpoints hide the complexity of the of the underlying message systems many times only requiring the proper configuration settings. This allows developers to focus on the business logic instead of the messaging API. Finally, this chapter covered how to secure a message channel and send to a message to a secure message channel.

CHAPTER 10

Monitoring and Management

Monitoring and management support is one of the most important requirements for maintaining enterprise integration. As discussed throughout this book, integration implementations have the potential to span completely different business areas across the enterprise, touching various services and applications that may be supported by different groups and technologies. The potential of taking the entire enterprise down as a result of a single application going down has lead to asynchronous, loosely coupled communication between the various endpoints. Thus, a single application's failure will not adversely affect all the other systems in an enterprise due to direct dependences. However, as a result, management and monitoring support must move beyond simple exception handling to a more comprehensive monitoring and feedback mechanism.

This chapter will introduce the support for management and monitoring provided by Spring Integration and other available open source systems. Spring Integration support for error handling, monitoring leveraging JMX (Java Management Extensions), and performance measurement using JAMon will be covered. In addition, Spring Integration's support for capturing message history and the Spring Integration control bus will be introduced. Finally, the Hyperic enterprise monitoring and management tool will be discussed.

Error Handling

In traditional applications, errors are signaled through exceptions. An exception aborts current execution, and forwards control to handler logic that can react to the exception. In an enterprise integration implementation, error handling is not so straightforward. Each of the application endpoints may have its own error handling process. Errors that occur between multiple systems are very difficult to diagnose. Components in a loosely coupled system should be resilient to any errors caused by a single component. Communication between components in a system is typically asynchronous, and exceptions are hard to diagnose because responses may not arrive in the same thread as a request. A typical integration process flow is shown in Figure 10–1. If an error occurs in process 2, there is no simple way to notify process 1 since it is in a separate thread and maybe running on a different host. The error handling will need to be handled by a completely different process.

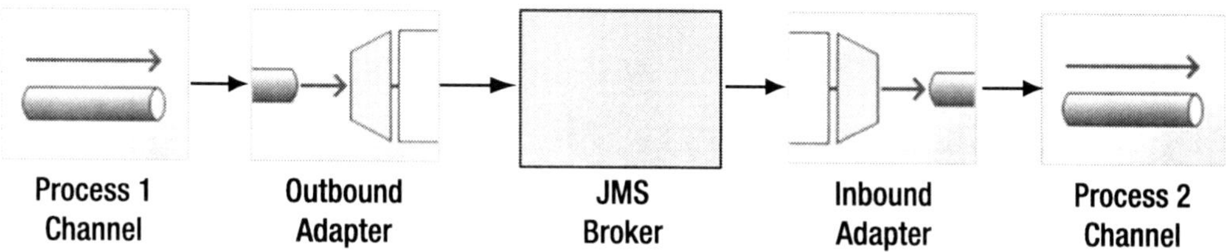

Figure 10–1. Typical Integration Process Flow

History in EAI and MOM: The Dead Letter Queue

There are a number of approaches to handling errors in EAI and message-oriented middleware (MOM). In a typical EAI implementation, several endpoints may be interested in the same message. If one of the endpoints is down, the other endpoints should still be able to process the message. Most message brokers support the concept of a transaction across the broker, but this is not a best practice, since if any one of the endpoints fails, it will roll back the other endpoints. In addition, running a transaction across the message broker will only allow for synchronous processing. The usual approach to this scenario is to have the message broker handle the transaction. Once the message has been delivered to the message broker, it sends back an acknowledgment to the client. Then the message broker is responsible for sending the message to the endpoint and ensuring that the delivery takes place without any errors.

One approach is to add a transaction manager that handles the message any time it cannot be delivered, or when the endpoint returns an error. It can be set up for retry and/or error handling logic. Another approach that is usually supported by the message broker or integration framework is the *dead letter queue*. Any time a message cannot be successfully delivered, it is added to the dead letter queue. Most implementations allow a configurable amount of retries before handing the message off to a dead letter queue. From there, the message may be managed by a manual or automatic process to deal with the undeliverable message.

The dead letter queue approach is shown in Figure 10–2. If, for whatever reason, the JMS broker is not able to deliver the message to the inbound channel adapter, the message will be sent to the dead letter queue for later processing. Therefore, any downtime for the inbound adapter will not affect the upstream process.

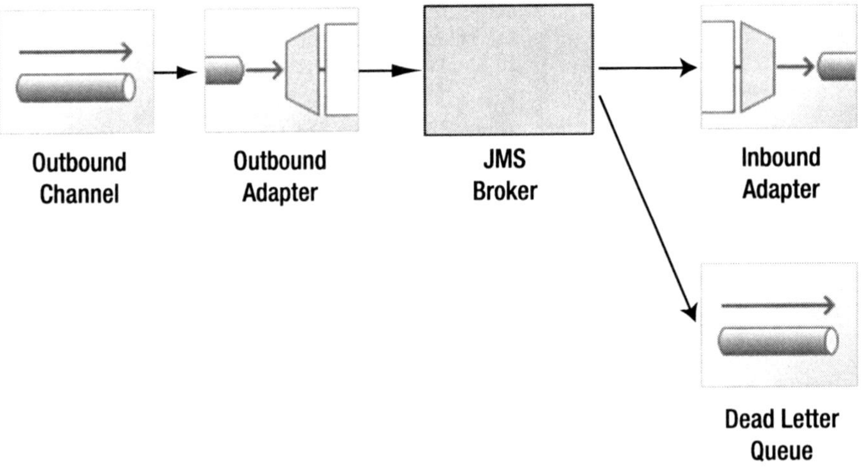

Figure 10–2. *The Dead Letter Queue*

The Error Channel in Spring Integration

Spring Integration supports the concept of an error channel. If the thread sending the message to the channel is not the same as the thread of the one of the downstream handlers, any exception thrown by the handler will cause an error message to be sent to the error channel. If the message handler is in the same thread as the message sender, the exception will be thrown back to the sender, as is usual for a normal method call. For example, if a message is sent to the default DirectChannel, any exception will be thrown back to the message sender.

In the case where a queue element is added to the channel to allow for polling, the message handler will be in a separate thread, making it impossible for the handler to throw an exception back to the message sender. In this case, if an exception is thrown, it will become the payload of an error message sent to a message channel. The channel is determined from the message header value, with the key defined by the constant MessageHeaders.ERROR_CHANNEL. If this message header is undefined, the error will be sent to the default error channel with the name errorChannel.

Setting Up a Default Error Channel

By default, an error channel with the name errorChannel is created when using the Spring Integration XML namespace. The default error channel is a PublishSubscribeChannel that may be modified by defining it explicitly. For example, a default QueueChannel may be created using the configuration in Listing 10–1.

Listing 10–1. *Setting Up a Default Error Channel*

```
<int:channel id="errorChannel">
    <int:queue capacity="25"/>
</int:channel>
```

To demonstrate the usage of the default error channel, a simple example configuration is shown in Listing 10–2.

Listing 10–2. *Simple Default Error Channel Spring Configuration*

```
<?xml version="1.0" encoding="UTF-8"?>
<beans xmlns="http://www.springframework.org/schema/beans"
       xmlns:xsi="http://www.w3.org/2001/XMLSchema-instance"
       xmlns:int="http://www.springframework.org/schema/integration"
       xmlns:context="http://www.springframework.org/schema/context"
       xsi:schemaLocation="http://www.springframework.org/schema/beans
    http://www.springframework.org/schema/beans/spring-beans-3.0.xsd
    http://www.springframework.org/schema/integration
    http://www.springframework.org/schema/integration/spring-integration-2.0.xsd
    http://www.springframework.org/schema/context
    http://www.springframework.org/schema/context/spring-context-3.0.xsd">

  <context:component-scan base-package="com.apress.prospringintegration.errorhandling"/>

  <int:poller default="true" max-messages-per-poll="1">
    <int:interval-trigger interval="1000"/>
  </int:poller>

  <int:channel id="input">
    <int:queue capacity="10"/>
  </int:channel>

  <int:chain input-channel="input">
    <int:service-activator ref="mockException" method="processMessage"/>
  </int:chain>
```

```
  <int:service-activator input-channel="errorChannel"
                         ref="errorLogger">

</beans>
```

In this example, a QueueChannel is created with a capacity of ten messages so that the message handler operates in a thread separate from the sender. A default poller is configured to pull the message off the queue every second, and a message handler chain forwards the message to the MockException class. As shown in Listing 10–3, the method processMessage is hard-coded to throw an exception.

Listing 10–3. *MockException Class Used to Replicate an Exception Being Thrown*

```
package com.apress.prospringintegration.errorhandling;

import org.springframework.stereotype.Component;

@Component
public class MockException {
    public String processMessage(String s) throws Exception {
        throw new Exception("Test");
    }
}
```

Because a message header error channel has not been set, the exception becomes the payload of a message sent to the errorChannel. A service activator has been configured to log the error message using the ErrorLogger class, as shown in Listing 10–4. This allows the message sent to the errorChannel to be sent to the service activator class.

Listing 10–4. *ErrorLogger Service Activator Class*

```
package com.apress.prospringintegration.errorhandling;

import org.springframework.integration.Message;
import org.springframework.integration.annotation.ServiceActivator;
import org.springframework.stereotype.Component;

@Component
public class ErrorLogger {
    @ServiceActivator
    public void logError(Message message) {
        System.out.println("Error: " + message);
    }
}
```

Setting Up a Per-Integration Error Channel

Sending all exceptions to a single error channel may not always be the best approach. In order to make the error handling more tractable, exceptions can be directed to a specific error channel. Similar to the reply header specifying the channel of the reply message, the message header specified by the key MessageHeaders.ERROR_CHANNEL may be set to the channel where the exceptions are sent. Thus, if the message causes any exceptions during processing, a message will be sent to the specified channel with the exception as the payload. For example, in Listing 10–5, the message handler chain enriches the header using the error-channel element to send all exception messages to the channel myErrorChannel.

***Listing 10–5.** Error Handler with Custom Error Channel*

```
<?xml version="1.0" encoding="UTF-8"?>
<beans xmlns="http://www.springframework.org/schema/beans"
       xmlns:xsi="http://www.w3.org/2001/XMLSchema-instance"
       xmlns:int="http://www.springframework.org/schema/integration"
       xmlns:stream="http://www.springframework.org/schema/integration/stream"
       xmlns:context="http://www.springframework.org/schema/context"
       xsi:schemaLocation="http://www.springframework.org/schema/beans
    http://www.springframework.org/schema/beans/spring-beans-3.0.xsd
    http://www.springframework.org/schema/integration
    http://www.springframework.org/schema/integration/spring-integration-2.0.xsd
    http://www.springframework.org/schema/integration/stream
    http://www.springframework.org/schema/integration/stream/spring-integration-stream-2.0.xsd
    http://www.springframework.org/schema/context
    http://www.springframework.org/schema/context/spring-context-3.0.xsd">

  <context:component-scan base-package="com.apress.prospringintegration.errorhandling"/>

  <int:poller default="true" max-messages-per-poll="1">
    <int:interval-trigger interval="1000"/>
  </int:poller>

  <int:channel id="input">
    <int:queue capacity="10"/>
  </int:channel>

  <int:channel id="myErrorChannel"/>

  <int:chain input-channel="input">
    <int:header-enricher>
      <int:error-channel ref="myErrorChannel"/>
    </int:header-enricher>
    <int:service-activator ref="mockException" method="processMessage"/>
  </int:chain>

  <int:service-activator input-channel="myErrorChannel"
                         ref="errorLogger"/>

  <stream:stderr-channel-adapter channel="myErrorChannel" append-newline="true"/>

</beans>
```

Note the `stderr-channel-adapter`, which is added as a generic error handler. This is recommended, since any exceptions cannot be sent back to the sender.

JMX

JMX has become ubiquitous with managing and monitoring Java applications. Most open source and commercial Java frameworks and applications come with some amount of JMX support. The ability to manage the application is exposed through a management interface defined by a set of Management Beans (MBeans). These MBeans are registered in an MBean server with a name or ObjectName. The

MBean may be accessed within the MBean server through a variety of protocols, including RMI, SNMP, and HTML. There are various tools and consoles available to monitor an application using JMX, including JConsole and MC4J. Spring integration has support for both monitoring and managing other applications that leverage JMX, as well as for exposing its own components as MBeans. Both of these features will be discussed in the following section.

Basic Monitoring for Your Application

Spring Integration has several channel adapters for interacting with JMX. This includes a channel adapter for sending and receiving JMX notifications as well as adapters for monitoring MBean attributes values and invoking MBean operations. These various adapters are listed here:

- Notification Listening channel adapter
- Notification Publishing channel adapter
- Attribute Polling channel adapter
- Operation Invoking channel adapter
- Operation Invoking outbound gateway

To test the different JMX adapters, a simple MBean will be created using Spring's general JMX support. By adding a few lines to the Spring configuration files leveraging the context namespace, as shown in Listing 10–6, MBeans may be created using simple annotations.

Listing 10–6. *Spring Configuration File for Creating MBeans*

```
<context:mbean-export/>
<context:mbean-server/>

<context:component-scan base-package="com.apress.prospringintegration.jmx"/>
```

The `mbean-server` element declares the default MBean server with the ID `mbeanServer`, and the `mbean-export` element exports any MBeans to the server. The `component-scan` element supports the annotation-based MBean declarations.

A simple MBean may be created using annotations, as shown in Listing 10–7. This MBean will be used to demonstrate the different Spring Integration JMX adapters.

Listing 10–7. *Simple MBean for Spring Integration JMX Examples*

```
package com.apress.prospringintegration.jmx;

import org.springframework.jmx.export.annotation.ManagedAttribute;
import org.springframework.jmx.export.annotation.ManagedOperation;
import org.springframework.jmx.export.annotation.ManagedResource;
import org.springframework.jmx.export.notification.NotificationPublisher;
import org.springframework.jmx.export.notification.NotificationPublisherAware;
import org.springframework.stereotype.Component;

import javax.management.Notification;

@Component
@ManagedResource
public class BasicMBean implements NotificationPublisherAware {
```

```
    private NotificationPublisher notificationPublisher;
    private String data;

    @ManagedAttribute
    public String getData() {
        return data;
    }

    @ManagedAttribute
    public void setData(String data) {
        this.data = data;
    }

    @ManagedOperation
    public Integer add(Integer a, Integer b) {
        notificationPublisher.sendNotification(new Notification("add", this, 0));
        return a + b;
    }

    @Override
    public void setNotificationPublisher(NotificationPublisher notificationPublisher) {
        this.notificationPublisher = notificationPublisher;
    }
}
```

The `Component` annotation causes the class to be scanned for context-based annotations. The `ManagedResource` annotation declares the class as an MBean. Adding the `ManagedAttribute` annotation to both the setter and getter of the data properties causes this property to be an MBean attribute with read and write privileges. The last annotation used is `ManageOperation`, which causes the `add` method to be exposed as an MBean operation. In addition, this operation also sends an MBean notification using `org.springframework.jmx.export.notification. NotificationPublisher`. Note the implementation of the interface `org.springframework.jmx.export.notification. NotificationPublisherAware`, which declares the `NotificationPublisher` instance for sending MBean notifications.

The Notification Listening channel adapter will listen for an MBean notification and forward it to the specified message channel. Using the configuration shown in Listing 10–8, a message will be sent to the notification channel if the add operation is invoked. Note the addition of the Spring Integration `jmx` namespace for JMX support and the `stream` namespace to log the notification messages.

***Listing 10–8.** Notification Listening Channel Adapter notification-listener.xml Configuration File*

```
<?xml version="1.0" encoding="UTF-8"?>
<beans xmlns="http://www.springframework.org/schema/beans"
       xmlns:xsi="http://www.w3.org/2001/XMLSchema-instance"
       xmlns:int="http://www.springframework.org/schema/integration"
       xmlns:context="http://www.springframework.org/schema/context"
       xmlns:jmx="http://www.springframework.org/schema/integration/jmx"
       xmlns:stream="http://www.springframework.org/schema/integration/stream"
       xsi:schemaLocation="http://www.springframework.org/schema/beans
    http://www.springframework.org/schema/beans/spring-beans-3.0.xsd
    http://www.springframework.org/schema/integration
    http://www.springframework.org/schema/integration/spring-integration-2.0.xsd
    http://www.springframework.org/schema/integration/jmx
    http://www.springframework.org/schema/integration/jmx/spring-integration-jmx-2.0.xsd
```

```
    http://www.springframework.org/schema/integration/stream
    http://www.springframework.org/schema/integration/stream/spring-integration-stream.xsd
    http://www.springframework.org/schema/context
    http://www.springframework.org/schema/context/spring-context-3.0.xsd">

  <context:mbean-export/>
  <context:mbean-server/>

  <context:component-scan base-package="com.apress.prospringintegration.jmx"/>

  <int:channel id="notification"/>

  <jmx:notification-listening-channel-adapter
      channel="notification"
      object-name="com.apress.prospringintegration.jmx:name=basicMBean,type=BasicMBean"/>

  <stream:stdout-channel-adapter channel="notification" append-newline="true"/>

</beans>
```

To test the different JMX examples, a simple JmxExample test class is created to load the Spring configuration file and wait to allow testing, as shown in Listing 10–9.

***Listing 10–9.** Example Class JmxNotificationListener to Load the Spring Configuration File and Wait*

```
package com.apress.prospringintegration.jmx;

import org.springframework.context.support.ClassPathXmlApplicationContext;

public class JmxNotificationListener {
    public static void main(String[] args) {
        ClassPathXmlApplicationContext context = new ClassPathXmlApplicationContext(
                "jmx/notification-listener.xml");

        try {
            Thread.sleep(180000);
        } catch (InterruptedException e) {
            //do nothing
        }
        context.stop();
    }
}
```

The example may be tested using JConsole, which comes with the Java JDK. Simply invoke the add operation of the BasicMBean object, as shown in Figure 10–3 . JConsole must be run within the 3-minute delay created by the example program.

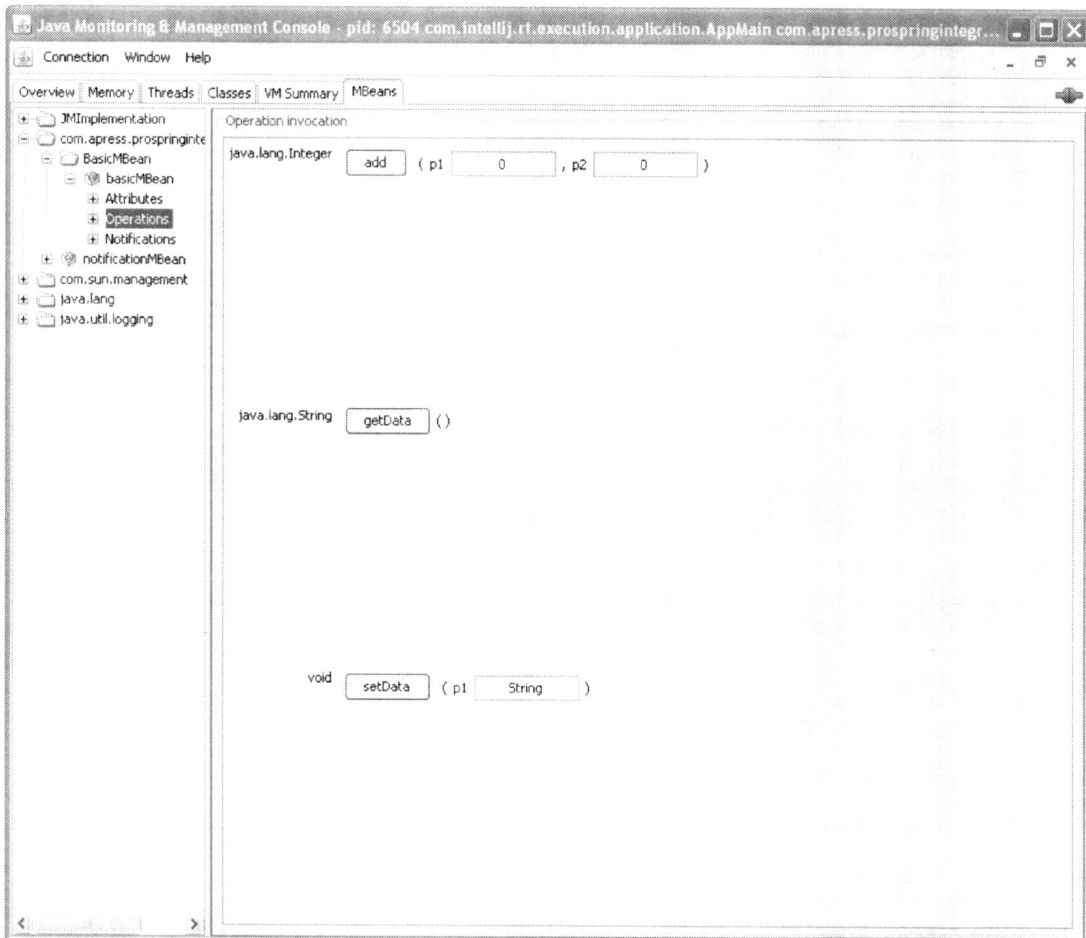

Figure 10–3. JConsole

Spring Integration may also publish an MBean notification using the Notification Publishing channel adapter. The example will be augmented to publish an MBean notification when a message is sent to the send channel. The additional configurations are shown in Listing 10–10. Note that the `mbean-export` element is required for this adapter. The object name will be set to the `notificationMBean` in the same package as the `BasicMBean` so it can be easily found in JConsole.

Listing 10–10. *Notification Publishing Channel Adapter notification-publisher.xml Spring Configuration*

```
<?xml version="1.0" encoding="UTF-8"?>
<beans xmlns="http://www.springframework.org/schema/beans"
       xmlns:xsi="http://www.w3.org/2001/XMLSchema-instance"
       xmlns:int="http://www.springframework.org/schema/integration"
       xmlns:context="http://www.springframework.org/schema/context"
       xmlns:jmx="http://www.springframework.org/schema/integration/jmx"
```

```
    xsi:schemaLocation="http://www.springframework.org/schema/beans
  http://www.springframework.org/schema/beans/spring-beans-3.0.xsd
  http://www.springframework.org/schema/integration
  http://www.springframework.org/schema/integration/spring-integration-2.0.xsd
  http://www.springframework.org/schema/integration/jmx
  http://www.springframework.org/schema/integration/jmx/spring-integration-jmx-2.0.xsd
  http://www.springframework.org/schema/context
  http://www.springframework.org/schema/context/spring-context-3.0.xsd">

<context:mbean-export/>
<context:mbean-server/>

<context:component-scan base-package="com.apress.prospringintegration.jmx"/>

<int:channel id="send"/>

<jmx:notification-publishing-channel-adapter
    channel="send"
    object-name="com.apress.prospringintegration.jmx:name=notificationMBean"
    default-notification-type="default.notification.type"/>

</beans>
```

The `JmxNotificationPublisher` test class is modified to wait for 1 minute and then send a message to the send channel, as shown in Listing 10–11.

Listing 10–11. *Example main Class That Sends a Message to the send Channel*

```
package com.apress.prospringintegration.jmx;

import org.springframework.context.support.ClassPathXmlApplicationContext;
import org.springframework.integration.MessageChannel;
import org.springframework.integration.support.MessageBuilder;

public class JmxNotificationPublisher {
    public static void main(String[] args) {
        ClassPathXmlApplicationContext context = new ClassPathXmlApplicationContext(
                "jmx/notification-publisher.xml");

        try {
            Thread.sleep(60000);
        } catch (InterruptedException e) {
            //do nothing
        }

        System.out.println("Sending message");
        MessageChannel send = context.getBean("send", MessageChannel.class);
        send.send(MessageBuilder.withPayload("Sample Message").build());

        try {
            Thread.sleep(180000);
        } catch (InterruptedException e) {
            //do nothing
        }
```

```
        context.stop();
    }
}
```

Note that a long delay is added to the main class before stopping the context. This should give sufficient time to connect to the MBean server with JConsole and subscribe to the notification, as shown in Figure 10–4.

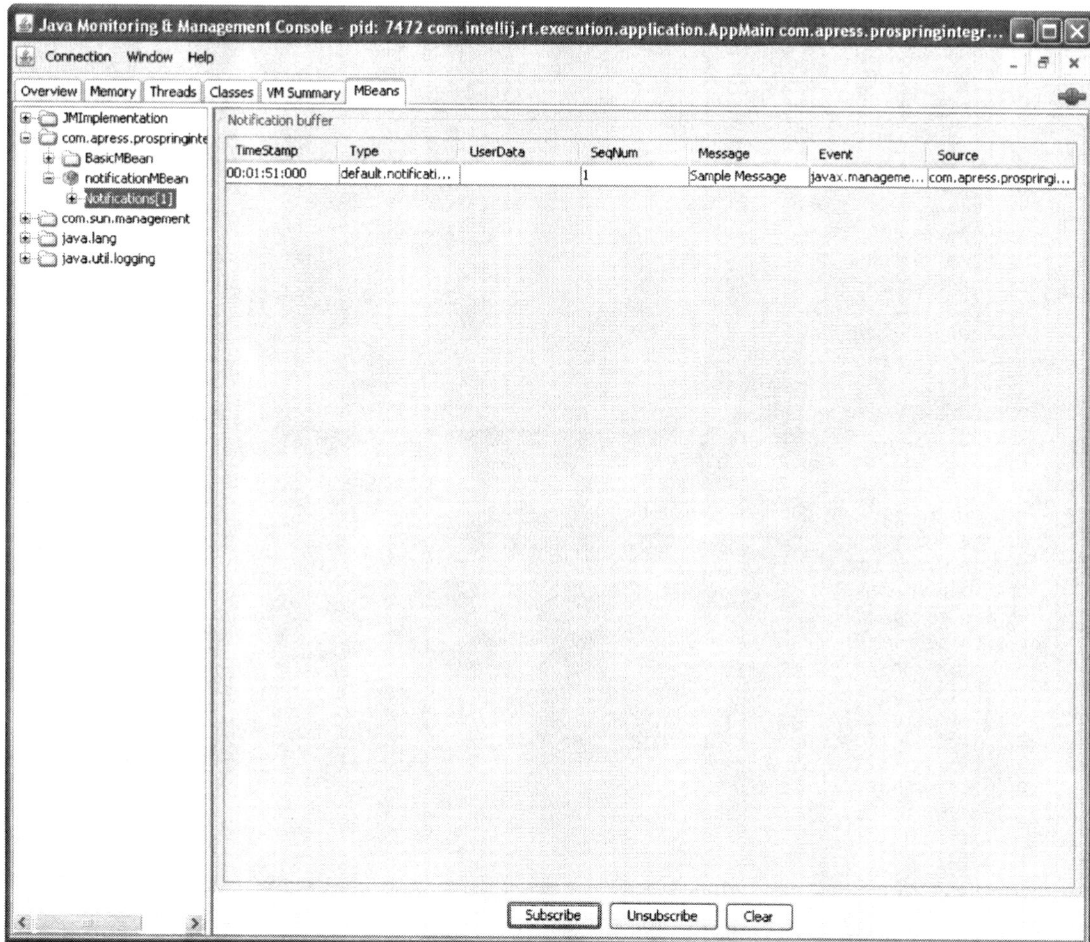

***Figure 10–4.** JConsole Showing MBean Notification*

The next JMX adapter is the Attribute Polling channel adapter. This adapter allows monitoring an attribute at a fixed rate. This is useful for monitoring a particular attribute value. The example is modified to monitor the data property every 5 seconds. The value will be published to the attribute channel and logged using the Spring Integration stream support. The additional Spring configurations are shown in Listing 10–12.

Listing 10–12. *Attribute Polling Channel Adapter attribute-polling.xml Spring Configuration*

```
<?xml version="1.0" encoding="UTF-8"?>
<beans xmlns="http://www.springframework.org/schema/beans"
       xmlns:xsi="http://www.w3.org/2001/XMLSchema-instance"
       xmlns:int="http://www.springframework.org/schema/integration"
       xmlns:context="http://www.springframework.org/schema/context"
       xmlns:jmx="http://www.springframework.org/schema/integration/jmx"
       xmlns:stream="http://www.springframework.org/schema/integration/stream"
       xsi:schemaLocation="http://www.springframework.org/schema/beans
    http://www.springframework.org/schema/beans/spring-beans-3.0.xsd
    http://www.springframework.org/schema/integration
    http://www.springframework.org/schema/integration/spring-integration-2.0.xsd
    http://www.springframework.org/schema/integration/jmx
    http://www.springframework.org/schema/integration/jmx/spring-integration-jmx-2.0.xsd
    http://www.springframework.org/schema/integration/stream
    http://www.springframework.org/schema/integration/stream/spring-integration-stream.xsd
    http://www.springframework.org/schema/context
    http://www.springframework.org/schema/context/spring-context-3.0.xsd">

  <context:mbean-export/>
  <context:mbean-server/>

  <context:component-scan base-package="com.apress.prospringintegration.jmx"/>

  <int:channel id="attribute"/>

  <jmx:attribute-polling-channel-adapter
      channel="attribute"
      object-name="com.apress.prospringintegration.jmx:name=basicMBean,type=BasicMBean"
      attribute-name="Data">
    <int:poller max-messages-per-poll="1" fixed-rate="5000"/>
  </jmx:attribute-polling-channel-adapter>

  <stream:stdout-channel-adapter channel="attribute" append-newline="true"/>

</beans>
```

Note the required poller element, which sets the number of message and rate that the attribute is checked. Start up the Spring context using the JmxAttributePolling class, shown in Listing 10–13. Then modify the attribute using JConsole, and it should be reflected in the log output.

Listing 10–13. *Attribute Polling Example JmxAttributePolling*

```
package com.apress.prospringintegration.jmx;

import org.springframework.context.support.ClassPathXmlApplicationContext;

public class JmxAttributePolling {
    public static void main(String[] args) {
        ClassPathXmlApplicationContext context = new ClassPathXmlApplicationContext(
                "jmx/attribute-polling.xml");

        try {
```

```
            Thread.sleep(180000);
        } catch (InterruptedException e) {
            //do nothing
        }
        context.stop();
    }
}
```

An adapter is also available for invoking MBean operations. The Operation Invoking channel adapter allows you to invoke an MBean operation whenever a message is published to a specified channel. For example, the setter method for the data property can be invoked as an operation. As shown in Listing 10–14, the adapter is configured to invoke the `setData` operation. The operation channel payload will be passed to the method.

Listing 10–14. *Operation Invoking Channel Adapter operation-invoking.xml Spring Configuration*

```
<?xml version="1.0" encoding="UTF-8"?>
<beans xmlns="http://www.springframework.org/schema/beans"
       xmlns:xsi="http://www.w3.org/2001/XMLSchema-instance"
       xmlns:int="http://www.springframework.org/schema/integration"
       xmlns:context="http://www.springframework.org/schema/context"
       xmlns:jmx="http://www.springframework.org/schema/integration/jmx"
       xsi:schemaLocation="http://www.springframework.org/schema/beans
    http://www.springframework.org/schema/beans/spring-beans-3.0.xsd
    http://www.springframework.org/schema/integration
    http://www.springframework.org/schema/integration/spring-integration-2.0.xsd
    http://www.springframework.org/schema/integration/jmx
    http://www.springframework.org/schema/integration/jmx/spring-integration-jmx-2.0.xsd
    http://www.springframework.org/schema/context
    http://www.springframework.org/schema/context/spring-context-3.0.xsd">

  <context:mbean-export/>
  <context:mbean-server/>

  <context:component-scan base-package="com.apress.prospringintegration.jmx"/>

  <int:channel id="operation"/>

  <jmx:operation-invoking-channel-adapter
      channel="operation"
      object-name="com.apress.prospringintegration.jmx:name=basicMBean,type=BasicMBean"
      operation-name="setData"/>

</beans>
```

The example `main` class is modified to send a message to the operation channel with a string payload, as shown in Listing 10–15. The data properties will be set to this string and logged with the previous Attribute Polling channel adapter.

Listing 10–15. *JmxOperationInvoking Class for the Operation Invoking Channel Adapter*

```
package com.apress.prospringintegration.jmx;

import org.springframework.context.support.ClassPathXmlApplicationContext;
import org.springframework.integration.MessageChannel;
```

```
import org.springframework.integration.support.MessageBuilder;

public class JmxOperationInvoking {
    public static void main(String[] args) {
        ClassPathXmlApplicationContext context = new ClassPathXmlApplicationContext(
                "jmx/operation-invoking.xml");

        MessageChannel add = context.getBean("operation", MessageChannel.class);
        add.send(MessageBuilder.withPayload("Hello").build());

        try {
            Thread.sleep(180000);
        } catch (InterruptedException e) {
            //do nothing
        }
        context.stop();
    }
}
```

The last adapter to be discussed is the Operation Invoking Outbound Gateway. This adapter is similar to the Operation Invoking channel adapter discussed just discussed, but allows for a reply message with the return value as the payload. This adapter will be used to invoke the add operation, and is configured as shown in Listing 10–16.

Listing 10–16. *Operation Invoking Outbound Gateway Configuration Example*

```
<?xml version="1.0" encoding="UTF-8"?>
<beans xmlns="http://www.springframework.org/schema/beans"
       xmlns:xsi="http://www.w3.org/2001/XMLSchema-instance"
       xmlns:int="http://www.springframework.org/schema/integration"
       xmlns:context="http://www.springframework.org/schema/context"
       xmlns:jmx="http://www.springframework.org/schema/integration/jmx"
       xmlns:stream="http://www.springframework.org/schema/integration/stream"
       xsi:schemaLocation="http://www.springframework.org/schema/beans
    http://www.springframework.org/schema/beans/spring-beans-3.0.xsd
    http://www.springframework.org/schema/integration
    http://www.springframework.org/schema/integration/spring-integration-2.0.xsd
    http://www.springframework.org/schema/integration/jmx
    http://www.springframework.org/schema/integration/jmx/spring-integration-jmx-2.0.xsd
    http://www.springframework.org/schema/integration/stream
    http://www.springframework.org/schema/integration/stream/spring-integration-stream.xsd
    http://www.springframework.org/schema/context
    http://www.springframework.org/schema/context/spring-context-3.0.xsd">

  <context:mbean-export/>
  <context:mbean-server/>

  <context:component-scan base-package="com.apress.prospringintegration.jmx"/>

  <int:channel id="request"/>
  <int:channel id="reply"/>

  <jmx:operation-invoking-outbound-gateway
      request-channel="request"
```

```
        object-name="com.apress.prospringintegration.jmx:name=basicMBean,type=BasicMBean"
        operation-name="add"
        reply-channel="reply"/>

    <stream:stdout-channel-adapter channel="reply" append-newline="true"/>

</beans>
```

The request message payload is a Map with a string-type key containing the parameter name. The return value will be the payload of the reply message. The example main class is modified as shown in Listing 10–17 to invoke the add operation.

Listing 10–17. *JmxOperationGateway Example Class for the Operation Invoking Outbound Gateway*

```
package com.apress.prospringintegration.jmx;

import org.springframework.context.support.ClassPathXmlApplicationContext;
import org.springframework.integration.MessageChannel;
import org.springframework.integration.support.MessageBuilder;

import java.util.HashMap;
import java.util.Map;

public class JmxOperationGateway {
    public static void main(String[] args) {
        ClassPathXmlApplicationContext context = new ClassPathXmlApplicationContext(
                "jmx/operation-gateway.xml");

        Map<String, Integer> parameters = new HashMap<String, Integer>();
        parameters.put("p1", 5);
        parameters.put("p2", 7);
        MessageChannel request = (MessageChannel) context.getBean("request");
        request.send(MessageBuilder.withPayload(parameters).build());

        try {
            Thread.sleep(180000);
        } catch (InterruptedException e) {
            //do nothing
        }
        context.stop();
    }
}
```

Exposing Your Services Through JMX

The Spring Integration components may be exposed as MBeans using the IntegrationMBeanExporter. This is done using the mbean-exporter element of the jmx namespace, as shown in Listing 10–18.

Listing 10–18. *Configuring the MBean Exporter for the Spring Integration Components*

```
<?xml version="1.0" encoding="UTF-8"?>
<beans xmlns="http://www.springframework.org/schema/beans"
       xmlns:xsi="http://www.w3.org/2001/XMLSchema-instance"
```

```
       xmlns:int="http://www.springframework.org/schema/integration"
       xmlns:jmx="http://www.springframework.org/schema/integration/jmx"
       xmlns:context="http://www.springframework.org/schema/context"
       xsi:schemaLocation="http://www.springframework.org/schema/beans
    http://www.springframework.org/schema/beans/spring-beans-3.0.xsd
    http://www.springframework.org/schema/integration
    http://www.springframework.org/schema/integration/spring-integration-2.0.xsd
    http://www.springframework.org/schema/integration/jmx
    http://www.springframework.org/schema/integration/jmx/spring-integration-jmx-2.0.xsd
    http://www.springframework.org/schema/context
    http://www.springframework.org/schema/context/spring-context-3.0.xsd">

  <context:component-scan base-package="com.apress.prospringintegration.errorhandling"/>

  <int:poller default="true" max-messages-per-poll="1">
    <int:interval-trigger interval="1000"/>
  </int:poller>

  <int:channel id="input">
    <int:queue capacity="10"/>
  </int:channel>

  <int:chain input-channel="input">
    <int:service-activator ref="mockException" method="processMessage"/>
  </int:chain>

  <int:service-activator input-channel="errorChannel"
                         ref="errorLogger"/>

  <jmx:mbean-export default-domain="com.apress.prospringintegration"
                    server="mbeanServer"/>

</beans>
```

The MBeans for the various Spring Integration components will appear under the package `com.apress.prospringintegration`. An example of this feature is shown in Figure 10–5, for the `ErrorHandlingDefault` example discussed previously.

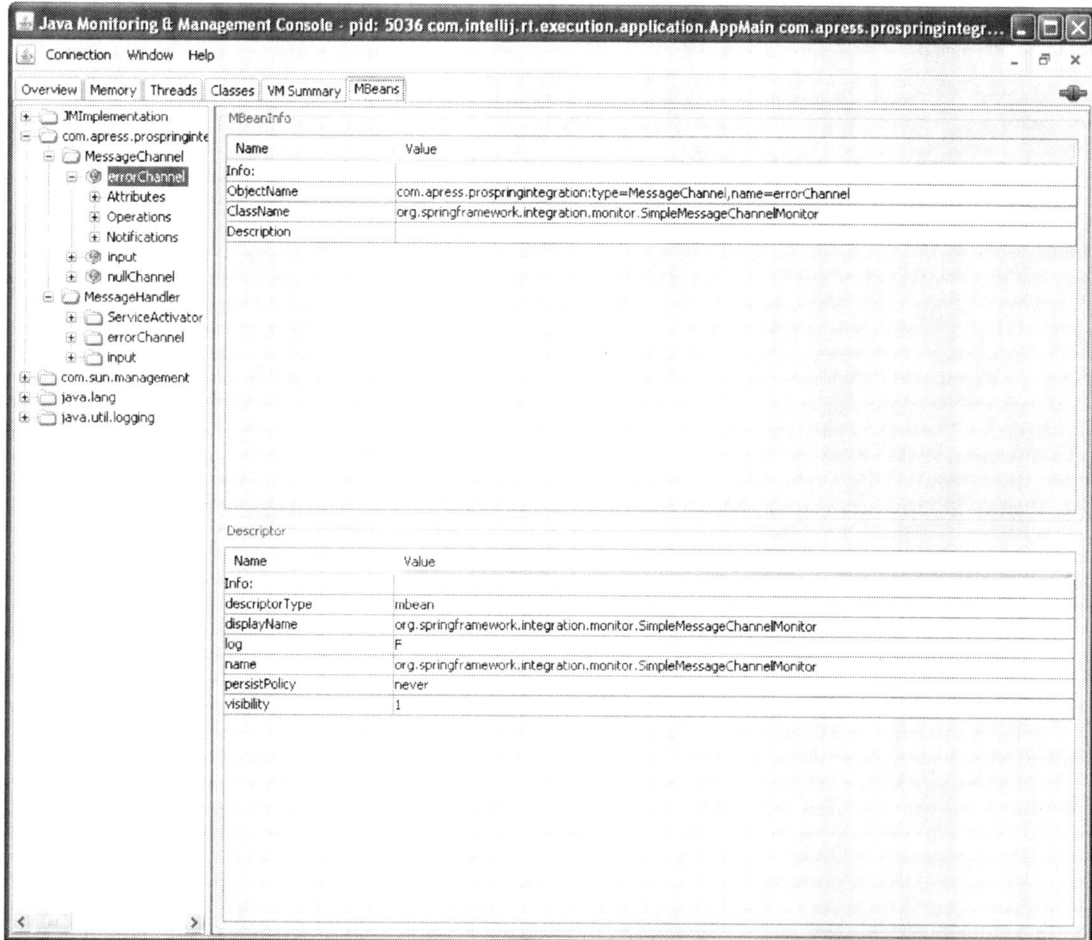

Figure 10–5. JConsole Displaying Spring Integration Components

NAGIOS

There are not many open source tools that allow monitoring applications via JMX for a production environment. JConsole and MX4J are good for diagnostics, but are not really well suited for monitoring in an enterprise environment. One open source project does exist that allows for monitoring JMX attributes and setting alerts that will send out notifications when any attribute reaches a certain value. Nagios (`www.nagios.org`) monitors such attributes as memory, CPU load, and disk usage, and leveraging the plug-in check_jmx (`http://code.google.com/p/jmxquery`) can also monitor JMX attributes. If any JMX attributes go out of range, an alert can be sent to the required personnel to address problems before they become critical.

Measuring Performance

Spring Integration exposes a number of performance metrics through component-level MBeans. They are exposed as discussed previously. For example, message channels and message handlers expose a number of performance measurements, as shown in Figures 10–6 and 10–7.

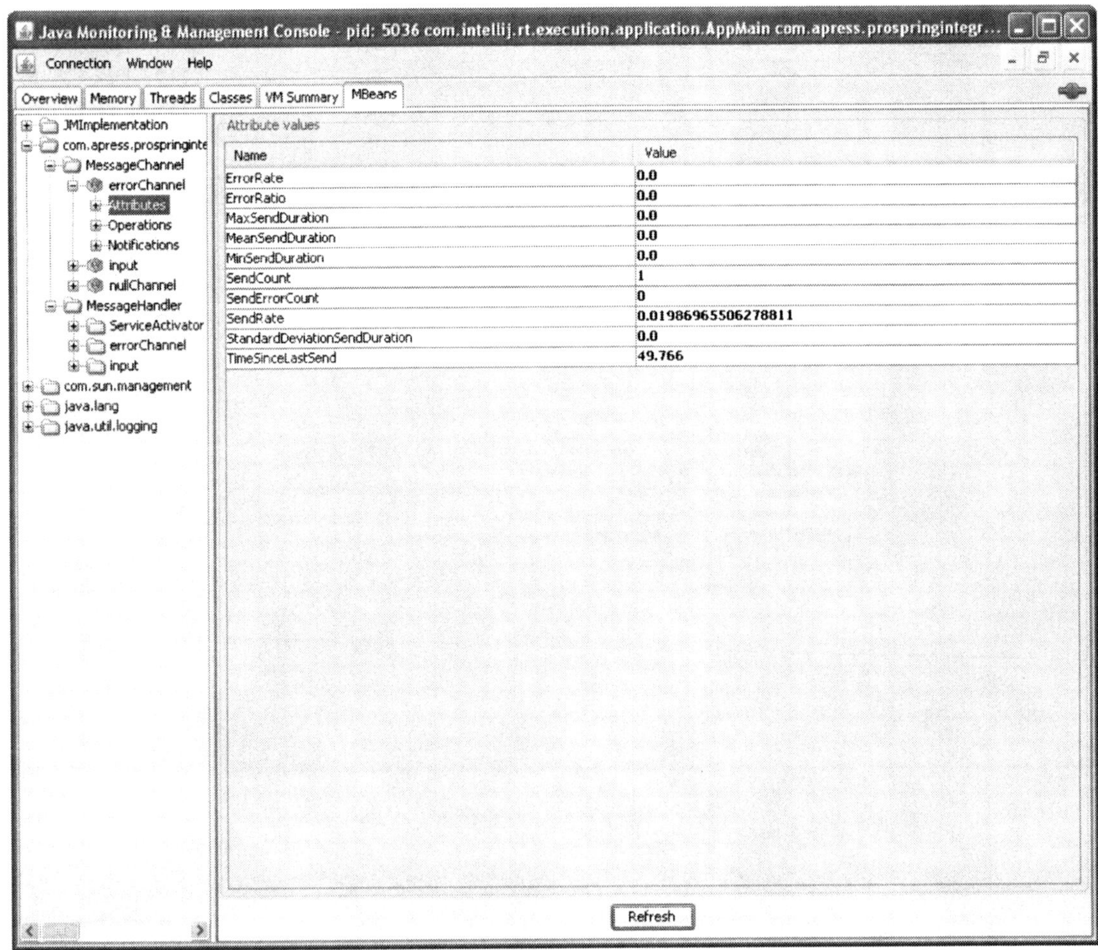

***Figure 10–6.** Example of Message Channel MBean Performance Attributes*

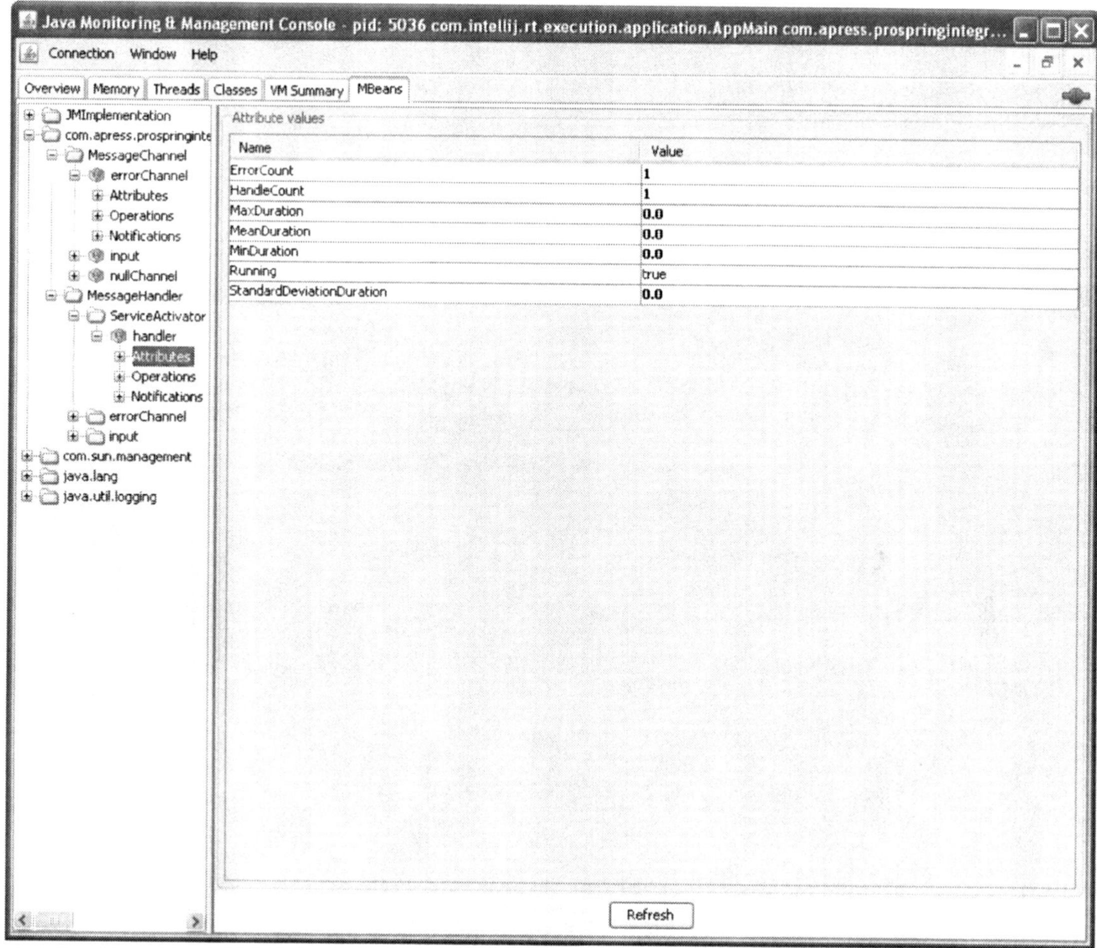

***Figure 10–7.** Example of Message Handler MBean Performance Attributes*

Another method of monitoring performance is to leverage the JAMon project (`http://jamonapi.sourceforge.net`). JAMon is a lightweight, thread-safe Java API that can be used to monitor performance in a production environment. JAMon records aggregated performance statistics such as hits, execution times, and concurrency information. Spring provides an AOP interception, `org.springframework.aop.interceptor.JamonPerformanceMonitorInterceptor`, which simplifies the process of adding JAMon to a Spring application. Using the `org.springframework.aop.framework.autoproxy.BeanNameAutoProxyCreator`, the Spring bean to be monitored may be defined. All public methods of the bean will be instrumented using this approach. Monitoring only specific methods requires customer coding, usually leveraging an AOP package such as Spring AOP. Two Maven dependencies must be added, JAMon and `cglib` required for Spring AOP. The additional dependencies are shown in Listing 10–19.

Listing 10–19. *Maven Dependencies Needed for JAMon and Spring AOP*

```
<dependency>
  <groupId>com.jamonapi</groupId>
  <artifactId>jamon</artifactId>
  <version>2.4</version>
</dependency>
<dependency>
  <groupId>cglib</groupId>
  <artifactId>cglib</artifactId>
  <version>2.2</version>
</dependency>
```

As an example of using JAMon for measuring performance, a basic two-method class will be created, as shown in Listing 10–20. The two methods simply log an input string argument.

Listing 10–20. *Process Message Class Used to Demonstrate Performance Monitoring Using JAMon*

```
package com.apress.prospringintegration.monitoring;

import org.springframework.stereotype.Component;

@Component
public class ProcessMessage {

    public void processMessage(String message) {
        System.out.println(message);
    }

    public void checkMessage(String message) {
        System.out.println(message);
    }

}
```

JAMon requires that a `com.jamonapi.Monitor` instance is started with a name for future reference when entering a method and stop after exiting the method. If this were done within the code, it would look something like Listing 10–21 .

Listing 10–21. *Adding JAMon Directly in the Code*

```
package com.apress.prospringintegration.monitoring;

import com.jamonapi.Monitor;
import com.jamonapi.MonitorFactory;

public class ProcessMessage {

    public void processMessage(String message) {
        Monitor monitor = MonitorFactory.start("process");
        System.out.println(message);
        monitor.stop();
    }
```

```
    public void checkMessage(String message) {
        Monitor monitor = MonitorFactory.start("check");
        System.out.println(message);
        monitor.stop();
    }

}
```

This approach requires quite a bit of additional coding, and is quite invasive if the code has already been written. But using the magic of Spring AOP, the same monitors may be added through the Spring configuration file, as shown in Listing 10–22, and the Java configuration file, as shown in Listing 10–23.

Listing 10–22. *Spring Configuration File for add JAMon*

```
<?xml version="1.0" encoding="UTF-8"?>
<beans xmlns="http://www.springframework.org/schema/beans"
       xmlns:xsi="http://www.w3.org/2001/XMLSchema-instance"
       xmlns:jmx="http://www.springframework.org/schema/integration/jmx"
       xmlns:context="http://www.springframework.org/schema/context"
       xsi:schemaLocation="http://www.springframework.org/schema/beans
    http://www.springframework.org/schema/beans/spring-beans-3.0.xsd
    http://www.springframework.org/schema/integration/jmx
    http://www.springframework.org/schema/integration/jmx/spring-integration-jmx-2.0.xsd
    http://www.springframework.org/schema/context
    http://www.springframework.org/schema/context/spring-context-3.0.xsd">

  <context:mbean-export/>
  <context:mbean-server/>

  <context:component-scan base-package="com.apress.prospringintegration.monitoring"/>

</beans>
```

Listing 10–23. *Java Configuration File MonitoringConfiguration*

```
package com.apress.prospringintegration.monitoring;

import org.springframework.aop.framework.autoproxy.BeanNameAutoProxyCreator;
import org.springframework.aop.interceptor.JamonPerformanceMonitorInterceptor;
import org.springframework.context.annotation.Bean;
import org.springframework.context.annotation.Configuration;

@Configuration
public class MonitoringConfiguration {

    final private static String JAMON_ID = "jamon";

    @Bean(name = JAMON_ID)
    public JamonPerformanceMonitorInterceptor jamonPerformanceMonitorInterceptor() {
        JamonPerformanceMonitorInterceptor interceptor =
                new JamonPerformanceMonitorInterceptor();
        interceptor.setTrackAllInvocations(true);
        interceptor.setUseDynamicLogger(true);
        return interceptor;
    }
```

```
    @Bean
    public BeanNameAutoProxyCreator autoProxyCreator() {
        BeanNameAutoProxyCreator proxyCreator = new BeanNameAutoProxyCreator();
        proxyCreator.setBeanNames(new String[]{"processMessage"});
        proxyCreator.setInterceptorNames(new String[]{"jamon"});
        return proxyCreator;
    }
}
```

The `BeanNameAutoProxyCreator` proxy creator adds the `JamonPerformanceMonitoringInterceptor` interceptor to the list of Spring beans through the `beanNames` property. This is equivalent to the code added in Listing 10–21.

Once the monitoring has been added, the performance information may be obtained through logging by setting the level to `TRACE`, or more elegantly with JMX using the techniques described early in this chapter. Note the context elements `mbean-server`, `mbean-export`, and `component-scan`, which will export any Java class with the proper annotations as an MBean. An MBean is created that will expose the JAMon monitor data as an attribute. This will allow the performance information to be accessed at any time using JMX. The MBean is shown in Listing 10–24.

Listing 10–24. *MBean for Accessing JAMon Performance Data*

```
package com.apress.prospringintegration.monitoring;

import com.jamonapi.MonitorFactory;
import org.springframework.jmx.export.annotation.ManagedAttribute;
import org.springframework.jmx.export.annotation.ManagedResource;
import org.springframework.stereotype.Component;

@Component
@ManagedResource
public class MonitorMBean {

    @ManagedAttribute
    public String[] getData() {
        String[] header = MonitorFactory.getHeader();
        Object[][] data = MonitorFactory.getData();
        String[] result = new String[data.length];

        for (int i = 0; i < data.length; i++) {
            StringBuffer dataValue = new StringBuffer();
            boolean isFirst = true;
            for (int j = 0; j < header.length; j++) {
                if (isFirst) {
                    isFirst = false;
                } else {
                    dataValue.append(",");
                }
                dataValue.append(header[j]).append(":");
                dataValue.append(data[i][j]);
            }
            result[i] = dataValue.toString();
        }
        return result;
```

```
    }

}
```

In order to test the performance monitoring code, a simple main class is created, as shown in Listing 10–25. The example class simply exercises the methods processMessage and checkMessage on the Spring bean ProcessMessage.

***Listing 10–25.** MonitoringExample main Class for Testing Performance Monitoring*

```
package com.apress.prospringintegration.monitoring;

import org.springframework.context.support.ClassPathXmlApplicationContext;

public class MonitoringExample {
    public static void main(String[] args) {
        ClassPathXmlApplicationContext context =
                new ClassPathXmlApplicationContext("classpath:monitoring/monitoring.xml");

        ProcessMessage processMessage =
            context.getBean("processMessage", ProcessMessage.class);

        for (int i = 0; i < 10; i++) {
            processMessage.processMessage("Process");
            processMessage.checkMessage("Check");
        }

        while(true) {
            try {
                Thread.sleep(60000);
            } catch (InterruptedException e) {
                //do nothing
            }
            context.stop();
        }
    }
}
```

Any time the data attribute is checked, the MBean will compile the performance data, as shown in Figure 10–8. Note that this is a simple example, and with further customization, individual MBeans may be created for each monitored Spring class. The attribute value may need to be double-clicked in JConsole for the detailed version of the data.

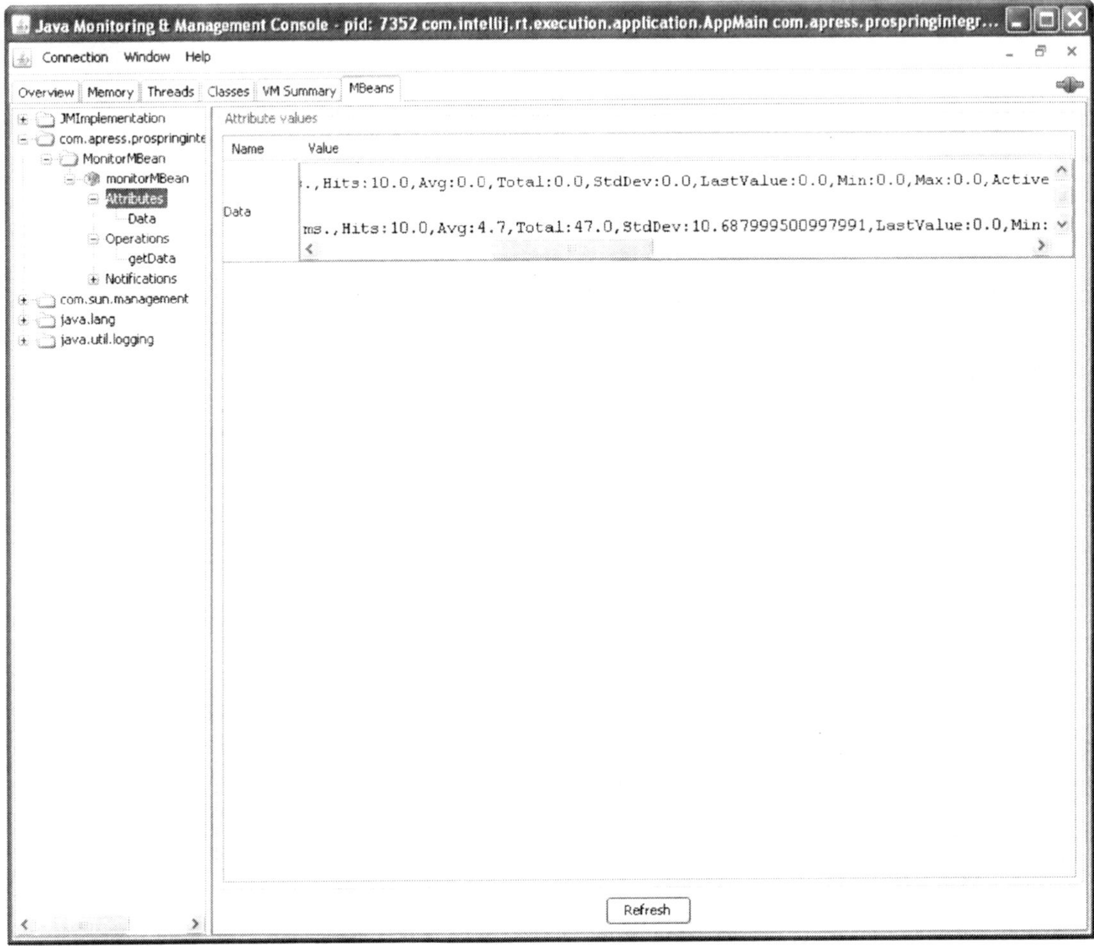

Figure 10–8. JConsole for JAMon Monitoring Data

Hyperic

Hyperic is an enterprise management and monitoring tool from Spring Source with an open source and enterprise edition. The open source version will be used for this example. Where it comes into play with Spring Integration is through its application management support using JMX. The current version will autodiscover any MBean servers configured for remote connections. The current JMX plug-in will allow monitoring basic attributes, such as number of classes loaded per minute, thread count, availability, and uptime. Monitoring other attributes requires customization of the JMX plug-in.

To install Hyperic, download both the server and agent from `www.hyperic.com/downloads`. There are different installation packages for the various operating systems. Install both the server and agent using the installation scripts. To enable autodiscovery of the JVM MBean server, add the property shown in Listing 10–26 to the `agent.properties` file in the `conf` directory in the agent installation location.

Listing 10–26. *Additional Property Needed for MBean Server Autodiscovery*

```
jmx.sun.discover=true
```

Using the monitoring example discussed previously, add the JVM parameters shown in Listing 10–27 to enable remote JMX with security disabled. Start the monitoring example before starting the agent so that the agent can find the remote JMX connection.

Listing 10–27. *Enabling Remote JMX Coonectivity*

```
-Dcom.sun.management.jmxremote
-Dcom.sun.management.jmxremote.port=9999
-Dcom.sun.management.jmxremote.authenticate=false
-Dcom.sun.management.jmxremote.ssl=false
```

To start up Hyperic, the database, server, and agent must be started (in that order). The startup script `db-startup` for starting the default PostgreSQL database is in the `bin` directory of the server installation. After starting the database, you can start the server using the `hq-server start` command. Once the server has started, the dashboard may be accessed at `http://localhost:7080` with the default username `hqadmin` and password `hqadmin`. You can start the agent by issuing the command `hq-agent install` and `hq-agent start`. Accept the default settings as required. The initial screen should look something like Figure 10–9 after the agent discovers the various applications and servers. Click the Add to Inventory button to add the resources to Hyperic.

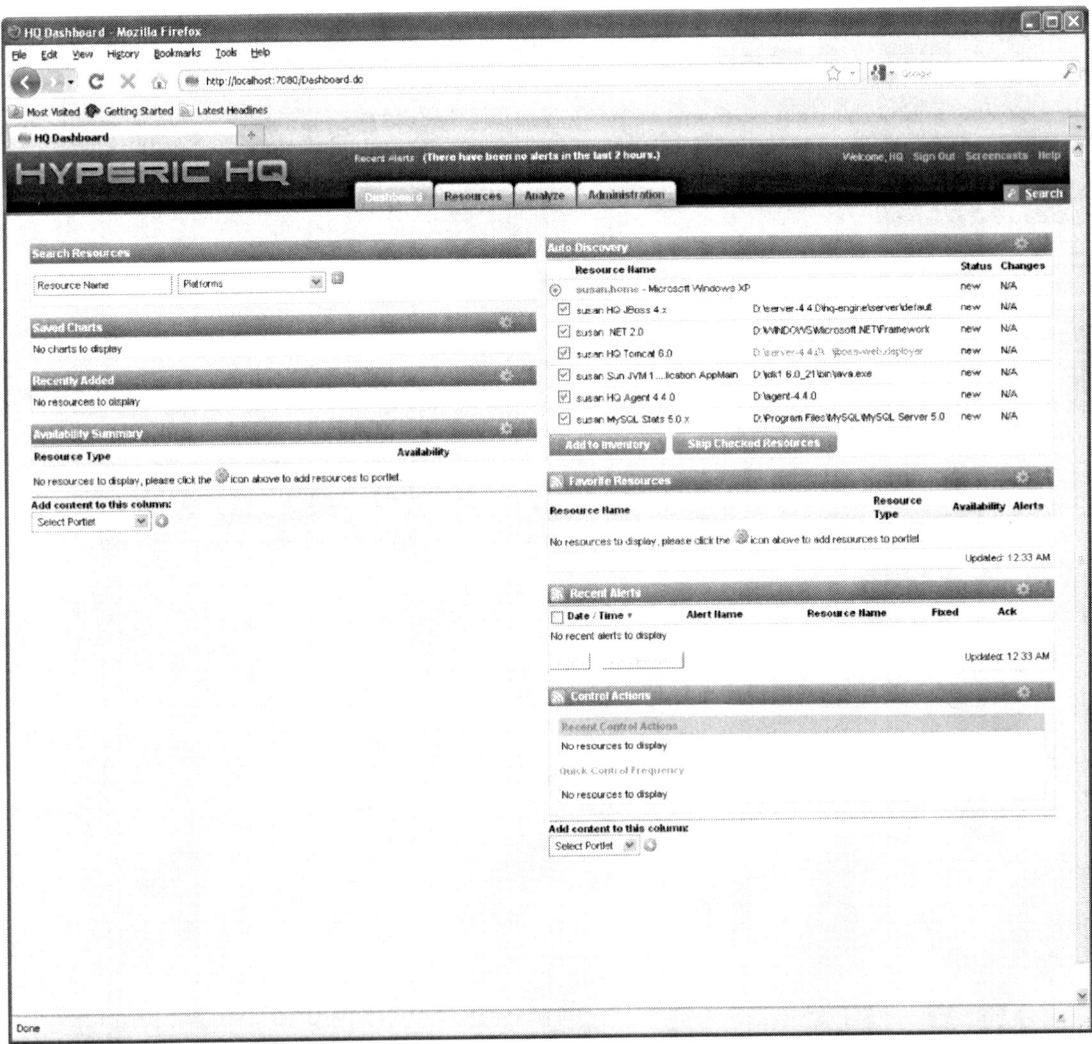

Figure 10–9. Hyperic Dashboard

Select the discovered resource link under the Recently Added resource name to go to the Resources page. Find the Sun JVM 1.5 link on the Resources tab to display the basic MBean attributes for the monitoring example. This is shown in Figure 10–10. Further MBeans may be added by customizing the JMX plug-in.

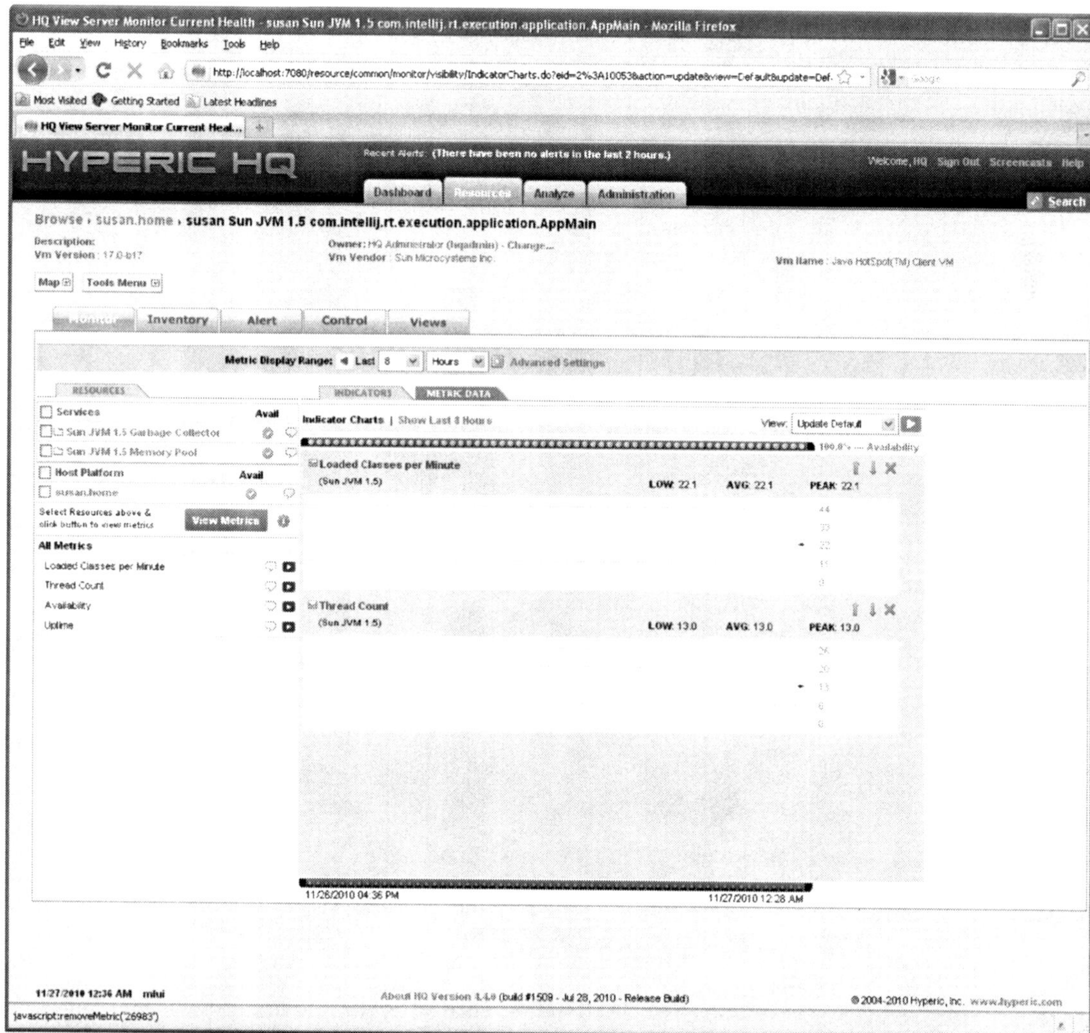

Figure 10–10. Hyperic MBeanMmonitoring

Wire Tap

As used in previous chapters, the Wire Tap interceptor provides a nice way to monitor any message channel without interfering with any currently defined message flows. By adding the `wire-tap` element as an interceptor to any message channel, the message can be captured without affecting any downstream message handlers. For example, as shown in Listing 10–28, any message passing through the input channel will be also sent to the `logging-channel-adapter`. This provides a means of debugging or simply monitoring a Spring Integration application. In addition, the message can be routed to any downstream message handler.

Listing 10–28. Wire Tap Example

```
<?xml version="1.0" encoding="UTF-8"?>
<beans xmlns="http://www.springframework.org/schema/beans"
       xmlns:xsi="http://www.w3.org/2001/XMLSchema-instance"
       xmlns:int="http://www.springframework.org/schema/integration"
       xsi:schemaLocation="http://www.springframework.org/schema/beans
    http://www.springframework.org/schema/beans/spring-beans-3.0.xsd
    http://www.springframework.org/schema/integration
    http://www.springframework.org/schema/integration/spring-integration-2.0.xsd">


  <int:bridge input-channel="input" output-channel="output"/>

  <int:channel id="input">
    <int:interceptors>
      <int:wire-tap channel="logger"/>
    </int:interceptors>
  </int:channel>

  <int:logging-channel-adapter log-full-message="true" id="logger" level="INFO"/>

  <int:channel id="output">
    <int:queue capacity="10"/>
  </int:channel>

</beans>
```

Message History

One feature introduced in Spring Integration 2.0 is recording the message history. This can be important in a messaging environment where each component does not necessarily know about the other's existence. Message history can be leverage for both debugging and auditing purposes. Spring Integration provides a simple way to update the message header each time a message is passed through a tracked component.

To demonstrate how to use message history, the simple example from Chapter 5 will be used, where a message is sent from an outbound JMS channel adapter and received by an inbound channel adapter. Message history is added to track the message after is it is received by the inbound channel and sent to the message channel output. The Spring configuration file is shown in Listing 10–29.

Listing 10–29. Message History Configuration File message-history-context.xml

```
<?xml version="1.0" encoding="UTF-8"?>
<beans xmlns="http://www.springframework.org/schema/beans"
       xmlns:xsi="http://www.w3.org/2001/XMLSchema-instance"
       xmlns:int="http://www.springframework.org/schema/integration"
       xmlns:jms="http://www.springframework.org/schema/integration/jms"
       xmlns:context="http://www.springframework.org/schema/context"
       xsi:schemaLocation="http://www.springframework.org/schema/beans
    http://www.springframework.org/schema/beans/spring-beans-3.0.xsd
    http://www.springframework.org/schema/integration
    http://www.springframework.org/schema/integration/spring-integration-2.0.xsd
```

```
    http://www.springframework.org/schema/integration/jms
    http://www.springframework.org/schema/integration/jms/spring-integration-jms-2.0.xsd
    http://www.springframework.org/schema/context
    http://www.springframework.org/schema/context/spring-context-3.0.xsd">

  <int:message-history/>

  <context:component-scan
      base-package="com.apress.prospringintegration.messagehistory"/>

  <int:channel id="input"/>

  <jms:outbound-channel-adapter id="outboundAdapter"
                                channel="input"
                                destination-name="requestQueue"/>

  <jms:message-driven-channel-adapter id="inboundAdapter"
                                      channel="output"
                                      destination-name="requestQueue"/>

  <int:channel id="output">
    <int:queue capacity="10"/>
  </int:channel>

</beans>
```

When adding the message-history element, any named component with an id defined will be tracked. For this example, the components downstream from the message-driven-channel-adapter will be monitored. The example main class MessageHistoryApp is shown in Listing 10–30.

Listing 10–30. MessageHistoryApp Class Demonstrating Message History

```
package com.apress.prospringintegration.messagehistory;

import org.springframework.context.support.ClassPathXmlApplicationContext;
import org.springframework.integration.Message;
import org.springframework.integration.MessageChannel;
import org.springframework.integration.core.PollableChannel;
import org.springframework.integration.history.MessageHistory;
import org.springframework.integration.support.MessageBuilder;

import java.util.Iterator;
import java.util.Properties;

public class MessageHistoryApp {
    public static void main(String[] args) {
        ClassPathXmlApplicationContext context =
                new ClassPathXmlApplicationContext(
                        "classpath:messagehistory/message-history-context.xml");

        MessageChannel input = context.getBean("input", MessageChannel.class);

        PollableChannel output = context.getBean("output", PollableChannel.class);
        input.send(MessageBuilder.withPayload("Pro Spring Integration Example").build());
```

```
        Message<?> reply = output.receive();

        Iterator<Properties> historyIterator =
            reply.getHeaders().get(MessageHistory.HEADER_NAME,
                    MessageHistory.class).iterator();

        while(historyIterator.hasNext()) {
            Properties properties = historyIterator.next();
            System.out.println(properties);
        }

        System.out.println("received: " + reply);

    }
}
```

As the message goes through the components inboundAdapter and output, the header with the key value MessageHistory.HEADER_NAME is updated with the message history. The example code logs the header values, as shown in Listing 10–31.

Listing 10–31. *Output from Running the Message History Example*

```
{name=inboundAdapter, type=jms:message-driven-channel-adapter, timestamp=1294026893876}
{name=output, type=channel, timestamp=1294026893876}
```

Control Bus

The concept of a control bus is that the same messaging system used for managing and monitoring can be used for application-level control. Spring Integration supports exposing operation invocation via messaging. Thus, a method may be invoked by sending a message.

To demonstrate this ability, a simple example will be created where a method call will be invoked by sending a message. Any Spring component with its method annotated with @ManagedAttribute or @ManagedOperation may be invoked. The example Spring component is shown in Listing 10–32.

Listing 10–32. *Spring Component ControlBean Demonstrating the Control Bus*

```
package com.apress.prospringintegration.controlbus;

import org.springframework.jmx.export.annotation.ManagedOperation;
import org.springframework.stereotype.Component;

@Component
public class ControlBean {

    @ManagedOperation
    public void performOperation() {
        System.out.println("running operation");
    }
}
```

The method performOperation will be invoked by sending a message through the control-bus. The Spring configuration file is shown in Listing 10–33. The control-bus element sets up the operationChannel message channel as a control bus, and a message sent down this channel can invoke an annotated method.

Listing 10–33. Control Bus Spring Configuration File

```
<?xml version="1.0" encoding="UTF-8"?>
<beans xmlns="http://www.springframework.org/schema/beans"
       xmlns:xsi="http://www.w3.org/2001/XMLSchema-instance"
       xmlns:int="http://www.springframework.org/schema/integration"
       xmlns:context="http://www.springframework.org/schema/context"
       xsi:schemaLocation="http://www.springframework.org/schema/beans
    http://www.springframework.org/schema/beans/spring-beans-3.0.xsd
    http://www.springframework.org/schema/integration
    http://www.springframework.org/schema/integration/spring-integration-2.0.xsd
    http://www.springframework.org/schema/context
    http://www.springframework.org/schema/context/spring-context-3.0.xsd">

  <context:component-scan
      base-package="com.apress.prospringintegration.controlbus"/>

  <int:channel id="operationChannel"/>

  <int:control-bus input-channel="operationChannel"/>

</beans>
```

To test the control bus example, we send a message to the operationChannel message channel with a payload specifying the intended method using the Spring expression language, as shown in Listing 10–34. The message payload @controlBean.performOperation will invoke the performOperation method of the Spring bean controlBean.

Listing 10–34. ControlBusApp Example main Class for Invoking the Method Using the Control Bus

```
package com.apress.prospringintegration.controlbus;

import org.springframework.context.support.ClassPathXmlApplicationContext;
import org.springframework.integration.Message;
import org.springframework.integration.MessageChannel;
import org.springframework.integration.support.MessageBuilder;

public class ControlBusApp {
    public static void main(String[] args) {
        ClassPathXmlApplicationContext context =
                new ClassPathXmlApplicationContext("controlbus/control-bus.xml");

        MessageChannel input = context.getBean("operationChannel", MessageChannel.class);

        String message = "@controlBean.performOperation()";
        System.out.println("Sending message: " + message);
        Message operation = MessageBuilder.withPayload(message).build();
        input.send(operation);

    }
}
```

The results of running the ControlBusApp main class are shown in Listing 10–35. The message is sent to the message channel operationChannel, resulting in a call to the method performOperation.

Listing 10–35. *Result of Running the Control Bus Example Code*

```
Sending message: @controlBean.performOperation()
running operation
```

Summary

Monitoring and management support is one of the most important requirements for maintaining an enterprise integration. Since integrations touch applications across the enterprise often managed by different business groups, monitoring and management is essential to pinpoint issues that may be occurring outside of the particular area having the problem. Spring Integration provides this support, and integrates well with external applications to provide this functionality.

This chapter has shown Spring Integration's support for error handling, monitoring using JMX, and performance measurement using Spring Integration and the JAMon project. In addition, it covered Spring Integration support for capturing message history and creating a control bus that allows application-level messaging. Finally, we discussed the Hyperic enterprise monitoring and management tool.

CHAPTER 11

Talking to the Metal

Spring Integration supports basic computer (the metal) integration with message sources and handlers for files, socket-level communication using TCP and UDP, and input and output streaming. In addition, Spring Integration supports sending and receiving files using the FTP and SFTP protocols. Moreover, Spring Integration can talk to a database using the JDBC adapters. The channel adapters used to communicate with files, sockets, streams, file servers, and databases will be discussed.

File System Integration

Using files is one of the most basic and simple approach to enterprise integration. If the format (and structure) of the file is agreed upon by the different parties in an exchange, integration is simply a matter of producing a file and sending it. It is not quite that simple, as you still have to determine the file format and structure, the means of transferring the file, when to transfer it, and how to handle mistakes. In the end, files are an integral part of integration within and between businesses. Spring Integration provides inbound and outbound channel adapters for files.

File Adapter

The `org.springframework.integration.core.MessageSource<T>` implementation `org.springframework.integration.file.FileReadingMessageSource` is used to consume files from the file system directory. This is an inbound adapter. This message source can be used directly, but is typically employed through the Spring Integration file namespace. The first step in using the file channel adapter is adding the Maven dependencies, as shown in Listing 11–1.

Listing 11–1. *Maven Dependencies for the File Channel Adapter*

```
<dependency>
  <groupId>org.springframework.integration</groupId>
  <artifactId>spring-integration-file</artifactId>
  <version>2.0.1.RELEASE</version>
</dependency>
```

The next step is to add the file-specific namespace, as shown in Listing 11–2.

Listing 11–2. *Spring Integration File Namespace*

```
<?xml version="1.0" encoding="UTF-8"?>
<beans xmlns="http://www.springframework.org/schema/beans"
       xmlns:xsi="http://www.w3.org/2001/XMLSchema-instance"
       xmlns:int="http://www.springframework.org/schema/integration"
```

```
       xmlns:file="http://www.springframework.org/schema/integration/file"
       xsi:schemaLocation="http://www.springframework.org/schema/beans
    http://www.springframework.org/schema/beans/spring-beans-3.0.xsd
    http://www.springframework.org/schema/integration
    http://www.springframework.org/schema/integration/spring-integration-2.0.xsd
    http://www.springframework.org/schema/integration/file
    http://www.springframework.org/schema/integration/file/spring-integration-file-➥
2.0.xsd">
</bean>
```

The most basic file adapter configuration is shown in Listing 11–3. The directory of the files to be consumed is directly named, and the `prevent-duplicates` property is set to `true` so that the file will only be consumed once per session; if you kill the Spring Integration process, and files are still present in the directory that have already been delivered, they will be redelivered. No other filters have been configured, so as soon as the file appears, it will be picked up by the periodic scan regardless of whether the file has been completely written to the directory. The example code reads all files from the directory specified, pushes the file to the `files` channel, and writes the file to the directory.

Listing 11–3. *Basic File Channel Adapter Configuration file-context.xml*

```
<?xml version="1.0" encoding="UTF-8"?>
<beans xmlns="http://www.springframework.org/schema/beans"
       xmlns:xsi="http://www.w3.org/2001/XMLSchema-instance"
       xmlns:int="http://www.springframework.org/schema/integration"
       xmlns:file="http://www.springframework.org/schema/integration/file"
       xsi:schemaLocation="http://www.springframework.org/schema/beans
    http://www.springframework.org/schema/beans/spring-beans-3.0.xsd
    http://www.springframework.org/schema/integration
    http://www.springframework.org/schema/integration/spring-integration-2.0.xsd
    http://www.springframework.org/schema/integration/file
    http://www.springframework.org/schema/integration/file/spring-integration-file-2.0.xsd">

  <int:channel id="files"/>

  <file:inbound-channel-adapter id="filesIn" channel="files"
                                directory="file:input" prevent-duplicates="true">
    <int:poller fixed-rate="1000" max-messages-per-poll="100"/>
  </file:inbound-channel-adapter>

  <file:outbound-channel-adapter id="filesOut" channel="files" directory="file:output"/>

</beans>
```

A file-matching pattern can be applied as a mask—each scan will pick up only files whose name matches the pattern. You can use a standard pattern-matching filter by setting the `filename-pattern` property. An example of this filter is shown in Listing 11–4. Only files with `onlyThisFile` as the beginning part of its file name and the extension `txt` will be consumed.

Listing 11–4. *File Channel Adapter Using the Pattern-Matching Filter file-pattern-context.xml*

```
<?xml version="1.0" encoding="UTF-8"?>
<beans xmlns="http://www.springframework.org/schema/beans"
       xmlns:xsi="http://www.w3.org/2001/XMLSchema-instance"
       xmlns:int="http://www.springframework.org/schema/integration"
```

```
       xmlns:file="http://www.springframework.org/schema/integration/file"
       xsi:schemaLocation="http://www.springframework.org/schema/beans
    http://www.springframework.org/schema/beans/spring-beans-3.0.xsd
    http://www.springframework.org/schema/integration
    http://www.springframework.org/schema/integration/spring-integration-2.0.xsd
    http://www.springframework.org/schema/integration/file
    http://www.springframework.org/schema/integration/file/spring-integration-file-2.0.xsd">

  <si:channel id="files"/>

  <file:inbound-channel-adapter id="filesIn" channel="files"
                                directory="file:input" filename-pattern="onlyThisFile*.txt">
    <int:poller fixed-rate="1000"/>
  </file:inbound-channel-adapter>

  <file:outbound-channel-adapter id="filesOut" channel="files" directory="file:output"/>

</beans>
```

The last out-of-the-box file filter allows using a regular expression (regex) pattern to match the file name. An example of this filter is shown in Listing 11–5. The file must match the regex pattern `test[0-9]+\.txt` to be consumed. In addition to the out-of-the-box filters, you can write a custom one by implementing the interface `org.springframework.integration.file.filters.FileListFilter` and setting the `filter` property to the custom filter class.

Listing 11–5. *File Channel Adapter Using the Regex Filter file-regex-context.xml*

```
<?xml version="1.0" encoding="UTF-8"?>
<beans xmlns="http://www.springframework.org/schema/beans"
       xmlns:xsi="http://www.w3.org/2001/XMLSchema-instance"
       xmlns:int="http://www.springframework.org/schema/integration"
       xmlns:file="http://www.springframework.org/schema/integration/file"
       xsi:schemaLocation="http://www.springframework.org/schema/beans
    http://www.springframework.org/schema/beans/spring-beans-3.0.xsd
    http://www.springframework.org/schema/integration
    http://www.springframework.org/schema/integration/spring-integration-2.0.xsd
    http://www.springframework.org/schema/integration/file
    http://www.springframework.org/schema/integration/file/spring-integration-file-2.0.xsd">

  <si:channel id="files"/>

  <file:inbound-channel-adapter id="filesIn" channel="files"
                                directory="file:input" filename-regex="test[0-9]+\.txt">
    <int:poller fixed-rate="1000"/>
  </file:inbound-channel-adapter>

  <file:outbound-channel-adapter id="filesOut" channel="files" directory="file:output"/>

</beans>
```

All the file adapters examples above use the file `outbound-channel-adapter` to write the file. It is straightforward to use this channel adapter, and it will accept file, string, or byte array payload as input. The additional attribute `delete-source-files` will delete the input file once the file has been delivered.

This property setting will only work if the inbound message has a file as the payload or if the header `FileHeaders.ORIGINAL_FILE` contains the source file or file path.

Finally, there is an outbound gateway file adapter, as shown in Listing 11–6. This gateway will send the file as a payload to the reply channel as soon as it is written. This gateway supports cases where further message processing is required based on the adapter successfully writing a file.

Listing 11–6. *An Example of a File Outbound gateway file-gateway-context.xml*

```
<?xml version="1.0" encoding="UTF-8"?>
<beans xmlns="http://www.springframework.org/schema/beans"
       xmlns:xsi="http://www.w3.org/2001/XMLSchema-instance"
       xmlns:context="http://www.springframework.org/schema/context"
       xmlns:int="http://www.springframework.org/schema/integration"
       xmlns:file="http://www.springframework.org/schema/integration/file"
       xsi:schemaLocation="http://www.springframework.org/schema/beans
    http://www.springframework.org/schema/beans/spring-beans-3.0.xsd
    http://www.springframework.org/schema/context
    http://www.springframework.org/schema/context/spring-context-3.0.xsd
    http://www.springframework.org/schema/integration
    http://www.springframework.org/schema/integration/spring-integration-2.0.xsd
    http://www.springframework.org/schema/integration/file
    http://www.springframework.org/schema/integration/file/spring-integration-file-2.0.xsd">

  <context:component-scan base-package="com.apress.prospringintegration.file"/>

  <int:channel id="files"/>

  <file:inbound-channel-adapter id="filesIn"
                                channel="moveInput"
                                directory="file:input" prevent-duplicates="true">
    <int:poller fixed-rate="1000"/>
  </file:inbound-channel-adapter>

  <file:outbound-gateway id="mover" request-channel="moveInput"
                         reply-channel="output"
                         directory="file:output"/>

  <int:service-activator id="handler" input-channel="output" ref="replyHandler"/>

</beans>
```

The `file` namespace also includes two transformers, `file-to-byte-transformer` and `file-to-string-transformer`, which support conversion between files, strings, and byte arrays. These are the two most common transformations used when dealing with file payloads. An example of using the file byte array transformer is shown in Listing 11–7. The example reads in the files from the `input` directory and converts the contents into a byte array. A byte array retains all character encodings, and usually provides the first step in converting to a different format. In Listing 11–8, which demonstrates the use of the transformer, the byte array is sent to the service activator class `ByteHandler`, which logs the length of the byte array.

Listing 11–7. Example of Using the File-to–Byte Array transformer file-transform-byte.xml

```
<?xml version="1.0" encoding="UTF-8"?>
<beans xmlns="http://www.springframework.org/schema/beans"
       xmlns:xsi="http://www.w3.org/2001/XMLSchema-instance"
       xmlns:context="http://www.springframework.org/schema/context"
       xmlns:int="http://www.springframework.org/schema/integration"
       xmlns:file="http://www.springframework.org/schema/integration/file"
       xsi:schemaLocation="http://www.springframework.org/schema/beans
    http://www.springframework.org/schema/beans/spring-beans-3.0.xsd
    http://www.springframework.org/schema/context
    http://www.springframework.org/schema/context/spring-context-3.0.xsd
    http://www.springframework.org/schema/integration
    http://www.springframework.org/schema/integration/spring-integration-2.0.xsd
    http://www.springframework.org/schema/integration/file
    http://www.springframework.org/schema/integration/file/spring-integration-file-2.0.xsd">

  <context:component-scan base-package="com.apress.prospringintegration.file"/>

  <int:channel id="fileOut"/>

  <file:inbound-channel-adapter id="filesIn" channel="input"
                                directory="file:input" prevent-duplicates="true">
    <int:poller fixed-rate="1000"/>
  </file:inbound-channel-adapter>

  <file:file-to-bytes-transformer id="transformer" input-channel="input"
                                  output-channel="output"/>

  <int:service-activator id="handler" input-channel="output"
                         output-channel="fileOut" ref="byteHandler"/>

  <file:outbound-channel-adapter id="filesOut" channel="fileOut" directory="file:output"/>

</beans>
```

Listing 11–8. Service Activator Class That Logs Byte Array Length

```
package com.apress.prospringintegration.file;

import org.springframework.integration.annotation.ServiceActivator;
import org.springframework.stereotype.Component;

@Component
public class ByteHandler {
    @ServiceActivator
    public byte[] handleBytes(byte[] input) {
        System.out.println("Copying " + input.length + " bytes");
        return input;
    }
}
```

The other file transformer converts the file payload into a string. This example is similar to the byte array transformer, and is shown in Listing 11–9. The files are read in from the `input` directory and contents converted into a string. This is useful when string output is desired, or for debugging purposes. A service activator, shown in Listing 11–10, is used to direct the string payload to the class `StringHandler`, in which the contents are logged.

Listing 11–9. *Example of a File-to-String Transfomer file-transform-string.xml*

```
<?xml version="1.0" encoding="UTF-8"?>
<beans xmlns="http://www.springframework.org/schema/beans"
       xmlns:xsi="http://www.w3.org/2001/XMLSchema-instance"
       xmlns:context="http://www.springframework.org/schema/context"
       xmlns:int="http://www.springframework.org/schema/integration"
       xmlns:file="http://www.springframework.org/schema/integration/file"
       xsi:schemaLocation="http://www.springframework.org/schema/beans
    http://www.springframework.org/schema/beans/spring-beans-3.0.xsd
    http://www.springframework.org/schema/context
    http://www.springframework.org/schema/context/spring-context-3.0.xsd
    http://www.springframework.org/schema/integration
    http://www.springframework.org/schema/integration/spring-integration-2.0.xsd
    http://www.springframework.org/schema/integration/file
    http://www.springframework.org/schema/integration/file/spring-integration-file-2.0.xsd">

  <context:component-scan base-package="com.apress.prospringintegration.file"/>

  <si:channel id="fileOut"/>

  <file:inbound-channel-adapter id="filesIn" channel="input"
                                directory="file:input" prevent-duplicates="true">
    <int:poller fixed-rate="1000"/>
  </file:inbound-channel-adapter>

  <file:file-to-string-transformer id="transformer" input-channel="input"
                                   output-channel="output" charset="UTF-8"/>

  <int:service-activator id="handler" input-channel="output"
                                      output-channel="fileOut"
                                      ref="stringHandler"/>

  <file:outbound-channel-adapter id="filesOut" channel="fileOut" directory="file:output"/>

</beans>
```

Listing 11–10. *Service Activator Class That Logs File Content*

```
package com.apress.prospringintegration.file;

import org.springframework.integration.annotation.ServiceActivator;
import org.springframework.stereotype.Component;

@Component
public class StringHandler {
    @ServiceActivator
    public String handleString(String input) {
```

```
        System.out.println("*** Copying text: " + input);
        return input;
    }
}
```

Native Event File Adapter

The default Spring Integration inbound file adapter polls the input directory for any new file. Depending on the polling rate, there can be a lag between when a new file is written and when the inbound channel adapter consumes the file. There is currently development on a native event file adapter that uses the file system kernel APIs on Linux, Mac, and Windows operating systems for notifications of new files, instead of adapter constantly polling for a new file. This will eliminate the lag time between when a file is written to the source directory and subsequently picked up by the normal file adapter's polling scans. As soon as the operating system or kernel sees the file, it publishes the notification to the channel and delivers it to consumers in Spring Integration. This code is in the Spring Integration sandbox at the time of this writing. To see how a version of the Linux native adapter might be implemented, consult Chapter 15. Ideally, the final version will be available with the Mac and Windows version in the 2.1 Spring Integration release.

TCP and UDP Integration

Spring Integration supports both UDP- and TCP-based communication. Both one-way and two-way communication are supported, using the channel adapters and message gateways, respectively. The maven dependencies for the UDP and TCP/IP adapters are shown in Listing 11–11.

Listing 11–11. *Maven Dependencies for the UDP and TCP Adapters*

```
<dependency>
  <groupId>org.springframework.integration</groupId>
  <artifactId>spring-integration-ip</artifactId>
  <version>2.0.1.RELEASE</version>
</dependency>
```

Spring Integration supports both sending and receiving a datagram packet to a single destination and to a multicast address. The message handler class for sending a datagram packet is `org.springframework.integration.ip.udp.UnicastSendingMessageHandler`, and the message adapter class for receiving the datagram packet is `org.springframework.integration.ip.udp.Unicast ReceivingChannelAdapter`. To simplify configuring these components, Spring Integration provides an XML `ip` namespace, as shown in Listing 11–12.

Listing 11–12. *Internet Protocol (IP) Namespace*

```
<?xml version="1.0" encoding="UTF-8"?>
<beans xmlns="http://www.springframework.org/schema/beans"
       xmlns:xsi="http://www.w3.org/2001/XMLSchema-instance"
       xmlns:context="http://www.springframework.org/schema/context"
       xmlns:int="http://www.springframework.org/schema/integration"
       xmlns:ip="http://www.springframework.org/schema/integration/ip"
       xsi:schemaLocation="http://www.springframework.org/schema/beans
    http://www.springframework.org/schema/beans/spring-beans-3.0.xsd
    http://www.springframework.org/schema/context
```

```
    http://www.springframework.org/schema/context/spring-context-3.0.xsd
    http://www.springframework.org/schema/integration
    http://www.springframework.org/schema/integration/spring-integration-2.0.xsd
    http://www.springframework.org/schema/integration/ip
    http://www.springframework.org/schema/integration/ip/spring-integration-ip-2.0.xsd">
</beans>
```

A basic example of using UDP with Spring Integration is shown in Listing 11–13. The udp-outbound-channel-adapter sends a UDP datagram packet out on port 1234 based on the message payload sent to the channel sendUdp. The datagram is received by the udp-inbound-channel-adapter and sent to the class UdpListener using the service activator configuration. The service activator logs the datagram message, as shown in Listing 11–14.

Listing 11–13. *Basic Spring Integration UDP Configuration udp-context.xml*

```
<?xml version="1.0" encoding="UTF-8"?>
<beans xmlns="http://www.springframework.org/schema/beans"
       xmlns:xsi="http://www.w3.org/2001/XMLSchema-instance"
       xmlns:context="http://www.springframework.org/schema/context"
       xmlns:int="http://www.springframework.org/schema/integration"
       xmlns:ip="http://www.springframework.org/schema/integration/ip"
       xsi:schemaLocation="http://www.springframework.org/schema/beans
    http://www.springframework.org/schema/beans/spring-beans-3.0.xsd
    http://www.springframework.org/schema/context
    http://www.springframework.org/schema/context/spring-context-3.0.xsd
    http://www.springframework.org/schema/integration
    http://www.springframework.org/schema/integration/spring-integration-2.0.xsd
    http://www.springframework.org/schema/integration/ip
    http://www.springframework.org/schema/integration/ip/spring-integration-ip-2.0.xsd">

  <context:component-scan base-package="com.apress.prospringintegration.ip"/>

  <int:channel id="sendUdp"/>

  <ip:udp-outbound-channel-adapter id="udpOut" host="localhost" port="12345"
                                   multicast="false" check-length="true"
                                   channel="sendUdp"/>

  <ip:udp-inbound-channel-adapter id="udpIn" port="12345" receive-buffer-size="500"
                                  multicast="false" check-length="true"
                                  channel="receiveUdp" />

  <int:service-activator id="updHandler" input-channel="receiveUdp" ref="udpListener"/>

</beans>
```

Listing 11–14. *UdpListener Service Activator Class*

```
package com.apress.prospringintegration.ip;

import org.springframework.integration.Message;
import org.springframework.integration.annotation.ServiceActivator;
import org.springframework.stereotype.Component;
```

```
@Component
public class UdpListener {
    @ServiceActivator
    public void handleUdp(Message<?> message) {
        System.out.println("*** UDP Message: " + message);
        System.out.println("*** UDP Message Payload: "
                + new String((byte[])message.getPayload()));
    }
}
```

UDP is an unreliable protocol, and thus Spring Integration provides two options to improve its reliability. One option used in the example in Listing 11–13 is setting the property `check-length` to `true`. This causes the adapter to prepend the length of the message to the message data. This allows the message to be checked for completeness. However, this requires that the receiving endpoint know about this check.

Another option is the `acknowledge` property. When set to `true`, this property causes the sending to wait for an acknowledgement from the receiving destination. Again, the destination endpoint must be set up to send an acknowledgement to the sender for this check to work. The configuration for this option is shown in Listing 11–15.

Listing 11–15. *Using UDP Application-Level Acknowledgement*

```
  <ip:udp-outbound-channel-adapter id="udpOut" host="localhost" port="12345"
                                   multicast="false" check-length="true"
                                   channel="sendUdp" acknowledge="true"
                                   ack-host="localhost" ack-port="12312"
                                   ack-timeout="5000"/>
```

A UDP multicast example is shown in Listing 11–16. The adapter configuration is similar to the single-destination configuration, except that the `multicast` property is set to `true`.

Listing 11–16. *UDP Multicast udp-multicast.xml*

```
<?xml version="1.0" encoding="UTF-8"?>
<beans xmlns="http://www.springframework.org/schema/beans"
       xmlns:xsi="http://www.w3.org/2001/XMLSchema-instance"
       xmlns:context="http://www.springframework.org/schema/context"
       xmlns:int="http://www.springframework.org/schema/integration"
       xmlns:ip="http://www.springframework.org/schema/integration/ip"
       xsi:schemaLocation="http://www.springframework.org/schema/beans
    http://www.springframework.org/schema/beans/spring-beans-3.0.xsd
    http://www.springframework.org/schema/context
    http://www.springframework.org/schema/context/spring-context-3.0.xsd
    http://www.springframework.org/schema/integration
    http://www.springframework.org/schema/integration/spring-integration-2.0.xsd
    http://www.springframework.org/schema/integration/ip
    http://www.springframework.org/schema/integration/ip/spring-integration-ip-2.0.xsd">

  <context:component-scan base-package="com.apress.prospringintegration.ip"/>

  <int:channel id="sendUdp"/>

  <ip:udp-outbound-channel-adapter id="udpOut" host="localhost" port="12345"
                                   multicast="true" check-length="true"
                                   channel="sendUdp"/>
```

```
    <ip:udp-inbound-channel-adapter id="udpIn" port="12345" receive-buffer-size="500"
                                    multicast="true" check-length="true"
                                    channel="receiveUdp" multicast-address="225.6.7.8"/>

    <int:service-activator id="updHandler" input-channel="receiveUdp" ref="udpListener"/>

</beans>
```

The basis for the underlying connection used by the TCP adapters can be configured using a connection factory. Spring Integration provides two TCP connections factories, one for the client and one for the server. A client factory is used for creating an outgoing connection, whereas a server factory is used to listen for an incoming connection. The TCP connection factories support both a `java.net.Socket` and `java.nio.channel.SocketChannel` connection set via the property `using-nio`, which when set to `true` uses the NIO (native input/output) connection introduced in Java 5. The TCP example shown in Listing 11–17 uses the `Socket` connection.

Listing 11–17. *TCP Channel Adapter tcp-context.xml*

```
<?xml version="1.0" encoding="UTF-8"?>
<beans xmlns="http://www.springframework.org/schema/beans"
       xmlns:xsi="http://www.w3.org/2001/XMLSchema-instance"
       xmlns:context="http://www.springframework.org/schema/context"
       xmlns:int="http://www.springframework.org/schema/integration"
       xmlns:ip="http://www.springframework.org/schema/integration/ip"
       xsi:schemaLocation="http://www.springframework.org/schema/beans
    http://www.springframework.org/schema/beans/spring-beans-3.0.xsd
    http://www.springframework.org/schema/context
    http://www.springframework.org/schema/context/spring-context-3.0.xsd
    http://www.springframework.org/schema/integration
    http://www.springframework.org/schema/integration/spring-integration-2.0.xsd
    http://www.springframework.org/schema/integration/ip
    http://www.springframework.org/schema/integration/ip/spring-integration-ip-2.0.xsd">

  <context:component-scan base-package="com.apress.prospringintegration.ip"/>

  <int:channel id="tcpSend"/>

  <ip:tcp-connection-factory id="client" type="client" host="localhost"
                             port="1234" single-use="true" so-timeout="10000"/>

  <ip:tcp-connection-factory id="server" type="server" host="localhost" port="1234"/>

  <ip:tcp-outbound-channel-adapter id="tcpOutbound" channel="tcpSend"
                                   connection-factory="client"/>

  <ip:tcp-inbound-channel-adapter id="tcpInbound" channel="tcpReceive"
                                  connection-factory="server"/>

  <int:service-activator id="tcpHandler" input-channel="tcpReceive"
                         ref="tcpListener"/>

</beans>
```

This basic example takes messages sent to the message channel tcpSend and sends it out using the tcp-outbound-channel-adapter. The channel adapter configuration is quite simple, only requiring a message channel and connection factory. Note that the inbound and outbound channel adapter can share the same connection factory; however, the inbound adapter owns the server connection factory, and the outbound adapter owns the client adapter. Only one adapter of each type can reference a single connection factory.

There are numerous properties for the connection factories, and only the pertinent ones will be mentioned here. The client or server is set through the type property. The hostname is set using the host property, and the port is set using the port property. If the single-use property is set to true, a new connection will be created each time a message is sent. The so-timeout property determines the socket timeout in milliseconds.

Following the previous example, a new TCP connection is made to localhost port 1234 of the tcp-inbound-channel-adapter. The message payload is sent to the tcpReceive channel and handled by the TcpListener service activator class shown in Listing 11–18. The service activator class logs the message payload.

Listing 11–18. *TcpListener Service Activator Class*

```
package com.apress.prospringintegration.ip;

import org.springframework.integration.Message;
import org.springframework.integration.annotation.ServiceActivator;
import org.springframework.stereotype.Component;

@Component
public class TcpListener {
    @ServiceActivator
    public void handleTcp(Message<?> message) {
        System.out.println("*** TCP Message: " + message);
        System.out.println("*** TCP Message Payload: "
                + new String((byte[]) message.getPayload()));
    }
}
```

TCP is a streaming protocol, and the message payload must be serialized and broken into discrete messages. At the protocol level, this is called a *frame*. Spring Integration provides several (de)serializers for this purpose. All serializers accept either a byte array or a string as input. All deserializers produce a byte array.

- The default (de)serializer org.springframework.integration.ip.tcp.serializer .ByteArrayCrlfSerializer converts the byte array into a stream of bytes followed by a carriage return and line feed. This serializer is used when none is explicitly specified, and will support a telnet client.
- The second (de)serializer is org.springframework.integration.ip.tcp.serializer .ByteArrayStxEtxSerializer, which converts the byte array into a stream of bytes preceded by a STX (Start of TeXt) and followed by an ETX (End of TeXt).
- The third (de)serializer is org.springframework.integration.ip.tcp.serializer .ByteArrayLengthHeaderSerializer, which converts the byte array into a stream of bytes preceded by a 4-byte binary length.

There are also inbound and outbound TCP gateways that use the same TCP connection factories described previously. They allow for request/reply scenarios using a TCP connection. An example of using the TCP gateways is shown in Listing 11–19.

Listing 11–19. TCP Gateway tcp-gateway.xml

```
<?xml version="1.0" encoding="UTF-8"?>
<beans xmlns="http://www.springframework.org/schema/beans"
       xmlns:xsi="http://www.w3.org/2001/XMLSchema-instance"
       xmlns:context="http://www.springframework.org/schema/context"
       xmlns:int="http://www.springframework.org/schema/integration"
       xmlns:ip="http://www.springframework.org/schema/integration/ip"
       xsi:schemaLocation="http://www.springframework.org/schema/beans
    http://www.springframework.org/schema/beans/spring-beans-3.0.xsd
    http://www.springframework.org/schema/context
    http://www.springframework.org/schema/context/spring-context-3.0.xsd
    http://www.springframework.org/schema/integration
    http://www.springframework.org/schema/integration/spring-integration-2.0.xsd
    http://www.springframework.org/schema/integration/ip
    http://www.springframework.org/schema/integration/ip/spring-integration-ip-2.0.xsd">

  <context:component-scan base-package="com.apress.prospringintegration.ip"/>

  <int:gateway id="tcpGateway" default-request-channel="outboundRequest"
             service-interface="com.apress.prospringintegration.ip.TcpGateway"/>

  <ip:tcp-connection-factory id="client" type="client" host="localhost"
                             port="1234" single-use="true"
                             so-timeout="10000"/>

  <ip:tcp-connection-factory id="server" type="server" host="localhost" port="1234"/>

  <ip:tcp-inbound-gateway id="inGateway" request-channel="inboundRequest"
                          connection-factory="server"/>

  <ip:tcp-outbound-gateway id="outGateway" request-channel="outboundRequest"
                           reply-channel="outboundReply"
                           connection-factory="client"/>

  <int:transformer id="bytes2String" input-channel="outboundReply"
                   expression="new String(payload)"/>

  <si:service-activator id="tcpHandler" input-channel="inboundRequest" ref="tcpEcho"/>

</beans>
```

A gateway is used as the entry point for this example, based on the interface TcpGateway, as shown in Listing 11–20. A string message is sent with a string response. This gateway forwards the string payload to the tcp-outbound-gateway through the outboundRequest message channel. The outbound gateway using the client connection factory connects to localhost port 1234 of the tcp-inbound-gateway. The inbound gateway forwards the message payload to the TcpEcho service activator via the inboundRequest message channel. The TcpEcho class shown in Listing 11–21 simply echoes the payload prepended with Reply:. Finally, the reply message is passed back through the outboundReply message channel, using a transformer to convert the byte array used by the TCP protocol to a string, and then sent back to the initial gateway.

***Listing 11–20.** Gateway Interface TcpGateway*

```
package com.apress.prospringintegration.ip;

public interface TcpGateway {
    public String sendTcp(String message);
}
```

***Listing 11–21.** TcpEcho Service Activator*

```
package com.apress.prospringintegration.ip;

import org.springframework.integration.annotation.ServiceActivator;
import org.springframework.stereotype.Component;

@Component
public class TcpEcho {
    @ServiceActivator
    public String echo(byte[] bytes) {
        return "reply: " + new String(bytes);
    }
}
```

Stream Processing

Spring Integration provides two adapters for reading from streams: org.springframework.integration .stream.ByteStreamReadingMessageSource for a byte stream and org.springframework.integration .stream.CharacterStreamReadingMessageSource for a character stream. The byte stream version requires an InputStream and the character version requires a Reader; both are specified through the constructor. The byte stream version has the optional property bytesPerMessage, which specifies how many bytes it will attempt to read in for each message; the default is 1024. The required Maven dependencies are shown in Listing 11–22 and sample configurations are shown in Listing 11–23.

***Listing 11–22.** Maven Dependencies for the Stream Adapters*

```
    <dependency>
      <groupId>org.springframework.integration</groupId>
      <artifactId>spring-integration-stream</artifactId>
      <version>2.0.1.RELEASE</version>
    </dependency>
```

***Listing 11–23.** Reading from a Stream*

```
<bean class="org.springframework.integration.stream.ByteStreamReadingMessageSource">
  <constructor-arg ref="inputStream"/>
  <property name="bytesPerMessage" value="4096"/>
</bean>

<bean class="org.springframework.integration.stream.CharacterStreamReadingMessageSource">
  <constructor-arg ref="reader"/>
</bean>
```

Two adapters are provided for writing to a stream, `org.springframework.integration.stream.ByteStreamWritingMessageHandler` for writing to a byte stream and `org.springframework.integration.stream.CharacterStreamWritingMessageHandler` for writing to a character stream. Similar to the stream readers, the byte stream version requires an `OutputStream` and the character version requires a `Writer`, again specified through the constructor. Both adapters have an optional second constructor argument for the buffer size. Sample configurations are shown in Listing 11–24.

***Listing 11–24.** Writing to a Stream in a Java Configuration*

```
@Bean
public org.springframework.integration.stream.ByteStreamWritingMessageHandler➥
 byteStreamWritingMessageHandler () {
    java.io.OutputStream os =  … ; // accquire this as appropriate to your application
    return new ByteStreamWritingMessageHandler(os, 1024) ;
}

@Bean
public CharacterStreamWritingMessageHandler characterStreamWritingMessageHandler () {
    java.io.Writer w = … ; // accquire this as appropriate to your application
    return new CharacterStreamWritingMessageHandler(w) ;
}
```

Stdin and Stdout

Spring Integration currently only provides namespace support for stdin and stdout streaming. The stdin adapter reads from the system's `STDIN` input stream (typically, this describes the content available when somebody writes to a command line or types something; in Java, this can be accessed from the `System.in` object). The stdout adapter writes to the system's `STDOUT` output stream (typically, this describes the stream that controls what shows up on the system's command line; in Java this can be accessed from the `System.out` object). A simple example that echoes any character sent to the console is shown in Listing 11–25.

***Listing 11–25.** Simple Stdin and Stdout Namespace Configuration input-stream.xml*

```
<?xml version="1.0" encoding="UTF-8"?>
<beans xmlns="http://www.springframework.org/schema/beans"
       xmlns:xsi="http://www.w3.org/2001/XMLSchema-instance"
       xmlns:context="http://www.springframework.org/schema/context"
       xmlns:int="http://www.springframework.org/schema/integration"
       xmlns:stream="http://www.springframework.org/schema/integration/stream"
       xsi:schemaLocation="http://www.springframework.org/schema/beans
    http://www.springframework.org/schema/beans/spring-beans-3.0.xsd
    http://www.springframework.org/schema/context
    http://www.springframework.org/schema/context/spring-context-3.0.xsd
    http://www.springframework.org/schema/integration
    http://www.springframework.org/schema/integration/spring-integration-2.0.xsd
    http://www.springframework.org/schema/integration/stream
    http://www.springframework.org/schema/integration/stream/spring-integration-stream➥
-2.0.xsd">

  <si:poller default="true" fixed-rate="50"/>
```

```
  <int:channel id="input"/>

  <stream:stdin-channel-adapter id="stdin" channel="input"/>

  <stream:stdout-channel-adapter id="stdout" channel="input" append-newline="true"/>

</beans>
```

Following a Log File

To demonstrate the power of Spring Integration's stream adapters, an example of following a log file is shown in Listing 11–26. This example allows monitoring a log file by creating an input stream, which is read into a message channel. An input stream of a logging file is passed to the `ByteStreamReadingMessageSource` adapter. An inbound channel adapter is configured to reference the input stream adapter. The input stream is polled and pushed to the message channel input. The service activator class `LogHandler`, shown in Listing 11–27, takes the incoming message payload and prints it to the console. This is a powerful technique that allows Spring Integration full access to an application log file.

Listing 11–26. *Spring Configuration for Following a Log File stream-log.xml*

```
<?xml version="1.0" encoding="UTF-8"?>
<beans xmlns="http://www.springframework.org/schema/beans"
       xmlns:xsi="http://www.w3.org/2001/XMLSchema-instance"
       xmlns:context="http://www.springframework.org/schema/context"
       xmlns:si="http://www.springframework.org/schema/integration"
       xmlns:stream="http://www.springframework.org/schema/integration/stream"
       xsi:schemaLocation="http://www.springframework.org/schema/beans
    http://www.springframework.org/schema/beans/spring-beans-3.0.xsd
    http://www.springframework.org/schema/context
    http://www.springframework.org/schema/context/spring-context-3.0.xsd
                http://www.springframework.org/schema/integration
                http://www.springframework.org/schema/integration/spring-integration-2.0.xsd
                http://www.springframework.org/schema/integration/stream
                http://www.springframework.org/schema/integration/stream/spring-integration➥
-stream-2.0.xsd">

  <context:component-scan base-package="com.apress.prospringintegration.stream"/>

  <bean id="loggingSource"
        class="org.springframework.integration.stream.ByteStreamReadingMessageSource">
    <constructor-arg ref="inputStream"/>
  </bean>

  <bean id="inputStream" class="java.io.FileInputStream">
    <constructor-arg type="java.lang.String" value="example.log"/>
  </bean>

  <si:inbound-channel-adapter id="inboundChannel" channel="input" ref="loggingSource">
    <si:poller fixed-rate="1000" max-messages-per-poll="100"/>
  </si:inbound-channel-adapter>

  <si:service-activator id="logProcess" ref="logHandler" input-channel="input"/>
</beans>
```

Listing 11–27. Log Handler Service Activator

```
package com.apress.prospringintegration.stream;

import org.springframework.integration.Message;
import org.springframework.integration.annotation.ServiceActivator;
import org.springframework.stereotype.Component;

@Component
public class LogHandler {
    @ServiceActivator
    public void handleLog(Message<?> message) {
        System.out.println("Log Payload: "
                + new String((byte[])message.getPayload()));
    }
}
```

FTP/FTPS and SFTP

Spring Integration supports file transfer operations using File Transfer Protocol (FTP), FTP Secure (FTPS), and Secure File Transfer Protocol (SFTP). Spring Integration allows sending and receiving files to and from a server using all of these protocols.

FTP

Spring Integration supports sending and receiving files over FTP by providing inbound and outbound channel adapters. As usual, the Spring Integration FTP adapter requires the additional Maven dependency:

```
<dependency>
  <groupId>org.springframework.integration</groupId>
  <artifactId>spring-integration-ftp</artifactId>
  <version>2.0.1.RELEASE</version>
</dependency>
```

In addition, you can provide namespace support for these adapters by adding the following header to your Spring configuration file:

```
<beans xmlns:int-ftp="http://www.springframework.org/schema/integration/ftp"
      xsi:schemaLocation="http://www.springframework.org/schema/integration/ftp
    http://www.springframework.org/schema/integration/ftp/spring-integration-ftp-2.0.xsd">
```

The first step in using the FTP adapters is creating an FTP session factory based on the class `org.springframework.integration.ftp.session.DefaultFtpSessionFactory`. The session factory is easily created using a Java configuration class, as shown in Listing 11–28.

Listing 11–28. Java Configuration for Creating an FTP Session

```
package com.apress.prospringintegration.ftp;

import org.apache.commons.net.ftp.FTPClient;
import org.springframework.beans.factory.annotation.Value;
```

```
import org.springframework.context.annotation.Bean;
import org.springframework.context.annotation.Configuration;
import org.springframework.integration.ftp.session.DefaultFtpSessionFactory;

@Configuration
public class FtpConfiguration {

    @Value("${host}")
    private String host;

    @Value("${username}")
    private String username;

    @Value("${password}")
    private String password;

    @Bean
    public DefaultFtpSessionFactory ftpClientFactory() {
        DefaultFtpSessionFactory ftpSessionFactory =
                new DefaultFtpSessionFactory();
        ftpSessionFactory.setHost(host);
        ftpSessionFactory.setUsername(username);
        ftpSessionFactory.setPassword(password);
        ftpSessionFactory.setClientMode(
                FTPClient.PASSIVE_LOCAL_DATA_CONNECTION_MODE);
        return ftpSessionFactory;
    }
}
```

The required parameters are the host, username, and password. These parameters are set via a properties files shown in Listing 11–29.

Listing 11–29. *FTP Configuration Properties File ftp.properties*

```
host=localhost
username=[username]
password=[password]
```

Note that you can support FTPS simply by configuring a different FTP session factory. FTPS is like FTP, except it uses SSL to communicate data privately. To use it, you need to have the key for the remote host in your Java key store. It is up to the implementer to install the FTP server's certificate. There are many ways to do this, but they are all painful. Instead, you might have an easier time using a key management tool, such as Portecle, from SourceForge (see `http://sourceforge.net/projects/portecle/files/portecle/1.7/portecle-1.7.zip/download`). Portecle is an open source Java UI for key management, and is very simple. Run `java -jar portecle.jar`, and when the UI shows up, go to Tools ➤ Import Trusted Certificate. If your certificate is a `.cert` file, then choose the `.cert` file or choose the appropriate format. Then your FTPS-based communication (including the Spring Integration adapter) should work.

Substitute the configuration in Listing 11–30 for the `DefaultFtpSessionFactory` bean configured in 11–28. The rest of the examples can use either FTP session factory implementation—they do not care whether you are using FTP or FTPS.

Listing 11–30. FTPS Java Configuration

```
package com.apress.prospringintegration.ftp;

import org.springframework.beans.factory.annotation.Value;
import org.springframework.context.annotation.Bean;
import org.springframework.context.annotation.Configuration;
import org.springframework.integration.sftp.session.DefaultSftpSessionFactory;

@Configuration
public class FtpConfiguration {

    @Value("${host}")
    private String host;

    @Value("${username}")
    private String username;

    @Value("${password}")
    private String password;

    @Bean
    public DefaultSftpSessionFactory ftpClientFactory() {
        DefaultSftpSessionFactory ftpSessionFactory =
                new DefaultSftpSessionFactory();
        ftpSessionFactory.setHost(host);
        ftpSessionFactory.setUser(username);
        ftpSessionFactory.setPrivateKeyPassphrase(password);
        return ftpSessionFactory;
    }
}
```

FTP Inbound Channel Adapter

The FTP inbound channel adapter is a listener adapter that connects to an FTP server based on the session factory, and checks for new files created, at which point it initiates a file transfer. The adapter then publishes a message containing a `File` instance of the file just transferred. An example of the Spring configuration file using the inbound FTP adapter is shown in Listing 11–31.

Listing 11–31. Spring Configuration for the Inbound FTP Adapter ftp-inbound-context.xml

```
<?xml version="1.0" encoding="UTF-8"?>
<beans xmlns="http://www.springframework.org/schema/beans"
       xmlns:xsi="http://www.w3.org/2001/XMLSchema-instance"
       xmlns:int="http://www.springframework.org/schema/integration"
       xmlns:int-ftp="http://www.springframework.org/schema/integration/ftp"
       xmlns:context="http://www.springframework.org/schema/context"
       xsi:schemaLocation="http://www.springframework.org/schema/beans
       http://www.springframework.org/schema/beans/spring-beans-3.0.xsd
    http://www.springframework.org/schema/integration
    http://www.springframework.org/schema/integration/spring-integration-2.0.xsd
    http://www.springframework.org/schema/context
```

```
    http://www.springframework.org/schema/context/spring-context-3.0.xsd
    http://www.springframework.org/schema/integration/ftp
    http://www.springframework.org/schema/integration/ftp/spring-integration-ftp-2.0.xsd">

  <context:property-placeholder location="/spring/ftp/ftp.properties"/>
  <context:component-scan base-package="com.apress.prospringintegration.ftp"/>

  <int-ftp:inbound-channel-adapter id="ftpInbound"
                                   channel="ftpChannel"
                                   session-factory="ftpClientFactory"
                                   filename-regex=".*\.txt$"
                                   auto-create-local-directory="true"
                                   delete-remote-files="false"
                                   remote-directory="."
                                   local-directory="file:output">
    <int:poller fixed-rate="1000"/>
  </int-ftp:inbound-channel-adapter>

  <int:channel id="ftpChannel">
    <int:queue/>
  </int:channel>

</beans>
```

The component-scan element is used to support the session factory Java configuration, and the property-placeholder element is used to read the properties file. The FTP inbound channel adapter is a polling consumer requiring a poller to initiate the FTP connection and check for any new files that may have been created. Once a file has been transferred, the adapter will publish a message with a java.io.File based on the newly transferred file as its payload, and send the message to the message channel ftpChannel. This adapter allows file filtering based on the file name, pattern, or regex, similar to the file adapter discussed previously in this chapter. For this example, a regex expression specified through the filename-regex attribute is used to pick up any file with the extension txt.

Additional attributes include delete-remote-files, which when set to true will delete the file at the remote server after the file has been transferred; remote-directory, which allows selecting the remote directory from which to transfer the file; and local-directory, which allows specifying the directory to transfer the file to. A simple main class to run this example is shown in Listing 11–32. This main class creates the Spring context and listens for an incoming message when a file is transferred.

Listing 11–32. *FTP Inbound Channel Adapter Example main Class*

```
package com.apress.prospringintegration.ftp;

import org.springframework.context.ApplicationContext;
import org.springframework.context.support.ClassPathXmlApplicationContext;
import org.springframework.integration.Message;
import org.springframework.integration.core.PollableChannel;

public class FtpInbound {

    public static void main(String[] args) {
        ApplicationContext context =
                new ClassPathXmlApplicationContext("/spring/ftp/ftp-inbound-context.xml");
        PollableChannel ftpChannel = context.getBean("ftpChannel", PollableChannel.class);
```

```
            Message<?> message =  ftpChannel.receive();
            System.out.println("message: " + message);
        }
    }
```

FTP Outbound Channel Adapter

The FTP outbound channel adapter supports connecting to a remote FTP server and transferring a file based on the incoming payload. The adapter supports the following payloads:

- `java.io.File`: The actual file object
- `byte[]`: A byte array that represents the file context
- `java.lang.String`: Text that represents the file context

This adapter uses the same FTP session factory as the inbound adapter discussed previously. An example Spring configuration file for a FTP outbound channel adapter is shown in Listing 11–33.

Listing 11–33. *Spring Configuration for the FTP Outbound Channel Adapter ftp-outbound-context.xml*

```
<?xml version="1.0" encoding="UTF-8"?>
<beans xmlns="http://www.springframework.org/schema/beans"
       xmlns:xsi="http://www.w3.org/2001/XMLSchema-instance"
       xmlns:int="http://www.springframework.org/schema/integration"
       xmlns:int-ftp="http://www.springframework.org/schema/integration/ftp"
       xmlns:context="http://www.springframework.org/schema/context"
       xsi:schemaLocation="http://www.springframework.org/schema/beans
       http://www.springframework.org/schema/beans/spring-beans-3.0.xsd
    http://www.springframework.org/schema/integration
    http://www.springframework.org/schema/integration/spring-integration-2.0.xsd
    http://www.springframework.org/schema/context
    http://www.springframework.org/schema/context/spring-context-3.0.xsd
    http://www.springframework.org/schema/integration/ftp
    http://www.springframework.org/schema/integration/ftp/spring-integration-ftp-2.0.xsd">

  <context:property-placeholder location="/spring/ftp/ftp.properties"/>
  <context:component-scan base-package="com.apress.prospringintegration.ftp"/>

  <int:channel id="ftpChannel"/>

  <int-ftp:outbound-channel-adapter id="ftpOutbound"
                                    channel="ftpChannel"
                                    remote-directory="."
                                    session-factory="ftpClientFactory"/>

</beans>
```

The FTP outbound channel adapter will take an incoming message on the channel `ftpOutbound`, initiate a connection to the FTP server based on the `session-factory` attribute, and transfer the file based on the message payload. The file will be transferred to the directory specified by the `remote-directory` attribute. An example `main` class that uses the FTP outbound channel adapter is shown in Listing 11–34.

Listing 11–34. *FTP Outbound Channel Adapter Example main Class*

```
package com.apress.prospringintegration.ftp;

import org.springframework.context.ApplicationContext;
import org.springframework.context.support.ClassPathXmlApplicationContext;
import org.springframework.integration.Message;
import org.springframework.integration.MessageChannel;
import org.springframework.integration.support.MessageBuilder;

import java.io.File;

public class FtpOutbound {

    public static void main(String[] args) {
        ApplicationContext context =
                new ClassPathXmlApplicationContext("/spring/ftp/ftp-outbound-context.xml");
        MessageChannel ftpChannel = context.getBean("ftpChannel", MessageChannel.class);
        File file = new File("readme.txt");
        Message<File> message = MessageBuilder.withPayload(file).build();
        ftpChannel.send(message);
    }
}
```

This example class creates the Spring context and sends a message to the `ftpChannel` message channel. The payload is the `File` instance representing the file `readme.txt`. This will cause the FTP adapter to connect to the remote FTP server and transfer the `readme.txt` file.

SFTP

Spring Integration also provides support for SFTP when file transfer is required to be over a secure stream. SFTP is a file system–like view over an SSH connection, and most of the time having SSH access to a server is enough to be able to use SFTP. The SFTP protocol requires a secure channel like SSH, as well visibility to the client's identity throughout the SFTP session. Similar to the FTP adapters, Spring Integration supports sending and receiving files over SFTP by providing inbound and outbound channel adapters. The following Maven dependency is required for the SFTP adapter:

```
<dependency>
  <groupId>org.springframework.integration</groupId>
  <artifactId>spring-integration-sftp</artifactId>
  <version>2.0.1.RELEASE</version>
</dependency>
```

You can provide namespace support for these adapters by adding the following header to your Spring configuration file:

```
<beans xmlns:int-sftp="http://www.springframework.org/schema/integration/sftp"
       xsi:schemaLocation="http://www.springframework.org/schema/integration/sftp
    http://www.springframework.org/schema/integration/sftp/spring-integration-sftp-➥
2.0.xsd">
```

Like the FTP adapters, the first step in using the SFTP adapters is to create an SFTP session factory based on the class `org.springframework.integration.sftp.session.DefaultSftpSessionFactory`. The session factory is again created using a Java configuration class, as shown in Listing 11–35.

Listing 11–35. *Java Configuration for Creating the SFTP Session Factory*

```
package com.apress.prospringintegration.ftp;

import org.springframework.beans.factory.annotation.Value;
import org.springframework.context.annotation.Bean;
import org.springframework.context.annotation.Configuration;
import org.springframework.integration.sftp.session.DefaultSftpSessionFactory;

@Configuration
public class SftpConfiguration {

    @Value("${host}")
    private String host;

    @Value("${username}")
    private String username;

    @Value("${password}")
    private String password;

    @Bean
    public DefaultSftpSessionFactory sftpSessionFactory() {
        DefaultSftpSessionFactory sessionFactory = new DefaultSftpSessionFactory();
        sessionFactory.setHost(host);
        sessionFactory.setUser(username);
        sessionFactory.setPassword(password);

        return sessionFactory;
    }
}
```

This session factory also supports using SSH keys (and keys that themselves are locked with a password), which can be set through the `DefaultSftpSessionFactory` session factory instance. The essential `host`, `username`, and `password` parameters used in this example are set through the same properties file as the FTP adapter.

SFTP Inbound Channel Adapter

The SFTP inbound channel adapter is a listener adapter that connects to an SFTP server based on the session factory, and checks for new files created, at which point it initiates a file transfer. The adapter then publishes a message containing a file instance of the file just transferred. The Spring configuration file for an example using the inbound SFTP adapter is shown in Listing 11–36.

Listing 11–36. *Spring Configuration for Inbound SFTP Adapter sftp-inbound-context.xml*

```
<?xml version="1.0" encoding="UTF-8"?>
<beans xmlns="http://www.springframework.org/schema/beans"
       xmlns:xsi="http://www.w3.org/2001/XMLSchema-instance"
       xmlns:int="http://www.springframework.org/schema/integration"
       xmlns:int-sftp="http://www.springframework.org/schema/integration/sftp"
       xmlns:context="http://www.springframework.org/schema/context"
```

```
        xsi:schemaLocation="http://www.springframework.org/schema/beans
        http://www.springframework.org/schema/beans/spring-beans-3.0.xsd
    http://www.springframework.org/schema/integration
    http://www.springframework.org/schema/integration/spring-integration-2.0.xsd
    http://www.springframework.org/schema/context
    http://www.springframework.org/schema/context/spring-context-3.0.xsd
    http://www.springframework.org/schema/integration/sftp
    http://www.springframework.org/schema/integration/sftp/spring-integration-sftp-2.0.xsd">

  <context:property-placeholder location="/spring/ftp/ftp.properties"/>
  <context:component-scan base-package="com.apress.prospringintegration.ftp"/>

  <int-sftp:inbound-channel-adapter id="ftpInbound"
                                    channel="ftpChannel"
                                    session-factory="sftpSessionFactory"
                                    filename-regex=".*\.txt$"
                                    auto-create-local-directory="true"
                                    delete-remote-files="false"
                                    remote-directory="."
                                    local-directory="file:output">
    <int:poller fixed-rate="1000"/>
  </int-sftp:inbound-channel-adapter>

  <int:channel id="ftpChannel">
    <int:queue/>
  </int:channel>

</beans>
```

Again, the context component-scan element is used to scan the configured package and find the session factory Java configuration. The property-placeholder element is used to read the properties file, and resolve and replace placeholder expressions in the configuration. The SFTP inbound channel adapter is also a polling consumer requiring a poller to initiate the SFTP connection and check for any new files that may have been created. Once the file has been transferred, the adapter will publish a message with a java.io.File based on the newly transferred file as its payload and send the message to the message channel ftpChannel. This adapter allows file filtering based on the file name, pattern, or regex, similar to the file adapter discussed previously in this chapter. For this example, a regex expression specified through the filename-regex attribute is used to pick up any file with the extension txt.

Additional attributes include delete-remote-files, which when set to true will delete the file at the remote server after the file has been transferred; remote-directory, which allows selecting the remote directory from which to transfer the file; and local-directory, which allows specifying the directory to transfer the file to. A simple main class to run this example is shown in Listing 11–37. This main class creates the Spring context and listens for an incoming message when a file is transferred.

Listing 11–37. *SFTP Inbound Channel Adapter Example main Class*

```
package com.apress.prospringintegration.ftp;

import org.springframework.context.ApplicationContext;
import org.springframework.context.support.ClassPathXmlApplicationContext;
import org.springframework.integration.Message;
import org.springframework.integration.core.PollableChannel;
```

```
public class SftpInbound {
    public static void main(String[] args) {
        ApplicationContext context =
                new ClassPathXmlApplicationContext("/spring/ftp/sftp-inbound-context.xml");
        PollableChannel ftpChannel = context.getBean("ftpChannel", PollableChannel.class);

        Message<?> message = ftpChannel.receive();
        System.out.println("message: " + message);
    }
}
```

SFTP Outbound Channel Adapter

The SFTP outbound channel adapter supports connecting to a remote SFTP server and transferring a file based on the incoming payload. Similar to the FTP adapter, the SFTP adapter supports the following payloads:

- `java.io.File`: The actual file object
- `byte[]`: A byte array that represents the file context
- `java.lang.String`: Text that represents the file context

This adapter uses the same SFTP session factory as the inbound adapter discussed previously. An example Spring configuration file for an SFTP outbound channel adapter is shown in Listing 11–38.

Listing 11–38. *Spring Configuration for the SFTP Outbound Channel Adapter sftp-outbound-context.xml*

```
<?xml version="1.0" encoding="UTF-8"?>
<beans xmlns="http://www.springframework.org/schema/beans"
       xmlns:xsi="http://www.w3.org/2001/XMLSchema-instance"
       xmlns:int="http://www.springframework.org/schema/integration"
       xmlns:int-sftp="http://www.springframework.org/schema/integration/sftp"
       xmlns:context="http://www.springframework.org/schema/context"
       xsi:schemaLocation="http://www.springframework.org/schema/beans
       http://www.springframework.org/schema/beans/spring-beans-3.0.xsd
    http://www.springframework.org/schema/integration
    http://www.springframework.org/schema/integration/spring-integration-2.0.xsd
    http://www.springframework.org/schema/context
    http://www.springframework.org/schema/context/spring-context-3.0.xsd
    http://www.springframework.org/schema/integration/sftp
    http://www.springframework.org/schema/integration/sftp/spring-integration-sftp-2.0.xsd">

  <context:property-placeholder location="/spring/ftp/ftp.properties"/>
  <context:component-scan base-package="com.apress.prospringintegration.ftp"/>

  <int:channel id="ftpChannel"/>

  <int-sftp:outbound-channel-adapter id="ftpOutbound"
                                     channel="ftpChannel"
                                     remote-directory="."
                                     session-factory="sftpSessionFactory"/>

</beans>
```

The SFTP outbound channel adapter will take an incoming message on the ftpOutbound channel, initiate a connection to the SFTP server based on the session-factory attribute, and transfer the file based on the message payload. The file will be transferred to the directory specified by the remote-directory attribute. An example main class that uses the SFTP outbound channel adapter is shown in Listing 11–39.

Listing 11–39. *FTP Outbound Channel Adapter Example main Class*

```
package com.apress.prospringintegration.ftp;

import org.springframework.context.ApplicationContext;
import org.springframework.context.support.ClassPathXmlApplicationContext;
import org.springframework.integration.Message;
import org.springframework.integration.MessageChannel;
import org.springframework.integration.support.MessageBuilder;

import java.io.File;

public class SftpOutbound {

    public static void main(String[] args) {
        ApplicationContext context =
                new ClassPathXmlApplicationContext("/spring/ftp/sftp-outbound-context.xml");
        MessageChannel ftpChannel = context.getBean("ftpChannel", MessageChannel.class);
        File file = new File("readme.txt");
        Message<File> message = MessageBuilder.withPayload(file).build();
        ftpChannel.send(message);
    }
}
```

This example class creates the Spring context and sends a message to the ftpChannel message channel. The payload is the java.io.File instance representing the file readme.txt. This will cause the SFTP adapter to connect to the remote SFTP server and transfer the readme.txt file.

Spring Integration's Remote File System Abstractions

The examples introduced thus far supporting inbound and outbound File, FTP/FTPS, and SFTP adapters are similar, and indeed, the only thing that needed to change besides the XML namespace used was the SessionFactory implementation. This is intentional—all the adapters share a number of common abstractions. The SessionFactory instances are in reality all implementations of the org.springframework.integration.file.remote.session.SessionFactory interface, which is responsible for producing a Session instance specific to each of the adapters. The Session interface is a generic view on top of the file system APIs that the adapters work with. The interface is reproduced here:

```
package org.springframework.integration.file.remote.session;

import java.io.IOException;
import java.io.InputStream;
import java.io.OutputStream;

public interface Session {

    boolean remove(String path) throws IOException;
```

```
    <F> F[] list(String path) throws IOException;

    void read(String source, OutputStream outputStream) throws IOException;

    void write(InputStream inputStream, String destination) throws IOException;

    void rename(String pathFrom, String pathTo) throws IOException;

    void close();

    boolean isOpen();

}
```

The Session (which surfaces an adapter-specific view of the file system) and the type of file being transmitted are the only things that really change in the various file transfer adapters. Each adapter uses an underlying abstraction that handles common operations such as listing files, getting file names and byte sizes, and moving files differently. So, the Session extracts this common functionality into a hierarchy that can be reused. It follows then that the adapters themselves can all share the same base code, as they all support writing to a remote file system and receiving remote files into a local directory. The inbound adapters descend from org.springframework.integration.file.remote.synchronizer .AbstractInboundFileSynchronizingMessageSource<F>. The AbstractInboundFileSynchronizing MessageSource<F> in turn delegates to implementations of org.springframework.integration.file .remote.synchronizer.AbstractInboundFileSynchronizer<F> to do the file system–specific work. These are strategy interfaces—if you want to write an inbound adapter that behaves in exactly the same way as these adapters, you need only implement the relatively trivial abstract methods on these classes. The inbound adapters support ways to poll the remote file system, download the new files to a local directory, and then deliver those new files as Spring Integration messages with a payload of type java.io.File. All the adapters support the option to delete the received file from the remote file system once it has been delivered. All the remote file system inbound adapters also support specifying a remote directory path to monitor and automatically create the directories that are used on startup. It is important to note that the remote file system adapters have two important components: the file system–specific synchronizer, which polls the remote file system for new files and downloads them, and the org.springframework.integration.file.FileReadingMessageSource (this is the class behind the inbound file adapter discussed previously), which actually delivers the java.io.File objects from the local download folder.

This design has several redeeming qualities. First, the adapters synchronize files to a local directory and then deliver *those* files to the consumers. If the Spring Integration process is killed during delivery, but there are still files in the local download directory, then these files will be still be delivered correctly when the adapter is restarted, because it is the local directory that is in fact the source of the delivered messages, not the remote file system. Additionally, consumers of these files can transform their contents and perform operations on them without fear of network I/O costs when using the normal java.io.File references.

The remote file system outbound adapters also share a common hierarchy of collaborating objects. In practice, all remote file system adapters are instances of org.springframework.integration.file .remote.handler.FileTransferringMessageHandler, and thus share common operations and features. All adapters support the configuration of an output character set, the local temporary directory to use for files being transferred, and a org.springframework.integration.file.FileNameGenerator implementation to customize how remotely written file names are generated from a Spring Integration message.

Spring Integration's File System Abstractions

There are abstractions common to both the remote file system adapters and the local file system adapter. Common to all the inbound adapters is support for limiting which files are detected during scans of the directory. There are three common but mutually exclusive attributes available in all the adapters' namespace-based configurations: `filename-pattern`, `filename-regex`, and `filter`. The first two attributes, `filename-pattern` and `filename-regex`, are convenience attributes. The `filename-pattern` attribute lets the user specify an Ant-style path or a matching expression to filter which files to use. The `filename-regex` attributes instead takes a regular expression, which, while more powerful, can also be a bit trickier to use. Both of these attributes ultimately result in the configuration of an implementation of `org.springframework.integration.file.filters.FileListFilter`. This interface is reproduced here:

```
package org.springframework.integration.file.filters;

import java.util.List;

public interface FileListFilter<F> {

    List<F> filterFiles(F[] files);
}
```

Most of the implementations of this interface are algorithmic, and do not depend on any specific file system APIs to do their jobs. Where required, there are file system–specific subclasses. One file system–specific feature commonly required is the derivation of a file's file name: the APIs are different for `java.io.File`, `org.apache.commons.net.ftp.FTPFile` (used in the FTP and FTPS adapters), and `com.jcraft.jsch.LsEntry` (used in SFTP adapters).

When you configure the `filename-pattern` attribute, an instance of a subclass of `AbstractSimplePatternFileListFilter<F>` (which in turn is an implementation of `org.springframework.integration.file.filters.FileListFilter<F>`) is configured as a filter on the adapter. When you configure a `filename-regex` attribute, an instance of a subclass of `AbstractRegexPatternFileListFilter<F>` (which in turn is an implementation of `FileListFilter<F>`) is configured as a filter on the adapter. If you require neither a regular expression–based nor an Ant-style expression-based filter, then you can configure the `filter` attribute. The `filter` attribute takes a reference to an instance of `FileListFilter<F>`. There are numerous implementations provided out of the box, and of course you are free to provide your own implementation. To compose multiple filters, use the `CompositeFileListFilter`.

All the outbound adapters support messages with payloads of type `byte[]`, `java.io.File`, and `java.lang.String`, and can correctly write them to a target directory (local or remote).

JDBC

The JDBC adapters provide a good solution to a very common requirement in integration. Most enterprise applications require some sort of interaction with a database. The JDBC channel adapters support sending and receiving messages via database queries. To support the JDBC example, the embedded database HyperSQL (`http://hsqldb.org`) will be used, since Spring JDBC supports it by default. The Spring `jdbc` namespace initializes and creates a simple table using HyperSQL. The Spring configuration file is shown in Listing 11–40.

Listing 11–40. Spring Configuration That Initializies the HyperSQL Database

```
<?xml version="1.0" encoding="UTF-8"?>
<beans xmlns:jdbc="http://www.springframework.org/schema/jdbc"
       xsi:schemaLocation="http://www.springframework.org/schema/jdbc
    http://www.springframework.org/schema/jdbc/spring-jdbc-3.0.xsd">

  <jdbc:embedded-database id="dataSource">
    <jdbc:script location="/spring/jdbc/hsqldb.sql"/>
  </jdbc:embedded-database>

</beans>
```

The `jdbc:script` element used to set the SQL script `hsqldb.sql` shown in Listing 11–41 which will be run after the database has initialized. This script creates a sample table used in all the JDBC adapter examples.

Listing 11–41. SQL Script hsqldb.sql

```
CREATE TABLE t (id INTEGER PRIMARY KEY,
   firstname VARCHAR(20),
   lastname VARCHAR(20),
   status INTEGER);
INSERT INTO t (id, firstname, lastname, status) VALUES (1, 'Felix', 'the Cat', 0);
INSERT INTO t (id, firstname, lastname, status) VALUES (2, 'Pink', 'Panther', 0);
```

JDBC Inbound Channel Adapter

The JDBC inbound channel adapter's basic function is to execute a SQL query, and then return the result set as the message payload. The message payload will contain the entire result set as a `List`. Using the default row-mapping strategy, the column values will be returned as a `Map` with the column name being the key values. You can customize the mapping strategy by implementing the `org.springframework.jdbc.core.RowMapper<T>` interface and referencing this class through the `row-mapper` attribute. A downstream splitter component can be used if individual messages per row are desired. The JDBC inbound channel adapter requires a reference either to a `JdbcTemplate` or `DataSource` instance.

An update statement can be added to the JDBC inbound channel adapter to mark rows as read to prevent the rows from showing up in the next poll. The update statement has access to a parameterized list of values from the original select statement. The list of values follow a default naming convention where a column in the input result set is translated into a list in the parameter map for the update called by the column name. The parameters are specified by a colon (:) prefixed to the name of a parameter. The parameter generation strategy can be overridden by creating a custom class implementing the `org.springframework.integration.jdbc.SqlParameterSourceFactory` interface by reference by the adapter attribute `sql-parameter-source-factory`. The Spring configuration file for an example using the JDBC inbound channel adapter is shown in Listing 11–42.

Listing 11–42. Spring Configuration for the JDBC Inbound Channel Adapter jdbc-inbound-context.xml

```
<?xml version="1.0" encoding="UTF-8"?>
<beans xmlns="http://www.springframework.org/schema/beans"
       xmlns:xsi="http://www.w3.org/2001/XMLSchema-instance"
       xmlns:context="http://www.springframework.org/schema/context"
```

```
       xmlns:int="http://www.springframework.org/schema/integration"
       xmlns:int-jdbc="http://www.springframework.org/schema/integration/jdbc"
       xmlns:jdbc="http://www.springframework.org/schema/jdbc"
       xsi:schemaLocation="http://www.springframework.org/schema/beans
    http://www.springframework.org/schema/beans/spring-beans-3.0.xsd
    http://www.springframework.org/schema/context
    http://www.springframework.org/schema/context/spring-context-3.0.xsd
    http://www.springframework.org/schema/integration
    http://www.springframework.org/schema/integration/spring-integration-2.0.xsd
    http://www.springframework.org/schema/integration/jdbc
    http://www.springframework.org/schema/integration/jdbc/spring-integration-jdbc-2.0.xsd
    http://www.springframework.org/schema/jdbc
    http://www.springframework.org/schema/jdbc/spring-jdbc-3.0.xsd">

  <context:component-scan base-package="com.apress.prospringintegration.jdbc"/>

  <int:channel id="target"/>

  <int-jdbc:inbound-channel-adapter channel="target"
                                    data-source="dataSource"
                                    query="select * from t where status = 0"
                                    update="update t set status = 1 where id in (:id)">
    <int:poller fixed-rate="1000">
      <int:transactional/>
    </int:poller>
  </int-jdbc:inbound-channel-adapter>

  <jdbc:embedded-database id="dataSource">
    <jdbc:script location="/spring/jdbc/hsqldb.sql"/>
  </jdbc:embedded-database>

  <int:service-activator input-channel="target" ref="jdbcMessageHandler"/>

</beans>
```

The example uses the embedded HyperSQL database and table discussed previously. Using the namespace support, the JDBC inbound channel adapter is configured to select all rows from table `t` where the `status` is 0, and then update the `status` to 1 so that the next poll will not pull the data again. The result set is then sent as a message payload to the message channel `target`.

The inbound channel adapter is set to poll at a fixed rate of 1,000 ms (once every second). Note the addition of the `transactional` element to the `poller`. This will cause the update and select queries to occur in the same transaction. The default transaction manager is configured using a Java configuration file, as shown in Listing 11–43. It is a common use case for the downstream channel to be a direct channel so that the endpoints are in the same thread and thus in the same transaction.

Listing 11–43. *Java Configuration for the Database Transaction Manager*

```
package com.apress.prospringintegration.jdbc;

import org.springframework.beans.factory.annotation.Value;
import org.springframework.context.annotation.Bean;
import org.springframework.context.annotation.Configuration;
import org.springframework.jdbc.datasource.DataSourceTransactionManager;
```

```
import javax.sql.DataSource;

@Configuration
public class JdbcConfiguration {

    @Value("#{dataSource}")
    private DataSource dataSource;

    @Bean
    public DataSourceTransactionManager transactionManager() {
        DataSourceTransactionManager transactionManager =
                new DataSourceTransactionManager();
        transactionManager.setDataSource(dataSource);
        return transactionManager;
    }
}
```

As shown in Listing 11–44, a service activator class is added that will log all the data in the result set of the query. This service activator is subscribed to the target message channel.

***Listing 11–44.** JDBC Example Message Handler*

```
package com.apress.prospringintegration.jdbc;

import org.springframework.integration.annotation.ServiceActivator;
import org.springframework.stereotype.Component;

import java.util.List;
import java.util.Map;

@Component
public class JdbcMessageHandler {

    @ServiceActivator
    public void handleJdbcMessage(List<Map<String, Object>> message) {
        for(Map<String, Object> resultMap: message) {
            System.out.println("Row");
            for(String column: resultMap.keySet()) {
                System.out.println("column: " + column + " value: " +
                        resultMap.get(column));
            }
        }
    }
}
```

To run the JDBC inbound channel adapter example, a main class is created, as shown in Listing 11–45. This class will kick off the Spring Integration flow, and then block for enough time to allow us to see the adapter in action.

***Listing 11–45.** JDBC Inbound Channel Adapter Example main Class*

```
package com.apress.prospringintegration.jdbc;

import org.springframework.context.ApplicationContext;
```

```
import org.springframework.context.support.ClassPathXmlApplicationContext;

public class JdbcInbound {

    public static void main(String[] args) throws Exception {
        ApplicationContext context =
                new ClassPathXmlApplicationContext("/spring/jdbc/jdbc-inbound-context.xml");
    }
}
```

The results of running the JDBC inbound channel adapter example are shown in Listing 11–46. Note that the query occurs before the update, so the status is equal to zero for alls rows.

Listing 11–46. *Results of Running the JDBC Inbound Channel Adapter Example*

```
Row
column: ID value: 1
column: FIRSTNAME value: Felix
column: LASTNAME value: the Cat
column: STATUS value: 0
Row
column: ID value: 2
column: FIRSTNAME value: Pink
column: LASTNAME value: Panther
column: STATUS value: 0
```

JDBC Outbound Channel Adapter

The JDBC outbound channel adapter supports handling an incoming message and using it to execute an SQL query—usually an update or insert statement. The message payload and header are accessible by default as input parameters. Using a Map as the incoming message payload, the values can be obtained using the expression :payload[<key>], where <key> is the Map key. The headers are also available using a similar expression, :headers[<key>]. As with the inbound adapter, the parameter generation can be overridden by using a custom SqlParameterSourceFactory. This adapter also requires a reference to either a JdbcTemplate or DataSource. If the input channel is a direct channel, then the outbound adapter will be in the same transaction as the sender.

The Spring configuration file for an example using the JDBC outbound channel adapter is shown in Listing 11–47. This example uses the previous inbound adapter to monitor any inserts to the database table. The JDBC outbound channel adapter is configured to listen to the message channel input. Based on the Map payload message, this adapter will perform an insert into table t.

Listing 11–47. *Spring Configuration for the JDBC Outbound Channel Adapter jdbc-outbound-context.xml*

```
<?xml version="1.0" encoding="UTF-8"?>
<beans xmlns="http://www.springframework.org/schema/beans"
       xmlns:xsi="http://www.w3.org/2001/XMLSchema-instance"
       xmlns:context="http://www.springframework.org/schema/context"
       xmlns:int="http://www.springframework.org/schema/integration"
       xmlns:int-jdbc="http://www.springframework.org/schema/integration/jdbc"
       xmlns:jdbc="http://www.springframework.org/schema/jdbc"
       xsi:schemaLocation="http://www.springframework.org/schema/beans
    http://www.springframework.org/schema/beans/spring-beans-3.0.xsd
    http://www.springframework.org/schema/context
```

```
    http://www.springframework.org/schema/context/spring-context-3.0.xsd
    http://www.springframework.org/schema/integration
    http://www.springframework.org/schema/integration/spring-integration-2.0.xsd
    http://www.springframework.org/schema/integration/jdbc
    http://www.springframework.org/schema/integration/jdbc/spring-integration-jdbc-2.0.xsd
    http://www.springframework.org/schema/jdbc
    http://www.springframework.org/schema/jdbc/spring-jdbc-3.0.xsd">

  <context:component-scan base-package="com.apress.prospringintegration.jdbc"/>

  <int:channel id="input"/>

  <int:channel id="target"/>

  <int-jdbc:outbound-channel-adapter channel="input"
                                     query="insert into t (id, firstname, lastname, status)
                                            values(:payload[id], :payload[firstname],
                                            :payload[lastname], :payload[status])"
                                     data-source="dataSource"/>

  <int-jdbc:inbound-channel-adapter channel="target"
                                    data-source="dataSource"
                                    query="select * from t where status = 0"
                                    update="update t set status = 1 where id in (:id)">
    <int:poller fixed-rate="1000">
      <int:transactional/>
    </int:poller>
  </int-jdbc:inbound-channel-adapter>

  <jdbc:embedded-database id="dataSource">
    <jdbc:script location="/spring/jdbc/hsqldb.sql"/>
  </jdbc:embedded-database>

  <int:service-activator input-channel="target" ref="jdbcMessageHandler"/>

</beans>
```

The main class for the JDBC outbound adapter is shown in Listing 11–48. This class creates a message with a Map payload containing the column values to insert. This will cause the outbound adapter to perform an insert into table t. The JDBC inbound adapter will then log the newly inserted row.

Listing 11–48. *JDBC Outbound Channel Adapter Example main Class*

```
package com.apress.prospringintegration.jdbc;

import org.springframework.context.ApplicationContext;
import org.springframework.context.support.ClassPathXmlApplicationContext;
import org.springframework.integration.Message;
import org.springframework.integration.MessageChannel;
import org.springframework.integration.support.MessageBuilder;

import java.util.HashMap;
import java.util.Map;
```

```
public class JdbcOutbound {
    public static void main(String[] args) throws Exception {
        ApplicationContext context =
                new ClassPathXmlApplicationContext(
                        "/spring/jdbc/jdbc-outbound-context.xml");

        MessageChannel input = context.getBean("input", MessageChannel.class);

        Map<String, Object> rowMessage = new HashMap<String, Object>();

        rowMessage.put("id", 3);
        rowMessage.put("firstname", "Mr");
        rowMessage.put("lastname", "Bill");
        rowMessage.put("status", 0);

        Message<Map<String, Object>> message =
                MessageBuilder.withPayload(rowMessage).build();
        input.send(message);

    }
}
```

The results of running the JDBC outbound channel adapter are shown in Listing 11–49. The first two rows are the preexisting data. The third row is from the insert done by the outbound adapter.

Listing 11–49. *Results of Running the JDBC Outbound Channel Adapter Example*

```
Row
column: ID value: 1
column: FIRSTNAME value: Felix
column: LASTNAME value: the Cat
column: STATUS value: 0
Row
column: ID value: 2
column: FIRSTNAME value: Pink
column: LASTNAME value: Panther
column: STATUS value: 0
Row
column: ID value: 3
column: FIRSTNAME value: Mr
column: LASTNAME value: Bill
column: STATUS value: 0
```

JDBC Outbound Gateway

The JDBC outbound gateway combines both an inbound and an outbound adapter. Similar to the JDBC outbound channel adapter, the gateway supports using the message payload and headers using the same conventions (i.e., `:payload[<key>]` and `:headers[<key>]`). As with the channel adapters, there is also an option to provide a custom `SqlParameterSourceFactory` for the request and reply. The gateway also requires a reference to a `JdbcTemplate` or `DataSource`.

There are three options for specifying what the reply message should contain:

- By default, an insert statement will return the following message to the output channel with the number of rows affect as a `Map`: `{UPDATED=1}`.
- Using the autogenerated keys option, the reply message will be populated with the generated key values. You can enabled this by setting the attribute `keys-generated` to `true`.
- The last option is to provide a query to execute and populate the reply message with the result set of the query.

The Spring configuration file for a JDBC outbound gateway example is shown in Listing 11–50. This example uses the third option, where a row is inserted and the reply message is a query of the newly added row. The `id` of the insert row is passed to the query to select only the inserted row.

***Listing 11–50.** Spring Configuration for the JDBC Outbound Gateway jdbc-gateway-context.xml*

```
<?xml version="1.0" encoding="UTF-8"?>
<beans xmlns="http://www.springframework.org/schema/beans"
       xmlns:xsi="http://www.w3.org/2001/XMLSchema-instance"
       xmlns:context="http://www.springframework.org/schema/context"
       xmlns:int="http://www.springframework.org/schema/integration"
       xmlns:int-jdbc="http://www.springframework.org/schema/integration/jdbc"
       xmlns:jdbc="http://www.springframework.org/schema/jdbc"
       xsi:schemaLocation="http://www.springframework.org/schema/beans
    http://www.springframework.org/schema/beans/spring-beans-3.0.xsd
    http://www.springframework.org/schema/context
    http://www.springframework.org/schema/context/spring-context-3.0.xsd
    http://www.springframework.org/schema/integration
    http://www.springframework.org/schema/integration/spring-integration-2.0.xsd
    http://www.springframework.org/schema/integration/jdbc
    http://www.springframework.org/schema/integration/jdbc/spring-integration-jdbc-2.0.xsd
    http://www.springframework.org/schema/jdbc
    http://www.springframework.org/schema/jdbc/spring-jdbc-3.0.xsd">

  <context:component-scan base-package="com.apress.prospringintegration.jdbc"/>

  <int:channel id="input"/>

  <int:channel id="output">
    <int:queue capacity="10"/>
  </int:channel>

  <int-jdbc:outbound-gateway request-channel="input"
                             reply-channel="output"
                             update="insert into t (id, firstname, lastname, status)
                                    values(:payload[id], :payload[firstname],
                                    :payload[lastname], :payload[status])"
                             query="select * from t where id = :payload[id]"
                             data-source="dataSource"/>

  <jdbc:embedded-database id="dataSource">
    <jdbc:script location="/spring/jdbc/hsqldb.sql"/>
  </jdbc:embedded-database>

</beans>
```

The main class for running the JDBC outbound gateway example is shown in Listing 11–51. The main class is similar to the outbound channel adapter, with the exception of additional code to receive the reply message.

Listing 11–51. JDBC Outbound Gateway Example main Class

```
package com.apress.prospringintegration.jdbc;

import org.springframework.context.ApplicationContext;
import org.springframework.context.support.ClassPathXmlApplicationContext;
import org.springframework.integration.Message;
import org.springframework.integration.MessageChannel;
import org.springframework.integration.core.PollableChannel;
import org.springframework.integration.support.MessageBuilder;

import java.util.HashMap;
import java.util.Map;

public class JdbcGateway {
    public static void main(String[] args) throws Exception {
        ApplicationContext context =
                new ClassPathXmlApplicationContext("/spring/jdbc/jdbc-gateway-context.xml");

        MessageChannel input = context.getBean("input", MessageChannel.class);
        PollableChannel output = context.getBean("output", PollableChannel.class);

        Map<String, Object> rowMessage = new HashMap<String, Object>();

        rowMessage.put("id", 3);
        rowMessage.put("firstname", "Mr");
        rowMessage.put("lastname", "Bill");
        rowMessage.put("status", 0);

        Message<Map<String, Object>> message =
                MessageBuilder.withPayload(rowMessage).build();
        input.send(message);

        Message<?> reply = output.receive();

        System.out.println("Reply message: " + reply);

        Map<String, Object> rowMap = (Map<String, Object>) reply.getPayload();

        for (String column : rowMap.keySet()) {
            System.out.println("column: " + column + " value: " + rowMap.get(column));
        }

    }
}
```

The results of running the JDBC outbound gateway example are shown in Listing 11–52. The reply message is returned, as well as the JdbcMessageHandler class and the inbound channel adapter.

Listing 11–52. Results of Running the JDBC Outbound Gateway Example

```
Reply message: [Payload={ID=3, FIRSTNAME=Mr, LASTNAME=Bill,➥
STATUS=0}][Headers={timestamp=1296538850203, id=9ff84cd9-38ec-4533-8f43-3faedb213d44}]
column: ID value: 3
column: FIRSTNAME value: Mr
column: LASTNAME value: Bill
column: STATUS value: 0
```

Summary

There are many means for communication and storage, including storing data as files, communication with other computers over the network using TCP and UDP, interacting with users using input and output streaming, transferring files using FTP/FTPS and SFTP, and storing and retrieving information held within a database. Spring Integration supports these different talk-to-the-metal endpoints with message sources and handlers for files, socket-level communication using TCP and UDP, input and output streaming, file transfer adapters, and JDBC adapters. These adapters are essential to integrating with the rest of the world.

CHAPTER 12

Enterprise Messaging with JMS and AMQP

Spring Integration enables applications to share data and processes using different integration styles, such as shared file systems, shared databases, remote procedure invocation, and messaging. This chapter will focus on enterprise messaging using transports such as Java Message Service (JMS) and Advanced Message Queuing Protocol (AMQP). Other message brokers, such as Simple Queue Service (SQS) and Kestrel MQ, will be discussed at the end of the chapter.

JMS Integration

JMS was originally part of the Java 2 Enterprise Edition (J2EE) specification, and was defined in the Java Community Process Java Specification Request (JSR) 914. It is the current standard for the Java Platform Standard Edition (Java SE) and Java Platform Enterprise Edition (Java EE). It allows applications to connect to each other using message-oriented communication. Using JMS, applications can communicate with each other in a loosely coupled and reliable way.

Spring Integration comes with JMS support out of the box. Before Spring Framework 1.1, applications needed to handle JMS connection management, session management, message creation, synchronous and asynchronous message delivery, and error handling manually. Spring Framework 1.1 provided limited support for JMS 1.1. Spring Framework 2.0 offered complete support for JMS, allowing asynchronous communication between applications. Spring Integration 1.0 provided inbound and outbound JMS adapters, and Spring Integration 2.0 furthers this support with JMS-backed message channels.

In JMS, there are two types of destinations: *queue* and *topic*. A JMS queue (`javax.jms.Queue`) is a point-to-point destination that allows one consumer to receive a message at any given time. A JMS topic (`javax.jms.Topic`) is a publish/subscribe-style destination that allows messages to be delivered to multiple consumers. Both classes extend `javax.jms.Destination`. Figure 12–1 illustrates the difference between the two.

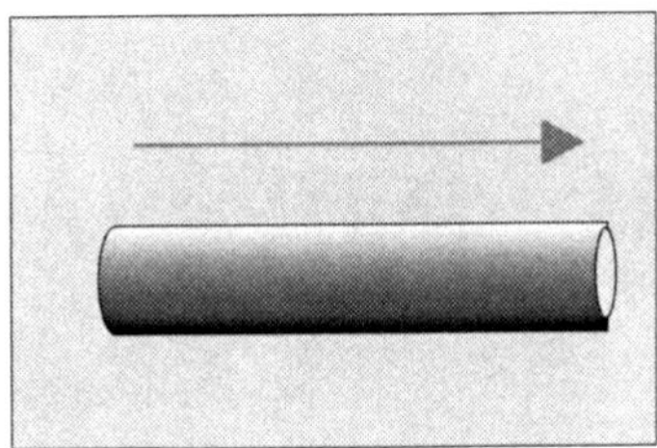

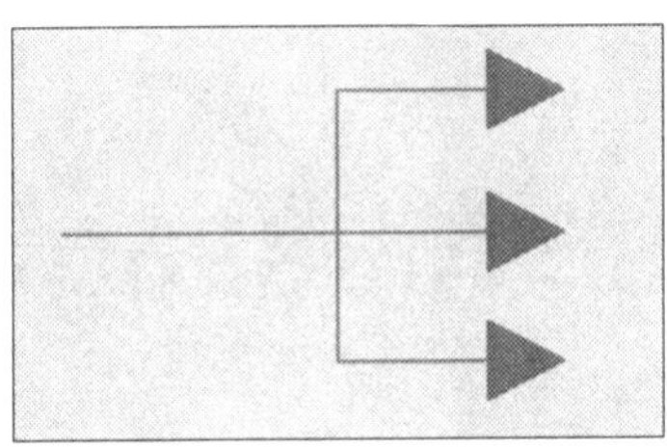

Figure 12–1. A JMS Queue (left) and a JMS Topic (right)

JMS Brokers

There are many JMS brokers available on the market. However, this chapter will mainly focus on two of the more popular open source JMS brokers: the Apache foundation's ActiveMQ and JBoss's HornetQ.

Apache ActiveMQ

Apache ActiveMQ (`http://activemq.apache.org`) is one of the more popular open source messaging brokers. It implements support for J2EE 1.4's JMS 1.1 specification, which supports transient, persistent, transactional, and distributed transactional (XA) messaging. Although ActiveMQ implements JMS 1.1, it also supports a variety of non-Java programming and scripting languages , including C, C++, C#, Erlang, Perl, PHP, Python, and Ruby. It also includes several transport protocols, including VM, TCP, SSL, Zeroconf, HTTP, UDP, multicast, and JXTA. (For more details on the list of supported protocols, see `http://activemq.apache.org/uri-protocols.html`.) ActiveMQ provides message persistence by using a high-speed journal, KahaDB. In addition, ActiveMQ provides Spring namespace support for configuring clients. The latest version of the ActiveMQ binary distribution (5.4.2 at the time of this writing) can be downloaded from `http://activemq.apache.org/download.html`.

ActiveMQ has two types of distribution: Windows and Unix/Linux/Cygwin. For the Windows platform, download `apache-activemq-5.4.2-bin.zip`, and for the Unix/Linux/Cygwin platform, download `apche-activemq-5.4.2-bin.tar.gz`. This chapter will use the Unix/Linux/Cygwin distribution.

To install ActiveMQ, simply unzip the distribution tarball, like so:

```
$ tar -zxf apache-activemq-5.4.2-bin.tar.gz
```

In order to start ActiveMQ on 32-bit Linux, run the following command:

```
$ apache-activemq-5.4.2/bin/linux-x86-32/activemq start
Starting ActiveMQ Broker...
```

In order to start ActiveMQ on 64-bit Linux, run the following:

```
$ apache-activemq-5.4.2/bin/linux-x86-64/activemq start
Starting ActiveMQ Broker...
```

In order to start ActiveMQ on Mac OS X, run the following:

```
$ apache-activemq-5.4.2/bin/macosx/activemq start
Starting ActiveMQ Broker...
```

In order to stop the ActiveMQ broker on 32-bit Linux, use the following:

```
$ apache-activemq-5.4.2/bin/linux-x86-32/activemq stop
Stopping ActiveMQ Broker...
Waiting for ActiveMQ Broker to exit...
Stopped ActiveMQ Broker.
```

In order to stop the ActiveMQ broker on 64-bit Linux, use the following:

```
$ apache-activemq-5.4.2/bin/linux-x86-64/activemq stop
Stopping ActiveMQ Broker...
Waiting for ActiveMQ Broker to exit...
Stopped ActiveMQ Broker.
```

In order to stop the ActiveMQ broker on Mac OS X, use the following:

```
$ apache-activemq-5.4.2/bin/macosx/activemq stop
Stopping ActiveMQ Broker...
Waiting for ActiveMQ Broker to exit...
Stopped ActiveMQ Broker.
```

If the ActiveMQ broker is running on the 32-bit Linux environment, use the following:

```
$ cd apache-activemq-5.4.2/bin/linux-x86-32/activemq status
ActiveMQ Broker is running (86610).
```

If the ActiveMQ broker is not running on the 32-bit Linux environment, use the following:

```
$ cd apache-activemq-5.4.2/bin/linux-x86-32/activemq status
ActiveMQ Broker is not running.
```

ActiveMQ 4.2 and later comes with a web console for easy monitoring as shown in Figure 12–2. The ActiveMQ console can be reached by using a web browser and pointing to `http://localhost:8161/admin/`.

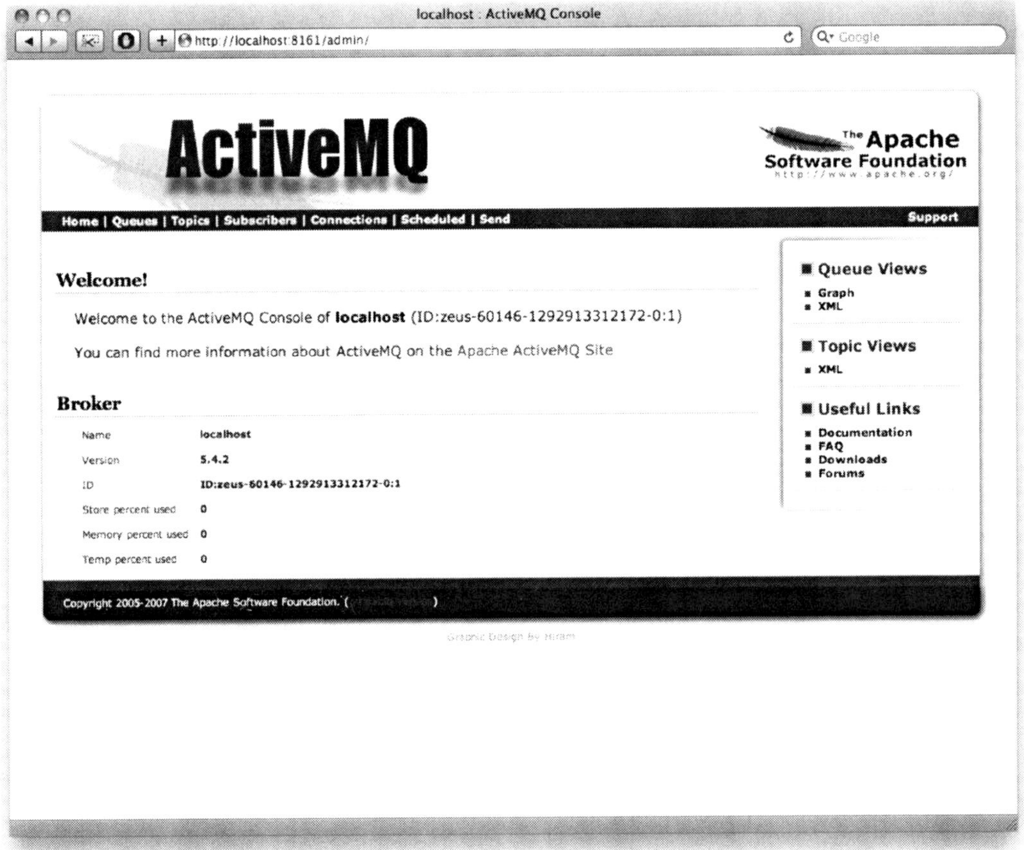

Figure 12–2. The ActiveMQ Web Console

Besides using the web console, ActiveMQ may also be modified by using a JMX console. By default, JMX support is disabled if ActiveMQ is launched with the wrapper. In order to enable JMX, the `wrapper.conf` file must be modified. On the Mac OS X platform, modify `apache-activemq-5.4.2/bin/macosx/wrapper.conf` using a text editor. Remove the comments and modify the configuration file as shown in Listing 12–1.

Listing 12–1. *wrapper.conf*

```
# ------------------------------------------------------------------------
# Licensed to the Apache Software Foundation (ASF) under one or more
# contributor license agreements.  See the NOTICE file distributed with
# this work for additional information regarding copyright ownership.
# The ASF licenses this file to You under the Apache License, Version 2.0
# (the "License"); you may not use this file except in compliance with
# the License.  You may obtain a copy of the License at
```

```
#
# http://www.apache.org/licenses/LICENSE-2.0
#
# Unless required by applicable law or agreed to in writing, software
# distributed under the License is distributed on an "AS IS" BASIS,
# WITHOUT WARRANTIES OR CONDITIONS OF ANY KIND, either express or implied.
# See the License for the specific language governing permissions and
# limitations under the License.
# ------------------------------------------------------------------------

#********************************************************************
# Wrapper Properties
#********************************************************************

#wrapper.debug=TRUE
set.default.ACTIVEMQ_HOME=../..
set.default.ACTIVEMQ_BASE=../..
wrapper.working.dir=.

# Java Application
wrapper.java.command=java

# Java Main class.  This class must implement the WrapperListener interface
#  or guarantee that the WrapperManager class is initialized.  Helper
#  classes are provided to do this for you.  See the Integration section
#  of the documentation for details.
wrapper.java.mainclass=org.tanukisoftware.wrapper.WrapperSimpleApp

# Java Classpath (include wrapper.jar)  Add class path elements as
#  needed starting from 1
wrapper.java.classpath.1=%ACTIVEMQ_HOME%/bin/wrapper.jar
wrapper.java.classpath.2=%ACTIVEMQ_HOME%/bin/run.jar

# Java Library Path (location of Wrapper.DLL or libwrapper.so)
wrapper.java.library.path.1=%ACTIVEMQ_HOME%/bin/macosx/

# Java Additional Parameters
# note that n is the parameter number starting from 1.
wrapper.java.additional.1=-Dactivemq.home=%ACTIVEMQ_HOME%
wrapper.java.additional.2=-Dactivemq.base=%ACTIVEMQ_BASE%
wrapper.java.additional.3=-Djavax.net.ssl.keyStorePassword=password
wrapper.java.additional.4=-Djavax.net.ssl.trustStorePassword=password
wrapper.java.additional.5=-Djavax.net.ssl.keyStore=%ACTIVEMQ_BASE%/conf/broker.ks
wrapper.java.additional.6=-Djavax.net.ssl.trustStore=%ACTIVEMQ_BASE%/conf/broker.ts
wrapper.java.additional.7=-Dcom.sun.management.jmxremote
wrapper.java.additional.8=-Dorg.apache.activemq.UseDedicatedTaskRunner=true
wrapper.java.additional.9=-Djava.util.logging.config.file=logging.properties

# Uncomment to enable jmx
wrapper.java.additional.10=-Dcom.sun.management.jmxremote.port=1616
wrapper.java.additional.11=-Dcom.sun.management.jmxremote.authenticate=false
wrapper.java.additional.12=-Dcom.sun.management.jmxremote.ssl=false
```

```
# Uncomment to enable YourKit profiling
#wrapper.java.additional.n=-Xrunyjpagent

# Uncomment to enable remote debugging
#wrapper.java.additional.n=-Xdebug -Xnoagent -Djava.compiler=NONE
#wrapper.java.additional.n=-Xrunjdwp:transport=dt_socket,server=y,suspend=n,address=5005

# Initial Java Heap Size (in MB)
#wrapper.java.initmemory=3

# Maximum Java Heap Size (in MB)
wrapper.java.maxmemory=512

# Application parameters.  Add parameters as needed starting from 1
wrapper.app.parameter.1=org.apache.activemq.console.Main
wrapper.app.parameter.2=start

#********************************************************************
# Wrapper Logging Properties
#********************************************************************
# Format of output for the console.  (See docs for formats)
wrapper.console.format=PM

# Log Level for console output.  (See docs for log levels)
wrapper.console.loglevel=INFO

# Log file to use for wrapper output logging.
wrapper.logfile=%ACTIVEMQ_BASE%/data/wrapper.log

# Format of output for the log file.  (See docs for formats)
wrapper.logfile.format=LPTM

# Log Level for log file output.  (See docs for log levels)
wrapper.logfile.loglevel=INFO

# Maximum size that the log file will be allowed to grow to before
#  the log is rolled. Size is specified in bytes.  The default value
#  of 0, disables log rolling.  May abbreviate with the 'k' (kb) or
#  'm' (mb) suffix.  For example: 10m = 10 megabytes.
wrapper.logfile.maxsize=0

# Maximum number of rolled log files which will be allowed before old
#  files are deleted.  The default value of 0 implies no limit.
wrapper.logfile.maxfiles=0

# Log Level for sys/event log output.  (See docs for log levels)
wrapper.syslog.loglevel=NONE

#********************************************************************
# Wrapper Windows Properties
#********************************************************************
# Title to use when running as a console
wrapper.console.title=ActiveMQ
```

```
#********************************************************************
# Wrapper Windows NT/2000/XP Service Properties
#********************************************************************
# WARNING - Do not modify any of these properties when an application
#  using this configuration file has been installed as a service.
#  Please uninstall the service before modifying this section.  The
#  service can then be reinstalled.

# Name of the service
wrapper.ntservice.name=ActiveMQ

# Display name of the service
wrapper.ntservice.displayname=ActiveMQ

# Description of the service
wrapper.ntservice.description=ActiveMQ Broker

# Service dependencies.  Add dependencies as needed starting from 1
wrapper.ntservice.dependency.1=

# Mode in which the service is installed.  AUTO_START or DEMAND_START
wrapper.ntservice.starttype=AUTO_START

# Allow the service to interact with the desktop.
wrapper.ntservice.interactive=false
```

Restart the ActiveMQ broker to have the new configuration takes effect,

```
$ apache-activemq-5.4.2/bin/macosx/activemq restart
Stopping ActiveMQ Broker...
Stopped ActiveMQ Broker.
Starting ActiveMQ Broker...
```

Now launch the JMX console (see Figure 12–3):

```
$ jconsole localhost:1616
```

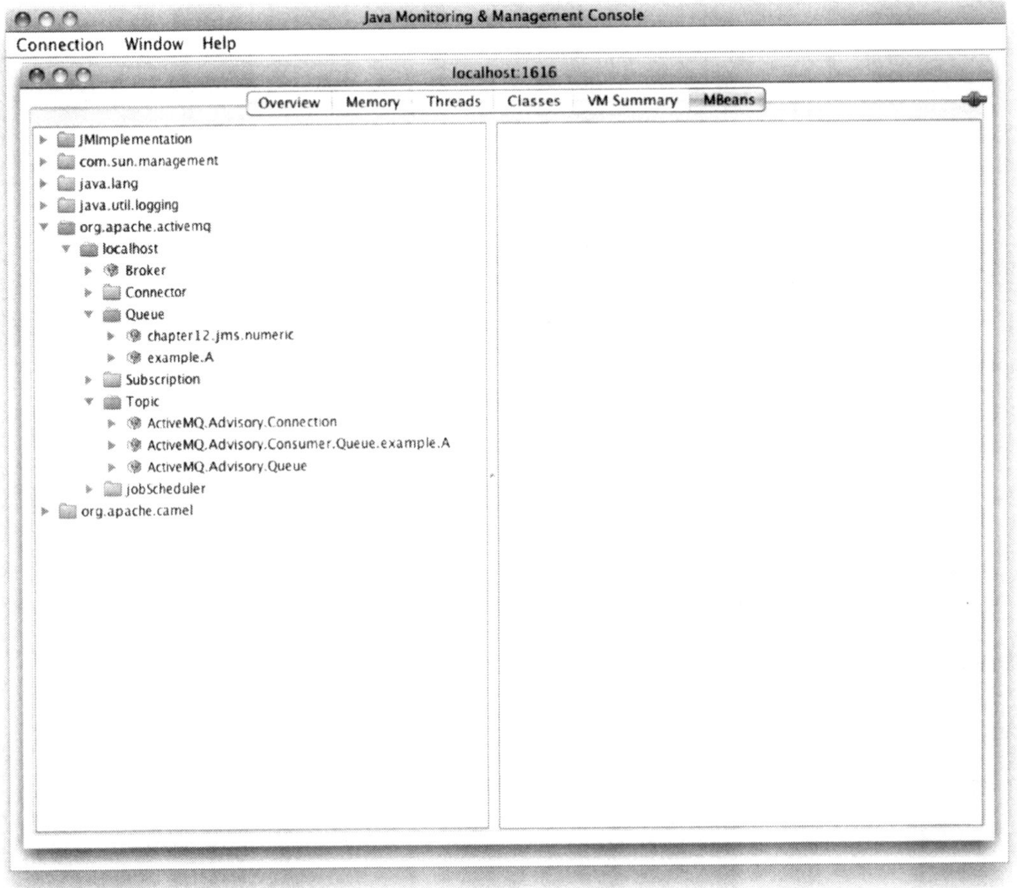

Figure 12–3. *The ActiveMQ JMX Console*

The ActiveMQ web and JMX consoles provide a lot of useful information regarding the message broker, message queue, message topic, and topic subscription. In addition, the consoles allow the administrator to operate and manage the ActiveMQ broker.

The ActiveMQ web console Queue page (see Figure 12–4) allows an administrator to create queues on the fly without modifying the ActiveMQ configuration file. It also shows statistics, including number of pending messages, number of consumers, messages enqueued, and messages dequeued. The web console also provides basic operations such as send, purge, and delete to allow the administrator to manage the message queue.

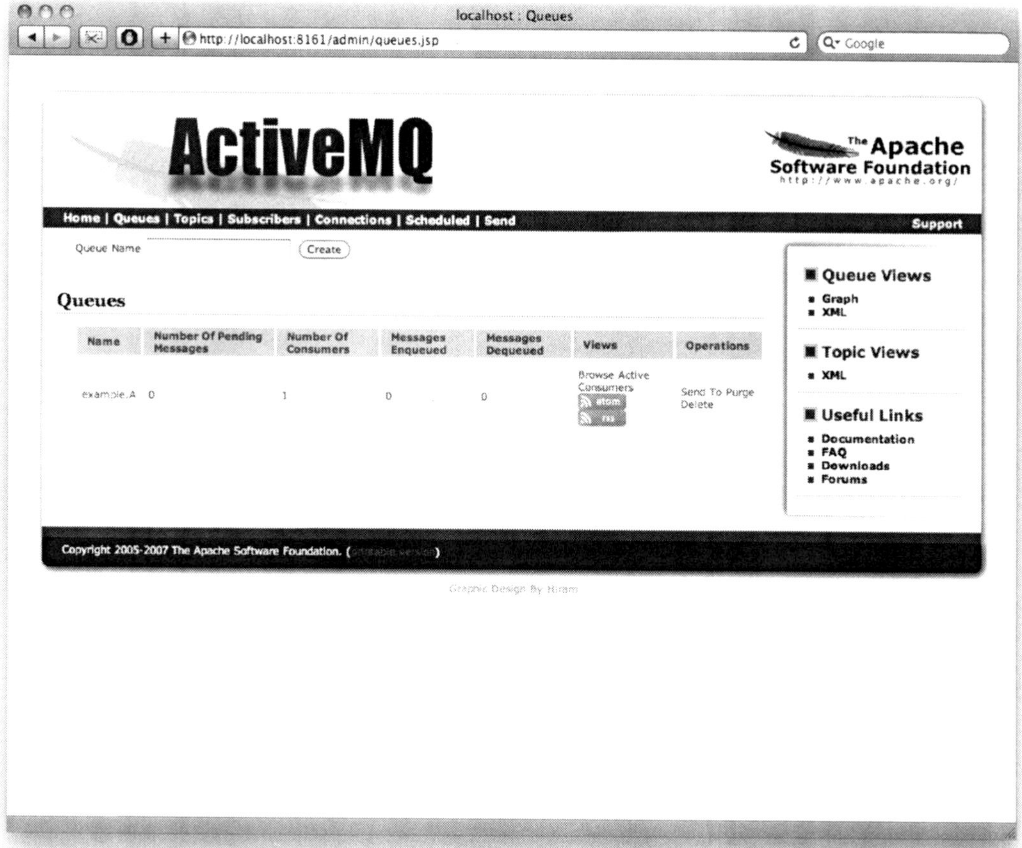

Figure 12–4. The Queue Page of the ActiveMQ Web Console

The JMX console also provides similar functionality to the web console as shown in Figures 12–5 and 12–6. The queue statistics are represented by JMX MBean attributes. The queue management operations can be invoked by using the JMX MBean methods.

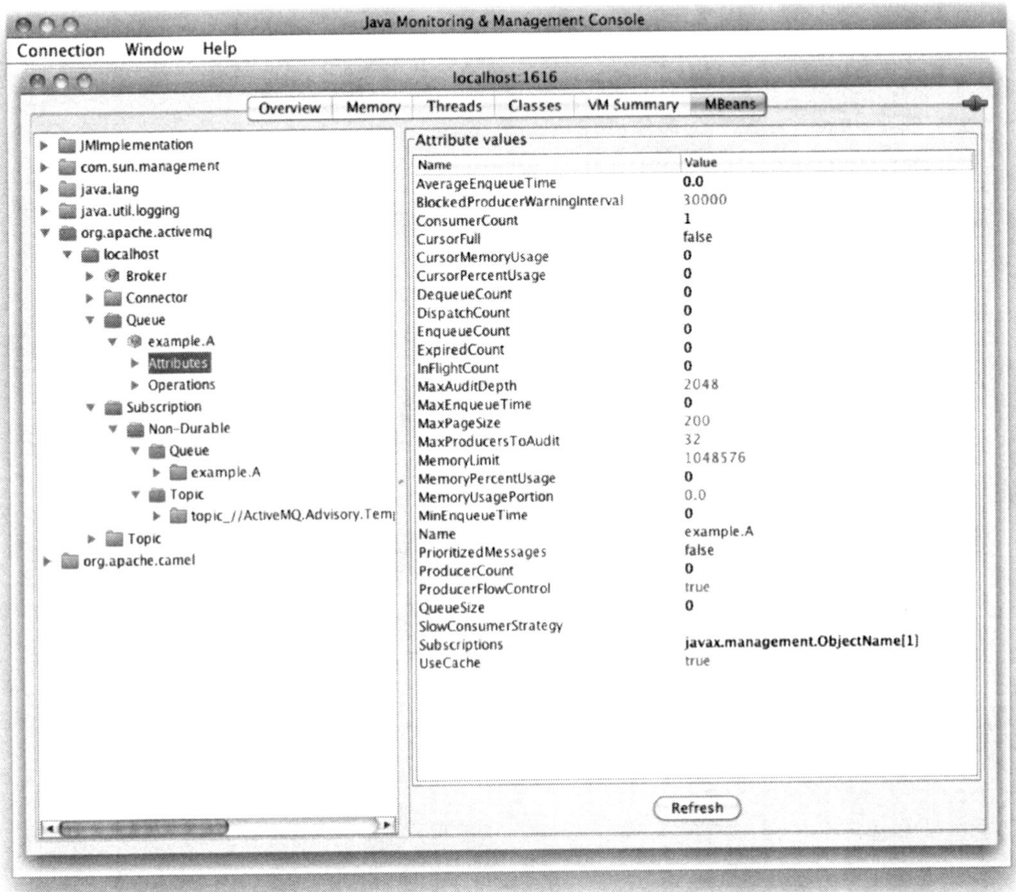

Figure 12–5. Queue MBean Attributes

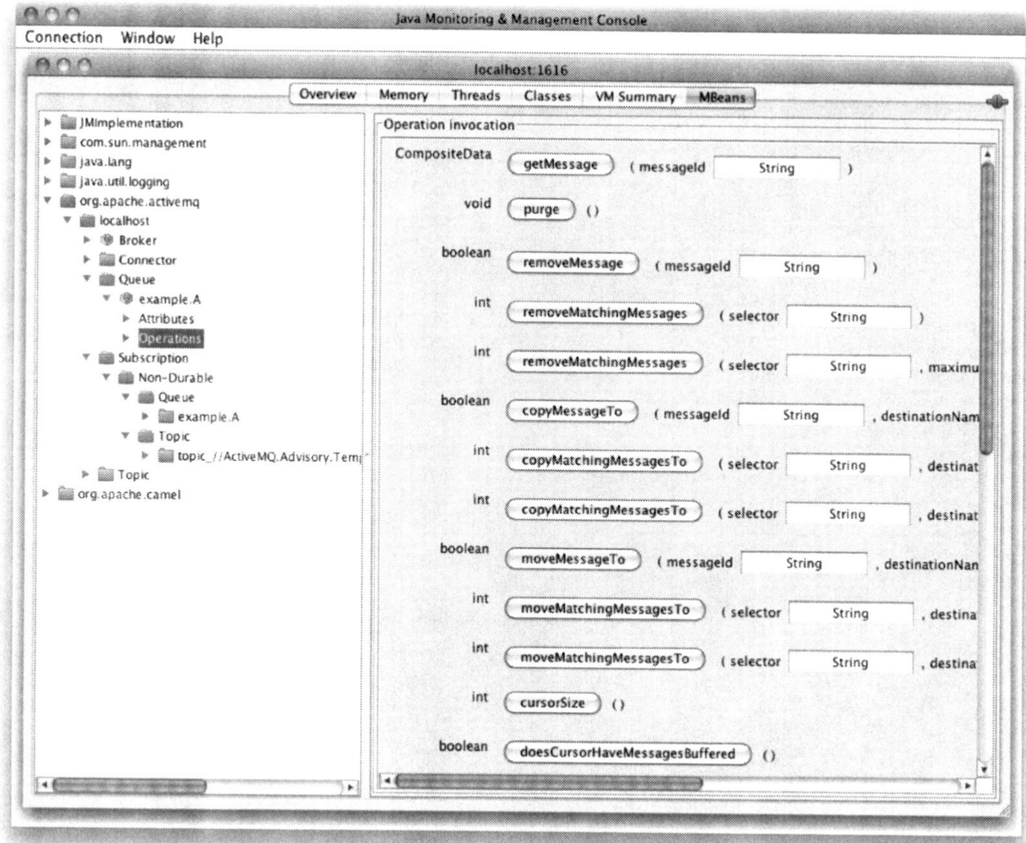

Figure 12–6. Queue MBean Operations

To use ActiveMQ, add the following dependency in your Maven `pom.xml` file:

```
<dependency>
  <groupId>org.apache.activemq</groupId>
  <artifactId>activemq-all</artifactId>
  <version5.4.2</version>
</dependency>
```

You'll need to configure a JMS connection factory. There are many ways to do this, including the ActiveMQ specific Spring namespace. However, to keep things simple, we'll use a Java configuration here:

```
@Bean
public ActiveMQConnectionFactory activeMqConnectionFactory() {
    ActiveMQConnectionFactory activeMQConnectionFactory =
            new ActiveMQConnectionFactory();
    activeMQConnectionFactory.setBrokerURL("tcp://localhost:61616");
```

```
        return activeMQConnectionFactory;
    }

    @Bean
    public CachingConnectionFactory connectionFactory() {
        CachingConnectionFactory cachingConnectionFactory =
                new CachingConnectionFactory();
        cachingConnectionFactory.setSessionCacheSize(10);
        cachingConnectionFactory.setCacheProducers(false);
        cachingConnectionFactory.setTargetConnectionFactory( activeMqConnectionFactory() );
        return cachingConnectionFactory;
    }
```

The preceding configuration example creates a connection factory which connects to the ActiveMQ broker on the localhost on port 61616. In addition, an instance of a Spring Framework class, `CachingConnectionFactory`, is defined, which makes working with JMS connection factories more sane in a Spring environment. Spring's support for JMS assumes that all connection factories belong to a pool (as is typical in a Java EE environment), and closes all resources after the client is done with it. Once closed, a pooled resource is simply returned to the pool—an inexpensive operation. If the connection factory is used directly, as in this example, then Spring will end up closing heavyweight connections that are actually used by the container, which will yield devastating performance. So, the connection factory is wrapped with a caching implementation that will in effect pool the instance and provide the expected performance.

In order to use ActiveMQ message destinations, the topic or queue needs to be defined in Spring. If the ActiveMQ message queue and topic have never been created in the broker, they can be created programmatically, as shown following:

```
    @Bean
    public ActiveMQQueue ticketQueue() {
        ActiveMQQueue activeMQQueue = new ActiveMQQueue("ticket.queue");
        return activeMQQueue;
    }

    @Bean
    public ActiveMQTopic ticketTopic() {
        ActiveMQTopic activeMQTopic = new ActiveMQTopic("ticket.topic");
        return activeMQTopic;
    }
```

If the message queue and topic are precreated (they can be created by using the web console, JMX console, or configuration file), the message destination can be referenced by name instead of the actual bean. How to reference these will be discussed later in this chapter.

JBoss HornetQ

JBoss HornetQ (`www.jboss.org/hornetq`) is an open source message broker under the Apache Software License 2.0. As of August 26, 2010, it is the fastest JMS message broker—faster than Apache ActiveMQ by 300 percent, according to SPECjms2007 (`www.spec.org/jms2007/results/jms2007.html`). The HornetQ project was launched by Tim Fox in 2009 and was originally intended to be the JBoss Messaging 2.0 project. HornetQ supports the JMS 1.1 specification, as well.

The latest version of HornetQ can be downloaded from `www.jboss.org/hornetq/downloads.html`. As of this writing, the latest release version is 2.1.2 (`http://sourceforge.net/projects/hornetq/files/2.1.2.FINAL/hornetq-2.1.2.Final.tar.gz/download`).

You can install HornetQ by simply decompressing the downloaded ZIP or tarball file, like so:

```
$ tar -zxf hornetq-2.1.2.Final.tar.gz
```

To start HornetQ in standalone mode on the Linux platform, run the following command:

```
$ hornetq-2.1.2.Final/bin/run.sh
```

Running this command will produce the following output:

```
********************************************************************************
java  -XX:+UseParallelGC -XX:+AggressiveOpts -XX:+UseFastAccessorMethods -Xms512M -Xmx1024M -
Dhornetq.config.dir=../config/stand-alone/non-clustered -
Djava.util.logging.config.file=../config/stand-alone/non-clustered/logging.properties -
Djava.library.path=. -classpath ../lib/twitter4j-
core.jar:../lib/netty.jar:../lib/jnpserver.jar:../lib/jnp-client.jar:../lib/jboss-
mc.jar:../lib/jboss-jms-api.jar:../lib/hornetq-twitter-integration.jar:../lib/hornetq-
logging.jar:../lib/hornetq-jms.jar:../lib/hornetq-jms-client.jar:../lib/hornetq-jms-client-
java5.jar:../lib/hornetq-jboss-as-integration.jar:../lib/hornetq-core.jar:../lib/hornetq-core-
client.jar:../lib/hornetq-core-client-java5.jar:../lib/hornetq-bootstrap.jar:../config/stand-
alone/non-clustered:../schemas/ org.hornetq.integration.bootstrap.HornetQBootstrapServer
hornetq-beans.xml
********************************************************************************
[main] 16:21:04,477 INFO [org.hornetq.integration.bootstrap.HornetQBootstrapServer]  Starting
HornetQ Server
[main] 16:21:05,707 WARNING [org.hornetq.core.deployers.impl.FileConfigurationParser]  AIO
wasn't located on this platform, it will fall back to using pure Java NIO. If your platform is
Linux, install LibAIO to enable the AIO journal
[main] 16:21:05,770 INFO [org.hornetq.core.server.impl.HornetQServerImpl]  live server is
starting..
[main] 16:21:05,798 INFO [org.hornetq.core.persistence.impl.journal.JournalStorageManager]
Using NIO Journal
[main] 16:21:05,823 WARNING [org.hornetq.core.server.impl.HornetQServerImpl]  Security risk!
It has been detected that the cluster admin user and password have not been changed from the
installation default. Please see the HornetQ user guide, cluster chapter, for instructions on
how to do this.
[main] 16:21:08,571 INFO [org.hornetq.core.remoting.impl.netty.NettyAcceptor]  Started Netty
Acceptor version 3.2.1.Final-r2319 localhost:5445 for CORE protocol
[main] 16:21:08,574 INFO [org.hornetq.core.remoting.impl.netty.NettyAcceptor]  Started Netty
Acceptor version 3.2.1.Final-r2319 localhost:5455 for CORE protocol
[main] 16:21:08,576 INFO [org.hornetq.core.server.impl.HornetQServerImpl]  HornetQ Server
version 2.1.2.Final (Colmeia, 120) started
```

HornetQ may also be run in the background by using nohup, as follows:

```
$ nohup hornetq-2.1.2.Final/bin/run.sh &
```

To stop HornetQ, enter the following command:

```
$ hornetq-2.1.2.Final/bin/stop.sh
```

HornetQ can be monitored using the JMX console. By default, JMX monitoring is only available on `localhost`. In order to enable remote JMX, modify `hornet-2.1.2.Final/bin/run.sh` as shown in Listing 12–2.

Listing 12–2. *hornet-2.1.2.Final/bin/run.sh*

```
#!/bin/sh

export HORNETQ_HOME=..
mkdir -p ../logs
# By default, the server is started in the non-clustered standalone configuration

if [ a"$1" = a ]; then CONFIG_DIR=$HORNETQ_HOME/config/stand-alone/non-clustered; else
CONFIG_DIR="$1"; fi
if [ a"$2" = a ]; then FILENAME=hornetq-beans.xml; else FILENAME="$2"; fi

export CLASSPATH=$CONFIG_DIR:$HORNETQ_HOME/schemas/
#you can use the following line if you want to run with different ports
#export CLUSTER_PROPS="-Djnp.port=1099 -Djnp.rmiPort=1098 -Djnp.host=localhost -
Dhornetq.remoting.netty.host=localhost -Dhornetq.remoting.netty.port=5445"
export JVM_ARGS="$CLUSTER_PROPS -XX:+UseParallelGC -XX:+AggressiveOpts -
XX:+UseFastAccessorMethods -Xms512M -Xmx1024M -Dhornetq.config.dir=$CONFIG_DIR -
Djava.util.logging.config.file=$CONFIG_DIR/logging.properties -Djava.library.path=."
#export JVM_ARGS="-Xmx512M -Djava.util.logging.config.file=$CONFIG_DIR/logging.properties -
Dhornetq.config.dir=$CONFIG_DIR -Djava.library.path=. -Xdebug -
Xrunjdwp:transport=dt_socket,server=y,suspend=y,address=5005"

for i in `ls $HORNETQ_HOME/lib/*.jar`; do
        CLASSPATH=$i:$CLASSPATH
done

echo "***********************************************************************************"
echo "java $JVM_ARGS -classpath $CLASSPATH
org.hornetq.integration.bootstrap.HornetQBootstrapServer $FILENAME"
echo "***********************************************************************************"
java $JVM_ARGS -classpath $CLASSPATH -Dcom.sun.management.jmxremote -
Dcom.sun.management.jmxremote.port=5000 -Dcom.sun.management.jmxremote.authenticate=false
org.hornetq.integration.bootstrap.HornetQBootstrapServer $FILENAME
```

Restart HornetQ after the running script has been modified, by entering the following:

```
$ hornet-2.1.2.Final/bin/stop.sh
$ nohup hornet-2.1.2.Final/bin/run.sh &
$ jconsole localhost:5000
```

The JMX console (see Figure 12–7) exposes the statistics for the individual message queue or topic. The console also allows the administrator to operate the message queue and topic via the JMX operations as shown in Figure 12–8.

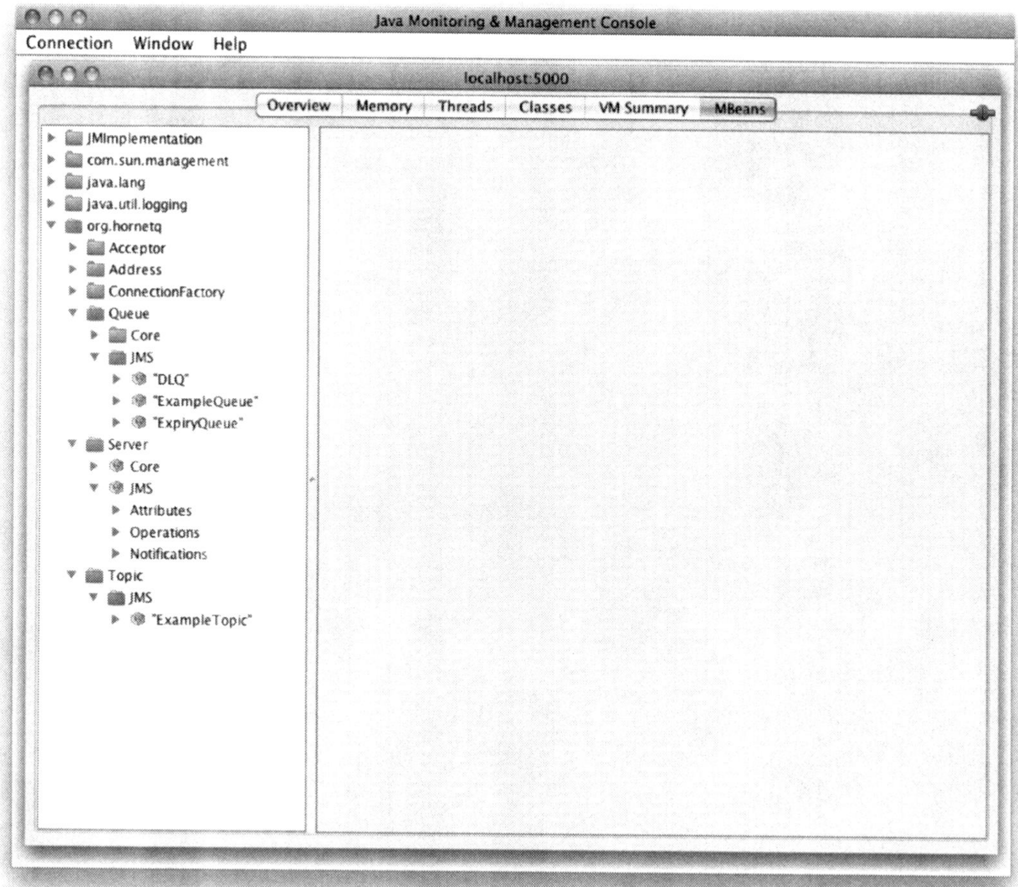

Figure 12–7. The HornetQ JMX Console

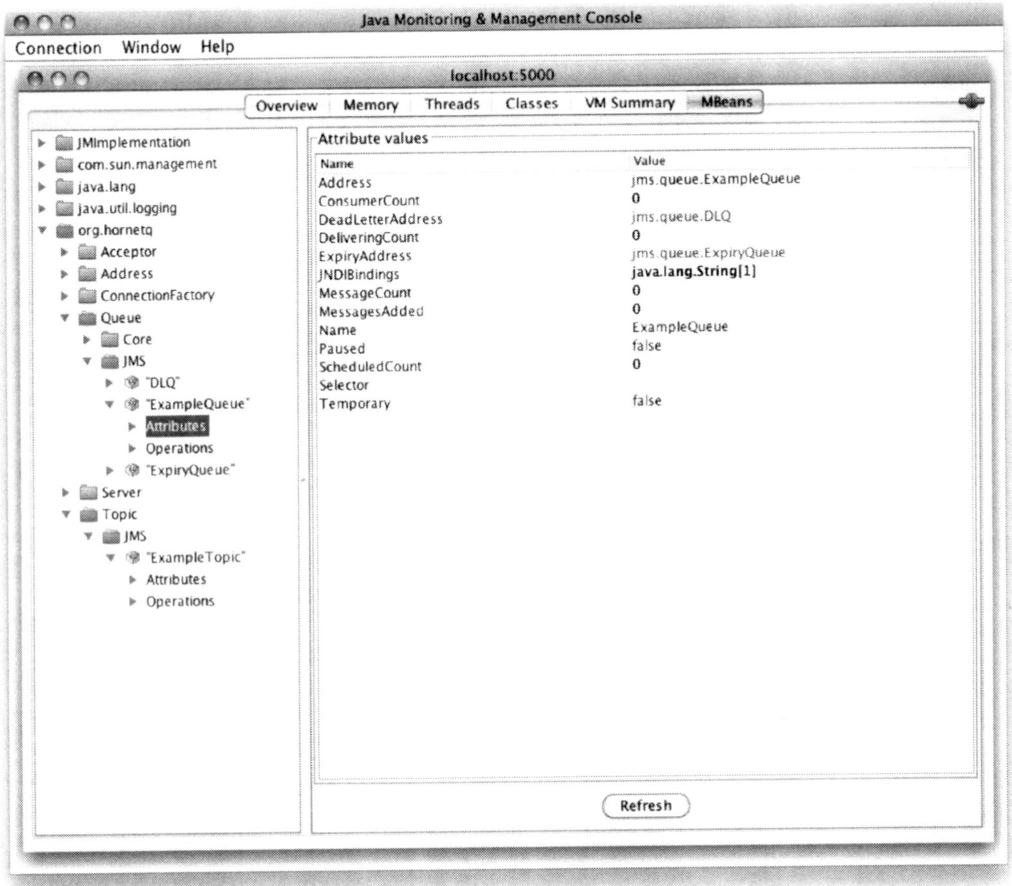

Figure 12–8. *Queue Attributes in the HornetQ JMX Console*

HornetQ comes with three point-to-point message queues out of the box: `ExampleQueue`, `ExpiryQueue`, and `DLQ` (which stands for "dead letter queue"). `DLQ` is used when HornetQ fails to deliver a message to a destination. Additionally, HornetQ also includes a sample topic, `ExampleTopic`. This queue can be seen in JConsole as shown in Figure 12–9.

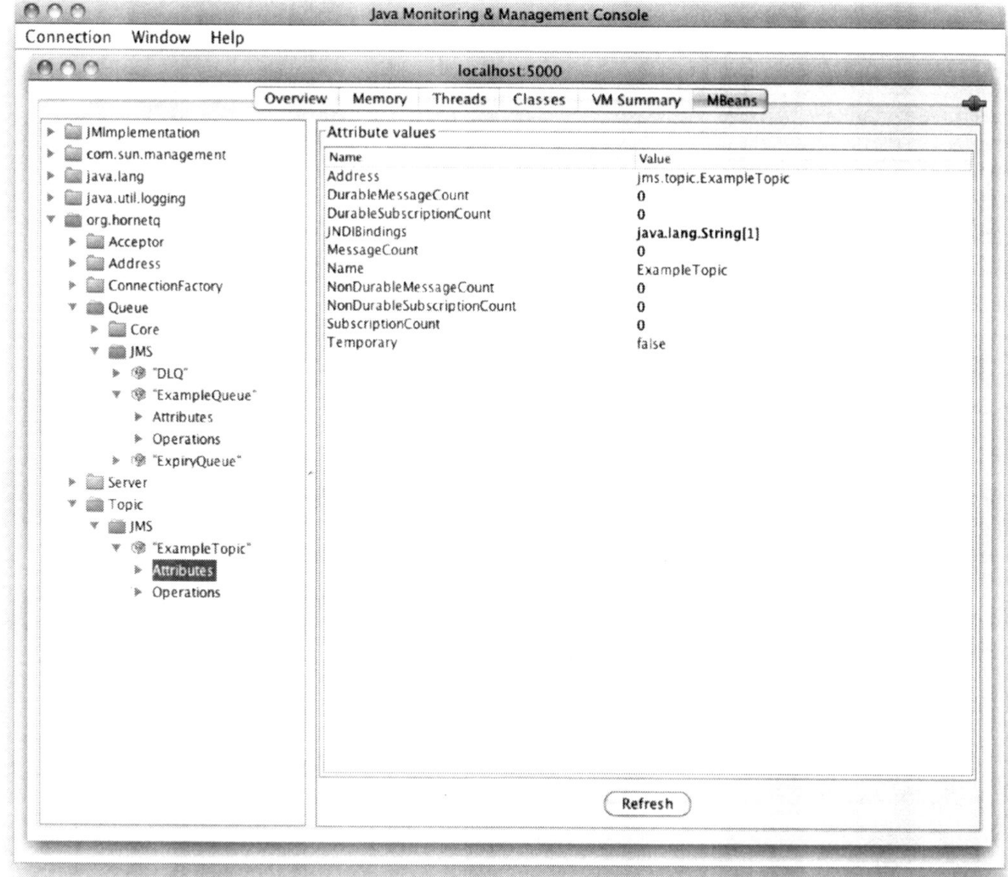

Figure 12–9. *Topic Attributes in the HornetQ JMX Console*

In order to use JBoss HornetQ with Spring Integration, you have to include the following dependencies in the Maven pom.xml configuration file:

```
<dependency>
  <groupId>org.hornetq</groupId>
  <artifactId>hornetq-core</artifactId>
  <version>2.1.2.Final</version>
</dependency>
<dependency>
  <groupId>org.hornetq</groupId>
  <artifactId>hornetq-core-client</artifactId>
  <version>2.1.2.Final</version>
</dependency>
<dependency>
```

```
    <groupId>org.hornetq</groupId>
    <artifactId>hornetq-jms-client</artifactId>
    <version>2.1.2.Final</version>
  </dependency>
  <dependency>
    <groupId>org.jboss.netty</groupId>
    <artifactId>netty</artifactId>
    <version>3.2.2.Final</version>
  </dependency>
```

Also, do not forget to add the JBoss Maven repositories:

```
<repository>
  <id>JBoss Repository</id>
  <url>https://repository.jboss.org/nexus/content/repositories/releases</url>
</repository>
<repository>
  <id>JBoss Maven2 Repository</id>
  <url>http://repository.jboss.org/maven2</url>
</repository>
```

Next, Spring requires a ConnectionFactory for HornetQ. Note that you can use a reference to a JMS topic, or the ID (a string) of the topic itself. In the following configuration, a CachingConnectionFactory is used, just as with ActiveMQ. Additionally, some HornetQ-specific configurations are used to help correctly set up the ConnectionFactory.

```
@Bean
public CachingConnectionFactory connectionFactory() {
    CachingConnectionFactory cachingConnectionFactory =
            new CachingConnectionFactory();
    cachingConnectionFactory.setSessionCacheSize(10);
    cachingConnectionFactory.setCacheProducers(false);
    cachingConnectionFactory.setTargetConnectionFactory(hornetQConnectionFactory());
    return cachingConnectionFactory;
}

@Bean
public HornetQConnectionFactory hornetQConnectionFactory() {
    HornetQConnectionFactory connectionFactory =
            new HornetQConnectionFactory(transportConfiguration());
    return connectionFactory;
}

@Bean
public TransportConfiguration transportConfiguration() {
    Map<String, Object> map = new HashMap<String, Object>();
    map.put("host", "localhost");
    map.put("port", 5445);
    TransportConfiguration configuration =
            new TransportConfiguration(
                    "org.hornetq.core.remoting.impl.netty.NettyConnectorFactory", map);
    return configuration;
}
```

JMS Channel Adapters

Referring back to the Ticket system example in Chapter 6, there is a single process that contains two threads: the main thread produces tickets with different priorities, and a separate thread receives the tickets. In Chapter 6, the examples are using different types of in-memory channels to connect the ticket producer and consumer. What if the ticket producer and ticket receiver are running in two different processes or two different servers in different locations? How can Spring Integration connect them together?

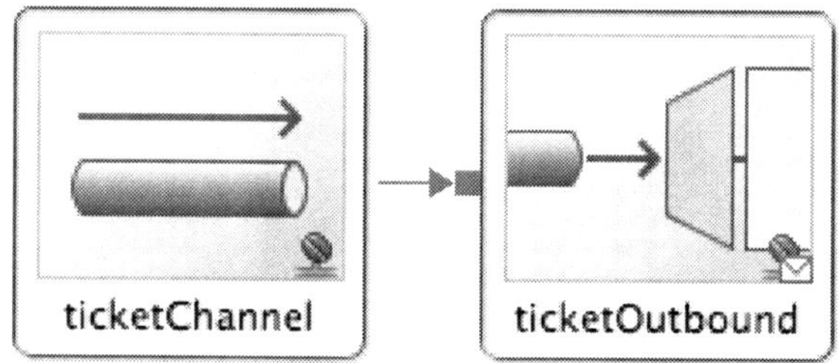

Figure 12–10. *Ticket reporter Enterprise Integration Pattern (EIP) Diagram*

The `ProblemReporter` will generate tickets with different priorities and send them to the `ticketChannel` message channel. In order to send the message to a different process outside of the JVM, an outbound JMS channel adapter is used to connect the `ticketChannel` with a JMS message queue, `ticket.queue`.

In order to use Spring JMS Integration, make sure the Spring configuration file contains the necessary namespaces as shown in Listing 12–3.

Listing 12–3. *ticket-reporter.xml*

```
<?xml version="1.0" encoding="UTF-8"?>
<beans xmlns="http://www.springframework.org/schema/beans"
       xmlns:xsi="http://www.w3.org/2001/XMLSchema-instance"
       xmlns:int="http://www.springframework.org/schema/integration"
       xmlns:int-jms="http://www.springframework.org/schema/integration/jms"
       xmlns:context="http://www.springframework.org/schema/context"
       xsi:schemaLocation="http://www.springframework.org/schema/integration
    http://www.springframework.org/schema/integration/spring-integration-2.0.xsd
    http://www.springframework.org/schema/integration/jms
    http://www.springframework.org/schema/integration/jms/spring-integration-jms-2.0.xsd
    http://www.springframework.org/schema/beans
    http://www.springframework.org/schema/beans/spring-beans-3.0.xsd
    http://www.springframework.org/schema/context
    http://www.springframework.org/schema/context/spring-context-3.0.xsd">

  <context:component-scan
      base-package="com.apress.prospringintegration.messaging.activemq.jms.adapter"/>

  <int-jms:outbound-channel-adapter id="ticketOutbound"
                                    destination="ticketQueue"
                                    channel="ticketChannel"/>

</beans>
```

The JMS channel adapter contains the attribute extract-payload. If the extract-payload attribute is true, which is the default, the adapter will try to extract the Spring Integration message payload by passing the message into the message converter SimpleMessageConverter. The SimpleMessageConverter will convert the incoming message into a JMS message payload. For example, if the Spring Integration message contains a string, the SimpleMessageConverter will convert the payload into a JMS TextMessage. Therefore, the Ticket object needs to implement the java.io.Serializable interface.

If the extract-payload value is set to false, then the whole Spring Integration message will be sent as a byte array and converted into a JMS message. This option can only be used if all the systems are using Spring Integration.

ActiveMQ will be used for these examples. Messages will travel through an ActiveMQ queue called ticket.queue. The JMS adapters require either a reference to a Spring JmsTemplate instance, or both a ConnectionFactory and java.jms.Destination reference. Directly specifying a destination name works as well:

```
<int-jms:outbound-channel-adapter id="ticketOutbound"
                                  destination-name="ticket.queue"
                                  channel="ticketChannel"/>
```

The outbound channel adapter sends a JMS message to the ticket.queue destination any time a message is sent to the message channel ticketOutbound. The rest of the source code for the Ticket reporter example is shown below. The Ticket class is shown in Listing 12–4.

Listing 12–4. *Ticket.java*

```
package com.apress.prospringintegration.messaging;

import java.io.Serializable;
import java.util.Calendar;

public class Ticket implements Serializable {
    private static final long serialVersionUID = 7216482616400695821;

    public enum Priority    {
        low,
        medium,
        high,
        emergency
    }

    private long ticketId;
    private Calendar issueDateTime;
    private String description;
    private Priority priority;

    public long getTicketId() {
        return ticketId;
    }

    public void setTicketId(long ticketId) {
        this.ticketId = ticketId;
    }

    public Calendar getIssueDateTime() {
        return issueDateTime;
```

```
    }

    public void setIssueDateTime(Calendar issueDateTime) {
        this.issueDateTime = issueDateTime;
    }

    public String getDescription()  {
        return description;
    }

    public void setDescription(String description)  {
        this.description = description;
    }

    public Priority getPriority()  {
        return priority;
    }

    public void setPriority(Priority priority) {
        this.priority = priority;
    }

    public String toString() {
        return String.format("Ticket# %d: [%s] %s", ticketId, priority, description);
    }
}
```

The ProblemReporter class is shown in Listing 12–5. This component publishes a message with a Ticket object as the payload to the ticketChannel message channel.

Listing 12–5. *ProblemReporter.java*

```
package com.apress.prospringintegration.messaging.activemq.jms.adapter;

import org.springframework.beans.factory.annotation.Value;
import org.springframework.integration.MessageChannel;
import org.springframework.integration.support.MessageBuilder;
import org.springframework.stereotype.Component;

@Component
public class ProblemReporter {

    private MessageChannel channel;

    @Value("#{ticketChannel}")
    public void setChannel(MessageChannel channel) {
        this.channel = channel;
    }

    public void openTicket(Ticket ticket) {
        channel.send(MessageBuilder.withPayload(ticket).build());
        System.out.println("Ticket Sent - " + ticket.toString());
    }
}
```

The TicketGenerator class shown in Listing 12–6 generates the Ticket objects with different priority levels.

Listing 12–6. *TicketGenerator.java*

```
package com.apress.prospringintegration.messaging.activemq.jms.adapter;

import com.apress.prospringintegration.messaging.activemq.jms.adapter.Ticket.Priority;
import org.springframework.stereotype.Component;

import java.util.ArrayList;
import java.util.GregorianCalendar;
import java.util.List;

@Component
public class TicketGenerator {

    private long nextTicketId;

    public TicketGenerator() {
        this.nextTicketId = 1000l;
    }

    public List<Ticket> createTickets() {
        List<Ticket> tickets = new ArrayList<Ticket>();

        tickets.add(createLowPriorityTicket());
        tickets.add(createLowPriorityTicket());
        tickets.add(createLowPriorityTicket());
        tickets.add(createLowPriorityTicket());
        tickets.add(createLowPriorityTicket());
        tickets.add(createMediumPriorityTicket());
        tickets.add(createMediumPriorityTicket());
        tickets.add(createMediumPriorityTicket());
        tickets.add(createMediumPriorityTicket());
        tickets.add(createMediumPriorityTicket());
        tickets.add(createHighPriorityTicket());
        tickets.add(createHighPriorityTicket());
        tickets.add(createHighPriorityTicket());
        tickets.add(createHighPriorityTicket());
        tickets.add(createHighPriorityTicket());
        tickets.add(createEmergencyTicket());
        tickets.add(createEmergencyTicket());
        tickets.add(createEmergencyTicket());
        tickets.add(createEmergencyTicket());
        tickets.add(createEmergencyTicket());

        return tickets;
    }

    Ticket createEmergencyTicket() {
        return createTicket(Priority.emergency,
                " Urgent problem. Fix immediately or revenue will be lost! ");
    }
```

```
    Ticket createHighPriorityTicket() {
        return createTicket(Priority.high,
                " Serious issue. Fix immediately.");
    }

    Ticket createMediumPriorityTicket() {
        return createTicket(Priority.medium,
                " There is an issue; take a look whenever you have time.");
    }

    Ticket createLowPriorityTicket() {
        return createTicket(Priority.low,
                " Some minor problems have been found.");
    }

    Ticket createTicket(Priority priority, String description) {
        Ticket ticket = new Ticket();
        ticket.setTicketId(nextTicketId++);
        ticket.setPriority(priority);
        ticket.setIssueDateTime(GregorianCalendar.getInstance());
        ticket.setDescription(description);

        return ticket;
    }
}
```

The main class that runs the Ticket reporter application is shown in Listing 12–27. This class creates the Spring context uses the `TicketGenerator` and `ProblemReporter` class to publish the Ticket objects with different priority levels to the JMS queue.

Listing 12–7. *TicketReporterMain.java*

```
package com.apress.prospringintegration.messaging.activemq.jms.adapter;

import org.springframework.context.support.ClassPathXmlApplicationContext;

import java.util.List;

public class TicketReporterMain {

    public static void main(String[] args)
            throws Throwable {
        String contextName = "ticket-reporter.xml";

        ClassPathXmlApplicationContext applicationContext =
                new ClassPathXmlApplicationContext(contextName);
        applicationContext.start();

        ProblemReporter problemReporter =
                applicationContext.getBean(ProblemReporter.class);
        TicketGenerator ticketGenerator =
                applicationContext.getBean(TicketGenerator.class);
```

```
            while (true) {
                List<Ticket> tickets = ticketGenerator.createTickets();
                for (Ticket ticket : tickets) {
                    problemReporter.openTicket(ticket);
                }

                Thread.sleep(5000);
            }
        }
    }
```

In order to run this example, the ActiveMQ broker needs to be started first. To start it, use the following command:

```
$ apache-activemq-5.4.2/bin/macosx/activemq start
Starting ActiveMQ Broker...
```

Next, start the JMX console so you can monitor the activity on the JMS broker:

```
$ jconsole localhost:1616
```

Launch the example using the following command:

```
$ cd prospringintegration/messaging/activemq-jmschanneladapter
$ mvn exec:java -
Dexec.mainClass="com.apress.prospringintegration.mesging.activemq.jms.adapter.TicketReporterMa
in"
```

The source code should be compiled and running. The following output will appear on the console:

```
12-25-2010 14:45:05 [INFO] Initializing ExecutorService  'taskScheduler'
12-25-2010 14:45:05 [INFO] Starting beans in phase -2147483648
12-25-2010 14:45:05 [INFO] started _org.springframework.integration.errorLogger
12-25-2010 14:45:05 [INFO] Starting beans in phase 2147483647
12-25-2010 14:45:05 [INFO] started ticketOutbound
12-25-2010 14:45:05 [INFO] Starting beans in phase -2147483648
12-25-2010 14:45:05 [INFO] Starting beans in phase 2147483647
Ticket Sent - Ticket# 1000: [low] Some minor problems have been found.
Ticket Sent - Ticket# 1001: [low] Some minor problems have been found.
Ticket Sent - Ticket# 1002: [low] Some minor problems have been found.
Ticket Sent - Ticket# 1003: [low] Some minor problems have been found.
Ticket Sent - Ticket# 1004: [low] Some minor problems have been found.
Ticket Sent - Ticket# 1005: [medium] There is an issue; take a look whenever you have time.
Ticket Sent - Ticket# 1006: [medium] There is an issue; Take a look whenever you have time.
Ticket Sent - Ticket# 1007: [medium] There is an issue; Take a look whenever you have time.
Ticket Sent - Ticket# 1008: [medium] There is an issue; Take a look whenever you have time.
Ticket Sent - Ticket# 1009: [medium] There is an issue; Take a look whenever you have time.
Ticket Sent - Ticket# 1010: [high] Serious issue. Fix immediately.
Ticket Sent - Ticket# 1011: [high] Serious issue. Fix immediately.
Ticket Sent - Ticket# 1012: [high] Serious issue. Fix immediately.
Ticket Sent - Ticket# 1013: [high] Serious issue. Fix immediately.
Ticket Sent - Ticket# 1014: [high] Serious issue. Fix immediately.
Ticket Sent - Ticket# 1016: [emergency] Urgent problem. Fix immediately or revenue will be lost!
Ticket Sent - Ticket# 1016: [emergency] Urgent problem. Fix immediately or revenue will be lost!
Ticket Sent - Ticket# 1017: [emergency] Urgent problem. Fix immediately or revenue will be lost!
Ticket Sent - Ticket# 1018: [emergency] Urgent problem. Fix immediately or revenue will be lost!
Ticket Sent - Ticket# 1019: [emergency] Urgent problem. Fix immediately or revenue will be lost!
```

Take a look at the JMX console that connects with the ActiveMQ broker. Switch to the MBeans tab and expand the MBean `org.apache.activemq.localhost.Queue` as shown in Listing 12–11. In addition to the default queue example, a new queue, `ticket.queue`, is created.

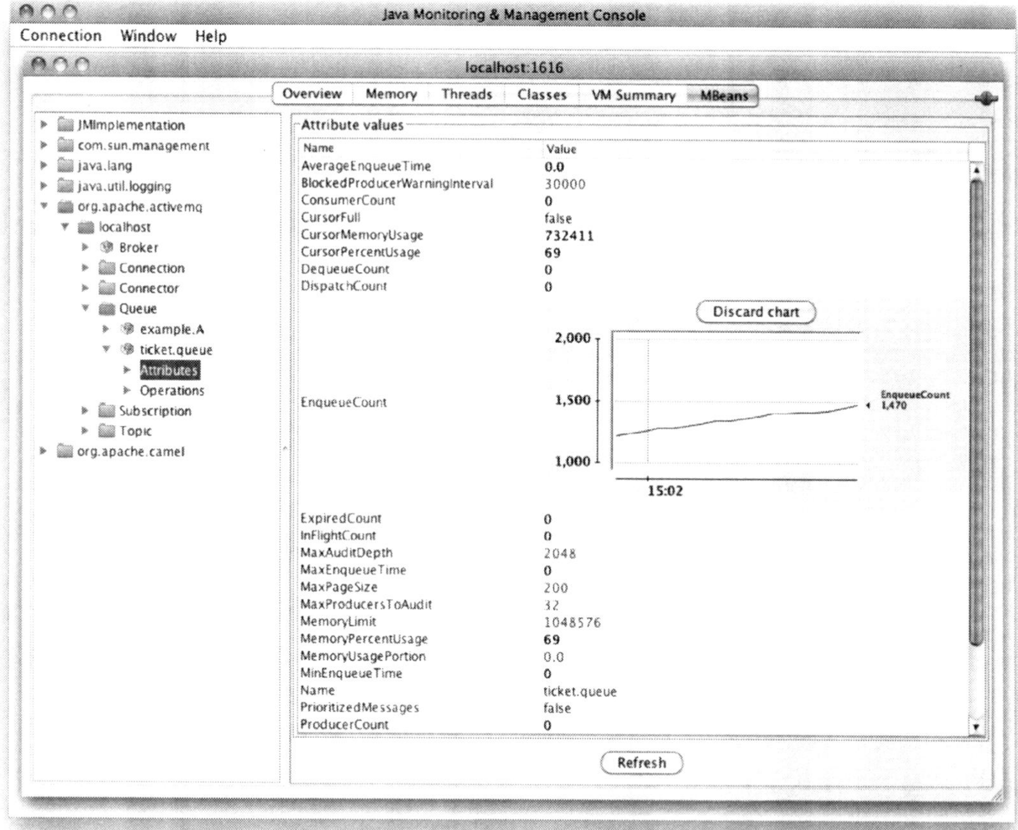

Figure 12–11. *ticket.queue Attributes*

Take a look at the MBean attributes of `ticket.queue` and double-click the `EnqueueCount` attribute. The count is increasing because the `TicketReporter` is generating messages and sending them to the JMS broker via the outbound channel adapter. Now stop the application by pressing Ctrl+C in the console window.

The Ticket receiver application will receive messages by using the inbound JMS message-driven adapter and connecting with the other message channel. The EIP diagram is illustrated in Figure 12–12.

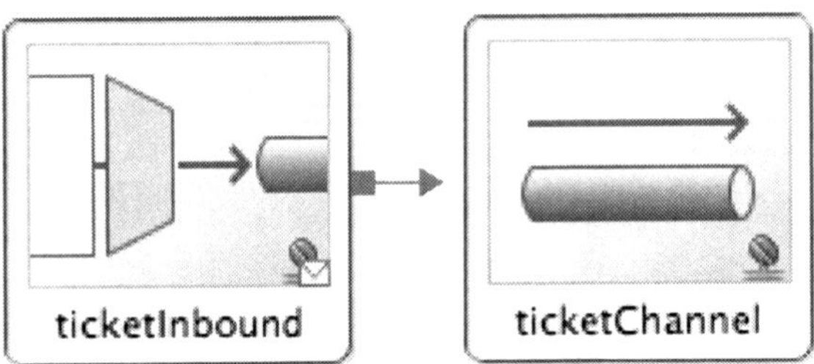

Figure 12–12. Ticket Receiver EIP diagram

The Spring configuration, as shown in Listing 12–8, is very similar to the Ticket reporter application.

***Listing 12–8.** ticket-receiver.xml*

```
<?xml version="1.0" encoding="UTF-8"?>
<beans xmlns="http://www.springframework.org/schema/beans"
       xmlns:xsi="http://www.w3.org/2001/XMLSchema-instance"
       xmlns:int="http://www.springframework.org/schema/integration"
       xmlns:int-jms="http://www.springframework.org/schema/integration/jms"
       xmlns:context="http://www.springframework.org/schema/context"
       xsi:schemaLocation="http://www.springframework.org/schema/integration
    http://www.springframework.org/schema/integration/spring-integration-2.0.xsd
    http://www.springframework.org/schema/integration/jms
    http://www.springframework.org/schema/integration/jms/spring-integration-jms-2.0.xsd
    http://www.springframework.org/schema/beans
    http://www.springframework.org/schema/beans/spring-beans-3.0.xsd
    http://www.springframework.org/schema/context
    http://www.springframework.org/schema/context/spring-context-3.0.xsd">

  <context:component-scan
      base-package="com.apress.prospringintegration.messaging.activemq.jms.adapter"/>

  <int:channel id="receiveChannel"/>

  <int:service-activator input-channel="receiveChannel" ref="ticketReceiver"/>

  <int-jms:message-driven-channel-adapter id="ticketInbound"
                                          destination="ticketQueue"
                                          channel="receiveChannel"/>
</beans>
```

There are two types of inbound channel adapters: *polling* and *message-driven*. The polling channel adapter uses `JmsTemplate` internally while the message-driven inbound channel adapter uses the Spring `MessageListener` container abstraction.

The preceding example uses the message-driven JMS channel adapters. In order to use the inbound JMS channel adapters, a poller must be configured, as shown following:

```
<int-jms:inbound-channel-adapter id="ticketInbound"
                                 channel="receiveChannel"
                                 destination="ticketQueue"
                                 connection-factory="connectionFactory">
```

```
    <int:poller fixed-rate="1000"/>
  </int-jms:inbound-channel-adapter>
```

The inbound JMS channel adapter also contains the attribute `extract-payload`. If the `extract-payload` attribute is `true`, which is the default, the adapter will try to extract the JMS message body by passing the message into the message converter `SimpleMessageConverter`. The `SimpleMessageConverter` will convert the incoming message body into a Spring message payload. For example, an incoming JMS `TextMessage` will be converted using the `SimpleMessageConverter` in a Spring Message with a string payload. If the `extract-payload` value is set to `false`, then the raw JMS message will become the Spring message payload

In inbound JMS message is routed to the `receiveChannel` message channel and forward to the `TicketReceiver` service activator shown in Listing 12–9. The `TicketReceiver` simply logs the Ticket object.

Listing 12–9. *TicketReceiver.java*

```
package com.apress.prospringintegration.messaging.activemq.jms.adapter;

import org.springframework.integration.annotation.ServiceActivator;
import org.springframework.stereotype.Component;

@Component
public class TicketReceiver {

    @ServiceActivator
    public void handleTicket(Ticket ticket) {
        System.out.println("Received ticket - " + ticket.toString());
    }

}
```

The main class for running the example is shown in Listing 12–10. The class will create the Spring context and the message driven bean which will listener for incoming JMS messages.

Listing 12–10. *TicketReceiverMain.java*

```
package com.apress.prospringintegration.messaging.activemq.jms.adapter;

import org.springframework.context.support.ClassPathXmlApplicationContext;

public class TicketReceiverMain {

    public static void main(String[] args) {
        String contextName = "ticket-receiver.xml";

        ClassPathXmlApplicationContext applicationContext =
            new ClassPathXmlApplicationContext(contextName);
        applicationContext.start();
    }
}
```

Run the TicketReceiver application by issuing the following command:

```
$ mvn exec:java -
Dexec.mainClass="com.apress.prospringintegration.mesging.activemq.jms.adapter.TicketReceiverMa
in"
```

Running the command will result in the following output:

```
12-25-2010 15:33:46 [INFO] Initializing ExecutorService  'taskScheduler'
12-25-2010 15:33:46 [INFO] Starting beans in phase -2147483648
12-25-2010 15:33:46 [INFO] started _org.springframework.integration.errorLogger
12-25-2010 15:33:46 [INFO] Starting beans in phase 2147483647
12-25-2010 15:33:46 [INFO] started ticketInbound
12-25-2010 15:33:46 [INFO] Starting beans in phase -2147483648
12-25-2010 15:33:46 [INFO] Starting beans in phase 2147483647
Received ticket - Ticket# 1000: [low] Some minor problems have been found.
Received ticket - Ticket# 1001: [low] Some minor problems have been found.
Received ticket - Ticket# 1002: [low] Some minor problems have been found.
Received ticket - Ticket# 1003: [low] Some minor problems have been found.
Received ticket - Ticket# 1004: [low] Some minor problems have been found.
Received ticket - Ticket# 1005: [medium] There is an issue; take a look whenever you have
time.
Received ticket - Ticket# 1006: [medium] There is an issue; Take a look whenever you have
time.
Received ticket - Ticket# 1007: [medium] There is an issue; Take a look whenever you have
time.
Received ticket - Ticket# 1008: [medium] There is an issue; Take a look whenever you have
time.
Received ticket - Ticket# 1009: [medium] There is an issue; Take a look whenever you have
time.
Received ticket - Ticket# 1010: [high] Serious issue. Fix immediately.
Received ticket - Ticket# 1011: [high] Serious issue. Fix immediately.
Received ticket - Ticket# 1012: [high] Serious issue. Fix immediately.
Received ticket - Ticket# 1013: [high] Serious issue. Fix immediately.
Received ticket - Ticket# 1014: [high] Serious issue. Fix immediately.
Received ticket - Ticket# 1015: [emergency] Urgent problem. Fix immediately or revenue will be
lost!
Received ticket - Ticket# 1016: [emergency] Urgent problem. Fix immediately or revenue will be
lost!
Received ticket - Ticket# 1017: [emergency] Urgent problem. Fix immediately or revenue will be
lost!
Received ticket - Ticket# 1018: [emergency] Urgent problem. Fix immediately or revenue will be
lost!
Received ticket - Ticket# 1019: [emergency] Urgent problem. Fix immediately or revenue will be
lost!
```

The JMX console also shows that the JMS message queue is draining by observing the decreasing DequeueCount MBean attribute (see Figure 12–13).

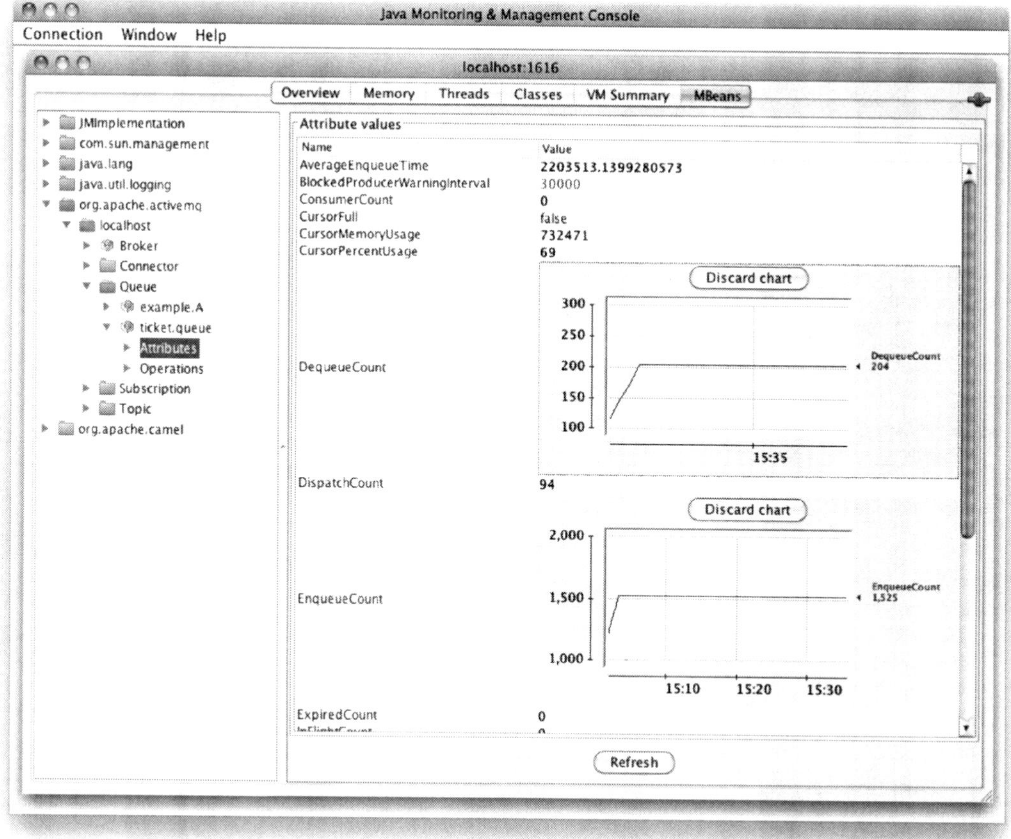

Figure 12–13. ticket.queue Attributes for Monitroing the Decreasing Queue Count

The preceding examples use ActiveMQ as the JMS broker. However, using HornetQ as the JMS broker instead is very simple. All Spring Integration requires is that the `connectionFactory` bean modified to use HornetQ. The new Java configuration file is shown in Listing 12–11.

Listing 12–11. HornetqConfiguration.java

```
package com.apress.prospringintegration.messaging.hornetq.jms.adapter;

import org.hornetq.api.core.TransportConfiguration;
import org.hornetq.jms.client.HornetQConnectionFactory;
import org.springframework.context.annotation.Bean;
import org.springframework.context.annotation.Configuration;
import org.springframework.integration.MessageChannel;
import org.springframework.integration.channel.DirectChannel;
import org.springframework.jms.connection.CachingConnectionFactory;
```

```
import java.util.HashMap;
import java.util.Map;

@Configuration
public class HornetqConfiguration {

    @Bean
    public CachingConnectionFactory connectionFactory() {
        CachingConnectionFactory cachingConnectionFactory =
                new CachingConnectionFactory();
        cachingConnectionFactory.setSessionCacheSize(10);
        cachingConnectionFactory.setCacheProducers(false);
        cachingConnectionFactory.setTargetConnectionFactory(hornetQConnectionFactory());
        return cachingConnectionFactory;
    }

    @Bean
    public HornetQConnectionFactory hornetQConnectionFactory() {
        HornetQConnectionFactory connectionFactory =
                new HornetQConnectionFactory(transportConfiguration());
        return connectionFactory;
    }

    @Bean
    public TransportConfiguration transportConfiguration() {
        Map<String, Object> map = new HashMap<String, Object>();
        map.put("host", "localhost");
        map.put("port", 5445);
        TransportConfiguration configuration =
                new TransportConfiguration(
                        "org.hornetq.core.remoting.impl.netty.NettyConnectorFactory", map);
        return configuration;
    }

    @Bean
    public MessageChannel ticketChannel() {
        MessageChannel channel = new DirectChannel();
        return channel;
    }
}
```

The HornetQ JMS destination can be monitored by using the JMX console, as shown in Figure 12–14.

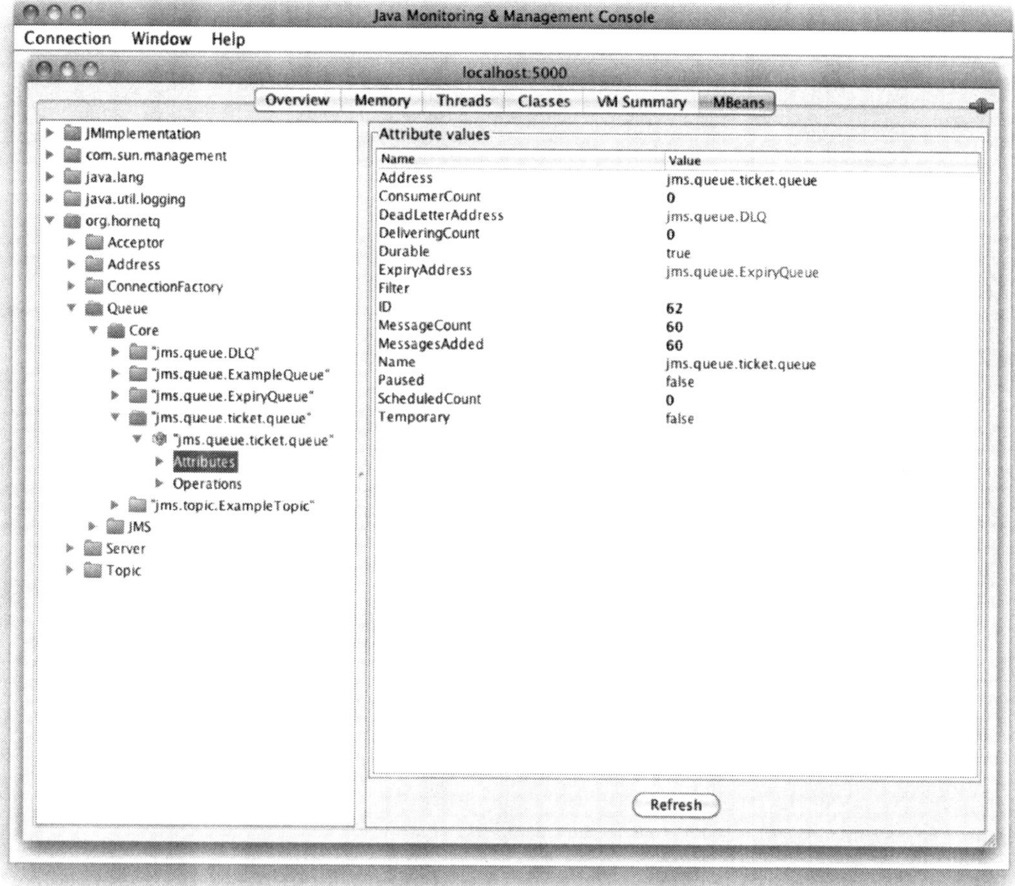

Figure 12–14. *ticket.queue Attributes using HornetQ*

JMS Gateway

The Spring Integration outbound JMS gateway creates a JMS message from a Spring Integration message, and sends it to the `request-destination`. The outbound JMS gateway handles the reply JMS message from the `reply-destination`. If no `reply-destination` is configured, the JMS gateway will create a `TemporaryQueue` in the JMS broker, and expect replies for the request to be sent to that queue. The outbound JMS gateway requires a reference to a `ConnectionFactory`. The inbound JMS gateway requires a reference to a `ConnectionFactory` and a `request-destination` as well.

```
<int-jms:inbound-gateway id="inGateway"
                         request-destination="ticketQueue"
                         request-channel="ticketChannel"
```

```
                                    connectionFactory="connectionFactory"/>

  <int-jms:outbound-gateway id="outGateway"
                            request-destination="ticketQueue"
                            request-channel="ticketChanne"
                            reply-destination="replyQueue"
                            reply-channel="jmsReply"/>
```

The inbound JMS gateway has an `extract-reply-payload` property, which works very similarly to the JMS channel adapter's `extract-payload` property. When `extract-reply-payload` is set to `true`, which is the default setting, the Spring Integration message payload will be extracted and converted into a JMS message. If the `extract-reply-payload` property is set to `false`, the whole Spring Integration message will become the JMS message payload. The outbound JMS gateway has the `extract-request-payload` property. Again, this works just like the outbound JMS channel adapter's `extract-payload` property.

JMS-Backed Message Channel

Spring Integration comes with a variety of in-memory message channels, which are discussed in Chapter 6. Since the messages are stored in memory, it could be a potential problem if the application were shut down accidentally. All the messages waiting in the message channel would be lost, and the message channel would become empty when the application restarts.

One solution to this problem is to have the message producer store the messages and redeliver them when the consumer (the application) is available. However, this requires additional work, and not all systems support message redelivery.

Another option is to use the JMS channel adapters, as described earlier in this chapter. However, this assumes that JMS is being used as the publisher and consumer. If a non-JMS endpoint is being used, then this will require an alternative way of providing durability and message redelivery to the application.

Here where Spring Integration 2.0 JMS-backed message channels come to the rescue. If a JMS-backed channel is being used, the messages between two endpoints (whether transactional or not) benefit from the guarantees that JMS provides—that is, messages will not be lost if the application crashes or is shut down. Let's revisit the ticket example from Chapter 6, this time using JMS backed channels. The Spring configuration file is shown in Listing 12–12.

Listing 12–12. *jms-backedchannel.xml*

```
<?xml version="1.0" encoding="UTF-8"?>
<beans xmlns="http://www.springframework.org/schema/beans"
       xmlns:xsi="http://www.w3.org/2001/XMLSchema-instance"
       xmlns:int-jms="http://www.springframework.org/schema/integration/jms"
       xmlns:context="http://www.springframework.org/schema/context"
       xsi:schemaLocation=" http://www.springframework.org/schema/integration/jms
    http://www.springframework.org/schema/integration/jms/spring-integration-jms-2.0.xsd
    http://www.springframework.org/schema/beans
    http://www.springframework.org/schema/beans/spring-beans-3.0.xsd
    http://www.springframework.org/schema/context
    http://www.springframework.org/schema/context/spring-context-3.0.xsd">

  <context:component-scan
      base-package="com.apress.prospringintegration.messaging.activemq.jms.backedchannel"/>

  <int-jms:channel id="ticketChannel"
                   queue-name="ticket.queue"
```

```
                    connection-factory="connectionFactory"/>

</beans>
```

In this case, a point-to-point message channel is used. A corresponding JMS message queue is used to support the point-to-point message channel. If the message channel is a `publish-subscribe` channel, a JMS message topic should be used instead, as follows:

```
<int-jms:publish-subscribe-channel id="ticketChannel" topic-name="ticket.topic" />
```

Spring Integration's JMS-based support looks for a well-known connection factory in the Spring application context, `connectionFactory`, and uses it if available. Otherwise, one must be specified on the adapter or endpoint. Again the Ticket class is shown in Listing 12–13.

Listing 12–13. *Ticket.java*

```
package com.apress.prospringintegration.messaging.activemq.jms.backedchannel;

import org.springframework.stereotype.Component;

import java.io.Serializable;
import java.util.Calendar;

@Component
public class Ticket implements Serializable {
    private static final long serialVersionUID = 721648261640069582L;

    public enum Priority {
        low,
        medium,
        high,
        emergency
    }

    private long ticketId;
    private Calendar issueDateTime;
    private String description;
    private Priority priority;

    public Ticket() {
    }

    public long getTicketId() {
        return ticketId;
    }

    public void setTicketId(long ticketId) {
        this.ticketId = ticketId;
    }

    public Calendar getIssueDateTime() {
        return issueDateTime;
    }

    public void setIssueDateTime(Calendar issueDateTime) {
```

```
        this.issueDateTime = issueDateTime;
    }

    public String getDescription() {
        return description;
    }

    public void setDescription(String description) {
        this.description = description;
    }

    public Priority getPriority() {
        return priority;
    }

    public void setPriority(Priority priority) {
        this.priority = priority;
    }

    public String toString() {
        return String.format("Ticket# %d: [%s] %s", ticketId, priority, description);
    }
}
```

The TicketCreator class shown in Listing 12–14 will send the Ticket object to the message channel ticketChannel.

Listing 12–14. *TicketCreator.java*

```
package com.apress.prospringintegration.messaging.activemq.jms.backedchannel;

import org.springframework.beans.factory.annotation.Value;
import org.springframework.integration.core.SubscribableChannel;
import org.springframework.integration.support.MessageBuilder;
import org.springframework.stereotype.Component;

@Component
public class TicketCreator {

    private SubscribableChannel channel;

    @Value("#{ticketChannel}")
    public void setChannel(SubscribableChannel channel) {
        this.channel = channel;
    }

    void openTicket(Ticket ticket) {
        channel.send(MessageBuilder.withPayload(ticket).build());
        System.out.println("Ticket Sent - " + ticket.toString());
    }
}
```

Even though the JMS-backed message channel is a point-to-point message channel, it implements the SubscribableChannel interface. Your messaging code need not be aware of the makeup or capabilities of a given channel, and can in the general case simply depend on the core MesssageChannel interface. Whether it's subscribable, publish/subscribe, or backed by JMS, it's ultimately a MessageChannel reference. The ProblemReport class shown in Listing 12–15 will also work with a JMS-backed channel.

***Listing 12–15.** ProblemReporter.java*

```
package com.apress.prospringintegration.messaging.activemq.jms.backedchannel;

import org.springframework.beans.factory.annotation.Value;
import org.springframework.integration.core.SubscribableChannel;
import org.springframework.integration.support.MessageBuilder;
import org.springframework.stereotype.Component;

@Component
public class ProblemReporter {
    private SubscribableChannel channel;

    @Value("#{ticketChannel}")
    public void setChannel(SubscribableChannel channel) {
        this.channel = channel;
    }

    public void openTicket(Ticket ticket) {
        channel.send(MessageBuilder.withPayload(ticket).build());
        System.out.println("Ticket Sent - " + ticket.toString());
    }
}
```

The Ticket objects with different priorities are again created using the TicketGenerator class shown in Listing 12–16.

***Listing 12–16.** TicketGenerator.java*

```
package com.apress.prospringintegration.messaging.activemq.jms.backedchannel;

import com.apress.prospringintegration.messaging.activemq.jms.backedchannel.Ticket.Priority;
import org.springframework.stereotype.Component;

import java.util.ArrayList;
import java.util.GregorianCalendar;
import java.util.List;

@Component
public class TicketGenerator {

    private long nextTicketId;

    public TicketGenerator() {
        this.nextTicketId = 1000l;
    }

    public List<Ticket> createTickets() {
        List<Ticket> tickets = new ArrayList<Ticket>();

        tickets.add(createLowPriorityTicket());
```

```
        tickets.add(createLowPriorityTicket());
        tickets.add(createLowPriorityTicket());
        tickets.add(createLowPriorityTicket());
        tickets.add(createLowPriorityTicket());
        tickets.add(createMediumPriorityTicket());
        tickets.add(createMediumPriorityTicket());
        tickets.add(createMediumPriorityTicket());
        tickets.add(createMediumPriorityTicket());
        tickets.add(createMediumPriorityTicket());
        tickets.add(createHighPriorityTicket());
        tickets.add(createHighPriorityTicket());
        tickets.add(createHighPriorityTicket());
        tickets.add(createHighPriorityTicket());
        tickets.add(createHighPriorityTicket());
        tickets.add(createEmergencyTicket());
        tickets.add(createEmergencyTicket());
        tickets.add(createEmergencyTicket());
        tickets.add(createEmergencyTicket());
        tickets.add(createEmergencyTicket());

        return tickets;
    }

    Ticket createEmergencyTicket() {
        return createTicket(Priority.emergency,
                " Urgent problem. Fix immediately or revenue will be lost!");
    }

    Ticket createHighPriorityTicket() {
        return createTicket(Priority.high,
                " Serious issue. Fix immediately.");
    }

    Ticket createMediumPriorityTicket() {
        return createTicket(Priority.medium,
                " There is an issue; take a look whenever you have time.");
    }

    Ticket createLowPriorityTicket() {
        return createTicket(Priority.low,
                " Some minor problems have been found.");
    }

    Ticket createTicket(Priority priority, String description) {
        Ticket ticket = new Ticket();
        ticket.setTicketId(nextTicketId++);
        ticket.setPriority(priority);
        ticket.setIssueDateTime(GregorianCalendar.getInstance());
        ticket.setDescription(description);

        return ticket;
    }
}
```

The incoming messages are logged using the TicketMessageHandler class shown in Listing 12–17.

Listing 12–17. *TicketMessageHandler.java*

```
package com.apress.prospringintegration.messaging.activemq.jms.backedchannel;

import org.springframework.integration.Message;
import org.springframework.integration.MessageRejectedException;
import org.springframework.integration.MessagingException;
import org.springframework.integration.core.MessageHandler;
import org.springframework.stereotype.Component;

@Component
public class TicketMessageHandler implements MessageHandler {

    @Override
    public void handleMessage(Message<?> message) throws MessagingException {
        Object payload = message.getPayload();

        if (payload instanceof Ticket) {
            handleTicket((Ticket) payload);
        } else {
            throw new MessageRejectedException(message,
                    "Unknown data type has been received.");
        }
    }

    void handleTicket(Ticket ticket) {
        System.out.println("Received ticket - " + ticket.toString());
    }
}
```

The main class TicketMain is shown in Listing 12–18. The class creates the Spring context, initialized the message handler and send the Ticket objects with different priorities to the message channel.

Listing 12–18. *TicketMain.java*

```
package com.apress.prospringintegration.messaging.activemq.jms.backedchannel;

import org.springframework.context.support.ClassPathXmlApplicationContext;
import org.springframework.integration.core.SubscribableChannel;

import java.util.List;

public class TicketMain {

    public static void main(String[] args) {

        String contextName = "jms-backedchannel.xml";

        ClassPathXmlApplicationContext applicationContext =
                new ClassPathXmlApplicationContext(contextName);
        applicationContext.start();

        TicketCreator ticketCreator =
```

```
                applicationContext.getBean(TicketCreator.class);
        TicketGenerator ticketGenerator =
                applicationContext.getBean(TicketGenerator.class);
        TicketMessageHandler ticketMessageHandler =
                applicationContext.getBean(TicketMessageHandler.class);

        SubscribableChannel channel =
                applicationContext.getBean("ticketChannel", SubscribableChannel.class);
        channel.subscribe(ticketMessageHandler);

        while (true) {
            List<Ticket> tickets = ticketGenerator.createTickets();
            for (Ticket ticket : tickets) {
                ticketCreator.openTicket(ticket);
            }
        }
    }
}
```

Once again, the preceding example uses ActiveMQ as the JMS broker to back the Spring Integration message channel. In order to use a different JMS broker such as HornetQ, simply change the `connectionFactory` to point to the HornetQ instance.

AMQP Integration

AMQP is an open standard for messaging protocol. AMQP also allows applications to communicate asynchronously, reliably, and securely. Unlike JMS, AMQP is a wire-level format, which provides network message framing; JMS, on the other hand, is a Java API. By complying with the AMQP standard, middleware products written for different platforms and programming languages can send and receive messages to and from each other. In other words, applications do not need to be written in Java in order to use AMQP as their enterprise integration broker.

In order to integrate an AMQP-compatible message broker with Spring Integration, AMQP channel adapters are used. At the time of writing, the Spring Integration AMQP channel adapters are still under development. Therefore, the source code needs to be downloaded, compiled, and installed.

The source code may be downloaded from `http://git-scm.com/download` using Git. Use the following command to clone the Spring Integration sandbox source code from Spring Source Git Repository:

```
$ git clone git://git.springsource.org/spring-integration/sandbox
$ cd sandbox/spring-integration-amqp
$ mvn -DskipTests=true clean install
```

Add the following to the `dependencies` section of the Maven `pom.xml` configuration file:

```
<dependency>
  <groupId>org.springframework.integration</groupId>
  <artifactId>spring-integration-amqp</artifactId>
  <version>2.0.0.BUILD-SNAPSHOT</version>
</dependency>
```

In addition, make sure the Spring Integration AMQP namespaces are added to the Spring configuration file, as follows:

```
<?xml version="1.0" encoding="UTF-8"?>
<beans xmlns="http://www.springframework.org/schema/beans"
       xmlns:xsi="http://www.w3.org/2001/XMLSchema-instance"
       xmlns:int="http://www.springframework.org/schema/integration"
       xmlns:context="http://www.springframework.org/schema/context"
       xmlns:int-amqp="http://www.springframework.org/schema/integration/amqp"
       xmlns:amqp="http://www.springframework.org/schema/amqp"
       xsi:schemaLocation="http://www.springframework.org/schema/integration
    http://www.springframework.org/schema/integration/spring-integration-2.0.xsd
    http://www.springframework.org/schema/beans
    http://www.springframework.org/schema/beans/spring-beans-3.0.xsd
    http://www.springframework.org/schema/context
    http://www.springframework.org/schema/context/spring-context-3.0.xsd
    http://www.springframework.org/schema/integration/amqp
    http://www.springframework.org/schema/integration/amqp/spring-integration-amqp-2.0.xsd">
</beans>
```

The *AMQP exchange* is the target destination for a message sender to send messages. The *AMQP queue* is the staging area for the message receiver to fetch messages. The *AMQP binding* is the link between the AMQP exchange and the AMQP queue.

There are three different types of AMQP exchange: direct, topic, and fanout as shown in Table 12–1.

***Table 12–1.** AMQP Exchanges*

	Direct Exchange	Topic Exchange	Fanout Exchange
Message Channel Type	Point-to-point	Publish/subscribe	Publish/subscribe
Routing Key	Absolute	Absolute, *, #	n/a
Example	`ticket.queue`	`ticket#`, `ticket*`	n/a

Since the direct exchange has a routing key, the queue needs to be configured using the same routing key; otherwise, messages will not be delivered to the queue. For example, if the exchange creates with the routing key "`ticket.queue`, then the queue that links with this exchange is required to have the queue name "`ticket.queue` as well. In other words, the direct exchange works like a point-to-point message channel.

The topic exchange can specify that the routing key contains wildcard, such as * (matching one character) and # (matching any character), so the queue that is configured with the routing key that matches the pattern can deliver the messages. For example, if the exchange is created with the routing key "`ticket*`, then the queue that links with this exchange is required to have the queue name "`ticket*`, where "`ticket*` can receive the message.

The fanout exchange is the simplest AMQP exchange type. It works very similar to the publish/subscribe message channel pattern, so a producer can send a message to multiple consumers. In addition, a fanout exchange does not need a routing key defined. Any queues that are bound with the exchange will have the message delivered.

Similar to how Spring Integration JMS works, that Spring Integration AMQP namespace supports inbound/outbound AMQP channel adapter as follows:

```
<int-amqp:inbound-channel-adapter connection-factory="connectionFactory"
                                  queue-name="ticket.queue"
                                  channel="ticketChannel" />
```

```
<int-amqp:outbound-channel-adapter amqp-template="amqpTemplate"
                                   channel="ticketChannel" />
```

SpringSource RabbitMQ

RabbitMQ (www.rabbitmq.com) is an open source message broker software that supports the AMQP standard. It is written in the Erlang language on top of the Open Telecom Platform (OTP), which is a library that promotes high performance, reliability, scalability, and availability through the use of many approaches, not the least of which is a job supervisor that respawns failed processes. RabbitMQ was originally written by Rabbit Technologies, and was acquired by SpringSource in early 2010. RabbitMQ is available under the Mozilla Public License.

Erlang needs to be installed in order to run RabbitMQ. The latest version of Erlang (R14B01at the time of this writing) can be downloaded from www.erlang.org/download.html. For Windows users, there is a binary version for download at www.erlang.org/download/otp_win32_R14B01.exe. For Mac OS X users, Erlang can be installed by using MacPorts. The latest version of MacPorts can be downloaded from www.macports.org/install.php. However, the MacPorts version (R13B03 at the time of writing) is up to date with the latest version on the Erlang official web site. After MacPorts is installed, Erlang may be installed as follows:

```
$ port list erlang
erlang                         @R13B03          lang/erlang
$ sudo port install erlang
```

After installing Erlang on Mac OS X, try to launch the Erlang shell to make sure everything is fine:

```
$ erl
Erlang R13B03 (erts-5.7.4) [source] [64-bit] [smp:2:2] [rq:2] [async-threads:0] [hipe]
[kernel-poll:false]

Eshell V5.7.4  (abort with ^G)
1>
```

To quit the Erlang shell, simply enter Ctrl-C from the shell and choose the "(a)bort" option. For the other Linux platforms, only source code is available for download. Enter the following commands to download and build Erlang from the source code:

```
$ wget http://www.erlang.org/download/otp_src_R14B01.tar.gz
$ tar -zxf otp_src_R14B01.tar.gz
$ cd otp_src_R14B01
$ ./configure
$ make
$ sudo make install
```

After Erlang has been installed, launch the Erlang shell to make sure everything is fine:

```
$ erl
Erlang R14B01 (erts-5.8.2) [source] [smp:2:2] [rq:2] [async-threads:0] [hipe] [kernel-
poll:false]

Eshell V5.8.2  (abort with ^G)
1>
```

Once Erlang is installed, the latest version of RabbitMQ Server (2.2.0 at the time of writing) may be downloaded from www.rabbitmq.com/download.html. Once again, RabbitMQ provides different compiled forms for different platform. Note that many Linux systems already provide binaries for both Erlang and RabbitMQ. So, for example, on the latest stable versions of Ubuntu, you can get both RabbitMQ and Erlang by using the following command: `sudo apt-get install rabbitmq-server`. For this book, the generic Unix system distribution will be used. Enter the following commands:

```
$ wget http://www.rabbitmq.com/releases/rabbitmq-server/v2.2.0/rabbitmq-server-generic-unix-
2.2.0.tar.gz
$ tar -zxf rabbitmq-server-generic-unix-2.2.0.tar.gz
$ cd rabbitmq_server-2.2.0
$ cd sbin
$ sudo ./rabbitmq-server
```

The commands result in the output below:

```
Activating RabbitMQ plugins ...
0 plugins activated:
```

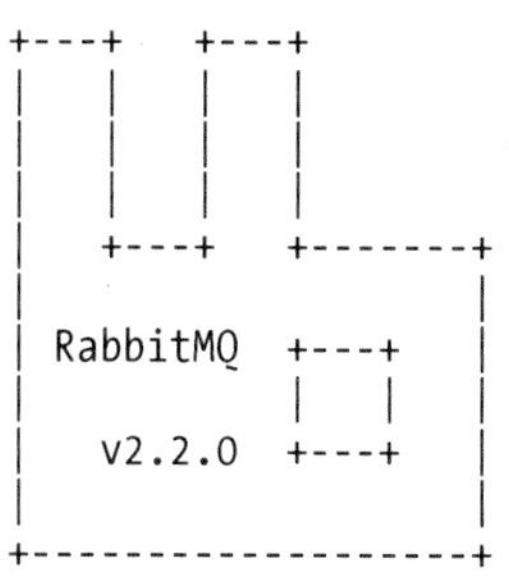

```
+---+   +---+
|   |   |   |
|   |   |   |
|   |   |   |
|   +---+   +-------+
|                   |
| RabbitMQ  +---+   |
|           |   |   |
|   v2.2.0  +---+   |
|                   |
+-------------------+
AMQP 0-9-1 / 0-9 / 0-8
Copyright (C) 2007-2010 LShift Ltd., Cohesive Financial Technologies LLC., and Rabbit
Technologies Ltd.
Licensed under the MPL.  See http://www.rabbitmq.com/

node           : rabbit@zeus
app descriptor : /Users/prospringintegration/rabbitmq_server-2.2.0/sbin/../ebin/rabbit.app
home dir       : /Users/prospringintegration
cookie hash    : fYhvVkawwYRTZihsIhXUuQ==
log            : /var/log/rabbitmq/rabbit@zeus.log
sasl log       : /var/log/rabbitmq/rabbit@zeus-sasl.log
database dir   : /var/lib/rabbitmq/mnesia/rabbit@zeus
erlang version : 5.7.4

starting file handle cache server                                     ...done
starting worker pool                                                  ...done
starting database                                                     ...done
starting codec correctness check                                      ...done
-- external infrastructure ready
starting statistics event manager                                     ...done
starting logging server                                               ...done
starting exchange type registry                                       ...done
starting exchange type direct                                         ...done
starting exchange type fanout                                         ...done
```

```
starting exchange type headers                                  ...done
starting exchange type topic                                    ...done
-- kernel ready
starting alarm handler                                          ...done
starting node monitor                                           ...done
starting cluster delegate                                       ...done
starting guid generator                                         ...done
starting memory monitor                                         ...done
-- core initialized
starting empty DB check                                         ...done
starting exchange recovery                                      ...done
starting queue supervisor and queue recovery                    ...done
-- message delivery logic ready
starting error log relay                                        ...done
starting networking                                             ...done
-- network listeners available

broker running
```

Since RabbitMQ is not written in Java, it does not come with JMX support. Luckily, RabbitMQ Server comes with a command-line monitoring tool, `rabbitmqctl`, out of the box. However, it is difficult to use. A better alternative is to use the RabbitMQ server management plug-in. In order to install the management plug-in, enter the following commands:

```
$ cd rabbitmq_server-2.2.0/plugins
$ wget http://www.rabbitmq.com/releases/plugins/v2.2.0/mochiweb-2.2.0.ez
$ wget http://www.rabbitmq.com/releases/plugins/v2.2.0/webmachine-2.2.0.ez
$ wget http://www.rabbitmq.com/releases/plugins/v2.2.0/amqp_client-2.2.0.ez
$ wget http://www.rabbitmq.com/releases/plugins/v2.2.0/rabbitmq-mochiweb-2.2.0.ez
$ wget http://www.rabbitmq.com/releases/plugins/v2.2.0/rabbitmq-management-agent-2.2.0.ez
$ wget http://www.rabbitmq.com/releases/plugins/v2.2.0/rabbitmq-management-2.2.0.ez
$ sudo rabbitmq_server-2.2.0/sbin/rabbitmq-server
```

These commands will result in the following ouput:

```
Activating RabbitMQ plugins ...
*WARNING* Undefined function fdsrv:bind_socket/2
*WARNING* Undefined function fdsrv:start/0
*WARNING* Undefined function fdsrv:stop/0
*WARNING* Undefined function webmachine_resource:start_link/2
6 plugins activated:
* amqp_client-2.2.0
* mochiweb-1.3
* rabbit_management-2.2.0
* rabbit_management_agent-2.2.0
* rabbit_mochiweb-2.2.0
* webmachine-1.7.0
.
.
.
```

The RabbitMQ server should restart and show six plug-ins activated. Next, open the web browser and go to `http://localhost:55672/mgmt/`. Enter the default username and password, which are `guest` and `guest`. The management console is shown in Figure 12–15.

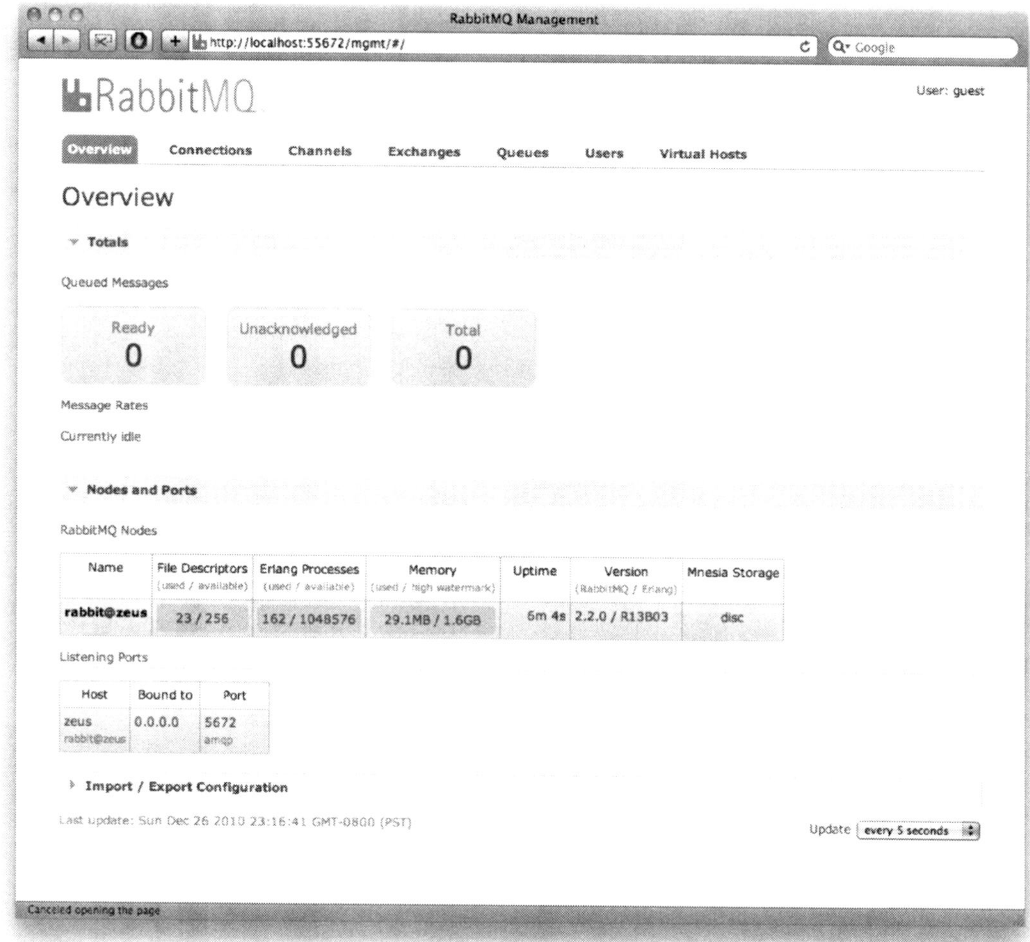

Figure 12-15. The RabbitMQ Management Console

Try to navigate to the Queues tab and create a new queue as shown in Figure 12-16.

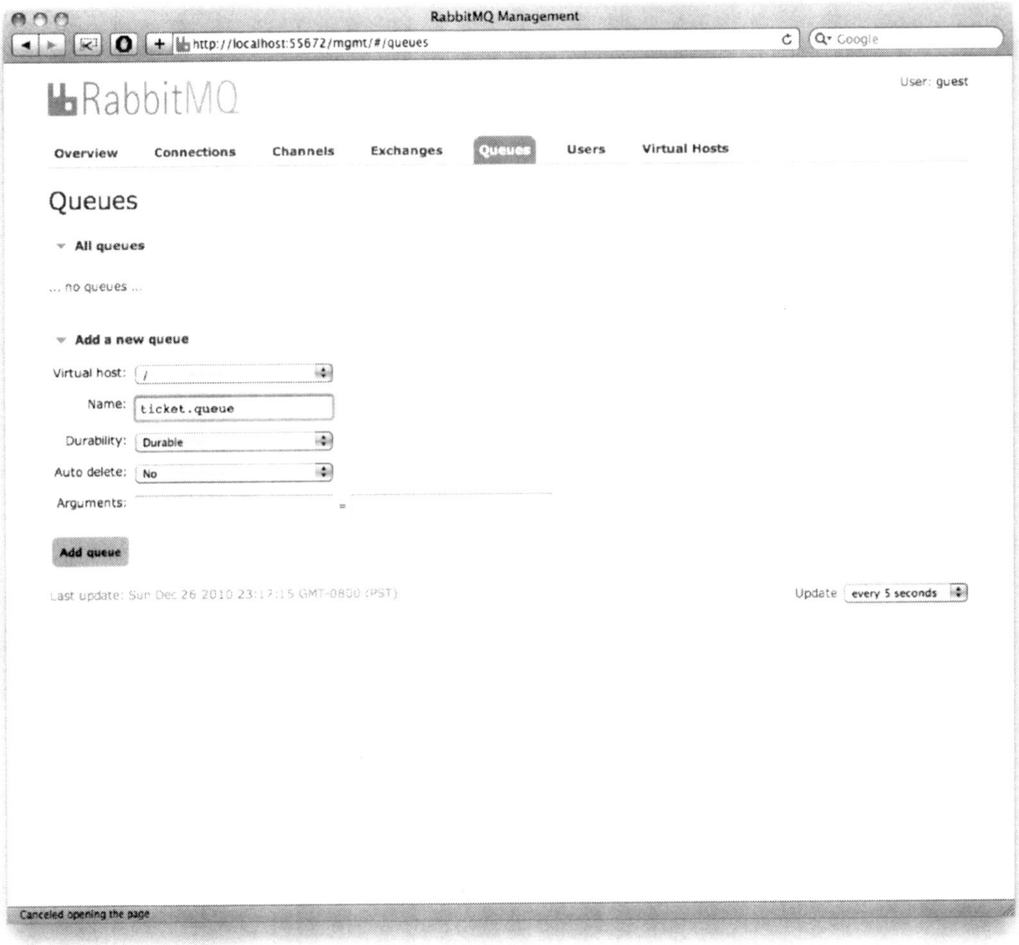

Figure 12–16. Creating a Queue in the RabbitMQ Management Console

Now returning to the Ticket system example described earlier in this chapter, the only code that needs to be changed in order to have the Ticket Reporter and Ticket Receiver applications work with RabbitMQ is in the Spring Java configuration file shown in Listing 12–19.

Listing 12–19. RabbitmqConfiguration.java Configuration File

```
package com.apress.prospringintegration.messaging.rabbitmq.jms.adapter;

import org.springframework.amqp.core.Queue;
import org.springframework.amqp.rabbit.connection.SingleConnectionFactory;
import org.springframework.amqp.rabbit.core.RabbitAdmin;
import org.springframework.amqp.rabbit.core.RabbitTemplate;
```

```
import org.springframework.context.annotation.Bean;
import org.springframework.context.annotation.Configuration;
import org.springframework.integration.MessageChannel;
import org.springframework.integration.channel.DirectChannel;

@Configuration
public class RabbitmqConfiguration {

    @Bean
    public SingleConnectionFactory connectionFactory() {
        SingleConnectionFactory connectionFactory =
                new SingleConnectionFactory("localhost");
        connectionFactory.setPort(5672);
        connectionFactory.setUsername("guest");
        connectionFactory.setPassword("guest");

        return connectionFactory;
    }

    @Bean
    public RabbitTemplate amqpTemplate() {
        RabbitTemplate rabbitTemplate = new RabbitTemplate();
        rabbitTemplate.setConnectionFactory(connectionFactory());
        rabbitTemplate.setRoutingKey("ticket.queue");
        rabbitTemplate.setQueue("ticket.queue");

        return rabbitTemplate;
    }

    @Bean
    public RabbitAdmin rabbitAdmin() {
        RabbitAdmin rabbitAdmin = new RabbitAdmin(connectionFactory());
        return rabbitAdmin;
    }

    @Bean
    public Queue ticketQueue() {
        Queue queue = new Queue("ticket.queue");
        return queue;
    }

    @Bean
    public MessageChannel ticketChannel() {
        MessageChannel channel = new DirectChannel();
        return channel;
    }
}
```

The Spring configuration file modified for RabbitMQ is shown in Listing 12–20.

Listing 12–20. *ticket-reporter.xml*

```
<?xml version="1.0" encoding="UTF-8"?>
<beans xmlns="http://www.springframework.org/schema/beans"
       xmlns:xsi="http://www.w3.org/2001/XMLSchema-instance"
       xmlns:context="http://www.springframework.org/schema/context"
       xmlns:int-amqp="http://www.springframework.org/schema/integration/amqp"
       xsi:schemaLocation="http://www.springframework.org/schema/beans
    http://www.springframework.org/schema/beans/spring-beans-3.0.xsd
    http://www.springframework.org/schema/context
    http://www.springframework.org/schema/context/spring-context-3.0.xsd
    http://www.springframework.org/schema/integration/amqp
    http://www.springframework.org/schema/integration/amqp/spring-integration-amqp-2.0.xsd">

  <context:component-scan
     base-package="com.apress.prospringintegration.messaging.rabbitmq.jms.adapter"/>

  <int-amqp:outbound-channel-adapter routing-key="ticket.queue"
                                     amqp-template="amqpTemplate"
                                     channel="ticketChannel"/>

</beans>
```

Spring allows moving from JMS to RabbitMQ with a configuration change alone, insolating the business logic from any change. Again, as the Spring Integration AMQP support is still under heavy development, the outbound AMQP channel adapter currently only supports the AMQP protocol for RabbitMQ at this time; there is no option to specify lower-level primitives, as there is with the JMS adapters. The Ticket reporter application using RabbitMQ may run by using the following command.

```
$ mvn exec:java -
Dexec.mainClass="com.apress.prospringintegration.mesging.rabbitmq.jms.adapter.TicketReporter
```

The command should result in the following output.

```
Main"
[INFO] Scanning for projects...
[INFO] Searching repository for plugin with prefix: 'exec'.
[INFO] ------------------------------------------------------------------------
[INFO] Building messaging-rabbitmq
[INFO]    task-segment: [exec:java]
[INFO] ------------------------------------------------------------------------
[INFO] Preparing exec:java
[INFO] No goals needed for project - skipping
[INFO] [exec:java {execution: default-cli}]
SLF4J: This version of SLF4J requires log4j version 1.2.12 or later. See also
http://www.slf4j.org/codes.html#log4j_version
12-26-2010 23:13:24 [INFO] Refreshing
org.springframework.context.support.ClassPathXmlApplicationContext@7d59ea8e: startup date [Sun
Dec 26 23:13:24 PST 2010]; root of context hierarchy
12-26-2010 23:13:24 [INFO] Loading XML bean definitions from class path resource [ticket-
reporter.xml]
12-26-2010 23:13:24 [WARN] Configuration problem: Poller configuration via 'interval-trigger'
subelements is deprecated, use the 'fixed-delay' or 'fixed-rate' attribute instead.
Offending resource: class path resource [ticket-reporter.xml]
```

```
12-26-2010 23:13:24 [INFO] No bean named 'errorChannel' has been explicitly defined.
Therefore, a default PublishSubscribeChannel will be created.
12-26-2010 23:13:24 [INFO] No bean named 'taskScheduler' has been explicitly defined.
Therefore, a default ThreadPoolTaskScheduler will be created.
12-26-2010 23:13:24 [INFO] Pre-instantiating singletons in
org.springframework.beans.factory.support.DefaultListableBeanFactory@5a4fdf11: defining beans
[problemReporter,ticketGenerator,ticketReceiver,org.springframework.context.annotation.interna
lConfigurationAnnotationProcessor,org.springframework.context.annotation.internalAutowiredAnno
tationProcessor,org.springframework.context.annotation.internalRequiredAnnotationProcessor,org
.springframework.context.annotation.internalCommonAnnotationProcessor,org.springframework.inte
gration.internalDefaultConfiguringBeanFactoryPostProcessor,org.springframework.scheduling.supp
ort.PeriodicTrigger#0,defaultPoller,ticketChannel,connectionFactory,amqpTemplate,org.springfra
mework.integration.amqp.AmqpOutboundEndpoint#0,org.springframework.integration.config.Consumer
EndpointFactoryBean#0,nullChannel,errorChannel,_org.springframework.integration.errorLogger,ta
skScheduler]; root of factory hierarchy
12-26-2010 23:13:25 [INFO] Initializing ExecutorService  'taskScheduler'
12-26-2010 23:13:25 [INFO] Starting beans in phase -2147483648
12-26-2010 23:13:25 [INFO] started _org.springframework.integration.errorLogger
12-26-2010 23:13:25 [INFO] Starting beans in phase 2147483647
12-26-2010 23:13:25 [INFO] started
org.springframework.integration.config.ConsumerEndpointFactoryBean#0
12-26-2010 23:13:25 [INFO] Starting beans in phase -2147483648
12-26-2010 23:13:25 [INFO] Starting beans in phase 2147483647
Ticket Sent - Ticket# 1000: [low] Some minor problems have been found.
Ticket Sent - Ticket# 1001: [low] Some minor problems have been found.
Ticket Sent - Ticket# 1002: [low] Some minor problems have been found.
Ticket Sent - Ticket# 1003: [low] Some minor problems have been found.
Ticket Sent - Ticket# 1004: [low] Some minor problems have been found.
Ticket Sent - Ticket# 1005: [medium] There is an issue; take a look whenever you have time.
Ticket Sent - Ticket# 1006: [medium] There is an issue; Take a look whenever you have time.
Ticket Sent - Ticket# 1007: [medium] There is an issue; Take a look whenever you have time.
Ticket Sent - Ticket# 1008: [medium] There is an issue; Take a look whenever you have time.
Ticket Sent - Ticket# 1009: [medium] There is an issue; Take a look whenever you have time.
Ticket Sent - Ticket# 1010: [high] Serious issue. Fix immediately.
Ticket Sent - Ticket# 1011: [high] Serious issue. Fix immediately.
Ticket Sent - Ticket# 1012: [high] Serious issue. Fix immediately.
Ticket Sent - Ticket# 1013: [high] Serious issue. Fix immediately.
Ticket Sent - Ticket# 1014: [high] Serious issue. Fix immediately.
Ticket Sent - Ticket# 1015: [emergency] Urgent problem. Fix immediately or revenue will be
lost!
Ticket Sent - Ticket# 1016: [emergency] Urgent problem. Fix immediately or revenue will be
lost!
Ticket Sent - Ticket# 1017: [emergency] Urgent problem. Fix immediately or revenue will be
lost!
Ticket Sent - Ticket# 1018: [emergency] Urgent problem. Fix immediately or revenue will be
lost!
Ticket Sent - Ticket# 1019: [emergency] Urgent problem. Fix immediately or revenue will be
lost!
```

Listing 12–21 shows the Spring bean configuration file for the Ticket receiver application.

***Listing 12–21.** ticket-receiver.xml*

```
<?xml version="1.0" encoding="UTF-8"?>
<beans xmlns="http://www.springframework.org/schema/beans"
       xmlns:xsi="http://www.w3.org/2001/XMLSchema-instance"
       xmlns:int="http://www.springframework.org/schema/integration"
       xmlns:context="http://www.springframework.org/schema/context"
       xmlns:int-amqp="http://www.springframework.org/schema/integration/amqp"
       xmlns:rabbit="http://www.springframework.org/schema/rabbit"
       xsi:schemaLocation="http://www.springframework.org/schema/integration
    http://www.springframework.org/schema/integration/spring-integration-2.0.xsd
    http://www.springframework.org/schema/beans
    http://www.springframework.org/schema/beans/spring-beans-3.0.xsd
    http://www.springframework.org/schema/context
    http://www.springframework.org/schema/context/spring-context-3.0.xsd
    http://www.springframework.org/schema/integration/amqp
    http://www.springframework.org/schema/integration/amqp/spring-integration-amqp-2.0.xsd
    http://www.springframework.org/schema/rabbit
    http://www.springframework.org/schema/rabbit/spring-rabbit-1.0.xsd">

  <context:component-scan
      base-package="com.apress.prospringintegration.messaging.rabbitmq.jms.adapter"/>

  <int:channel id="receiveChannel"/>

  <int:service-activator input-channel="receiveChannel" ref="ticketReceiver"/>

  <int-amqp:inbound-channel-adapter connection-factory="connectionFactory"
                                    queue-name="ticket.queue"
                                    channel="receiveChannel"/>

</beans>
```

The inbound AMQP channel adapter is different from the outbound AMQP channel adapter. Instead of accepting the `AmqpTemplate` reference, the inbound channel adapter accepts a reference to the `ConnectionFactory` instead. In addition, it takes the AMQP queue name only. This is somewhat inconsistent, but the AMQP integration is still in sandbox development at the time of writing, so it may be fixed later.

Apache Qpid

Apache Qpid (`http://qpid.apache.org`) is another open source AMQP messaging system. Qpid has both a Java and a C++ broker implementation. The latest version (0.8) can be downloaded from `http://qpid.apache.org/download.cgi`. The commands for downloading and running Qpid are shown below:

```
$ wget http://www.poolsaboveground.com/apache/qpid/0.8/qpid-java-0.8.tar.gz
$ tar -zxf qpid-java-0.8.tar.gz
$ cd qpid-0.8/bin
$ ./qpid-servers
```

Running the command will have the following output:

```
Setting QPID_WORK to /Users/psi as default
System Properties set to -Damqj.logging.level=info -DQPID_HOME=/Users/psi/ qpid-0.8 -
DQPID_WORK=/Users/psi
QPID_OPTS set to -Damqj.read_write_pool_size=32 -DQPID_LOG_APPEND=
Using QPID_CLASSPATH /Users/psi/qpid-0.8/lib/qpid-all.jar
Info: QPID_JAVA_GC not set. Defaulting to JAVA_GC -XX:+UseConcMarkSweepGC -
XX:+HeapDumpOnOutOfMemoryError
Info: QPID_JAVA_MEM not set. Defaulting to JAVA_MEM -Xmx1024m
[Broker] BRK-1006 : Using configuration : /Users/psi/qpid-0.8/etc/config.xml
[Broker] BRK-1007 : Using logging configuration : /Users/psi/qpid-0.8/etc/log4j.xml
[Broker] BRK-1001 : Startup : Version: 0.8 Build: 1037942
[Broker] MNG-1001 : Startup
[Broker] MNG-1002 : Starting : RMI Registry : Listening on port 8999
[Broker] MNG-1002 : Starting : JMX RMIConnectorServer : Listening on port 9099
[Broker] MNG-1004 : Ready
[Broker] BRK-1002 : Starting : Listening on TCP port 5672
[Broker] BRK-1004 : Qpid Broker Ready
```

Apache Qpid does not come with any management console for monitoring purpose. However, there is a JMX management console that can be downloaded from Qpid web site. There are different distributions for different running platforms. For Windows, Qpid can be downloaded from http://ftp.wayne.edu/apache//qpid/0.8/qpid-jmx-management-console-0.8-win32-win32-x86.zip; for Mac OS X, Qpid can downloaded from http://ftp.wayne.edu/apache//qpid/0.8/qpid-jmx-management-console-0.8-macosx.zip.

Once the compressed binary file has been downloaded, unzip it and run the qpidmc executable. Since this will be the first time JMX management console is run, you'll need to add the Qpid broker. The Qpid management console is shown in Figure 12–17. For details on using the Qpid JMX management console, refer to the Qpid web site (http://qpid.apache.org/books/0.8/AMQP-Messaging-Broker-Java-Book/html/ch03.html).

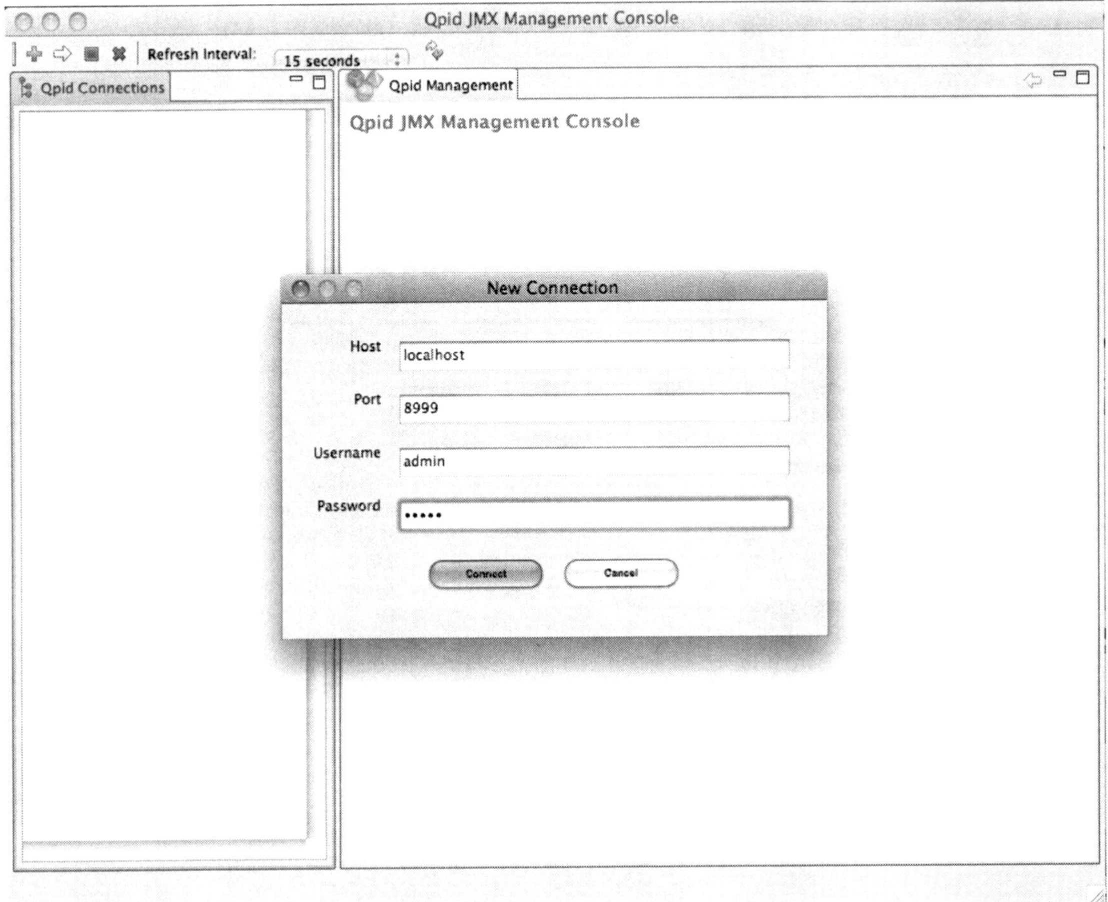

Figure 12–17. The Apache Qpid JMX Management Console

Although Apache Qpid is an AMQP messaging broker, it supports JMS 1.1 as well. The Spring Integration adapter uses the Spring AMQP project, and the Spring AMQP project itself provides the AMQP abstraction. At the time of this writing, there is no Qpid-specific client, so Spring AMQP might not offer a compelling way to approach using Qpid. This is sure to change as the projects move closer to a final release, though. In the meantime, Spring Integration's JMS supports may be used with Apache Qpid.

Much like the other messaging brokers described in this chapter, using Qpid is simply a matter of changing the configuration. The Qpid Java configuration file is shown in Listing 12–22.

Listing 12–22. QpidConfiguration Java Configuration

```
package com.apress.prospringintegration.messaging.qpid.jms.adapter;

import org.apache.qpid.client.AMQQueue;
import org.springframework.beans.factory.annotation.Value;
import org.springframework.context.annotation.Bean;
```

```
import org.springframework.context.annotation.Configuration;
import org.springframework.integration.MessageChannel;
import org.springframework.integration.channel.DirectChannel;
import org.springframework.jms.connection.CachingConnectionFactory;
import org.springframework.jndi.JndiObjectFactoryBean;
import org.springframework.jndi.JndiTemplate;

import javax.jms.ConnectionFactory;
import java.net.URISyntaxException;
import java.util.Properties;

@Configuration
public class QpidConfiguration {

    @Value("#{qpidConnectionFactory}")
    private ConnectionFactory connectionFactory;

    @Bean
    public JndiTemplate jndiTemplate() {
        JndiTemplate jndiTemplate = new JndiTemplate();
        Properties properties = new Properties();
        properties.setProperty("java.naming.factory.initial",
                "org.apache.qpid.jndi.PropertiesFileInitialContextFactory");
        jndiTemplate.setEnvironment(properties);

        return jndiTemplate;
    }

    @Bean
    public JndiObjectFactoryBean qpidConnectionFactory() {
        JndiObjectFactoryBean jndiObjectFactoryBean = new JndiObjectFactoryBean();
        jndiObjectFactoryBean.setJndiTemplate(jndiTemplate());
        jndiObjectFactoryBean.setJndiName("amqpConnectionfactory");

        return jndiObjectFactoryBean;
    }

    @Bean
    public CachingConnectionFactory connectionFactory() {
        CachingConnectionFactory cachingConnectionFactory = new CachingConnectionFactory();
        cachingConnectionFactory.setTargetConnectionFactory(connectionFactory);
        cachingConnectionFactory.setSessionCacheSize(10);

        return cachingConnectionFactory;
    }

    @Bean
    public AMQQueue ticketQueue() throws URISyntaxException {
        AMQQueue amqQueue = new AMQQueue("ticket.queue");
        return amqQueue;
    }

    @Bean
    public MessageChannel ticketChannel() {
```

```
        MessageChannel channel = new DirectChannel();
        return channel;
    }
}
```

The Spring configuration file for the Ticket reporter application will look similar to the previous examples using different message brokers as shown in Listing 12–23.

Listing 12–23. *ticket-reporter.xml*

```
<?xml version="1.0" encoding="UTF-8"?>
<beans xmlns="http://www.springframework.org/schema/beans"
       xmlns:xsi="http://www.w3.org/2001/XMLSchema-instance"
       xmlns:int-jms="http://www.springframework.org/schema/integration/jms"
       xmlns:context="http://www.springframework.org/schema/context"
       xsi:schemaLocation="http://www.springframework.org/schema/integration/jms
    http://www.springframework.org/schema/integration/jms/spring-integration-jms-2.0.xsd
    http://www.springframework.org/schema/beans
    http://www.springframework.org/schema/beans/spring-beans-3.0.xsd
    http://www.springframework.org/schema/context
    http://www.springframework.org/schema/context/spring-context-3.0.xsd">

  <context:component-scan
     base-package="com.apress.prospringintegration.messaging.qpid.jms.adapter"/>

  <int-jms:outbound-channel-adapter id="ticketOutbound"
                                    destination="ticketQueue"
                                    channel="ticketChannel"/>

</beans>
```

The ConnectionFactory for Apache Qpid is a bit complicated since the messaging broker uses JNDI for property discovery. In order to work, it needs a jndi.properties file as shown in Listing 12–24.

Listing 12–24. *jndi.properties*

```
java.naming.factory.initial=org.apache.qpid.jndi.PropertiesFileInitialContextFactory
connectionfactory.amqpConnectionfactory=amqp://guest:guest@clientid/test?brokerlist='tcp://loc
alhost:5672'&maxprefetch='1'
```

The changes required for the ticket-receiver.xml file are the same as for ticket-reporter.xml configuration file. All that is required is changing the ConnectionFactory configuration and the message queue configuration as shown in Listing 12–25.

Listing 12–25. *ticket-receiver.xml*

```
<?xml version="1.0" encoding="UTF-8"?>
<beans xmlns="http://www.springframework.org/schema/beans"
xmlns:xsi="http://www.w3.org/2001/XMLSchema-instance"
       xmlns:int="http://www.springframework.org/schema/integration"
       xmlns:int-jms="http://www.springframework.org/schema/integration/jms"
       xmlns:context="http://www.springframework.org/schema/context"
       xsi:schemaLocation="http://www.springframework.org/schema/integration
    http://www.springframework.org/schema/integration/spring-integration-2.0.xsd
    http://www.springframework.org/schema/integration/jms
    http://www.springframework.org/schema/integration/jms/spring-integration-jms-2.0.xsd
```

```
    http://www.springframework.org/schema/beans
    http://www.springframework.org/schema/beans/spring-beans-3.0.xsd
    http://www.springframework.org/schema/context
    http://www.springframework.org/schema/context/spring-context-3.0.xsd">

  <context:component-scan
      base-package="com.apress.prospringintegration.messaging.qpid.jms.adapter"/>

  <int:channel id="receiveChannel"/>

  <int:service-activator input-channel="receiveChannel" ref="ticketReceiver"/>

  <int-jms:message-driven-channel-adapter id="ticketInbound"
                                          destination="ticketQueue"
                                          channel="receiveChannel"
                                          connection-factory="connectionFactory"/>
</beans>
```

Qpid requires that the message queue be declared before starting the broker. You can do this by adding the following lines to the `virtualhosts.xml` file in the `etc` directory of the Qpid installation:

```
<queue>
  <name>ticket.queue</name>
  <queue>
    <exchange>amq.direct</exchange>
    <maximumQueueDepth>4235264</maximumQueueDepth>
    <!-- 4Mb -->
    <maximumMessageSize>2117632</maximumMessageSize>
    <!-- 2Mb -->
    <maximumMessageAge>600000</maximumMessageAge>
    <!-- 10 mins -->
    </queue>
</queue>
```

Other Messaging Systems

Besides JMS and AMQP, there are some other messaging systems that use different communication protocols. Although Spring Integration may not support these messaging systems out of box, custom channel adapters can be written to work with them.

Amazon SQS

Amazon Simple Queue Service (SQS) (`http://aws.amazon.com/sqs`) is part of the Amazon Web Services (AWS) infrastructure. In conjunction with Amazon's Elastic Compute Cloud (EC2), SQS provides a reliable and scalable messaging solution for cloud computing. In order to integrate with SQS, the application needs to be running in the EC2 stack inside the Amazon cloud environment. Since the SQS API is REST-based, the Spring Integration HTTP/Web Service channel adapter can be used to integrate with SQS. Alternatively, a quick search on the Internet reveals a couple SQS adapters already written by community members. Also note that RabbitMQ is more commonly used to meet cloud-scale messaging, even in the AWS environment.

Kestrel MQ

Kestrel MQ (`http://github.com/robey/kestrel`) is the messaging system used by Twitter, the popular social networking and microblogging web site. According to statistics, each user has 126 followers. This means that each tweet (message) will result in 126 messages in the message queue. During Obama's inauguration, the system received several hundreds of tweets per second, resulting in tens of thousands of messages in the message queue. Because of events like this, Twitter's messaging system needs to be very fast and memory-based.

Kestrel MQ is written in Scala. According to Kestrel's README file, Kestrel is based on Blaine Cook's "starling" simple distributed message queue, although it has added features and bulletproofing, as well as the scalability offered by clustering the Kestrel servers.

Kestrel MQ is a fast, small footprint message broker that's durable and reliable. In order for Spring Integration to integrate Kestrel MQ, a custom channel adapter is required to tie the Kestrel MQ API together with Spring Integration framework.

Kafka

Kafka (`http://sna-projects.com/kafka`) is an open source message broker originally built by LinkedIn. It has similar scalability characteristics to Kestrel. It was engineered to handle activity stream data (news feeds, page views, searches, etc.). Think of Kafka as a highly scalable way to log (and process) important business events in a system.

Kafka, Kestrel, and SQS all require custom adapters to work with the Spring Integration Framework. It's convenient that message-based solutions written against these brokers need not be aware of them, thanks to the indirection afforded by Spring Integration's channel abstraction as demonstrated by the above examples.

Summary

This chapter covered a number of popular messaging systems based on the JMS and AMQP standards. Spring Integration provides JMS channel adapters, the JMS gateway, and the JMS-backed message channel out of the box so that developers can integrate Spring Integration with JMS messaging brokers very easy. This chapter also discussed the Spring Integration support of the AMQP messaging system. With Spring IoC, it is very easy to switch from one messaging system to another one by simply changing the Spring bean configuration; you don't have to modify any Java code. Finally, this chapter discussed some new types of messaging systems that don't use JMS or AMQP. Although these aren't supported by Spring Integration out of the box, custom channel adapters may be written to allow them to work with Spring Integration.

CHAPTER 13

Social Messaging

Social computing is taking the Internet by storm. With the rising popularity of e-mail, Instant Messaging (IM), Facebook, and Twitter, social computing has become mainstream. Social computing technologies use a large part of the current Internet bandwidth and are continuing to grow.

Part of the appeal of these technologies is that they help connect applications with real users. They enable a whole realm of applications to become part of the users' world and workflow. Applications that ingratiate themselves with their users by becoming a natural extension of the tools and workflows with which the world is already familiar will be used more than similar tools that are less intuitive. Some of these technologies, like chat and news streams, trade on the data most interesting to a most people: their own. These technologies, which foster active interest from their users, encourage them to invest in it. In a sense, an application that succeeds in making itself relevant to its user base will grow on the strength of its community, not just on the efforts of a marketing team.

Spring Integration social messaging adapters are different from many of the other adapters discussed in this book because these are all about bringing an application's data and services to an external user, not necessarily another system. Spring Integration currently supports integrating with e-mail, XMPP (Jabber, GTalk, Facebook Chat), news feeds (RSS, ATOM), and Twitter. The Spring Integration adapter supporting these protocols will be discussed in this chapter.

E-mail

Spring Integration supports the usual e-mail protocol, allowing the sending of e-mail based on incoming channel messages and the receiving of e-mails as channel messages. IMAP, IMAP-IDLE, POP3, and SMTP examples are discussed in the following sections. First, the required Maven dependencies must be added to support the Spring Integration e-mail adapters. The dependencies are shown in Listing 13–1.

Listing 13–1. *Maven Dependencies for E-mail Support*

```
<dependency>
  <groupId>org.springframework.integration</groupId>
  <artifactId>spring-integration-mail</artifactId>
  <version>2.0.1.RELEASE</version>
</dependency>
<dependency>
  <groupId>javax.activation</groupId>
  <artifactId>activation</artifactId>
  <version>1.1.1</version>
  <optional>true</optional>
</dependency>
<dependency>
  <groupId>javax.mail</groupId>
  <artifactId>mail</artifactId>
```

```
    <version>1.4.1</version>
  </dependency>
```

IMAP and IMAP-IDLE

Spring Integration supports IMAP and IMAP-IDLE for incoming e-mails. IMAP-IDLE allows for asynchronous (push) reception of e-mail if the e-mail server supports it. The standard IMAP adapter requires polling to pull the e-mails from the server.

The Spring configuration for an IMAP polling channel adapter is shown in Listing 13–2. The Spring Integration `mail` namespace has been added, as well as the Spring utility namespace to support configuring the Java mail properties. The mail inbound channel adapter support both the IMAP and POP3 mail protocol. For this example, the inbound adapter is configured for Gmail receiving the e-mail using IMAP protocol. The POP3 protocol configuration will be shown in the next section. Use the `store-uri` attribute to configure the protocol, host, port, and username/password if required. The `poller` element has been added to check for e-mail every five seconds, downloading one e-mail with each poll. The e-mail message is sent to the `inputMail` channel. The `mail-to-spring` transformer is used to convert the incoming mail payload into a string representation. The two attribute options worth mentioning are `should-delete-messages`, which removes the message from the server after downloading, and `should-mark-messages-as-read`, which marks the message on the server so it is only downloaded once. Note that the latter attribute is only supported for IMAP, not for POP3. Thus the `should-delete-messages` is the only way to prevent multiple downloads of the e-mail message if the adapter is restarted for the POP3 protocol. This will be discussed in more detail in the POP3 section.

***Listing 13–2.** Receiving E-mail with IMAP Spring Configuration imap-mail.xml*

```
<?xml version="1.0" encoding="UTF-8"?>
<beans xmlns="http://www.springframework.org/schema/beans"
       xmlns:xsi="http://www.w3.org/2001/XMLSchema-instance"
       xmlns:int="http://www.springframework.org/schema/integration"
       xmlns:mail="http://www.springframework.org/schema/integration/mail"
       xmlns:util="http://www.springframework.org/schema/util"
       xsi:schemaLocation="http://www.springframework.org/schema/integration
    http://www.springframework.org/schema/integration/spring-integration-2.0.xsd
    http://www.springframework.org/schema/beans
    http://www.springframework.org/schema/beans/spring-beans-3.0.xsd
    http://www.springframework.org/schema/integration/mail
    http://www.springframework.org/schema/integration/mail/spring-integration-mail-2.0.xsd
    http://www.springframework.org/schema/util
    http://www.springframework.org/schema/util/spring-util-3.0.xsd">

  <int:channel id="inputChannel"/>

  <int:channel id="inputMail"/>

  <mail:mail-to-string-transformer input-channel="inputMail" output-channel="inputChannel"/>

  <mail:inbound-channel-adapter id="customAdapter"
                                store-uri=
                                    "imaps://[usename]:[password]@imap.gmail.com:993/inbox"
                                channel="inputMail"
                                should-delete-messages="false"
                                should-mark-messages-as-read="false"
                                java-mail-properties="javaMailProperties">
```

```
    <int:poller max-messages-per-poll="1" fixed-rate="5000"/>
  </mail:inbound-channel-adapter>

  <util:properties id="javaMailProperties">
    <prop key="mail.imap.socketFactory.class">javax.net.ssl.SSLSocketFactory</prop>
    <prop key="mail.imap.socketFactory.fallback">false</prop>
    <prop key="mail.store.protocol">imaps</prop>
    <prop key="mail.debug">false</prop>
  </util:properties>

</beans>
```

Note that the Spring `util` namespace is used to populate the java mail properties required by the mail adapter with parameters needed to support SSL security. This example is using Gmail IMAP support.

In order to the test the inbound e-mail adapters, a simple main class is required, as shown in Listing 13–3. This test class loads the Spring configuration file and subscribes to the `inputChannel` message channel. The message handler will log any new e-mail message.

Listing 13–3. *IMAP E-mail Receiving main Class ImapMail*

```
package com.apress.prospringintegration.social.mail;

import org.apache.log4j.Logger;
import org.springframework.context.ApplicationContext;
import org.springframework.context.support.ClassPathXmlApplicationContext;
import org.springframework.integration.Message;
import org.springframework.integration.MessagingException;
import org.springframework.integration.channel.DirectChannel;
import org.springframework.integration.core.MessageHandler;

public class ImapMail {
    private static Logger LOG = Logger.getLogger(ImapMail.class);

    public static void main(String[] args) throws Exception {
        ApplicationContext context =
                new ClassPathXmlApplicationContext("/spring/mail/imap-mail.xml");

        DirectChannel inputChannel = context.getBean("inputChannel", DirectChannel.class);

        inputChannel.subscribe(new MessageHandler() {
            public void handleMessage(Message<?> message) throws MessagingException {
                LOG.info("Message: " + message);
            }
        });
    }
}
```

If the e-mail server supports IMAP idle, the `imap-idle-channel-adapter` may be used to support event-driven notifications. This adapter will send the e-mail message to the specified channel any time a notification is received. This eliminates the need for a poller element. Except for the missing `poller` element and using the `imap-idle-channel-adapter`, the configuration is identical to the standard IMAP adapter. An example of the Spring configuration for this adapter, specifically for a Gmail e-mail server, is shown in Listing 13–4.

Listing 13–4. Receiving E-mail with IMAP-IDLE Spring Configuration imap-idle-mail.xml

```
<?xml version="1.0" encoding="UTF-8"?>
<beans xmlns="http://www.springframework.org/schema/beans"
       xmlns:xsi="http://www.w3.org/2001/XMLSchema-instance"
       xmlns:int="http://www.springframework.org/schema/integration"
       xmlns:mail="http://www.springframework.org/schema/integration/mail"
       xmlns:util="http://www.springframework.org/schema/util"
       xsi:schemaLocation="http://www.springframework.org/schema/integration
    http://www.springframework.org/schema/integration/spring-integration-2.0.xsd
    http://www.springframework.org/schema/beans
    http://www.springframework.org/schema/beans/spring-beans-3.0.xsd
    http://www.springframework.org/schema/integration/mail
    http://www.springframework.org/schema/integration/mail/spring-integration-mail-2.0.xsd
    http://www.springframework.org/schema/util
    http://www.springframework.org/schema/util/spring-util-3.0.xsd">

  <int:channel id="inputChannel"/>

  <int:channel id="inputMail"/>

  <mail:mail-to-string-transformer input-channel="inputMail" output-channel="inputChannel"/>

  <mail:imap-idle-channel-adapter id="customAdapter"
                                  store-uri=
                                      "imaps://[username]:[password]@imap.gmail.com:993/inbox"
                                  channel="inputMail"
                                  should-delete-messages="false"
                                  should-mark-messages-as-read="false"
                                  java-mail-properties="javaMailProperties"/>

  <util:properties id="javaMailProperties">
    <prop key="mail.imap.socketFactory.class">javax.net.ssl.SSLSocketFactory</prop>
    <prop key="mail.imap.socketFactory.fallback">false</prop>
    <prop key="mail.store.protocol">imaps</prop>
    <prop key="mail.debug">false</prop>
  </util:properties>

</beans>
```

To test the IMAP-IDLE mail adapter, a simple main class is created, as shown in Listing 13–5. This class is similar to the previous IMAP example. A message handler is added to the inputChannel message channel and will log any new e-mail message on the server.

Listing 13–5. IMAP-IDLE mail receiving main class ImapIdle-mail

```
package com.apress.prospringintegration.social.mail;

import org.apache.log4j.Logger;
import org.springframework.context.ApplicationContext;
import org.springframework.context.support.ClassPathXmlApplicationContext;
import org.springframework.integration.Message;
import org.springframework.integration.MessagingException;
import org.springframework.integration.channel.DirectChannel;
```

```
import org.springframework.integration.core.MessageHandler;

public class ImapIdle-mail {
    private static Logger LOG = Logger.getLogger(ImapMail.class);

    public static void main(String[] args) throws Exception {
        ApplicationContext context =
                new ClassPathXmlApplicationContext("/spring/mail/imap-idle-mail.xml");

        DirectChannel inputChannel = context.getBean("inputChannel", DirectChannel.class);

        inputChannel.subscribe(new MessageHandler() {
            public void handleMessage(Message<?> message) throws MessagingException {
                LOG.info("Message: " + message);
            }
        });
    }
}
```

POP3

The inbound-channel-adapter also supports the POP3 e-mail protocol. The configuration is identical to the IMAP configuration except for the `store-uri` attribute. This attribute must be prefaced with `pop3` as opposed to `imaps`. The most important difference between the POP3 adapter and IMAP is the lack of the `should-mark-messages-as-read` attribute. POP3 protocol has no concept of what messages have been read. POP3 only keeps track of which messages were downloaded on a per-session basis. If a new session has been started, all previously downloaded e-mails will be downloaded again. The only option is to delete the message on the server after downloading using the `should-delete-messages` attribute. This is one of the reasons this is a required attribute. However, if this attribute is set to true, any other client will be unable to access the downloaded messages. The setting of this attribute should be carefully selected. An example of the Spring configuration for POP3 protocol is shown in Listing 13–6.

***Listing 13–6.** Receiving e-mail with POP3 Spring configuration pop-mail.xml*

```
<?xml version="1.0" encoding="UTF-8"?>
<beans xmlns="http://www.springframework.org/schema/beans"
       xmlns:xsi="http://www.w3.org/2001/XMLSchema-instance"
       xmlns:int="http://www.springframework.org/schema/integration"
       xmlns:mail="http://www.springframework.org/schema/integration/mail"
       xmlns:util="http://www.springframework.org/schema/util"
       xsi:schemaLocation="http://www.springframework.org/schema/integration
    http://www.springframework.org/schema/integration/spring-integration-2.0.xsd
    http://www.springframework.org/schema/beans
    http://www.springframework.org/schema/beans/spring-beans-3.0.xsd
    http://www.springframework.org/schema/integration/mail
    http://www.springframework.org/schema/integration/mail/spring-integration-mail-2.0.xsd
    http://www.springframework.org/schema/util
    http://www.springframework.org/schema/util/spring-util-3.0.xsd">

  <int:channel id="inputChannel"/>

  <int:channel id="inputMail"/>
```

```
  <mail:mail-to-string-transformer input-channel="inputMail" output-channel="inputChannel"/>

  <mail:inbound-channel-adapter id="customAdapter"
                                store-uri="pop3://[username]:[password]@pop.gmail.com/inbox"
                                channel="inputMail"
                                should-delete-messages="false"
                                java-mail-properties="javaMailProperties">
    <int:poller max-messages-per-poll="1" fixed-rate="5000"/>
  </mail:inbound-channel-adapter>

  <util:properties id="javaMailProperties">
    <prop key="mail.pop3.socketFactory.fallback">false</prop>
    <prop key="mail.debug">true</prop>
    <prop key="mail.pop3.port">995</prop>
    <prop key="mail.pop3.socketFactory.class">javax.net.ssl.SSLSocketFactory</prop>
    <prop key="mail.pop3.socketFactory.port">995</prop>
  </util:properties>

</beans>
```

Again, note the use of the Spring util namespace to populate the Java mail properties to enable SSL protocol. Similar to the other inbound mail adapter examples, a simple main class is created to demonstrate the POP3 mail adapter. The example class is shown in Listing 13–7, where the Spring context is created and used to subscribe to the inputChannel message channel. Any incoming e-mail messages will be logged by this code.

Listing 13–7. *POP3 E-mail Receiving main Class PopMail*

```
package com.apress.prospringintegration.social.mail;

import org.apache.log4j.Logger;
import org.springframework.context.ApplicationContext;
import org.springframework.context.support.ClassPathXmlApplicationContext;
import org.springframework.integration.Message;
import org.springframework.integration.MessagingException;
import org.springframework.integration.channel.DirectChannel;
import org.springframework.integration.core.MessageHandler;

public class PopMail {
    private static Logger LOG = Logger.getLogger(PopMail.class);

    public static void main(String[] args) throws Exception {
        ApplicationContext context =
                new ClassPathXmlApplicationContext("/spring/mail/pop-mail.xml");

        DirectChannel inputChannel = context.getBean("inputChannel", DirectChannel.class);

        inputChannel.subscribe(new MessageHandler() {
            public void handleMessage(Message<?> message) throws MessagingException {
                LOG.info("Message: " + message);
            }
        });
    }
}
```

SMTP

The e-mail outbound-channel-adapter uses the SMTP protocol to send e-mail messages. One of the most important concepts to grasp when using this adapter is the default message mapping strategies. If the input message payload is an instance of the `org.springframework.mail.MailMessage` interface, it will be sent directly. A byte array message payload will be sent as an e-mail attachment. A string payload will be mapped to text-based e-mail content. More complex e-mail content will require a message transformation as discussed earlier in the book.

The different e-mail parameters are configured through the message header. An e-mail-specific header-enricher transformer is available in the mail namespace. This enricher allows setting e-mail parameters such as to, cc, bcc, from, and reply-to. An example of the e-mail `outbound-channel-adapter` is shown in Listing 13–8. This example is configured for the Gmail server.

Listing 13–8. *Sending E-mail with SMTP Spring Configuration smtp-mail.xml*

```
<?xml version="1.0" encoding="UTF-8"?>
<beans xmlns="http://www.springframework.org/schema/beans"
       xmlns:xsi="http://www.w3.org/2001/XMLSchema-instance"
       xmlns:int="http://www.springframework.org/schema/integration"
       xmlns:mail="http://www.springframework.org/schema/integration/mail"
       xmlns:util="http://www.springframework.org/schema/util"
       xmlns:context="http://www.springframework.org/schema/context"
       xsi:schemaLocation="http://www.springframework.org/schema/integration
    http://www.springframework.org/schema/integration/spring-integration-2.0.xsd
    http://www.springframework.org/schema/beans
    http://www.springframework.org/schema/beans/spring-beans-3.0.xsd
    http://www.springframework.org/schema/integration/mail
    http://www.springframework.org/schema/integration/mail/spring-integration-mail-2.0.xsd
    http://www.springframework.org/schema/util
    http://www.springframework.org/schema/util/spring-util-3.0.xsd
    http://www.springframework.org/schema/context
    http://www.springframework.org/schema/context/spring-context-3.0.xsd">

  <context:component-scan base-package="com.apress.prospringintegration.social.mail"/>

  <int:channel id="input"/>

  <int:channel id="outboundMail"/>

  <mail:outbound-channel-adapter channel="outboundMail"
                                 mail-sender="mailSender"/>

  <mail:header-enricher input-channel="input" output-channel="outboundMail">
    <mail:to value="[username]@gmail.com"/>
    <mail:from value="[username]@gmail.com"/>
    <mail:subject value="Test"/>
  </mail:header-enricher>

</beans>
```

The outbound adapter requires an instance of Spring's `org.springframework.mail.javamail.JavaMailSender`. Spring Java configuration is used to create the instance as shown in Listing 13–9. This configuration is specifically set up for Gmail's security requirements.

Listing 13–9. *Java Configuration MailConfiguration for Creating the JavaMailSender Instance*

```
package com.apress.prospringintegration.social.mail;

import org.springframework.context.annotation.Bean;
import org.springframework.context.annotation.Configuration;
import org.springframework.mail.javamail.JavaMailSender;
import org.springframework.mail.javamail.JavaMailSenderImpl;

import java.util.Properties;

@Configuration
public class MailConfiguration {

    @Bean
    public JavaMailSenderImpl mailSender() {
        JavaMailSenderImpl mailSender = new JavaMailSenderImpl();
        mailSender.setHost("smtp.gmail.com");
        mailSender.setPort(587);
        mailSender.setUsername("[username]@gmail");
        mailSender.setPassword("[password]");
        Properties properties = new Properties();
        properties.setProperty("mail.smtp.starttls.enable", "true");
        properties.setProperty("mail.smtp.auth", "true");
        mailSender.setJavaMailProperties(properties);
        return mailSender;
    }
}
```

Listing 13–10 shows the test code for sending an e-mail using the Spring configuration file in Listing 13–9. The test code sends a message to the input channel with the text string "This is a test." The result will be an e-mail message sent with the previous text string.

Listing 13–10. *E-mail Sending Test Code*

```
package com.apress.prospringintegration.social.mail;

import org.springframework.context.support.ClassPathXmlApplicationContext;
import org.springframework.integration.Message;
import org.springframework.integration.MessageChannel;
import org.springframework.integration.support.MessageBuilder;

public class SmtpMail {

    public static void main(String[] args) {
        ClassPathXmlApplicationContext context = new ClassPathXmlApplicationContext(
                "/spring/mail/smtp-mail.xml", SmtpMail.class);

        MessageChannel input = context.getBean("input", MessageChannel.class);
        Message<String> message = MessageBuilder.withPayload("This is a test").build();
        input.send(message);

        context.stop();
    }
}
```

XMPP

Spring Integration enables sending and receiving XMPP messages supported by Instant Messaging (IM) networks such as GTalk and Facebook Chat. In addition, Spring Integration supports broadcasting and receiving state using the presence adapters. XMPP support requires an additional Maven dependency, as shown in Listing 13–11.

Listing 13–11. Maven Dependency for XMPP Support

```
<dependency>
  <groupId>org.springframework.integration</groupId>
  <artifactId>spring-integration-xmpp</artifactId>
  <version>2.0.1.RELEASE</version>
</dependency>
```

In order to communicate with an XMPP server, a connection factory must first be configured. This is best done with Spring Java configuration, as shown in Listing 13–12. This configuration is specifically directed at GTalk and SASL authentication mechanism. Spring XMPP support is based on the Smack 3.1 API (www.igniterealtime.org/downloads/index.jsp). Java configuration is well suited for the XMPP adapters, due to the large number of potential configuration parameters and the static initializers.

Listing 13–12. Java Configuration XmppConfiguration for XMPP Connection Factory

```
package com.apress.prospringintegration.social.xmpp;

import org.jivesoftware.smack.ConnectionConfiguration;
import org.jivesoftware.smack.SASLAuthentication;
import org.springframework.beans.factory.annotation.Value;
import org.springframework.context.annotation.Bean;
import org.springframework.context.annotation.Configuration;
import org.springframework.integration.xmpp.config.XmppConnectionFactoryBean;

@Configuration
public class XmppConfiguration {

    @Value("${host}")
    private String host;

    @Value("${port}")
    private int port;

    @Value("${service-name}")
    private String serviceName;

    @Value("${resource}")
    private String resource;

    @Value("${subscription-mode}")
    private String subscriptionMode;

    @Value("${user}")
    private String user;

    @Value("${password}")
```

```
    private String password;

    @Value("${sasl-mechanism-supported")
    private String saslMechanismSupported;

    @Value("${sasl-mechanism-supported-index}")
    private int saslMechanismSupportedIndex;

    @Bean
    public XmppConnectionFactoryBean xmppConnectionFactoryBean() {
        SASLAuthentication.supportSASLMechanism(saslMechanismSupported,
                saslMechanismSupportedIndex);
        ConnectionConfiguration connectionConfiguration =
                new ConnectionConfiguration(host, port, serviceName);
        XmppConnectionFactoryBean connectionFactoryBean =
                new XmppConnectionFactoryBean(connectionConfiguration);
        connectionFactoryBean.setResource(resource);
        connectionFactoryBean.setSubscriptionMode(subscriptionMode);
        connectionFactoryBean.setUser(user);
        connectionFactoryBean.setPassword(password);

        return connectionFactoryBean;
    }
}
```

The various configuration values are passed to the Java configuration using `@Value` attribute and a properties file. The specific properties for GTalk are shown in Listing 13–13.

***Listing 13–13.** XMPP Configuration Properties File xmpp.properties*

```
user=[username]@gmail.com
password=[password]
host=talk.google.com
port=5222
subscription-mode=accept_all
sasl-mechanism-supported=PLAIN
sasl-mechanism-supported-index=0
resource=resource
service-name=gmail.com
```

An example of configuration Spring Integration for receiving a XMPP message from the GTalk server is shown in Listing 13–14. Note the additional namespace element required to support XMPP. The `xmpp inbound-channel-adapter` is configured to use the `xmppConnectionFactoryBean` discussed previously. The inbound adapter is configured to extract the message as an `org.springframework.integration.twitter.core.Tweet` object and sent as a payload to the `xmppChannel`.

***Listing 13–14.** Receiving XMPP Message Spring Configuration xmpp-inbound.xml*

```
<?xml version="1.0" encoding="UTF-8"?>
<beans xmlns="http://www.springframework.org/schema/beans"
       xmlns:int="http://www.springframework.org/schema/integration"
       xmlns:xsi="http://www.w3.org/2001/XMLSchema-instance"
       xmlns:xmpp="http://www.springframework.org/schema/integration/xmpp"
       xmlns:context="http://www.springframework.org/schema/context"
       xsi:schemaLocation="http://www.springframework.org/schema/integration/xmpp
```

```
        http://www.springframework.org/schema/integration/xmpp/spring-integration-xmpp-2.0.xsd
        http://www.springframework.org/schema/beans
        http://www.springframework.org/schema/beans/spring-beans-3.0.xsd
        http://www.springframework.org/schema/integration
        http://www.springframework.org/schema/integration/spring-integration-2.0.xsd
        http://www.springframework.org/schema/context
        http://www.springframework.org/schema/context/spring-context-3.0.xsd">

    <context:component-scan base-package="com.apress.prospringintegration.social.xmpp"/>
    <context:property-placeholder location="/spring/xmpp/xmpp.properties"/>

    <int:channel id="xmppInbound"/>

    <xmpp:inbound-channel-adapter extract-payload="true"
                                  channel="xmppInbound"
                                  xmpp-connection="xmppConnectionFactoryBean"/>

    <int:service-activator input-channel="xmppInbound"
                           ref="xmppMessageConsumer"/>

</beans>
```

The message is received by the XmppMessageConsumer service activator, as shown in Listing 13–15. The service activator is configured using annotations and component scanning. The service activator extracts the payload and logs the message text and the sender of the message.

Listing 13–15. *XMPP Message Consumer Class XmppMessageConsumer*

```
package com.apress.prospringintegration.social.twitter;

import org.apache.log4j.Logger;
import org.springframework.integration.Message;
import org.springframework.integration.annotation.ServiceActivator;
import org.springframework.integration.twitter.core.Tweet;
import org.springframework.stereotype.Component;

@Component
public class TwitterMessageConsumer {
    private static Logger LOG = Logger.getLogger(TwitterMessageConsumer.class);

    @ServiceActivator
    public void consume(Message<Tweet> message) {
        Tweet tweet = message.getPayload();
        LOG.info(tweet.getText() + " from: " + tweet.getFromUser());
    }
}
```

The test code to load the Spring configuration and wait for the XMPP messages is shown in Listing 13–16. Any XMPP message that is sent to the account specified in the XmppConfiguration Java configuration file will be logged.

Listing 13–16. Receiving XMPP Message Test Code

```
package com.apress.prospringintegration.social.xmpp;

import org.springframework.context.ApplicationContext;
import org.springframework.context.support.ClassPathXmlApplicationContext;

public class XmppInbound {

    public static void main(String[] args) throws Exception {
        ApplicationContext context =
                new ClassPathXmlApplicationContext("/spring/xmpp/xmpp-inbound.xml");

        Thread.sleep(10 * 60 * 1000);
    }
}
```

In a similar fashion, messages can be sent to users on XMPP. The same `XmppConfiguration` Java configuration is used to connect to the GTalk server, as shown in Listing 13–17. The `xmpp outbound-channel-adapter` is configured to send the payload of the incoming message on the `xmppOutbound` channel. A specific XMPP `header-enricher` via the `message-to` element is used to specify the user that is to receive the XMPP message.

Listing 13–17. Sending XMPP Message Spring Configuration xmpp-outbound.xml

```
<?xml version="1.0" encoding="UTF-8"?>
<beans xmlns="http://www.springframework.org/schema/beans"
       xmlns:int="http://www.springframework.org/schema/integration"
       xmlns:xsi="http://www.w3.org/2001/XMLSchema-instance"
       xmlns:xmpp="http://www.springframework.org/schema/integration/xmpp"
       xmlns:context="http://www.springframework.org/schema/context"
       xsi:schemaLocation="http://www.springframework.org/schema/integration/xmpp
    http://www.springframework.org/schema/integration/xmpp/spring-integration-xmpp-2.0.xsd
    http://www.springframework.org/schema/beans
    http://www.springframework.org/schema/beans/spring-beans-3.0.xsd
    http://www.springframework.org/schema/integration
    http://www.springframework.org/schema/integration/spring-integration-2.0.xsd
    http://www.springframework.org/schema/context
    http://www.springframework.org/schema/context/spring-context-3.0.xsd">

  <context:component-scan base-package="com.apress.prospringintegration.social.xmpp"/>
  <context:property-placeholder location="/spring/xmpp/xmpp.properties"/>

  <int:channel id="xmppOutbound"/>
  <int:channel id="input"/>

  <xmpp:outbound-channel-adapter channel="xmppOutbound"
                                 xmpp-connection="xmppConnectionFactoryBean"/>

  <xmpp:header-enricher input-channel="input" output-channel="xmppOutbound">
    <xmpp:chat-to value="[username]@gmail.com"/>
  </xmpp:header-enricher>

</beans>
```

Listing 13–18 shows test code that will send a message to the XMPP user specified in the previous Spring configuration file. A message will be sent to the input message channel, the header message-to will set the user destination, and the message will be sent to the GTalk using xmpp outbound-channel-adapter.

***Listing 13–18.** Sending XMPP Message Test Code*

```
package com.apress.prospringintegration.social.xmpp;

import org.springframework.context.support.ClassPathXmlApplicationContext;
import org.springframework.integration.Message;
import org.springframework.integration.MessageChannel;
import org.springframework.integration.support.MessageBuilder;

public class XmppOutbound {

    public static void main(String[] args) {
        ClassPathXmlApplicationContext context = new ClassPathXmlApplicationContext(
                "/spring/xmpp/xmpp-outbound.xml", XmppOutbound.class);

        MessageChannel input = context.getBean("input", MessageChannel.class);
        Message<String> message = MessageBuilder.withPayload("This is a test").build();
        input.send(message);

        context.stop();
    }
}
```

Spring Integration also support broadcasting and receiving state. This allows IM users to let others on their roster know their current state. For example, if an IM user is unavailable to chat, they may broadcast an "away" state. This will be reflected in the roster status in everyone's IM client. The Spring Integration presence adapters are used to send and receive notifications of IM state changes.

To monitor what the current status of the others users in your roster, Spring Integration provides a presence-inboud-channel-adapter. The XMPP presence adapter shown in Listing 13–19 uses the same connection factory as the previous examples. The adapter sends the status of users in the roster as a org.jivesoftware.smack.packet.Presence object (see www.igniterealtime.org/builds/smack/docs/3.1.0/javadoc/org/jivesoftware/smack/packet/Presence.html) to the message channel xmppInbound.

***Listing 13–19.** Spring Configuration xmpp-presence-inbound.xml for Receiving State*

```
<?xml version="1.0" encoding="UTF-8"?>
<beans xmlns="http://www.springframework.org/schema/beans"
       xmlns:int="http://www.springframework.org/schema/integration"
       xmlns:xsi="http://www.w3.org/2001/XMLSchema-instance"
       xmlns:xmpp="http://www.springframework.org/schema/integration/xmpp"
       xmlns:context="http://www.springframework.org/schema/context"
       xsi:schemaLocation="http://www.springframework.org/schema/integration/xmpp
    http://www.springframework.org/schema/integration/xmpp/spring-integration-xmpp-2.0.xsd
    http://www.springframework.org/schema/beans
    http://www.springframework.org/schema/beans/spring-beans-3.0.xsd
    http://www.springframework.org/schema/integration
    http://www.springframework.org/schema/integration/spring-integration-2.0.xsd
    http://www.springframework.org/schema/context
    http://www.springframework.org/schema/context/spring-context-3.0.xsd">
```

```
    <context:component-scan base-package="com.apress.prospringintegration.social.xmpp"/>
    <context:property-placeholder location="/spring/xmpp/xmpp.properties"/>

    <int:channel id="xmppInbound"/>

    <xmpp:presence-inbound-channel-adapter channel="xmppInbound"
                                           xmpp-connection="xmppConnectionFactoryBean"/>

    <int:service-activator input-channel="xmppInbound"
                           ref="xmppMessageConsumer"/>

</beans>
```

A service activator is configured to send the message sent to the message channel `xmppInbound` to the Spring bean `xmppMessageConsumer`, which is shown in Listing 13–20. This service activator logs the status of the users on your roster.

Listing 13–20. *Service activator XmppMessageConsumer which Logs the XMPP Presence Message*

```
package com.apress.prospringintegration.social.xmpp;

import org.apache.log4j.Logger;
import org.springframework.integration.Message;
import org.springframework.integration.annotation.ServiceActivator;
import org.springframework.stereotype.Component;

@Component
public class XmppPresenceConsumer {
    private static Logger LOG = Logger.getLogger(XmppMessageConsumer.class);

    @ServiceActivator
    public void consume(Message<?> input) {
        LOG.info("Received message: " + input);
    }
}
```

The example may be run using the simple main class `XmppPresenceConsumer` shown in Listing 13–21. This will list the status of the various users on your roster and any status updates thereafter.

Listing 13–21. *Inbound Presence Example main Class XmppPresenceInbound*

```
package com.apress.prospringintegration.social.xmpp;

import org.springframework.context.ApplicationContext;
import org.springframework.context.support.ClassPathXmlApplicationContext;

public class XmppPresenceInbound {

    public static void main(String[] args) throws Exception {
        ApplicationContext context =
                new ClassPathXmlApplicationContext("/spring/xmpp/xmpp-presence-inbound.xml");

        Thread.sleep(10 * 60 * 1000);
    }
}
```

In the same manner, the user's status may be broadcasted to all the other users on the user's roster. This is done using the presence-outbound-channel-adapter. Again the XMPP configuration factory created by the Spring Java configuration file is used. The outbound adapter takes the same Presence object discussed for the inbound adapter and broadcasts the status to all the users on your roster. See Listing 13–22.

Listing 13–22. *Spring Configuration xmpp-presence-outbound.xml for Broadcasting Status*

```
<?xml version="1.0" encoding="UTF-8"?>
<beans xmlns="http://www.springframework.org/schema/beans"
       xmlns:int="http://www.springframework.org/schema/integration"
       xmlns:xsi="http://www.w3.org/2001/XMLSchema-instance"
       xmlns:xmpp="http://www.springframework.org/schema/integration/xmpp"
       xmlns:context="http://www.springframework.org/schema/context"
       xsi:schemaLocation="http://www.springframework.org/schema/integration/xmpp
    http://www.springframework.org/schema/integration/xmpp/spring-integration-xmpp-2.0.xsd
    http://www.springframework.org/schema/beans
    http://www.springframework.org/schema/beans/spring-beans-3.0.xsd
    http://www.springframework.org/schema/integration
    http://www.springframework.org/schema/integration/spring-integration-2.0.xsd
    http://www.springframework.org/schema/context
    http://www.springframework.org/schema/context/spring-context-3.0.xsd">

  <context:component-scan base-package="com.apress.prospringintegration.social.xmpp"/>
  <context:property-placeholder location="/spring/xmpp/xmpp.properties"/>

  <int:channel id="xmppOutbound"/>

  <xmpp:presence-outbound-channel-adapter channel="xmppOutbound"
                                          xmpp-connection="xmppConnectionFactoryBean"/>

</beans>
```

The XMPP outbound adapter may be tested using the example main class shown in Listing 13–23. A Presence object is instantiated with Presence.Type.available where the user is subscribed to the XMPP server, the message "Out to Lunch," which will appear in the other users' client, and a Presence.Mode.away, which will be the displayed status. Running this example will broadcast this status to all of the users on their roster.

Listing 13–23. *Outbound Presence Example main Class XmppPresenceOutbound*

```
package com.apress.prospringintegration.social.xmpp;

import org.jivesoftware.smack.packet.Presence;
import org.springframework.context.support.ClassPathXmlApplicationContext;
import org.springframework.integration.Message;
import org.springframework.integration.MessageChannel;
import org.springframework.integration.support.MessageBuilder;

public class XmppPresenceOutbound {

    public static void main(String[] args) throws Exception {
        ClassPathXmlApplicationContext context = new ClassPathXmlApplicationContext(
                "/spring/xmpp/xmpp-presence-outbound.xml", XmppOutbound.class);
```

```
        MessageChannel input = context.getBean("xmppOutbound", MessageChannel.class);

        Presence presence =
                new Presence(Presence.Type.available, "Out to lunch", 0, Presence.Mode.away);
        Message<Presence> message = MessageBuilder.withPayload(presence).build();

        input.send(message);

        Thread.sleep(10 * 60 * 1000);
    }
}
```

Twitter

Spring Integration can also send and receive "tweets." The Maven dependency is shown in Listing 13–24.

***Listing 13–24.** Maven Dependency for Twitter Support*

```
<dependency>
  <groupId>org.springframework.integration</groupId>
  <artifactId>spring-integration-twitter</artifactId>
  <version>2.0.1.RELEASE</version>
</dependency>
```

Spring Integration supports sending and receiving Twitter updates, direct messages (DM), and mentions (tweets that include somebody else's Twitter handle preceded by a "@"). Twitter updates are the standard tweet that users send out to all their followers. DMs are private messages sent directly to a user. A DM does not appear in the public timeline and the recipient of a DM must also be a follower of the sender. Mentions are tweets that are directed at or in response to a particular person using the familiar @username symbol. These messages can be seen by all, but show up in the reply tab of the intended recipient.

All of the Twitter adapters require a Twitter template that will be configured using Spring Java configuration, as shown in Listing 13–25. The `twitterTemplate` bean requires a set of authorization keys that may be obtained by request at `http://dev.twitter.com/pages/auth`. For the purpose of this example, the keys are provided for the Twitter account @prosibook.

***Listing 13–25.** Java Configuration TwitterConfiguration used to Configure Twitter Template*

```
package com.apress.prospringintegration.social.twitter;

import org.springframework.beans.factory.annotation.Value;
import org.springframework.context.annotation.Bean;
import org.springframework.context.annotation.Configuration;
import org.springframework.integration.twitter.core.Twitter4jTemplate;
import org.springframework.integration.twitter.core.TwitterOperations;

@Configuration
public class TwitterConfiguration {

    @Value("${consumer-key}")
    private String consumerKey;

    @Value("${consumer-secret}")
```

```
    private String consumerSecret;

    @Value("${access-token}")
    private String accessToken;

    @Value("${access-token-secret}")
    private String accessTokenSecret;

    @Bean
    public TwitterOperations twitterTemplate() {
        Twitter4jTemplate twitterOperations =
                new Twitter4jTemplate(
                        consumerKey, consumerSecret, accessToken, accessTokenSecret);
        return twitterOperations;

    }
}
```

The Twitter keys are defined in the properties file shown in Listing 13–26. These keys are used to authenticate and authorize the user.

Listing 13–26. *Properties File twitter.properties Defining Twitter Keys*

```
consumer-key=SZHVUR5O6Awq2cJJvPZEA
consumer-secret=iXwGDkJdWuCzsXFfZpAtqfFygPBB5QkdUhLsvbsyEA
access-token=184204629-C1cyGIrfmppJNu1WdASZ1bQaAvYrOYLzHxXPvEcQ
access-token-secret=Y25kBcxolzqu76wZI3D1iDSEloCGkcUtlDv9Q7K9wo
```

Using Spring Integration, a channel message may be converted into a Twitter update, DM, or mention using the Twitter outbound adapter. The `outbound-channel-adapter` is configured in Listing 13–27 to send the incoming channel message on `twitterOutbound` to Twitter as an updated to @prosibook. In addition, note the required twitter namespace that has been added to the configuration file.

Listing 13–27. *Sending Twitter Update Message Spring Configuration twitter-outbound.xml*

```
<?xml version="1.0" encoding="UTF-8"?>
<beans xmlns="http://www.springframework.org/schema/beans"
       xmlns:int="http://www.springframework.org/schema/integration"
       xmlns:xsi="http://www.w3.org/2001/XMLSchema-instance"
       xmlns:twitter="http://www.springframework.org/schema/integration/twitter"
       xmlns:context="http://www.springframework.org/schema/context"
       xsi:schemaLocation="http://www.springframework.org/schema/integration/twitter
    http://www.springframework.org/schema/integration/twitter/spring-integration-twitter↵
-2.0.xsd
    http://www.springframework.org/schema/beans
    http://www.springframework.org/schema/beans/spring-beans-3.0.xsd
    http://www.springframework.org/schema/integration
    http://www.springframework.org/schema/integration/spring-integration-2.0.xsd
    http://www.springframework.org/schema/context
    http://www.springframework.org/schema/context/spring-context-3.0.xsd">

  <context:component-scan base-package="com.apress.prospringintegration.social.twitter"/>
  <context:property-placeholder location="/spring/twitter/twitter.properties"/>

  <int:channel id="twitterOutbound"/>
```

```
    <twitter:outbound-channel-adapter twitter-template="twitterTemplate"
                                      channel="twitterOutbound"/>

</beans>
```

To test the Twitter update Spring configuration, a simple test class is required. This is shown in Listing 13–28. It simply sends a text message to the `twitterOutbound` message channel that will result in a tweet being posted to the @prosibook account. Note the addition of the current timestamp to the outbound message. This is required, because the same update cannot be sent twice to Twitter in a certain time window.

***Listing 13–28.** Sending Twitter Update Message Test Code TwitterOutbound*

```
package com.apress.prospringintegration.social.twitter;

import org.springframework.context.support.ClassPathXmlApplicationContext;
import org.springframework.integration.Message;
import org.springframework.integration.MessageChannel;
import org.springframework.integration.support.MessageBuilder;

import java.util.Calendar;

public class TwitterOutbound {

    public static void main(String[] args) {
        ClassPathXmlApplicationContext context = new ClassPathXmlApplicationContext(
                "/spring/twitter/twitter-outbound.xml", TwitterOutbound.class);

        MessageChannel input = context.getBean("twitterOutbound", MessageChannel.class);
        Message<String> message =
                MessageBuilder.withPayload("Only can send message once " +
                        Calendar.getInstance().getTimeInMillis()).build();
        input.send(message);

        context.stop();
    }
}
```

The next outbound adapter provides support for sending a DM to a Twitter account. This will send a private message to a specific user who is also a follower. The configuration is similar to update adapter, except it uses the `outbound-dm-channel` adapter. The Spring configuration file is shown in Listing 13–29.

***Listing 13–29.** Sending Twitter DM Spring Configuration twitter-dm-outbound.xml*

```
<?xml version="1.0" encoding="UTF-8"?>
<beans xmlns="http://www.springframework.org/schema/beans"
       xmlns:int="http://www.springframework.org/schema/integration"
       xmlns:xsi="http://www.w3.org/2001/XMLSchema-instance"
       xmlns:twitter="http://www.springframework.org/schema/integration/twitter"
       xmlns:context="http://www.springframework.org/schema/context"
       xsi:schemaLocation="http://www.springframework.org/schema/integration/twitter
    http://www.springframework.org/schema/integration/twitter/spring-integration-twitter➥
-2.0.xsd
    http://www.springframework.org/schema/beans
```

```
        http://www.springframework.org/schema/beans/spring-beans-3.0.xsd
        http://www.springframework.org/schema/integration
        http://www.springframework.org/schema/integration/spring-integration-2.0.xsd
        http://www.springframework.org/schema/context
        http://www.springframework.org/schema/context/spring-context-3.0.xsd">

    <context:component-scan base-package="com.apress.prospringintegration.social.twitter"/>
    <context:property-placeholder location="/spring/twitter/twitter.properties"/>

    <int:channel id="twitterOutbound"/>

    <twitter:dm-inbound-channel-adapter channel="twitterOutbound"
                                        twitter-template="twitterTemplate"/>

</beans>
```

The target user is set through the header TwitterHeaders.DM_TARGET_USER_ID. The test code shown in Listing 13–30 sets the header value programmatically to send a DM to @prosibook.

Listing 13–30. *Sending Twitter DM Test Code TwitterDmOutbound*

```
package com.apress.prospringintegration.social.twitter;

import org.springframework.context.support.ClassPathXmlApplicationContext;
import org.springframework.integration.Message;
import org.springframework.integration.MessageChannel;
import org.springframework.integration.support.MessageBuilder;
import org.springframework.integration.twitter.core.TwitterHeaders;

public class TwitterDmOutbound {

    public static void main(String[] args) {
        ClassPathXmlApplicationContext context = new ClassPathXmlApplicationContext(
                "/spring/twitter/twitter-outbound.xml", TwitterOutbound.class);

        MessageChannel input = context.getBean("twitterOutbound", MessageChannel.class);
        Message<String> message = MessageBuilder.withPayload("This is a test")
                .setHeader(TwitterHeaders.DM_TARGET_USER_ID, "@prosibook").build();
        input.send(message);

        context.stop();
    }
}
```

Spring Integration can also receive Twitter messages. The Spring configuration for receiving a Twitter update is shown in Listing 13–31. The inbound-update-channel-adapter is configured with the same twitter-template to send the Twitter update message to the twitterInbound channel. A poller element is required to pull the messages from the Twitter server.

Listing 13–31. *Receiving Twitter Update Message Spring Configuration twitter-inbound.xml*

```
<?xml version="1.0" encoding="UTF-8"?>
<beans xmlns="http://www.springframework.org/schema/beans"
       xmlns:int="http://www.springframework.org/schema/integration"
       xmlns:xsi="http://www.w3.org/2001/XMLSchema-instance"
```

```
       xmlns:twitter="http://www.springframework.org/schema/integration/twitter"
       xmlns:context="http://www.springframework.org/schema/context"
       xsi:schemaLocation="http://www.springframework.org/schema/integration/twitter
    http://www.springframework.org/schema/integration/twitter/spring-integration-twitter➥
-2.0.xsd
    http://www.springframework.org/schema/beans
    http://www.springframework.org/schema/beans/spring-beans-3.0.xsd
    http://www.springframework.org/schema/integration
    http://www.springframework.org/schema/integration/spring-integration-2.0.xsd
    http://www.springframework.org/schema/context
    http://www.springframework.org/schema/context/spring-context-3.0.xsd">

  <context:component-scan base-package="com.apress.prospringintegration.social.twitter"/>
  <context:property-placeholder location="/spring/twitter/twitter.properties"/>

  <int:channel id="twitterInbound"/>

  <twitter:inbound-channel-adapter channel="twitterInbound"
                                   twitter-template="twitterTemplate">
    <int:poller fixed-rate="5000" max-messages-per-poll="3"/>
  </twitter:inbound-channel-adapter>

  <int:service-activator input-channel="twitterInbound" ref="twitterMessageConsumer"/>

</beans>
```

The service activator class is used to receive the Twitter message, as shown in Listing 13–32. The same class may be used for the incoming Twitter update, DM, and mention.

Listing 13–32. *Twitter Message Consumer Class TwitterMessageConsumer*

```
package com.apress.prospringintegration.social.twitter;

import org.apache.log4j.Logger;
import org.springframework.integration.Message;
import org.springframework.integration.annotation.ServiceActivator;
import org.springframework.integration.twitter.core.Tweet;
import org.springframework.stereotype.Component;

@Component
public class TwitterMessageConsumer {
    private static Logger LOG = Logger.getLogger(TwitterMessageConsumer.class);

    @ServiceActivator
    public void consume(Message<Tweet> message) {
        Tweet tweet = message.getPayload();
        LOG.info(tweet.getText() + " from: " + tweet.getFromUser());
    }
}
```

All that is required to run the Twitter inbound message example is to load the Spring configuration file, as shown in Listing 13–33. A ten-minute delay is added to the code to wait for any new tweets.

Listing 13–33. *Twitter Message Consumer Test Code TwitterInbound*

```
package com.apress.prospringintegration.social.twitter;

import org.apache.log4j.Logger;
import org.springframework.context.ApplicationContext;
import org.springframework.context.support.ClassPathXmlApplicationContext;

public class TwitterInbound {
    private static Logger LOG = Logger.getLogger(TwitterInbound.class);

    public static void main(String[] args) throws Exception {
        ApplicationContext context =
                new ClassPathXmlApplicationContext("/spring/twitter/twitter-inbound.xml");

        Thread.sleep(10 * 60 * 1000);
    }
}
```

Receiving the Twitter DM is identical to receiving an update except for using the `inbound-dm-channel-adapter`. An example of a Spring configuration for receiving a Twitter DM is shown in Listing 13–34. Again, this adapter requires a poller element to pull the messages from Twitter.

Listing 13–34. *Receiving Twitter DM Spring Configuration*

```
<?xml version="1.0" encoding="UTF-8"?>
<beans xmlns="http://www.springframework.org/schema/beans"
       xmlns:int="http://www.springframework.org/schema/integration"
       xmlns:xsi="http://www.w3.org/2001/XMLSchema-instance"
       xmlns:twitter="http://www.springframework.org/schema/integration/twitter"
       xmlns:context="http://www.springframework.org/schema/context"
       xsi:schemaLocation="http://www.springframework.org/schema/integration/twitter
    http://www.springframework.org/schema/integration/twitter/spring-integration-twitter➥
-2.0.xsd
    http://www.springframework.org/schema/beans
    http://www.springframework.org/schema/beans/spring-beans-3.0.xsd
    http://www.springframework.org/schema/integration
    http://www.springframework.org/schema/integration/spring-integration-2.0.xsd
    http://www.springframework.org/schema/context
    http://www.springframework.org/schema/context/spring-context-3.0.xsd">

  <context:component-scan base-package="com.apress.prospringintegration.social.twitter"/>
  <context:property-placeholder location="/spring/twitter/twitter.properties"/>

  <int:channel id="twitterInbound"/>

  <twitter:dm-inbound-channel-adapter twitter-template="twitterTemplate"
                                      channel="twitterInbound">
    <int:poller fixed-rate="5000" max-messages-per-poll="3"/>
  </twitter:dm-inbound-channel-adapter>

  <int:service-activator input-channel="twitterInbound" ref="twitterMessageConsumer"/>

</beans>
```

The Twitter DM inbound example may be tested using the main class shown in Listing 13–35. Again a ten-minute delay is added to the code to wait for incoming DMs.

Listing 13–35. *Receiving Twitter DM Example main Class TwitterDmInbound*

```
package com.apress.prospringintegration.social.twitter;

import org.apache.log4j.Logger;
import org.springframework.context.ApplicationContext;
import org.springframework.context.support.ClassPathXmlApplicationContext;

public class TwitterDmInbound {
    private static Logger LOG = Logger.getLogger(TwitterDmInbound.class);

    public static void main(String[] args) throws Exception {
        ApplicationContext context =
                new ClassPathXmlApplicationContext("/spring/twitter/twitter-dm-inbound.xml");

        Thread.sleep(10 * 60 * 1000);
    }
}
```

An example of receiving Twitter mention messages is shown in Listing 13–36. The `inbound-mention-channel-adapter` is used to receive the mentions using a configuration identical to the other inbound Twitter adapters.

Listing 13–36. *Receiving Twitter Mention Message Spring Configuration twitter-mention-inbound.xml*

```
<?xml version="1.0" encoding="UTF-8"?>
<beans xmlns="http://www.springframework.org/schema/beans"
       xmlns:int="http://www.springframework.org/schema/integration"
       xmlns:xsi="http://www.w3.org/2001/XMLSchema-instance"
       xmlns:twitter="http://www.springframework.org/schema/integration/twitter"
       xmlns:context="http://www.springframework.org/schema/context"
       xsi:schemaLocation="http://www.springframework.org/schema/integration/twitter
    http://www.springframework.org/schema/integration/twitter/spring-integration-twitter↵
-2.0.xsd
    http://www.springframework.org/schema/beans
    http://www.springframework.org/schema/beans/spring-beans-3.0.xsd
    http://www.springframework.org/schema/integration
    http://www.springframework.org/schema/integration/spring-integration-2.0.xsd
    http://www.springframework.org/schema/context
    http://www.springframework.org/schema/context/spring-context-3.0.xsd">

  <context:component-scan base-package="com.apress.prospringintegration.social.twitter"/>
  <context:property-placeholder location="/spring/twitter/twitter.properties"/>

  <int:channel id="twitterInbound"/>

  <twitter:mentions-inbound-channel-adapter channel="twitterInbound"
                                            twitter-template="twitterTemplate">
    <int:poller fixed-rate="5000" max-messages-per-poll="3"/>
  </twitter:mentions-inbound-channel-adapter>

  <int:service-activator input-channel="twitterInbound" ref="twitterMessageConsumer"/>

</beans>
```

Again, a main class is used to create the Spring context and wait for ten minutes for any incoming Twitter mentions. The example main class is shown in Listing 13–37.

Listing 13–37. *Receiving Twitter Mentions Example class TwitterMentionInbound*

```
package com.apress.prospringintegration.social.twitter;

import org.apache.log4j.Logger;
import org.springframework.context.ApplicationContext;
import org.springframework.context.support.ClassPathXmlApplicationContext;

public class TwitterMentionInbound {
    private static Logger LOG = Logger.getLogger(TwitterMentionInbound.class);

    public static void main(String[] args) throws Exception {
        ApplicationContext context =
                new ClassPathXmlApplicationContext(
                        "/spring/twitter/twitter-mention-inbound.xml");

        Thread.sleep(10 * 60 * 1000);
    }
}}
```

The final Twitter adapter that will be discussed is inbound search adapter. This adapter can do Twitter searches based on a query. More information about Twitter queries may be found at `http://search.twitter.com/operators`. The Spring configuration file for an inbound Twitter search adapter is shown in Listing 13–38. Note that this adapter does not require a reference to a `twitter-template`, because a search is anonymous.

Listing 13–38. *Spring Configuration twitter-search-inbound.xml Demostrating a Twitter Search*

```
<?xml version="1.0" encoding="UTF-8"?>
<beans xmlns="http://www.springframework.org/schema/beans"
       xmlns:int="http://www.springframework.org/schema/integration"
       xmlns:xsi="http://www.w3.org/2001/XMLSchema-instance"
       xmlns:twitter="http://www.springframework.org/schema/integration/twitter"
       xmlns:context="http://www.springframework.org/schema/context"
       xsi:schemaLocation="http://www.springframework.org/schema/integration/twitter
    http://www.springframework.org/schema/integration/twitter/spring-integration-twitter➥
-2.0.xsd
    http://www.springframework.org/schema/beans
    http://www.springframework.org/schema/beans/spring-beans-3.0.xsd
    http://www.springframework.org/schema/integration
    http://www.springframework.org/schema/integration/spring-integration-2.0.xsd
    http://www.springframework.org/schema/context
    http://www.springframework.org/schema/context/spring-context-3.0.xsd">

  <context:component-scan base-package="com.apress.prospringintegration.social.twitter"/>

  <int:channel id="twitterInbound"/>

  <twitter:search-inbound-channel-adapter query="#springintegration"
                                          channel="twitterInbound">
    <int:poller fixed-rate="5000" max-messages-per-poll="3"/>
```

```
    </twitter:search-inbound-channel-adapter>

    <int:service-activator input-channel="twitterInbound" ref="twitterMessageConsumer"/>

</beans>
```

The inbound Twitter search adapter may be tested using the example main class shown in Listing 13–39. This example will list the search results from the query defined in the search-inbound-channel-adapter shown previously.

***Listing 13–39.** Example main Class TwitterSearchInbound Demostrating a Twitter Search*

```
package com.apress.prospringintegration.social.twitter;

import org.apache.log4j.Logger;
import org.springframework.context.ApplicationContext;
import org.springframework.context.support.ClassPathXmlApplicationContext;

public class TwitterSearchInbound {
    private static Logger LOG = Logger.getLogger(TwitterInbound.class);

    public static void main(String[] args) throws Exception {
        ApplicationContext context =
                new ClassPathXmlApplicationContext(
                        "/spring/twitter/twitter-search-inbound.xml");

        Thread.sleep(10 * 60 * 1000);
    }
}
```

News Feed

Spring Integration provides support for Web Syndication by supplying a feed adapter that enables subscribing to an RSS or ATOM feed. RSS and ATOM are useful for broadcasting events. Most often this takes the form of news feeds, but it could also be a system log of application events. for example. The following Maven dependency shown in Listing 13–41 is required for the feed adapter.

***Listing 13–40.** Addition Maven Dependency for RSS Feed*

```
    <dependency>
      <groupId>org.springframework.integration</groupId>
      <artifactId>spring-integration-feed</artifactId>
    </dependency>
```

The feed adapter is configured by supplying the URL of the RSS feed of interest and the channel where the feed will be sent. An example Spring configuration for a feed adapter is shown in Listing 13–41. Note the additional feed namespace used for the feed adapter. The feed adapter will listen to the RSS feed at http://feeds.nytimes.com/nyt/rss/Technolgy and will send a message to the channel feedChannel. The message will have a payload of the type com.sun.syndication.feed.syn.SyndEntry, which encapsulates information about the news item including content, dates, and authors. A poller element is required for the feed adapter, because it is a poller consumer.

Note that the feed adapter is slightly different than other polling consumers. When the feed adapter is first started and does its first poll, a com.sun.syndication.feed.synd.SyndEntryFeed instance is received. This object contains multiple SyndEntry objects and each entry is stored in a local entry queue and released based on the `max-messages-per-poll` property of the poller. This queue will be refreshed if it becomes empty and there are additional new entries available.

Listing 13–41. Spring Configuration feed-inbound.xml for Following a RSS Feed

```
<?xml version="1.0" encoding="UTF-8"?>
<beans xmlns="http://www.springframework.org/schema/beans"
       xmlns:xsi="http://www.w3.org/2001/XMLSchema-instance"
       xmlns:int="http://www.springframework.org/schema/integration"
       xmlns:feed="http://www.springframework.org/schema/integration/feed"
       xsi:schemaLocation="http://www.springframework.org/schema/beans
    http://www.springframework.org/schema/beans/spring-beans-3.0.xsd
    http://www.springframework.org/schema/integration
    http://www.springframework.org/schema/integration/spring-integration-2.0.xsd
    http://www.springframework.org/schema/integration/feed
    http://www.springframework.org/schema/integration/feed/spring-integration-feed-2.0.xsd">

  <int:channel id="feedChannel">
    <int:queue/>
  </int:channel>

  <feed:inbound-channel-adapter id="feedAdapter"
                                channel="feedChannel"
                                url="http://feeds.nytimes.com/nyt/rss/Technology">
    <int:poller fixed-rate="10000" max-messages-per-poll="100"/>
  </feed:inbound-channel-adapter>

</beans>
```

Spring Integration also provides a mechanism to prevent duplicate entries. Each feed entry has an associated published date field. Each time the feed adapter creates a new message object, the feed adapter stores the latest published date in an instance of `org.springframework.integration.core.store.MetadataStore`. The feed adapter will look at this data store before creating and sending a message to insure that no duplicate entries are sent. By default, Spring Integration will the `Metadatastore` implementation `SimpleMetadataStore`, which is an in-memory implementation. This datastore will be lost if the adapter is restarted. Otherwise the properties file based `PropertiesPersistingMetadataStore`. For example, the property-based persister may be configured using Java configuration as shown in Listing 13–42.

Listing 13–42. Property Base Persistence Configuration

```
package com.apress.prospringintegration.social.feed;

import org.springframework.context.annotation.Bean;
import org.springframework.context.annotation.Configuration;
import org.springframework.integration.store.PropertiesPersistingMetadataStore;

@Configuration
public class FeedConfiguration {

    @Bean
    public PropertiesPersistingMetadataStore metadataStore() {
        PropertiesPersistingMetadataStore metadataStore =
```

```
                new PropertiesPersistingMetadataStore();
        return metadataStore;
    }
}
```

The feed adapter may be tested using the main class shown in Listing 13–43. The Spring context is created and the messages are pulled from the message channel feedChannel. The payload coming from the feed adapter is of the type SyndEntry. The main class logs the published date and the title of the entry. Additional information such as the context may also be derived from the SyndEntry instance.

Listing 13–43. *Example main Class FeedInboundApp for Following an RSS Feed*

```
package com.apress.prospringintegration.social.feed;

import com.sun.syndication.feed.synd.SyndEntry;
import org.springframework.context.ApplicationContext;
import org.springframework.context.support.ClassPathXmlApplicationContext;
import org.springframework.integration.Message;
import org.springframework.integration.core.PollableChannel;

public class FeedInboundApp {

    public static void main(String[] args) {
        ApplicationContext context =
                new ClassPathXmlApplicationContext("/spring/feed/feed-inbound.xml");

        PollableChannel feedChannel = context.getBean("feedChannel", PollableChannel.class);

        for (int i = 0; i < 10; i++) {
            Message<SyndEntry> message = (Message<SyndEntry>) feedChannel.receive(1000);
            if (message != null) {
                SyndEntry entry = message.getPayload();
                System.out.println(entry.getPublishedDate() + " - " + entry.getTitle());
            } else {
                break;
            }
        }
    }
}
```

Summary

This chapter has covered the current support in Spring Integration for social computing. Social computing is becoming a part of everyone's life, and dominates a large part of the Internet bandwidth. Its growth is expanding with the mobile market. Spring Integration provides support for e-mail, XMPP, RSS, and Twitter, and this chapter has introduced how these technologies may become a part of enterprise integration.

CHAPTER 14

Web Services

Web services have emerged as a key technology for communication between web-based applications over the network. Web services typically leverage HTTP protocol for communication over the network, and use XML as the message payload format. Using web-related standards allows for application interoperability even between disparate applications and technologies. This chapter will focus on Spring Integration's support for Standard Object Access Protocol (SOAP) services using the Web Services Definition Language (WSDL) as a method of describing the service for external clients. Spring Integration's support for REST services will be covered in Chapter 18.

We will be taking a contract-first approach for creating web services using the document/literal style of SOAP messaging. This allows a web service to take advantage of the best of messaging and statelessness. The request-and-response XML message will be defined by an XML schema, and the web service will be based on this, adding the SOAP protocol. This allows the web services consumers and providers to be in any technology, since XML is a text-based messaging format. The SOAP RPC style is typically based on building a web services endpoint based on Java method call. Thus, SOAP RPC supports the concept of a method to be called and parameters to be passed. This causes SOAP RPC to be restrictive and not map well into a messaging framework.

Spring Integration provides two components for supporting web services: invoking a web service by sending a message to a channel using an outbound web service gateway, and sending a message to a channel upon receiving a web service invocation using an inbound web service gateway. Both the inbound and outbound gateways include support for adding an XML marshaller. We will cover how Spring Integration provides both client and server support for web services, and how to integrate web services with the Spring Integration messaging framework.

Maven Dependencies

Spring Integration builds upon the Spring Web Services project (`http://static.springsource.org/spring-ws/sites/1.5`). The required Maven dependencies for the Spring Integration web services gateways are shown in Listing 14–1. The `cglib` library is required to support Java configuration, as discussed in Chapter 3.

Listing 14–1. *Required Project Dependencies That Enable Spring WS pom.xml*

```
<dependencies>
  <dependency>
    <groupId>org.springframework.integration</groupId>
    <artifactId>spring-integration-xml</artifactId>
    <version>2.0.1.RELEASE</version>
  </dependency>
  <dependency>
    <groupId>org.springframework.integration</groupId>
    <artifactId>spring-integration-ws</artifactId>
```

```
      <version>2.0.1.RELEASE</version>
    </dependency>
    <dependency>
      <groupId>cglib</groupId>
      <artifactId>cglib</artifactId>
      <version>2.2</version>
    </dependency>
  </dependencies>
```

XML Schema

The standard message payload format for a web service is XML. XML is a plain-text format designed for data transfer and can be read by most application technologies. To ensure that both the web services client and server agree to the message payload format, a contract is usually enforced for the XML data using an XML schema. An XML schema is a description of the XML documents in terms of the constraints on the structure and the content.

To demonstrate, we'll create an XML schema to represent a ticket request and response of a web service endpoint representing a ticket-issuing system, similar to the examples used in previous chapters. The XML schema describes a ticket request with a `TicketRequest` element consisting of a description and priority property. The ticket response is represented by a `TicketResponse` element with the properties `ticketId` (a unique identifier) and `issueDateTime` (the time the ticket is issued), a priority, and a description. The priority property is limited to the values `low`, `medium`, `high`, and `emergency` based on an enumeration. Listing 14–2 shows the XML schema, which defines the request and response for the web service ticket-issuing endpoint.

Listing 14–2. *XML Schema Ticket.xsd*

```
<?xml version="1.0" encoding="UTF-8" standalone="yes"?>

<xs:schema version="1.0"
           attributeFormDefault="unqualified"
           elementFormDefault="qualified"
           targetNamespace="http://prospringintegration.com/tk/schemas"
           xmlns:xs="http://www.w3.org/2001/XMLSchema">

  <xs:element name="TicketRequest">
    <xs:complexType>
      <xs:sequence>
        <xs:element type="xs:string" name="description"/>
        <xs:element type="priorityType" name="priority"/>
      </xs:sequence>
    </xs:complexType>
  </xs:element>

  <xs:element name="TicketResponse">
    <xs:complexType>
      <xs:sequence>
        <xs:element type="ticketType" name="ticket"/>
      </xs:sequence>
    </xs:complexType>
  </xs:element>
```

```
  <xs:complexType name="ticketType">
    <xs:sequence>
      <xs:element name="description" type="xs:string" minOccurs="0"/>
      <xs:element name="issueDateTime" type="xs:dateTime" minOccurs="0"/>
      <xs:element name="priority" type="priorityType" minOccurs="0"/>
      <xs:element name="ticketId" type="xs:long"/>
    </xs:sequence>
  </xs:complexType>

  <xs:simpleType name="priorityType">
    <xs:restriction base="xs:string">
      <xs:enumeration value="low"/>
      <xs:enumeration value="medium"/>
      <xs:enumeration value="high"/>
      <xs:enumeration value="emergency"/>
    </xs:restriction>
  </xs:simpleType>

</xs:schema>
```

Configuring a Web Services Inbound Gateway

There are two Spring Integration implementations for an inbound web services gateway: `org.springframework.integration.ws.SimpleWebServiceInboundGateway` and `org.springframework.integration.ws.MarshallingWebServiceInboundGateway`. The `SimpleWebServiceInboundGateway` will extract a `javax.xml.tranform.Source` from the `org.springframework.ws.WebServiceMessage` and set it as the message payload. The `MarshallingServiceInboundGateway` provides support for defining an implementation of the `org.springframework.oxm.Marshaller` and `org.springframework.oxm.Unmarshaller` interfaces, and will be discussed in more detail following. The SOAP action header will be added to the headers of the messages that are forwarded to the request channel for both gateways.

Both gateway implementations implement the Spring Web Services `org.springframework.ws.server.endpoint.MessageEndpoint` interface, so they can be configured using an `org.springframework.ws.transport.http.MessageDispatcherServlet`, similar to a standard Spring Web Services configuration. As with a Spring Web Services, the inbound web services gateway must be deployed within a servlet container with the standard directory structure and configuration files. The `web.xml` file is shown in Listing 14–3. The servlet class is set to the `MessageDispacherServlet`, and all requests with the URL pattern `/ticketservice/*` will be directed to the servlet.

Listing 14–3. *Inbound Web Services Gateway web.xml*

```
<?xml version="1.0" encoding="UTF-8"?>
<web-app xmlns="http://java.sun.com/xml/ns/j2ee"
         xmlns:xsi="http://www.w3.org/2001/XMLSchema-instance"
         xsi:schemaLocation=
    "http://java.sun.com/xml/ns/j2ee http://java.sun.com/xml/ns/j2ee/web-app_2_4.xsd"
         version="2.4">

  <display-name>Pro Spring Integration Inbound SOAP Gateway Example</display-name>

  <servlet>
    <servlet-name>ticket-ws</servlet-name>
```

```
    <servlet-class>org.springframework.ws.transport.http.MessageDispatcherServlet</servlet-➥
class>
    <load-on-startup>1</load-on-startup>
  </servlet>

  <servlet-mapping>
    <servlet-name>ticket-ws</servlet-name>
    <url-pattern>/ticketservice/*</url-pattern>
  </servlet-mapping>

  <welcome-file-list>
    <welcome-file>index.html</welcome-file>
  </welcome-file-list>

</web-app>
```

By convention, the Spring configuration file should have the name `<servlet name>-servlet.xml` and be placed in the `webapp/WEB-INF` directory. In our example, the name will be `ticket-ws-servlet.xml`, which is shown in Listing 14–4. The component-scanning element is used to create the references to the Java configuration and component beans, which will be discussed following.

Listing 14–4. *Base Spring Configuration for Applying a Web Service Inbound Gateway service.xml*

```
<beans xmlns="http://www.springframework.org/schema/beans"
       xmlns:xsi="http://www.w3.org/2001/XMLSchema-instance"
       xmlns:int="http://www.springframework.org/schema/integration"
       xmlns:ws="http://www.springframework.org/schema/integration/ws"
       xmlns:context="http://www.springframework.org/schema/context"
       xsi:schemaLocation="http://www.springframework.org/schema/beans
    http://www.springframework.org/schema/beans/spring-beans-3.0.xsd
    http://www.springframework.org/schema/context
    http://www.springframework.org/schema/context/spring-context-3.0.xsd
    http://www.springframework.org/schema/integration/ws
    http://www.springframework.org/schema/integration/ws/spring-integration-ws-2.0.xsd
    http://www.springframework.org/schema/integration
    http://www.springframework.org/schema/integration/spring-integration-2.0.xsd">

  <context:component-scan
      base-package="com.apress.prospringintegration.webservice.web"/>

  <int:channel id="inboundDOMTicketRequest"/>

  <ws:inbound-gateway id="wsInboundGateway"
                      request-channel="inboundDOMTicketRequest"/>

  <int:service-activator input-channel="inboundDOMTicketRequest"
                         ref="ticketIssuerEndpoint"/>

</beans>
```

We will leverage the Spring Integration `ws` namespace to create the inbound web services gateway. The `inbound-gateway` element is configured to create a web services endpoint that forwards the web service invocation `Source` object containing the XML message to the `inboundDomTicketRequest` message channel defined by the `request-channel` attribute. The beauty of this example is that the underlying Spring Web Services libraries handle the SOAP protocol. Another option for the `inbound-gateway` is the reply-channel. By default, an anonymous channel is created and set through the REPLY_CHANNEL message header. Also, the extract-payload attribute can be set to false (it defaults to true) to pass the entire WebServicesMessage as the message payload sent to the request channel. Finally, the marshaller and unmarshaller can be set (this will be discussed in the next example).

A ticketIssuerEndpoint service activator is configured to receive the incoming XML message and to create a reply XML message. This service activator will be discussed following.

Configuring Web Services Endpoints

The web services endpoint is configured to send all incoming SOAP request invocations that match the URL pattern set in the web.xml file to the Spring Integration inbound gateway using the Java configuration file shown in Listing 14–5. An org.springframework.ws.server.endpoint.mapping.UriEndpointMapping instance is created, and the default endpoint is set to the Spring Integration gateway wsInboundGateway.

Listing 14–5. *Java Configuration for the Web Services Endpoint*

```
package com.apress.prospringintegration.webservice.web;

import com.apress.prospringintegration.webservice.CommonConfiguration;
import org.springframework.beans.factory.annotation.Value;
import org.springframework.context.annotation.Bean;
import org.springframework.context.annotation.Configuration;
import org.springframework.ws.server.endpoint.MessageEndpoint;
import org.springframework.ws.server.endpoint.mapping.UriEndpointMapping;

@Configuration
public class TicketIssuerConfiguration extends CommonConfiguration {

    //the ws:inbound-gateway is in fact a reference to this base Spring WS object
    @Value("#{wsInboundGateway}")
    private MessageEndpoint wsInboundGateway;

    @Bean
    public UriEndpointMapping uriEndpointMapping() {
        UriEndpointMapping uriEndpointMapping = new UriEndpointMapping();
        uriEndpointMapping.setDefaultEndpoint(wsInboundGateway);
        return uriEndpointMapping;
    }

}
```

Payload Extraction with DOM

Spring Web Services uses the org.springframework.ws.soap.saaj.SaajSoapMessageFactory to extract the XML payload from the incoming SOAP request. The request payload must be parsed with an XML parser. As shown in the service activator code in Listing 14–6, the XML payload is parsed using the Java default DOM parser. The description and priority are extracted from the incoming XML request and used to create the reply XML message. In this example, the XML reply payload is created by hand. A parser can be used to create the XML reply; however, this code is presented in contrast to the simplicity of using a marshaller, which will be demonstrated in the next example.

Listing 14–6. Service Activator Handling an Incoming Web Services Request

```
package com.apress.prospringintegration.webservice.web;

import com.apress.prospringintegration.webservice.CommonConfiguration;
import org.springframework.integration.annotation.ServiceActivator;
import org.springframework.integration.xml.source.DomSourceFactory;
import org.springframework.stereotype.Component;
import org.w3c.dom.Node;
import org.w3c.dom.NodeList;

import javax.xml.transform.Source;
import javax.xml.transform.dom.DOMSource;
import java.util.Date;
import java.util.Random;

@Component
public class TicketIssuerEndpoint {

    private String replyTemplate =
            "<TicketResponse xmlns=\"" + CommonConfiguration.NAMESPACE + "\">" +
                    "<ticket>" +
                    "<description>%s</description>" +
                    "<priority>%s</priority>" +
                    "<ticketId>%d</ticketId>" +
                    "<issueDateTime>%tc</issueDateTime>" +
                    "</ticket>" +
                    "</TicketResponse>";

    @ServiceActivator
    public Source handleRequest(DOMSource source)
            throws Exception {

        NodeList nodeList = source.getNode().getChildNodes();
        String description = "";
        String priority = "";

        for (int i = 0; i < nodeList.getLength(); i++) {
            Node node = nodeList.item(i);
            if (node.getNodeName().equals("priority")) {
                priority = node.getFirstChild().getNodeValue();
            } else if (node.getNodeName().equals("description")) {
                description = node.getFirstChild().getNodeValue();
            }
        }

        // transfer properties to an XML document
        String xml = String.format(replyTemplate, description, priority,
                new Random().nextLong() * 1000, new Date());

        return new DomSourceFactory().createSource(xml);
    }
}
```

This Spring Integration example can be built and then deployed to a servlet container such as Tomcat or Jetty. To build the war, simply execute `mvn install`, and copy the resulting war file within the `target` directory to the servlet container's `webapps` directory.

Invoking Web Services Using an Outbound Gateway

Spring Integration has two outbound web services gateway implementations: `org.springframework.integration.ws.SimpleWebServiceOutboundGateway` and `org.springframework.integration.ws.MarshallingWebServiceOutboundGateway`. `SimpleWebServiceOutboundGateway` takes either a `String` or a `Source` an inbound message payload. `MarshallingWebServiceOutboundGateway` provides support for any implementation of the `Marshaller` and `Unmarshaller` interfaces. Both gateways require a Spring Web Services `org.springframework.ws.client.support.destination.DestinationProvider` for determining the URI of the web service to be invoked. Luckily, this will be handled behind the scenes using the Spring Integration `ws` namespace.

The Spring configuration file for the outbound web services gateway is shown in Listing 14–7. Note that a `property-placeholder` element is used to leverage the `client.properties` properties file shown in Listing 14–8. The gateway is configured using the `outbound-gateway` element. The gateway will respond to the message channel `ticketRequest`, which is set through the `request-channel` attribute. The outbound gateway requires that the URL for the web service endpoint be specified using the `url` attribute. In this example, the `reply-channel` attribute is not set. If the web service were to return a nonempty response, it would be returned to the request message's `REPLY_CHANNEL` header. A specific reply channel can be set using the `reply-channel` attribute.

***Listing 14–7.** Spring Configuration for Outbound Gateway client.xml*

```
<?xml version="1.0" encoding="UTF-8"?>
<beans xmlns="http://www.springframework.org/schema/beans"
       xmlns:xsi="http://www.w3.org/2001/XMLSchema-instance"
       xmlns:ws="http://www.springframework.org/schema/integration/ws"
       xmlns:int="http://www.springframework.org/schema/integration"
       xmlns:context="http://www.springframework.org/schema/context"
       xsi:schemaLocation="http://www.springframework.org/schema/beans
    http://www.springframework.org/schema/beans/spring-beans-3.0.xsd
    http://www.springframework.org/schema/context
    http://www.springframework.org/schema/context/spring-context-3.0.xsd
    http://www.springframework.org/schema/integration
    http://www.springframework.org/schema/integration/spring-integration-2.0.xsd
    http://www.springframework.org/schema/integration/ws
    http://www.springframework.org/schema/integration/ws/spring-integration-ws-2.0.xsd">

  <context:property-placeholder location="client.properties"/>

  <int:channel id="ticketRequests"/>

  <ws:outbound-gateway id="ticketIssueGateway" request-channel="ticketRequests"
                       uri="http://${ws.host}:${ws.port}/${ws.context}/ticketservice/➥
tickets"/>


</beans>
```

Listing 14–8. Client Properties File client.properties

```
ws.host=127.0.0.1
ws.port=8080
ws.context=ticket-service-gateway-1.0
```

To construct an XML request message, either create a DOMSource instance or simply create a string representation of the XML structure. This example uses the latter approach, since is requires less code, and the XML request payload is rather short. The XML document is created to conform to the previous Ticket.xsd schema. The XML message is sent as a message payload to the ticketRequest message channel. The response message payload is logged to the console (Listing 14–9).

Listing 14–9. Client for Invoking Standard Web Services Endpoints

```
package com.apress.prospringintegration.webservice.client;

import com.apress.prospringintegration.webservice.CommonConfiguration;
import org.springframework.context.support.ClassPathXmlApplicationContext;
import org.springframework.integration.Message;
import org.springframework.integration.MessageChannel;
import org.springframework.integration.core.MessagingTemplate;
import org.springframework.integration.support.MessageBuilder;

public class TicketWebServiceDomClient {
    private static String bodyTemplate =
            "<TicketRequest xmlns=\"" + CommonConfiguration.NAMESPACE + "\">" +
                    "<description>%s</description>" +
                    "<priority>%s</priority>" +
                    "</TicketRequest>";

    public static void main(String[] args) throws Exception {
        ClassPathXmlApplicationContext context =
                new ClassPathXmlApplicationContext("client.xml");

        MessageChannel channel = context.getBean("ticketRequests", MessageChannel.class);

        String body = String.format(bodyTemplate, "Message Broker Down", "emergency");
        System.out.println(body);
        MessagingTemplate messagingTemplate = new MessagingTemplate();
        Message<?> message = messagingTemplate.sendAndReceive(
                channel, MessageBuilder.withPayload(body).build());

        System.out.println(message.getPayload());

    }

}
```

The results of running the web services gateway example are shown in Listing 14–10. The request XML message is shown, followed by the response message. Note the addition of the ticket ID and issue date time.

Listing 14–10. Results of Running the Web Services Gateway Example

```
<TicketRequest xmlns="http://prospringintegration.com/tk/schemas"><description>Message ➥
Broker Down</description><priority>emergency</priority></TicketRequest>
<?xml version="1.0" encoding="UTF-8"?><TicketResponse ➥
xmlns="http://prospringintegration.com/tk/schemas"><ticket><description>Message Broker ➥
Down</description><priority>emergency</priority><ticketId>-➥
7242698475708198496</ticketId><issueDateTime>Sun Feb 27 00:21:30 PST ➥
2011</issueDateTime></ticket></TicketResponse>
```

Web Services and XML Marshalling

Spring Integration supports supplying a marshaller and unmarshaller for the inbound and outbound web services gateways. This allows using domain objects instead of working directly with the XML documents. This technology is also known as *object/XML mapping (OXM)*. The marshalling library maps the domain object properties to the XML elements.

To implement gateway endpoints using XML marshalling, specify the `marshaller` and `unmarshaller` attributes on the `inbound-gateway` and `outbound-gateway`. Spring supports a variety of marshallers that leverage different XML-marshalling APIs, as shown in Table 14–1.

Table 14–1. Marshallers for Different XML-Marshalling APIs

API	Marshaller
JAXB 1.0	`org.springframework.oxm.jaxb.Jaxb1Marshaller`
JAXB 2.0	`org.springframework.oxm.jaxb.Jaxb2Marshaller`
Castor	`org.springframework.oxm.castor.CastorMarshaller`
XMLBeans	`org.springframework.oxm.xmlbeans.XmlBeansMarshaller`
JiBX	`org.springframework.oxm.jibx.JibxMarshaller`
XStream	`org.springframework.oxm.xstream.XStreamMarshaller`

In this example, we will use Castor (`www.castor.org`) as the marshaller. Using other XML marshalling APIs with Spring is very similar. Castor supports working from existing data models or generating the domain objects from the XML schema. For very simple cases, the mappings can be written by hand. However, since the web service contract is typically fixed by the XML schema, this will be the starting point for this example. First, the Castor Maven dependency must be added to the `pom.xml` file, as shown in Listing 14–11.

Listing 14–11. Castor Maven Dependency

```
<dependency>
  <groupId>org.codehaus.castor</groupId>
  <artifactId>castor-xml</artifactId>
  <version>1.3.1</version>
</dependency>
```

Castor provides a Maven plug-in that will generate the domain classes to support a marshaller between the object and XML representation. The Maven plug-in configuration is shown in Listing 14–12. The location of the XML schema and the target package name are configured for the plug-in.

Listing 14–12. *Castor Source Generation Plug-In pom.xml*

```
<build>
  <plugins>
    <plugin>
      <groupId>org.codehaus.mojo</groupId>
      <artifactId>castor-maven-plugin</artifactId>
      <version>2.0</version>
      <configuration>
        <schema>src/main/resources/Ticket.xsd</schema>
        <packaging>com.apress.prospringintegration.webservice.domain</packaging>
        <marshal>false</marshal>
      </configuration>
      <executions>
        <execution>
          <goals>
            <goal>generate</goal>
          </goals>
        </execution>
      </executions>
    </plugin>
  </plugins>
</build>
```

Castor has a number of options for specifying the mappings between the domain objects and the XML document. In this example, we will be using the descriptor class to define the mappings. The generated domain classes for the `TicketRequest` and `TicketResponse` are shown in Listings 14–13 and 14–14, respectively.

Listing 14–13. *TicketRequest Domain Class Created by Castor (Comments Removed for Brevity)*

```
package com.apress.prospringintegration.webservice.domain;

@SuppressWarnings("serial")
public class TicketRequest implements java.io.Serializable {
    private java.lang.String _description;
    private com.apress.prospringintegration.webservice.domain.types.PriorityType _priority;

    public TicketRequest() {
        super();
    }

    public java.lang.String getDescription(
    ) {
        return this._description;
    }

    public com.apress.prospringintegration.webservice.domain.types.PriorityType getPriority(
    ) {
        return this._priority;
    }
```

```
    public void setDescription(
            final java.lang.String description) {
        this._description = description;
    }

    public void setPriority(
            final com.apress.prospringintegration.webservice.domain.types.PriorityType ➥
priority) {
        this._priority = priority;
    }

}
```

Listing 14–14. TicketResponse Domain Class Created by Castor (Comments Removed for Brevity)

```
package com.apress.prospringintegration.webservice.domain;

@SuppressWarnings("serial")
public class TicketResponse implements java.io.Serializable {

    private com.apress.prospringintegration.webservice.domain.Ticket _ticket;

    public TicketResponse() {
        super();
    }

    public com.apress.prospringintegration.webservice.domain.Ticket getTicket(
    ) {
        return this._ticket;
    }

    public void setTicket(
            final com.apress.prospringintegration.webservice.domain.Ticket ticket) {
        this._ticket = ticket;
    }

}
```

An example of a generated Castor descriptor class for the TicketResponse domain class is shown in Listing 14–15.

Listing 14–15. Example of a Castor Descriptor Class (Some Comments Removed for Brevity)

```
package com.apress.prospringintegration.webservice.domain.descriptors;

import com.apress.prospringintegration.webservice.domain.TicketResponse;

public class TicketResponseDescriptor extends org.exolab.castor.xml.util➥
.XMLClassDescriptorImpl {

    private boolean _elementDefinition;
    private java.lang.String _nsPrefix;
    private java.lang.String _nsURI;
```

```
    private java.lang.String _xmlName;
    private org.exolab.castor.xml.XMLFieldDescriptor _identity;

    public TicketResponseDescriptor() {
        super();
        _nsURI = "http://prospringintegration.com/tk/schemas";
        _xmlName = "TicketResponse";
        _elementDefinition = true;

        //-- set grouping compositor
        setCompositorAsSequence();
        org.exolab.castor.xml.util.XMLFieldDescriptorImpl desc = null;
        org.exolab.castor.mapping.FieldHandler handler = null;
        org.exolab.castor.xml.FieldValidator fieldValidator = null;
        //-- initialize attribute descriptors

        //-- initialize element descriptors

        //-- _ticket
        desc = new org.exolab.castor.xml.util.XMLFieldDescriptorImpl(
                com.apress.prospringintegration.webservice.domain.Ticket.class, "_ticket", ➥
"ticket",
                org.exolab.castor.xml.NodeType.Element);
        handler = new org.exolab.castor.xml.XMLFieldHandler() {
            @Override
            public java.lang.Object getValue(java.lang.Object object)
                    throws IllegalStateException {
                TicketResponse target = (TicketResponse) object;
                return target.getTicket();
            }

            @Override
            public void setValue(java.lang.Object object, java.lang.Object value)
                    throws IllegalStateException, IllegalArgumentException {
                try {
                    TicketResponse target = (TicketResponse) object;
                    target.setTicket((
                        com.apress.prospringintegration.webservice.domain.Ticket) value);
                } catch (java.lang.Exception ex) {
                    throw new IllegalStateException(ex.toString());
                }
            }

            @Override
            @SuppressWarnings("unused")
            public java.lang.Object newInstance(java.lang.Object parent) {
                return new com.apress.prospringintegration.webservice.domain.Ticket();
            }
        };
        desc.setSchemaType("com.apress.prospringintegration.webservice.domain.Ticket");
        desc.setHandler(handler);
        desc.setNameSpaceURI("http://prospringintegration.com/tk/schemas");
        desc.setRequired(true);
        desc.setMultivalued(false);
```

```
        addFieldDescriptor(desc);
        addSequenceElement(desc);

        //-- validation code for: _ticket
        fieldValidator = new org.exolab.castor.xml.FieldValidator();
        fieldValidator.setMinOccurs(1);
        { //-- local scope
        }
        desc.setValidator(fieldValidator);
    }

    @Override()
    public org.exolab.castor.mapping.AccessMode getAccessMode(
    ) {
        return null;
    }

    @Override()
    public org.exolab.castor.mapping.FieldDescriptor getIdentity(
    ) {
        return _identity;
    }

    @Override()
    public java.lang.Class getJavaClass(
    ) {
        return com.apress.prospringintegration.webservice.domain.TicketResponse.class;
    }

    @Override()
    public java.lang.String getNameSpacePrefix(
    ) {
        return _nsPrefix;
    }

    @Override()
    public java.lang.String getNameSpaceURI(
    ) {
        return _nsURI;
    }

    @Override()
    public org.exolab.castor.xml.TypeValidator getValidator(
    ) {
        return this;
    }

    @Override()
    public java.lang.String getXMLName(
    ) {
        return _xmlName;
    }

    public boolean isElementDefinition(
```

```
    ) {
        return _elementDefinition;
    }

}
```

With the domain objects and mappings created, the Spring Integration gateway can be configured to use Castor as the marshaller. The Spring configuration for the gateway example using Castor as the marshalling library is shown in Listing 14–16. This configuration is identical to the previous example, with the exception that a reference is added to the Castor marshaller using the `inbound-gateway` attributes `mashaller` and `unmarshaller`.

Listing 14–16. *Spring Configuration File for the Web Services Example Using Marshalling ticket-ws-servlet.xml*

```
<beans xmlns="http://www.springframework.org/schema/beans"
       xmlns:xsi="http://www.w3.org/2001/XMLSchema-instance"
       xmlns:int="http://www.springframework.org/schema/integration"
       xmlns:ws="http://www.springframework.org/schema/integration/ws"
       xmlns:context="http://www.springframework.org/schema/context"
       xsi:schemaLocation="http://www.springframework.org/schema/beans
    http://www.springframework.org/schema/beans/spring-beans-3.0.xsd
    http://www.springframework.org/schema/context
    http://www.springframework.org/schema/context/spring-context-3.0.xsd
    http://www.springframework.org/schema/integration/ws
    http://www.springframework.org/schema/integration/ws/spring-integration-ws-2.0.xsd
    http://www.springframework.org/schema/integration
    http://www.springframework.org/schema/integration/spring-integration-2.0.xsd">

  <context:component-scan
      base-package="com.apress.prospringintegration.webservice.web"/>
  <context:component-scan
      base-package="com.apress.prospringintegration.webservice.service"/>

  <int:channel id="inboundOXMTicketRequest"/>

  <ws:inbound-gateway id="wsInboundGateway"
                      request-channel="inboundOXMTicketRequest"
                      marshaller="castorMarshaller"
                      unmarshaller="castorMarshaller"/>

  <int:service-activator input-channel="inboundOXMTicketRequest"
                         ref="ticketIssuerMarshallingEndpoint"/>

</beans>
```

The Castor marshaller will be used to handle the marshalling and unmarshalling processes. The `org.springframework.oxm.castor.CastorMarshaller` reference is created using Java configuration, as shown in Listing 14–17. The key property for the inbound gateway is setting the `targetClass` property with the base domain object that needs to be parsed `TicketRequest`. Once Castor knows the base object, it will find the child domain objects and descriptor files needed for parsing and mapping the XML request.

Listing 14–17. Java Configuration for Creating a Castor Marshaller Instance

```
package com.apress.prospringintegration.webservice.web;

import com.apress.prospringintegration.webservice.domain.TicketRequest;
import org.springframework.context.annotation.Bean;
import org.springframework.context.annotation.Configuration;
import org.springframework.oxm.castor.CastorMarshaller;

@Configuration
public class CastorConfiguration {
    @Bean
    public CastorMarshaller castorMarshaller() {
        CastorMarshaller castorMarshaller = new CastorMarshaller();
        castorMarshaller.setTargetClass(TicketRequest.class);
        return castorMarshaller;
    }


}
```

The inbound gateway uses the Castor marshaller to obtain the `TicketRequest` instance and forwards the instance on as a message payload to the `inboundOXMTicketRequest` channel. The message is then picked up by the service activator shown in Listing 14–18. Note that the incoming message to the service activator is the `TicketRequest` instance. Because of the Castor marshaller, there is no need to parse any XML document.

Listing 14–18. Gateway Service Activator That Issues Tickets

```
package com.apress.prospringintegration.webservice.web;

import com.apress.prospringintegration.webservice.domain.Ticket;
import com.apress.prospringintegration.webservice.domain.TicketRequest;
import com.apress.prospringintegration.webservice.domain.TicketResponse;
import com.apress.prospringintegration.webservice.service.TicketIssuerService;
import org.springframework.beans.factory.annotation.Autowired;
import org.springframework.integration.annotation.ServiceActivator;
import org.springframework.stereotype.Component;

@Component
public class TicketIssuerMarshallingEndpoint {

    @Autowired
    private TicketIssuerService ticketIssuerService;

    @ServiceActivator
    public TicketResponse handleRequest(TicketRequest tr) throws Exception {
        System.out.println("TicketRequest: " + tr);
        TicketResponse ticketResponse = new TicketResponse();
        Ticket t = ticketIssuerService.issueTicket(tr.getDescription(),
                tr.getPriority().name());
        ticketResponse.setTicket(t);
        return ticketResponse;
    }
}
```

The ticketIssuerService component shown in Listing 14–19 is used to generate the ticket with a unique ID and issue data time. The service activator then returns a TicketResponse object back to the gateway, and it is forwarded back to the client.

***Listing 14–19.** Ticket Issuer Service Component*

```
package com.apress.prospringintegration.webservice.service;

import com.apress.prospringintegration.webservice.domain.Ticket;
import com.apress.prospringintegration.webservice.domain.types.PriorityType;
import org.springframework.stereotype.Component;

import java.util.Date;
import java.util.Random;

@Component
public class TicketIssuerService {
    public Ticket issueTicket(String description, String priority) throws Exception {
        Ticket ticket = new Ticket();
        ticket.setDescription(description);
        ticket.setPriority(PriorityType.valueOf(priority));
        ticket.setTicketId(new Random().nextLong() * 1000);
        ticket.setIssueDateTime(new Date());

        return ticket;
    }
}
```

WSDL Options

A WSDL is a service contract between the web services provider (server) and service requestor (client), and is primarily used for SOAP services. It is similar to the contract created by an interface for a Java class. Spring Web Services provides support for exposing a WSDL using an instance of org.springframework.ws.wsdl.wsdl11.DefaultWsdl11Definition. DefaultWsdl11Definition, which autogenerates the WSDL based an instance of org.springframework.xml.xsd.SimpleXsdSchema. In our example, SimpleXsdSchema is used to expose Ticket.xsd as source schema for WSDL generation, as shown in the Java configuration in Listing 14–20. org.springframework.ws.server.endpoint.mapping.PayloadRootQNameEndpointMapping is used to map the incoming request to the service endpoints. In addition, org.springframework.web.servlet.handler.SimpleUrlHandlerMapping is used to specifically expose the WSDL file through the URI /tickets.wsdl.

***Listing 14–20.** Generating a WSDL File Using an XML Schema*

```
package com.apress.prospringintegration.webservice.web;

import com.apress.prospringintegration.webservice.domain.TicketRequest;
import org.springframework.beans.factory.annotation.Value;
import org.springframework.context.annotation.Bean;
import org.springframework.context.annotation.Configuration;
import org.springframework.core.io.ClassPathResource;
import org.springframework.oxm.castor.CastorMarshaller;
import org.springframework.web.servlet.handler.SimpleUrlHandlerMapping;
```

```
import org.springframework.ws.server.EndpointInterceptor;
import org.springframework.ws.server.endpoint.MessageEndpoint;
import org.springframework.ws.server.endpoint.interceptor.PayloadLoggingInterceptor;
import org.springframework.ws.server.endpoint.mapping.PayloadRootQNameEndpointMapping;
import org.springframework.ws.soap.server.SoapMessageDispatcher;
import org.springframework.ws.wsdl.wsdl11.DefaultWsdl11Definition;
import org.springframework.xml.xsd.SimpleXsdSchema;
import org.springframework.xml.xsd.XsdSchema;

import java.util.HashMap;
import java.util.Map;
import java.util.Properties;

@SuppressWarnings("unused")
@Configuration
public class TicketIssuerServiceConfiguration {
    public static String NAMESPACE = "http://prospringintegration.com/tk/schemas";

    // the ws:inbound-gateway is in fact a reference to this base Spring WS object
    @Value("#{wsInboundGateway}")
    private MessageEndpoint wsInboundGateway;

    @Bean
    public XsdSchema schema() {
        SimpleXsdSchema xsdSchema = new SimpleXsdSchema();
        xsdSchema.setXsd(new ClassPathResource("Ticket.xsd"));
        return xsdSchema;
    }

    @Bean
    public DefaultWsdl11Definition tickets() throws Throwable {
        DefaultWsdl11Definition defaultWsdl11Definition =
                new DefaultWsdl11Definition();
        defaultWsdl11Definition.setSchema(schema());
        defaultWsdl11Definition.setPortTypeName("TicketRequest");
        defaultWsdl11Definition.setLocationUri("/tickets");
        defaultWsdl11Definition.setTargetNamespace(NAMESPACE);

        return defaultWsdl11Definition;
    }

    @Bean
    public PayloadRootQNameEndpointMapping payloadRootQNameEndpointMapping() {
        String fqn = String.format("{%s}%s", NAMESPACE, "TicketRequest");
        Map<String, MessageEndpoint> endpoints = new HashMap<String, MessageEndpoint>();
        endpoints.put(fqn, wsInboundGateway);
        PayloadRootQNameEndpointMapping payloadRootQNameEndpointMapping =
                new PayloadRootQNameEndpointMapping();
        payloadRootQNameEndpointMapping.setEndpointMap(endpoints);
        payloadRootQNameEndpointMapping.setInterceptors(
                new EndpointInterceptor[]{new PayloadLoggingInterceptor()});
        return payloadRootQNameEndpointMapping;
    }
```

```
    @Bean
    public SimpleUrlHandlerMapping simpleUrlHandlerMapping() {
        SimpleUrlHandlerMapping simpleHandlerMapping = new SimpleUrlHandlerMapping();
        simpleHandlerMapping.setDefaultHandler(soapMessageDispatcher());
        Properties urlMap = new Properties();
        urlMap.setProperty("*.wsdl", "tickets");
        simpleHandlerMapping.setMappings(urlMap);
        return simpleHandlerMapping;
    }

    @Bean
    public SoapMessageDispatcher soapMessageDispatcher() {
        return new SoapMessageDispatcher();
    }
}
```

To test the inbound web services gateway example using Castor marshalling, the `ticket-service-marshaller` project must be built and deployed to a servlet container such as Tomcat or Jetty. To build the war, simply execute `mvn install` and copy the resulting war file within the `target` directory to the servlet container's `webapps` directory. Use a browser and go to the URL `http://localhost:8080/ticket-service-marshalling-1.0/ticketservice/tickets.wsdl`. The WSDL shown in Listing 14–21 will appear, describing the inbound gateway endpoint. You can also use this WSDL to create a client using one of the WSDL-to-Java tools available from projects such as Axis, CXF, or XFire.

***Listing 14–21.** Ouput of WSDL Generation tickets.wsdl*

```
<?xml version="1.0" encoding="UTF-8" standalone="no"?>
<wsdl:definitions xmlns:wsdl="http://schemas.xmlsoap.org/wsdl/"
                  xmlns:sch="http://prospringintegration.com/tk/schemas"
                  xmlns:soap="http://schemas.xmlsoap.org/wsdl/soap/"
                  xmlns:tns="http://prospringintegration.com/tk/schemas"
                  targetNamespace="http://prospringintegration.com/tk/schemas">
  <wsdl:types>
    <xs:schema xmlns:xs="http://www.w3.org/2001/XMLSchema"
               attributeFormDefault="unqualified"
               elementFormDefault="qualified"
               targetNamespace="http://prospringintegration.com/tk/schemas"
               version="1.0">

      <xs:element name="TicketRequest">
        <xs:complexType>
          <xs:sequence>
            <xs:element name="description" type="xs:string"/>
            <xs:element name="priority" type="priorityType"/>
          </xs:sequence>

        </xs:complexType>
      </xs:element>

      <xs:element name="TicketResponse">
        <xs:complexType>
          <xs:sequence>
            <xs:element name="ticket" type="ticketType"/>
          </xs:sequence>
```

```
      </xs:complexType>

    </xs:element>

    <xs:complexType name="ticketType">
      <xs:sequence>
        <xs:element minOccurs="0" name="description" type="xs:string"/>
        <xs:element minOccurs="0" name="issueDateTime" type="xs:dateTime"/>
        <xs:element minOccurs="0" name="priority" type="priorityType"/>
        <xs:element name="ticketId" type="xs:long"/>
      </xs:sequence>

    </xs:complexType>

    <xs:simpleType name="priorityType">
      <xs:restriction base="xs:string">
        <xs:enumeration value="low"/>
        <xs:enumeration value="medium"/>
        <xs:enumeration value="high"/>
        <xs:enumeration value="emergency"/>
      </xs:restriction>

    </xs:simpleType>

  </xs:schema>
</wsdl:types>
<wsdl:message name="TicketRequest">
  <wsdl:part element="tns:TicketRequest" name="TicketRequest">
  </wsdl:part>
</wsdl:message>
<wsdl:message name="TicketResponse">
  <wsdl:part element="tns:TicketResponse" name="TicketResponse">

  </wsdl:part>
</wsdl:message>
<wsdl:portType name="TicketRequest">
  <wsdl:operation name="Ticket">
    <wsdl:input message="tns:TicketRequest" name="TicketRequest">
    </wsdl:input>
    <wsdl:output message="tns:TicketResponse" name="TicketResponse">
    </wsdl:output>
  </wsdl:operation>

</wsdl:portType>
<wsdl:binding name="TicketRequestSoap11" type="tns:TicketRequest">
  <soap:binding style="document"
                transport="http://schemas.xmlsoap.org/soap/http"/>
  <wsdl:operation name="Ticket">
    <soap:operation soapAction=""/>
    <wsdl:input name="TicketRequest">
      <soap:body use="literal"/>
    </wsdl:input>
    <wsdl:output name="TicketResponse">
```

```
        <soap:body use="literal"/>
      </wsdl:output>
    </wsdl:operation>
  </wsdl:binding>
  <wsdl:service name="TicketRequestService">
    <wsdl:port binding="tns:TicketRequestSoap11" name="TicketRequestSoap11">
      <soap:address
          location="http://localhost:8080/ticket-service-marshalling-1.0/tickets"/>
    </wsdl:port>
  </wsdl:service>

</wsdl:definitions>
```

Outbound Web Services Gateway with XML Marshalling

The Castor marshaller can also be used with the outbound web services gateway. This example will use the same domain and descriptor mapping classes from the inbound gateway example. Similar to the inbound-gateway configuration, the Castor marshaller is set through the marshaller and unmarshaller attributes of the outbound-gateway element, as shown in Listing 14–22.

Listing 14–22. *Spring Configuration for Gateway Client Using the Castor Marshaller client.xml*

```
<?xml version="1.0" encoding="UTF-8"?>
<beans xmlns="http://www.springframework.org/schema/beans"
       xmlns:xsi="http://www.w3.org/2001/XMLSchema-instance"
       xmlns:ws="http://www.springframework.org/schema/integration/ws"
       xmlns:int="http://www.springframework.org/schema/integration"
       xmlns:context="http://www.springframework.org/schema/context"
       xsi:schemaLocation="http://www.springframework.org/schema/beans
    http://www.springframework.org/schema/beans/spring-beans-3.0.xsd
    http://www.springframework.org/schema/context
    http://www.springframework.org/schema/context/spring-context-3.0.xsd
    http://www.springframework.org/schema/integration
    http://www.springframework.org/schema/integration/spring-integration-2.0.xsd
    http://www.springframework.org/schema/integration/ws
    http://www.springframework.org/schema/integration/ws/spring-integration-ws-2.0.xsd">

  <context:component-scan base-package="com.apress.prospringintegration.webservice.client"/>
  <context:property-placeholder location="client.properties"/>

  <int:channel id="ticketRequests"/>

  <ws:outbound-gateway id="ticketIssueGateway"
           request-channel="ticketRequests"
           uri="http://${ws.host}:${ws.port}/${ws.context}/ticketservice/tickets"
           marshaller="castorMarshaller" unmarshaller="castorMarshaller"/>
</beans>
```

The Java configuration for the Castor marshaller is shown in Listing 14–23. Since the TicketRequest instance is sent first to the marshaller, Castor is able to get the reference to this instance and the related domain and descriptor mapping classes.

Listing 14–23. Java Configuration for the Outbound Gateway Client Using the Castor Marshaller

```
package com.apress.prospringintegration.webservice.client;

import org.springframework.context.annotation.Bean;
import org.springframework.context.annotation.Configuration;
import org.springframework.core.io.ClassPathResource;
import org.springframework.oxm.castor.CastorMarshaller;

@Configuration
public class TicketWebServiceMarshallingConfiguration {
    @Bean
    public CastorMarshaller castorMarshaller() {
        CastorMarshaller castorMarshaller = new CastorMarshaller();
        return castorMarshaller;
    }
}
```

The client code is similar to the first outbound gateway example, as shown in Listing 14–24. However, in this case XML document isn't created by hand; instead, all the interaction with the gateway occurs through the domain objects.

Listing 14–24. Outbound Gateway Using the Castor Marshaller Client Class

```
package com.apress.prospringintegration.webservice.client;

import com.apress.prospringintegration.webservice.domain.Ticket;
import com.apress.prospringintegration.webservice.domain.TicketRequest;
import com.apress.prospringintegration.webservice.domain.TicketResponse;
import com.apress.prospringintegration.webservice.domain.types.PriorityType;
import org.springframework.context.support.ClassPathXmlApplicationContext;
import org.springframework.integration.Message;
import org.springframework.integration.MessageChannel;
import org.springframework.integration.core.MessagingTemplate;
import org.springframework.integration.support.MessageBuilder;
import org.springframework.stereotype.Component;

@Component
public class TicketWebServiceMarshallingClient {

    public static void main(String[] args) throws Exception {
        ClassPathXmlApplicationContext context =
                new ClassPathXmlApplicationContext("client.xml");

        MessageChannel channel =
                context.getBean("ticketRequests", MessageChannel.class);

        MessagingTemplate messagingTemplate = new MessagingTemplate();

        TicketRequest tr = new TicketRequest();
        tr.setDescription("Message Broker Down");
        tr.setPriority(PriorityType.EMERGENCY);
        System.out.printf("Ticket Request: %s [priority: %s] %n", tr.getDescription(),
                tr.getPriority());
```

```
        Message<TicketRequest> ticketRequestMessage =
                MessageBuilder.withPayload(tr).build();

        @SuppressWarnings("unchecked")
        Message<TicketResponse> message =
                (Message<TicketResponse>) messagingTemplate.sendAndReceive(
                        channel, ticketRequestMessage);

        Ticket ticket = message.getPayload().getTicket();
        System.out.printf("Ticket Response: %s [id: %d] [priority: %s] [date: %s]%n",
                ticket.getDescription(), ticket.getTicketId(),
                ticket.getPriority(), ticket.getIssueDateTime());

    }
}
```

The results of running the outbound gateway client code are shown in Listing 14–25. The TicketRequest object is created and sent to the outbound gateway. Castor marshalling handles parsing the XML. The gateway invokes the web service endpoint and returns the TicketResponse object with the new ticket issued.

Listing 14–25. *Web Services Gateway Example Results Using the Castor Marshaller*

```
Ticket Request: Message Broker Down [priority: emergency]
Ticket Response: Message Broker Down [id: 5433537107850368600] [priority: emergency] [date:↵
Sun Feb 27 12:18:01 PST 2011]
```

Summary

Spring Integration provides two components for supporting web services: invoking a web service by sending a message to a channel using an outbound web service gateway and sending a message to a channel upon receiving a web service invocation using an inbound web service gateway. Both the inbound and outbound gateways include support for adding an XML marshaller. We have covered how Spring Integration provides both client and server support for web services and how to integrate web services with the Spring Integration messaging framework. We used the Castor project as an example of providing a marshaller for the Spring Integration gateways, and we explored how to use the Spring Web Services project to expose a WSDL providing a full description of the web service endpoints.

CHAPTER 15

Extending Spring Integration

The Spring Integration framework provides an extensive toolbox for integration problems. Spring Integration 2.0 ships with many new adapters, and lays the groundwork for many other adapters to come. The adapter support is also often very generic, providing support for a broad spectrum of concerns. For example, while the Twitter adapters speak specifically to Twitter and are considered very specific, the TCP/UDP support can speak to *any* system that speaks TCP or UDP, and the HTTP adapter can speak to *any* HTTP endpoint. In a sense, the TCP/UDP support is much broader than the HTTP support. If there is a problem that cannot be fixed with the HTTP support and feels like it can be tackled using raw TCP/UDP, then that is a viable route. In the other direction, Spring Integration also provides first-class support for SOAP-based web services, which can be thought of as a specialization of HTTP support. Spring Integration ships with SOAP support because SOAP as a protocol and specification exposes well-known request and response-specific payloads, and is used by many people. Wherever Spring Integration can provide specific, ready-to-use support for a system or protocol, it does. It is helpful to know that while some systems may lack specific support, there are more generic options.

On occasion, however, the Spring Integration toolbox may not have the tool that is needed or perhaps the task at hand is more readily addressed using higher-level abstractions. There are many reasons this might happen: perhaps the system that needs to be integrated with is proprietary to the business, or perhaps the system to be integrated with requires libraries whose license are incompatible with Spring Integration's Apache 2 license. Whenever this happens, the following approaches may be taken:

- *Check to see if the Spring Integration team is already working on it.* If this is an important endpoint, it is likely that it is already being worked on. Perhaps the support is already being checked into the Spring Integration sandbox, or the support is in the Spring Integration trunk, being prepared for the next release.
- *Check to see if somebody else in the community has already tackled the problem.* This is also very common. Google will often yield options, and as often as not some of these projects are mentioned in the Spring Integration forums.

If there is no existing solution, a custom adapter will be the answer. Even here, favor reuse or specialization of existing adapters where possible and convenient.

This chapter is about what to do when no solution already exists. Writing a custom adapter should be a decision made only as a last resort. Fortunately, Spring Integration makes it easy to do. If the support needed is something that can be of use to the community at large, consider filing a JIRA with the Spring Integration team, and maybe even donating your work. Often, writing adapters to support a specific scenario is as simple as wrapping an existing library, so it is very easy to provide valuable adapters with relative ease.

In this chapter, we will explore the support offered in the core Spring Integration framework to help you build your own adapters. Broadly, there are inbound and outbound adapters.

Inbound Adapters

An inbound adapter is a Spring Integration component that sits at the beginning of an integration flow. It receives messages from an external system and forwards them to components running in a Spring Integration framework flow, where it can be manipulated. One example of an inbound adapter shipped with the framework is the JMS inbound adapter support, which dequeues `javax.jms.Message` messages from a JMS destination and forwards them as Spring Integration messages. There are two types of inbound adapters: event-driven and polling adapters.

As discussed in Chapter 9, event-driven adapters produce messages as dictated by the events in an external system. Many systems meet this description. Some systems are naturally event-driven. These are characterized by their ability to "tell" Spring Integration when an event of interest has transpired. XMPP, which is the protocol underlying Google Talk and Facebook's chat mechanism, is event-driven. Spring Integration should be notified instantly whenever somebody sends an instant message.

Polling adapters, on the other hand, are used to talk to systems that don't have the ability to "tell" other systems about interesting events. They are also common. HTTP for example, is unidirectional: clients can ask HTTP servers questions, but servers cannot make requests of clients. Other examples of polling adapters that come with the framework are SFTP, FTP, and FTPS: a client must ask the server which files are newly available. "Polling" speaks to the requirement of these adapters to query the remote system on a schedule. Spring Integration provides support for CRON expression-based, interval-based, and fixed rate-based scheduling.

Many systems provide both polling- and event-driven-based support. JMS destinations on a JMS message broker can be queried manually, or can register a `MessageListenerContainer`, which is notified of messages instantly. For this reason, Spring Integration ships with both a polling adapter - `<jms:inbound-channel-adapter>` and an event-driven alternative called `<jms:message-driven-channel-adapter>` that uses a `MessageListenerContainer`. Another example is email. Email requires several protocols: two for receiving messages. POP3 is an older standard that requires clients to query (hence, *poll*) it for new email messages. There is a Spring Integration adapter for POP3-based message receipt, `<mail:inbound-channel-adapter>`, that requires a poller to be configured. IMAP-IDLE is a newer standard in which email messages are delivered to clients (hence, they are *pushed*, or event-driven). It is not surprising then that there is also a Spring Integration adapter for IMAP-IDLE – `<mail:imap-idle-channel-adapter>` – which can "push" messages to clients and does not need a poller to be configured.

When messages arrive, they typically have a payload that is specific to the eternal system. The file-system adapters produce `java.io.File` payloads, for example, and have specific message headers that provide details that the payload itself doesn't convey, or at least that the payload doesn't expose on the surface. Often, adapters also come with transformer implementations that can be used to transform input payloads into other, common payload types for subsequent consumption by other components. An example of this is various transformers that come with the file adapters for transforming `java.io.File` objects to `java.lang.Strings`, or `byte[]` arrays.

Writing an Event-Driven Adapter

An event-driven inbound adapter is the least ceremonious of the three types of adapters (inbound event-driven, inbound poller-driven, and outbound). The recipe is simple: acquire a reference to a `MessageChannel` and send a `Message` on it when some event in your system dictates that it should. At what time or rate the message is sent is up to the developer. Listing 15–1 shows a basic, skeletal inbound adapter that only sends one message, at startup. As can be seen, there is no particular API requirement.

Listing 15–1. Basic Inbound Adapter

```
package com.apress.prospringintegration.customadapters.inbound.eventdriven;

import org.springframework.beans.factory.InitializingBean;
import org.springframework.integration.Message;
import org.springframework.integration.MessageChannel;
import org.springframework.integration.core.MessagingTemplate;
import org.springframework.integration.support.MessageBuilder;

public class BasicEventDrivenInboundChannelAdapter implements InitializingBean {

    private MessagingTemplate template = new MessagingTemplate();

    private MessageChannel channel;

    public void setChannel(MessageChannel channel) {
        this.channel = channel;
    }

    @Override
    public void afterPropertiesSet() throws Exception {

        Message<?> msg = MessageBuilder.withPayload("hello, world!").build();
        this.template.send(this.channel, msg);
    }
}
```

This example does not particularly integrate with any other system; therefore, it has no "events" to create messages for. If there were events, then simply create a Spring Integration `Message` and send them through the `channel` when the adapter was notified of those events. In the example, the `MessagingTemplate` is leveraged. Though this example is simple, it is still a bit overdrawn by Spring Integration standards. Spring Integration provides an abstract class called `MessageProducerSupport`. The `MessageProducerSupport` class provides the `doStart()` lifecycle method as a convenient place to launch whatever listeners or loops are required to receive events from an external system. The class also provides a convenience method – `sendMessage(Message<?> msg)` – which negates the need for the `MessageChannel` and `MessagingTemplate` instance variables in the first example. The previous example rewritten to use `MessageProducerSupport` is shown in Listing 15–2.

Listing 15–2. Example using MessageProducerSupport

```
package com.apress.prospringintegration.customadapters.inbound.eventdriven;

import org.springframework.integration.Message;
import org.springframework.integration.endpoint.MessageProducerSupport;
import org.springframework.integration.support.MessageBuilder;

public class MessageProducerSupportEventDrivenInboundChannelAdapter
        extends MessageProducerSupport {

    @Override
    protected void doStart() {
        Message<?> msg = MessageBuilder.withPayload("hello, world!").build();
```

```
            this.sendMessage(msg);
        }
}
```

This is much cleaner and simpler – almost *too* simple.

Now that you understand the moving parts, let's build something more interesting. Spring Integration ships with an adapter for receiving events whenever a new file appears in a directory: the `<file:inbound-channel-adapter>` adapter. It is a polling adapter that runs on a timed loop and checks for new files in a given directory. It uses the `java.io.File` class in the JDK to list the files in a directory and then calculate the difference between the current listing and the listing from the previous run. Any "new" files are sent as Messages into Spring Integration.

Problems with the Adapter

This adapter works well, in a cross-platform manner. However, there are some caveats.

- First, because the scans occur on a schedule, it's possible for `java.io.File.listFiles` to pick up files that are not fully written. That is, if a process starts writing a terabyte file, and the scan is set to run every 10 seconds, it is possible that the file will not be fully written to the directory by the time the scan starts anew. A file that is not fully written will be delivered as a `Message`.
- Second, because the scans are scheduled, care must be taken to pick a frequency frequent enough to be effective, but to not overburden the system.

The first problem – having files that are not 100% written delivered as new files – has some well-known workarounds. A common approach is to have the inbound file adapter match (and only deliver) files that match a certain pattern (a "glob"). The process writing the file writes to a file whose name will not be picked up by the glob. Once the write is 100% complete, the process writing the file simply renames it to match the pattern expected by the inbound file adapter. However, this assumes that the writing process can be made to comply – something that cannot take for granted in the world of business-to-business integrations.

The second problem – of overly or under aggressive scanning cycles – has no workaround. The cycle simply has to be calibrated painstakingly to find a value appropriate to your application.

These problems are usually not insurmountable, but they betray an underlying problem: sometimes the JDK doesn't offer a better solution. Sometimes the facilities in external systems must be taken advantage of and used in Spring Integration. In the case of file detection, these limitations can be overcome by tapping into the facilities exposed by the underlying operating system. Many operating systems (Windows, Solaris, OS X, BSD, and Linux for example) offer APIs that can notify clients when new files appear in a directory. These APIs vary wildly from operating system to operating system. On Windows there exists a COM object (that is also exposed through .NET) that can be used, though it requires understanding of the nuances of COM threading. On BSD and OS X there exists KQueue, which is one way of solving the problem. On OS X, however, there are other APIs that are said to supersede the KQueue functionality. On Linux, there is the inotify kernel module.

Finally, it should be noted that JDK 7 (the NIO2 specification) is supposed to provide a solution for this problem. When it ships and is available in our environment over the next few years, we can switch to that. For now, we will simply leverage the operating system primitives to support our use case. The `inotify` API on Linux is the easiest to use and more likely than not you are going to be deploying to a Linux machine for your server environment. So for this example, we will demonstrate talking to Linux's inotify APIs to support receiving file notifications of new files in an event-oriented way. `Inotify` will solve both problems enumerated before: it only raises events when the file's entirely written, and it relieves the consumer of the burden of blindly scanning directories for changes.

Writing the Java Side

The functionality we are going to build is useful, and there is no reason to build it in terms of the Spring Integration framework. Let's build it as a standalone piece of functionality and then simply wrap it in Spring Integration. Thus, by definition, this will be pluggable. After all, in the future it may be desirable to support other operating systems and retrofit this functionality when JDK 7 ships. Either way, it will not hurt to provide a bit of interface indirection in the name of flexibility. Listing 15–3 shows the interface we will work with.

***Listing 15–3.** File Adapter Interface*

```
package com.apress.prospringintegration.customadapters.inbound.eventdriven.fsmon;

import java.io.File;

public interface DirectoryMonitor {

    void monitor(File file, FileAddedListener fal);

    interface FileAddedListener {

        void fileAdded(File dir, String fn);
    }
}
```

So, a `DirectoryMonitor` can be asked to monitor a directory (of type `java.io.File`) and will notify an instance of `FileAddedListener` when a file is added to a directory. The callback will have the directory in which the file appeared, and the name of the file, inside the directory.

The code will be required to connect the C code to some Java code. `Inotify` will be used to register a watch on a directory from Java. When the `inotify` watch "sees" a new file, the C code needs to tell the running Java code that the file has appeared. The Java Native Interface (JNI) will be used to both to initiate the watch from Java, and to talk to the Java code from the C code.

To tell the Java runtime that a method is to be handled by native code, the method prototype must be preceded with `native`, and then omit the body, very much like an abstract method. Code will be written that registers the `inotify` watch a native method. Finally, a well known method will be needed that the JNI code can use to call back into the executing Java code.

Listing 15–4 shows the Java class that will be used to implement `DirectoryMonitor`, and to provide the hooks for our native code integration.

***Listing 15–4.** DirectorMonitor Implementation Class for Linux*

```
package com.apress.prospringintegration.customadapters.inbound.eventdriven.fsmon;

import org.apache.commons.lang.exception.ExceptionUtils;
import org.apache.log4j.Logger;
import org.springframework.beans.factory.InitializingBean;
import org.springframework.util.Assert;

import java.io.File;
import java.util.Map;
import java.util.concurrent.ConcurrentHashMap;
import java.util.concurrent.Executor;
import java.util.concurrent.Executors;
```

```
public class LinuxInotifyDirectoryMonitor implements InitializingBean, DirectoryMonitor {
    private static Logger logger = Logger.getLogger(LinuxInotifyDirectoryMonitor.class);

    static {
        try {
            System.loadLibrary("sifsmon");
        } catch (Throwable t) {
            logger.error("Received exception " + ExceptionUtils.getFullStackTrace(t)
                    + " when trying to load the native library sifsmon");
        }
    }

    private volatile Executor executor;

    private Map<String, File> mapOfDirectoriesUnderMonitor =
            new ConcurrentHashMap<String, File>();

    private volatile ConcurrentHashMap<File, FileAddedListener> monitors =
            new ConcurrentHashMap<File, FileAddedListener>();

    private boolean autoCreateDirectory = true;

    protected boolean exists(File dir) {
        boolean goodDirToMonitor = (dir.isDirectory() && dir.exists());

        Assert.notNull(dir, "the 'dir' parameter must not be null");

        if (!goodDirToMonitor) {
            if (!dir.exists()) {
                if (this.autoCreateDirectory) {
                    if (!dir.mkdirs()) {
                        logger.debug(String.format("couldn't create directory %s",
                                dir.getAbsolutePath()));
                    }
                }
            }
        }

        Assert.state(dir.exists(), "the directory " + dir.getAbsolutePath()
                + " doesn't exist");

        return dir.exists();
    }

    public void fileReceived(String dir, String fileName) {
        File dirFile = mapOfDirectoriesUnderMonitor.get(dir);
        this.monitors.get(dirFile).fileAdded(dirFile, fileName);
    }

    @Override
    public void monitor(final File dir, final FileAddedListener fal) {
        if (exists(dir)) {
            mapOfDirectoriesUnderMonitor.put(dir.getAbsolutePath(), dir);
```

```
            monitors.putIfAbsent(dir, fal);
            executor.execute(new Runnable() {
                @Override
                public void run() {
                    monitor(dir.getAbsolutePath());
                }
            });
        }
    }

    native void monitor(String path);

    public void setExecutor(Executor executor) {
        this.executor = executor;
    }

    @Override
    public void afterPropertiesSet() throws Exception {
        if (this.executor == null) {
            this.executor = Executors.newFixedThreadPool(10);
        }
    }
}
```

Most of the code is pretty straightforward. InitializingBean is implemented to take advantage of the lifecycle hook to set up an executor.

At the top of the class is a static block to load a system library (on a Windows machine this is a .dll file; on Linux, a .so; on OS X, a .dylib, and so on). The String passed in to System.loadLibrary does not directly describe a library: the JVM has heuristics for discovering which library to load is based on the String. On Linux, given a parameter of sifsmon, the system will attempt to load libsifsmon.so. The JVM will look in the standard library path for your particular operating system (on Linux or Unix-based systems [Unixen], you can see what this is by echoing the shell variable, $LD_PATH). The directories to search may be specified with the JVM java.library.path system property. The JVM will consult those directories as it is looking for libraries.

It keeps a cache of which directories are monitored and which FileAddedListener to callback. It has two implementations of the monitor method: one that satisfies the interface requirement and in turn calls another monitor method, which takes a single String argument; and one that is a native method, and so lacks a body. The body will be implemented by native code.

When the interface version of monitor is called, it submits the invocation of the native monitor method to a java.util.concurrent.Executor implementation because the native code never returns. The method fileReceived expects two String parameters: the directory in which the event occurred and the name of the file that was detected. It is expected that the native code will invoke this method when it detects a file has appeared. Inside the method, a mapping of directories to FileAddedListener instances is consulted and then the FileAddedListener's fileAdded method is invoked, passing in the newly discovered file.

■ **Designing for Interop** Plain Strings are used as parameters for both the native method `monitor` and for the `fileReceived` method because it is easier to work with the core types (the primitive types, `java.lang.Object`, and `java.lang.String`) from JNI. If simple types can be used avoiding a complex Java object, do so. In this case, inotify expects an array of characters (a `char*`, or an array of chars, is *roughly* the C analog of a `java.lang.String`) representing a filesystem path when the monitor method is called. Similarly, it is easier to send a `char*` out from native code and back into the JVM as `java.lang.String`, so the `fileReceived` expects the simplest parameters possible.

Writing the Native Side

Next, let's look at the native code itself. Most of the native code is ceremonial JNI macro definitions. To obtain the correct definitions and stubs for the implementation of our native monitor method, use the `javah` command. Run `javah` in the following in the directory containing the `.class` file for the `LinuxInotifyDirectoryMonitor` as shown here.

```
javah -classpath . com.apress.prospringintegration.customadapters.inbound.➥
eventdriven.fsmon.LinuxInotifyDirectoryMonitor
```

This will write out C implementation and header files that can be used as the seed of the native code implementation. In the interest of expediency, a separate header file is not used. All the code is simply inline the whole thing into one code page file `fsmon.c`. The implementation is shown in Listing 15–5.

***Listing 15–5.** Native Code Implementation fsmon.c*

```
#include <jni.h>
#include <stdio.h>
#include <stdlib.h>
#include <errno.h>
#include <sys/types.h>
#include <sys/inotify.h>
#include <malloc.h>

#define EVENT_SIZE  ( sizeof (struct inotify_event) )
#define BUF_LEN     ( 1024 * ( EVENT_SIZE + 16 ) )

#ifndef _Included_com_apress_prospringintegration_customadapters_inbound_eventdriven➥
_fsmon_LinuxInotifyDirectoryMonitor
#define _Included_com_apress_prospringintegration_customadapters_inbound_eventdriven➥
_fsmon_LinuxInotifyDirectoryMonitor
#ifdef __cplusplus
extern "C" {
#endif

JNIEXPORT void JNICALL Java_com_apress_prospringintegration_customadapters_inbound➥
_eventdriven_fsmon_LinuxInotifyDirectoryMonitor_monitor(JNIEnv * env, jobject obj,➥
 jstring javaSpecifiedPath) {
```

```
int fd = inotify_init();
if ( fd < 0 ) {
 perror( "inotify_init" );
}

// variable extraction
char * path = (char *)(*env)->GetStringUTFChars( env, javaSpecifiedPath , NULL ) ;

// java reflection to obtain a reference to the fileReceived method in the currently➥
 running java object
jclass cls = ( *env)->GetObjectClass(env, obj);
jmethodID mid = (*env)->GetMethodID(env, cls, "fileReceived", "(Ljava/lang/String;➥
Ljava/lang/String;)V");
if( mid == 0 ) {
  printf( "method callback is not valid!") ;
  return ;
}

// setup inotify
int wd = inotify_add_watch( fd, path,  IN_MOVED_TO| IN_CLOSE_WRITE );
while( 1 > 0 ){
        int length = 0;
        int i = 0;
        char buffer[BUF_LEN];
        length = read( fd, buffer, BUF_LEN );

        if ( length < 0 ) {
          perror( "read" );
        }

        while ( i < length ) {
          struct inotify_event *event = ( struct inotify_event * ) &buffer[ i ];
          if ( event->len ) {
                if ( event->mask & IN_CLOSE_WRITE || event->mask & IN_MOVED_TO ) {
                  char *name = event->name;
                  const int mlen = event->len;
                  char nc[mlen];
                  int indx;
                  for(indx=0; indx < event->len; indx++) {
                    char c  =(char) name[indx];
                    nc[indx]=c;
                  }
                  jstring jpath = (*env)->NewStringUTF( env, (const char*) nc  );
                  (*env)->CallVoidMethod(env, obj, mid, javaSpecifiedPath, jpath );
                        }
          }
          i += EVENT_SIZE + event->len;
        }
}
( void ) inotify_rm_watch( fd, wd );
( void ) close( fd );

}
```

```
#ifdef __cplusplus
}
#endif
#endif
```

The following simple shell script may be used to build the native code on Linux:

```
# we need to make sure we have the Linux JNI headers from the JDK
export JDK_INCLUDE_DIR="$JAVA_HOME/include";

# make sure we delete the existing one
touch libsifsmon.so; rm libsifsmon.so;

# build the new one
gcc  -o libsifsmon.so -shared  -fPIC -I$JDK_INCLUDE_DIR -I$JDK_INCLUDE_DIR/linux fsmon.c -lc;
```

Using the Directory Monitor

This completes the native library. The directory monitor class can now be used in a stand-alone client, as shown in Listing 15–6.

Listing 15–6. *Directory Monitor Client Class*

```
package com.apress.prospringintegration.customadapters.inbound.eventdriven.fsmon;

import org.apache.commons.lang.SystemUtils;

import java.io.File;
import java.util.concurrent.Executor;
import java.util.concurrent.Executors;

public class DirectoryMonitorClient {
    public static void main(String[] args) throws Throwable {
        File[] files = {
                new File(new File(SystemUtils.getUserHome(), "Desktop"), "test2"),
                new File(new File(SystemUtils.getUserHome(), "Desktop"), "test1")};

        Executor ex = Executors.newFixedThreadPool(10);

        final LinuxInotifyDirectoryMonitor monitor = new LinuxInotifyDirectoryMonitor();
        monitor.setExecutor(ex);
        monitor.afterPropertiesSet();

        final DirectoryMonitor.FileAddedListener fileAddedListener =
                new DirectoryMonitor.FileAddedListener() {
                    @Override
                    public void fileAdded(File dir, String fn) {
                        System.out.println("A new file in " + dir.getAbsolutePath()
                                + " called " + fn + " has been noticed");
                    }
                };

        for (File f : files) {
```

```
            monitor.monitor(f, fileAddedListener);
        }
    }
}
```

The majority of this section has been about achieving the integration with a third-party API. Once the integration is achieved, or an existing one is understood, it is very easy to build a Spring Integration adapter that wraps the integration, as shown in Listing 15–7.

Listing 15–7. Directory Monitor Inbound File Adapter

```
package com.apress.prospringintegration.customadapters.inbound.eventdriven;

package com.apress.prospringintegration.customadapters.inbound.eventdriven;

import com.apress.prospringintegration.customadapters.inbound.eventdriven.fsmon.*;
import org.apache.commons.lang.SystemUtils;
import org.springframework.integration.Message;
import org.springframework.integration.endpoint.MessageProducerSupport;
import org.springframework.integration.file.FileHeaders;
import org.springframework.integration.support.MessageBuilder;
import org.springframework.util.Assert;

import java.io.File;
import java.util.concurrent.Executor;

public class DirectoryMonitorInboundFileEndpoint extends MessageProducerSupport {

    private File directoryToMonitor;
    private DirectoryMonitor monitor;
    private Executor executor;
    private int queueSize = 10;

    @Override
    protected void onInit() {
        try {
            if (SystemUtils.IS_OS_LINUX) {
                LinuxInotifyDirectoryMonitor mon = new LinuxInotifyDirectoryMonitor();
                if (executor != null) {
                    mon.setExecutor(executor);
                }
                mon.afterPropertiesSet();
                this.monitor = mon;
            }
        } catch (Exception e) {
            throw new RuntimeException("Exception thrown when trying to setup "
                    + DirectoryMonitorInboundFileEndpoint.class, e);
        }
    }

    @Override
    protected void doStart() {
        Assert.notNull(monitor, "the monitor can't be null");
        MessageProducingFileAddedListener messageProducingFileAddedListener =
```

```
                new MessageProducingFileAddedListener();
        monitor.monitor(directoryToMonitor, messageProducingFileAddedListener);
    }

    @Override
    protected void doStop() {
    }

    public void setDirectoryToMonitor(File directoryToMonitor) {
        this.directoryToMonitor = directoryToMonitor;
    }

    class MessageProducingFileAddedListener
            implements DirectoryMonitor.FileAddedListener {
        @Override
        public void fileAdded(File dir, String fn) {
            File fi = new File(dir, fn);
            Message<File> msg =
                    MessageBuilder.withPayload(fi).setHeader(
                            FileHeaders.FILENAME, fi.getPath()).build();
            sendMessage(msg);
        }
    }
}
```

This `DirectoryMonitorInboundFileEndpoint` class follows the form outlined at the beginning of this section: it extends the `MessageProdUcerSupport` class and uses the lifecycle hooks to set up the integration. The class reuses the `DirectoryMonitor` hierarchy described previously.

An inner class – `MessageProducingFileAddedListener` – receives notifications from the directory configured on the monitor and forwards the events as Spring Integration `Messages` with a header containing the file name. The header value is stored under the same key as the file name is stored when using the default Spring Integration `<file:inbound-channel-adapter>`. This implementation is already a drop-in replacement for many integration flows using the default file inbound channel adapter as the payload and one of the more visible, important headers keys and values are the same.

Using this adapter is as simple as instantiating the bean, and providing it with a reference to an output channel. In the example configuration file in Listing 15–8, the adapter and a service-activator is configured to simply print out the messages as files are detected.

Listing 15–8. *Spring Configuration for Custom File Adapter*

```
<?xml version="1.0" encoding="UTF-8"?>
<beans xmlns="http://www.springframework.org/schema/beans"
       xmlns:xsi="http://www.w3.org/2001/XMLSchema-instance"
       xmlns:int="http://www.springframework.org/schema/integration"
       xmlns:context="http://www.springframework.org/schema/context"
       xsi:schemaLocation="http://www.springframework.org/schema/beans
    http://www.springframework.org/schema/beans/spring-beans-3.0.xsd
    http://www.springframework.org/schema/integration
    http://www.springframework.org/schema/integration/spring-integration.xsd
    http://www.springframework.org/schema/context
    http://www.springframework.org/schema/context/spring-context-3.0.xsd">

  <context:property-placeholder location="test.properties"/>
```

```
  <bean class="com.apress.prospringintegration.customadapters.inbound.
              eventdriven.DirectoryMonitorInboundFileEndpoint">
    <property name="outputChannel" ref="fileChannel"/>
    <property name="directoryToMonitor" value="/home/${user.name}/Desktop/a"/>
  </bean>

  <bean id="loggingServiceActivator"
        class="com.apress.prospringintegration.customadapters.LoggingServiceActivator"/>

  <int:channel id="fileChannel"/>

  <int:service-activator ref="loggingServiceActivator" input-channel="fileChannel"/>

</beans>
```

Writing a Polling Adapter

Polling adapters are responsible for delivering one message when asked, whenever asked. There is much that has to happen to make a polling adapter work correctly. The first requirement in Spring Integration is the configuration of a *poller*, unsurprisingly. Pollers tell Spring Integration that the component on which they are configured should be re-queried according to the schedule dictated by the poller. A poller might query at a fixed-interval, fixed-rate, or according to a CRON expression. Configuring a query and wiring it up requires a lot of machinery that you would not want to write for every custom polling adapter.

Spring Integration makes it easy. First, an adapter writer must write a class that implements the `org.springframework.integration.core.MessageSource` interface. This interface has only one method:

```
Message<T> receive()
```

This method speaks for itself: it's expecting a Spring Integration message as its return value. Spring Integration provides the `inbound-channel-adapter>` element to take a bean that implements the `MessageSource` interface and wire it up to a channel and a poller. Suppose you had a bean that implemented `MessageSourcce` with the id `myMessageSource`. In Listing 15–9, the bean is not shown, but presumably it has been configured in a Java configuration class, or picked up by component scanning. To wire it up with a poller and a channel, you'd configure an XML file as shown here.

Listing 15–9. *Polling Adapter Configuration Example*

```
<?xml version="1.0" encoding="UTF-8"?>
<beans xmlns="http://www.springframework.org/schema/beans"
       xmlns:xsi="http://www.w3.org/2001/XMLSchema-instance"
       xmlns:int="http://www.springframework.org/schema/integration"
       xmlns:context="http://www.springframework.org/schema/context"
       xsi:schemaLocation="http://www.springframework.org/schema/beans
    http://www.springframework.org/schema/beans/spring-beans-3.0.xsd
    http://www.springframework.org/schema/integration
    http://www.springframework.org/schema/integration/spring-integration.xsd
    http://www.springframework.org/schema/context
    http://www.springframework.org/schema/context/spring-context-3.0.xsd">

  <context:component-scan
      base-package="com.apress.prospringintegration.customadapters.inbound.pollerdriven"/>
```

```
  <int:channel id="inbound"/>

  <int:inbound-channel-adapter ref="myMessageSource"
                               channel="inbbound">
    <int:poller cron="*/10 * * * * *"/>
  </int:inbound-channel-adapter>

</beans>
```

Let's build a more sophisticated example. Polling adapters are frequently used to provide a way to query a system and feed the results into a Spring Integration flow. They can be use for times where the process needs to be notified of events, but the system has no way of notifying process by itself.

In the next example an adapter for a stock service will be created that will notify us of a stock symbol's current price. This example will resort to old-fashioned screen scraping built on top of the Spring framework's `RestTemplate` class, which provides excellent support for interacting with HTTP-based resources. The adapter code is shown in Listing 15–10.

Listing 15–10. *Polling Adapter Example*

```
package com.apress.prospringintegration.customadapters.inbound.pollerdriven;

import org.apache.commons.io.IOUtils;
import org.springframework.beans.factory.InitializingBean;
import org.springframework.http.HttpMethod;
import org.springframework.http.client.ClientHttpResponse;
import org.springframework.integration.Message;
import org.springframework.integration.core.MessageSource;
import org.springframework.integration.support.MessageBuilder;
import org.springframework.web.client.ResponseExtractor;
import org.springframework.web.client.RestTemplate;

import java.io.IOException;
import java.util.regex.Matcher;
import java.util.regex.Pattern;

public class StockPollingMessageSource implements MessageSource<Stock>, InitializingBean {
    private String tickerSymbol;
    private String jsonFragmentTemplate = "u:\"/finance?q=NYSE:%s\",name:\"%s\"";
    private String stockServiceUrl = "http://www.google.com/finance?q=NYSE:%s";
    private RestTemplate restTemplate = new RestTemplate();
    private Pattern symbolSize = Pattern.compile(",p:\"(\\d+)\\.(\\d+)\"");

    protected Stock getStockInformationFor(final String symbol) {
        String url = String.format(this.stockServiceUrl, symbol);
        Stock stock = restTemplate.execute(url, HttpMethod.GET, null,
                new ResponseExtractor<Stock>() {
                    @Override
                    public Stock extractData(ClientHttpResponse clientHttpResponse)
                            throws IOException {
                        String fragPattern =
                                String.format(jsonFragmentTemplate, symbol, symbol);
                        String bodyAsText = IOUtils.toString(clientHttpResponse.getBody());
```

```
                    int indexOfMatch = bodyAsText.indexOf(fragPattern);

                    if (indexOfMatch != -1) {
                        String sectionContainingPrice =
                                bodyAsText.substring(indexOfMatch);
                        Matcher matcher = symbolSize.matcher(sectionContainingPrice);

                        StringBuilder stringBuilder = new StringBuilder();

                        while (matcher.find()) {
                            stringBuilder.append(matcher.group(1))
                                    .append(".").append(matcher.group(2));
                        }

                        String response = stringBuilder.toString();
                        Float fl = Float.parseFloat(response);

                        return new Stock(symbol, fl);
                    }

                    return null;
                }
            });

        return stock;
    }

    @Override
    public Message<Stock> receive() {
        Stock stock = getStockInformationFor(this.tickerSymbol);

        if (stock == null) {
            return null;
        }

        return MessageBuilder.withPayload(stock).setHeader("symbol", this.tickerSymbol)
                .setHeader("price", stock.getPrice()).build();
    }

    public void setTickerSymbol(String tickerSymbol) {
        this.tickerSymbol = tickerSymbol;
    }

    @Override
    public void afterPropertiesSet() throws Exception {
        this.tickerSymbol = this.tickerSymbol.trim().toUpperCase();
    }
}
```

As with the event driven adapter before, the very large majority of this adapter is code to handle the integration – the screen scraping of a stock and price. The stock price retrieval may be tested using `getStockInformationFor(String)` in isolation. The class requires a ticker symbol to be configured. The receive method simply delegates to that method. If the method returns `null`, then receive returns null. It is important to remember that Spring Integration does not proceed with integration flows with `null` payloads. Returning null here is a good way to abort processing if there is nothing interesting to deliver. While is has not been done so here, but it would be trivial to store the last retrieved stock and then compare the current request against the last one. If a new stock price is identical to the previous one, then it might make sense to stop subsequent, unnecessary processing by returning null. An example integration incorporating this adapter is shown in Listing 15–11.

Listing 15–11. *Spring Configuration Example for Polling Adapter*

```
<?xml version="1.0" encoding="UTF-8"?>
<beans xmlns="http://www.springframework.org/schema/beans"
       xmlns:xsi="http://www.w3.org/2001/XMLSchema-instance"
       xmlns:int="http://www.springframework.org/schema/integration"
       xmlns:context="http://www.springframework.org/schema/context"
       xsi:schemaLocation="http://www.springframework.org/schema/beans
    http://www.springframework.org/schema/beans/spring-beans-3.0.xsd
    http://www.springframework.org/schema/integration
    http://www.springframework.org/schema/integration/spring-integration.xsd
    http://www.springframework.org/schema/context
    http://www.springframework.org/schema/context/spring-context-3.0.xsd">

  <context:component-scan
     base-package="com.apress.prospringintegration.customadapters.inbound.pollerdriven"/>

  <context:property-placeholder location="test.properties"/>

  <int:channel id="stockChannel"/>

  <int:inbound-channel-adapter ref="stockPollingMessageSource"
                               channel="stockChannel">
    <int:poller cron="*/10 * * * * *"/>
  </int:inbound-channel-adapter>

</beans>
```

This example is using a Java configuration class (which will be picked up by the component-scan element) to configure the polling adapter and the logging service activator referenced in the example above. The Java configuration file is shown in Listing 15–12.

Listing 15–12. *Java Configuration for Polling Adapter*

```
package com.apress.prospringintegration.customadapters.inbound.pollerdriven;

import com.apress.prospringintegration.customadapters.inbound.IntegrationTestUtils;
import org.springframework.context.annotation.Bean;
import org.springframework.context.annotation.Configuration;

@Configuration
public class StockPollingMessageSourceConfiguration {

    @Bean
    public IntegrationTestUtils inboundMessageEndpointTestUtils() {
        return new IntegrationTestUtils();
    }
```

```
    @Bean
    public StockPollingMessageSource stockPollingMessageSource() {
        StockPollingMessageSource ms = new StockPollingMessageSource();
        ms.setTickerSymbol("VMW");
        return ms;
    }
}
```

Outbound Adapters

Outbound adapters are simpler than inbound adapters and are used to facilitate sending messages from a Spring Integration flow to an external system. Spring Integration provides outbound adapter support as a counterpart to the inbound adapter support where appropriate. Some systems are read-only or write-only in nature. Outbound adapters sit at the end of a Spring Integration message flow – once a message is sent to an outbound adapter, it has to renter it again through some other mechanism like an inbound adapter.

Spring Integration ships with about as many outbound adapters as inbound adapters. Some examples include using the outbound JMS adapter's to send messages using JMS, or using the JDBC adapter to write records into a database.

Spring Integration provides several outbound adapters for sending messages to systems such as XMPP, Twitter, or FTP. Often, messages sent into an outbound adapter need be of a well-known payload type, or have headers that aid the outbound adapter in doing its work. And many times adapters also provide transformers or message enrichers that can help transform messages of common payloads and headers into something that the outbound adapter can understand.

Outbound adapters are very easy to build. They must simply implement the `org.springframework.integration.core.essageHandler` interface. `MessageHandlers` are a generic component used throughout the framework. They can be though as being the workhorse of the framework. If the `service-activator` element did not make invoking Spring beans so easy, the `MessageHandler` interface would be the answer. `MessageHandlers` have one method, `handleMessage`, which takes a single parameter of type `Message`. The `outbound-channel-adapter` element can be used to automatically wire up a `MessageHandler` implementation to a channel.

Let's build a simple outbound adapter. On Unix systems, there are two commands that are commonly used to make announcements visible to users logged into a host via the shell: `write` and `wall`. So suppose `u1` and `u2` are two system accounts on host `integrationsvr1`. If `u1` is logged in and wants to send a message to `u2` who is also logged in, `u1` would use the `write` command. The `write` command sends messages to a single user. On a Unix-like system, the incantation looks like this:

```
u1@integrationsvr1$ echo "Hello." | write u2
```

User `u2` would receive the following prompt on their shell:

```
Message from u1@ integrationsvr1 on pts/0 at 01:33 ...
Hello.
EOF
```

If `u1` wants to announce something that should be seen by all users logged into the host, `u1` can use the `wall` ("`write` **`all`**") command. On a Unix-like system, the incantation looks like this:

```
u1@integrationsvr1$ echo "taking down the system in 10 minutes for maintenance. Emacs ↵
updates requires a new kernel" | wall
```

Anybody else logged into the system will see a message on their shell, like this:

```
Broadcast Message from u1@ integrationsvr1
```

```
        (/dev/pts/6) at 1:20 ...

taking down the system in 10 minutes for maintenance. Emacs updates requires a new kernel
```

Clearly, support for these functions is a crucially important to both today's applications and tomorrow's. The commands wall and write could be thought of as the first social networks. If you can't trust and be intimate with somebody else on 127.0.0.1, then whom can you trust?

In this example, the adapter will forward messages using write and wall. If there is a message header specifying a specific user, then write will be used to address just that user. If no user is specified, then wall will be used.

Note that this description of creating an outbound adapter using the MessageHandler interface may have been an over simplification. MessageHandler is indeed the root of a large part of the framework, but it is not the recommended approach. While MessageHandler can be implemented directly, the best approach would be to extend the org.springframework.integration.handler.AbstractMessageHandler class, which comes pre-packaged with support for specifying accessing common Spring Integration component services, as well as for tying into the Spring Integration message history framework. The requirements are basically the same as implementing MessageHandler. There is only one required method to be implemented.

```
protected void handleMessageInternal(Message<?> message) throws Exception
```

A simple, skeletal instance of an outbound will look like this:

```
import org.springframework.integration.Message;
import org.springframework.integration.handler.AbstractMessageHandler;

public class SimpleOutboundMessageWritingEndpoint extends AbstractMessageHandler {
    @Override
    protected void handleMessageInternal(Message<?> message) throws Exception {
        // takes a message and writes it to an external system
    }
}
```

What follows in Listing 15–13 is a complete outbound adapter implementation.

Listing 15–13. *Outbound Adapter Class*

```
package com.apress.prospringintegration.customadapters.outbound;

import org.apache.commons.io.IOUtils;
import org.apache.commons.lang.StringUtils;
import org.springframework.integration.Message;
import org.springframework.integration.MessageHeaders;
import org.springframework.integration.handler.AbstractMessageHandler;
import org.springframework.util.Assert;

import java.io.OutputStreamWriter;
import java.io.Writer;
import java.util.ArrayList;
import java.util.Arrays;
import java.util.List;

public class ShellMessageWritingMessageEndpoint extends AbstractMessageHandler {

    static public String USERID_HEADER = "shell-userid";
```

```
static public String TERMINALS_HEADER = "shell-terminal";

protected void write(String user, String msg, String terminal) {
    List<String> cmdList = new ArrayList<String>();
    cmdList.add("write");
    cmdList.add(user);

    if (!StringUtils.isEmpty(terminal)) {
        cmdList.add(terminal);
    }

    writeToShellCommand(cmdList.toArray(new String[cmdList.size()]), msg);
}

protected void wall(String msg) {
    writeToShellCommand(new String[]{"wall"}, msg);
}

@Override
protected void handleMessageInternal(Message<?> message) throws Exception {

    Assert.isInstanceOf(String.class, message.getPayload(),
            "the payload must be a String");

    String msg = (String) message.getPayload();

    MessageHeaders headers = message.getHeaders();

    try {
        if (headers.containsKey(USERID_HEADER)) {
            String ptys = headers.containsKey(TERMINALS_HEADER) ?
                    (String) headers.get(TERMINALS_HEADER) : null;
            String userid = (String) headers.get(USERID_HEADER);
            write(userid, msg, ptys);
        } else {
            wall(msg);
        }
    } catch (Throwable throwable) {
        throw new RuntimeException(throwable);
    }
}

protected int writeToShellCommand(String[] cmds, String msg) {
    try {
        ProcessBuilder processBuilder = new ProcessBuilder(Arrays.asList(cmds));
        Process proc = processBuilder.start();

        Writer streamWriter = null;

        try {
            streamWriter = new OutputStreamWriter(proc.getOutputStream());
            streamWriter.write(msg);
```

```
            } finally {
                IOUtils.closeQuietly(streamWriter);
            }

            int retVal = proc.waitFor();

            if (retVal != 0) {
                throw new RuntimeException("couldn't write message to 'write'");
            }

            return retVal;
        } catch (Throwable th) {
            throw new RuntimeException(th);
        }
    }
}
```

Most of the code in the class is dedicated to wrapping the `write` and `wall` commands and invoking them from Java. This class just wraps the functionality, making it available to Spring Integration. This is central to the core tenants of application integration, which espouses reuse of services and data in a clean way. In wrapping the integration logic with this class, it has been made available for other Spring Integration components to reuse in a clean, simple way, in terms of messages. There is also a natural place for indirection: if this class is to be made to work on multiple platforms, then consumers of the adapter would be undisturbed and their integration would continue to work.

The `handleMessageInternal` implementation detects which headers are present and delegates to the appropriate wrapper method. `AbstractMessageHandler` is an abstract class. If `MessageHandler` was implemented directly, this would have required implementing `handleMessage`. `AbstractMessageHandler` implements that method and makes it a final method and expects subclasses to override the abstract `handleMessageInternal` method instead.

Let's look at to use this outbound adapter in an application. First, the Spring Java configuration class for the outbound adapter is shown in Listing 15–14.

Listing 15–14. *Spring Java Configuration for Outbound Adapter*

```
package com.apress.prospringintegration.customadapters.outbound;

import org.springframework.context.annotation.Bean;
import org.springframework.context.annotation.Configuration;

@Configuration
public class ShellMessageWritingMessageEndpointConfiguration {
        @Bean
        public ShellMessageWritingMessageEndpoint shellMessageWritingMessageEndpoint(){
                return new ShellMessageWritingMessageEndpoint();
        }
}
```

Because the `ShellMessageWritingMessageEndpoint` has no dependencies, this configuration class is very simple. The next part is the actual Spring Integration flow. For the purposes of this example, the adapter will simply send a static message using a poller. On a Unix system with the `wall` and `write` commands installed, a console may be opened to see the output. The Spring configuration file is shown in Listing 15–15.

Listing 15–15. Spring Configuration for Outbound Adapter

```
<?xml version="1.0" encoding="UTF-8"?>
<beans xmlns="http://www.springframework.org/schema/beans"
       xmlns:xsi="http://www.w3.org/2001/XMLSchema-instance"
       xmlns:int="http://www.springframework.org/schema/integration"
       xmlns:context="http://www.springframework.org/schema/context"
       xsi:schemaLocation="http://www.springframework.org/schema/beans
    http://www.springframework.org/schema/beans/spring-beans-3.0.xsd
    http://www.springframework.org/schema/integration
    http://www.springframework.org/schema/integration/spring-integration.xsd
    http://www.springframework.org/schema/context
    http://www.springframework.org/schema/context/spring-context-3.0.xsd">

  <context:component-scan
      base-package="com.apress.prospringintegration.customadapters.outbound"/>

  <context:property-placeholder location="test.properties"/>

  <int:inbound-channel-adapter expression="'this message is going out through wall'"
                               channel="shellChannel">
    <int:poller cron="*/20 * * * * *"/>
  </int:inbound-channel-adapter>

  <int:channel id="shellChannel"/>

  <int:outbound-channel-adapter channel="shellChannel"
                                ref="shellMessageWritingMessageEndpoint"/>

</beans>
```

Spring Integration will connect your `MessageHandler` implementation with messages on an inbound channel using the `outbound-channel-adapter` element. It expects, at minimum, a `channel` attribute and a `ref` attribute. The bean used for the ref attribute is our `ShellWritingMessageEndpoint` instance. This completes the example of an outbound adapter and how to connect it to your messaging solution. It is reusable and requires very little code. It can easily support any enterprise `wall` requirement.

These examples have been simple, but that simplicity underscores Spring Integration's power. If writing an adapter is difficult, it is because the integration to the external system is difficult, for example connecting to CICS or SAP, not because Spring Integration makes it so.

Packaging Your Adapters for Reuse

So far, adapters have been written and reused them by configuring regular Spring beans. For the polling inbound adapters and for the outbound adapters, Spring Integration namespace support has been used to handle wiring those beans up to the integration pipeline correctly. This has left the adapter producers free to address the singular concern motivating developer to write the adapters in the first place. This has made the process very easy and indeed, assuming that the nature of the classes is known and how they are to be used; the reuse is easy for consumers of these adapters.

Integration with another system can be complex, which is precisely why being able to encapsulate their integrations is so valuable. It's not likely that third-party consumers will know what dependencies are expected to support the adapter without some innate knowledge of the integration itself. Interface contracts can carry a lot of information, and good documentation can go a long way, but it is still far away from being able to give somebody a `.jar` and say, "use this to talk to system X using Spring Integration."

Indeed, the previous examples are still far away from being able to support giving somebody *any* `.jar` with some expectation that the user will know what to do, especially for complex coordinating object graphs. The Spring Framework provides XML namespaces that can hide the construction of complex objects and provide more feedback to consumers of the objects about which fields are required, and when. This core support was discussed in Chapter 3. The Spring namespace mechanism relies on two things: XSDs to describe the structure of valid XML input, and Java-based namespace parsers interact with the XML DOM at runtime.

In Spring Integration, where components are often part of a very rich object graph, namespaces are used judiciously to reduce the burden on the consumer. When writing custom adapters, it is helpful to provide its own namespace so that consumers of the adapter have an easier time using it. Plus, a namespace provides the adapter producer, with a layer of indirection that will help the user to change the backend implementation as appropriate. A namespace provides the flexibility needed to build adapters that survive Spring Integration iterations, external system changes, and more.

Let's revisit the adapters that have been written so far in this chapter and create namespaces for them. An XSD file will be needed for each of our various adapters. Because there are three adapters, three XSD files will be required, as well as three pairs of `NamespaceHandlers` and `Parsers`. Additionally, two key files will be added that are key to the Spring framework's mechanism for resolving namespaces: `META-INF/spring.handlers`, and `META-INF/spring.schemas`. Figure 15–1 shows the structure of our project.

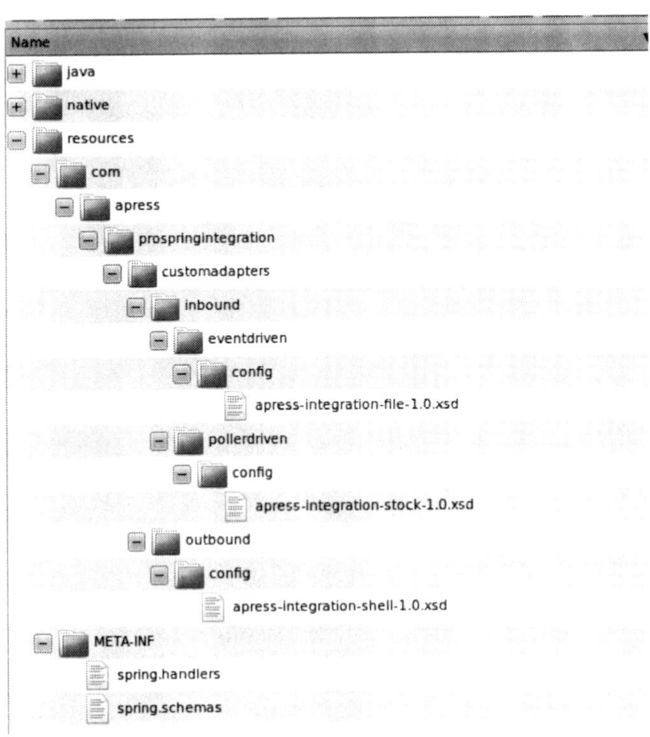

Figure 15–1. *The Structure of our Project and Location of the `.xsd` Schemas in the Directory Structure*

With the folder structure in place, the XSDs can be examined for the adapters, as well as the namespace handler code. Most of the XSDs are similar, and benefit from common XSD definitions provided by the core Spring Integration schema.

Building a Namespace for the File System Monitoring Adapter

First to support registration of the namespace, a declaration has been added to META-INF/spring.schemas:

```
http\://www.apress.com/schema/integration/file/apress-integration-file-1.0.xsd=➥
com/apress/prospringintegration/customadapters/inbound/eventdriven/config/➥
apress-integration-file-1.0.xsd
http\://www.apress.com/schema/integration/file/apress-integration-file.xsd=➥
com/apress/prospringintegration/customadapters/inbound/eventdriven/config/➥
apress-integration-file-1.0.xsd
```

This mapping establishes a custom namespace, `http://www.apress.com/schema/integration/file`, whose schema is defined in `apress-integration-file.xsd`. The event driven adapter is the easiest to build a namespace for, precisely because it has no specific requirements beyond that of a regular Spring bean. In spring.handlers, a mapping is defined between the aforementioned namespace and the Java class charged with parsing it.

```
http\://www.apress.com/schema/integration/file=com.apress.prospringintegration.➥
customadapters.inbound.eventdriven.config.DirectoryMonitorNamespaceHandler
```

The `DirectoryMonitorNamespaceHandler` registers a parser (the inline class at the bottom of the handler) for the `inbound-channel-adapter` element in the namespace. See Listing 15–16.

Listing 15–16. *Namespace Handler Class DirectoryMonitorNamespaceHandler*

```
package com.apress.prospringintegration.customadapters.inbound.eventdriven.config;

import com.apress.prospringintegration.customadapters.inbound.eventdriven.➥
DirectoryMonitorInboundFileEndpoint;
import org.springframework.beans.factory.support.BeanDefinitionBuilder;
import org.springframework.beans.factory.xml.AbstractSingleBeanDefinitionParser;
import org.springframework.beans.factory.xml.ParserContext;
import org.springframework.integration.config.xml.AbstractIntegrationNamespaceHandler;
import org.springframework.integration.config.xml.IntegrationNamespaceUtils;
import org.w3c.dom.Element;

public class DirectoryMonitorNamespaceHandler
        extends AbstractIntegrationNamespaceHandler {

    public void init() {
        registerBeanDefinitionParser("inbound-channel-adapter",
                new DirectoryMonitorInboundFileEndpointParser());
    }

    public class DirectoryMonitorInboundFileEndpointParser
            extends AbstractSingleBeanDefinitionParser {

        @Override
```

```
        protected String getBeanClassName(Element element) {
            return DirectoryMonitorInboundFileEndpoint.class.getName();
        }

        @Override
        protected boolean shouldGenerateIdAsFallback() {
            return true;
        }

        @Override
        protected boolean shouldGenerateId() {
            return false;
        }

        @Override
        protected void doParse(Element element, ParserContext parserContext,
                               BeanDefinitionBuilder builder) {
            IntegrationNamespaceUtils.setValueIfAttributeDefined(
                    builder, element, "directory", "directoryToMonitor");
            IntegrationNamespaceUtils.setReferenceIfAttributeDefined(
                    builder, element, "channel", "outputChannel");
        }
    }
}
```

The parser extends `AbstractSingleBeanDefinitionParser`, which is a core Spring class for bean parsing. In the parser, the `doParse` method is implemented. The `doParse` method is called when an element in a Spring XML application context file matches the element that the parser is registered under. In it, the Spring Integration convenience class `IntegrationNamespaceUtils` is leveraged. Two methods are used here: `IntegrationNamespaceUtils.setValueIfAttributeDefined`, and `IntegrationNamespaceUtils.setReferenceIfAttributeDefined`. The first method passes the value through to the appropriate JavaBean property on an instance of the class returned from the parser's `getBeanClassName` method. The penultimate parameter of this method is the XML attribute name from which the value should be taken. The ultimate parameter is the name of the JavaBean property to which the value should be passed.

Next the XSD file is created called `apress-integration-file.xsd`, as shown in Listing 15–17.

Listing 15–17. *XML Schema apress-integration-file.xsd.*

```
<?xml version="1.0" encoding="UTF-8"?>
<xsd:schema xmlns="http://www.apress.com/schema/integration/file"
            xmlns:xsd="http://www.w3.org/2001/XMLSchema"
            xmlns:beans="http://www.springframework.org/schema/beans"
            xmlns:tool="http://www.springframework.org/schema/tool"
            xmlns:integration="http://www.springframework.org/schema/integration"
            targetNamespace="http://www.apress.com/schema/integration/file"
            elementFormDefault="qualified"
            attributeFormDefault="unqualified">

  <xsd:import namespace="http://www.springframework.org/schema/beans"/>
  <xsd:import namespace="http://www.springframework.org/schema/tool"/>
  <xsd:import namespace="http://www.springframework.org/schema/integration"
              schemaLocation="http://www.springframework.org/schema/integration/➥
spring-integration-2.0.xsd"/>
```

```
  <xsd:element name="inbound-channel-adapter">
    <xsd:annotation>
      <xsd:documentation>
        Configures the event-driven, inbound file adapter
      </xsd:documentation>
    </xsd:annotation>
    <xsd:complexType>
      <xsd:attribute name="id" type="xsd:string"/>
      <xsd:attribute name="directory" type="xsd:string" use="required"/>
      <xsd:attribute name="channel" use="required" type="xsd:string">
        <xsd:annotation>
          <xsd:appinfo>
            <tool:annotation kind="ref">
              <tool:expected-type
                  type="org.springframework.integration.core.MessageChannel"/>
            </tool:annotation>
          </xsd:appinfo>
          <xsd:documentation>
            Identifies channel through which messages produced by this adapter are sent
          </xsd:documentation>
        </xsd:annotation>
      </xsd:attribute>
    </xsd:complexType>
  </xsd:element>
</xsd:schema>
```

The XML file might seem overwhelming, but look only at the `<xsd:element ...>` declaration - where this namespace will map to an element of inbound-channel-adapter, then look at the `<xsd:complexType>` element. The `<xsd:attribute>` elements define which attributes are expected on a correctly configured use of the namespace. In most adapters requires definitions for `id`, and `channel` that look like the ones shown here. Most of this is XML is not required – any `<tool:annotation>`, and the `<xsd:documentation>` element for example - but definitions are recommended as many modern IDEs can provide feedback based on the extra metadata provided.

Building a Namespace for the Polling Adapter

Next we will look at building a namespace for the stock inbound adapter. This has slightly different requirements because it must be designed to accept a `<poller>` element in the XML. At runtime care must be taken to correctly wire a poller to the Spring bean. Fortunately, as before, Spring Integration provides conveniences to make this easy and repeatable. First, to support registration of the namespace, a declaration is added to `META-INF/spring.schemas`:

```
http\://www.apress.com/schema/integration/stock/apress-integration-stock-1.0.xsd=➥
com/apress/prospringintegration/customadapters/inbound/eventdriven/config/➥
apress-integration-stock-1.0.xsd
http\://www.apress.com/schema/integration/stock/apress-integration-stock.xsd=➥
com/apress/prospringintegration/customadapters/inbound/eventdriven/config/➥
apress-integration-stock -1.0.xsd
```

This mapping establishes a custom namespace, `http://www.apress.com/schema/integration/stock`, whose schema is defined in `apress-integration-stock.xsd`. In `spring.handlers`, a mapping is defined between the aforementioned namespace and the Java class charged with parsing it.

```
http\://www.apress.com/schema/integration/stock=com.apress.prospringintegration.➥
customadapters.inbound.pollerdriven.config.StockNamespaceHandler
```

The StockNamespaceHandler is presented here in Listing 15–18. It simply registers a bean definition parser, as in the previous example.

Listing 15–18. *Namespace Handler for Stock Adapter.*

```
package com.apress.prospringintegration.customadapters.inbound.pollerdriven.config;

import com.apress.prospringintegration.customadapters.inbound.pollerdriven.➥
StockPollingMessageSource;
import org.springframework.beans.BeanMetadataElement;
import org.springframework.beans.factory.support.BeanDefinitionBuilder;
import org.springframework.beans.factory.xml.ParserContext;
import org.springframework.integration.config.xml.AbstractIntegrationNamespaceHandler;
import org.springframework.integration.config.xml.AbstractPollingInboundChannelAdapterParser;
import org.springframework.integration.config.xml.IntegrationNamespaceUtils;
import org.w3c.dom.Element;

public class StockNamespaceHandler extends AbstractIntegrationNamespaceHandler {

    public void init() {
        registerBeanDefinitionParser("inbound-channel-adapter",
                new StockPollingMessageSourceParser());
    }

    public class StockPollingMessageSourceParser
            extends AbstractPollingInboundChannelAdapterParser {
        @Override
        protected BeanMetadataElement parseSource(Element element,
                                                  ParserContext parserContext) {
            BeanDefinitionBuilder sourceBuilder =
                    BeanDefinitionBuilder.genericBeanDefinition(
                            StockPollingMessageSource.class.getName());
            IntegrationNamespaceUtils
                    .setValueIfAttributeDefined(sourceBuilder, element,
                            "stock", "tickerSymbol");
            return sourceBuilder.getBeanDefinition();
        }
    }
}
```

The inner class – the parser – is more interesting. This time, the Spring Integration specific parsing class, AbstractPollingInboundChannelAdapterParser, is extended which provides support for parsing and configuring a poller from XML, assuming it matches the definition used in the Spring Integration core XSD file. The abstract class only requires handling the parsing for the bean itself, just as last time. Here, the bean definition is simply instantiated, the stock ticker symbol is set using the IntegrationNamespaceUtils class, and the bean definition is returned from the abstract method parseSource. The base class used here is specifically intended to make the job of configuring polling adapters easier.

The XML schema file employed here, apress-integration-stock.xsd is shown in Listing 15–19 below.

Listing 15–19. *XML Schema for Stock Adapter Namespace.*

```
<?xml version="1.0" encoding="UTF-8"?>
<xsd:schema xmlns="http://www.apress.com/schema/integration/file"
            xmlns:xsd="http://www.w3.org/2001/XMLSchema"
            xmlns:beans="http://www.springframework.org/schema/beans"
            xmlns:tool="http://www.springframework.org/schema/tool"
            xmlns:integration="http://www.springframework.org/schema/integration"
            targetNamespace="http://www.apress.com/schema/integration/stock"
            elementFormDefault="qualified"
            attributeFormDefault="unqualified">

  <xsd:import namespace="http://www.springframework.org/schema/beans"/>
  <xsd:import namespace="http://www.springframework.org/schema/tool"/>
  <xsd:import namespace="http://www.springframework.org/schema/integration"
              schemaLocation="http://www.springframework.org/schema/integration/spring➥
-integration-2.0.xsd"/>

  <xsd:element name="inbound-channel-adapter">
    <xsd:annotation>
      <xsd:documentation>
        <![CDATA[
          Builds an inbound-channel-adapter that fetches stock data for a given stock symbol
        ]]></xsd:documentation>
    </xsd:annotation>
    <xsd:complexType>
      <xsd:sequence>
        <xsd:element ref="integration:poller" minOccurs="0" maxOccurs="1"/>
      </xsd:sequence>
      <xsd:attribute name="id" type="xsd:string"/>

      <xsd:attribute name="channel" use="required" type="xsd:string">
        <xsd:annotation>
          <xsd:appinfo>
            <tool:annotation kind="ref">
              <tool:expected-type
                  type="org.springframework.integration.core.MessageChannel"/>
            </tool:annotation>
          </xsd:appinfo>
          <xsd:documentation>
            the channel reference through which stock updates are to be sent
          </xsd:documentation>
        </xsd:annotation>
      </xsd:attribute>
      <xsd:attribute name="stock" type="xsd:string" use="required">
        <xsd:annotation>
          <xsd:documentation>
            Which stock symbol to query (e.g.: "VMW")
          </xsd:documentation>
        </xsd:annotation>
      </xsd:attribute>

    </xsd:complexType>
```

```
  </xsd:element>

</xsd:schema>
```

Most of this should look familiar, save for the attributes unique to this adapter and the poller configuration. The poller element is interesting:

```
<xsd:sequence>
    <xsd:element ref="integration:poller" minOccurs="0" maxOccurs="1"/>
</xsd:sequence>
```

It simply says that the encompassing element should expect a complex structure that matches the definition of a poller. The integration:poller element indicates that the poller schema itself came from another namespace, which can be reuse.

Building a Namespace for the Outbound Channel Adapter

Finally, the namespace for the outbound channel adapter will be built. This adapter published messages that came into it as messages broadcast using the Unix write and wall commands. This is one of the simpler parsers, since there are not any attributes to configure. First to support registration of the namespace, declarations have been added to META-INF/spring.schemas:

```
http\://www.apress.com/schema/integration/shell/apress-integration-shell.xsd=➥
com/apress/prospringintegration/customadapters/outbound/config/➥
apress-integration-shell-1.0.xsd
http\://www.apress.com/schema/integration/shell/apress-integration-shell-1.0.xsd=➥
com/apress/prospringintegration/customadapters/outbound/config/➥
apress-integration-shell-1.0.xsd
```

This mapping establishes a custom namespace, www.apress.com/schema/integration/shell, whose schema is defined in apress-integration-shell.xsd. In spring.handlers, a mapping is defined between the aforementioned namespace and the Java class charged with parsing it.

```
http\://www.apress.com/schema/integration/shell=com.apress.prospringintegration.➥
customadapters.outbound.config.ShellMessagingNamespaceHandler
```

The namespace handler StockNamespaceHandler is shown in Listing 15–20 below. It simply registers a bean definition parser, as done in the previous examples.

Listing 15–20. *Namespace Handler StockNamespaceHandler for Outbound Adapter.*

```
Package com.apress.prospringintegration.customadapters.outbound.config;

import com.apress.prospringintegration.customadapters.outbound.➥
ShellMessageWritingMessageEndpoint;
import org.springframework.beans.factory.support.AbstractBeanDefinition;
import org.springframework.beans.factory.support.BeanDefinitionBuilder;
import org.springframework.beans.factory.xml.ParserContext;
import org.springframework.integration.config.xml.AbstractIntegrationNamespaceHandler;
import org.springframework.integration.config.xml.AbstractOutboundChannelAdapterParser;
import org.w3c.dom.Element;

public class ShellMessagingNamespaceHandler
        extends AbstractIntegrationNamespaceHandler {
    @Override
```

```
    public void init() {
        registerBeanDefinitionParser("outbound-channel-adapter",
                new ShellMessagingOutboundChannelAdapterParser());
    }

    public class ShellMessagingOutboundChannelAdapterParser
            extends AbstractOutboundChannelAdapterParser {

        @Override
        protected AbstractBeanDefinition
        parseConsumer(Element element, ParserContext parserContext) {
            BeanDefinitionBuilder builder =
                    BeanDefinitionBuilder.genericBeanDefinition(
                            ShellMessageWritingMessageEndpoint.class);
            return builder.getBeanDefinition();
        }
    }

}
"
```

As before, the namespace handler simply registers the appropriate parser. The parser class extends the `AbstractOutboundChannelAdapterParser` class, which handles setting up the machinery so that a bean can receive `Messages` on channels. As before, the only requirement is to override the abstract base method and provide a definition for the endpoint class, `ShellMessageWritingMessageEndpoint`. Since there are no properties to set, the parser simply instantiates a bean definition and returns it. There is nothing of interest or novelty in the XSD file for this namespace, since it is attribute-less and establishes no new conventions. It is shown in Listing 15–21 mainly for completeness.

Listing 15–21. *Namespace XML Schema apress-integration-shell-1.0.xsd for Outbound Adapter.*

```
<?xml version="1.0" encoding="UTF-8"?>
<xsd:schema xmlns="http://www.apress.com/schema/integration/shell"
            xmlns:xsd="http://www.w3.org/2001/XMLSchema"
            xmlns:beans="http://www.springframework.org/schema/beans"
            xmlns:tool="http://www.springframework.org/schema/tool"
            xmlns:integration="http://www.springframework.org/schema/integration"
            targetNamespace="http://www.apress.com/schema/integration/shell"
            elementFormDefault="qualified"
            attributeFormDefault="unqualified">

  <xsd:import namespace="http://www.springframework.org/schema/beans"/>
  <xsd:import namespace="http://www.springframework.org/schema/tool"/>
  <xsd:import namespace="http://www.springframework.org/schema/integration"
              schemaLocation="http://www.springframework.org/schema/integration/➥
spring-integration-2.0.xsd"/>

  <xsd:element name="outbound-channel-adapter">
    <xsd:annotation>
      <xsd:documentation>
        Writes messages to other users on the same host using wall or write.
      </xsd:documentation>
    </xsd:annotation>
    <xsd:complexType>
```

```
        <xsd:sequence>
          <xsd:element ref="integration:poller" minOccurs="0" maxOccurs="1"/>
        </xsd:sequence>
        <xsd:attribute name="id" type="xsd:string"/>
        <xsd:attribute name="channel" type="xsd:string">
          <xsd:annotation>
            <xsd:appinfo>
              <tool:annotation kind="ref">
                <tool:expected-type
                    type="org.springframework.integration.core.MessageChannel"/>
              </tool:annotation>
            </xsd:appinfo>
            <xsd:documentation>
              Identifies channel attached to this adapter.
            </xsd:documentation>
          </xsd:annotation>
        </xsd:attribute>

      </xsd:complexType>
    </xsd:element>

</xsd:schema>
```

Summary

In this chapter we explored the extension points that Spring Integration provides for writing your own, custom adapters. We have learned how to create adapters for both inbound and outbound integration, and how to let Spring Integration handle much of the tedium required in many cases, leaving only writing the code that matters and is unique to the particular integration problem at hand. Finally, we looked at the options specifically available for packaging the up the adapters as Spring namespaces.

CHAPTER 16

Scaling Your Spring Integration Application

More than 40 years ago, Gordon Moore, the cofounder of Intel Corporation, published a paper that predicted the number of transistors on an integrated circuit would double every 18 months. Moore's prediction also implied that computer hardware performance would double and that the cost would decline every 18 months. This became known as Moore's Law, which still roughly holds true today (though processing power now doubles about every two years).

Since hardware performance can double every 18-24 months, software developers can develop very complex software system without worrying about performance bottlenecks. By switching to faster processors and adding more system memory, software developers have enjoyed almost unlimited computing power for the past four decades.

In order to increase speed, microprocessor manufacturers put more transistors within the same integrated circuit, resulting in increased density of the electronic components within the circuit. There is, however, a limitation as to how many components can be crammed into the same small space. Due to limitations of modern lithography techniques (and finally, the quantum tunneling limit), Moore's Law is becoming more difficult to uphold. In recent years, in order to address these restrictions, microprocessor manufacturers have instead focused on increasing the number of cores within the same microprocessor chip.

In much the same way, software today must scale out, not up, to achieve performance. This chapter will primarily focus on how to increase performance by adding additional hardware as opposed to faster hardware, and how Spring Integration applications can take advantage of concurrency.

Introducing Scalability

Scalability refers to the capability of a computing system to increase performance and accommodate additional load by adding hardware or software to the existing environment without making significant modifications. There are two types of scalability: vertical and horizontal. Vertical scaling, or *scaling up*, is the easiest way to increase the system capacity and capability. By simply upgrading the server hardware (e.g., switching to a faster microprocessor), software performance can be increased with relative ease. Unfortunately, microprocessor speed is not as fruitful a source of speed gains as it once was. In order to take advantage of the best microprocessor performance, most existing software applications must be modified to take advantage of multiple microprocessor cores. The modifications are usually complex and difficult due to the limitations of most mainstream programming languages, such as C++ and Java. Luckily, there are programming languages such as Erlang designed specifically for programming concurrent software systems.

Horizontal scaling, or *scaling out*, increases application performance by connecting multiple hardware or software entities to form a single working unit. Typically, horizontal scaling involves load balancing and clustering into a distributed system. Instead of being limited by microprocessor performance or memory consumption, horizontal scaling is limited by data center space, power consumption, and network latency.

There are always going to be some constraints to horizontal scaling, and very rarely is an entire system uniformly scalable. The cost of coordinating state between nodes, for example, might be high because of network or hard disk latency. In addition, some types of work are serial in nature. There are many ways to attempt to capture the efficiency of introducing parallelization into a system with a fixed, serial part. One formula, Gustafson's Law (or Gustafson's trend), is as follows:

$$\frac{S + N(1 - S)}{S + (1 - S)} - O_N$$

In the formula, N is the number of workers (processors, threads, computers, etc.), S is the serial part of the process (a percentage, expressed as a value between 0 and 1), and O_N is the parallelization overhead for threading (network latency, onboard communication, etc.). It describes the relationship between a solution's execution time when serially executed and when executed in parallel with the same problem set.

The Java code for this looks like this:

```
double gustafson( double n, double  s, double  o) {
    return (s + n * ( 1 - s )) / (s + ( 1 - s ) - ( o_n );
}
```

So, given a task with one processor and a runtime that's 10 percent serial, with threading or worker orchestration requiring 1 percent of time, the expected speed is (unsurprisingly) only 99 percent. If you ramp up the processors to ten workers, however, leaving thread synchronization and the serial percentage in place, you enjoy a 909 percent speedup. Not bad!

Spring and Spring Integration assist developers to resolve the scaling issue with enterprise software systems. Spring provides the task execution and scheduling framework to deal with concurrent programming. Spring Integration scales software systems by separating the functionalities into different components and connecting them by message channels. Once you've decoupled the components in your system, you are free to scale them out individually.

Most Spring Integration applications are compositions of multiple middleware components (such as messaging system, web services, databases, etc) as shown in Figure 16–1.

Figure 16–1. Typical Spring Integration application

If application A increases throughput, the channel between application A and web service B will need to increase capacity to handle the additional loads from application A. However, if we do not scale web service B, it will become the bottleneck of the software system. As a result, all the components within the Spring Integration application need to scale up to handle the increased throughput from application A. If one of the components within the system does not scale, the whole system will not scale appropriately. Put another way, a distributed system built like this is as slow as its slowest component.

Concurrency

In order to take advantage of current multicore microprocessors, we need to run multiple instances of the same application on the same server. As a result, each instance of the software will fully utilize each CPU core. However, memory overhead and threading contention make this inefficient. For example, when running Java-based applications, each Java Virtual Machine (JVM) will consume about 512 MB of memory. As a result, running four Java applications on the same server will consume about 2GB of memory just running the virtual machines. Therefore, software should be rewritten to utilize multiple threads in order to take full advantage of the hardware capabilities.

Concurrency allows software code to be executed simultaneously. In a single-core microprocessor system, software code is executed by using preemptive time-shared threads on the same microprocessor. Software performance can be increased if microprocessor clock speed is increased. On the other hand, concurrent software code can be executed on multiple threads on individual microprocessor cores within a multicore microprocessor system. Therefore, adding more cores into the same microprocessor can increase software performance even with constant CPU clock speed.

Threading is a difficult issue, and several difficult use cases remain unapproachable without a sizable amount of effort; others are at least very tedious to implement using standard threading in the Java SE environment. Concurrency is an important aspect of architectures when implementing server-side components, and enjoys no standardization in the Java EE space. In fact, it's quite the contrary: some parts of the Java EE specifications forbid the explicit creation and manipulation of threads!

Java SE

In the Java SE landscape, myriad options have been introduced over the years. First, there is the standard `java.lang.Thread` support in the Java Development Kit (JDK) 1.0. Java 1.3 saw the introduction of `java.util.TimerTask` to support running a portion of code periodically. Java 5 debuted the `java.util.concurrent` package as well as a reworked hierarchy for building thread pools, leveraging the `java.util.concurrent.Executor`.

The API for `Executor` is simple:

```
package java.util.concurrent;
public interface Executor {
    void execute(Runnable command);
}
```

`ExecutorService`, a subinterface, provides more functionality for managing threads and providing support for raising events to the threads, such as `shutdown`. There are several implementations of the `ExecutorService` that have shipped with the JDK since Java SE 5.0. Many of them are available via static factory methods on the `java.util.concurrent.Executors` class, in much the same way that utility methods for manipulating `java.util.Collection` instances are offered on the `java.util.Collections` class. `ExecutorService` also provides a `submit` method, which returns an instance of `Future<T>`. An instance of `Future<T>` can be used to track the progress of a thread that's executing—usually asynchronously. You can call `Future.isDone` or `Future.isCancelled` to determine whether the job is finished or cancelled, respectively. When you use the `ExecutorService` and submit a `Runnable`, whose `run` method has no return type, calling get on the returned `Future` will return `null`, or the value you specified on submission:

```
Runnable task = new Runnable() {
    public void run() {
        try {
            Thread.sleep(1000 * 60) ;
            System.out.println("Done sleeping for a minute, returning!");
        } catch (Exception ex) { /* ... */ }
```

```
    }
};

ExecutorService executorService = Executors.newCachedThreadPool();

if (executorService.submit(task, Boolean.TRUE).get().equals(Boolean.TRUE)) {
    System.out.println("Job has finished!");
}
```

Let's explore some the characteristics of the various implementations. As a basis for the example, we will use the Runnable instance shown in Listing 16–1.

***Listing 16–1.** Example Runnable Instance*

```
package com.apress.prospringintegration.concurrency;

import org.apache.commons.lang.exception.ExceptionUtils;

import java.util.Date;

public class DemonstrationRunnable implements Runnable {
    public void run() {
        try {
            Thread.sleep(1000);
        } catch (InterruptedException e) {
            System.out.println(
                    ExceptionUtils.getFullStackTrace(e));
        }
        System.out.println(Thread.currentThread().getName());
        System.out.printf("Hello at %s \n", new Date());
    }

}
```

The class is designed only to mark the passage of time. The same instance will be used to explore Java SE Executor and Spring's TaskExecutor support. Examples of the Java SE executors are shown in Listing 16–2.

***Listing 16–2.** Examples of Java SE Executors*

```
package com.apress.prospringintegration.concurrency;

import java.util.Date;
import java.util.concurrent.ExecutorService;
import java.util.concurrent.Executors;
import java.util.concurrent.ScheduledExecutorService;
import java.util.concurrent.TimeUnit;

public class ExecutorDemo {
    public static void main(String[] args) throws Throwable {
        Runnable task = new DemonstrationRunnable();

        // will create a pool of threads and attempt to
        // reuse previously created ones if possible
```

```
        ExecutorService cachedThreadPoolExecutorService = Executors
                .newCachedThreadPool();
        if (cachedThreadPoolExecutorService.submit(task).get() == null)
            System.out.printf("The cachedThreadPoolExecutorService "
                    + "has succeeded at %s \n", new Date());

        // limits how many new threads are created, queuing the rest
        ExecutorService fixedThreadPool = Executors.newFixedThreadPool(100);
        if (fixedThreadPool.submit(task).get() == null)
            System.out.printf("The fixedThreadPool has " +
                    "succeeded at %s \n",
                    new Date());

        // doesn't use more than one thread at a time
        ExecutorService singleThreadExecutorService = Executors
                .newSingleThreadExecutor();
        if (singleThreadExecutorService.submit(task).get() == null)
            System.out.printf("The singleThreadExecutorService "
                    + "has succeeded at %s \n", new Date());

        // support sending a job with a known result
        ExecutorService es = Executors.newCachedThreadPool();
        if (es.submit(task, Boolean.TRUE).get().equals(Boolean.TRUE))
            System.out.println("Job has finished!");

        // mimic TimerTask
        ScheduledExecutorService scheduledThreadExecutorService = Executors
                .newScheduledThreadPool(10);
        if (scheduledThreadExecutorService.schedule(
                task, 30, TimeUnit.SECONDS).get() == null)
            System.out.printf("The scheduledThreadExecutorService "
                    + "has succeeded at %s \n", new Date());

        // this doesn't stop until it encounters
        // an exception or it's cancel()ed
        scheduledThreadExecutorService.scheduleAtFixedRate(task, 0, 5,
                TimeUnit.SECONDS);

    }
}
```

If you use the version of the submit method on the ExecutorService that accepts a Callable<T>, then submitwill return whatever was returned from the Callable main method call. The interface for Callable is as follows:

```
package java.util.concurrent;

public interface Callable<V> {
     V call() throws Exception;
}
```

Java EE

In the Java EE landscape, different approaches for solving these sorts of problems have been created, often missing the point. Java EE has offered no threading issue help for a long time.

There are other solutions for these sorts of problems, though. Quartz (a job-scheduling framework) fills the gap by providing a solution that uses scheduling and concurrency. JCA 1.5 (or the J2EE Connector Architecture; the JCA acronym is most used when referring to this technology, even though it was supposed to be the acronym for the Java Cryptography Architecture) is a specification that supports concurrency in that it provides a primitive type of gateway for integration functionality. Components can be notified about incoming messages and respond concurrently. JCA 1.5 provides a primitive, limited enterprise service bus—similar to integration features, but without nearly as much finesse as the Spring Integration Framework. That said, if you had to tie a legacy application written in C to a Java EE application server and let it optionally participate in container services (and wanted to do it in a *reasonably* portable way before 2006), it worked well.

The requirement for concurrency was not lost on application server vendors, though. In 2003, IBM and BEA jointly created the Timer and WorkManager APIs. The APIs eventually became JSR-237, which was subsequently withdrawn and merged with JSR-236, with the focus being on how to implement concurrency in a managed (usually Java EE) environment. JSR-236 is still not final. The Service Data Object (SDO) specification, JSR-235, also had a similar solution in the works, although it is not final either. Both SDO and the WorkManager API were targeted for Java EE 1.4, although they are both progressed independently since. The Timer and WorkManager APIs (also known as the CommonJ WorkManager API) enjoys support on both WebLogic (9.0 and later) and WebSphere (6.0 and later), although they are not necessarily portable. Finally, open source implementations of the CommonJ API have sprung up in recent years.

The issue is that there's no portable, standard, simple way of controlling threads and providing concurrency for components in a managed environment (or an unmanaged environment). Even if the discussion is framed in terms of Java SE–specific solutions, you have an overwhelming plethora of choices to make.

Spring Framework

In Spring 2.0, a unifying solution was introduced in the `org.springframework.core.task.TaskExecutor` interface. The `TaskExecutor` abstraction served all concurrency requirements pretty well. Because Spring supported Java 1.4, `TaskExecutor` did not implement the `java.util.concurrent.Executor` interface, introduced in Java 1.5, although its interface was compatible. And any class implementing `TaskExecutor` could also implement the `Executor` interface, because it defined the exact same method signature. This interface exists even in Spring 3.0 for backward compatibility with JDK 1.4 in Spring 2.x. This means that people stuck on older JDKs can build applications with this sophisticated functionality without JDK 5. In Spring 3.0, with Java 5 the baseline, the `TaskExecutor` interface now extends `Executor`, which means that all the support provided by Spring now works with the core JDK support, too.

The `TaskExecutor` interface is used quite a bit internally in the Spring Framework. For example, the Quartz integration (which has threading, of course) and the message-driven POJO container support make use of `TaskExecutor`:

```
// the Spring abstraction
package org.springframework.core.task;

import java.util.concurrent.Executor;

public interface TaskExecutor extends Executor {
    void execute(Runnable task);
}
```

In some places, the various solutions mirror the functionality provided by the core JDK options. In others, they are unique, and provide integrations with other frameworks (e.g., as with CommonJ WorkManager). These integrations usually take the form of a class that can exist in the target framework, but that you can manipulate just like any other TaskExecutor abstraction. Although there is support for adapting an existing Java SE Executor or ExecutorService as a TaskExecutor, this is not so important in Spring 3.0, because the base class for TaskExecutor is Executor anyway. In this way, TaskExecutor in Spring bridges the gap between various solutions on Java EE and Java SE.

Let's see some of the simple support for TaskExecutor first, using the same Runnable defined previously. This code is a simple Spring bean, into which is injected various instances of TaskExecutor with the sole aim of submitting the Runnable (see Listing 16–3).

Listing 16–3. *Spring Bean Demonstrating TaskExectutor*

```
package com.apress.prospringintegration.concurrency;

import org.springframework.beans.factory.annotation.Autowired;
import org.springframework.core.task.SimpleAsyncTaskExecutor;
import org.springframework.core.task.SyncTaskExecutor;
import org.springframework.core.task.support.TaskExecutorAdapter;
import org.springframework.scheduling.concurrent.ThreadPoolTaskExecutor;
import org.springframework.scheduling.timer.TimerTaskExecutor;

import javax.annotation.Resource;

public class TaskExecutorExample {
    @Autowired
    private SimpleAsyncTaskExecutor asyncTaskExecutor;

    @Autowired
    private SyncTaskExecutor syncTaskExecutor;

    @Autowired
    private TaskExecutorAdapter taskExecutorAdapter;

    /*  No need, since the scheduling is already configured, in the application context
    @Resource(name = "timerTaskExecutorWithScheduledTimerTasks")
    private TimerTaskExecutor timerTaskExecutorWithScheduledTimerTasks;
    */

    @Resource(name = "timerTaskExecutorWithoutScheduledTimerTasks")
    private TimerTaskExecutor timerTaskExecutorWithoutScheduledTimerTasks;

    @Autowired
    private ThreadPoolTaskExecutor threadPoolTaskExecutor;

    @Autowired
    private DemonstrationRunnable task;

    public void submitJobs() {
        syncTaskExecutor.execute(task);
        taskExecutorAdapter.submit(task);
        asyncTaskExecutor.submit(task);
```

```
        timerTaskExecutorWithoutScheduledTimerTasks.submit(task);

        /* will do 100 at a time,
            then queue the rest, ie,
            should take around 5 seconds total
        */
        for (int i = 0; i < 500; i++)
            threadPoolTaskExecutor.submit(task);
    }
}
```

The application context demonstrates the creation of these various TaskExecutor implementations. Most are so simple that you could create them manually. Only in one case (the timerTaskExecutor) do you delegate to a factory bean (see Listing 16–4).

***Listing 16–4.** Java Configuration: TaskExecutorExampleConfiguration*

```
package com.apress.prospringintegration.concurrency.taskexecutorexample;

import com.apress.prospringintegration.concurrency.DemonstrationRunnable;
import org.springframework.context.annotation.Bean;
import org.springframework.context.annotation.Configuration;
import org.springframework.core.task.SimpleAsyncTaskExecutor;
import org.springframework.core.task.SyncTaskExecutor;
import org.springframework.core.task.support.TaskExecutorAdapter;
import org.springframework.scheduling.concurrent.ThreadPoolTaskExecutor;
import org.springframework.scheduling.timer.ScheduledTimerTask;
import org.springframework.scheduling.timer.TimerFactoryBean;
import org.springframework.scheduling.timer.TimerTaskExecutor;

import java.util.concurrent.Executors;

@Configuration
public class TaskExecutorExampleConfiguration {
    @Bean
    public TaskExecutorExample taskExecutorExample() {
        return new TaskExecutorExample();
    }

    @Bean
    public DemonstrationRunnable demonstrationRunnable() {
        return new DemonstrationRunnable();
    }

    @Bean
    public TaskExecutorAdapter taskExecutorAdapter() {
        return new TaskExecutorAdapter(Executors.newCachedThreadPool());
    }

    @Bean
    public SimpleAsyncTaskExecutor simpleAsyncTaskExecutor() {
        SimpleAsyncTaskExecutor simpleAsyncTaskExecutor = new SimpleAsyncTaskExecutor();
        simpleAsyncTaskExecutor.setDaemon(false);
        return simpleAsyncTaskExecutor;
```

```
    }

    @Bean(name = "timerTaskExecutorWithoutScheduledTimerTasks")
    public TimerTaskExecutor timerTaskExecutor() {
        TimerTaskExecutor timerTaskExecutor = new TimerTaskExecutor();
        timerTaskExecutor.setDelay(10000);
        return timerTaskExecutor;
    }

    @Bean
    public SyncTaskExecutor syncTaskExecutor() {
        return new SyncTaskExecutor();
    }

    @Bean(name = "timerTaskExecutorWithScheduledTimerTasks")
    public TimerTaskExecutor timerTaskExecutor1() {
        ScheduledTimerTask scheduledTimerTask = new ScheduledTimerTask();
        scheduledTimerTask.setDelay(10);
        scheduledTimerTask.setFixedRate(true);
        scheduledTimerTask.setPeriod(10000);
        scheduledTimerTask.setRunnable(this.demonstrationRunnable());

        TimerFactoryBean timerFactoryBean = new TimerFactoryBean();
        timerFactoryBean.setScheduledTimerTasks(
                new ScheduledTimerTask[] {scheduledTimerTask});
        timerFactoryBean.afterPropertiesSet();
        timerFactoryBean.setBeanName("timerFactoryBean");

        return new TimerTaskExecutor(timerFactoryBean.getObject());
    }

    @Bean
    public ThreadPoolTaskExecutor threadPoolTaskExecutor() {
        ThreadPoolTaskExecutor executor = new ThreadPoolTaskExecutor();
        executor.setCorePoolSize(50);
        executor.setDaemon(false);
        executor.setWaitForTasksToCompleteOnShutdown(true);
        executor.setMaxPoolSize(100);
        executor.setAllowCoreThreadTimeOut(true);
        return executor;
    }
}
```

The `main` class to create the Spring context and run the different `TaskExecutor` implementations is shown in Listing 16–5.

Listing 16–5. *TaskExecutor Example main Class*

```
package com.apress.prospringintegration.concurrency.taskexecutorexample;

import org.springframework.context.ApplicationContext;
import org.springframework.context.annotation.AnnotationConfigApplicationContext;
```

```
public class TaskExecutorExampleApp {
    public static void main(String[] args) {
        ApplicationContext ctx =
                New AnnotationConfigApplicationContext(
                    TaskExecutorExampleConfiguration.class);
        TaskExecutorExample demo = ctx.getBean(TaskExecutorExample.class);
        demo.submitJobs();
    }
}
```

The preceding code shows different implementations of the TaskExecutor interface. The first bean, the TaskExecutorAdapter instance, is a simple wrapper around a java.util.concurrence.Executors instance, which allows you to work in terms of the Spring TaskExecutor interface. This is only slightly useful, because you could conceptually use the Executor interface now, since Spring 3.0 updates the TaskExecutor interface to extend Executor. You use Spring here to configure an instance of an Executor and pass it in as the constructor argument.

SimpleAsyncTaskExecutor provides a new Thread for each job submitted. It does no thread pooling or reuse. Each job submitted runs asynchronously in a thread.

SyncTaskExecutor is the simplest of the implementations of TaskExecutor. Submission of a job is synchronous, and tantamount to launching a Thread, running it, and then use jointo connect it immediately. It's effectively the same as manually invoking the run method in the calling thread, skipping threading all together.

TimerTaskExecutor uses a java.util.Timer instance and manages jobs (java.util.concurrent.Callable<T> or java.lang.Runnable instances) for you by running them on the Timer. You can specify a delay when creating the TimerTaskExecutor, after which all submitted jobs will start running. Internally, the TimerTaskExecutor converts Callable<T> instances or Runnable instances that are submitted into TimerTasks, which it then schedules on the Timer. If you schedule multiple jobs, they will be run serialized on the same thread with the same Timer. If you don't specify a Timer explicitly, a default one will be created. If you want to explicitly register TimerTasks on the Timer, use the org.springframework.scheduling.timer.TimerFactoryBean's scheduledTimerTasks property. The TimerTaskExecutor doesn't surface methods for more advanced scheduling like the Timer class does. If you want to schedule at fixed intervals, at a certain Date (point in time), or for a certain period, you need to manipulate the TimerTask itself. You can do this with the org.springframework.scheduling.timer.ScheduledTimerTask class, which provides an easily configurable TimerTask that the TimerFactoryBean will schedule appropriately.

To submit jobs just as you have with other TaskExecutors, after a delay simply configure a TimerFactoryBean and then submit as usual:

```
@Bean(name = "timerTaskExecutorWithoutScheduledTimerTasks")
public TimerTaskExecutor timerTaskExecutor() {
    TimerTaskExecutor timerTaskExecutor = new TimerTaskExecutor();
    timerTaskExecutor.setDelay(10000);
    return timerTaskExecutor;
}
```

More complex scheduling, such as fixed interval execution, requires that you set the TimerTask explicitly. Here, it does little good to actually submit jobs manually. For more advanced functionality, you'll want to use something like Quartz, which can support cron expressions.

```
@Bean(name = "timerTaskExecutorWithScheduledTimerTasks")
public TimerTaskExecutor timerTaskExecutor1() {
    ScheduledTimerTask scheduledTimerTask = new ScheduledTimerTask();
    scheduledTimerTask.setDelay(10);
    scheduledTimerTask.setFixedRate(true);
    scheduledTimerTask.setPeriod(10000);
```

```
        scheduledTimerTask.setRunnable(this.demonstrationRunnable());

        TimerFactoryBean timerFactoryBean = new TimerFactoryBean();
        timerFactoryBean.setScheduledTimerTasks(
                new ScheduledTimerTask[]{scheduledTimerTask});
        timerFactoryBean.afterPropertiesSet();
        timerFactoryBean.setBeanName("timerFactoryBean");

        return new TimerTaskExecutor(timerFactoryBean.getObject());
    }
```

The last example uses `ThreadPoolTaskExecutor`, which is a full-on thread pool implementation building on `java.util.concurrent.ThreadPoolExecutor`.

If you want to build applications using the CommonJ WorkManager/TimerManager support available in IBM WebSphere 6.0 and BEA WebLogic 9.0, you can use `org.springframework.scheduling.commonj.WorkManagerTaskExecutor`. This class delegates to a reference to the CommonJ WorkManager available inside of WebSphere or WebLogic. Usually, you'll provide it with a JNDI reference to the appropriate resource. This works well enough with Geronimo, but extra effort is required with JBoss or GlassFish. Spring provides classes that delegate to the JCA support provided on those servers: for GlassFish, use `org.springframework.jca.work.glassfish.GlassFishWorkManagerTaskExecutor`; for JBoss, use `org.springframework.jca.work.jboss.JBossWorkManagerTaskExecutor`.

The `TaskExecutor` support provides a powerful way to access scheduling services on your application server via a unified interface. If you're looking for more robust support that can be deployed on any server (even Tomcat and Jetty), you might consider Spring's Quartz support (although keep in mind that this is much more heavyweight).

In addition to `TaskExecutor`, Spring 3.0 introduces `org.springframework.scheduling.TaskScheduler`, which allows a task to be executed at a scheduled time in the future. In addition to converting a single thread method into asynchronous task, you can use the Spring Framework to execute task scheduling in a separate thread by using the `TaskScheduler` interface, as shown in Listing 16–6.

Listing 16–6. *TaskScheduler.java*

```
package org.springframework.scheduling;

public interface TaskScheduler {

   ScheduledFuture schedule(Runnable task, Trigger trigger);
   ScheduledFuture schedule(Runnable task, Date startTime);
   ScheduledFuture scheduleAtFixedRate(Runnable task, Date startTime, long period);
   ScheduledFuture scheduleAtFixedRate(Runnable task, long period);
   ScheduledFuture scheduleWithFixedDelay(Runnable task, Date startTime, long delay);
   ScheduledFuture scheduleWithFixedDelay(Runnable task, long delay);

}
```

`TaskScheduler` executes a task at a specific date and time You can also use `TaskScheduler` to execute a task according to a specific condition by using the `Trigger` interface. There are two `Trigger` implementation in Spring Framework: `CronTrigger` and `PeriodicTrigger`. These two `Trigger` implementations were used in previous chapters for defining the time interval for the `PollingConsumer` endpoints. You can apply a fixed delay or fixed rate to `PeriodicTrigger`. `CronTrigger` creates trigger conditions by using standard `cron` expressions.

Spring 3 also debuted support for automatically proxying methods annotated with `@Async` and delegating their execution to a `TaskExecutor`. Thus, the annotated method will execute asynchronously.

A simple example is shown in Listing 16–7. When called, the runTask method will return immediately while the method code continues to run within the TaskExecutor.

Listing 16–7. *Example Using @Async Annotation*

```
package com.apress.prospringintegration.concurrency;

import org.springframework.scheduling.annotation.Async;
import org.springframework.stereotype.Component;

@Component
public class AsyncExample {

    @Async
    public void runTask() throws InterruptedException {
        for (int i = 0; i < 10; i++) {
            System.out.println("Processing: " + i);
            Thread.sleep(1000 * 5);
        }
    }
}
```

Listing 16–8 shows the Spring configuration file for the @Async example. Note the addition of the annotation-drive element required for supporting @Async.

Listing 16–8. *Spring Configuration for @Async Annotation Example async-context.xml*

```
<?xml version="1.0" encoding="UTF-8"?>
<beans xmlns="http://www.springframework.org/schema/beans"
       xmlns:xsi="http://www.w3.org/2001/XMLSchema-instance"
       xmlns:context="http://www.springframework.org/schema/context"
       xmlns:task="http://www.springframework.org/schema/task"
       xsi:schemaLocation="http://www.springframework.org/schema/context
    http://www.springframework.org/schema/context/spring-context-3.0.xsd
    http://www.springframework.org/schema/beans
    http://www.springframework.org/schema/beans/spring-beans-3.0.xsd
    http://www.springframework.org/schema/task
    http://www.springframework.org/schema/task/spring-task-3.0.xsd">

  <context:component-scan base-package="com.apress.prospringintegration.concurrency"/>

  <task:annotation-driven/>

</beans>
```

You can run this example using the main class shown in Listing 16–9. The Spring context is created and the asyncExample bean is accessed. When the runTask executed, it will return immediately and produce the output “Finished Submitting Job,” while the method code will continue to run asynchronously.

Listing 16–9. @Async Annotation Example main Class

```
package com.apress.prospringintegration.concurrency;

import org.springframework.context.support.ClassPathXmlApplicationContext;

public class AsyncExampleApp {

    public static void main(String[] args) throws Exception {
        ClassPathXmlApplicationContext ctx =
                new ClassPathXmlApplicationContext("async-context.xml");
        AsyncExample asyncExample = ctx.getBean(
                "asyncExample", AsyncExample.class);

        System.out.println("Submitting Job");
        asyncExample.runTask();
        System.out.println("Finish Submitting Job");
    }
}
```

By using concurrency, developers can increase the message throughput on producing and consuming messages within the Spring Integration system. For example, the Spring Integration `PublishSubscribeChannel` allows a developer passing in an `Executor` to order the message handler to be invoked concurrently. As a result, the consumer can handle more incoming messages at the same time. There are a number of places where the `TaskExecutor` can be used in Spring Integration to handle concurrency requirements, including the `PublishSubscribeChannel` just described. The `ExecutorChannel` uses the `TaskExecutor` to handles the rest of the message chain allowing the send method not to block. Polling support for channels and consumers leverages the `TaskExecutor`, as does the anonymous gateway.

Scaling the Middleware

Spring Integration allows developers to connect to external systems using channel adapters, and provides out-of-the-box support for various integration styles using—among other things—message brokers, databases, web services, and file systems. It is very difficult to achieve linear scalability across a multiple-tier system. External systems have different characteristic when scaled, and often run on different hardware systems in different geographic locations. In this chapter, we are going to focus on some of the common techniques to scale the transport layer and endpoints of a Spring Integration solution.

Message Broker

Scaling a message broker is all about how to keep constant message throughput within the messaging system when adding more message producers or consumers. When the number of message producers increases, the message broker needs to be able to sustain message consumption and delivery speeds. In addition, the message broker needs to make sure there is enough storage to handle message backlogs if the consumers cannot handle the increased number of messages.

The easiest solution is scaling vertically by adding more resources to the message broker hardware, such as a faster network interface, a faster hard drive or solid state drive (SSD), and more memory and disk storage. For example, the current fastest network interface is 100 GB Ethernet, and the latest Serial

Advanced Technology Attachment (SATA) interface can deliver up to 700 MB/s when using SSD. All these solutions require new infrastructure and are very expensive.

The alternative solution is scaling horizontally by combining multiple message brokers into a cluster. Most of the JMS- and AMQP-based message brokers such as RabbitMQ, ActiveMQ, and HornetQ support clustering.

RabbitMQ

As described in Chapter 12, RabbitMQ is an open source AMQP message broker. A cluster may be created by setting up a group of RabbitMQ nodes. Each cluster can share users, virtual hosts, queues, exchanges, and so on. The current version of RabbitMQ (2.2.0) replicates all the metadata across the nodes of the cluster for reliability and scaling. However, the message queues remain local to the nodes on which they are created. Future versions of RabbitMQ will allow message queue replication.

Each RabbitMQ node can run either as a RAM node or a disk node. RAM nodes have very fast performance because they keep all the data in memory. However, with RAM nodes, all the data will be lost if there is power failure. A disk node, by contrast, stores all the data on the disk, and disk speed can become a performance bottleneck. Optimum performance can be achieved with one disk node within the cluster, since the metadata is replicated across all the nodes.

By default, RabbitMQ runs in single node mode. You can set up a cluster by changing the RabbitMQ configuration file `rabbitmq.config`, as shown in Listing 16–10. The location of the file is defined in the `rabbitmq-server.sh(bat)` startup script in the `sbin` directory.

***Listing 16–10.** rabbitmq.config*

```
[
   {rabbit, [
      {cluster_nodes, ['rabbit@host1', 'rabbit@host2']}
   ]}
].
```

This example sets up a RabbitMQ cluster named `cluster`, which contains two RabbitMQ message brokers running on hosts `host1` and `host2`. The RabbitMQ nodes can join the existing cluster on the fly without using the configuration file. For example, a new RabbitMQ node may be added to the cluster using the `rabbitmqctl` command script is found in the `sbin` directory.

```
host3$ rabbitmqctl cluster rabbit@host1
host3$ rabbitmqctl start_app
```

The ability to dynamically add nodes to a cluster is very useful when throughput is saturated and new nodes are required to relieve load.

ActiveMQ

Apache ActiveMQ is a very popular open source JMS message broker. It also allows multiple ActiveMQ instances to form a cluster by running as a network of brokers. The cluster mechanism stores and forwards messages between multiple ActiveMQ instances to support distributed queues and topics. Instead of replicating all the messages and data across all of the brokers, each message only exists in an ActiveMQ broker at given time. The message travels from one broker to another until it reaches an available message consumer.

This is very different than RabbitMQ clustering; ActiveMQ does not maintain a single queue or shared metadata across the cluster. Thus, the order is not maintained within the queue across the cluster; messages are placed at the end of the queue even if they were not at the end of the queue on their node of origin. However, this clustering method allows messages to travel across brokers throughout the network (particularly wide-area networks) more efficiently.

There are two types of configurations for setting up ActiveMQ's network of brokers. The first uses well-known address (WKA) by modifying the `activemq.xml` file in the `conf` directory, as shown in Listing 16–11.

Listing 16–11. *activemq.xml*

```
<?xml version="1.0" encoding="UTF-8"?>

<beans xmlns="http://activemq.org/config/1.0">

  <broker name="broker1" persistent="false">
    <networkConnectors>
      <networkConnector uri="static:(tcp://host1:61616,tcp://host2:61616)"/>
    </networkConnectors>
  </broker>

</beans>
```

In the second scenario, ActiveMQ uses a discovery agent to detect remote brokers. There are two types of discovery agent using either the *multicast* or *Zeroconfig* discovery protocol. To use multicast discovery, you need to modify the ActiveMQ configuration file `activemq.xml` as shown in Listing 16–12.

Listing 16–12. *activemq.xml*

```
<?xml version="1.0" encoding="UTF-8"?>

<beans xmlns="http://activemq.org/config/1.0">

  <broker name="broker1" persistent="false">
    <networkConnectors>
      <networkConnector uri="multicast://default"/>
    </networkConnectors>
  </broker>

</beans>
```

ActiveMQ's network-of-brokers setup allows the message brokers to handle an increased number of message producers and consumers by distributing the load to multiple message brokers. However, due to the store-and-forward implementation, the consumers will receive messages in a different order than the sending order.

HornetQ

Similar to RabbitMQ and ActiveMQ, HornetQ is another open source message broker that supports clustering. HornetQ is unique in that it passes the message to one of the message brokers within the cluster in a round-robin fashion. The client is totally ignorant of the cluster topography, so it still connects to just one of the message brokers. The `hornet-configuration.xml` file (usually found in the `config/stand-alone/clustered`)directory needs to be modified for clustering as shown in Listing 16–13.

Listing 16–13. *hornetq-configuration.xml*

```
<discovery-groups>
   <discovery-group name="cluster-group">
      <group-address>192.0.0.0</group-address>
      <group-port>9876</group-port>
      <refresh-timeout>10000</refresh-timeout>
   </discovery-group>
</discovery-groups>

<cluster-connections>
    <cluster-connection name="cluster">
        <address>jms</address>
        <retry-interval>500</retry-interval>
        <use-duplicate-detection>true</use-duplicate-detection>
        <forward-when-no-consumers>false</forward-when-no-consumers>
        <max-hops>1</max-hops>
        <discovery-group-ref discovery-group-name="cluster-group"/>
    </cluster-connection>
</cluster-connections>
```

HornetQ cluster setup is very easy because of auto–broker group discovery. The `discovery-group` element defines a group for auto–message broker discovery. The `group-address` is the multicast IP address for the group to listen on. In the `cluster-connection` element, a cluster name is defined and the `discovery-group-name` is assigned to the cluster group. By using HornetQ server-side clustering and load balancing, messages are evenly distributed across every HornetQ instance within the cluster.

Regardless of what kind of message broker is used, there are still many constraints that a message system client might easily fail to comply with. In some software systems, it would be ideal to offload a time-consuming process to separate servers. By using the aggressive consumer pattern, you can achieve system scalability by adding more consumer servers to absorb the load from producers. As a result, the producer will not be blocked waiting for the time-consuming process to complete.

The ability to separate the instigation of a job from its actual completion timeline is called *temporal decoupling*. On the command line, in Unix-like environments, job operators like & can be used to send work to the background. Messaging brings that concept to your enterprise architecture.

By default, Spring Integration message channels are memory-backed. As a result, the size of the channel will be limited by the available JVM heap size or system memory. Luckily, Spring Integration 2.0 message channels can be backed by a JMS message broker. As a result, message channels can scale out to an external messaging system. By scaling out the messaging system, Spring Integration message channels can be backed by virtually unlimited storage.

Web Services

Clustering the message brokers is a technique for scaling the transport layer of an integration system. The endpoints can also be scaled to increase performance and capacity. The first external endpoint that we'll explore is a web service. Web service performance is usually measured by the number of web requests the server can handle per second. The web service throughput can usually be improved by adding more CPU and memory to allow more threads to handle additional web service requests on a single application server instance. A better approach is to horizontally scale the web service to run on multiple application servers to form a cluster. Thus, the service requests can be distributed across the cluster.

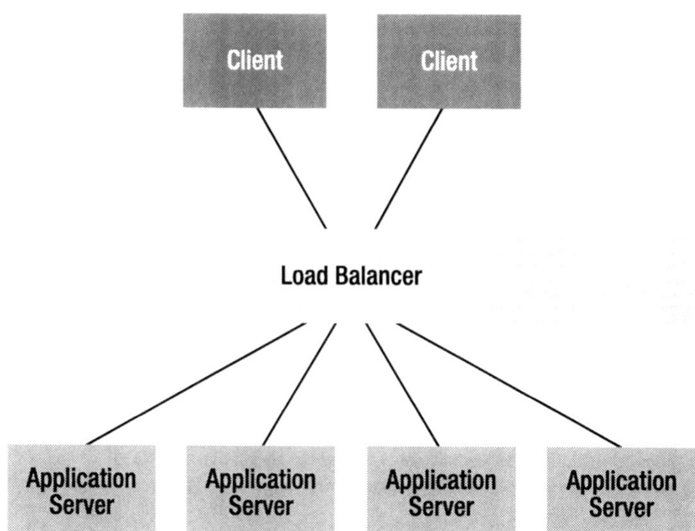

Figure 16–2. Web service application server clustering

In order to have the web service run on multiple application servers, the first step is to make the web application stateless, with no HTTP sessions. Without HTTP sessions, any of the application servers within the cluster can handle any HTTP requests from any clients. Some HTTP load balancers can make the HTTP session *sticky*, in which requests initiated on one server will generate a cookie that guarantees subsequent requests will be routed to the same server. However, it is very difficult to create true linear horizontal scalability using this approach. By using HTTP sessionless web services, web traffic can be load-balanced to any of the application servers in the cluster.

Caching is another technique that can be used to scale application servers. By using caching, web service clients can reuse the same copies of data without spending additional resources to connect to the originating system (be it the file system, database, or another service all together). Since caches store the majority of data in system memory, latency can be reduced dramatically. Caches can be implemented locally on each application server or using an application server cluster as distributed cache service.

A *read-through* cache (see Figure 16–3) retrieves data from the originating system (the store of record) if the requested data does not exist in the cache. The result is then cached, and subsequent reads will receive the cached version, avoiding a potentially expensive trip to the originating system. This type of cache minimizes the additional round-trip from the client to the store of record if the data is repeatedly requested.

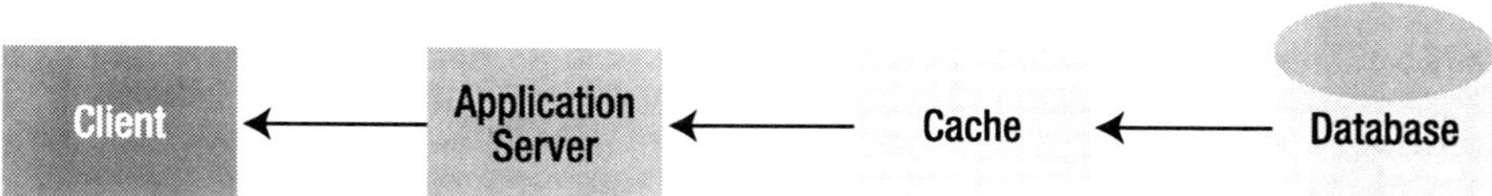

Figure 16–3. Read-through cache

A *write-through* cache allows the application to write to the cache first, and then synchronously write to the store of records. The write from the client's perspective isn't finished until both the cache and the store of records have been updated.

A *write-behind* cache allows clients to write to the cache first, and then the cache writes to the store of records asynchronously. From the client's perspective, the write is finished as soon as the write to the cache (a cheap operation) is finished.

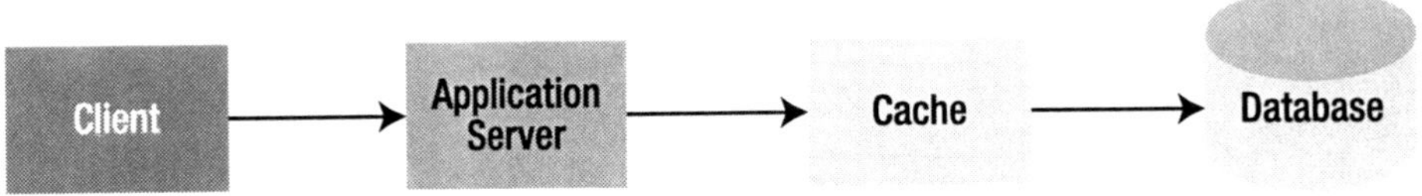

Figure 16–4. *Write-behind cache*

An additional type of caching—*write-aside* caching—occurs when the client ensures that both the store of records and the cache are updated. This has the same performance characteristics as write-behind and write-through caching, but imposes more on the client.

There are a number of caching technologies on the market, including Cassandra, Hazelcast, Coherence, Gemfire, and Ehcache. Your choice will depend on your particular needs in terms of performance, support, integration with your particular technology, and cost.

Database

The term *database server* usually refers to a traditional relational database management system (RDBMS). Most of the database systems used today are RDBMSs, including Oracle, SQL Server, Sybase, PostgreSQL, and MySQL.

RDBMSs can be easily scaled vertically. However, scaling out a RDBMS horizontally to tens or hundreds of server nodes is very complex and troublesome. There is no true solution to scale out a relational database system, since an RDBMS is fundamentally unscalable. However, there are solutions to help improve RDBMS performance and scaling. Since databases store data on disks, you can improve relational database server performance by improving the throughput of the storage unit. Database data can be partitioned either horizontally or vertically so that data can be stored on different storage devices. In other words, instead of scaling out the database server, we can scale out the database storage.

With horizontal data partitioning, database structure can be maintained across multiple database servers and storage devices. The only difference is the data each partition is holding. For example, data can be partitioned by dividing up odd and even numeric identifiers. Some database servers support *range partitioning* and *hash partitioning*. Range partitioning can be done with specific ranges of keys, while hash partitioning can be done by hashing keys into a finite set of partitions.

Vertical data partitioning is sometimes called data sharding. The actual database table is separated into multiple database instances. Each instance holds different sets of data. For example, employee data can be stored in database A while an employee's payroll could be stored in database B.

Horizontal and vertical data partitioning are designed to archive the same goal, which is making the database smaller. Smaller databases are easier to manage, faster, and cheaper to maintain. However, both methods require significant amount of business logic knowledge and database server tuning to meet the specific requirements of the software system. As a result, neither are true scaling solutions.

In early 2009, the *NoSQL* movement began promoting the use of nonrelational data stores. The term *NoSQL* refers to nonrelational distributed data stores that do not attempt to provide the traditional ACID guarantees of the classical relational databases. NoSQL comes in several flavors, including key/value stores (e.g., Hadoop and Regis), document databases (e.g., CouchDB and Cassandra), graph databases (e.g., Neo4J and AllegroGraph), and distributed caching systems (e.g., Coherence and Gemfire). Traditional RDBMSs can handle up to terabytes of data, but NoSQL is designed to be massively horizontally scalable and deal with petabytes of data. (This petabyte range of storage has become known as "big data.")

As they say, there's no such thing as a free lunch. Many of these NoSQL systems trade one thing for another, and you must be aware of the trade-offs when choosing one. One way to classify the different available options is according to Eric Brewer's CAP theorem (`http://www.julianbrowne.com/article/viewer/brewers-cap-theorem`), which says that a distributed system can only be any two of the following: partition-tolerant, available, or consistent. For example, a database is available and consistent—reads and writes can be fast, and data is guaranteed to be in a known state after a write. However, it is not partition-tolerant—you can't easily scale out the database without sacrificing one of those characteristics. It can be slow to replicate (and thus unavailable). You can insulate clients from this lack of availability by using background replication, but this implies that clients on one database node might see data that is out of sync. In such a case, consistency is usually what gets sacrificed. In a NoSQL system, that trade-off is explicit: NoSQL systems are designed to be partition-tolerant and available. They are usually said to be "eventually consistent;" data will eventually be synchronized across all partitions. Usually, "eventually" means "a few milliseconds to seconds." Stock trades that depend on pinprick precision probably can't afford to have invalid stock data from 10 seconds ago. A user's inbox, on the other hand, can be made to wait to be synchronized for 10 seconds.

If the NoSQL node on which the canonical data lives goes down before its contents are replicated to other nodes, then it's possible that data may be permanently lost, which may not be acceptable. Often, these systems will employ *quorum-based replication*, in which a write might be acknowledged if 10 percent of all available nodes have the replicated data. Thus, if any one node goes down, there's still no risk.

Scaling State in Spring Integration

Most of the components in Spring Integration are stateless, and so our examples have been stateless. This covers about 90 percent of the situations when implementing an integration solution. In about 10 percent of cases, however, the integration system needs to maintain state. An example of maintaining state in an integration is when a message is received with a very large payload that could potentially overwhelm downstream components and burden the system's memory. This is where the claim check pattern comes in.

Claim Check Pattern

The claim check pattern supports storing data in a well-known place while keeping a pointer, or *claim check* (so named for the token you're given when you deposit something in somebody else's care—perhaps luggage at a hotel or your car at a car wash—that can be redeemed for the original object), to the original object. The claim check can be passed along as the message payload until the message hits a component that needs access to the payload. The component can then retrieve the data via the claim check reference.

Spring Integration provides two claim check transformers: *the incoming claim check transformer* and the *outgoing claim check transformer*. Namespace configuration support is also provided for these transformers. Listing 16–14 shows the Spring configuration file for a simple example of using the claim check transformers.

Listing 16–14. *Spring Configuration for the Claim Check Example claimcheck-context.xml*

```
<?xml version="1.0" encoding="UTF-8"?>
<beans xmlns="http://www.springframework.org/schema/beans"
       xmlns:xsi="http://www.w3.org/2001/XMLSchema-instance"
       xmlns:int="http://www.springframework.org/schema/integration"
       xmlns:context="http://www.springframework.org/schema/context"
       xsi:schemaLocation="http://www.springframework.org/schema/integration
    http://www.springframework.org/schema/integration/spring-integration-2.0.xsd
```

```
        http://www.springframework.org/schema/beans
        http://www.springframework.org/schema/beans/spring-beans-3.0.xsd
        http://www.springframework.org/schema/context
        http://www.springframework.org/schema/context/spring-context-3.0.xsd">

  <context:component-scan base-package="com.apress.prospringintegration.claimcheck"/>

  <int:claim-check-in id="checkin"
                      input-channel="checkinChannel"
                      message-store="messageStore"
                      output-channel="process"/>

  <int:claim-check-out id="checkout"
                       input-channel="process"
                       message-store="messageStore"
                       output-channel="checkoutChannel"/>

  <int:channel id="checkinChannel">
    <int:interceptors>
      <int:wire-tap channel="logger"/>
    </int:interceptors>
  </int:channel>

  <int:channel id="process">
    <int:interceptors>
      <int:wire-tap channel="logger"/>
    </int:interceptors>
  </int:channel>

  <int:logging-channel-adapter log-full-message="true" id="logger" level="INFO"/>

  <int:channel id="checkoutChannel">
    <int:queue capacity="10"/>
  </int:channel>

</beans>
```

The claim-check-in element configuration receives a message on the checkinChannel channel. The incoming claim check transformer will take the payload of the inbound message and store it in the message store identified by the message-store attribute with a generated key ID. The ID will be set as the payload of the outgoing message sent on the channel process. The original payload can be retrieved from the message store at a later time using the key ID. The messageStore is configured using the Java configuration file ClaimCheckConfiguration shown in Listing 16–15. For this example, the map-based in-memory message store SimpeMessageStore is used. JdbcMessageStore is an alternative, relational-database implementation of MessageStore that can also be used (especially if the claim check will be used across multiple nodes in a distributed environment where the message is stored on one host and retrieved on a different host). Any map key/value store can be used to support the claim check transformer.

Listing 16–15. *Claim Check Java Configuration*

```
package com.apress.prospringintegration.claimcheck;

import org.springframework.context.annotation.Bean;
import org.springframework.context.annotation.Configuration;
import org.springframework.integration.store.SimpleMessageStore;

@Configuration
public class ClaimCheckConfiguration {

    @Bean
    public SimpleMessageStore messageStore() {
        SimpleMessageStore messageStore = new SimpleMessageStore();

        return messageStore;
    }

}
```

Spring Integration provides an outgoing claim check transformer to transform a message with a claim check payload back into a message with the original payload. This is configured with the `claim-check-out` element, as shown previously in Listing 16–14. The claim check message is received from the `process` channel. Using the claim check, the transformer retrieves the message from the message store and sends a message with the original payload to the `checkoutChannel` channel. A wire tap is added to the `process` channel to ensure that the message contains only the claim check as the payload. Listing 16–16 shows the creation of a simple `main` class to test this example.

Listing 16–16. *Claim Check Example main Class*

```
package com.apress.prospringintegration.claimcheck;

import org.springframework.context.support.ClassPathXmlApplicationContext;
import org.springframework.integration.Message;
import org.springframework.integration.MessageChannel;
import org.springframework.integration.core.PollableChannel;
import org.springframework.integration.support.MessageBuilder;

import java.util.HashMap;
import java.util.Map;

public class ClaimCheckExample {

    public static void main(String[] args) {
        ClassPathXmlApplicationContext context =
                new ClassPathXmlApplicationContext("spring/claimcheck-context.xml");

        MessageChannel input = context.getBean("checkinChannel", MessageChannel.class);
        PollableChannel output = context.getBean("checkoutChannel", PollableChannel.class);

        Map<String, String> customerMap = new HashMap<String, String>();
        customerMap.put("firstName", "John");
        customerMap.put("lastName", "Smith");
```

```
        customerMap.put("address", "100 State Street");
        customerMap.put("city", "Los Angeles");
        customerMap.put("state", "CA");
        customerMap.put("zip", "90064");

        Message<Map<String, String>> message =
                MessageBuilder.withPayload(customerMap).build();
        input.send(message);

        Message<?> reply = output.receive();
        System.out.println("received: " + reply.getPayload());
    }
}
```

This example creates a simple `Map` object and sends it to the `checkinChannel` channel. A message is then received from the `checkoutChannel` channel. Running this example shows that the `Map` class is converted to a claim check ID, and then retrieved back from the message store, as shown in Listing 16–17.

***Listing 16–17.** Results of Running the Claim Check Example*

```
INFO : org.springframework.integration.handler.LoggingHandler - [Payload={zip=90064,
lastName=Smith, address=100 State Street, state=CA, firstName=John, city=Los
Angeles}][Headers={timestamp=1295826995144, id=c5596f68-3c44-486a-88de-59b65e19b2e4}]

INFO : org.springframework.integration.handler.LoggingHandler - [Payload=c5596f68-3c44-486a-
88de-59b65e19b2e4][Headers={timestamp=1295826995144, id=ee6ea488-8a27-4d40-965e-3677a27127c6}]

received: {zip=90064, lastName=Smith, address=100 State Street, state=CA, firstName=John,
city=Los Angeles}
```

MessageGroupStore

Another stateful component in Spring Integration is the aggregator. Suppose some process is waiting for bids on a job from contractors before a decision can be made. Perhaps a simple majority of the contractors have to respond before work can proceed, or perhaps all of them need to respond. Either way, this could take hours—or weeks! Spring Integration would have to store the messages in-memory while they arrive.

In such a scenario, the integration would be flawed if it were set up on multiple nodes: perhaps one node consumes three of the nine messages being waited for, another node consumes three, and another node consumes three. They would all wait for eternity, expecting the other six to come! In this case, the state needs to be externalized and available to all of the Spring Integration instances so that they can "see" that all nine messages have indeed arrived, just on different machines. Luckily, Spring Integration provides support for this scenario. A message group store supports storage operations for a group of messages linked by a group ID. The `MessageGroupStore` interface has a number of implementations, including the `JdbcMessageStore`, which uses a database to store the information, as well as a Gemfire implementation. As discussed, the scalability of an RDBMS is limited. A distributed caching system such a Gemfire, on the other hand, can be elastically scaled at will. Again, any map (key/value) store may be used to back a `MessageGroupStore`.

To support the examples of a message group store using a database and distributed cache to maintain the state, the Maven dependencies shown in Listing 16–18 will be needed. The Gemfire adapter, used in this example, is still in development and only available as a snapshot version. Additional information about using this support is given following.

***Listing 16–18.** Maven Dependencies for the Message Group Store Example*

```
<dependencies>
  <dependency>
    <groupId>org.springframework.data.gemfire</groupId>
    <artifactId>spring-gemfire</artifactId>
    <version>1.0.0.M2-SNAPSHOT</version>
  </dependency>
  <dependency>
    <groupId>org.springframework.integration</groupId>
    <artifactId>spring-integration-gemfire</artifactId>
    <version>2.0.0.BUILD-SNAPSHOT</version>
  </dependency>
  <dependency>
    <groupId>org.springframework.integration</groupId>
    <artifactId>spring-integration-core</artifactId>
    <version>2.0.1.RELEASE</version>
  </dependency>
  <dependency>
    <groupId>org.springframework.integration</groupId>
    <artifactId>spring-integration-jdbc</artifactId>
    <version>2.0.1.RELEASE</version>
  </dependency>
  <dependency>
    <groupId>org.springframework</groupId>
    <artifactId>spring-core</artifactId>
    <version>3.0.5.RELEASE</version>
  </dependency>
  <dependency>
    <groupId>cglib</groupId>
    <artifactId>cglib</artifactId>
    <version>2.2</version>
  </dependency>
  <dependency>
    <groupId>hsqldb</groupId>
    <artifactId>hsqldb</artifactId>
    <version>1.8.0.7</version>
  </dependency>
</dependencies>
```

Database Message Group Store

The first example we will use is a JDBC message group store to maintain the state of the aggregation process. The general concept is that a series of messages will be sent to a message channel. The channel will forward the messages to an aggregator, which will be set up to wait for a specified number of messages with the same correlation value. Only after all the messages have arrived will they be forwarded on to the service activator endpoint. The current state, i.e., number of numbers that have arrived with the same correlation ID will be maintained in a database. By storing the state in a database instead of in memory, you can use multiple instances of Spring Integration to process the messages, and there is no risk of an aborted Spring Integration operating system process "losing" the messages. Thus, the process can be scaled out over multiple systems. The Spring configuration file is shown in Listing 16–19.

Listing 16–19. *Spring Configuration for the Message Group Store Example spring-context.xml*

```
<?xml version="1.0" encoding="UTF-8"?>
<beans xmlns="http://www.springframework.org/schema/beans"
       xmlns:xsi="http://www.w3.org/2001/XMLSchema-instance"
       xmlns:jdbc="http://www.springframework.org/schema/jdbc"
       xmlns:int="http://www.springframework.org/schema/integration"
       xmlns:context="http://www.springframework.org/schema/context"
       xsi:schemaLocation="http://www.springframework.org/schema/integration
    http://www.springframework.org/schema/integration/spring-integration-2.0.xsd
    http://www.springframework.org/schema/beans
    http://www.springframework.org/schema/beans/spring-beans-3.0.xsd
    http://www.springframework.org/schema/jdbc
    http://www.springframework.org/schema/jdbc/spring-jdbc-3.0.xsd
    http://www.springframework.org/schema/context
    http://www.springframework.org/schema/context/spring-context-3.0.xsd">

  <context:property-placeholder location="spring/jdbc/jdbc.properties"/>

  <context:component-scan base-package="com.apress.prospringintegration.messagestore">
    <context:exclude-filter type="regex"
            expression="com\.apress\.prospringintegration\.messagestore\.gemfire.*"/>
  </context:component-scan>

  <int:channel id="input"/>

  <int:channel id="output"/>

  <int:aggregator release-strategy="releaseStrategy"
                  correlation-strategy="correlationStrategy"
                  message-store="jdbcMessageGroupStore"
                  input-channel="input"
                  output-channel="output"/>

  <int:service-activator input-channel="output" ref="messageGroupStoreActivator"/>

  <jdbc:embedded-database id="dataSource">
    <jdbc:script
        location="classpath:org/springframework/integration/jdbc/schema-hsqldb.sql"/>
  </jdbc:embedded-database>

</beans>
```

The Spring context namespace is used to import the jdbc.properties file using the property-placeholder element, and annotation support is provided by the component-scan element. An input channel and an output channel are configured for sending and receiving the messages. The aggregator component has a number of properties to be configured. The release-strategy determines when the set of message will be forwarded on to the output channel. The correlation-strategy is the condition on which the messages are considered to be part of the same group. The message-store is where the state is stored. All of the properties will be configured using the Java configuration support described following. The next element is the actual database configuration used to back the message group store. In this example, an HSQLDB database is used to simplify the setup. The default SQL script to set up the base database tables is specified through the script element. Finally, the service activator component messageGroupStoreActivator is configured to log the series of messages that are part of a single group. The service activator class is shown in Listing 16–20.

Listing 16–20. *Service Activator Class for the Message Group Store Example*

```
package com.apress.prospringintegration.messagestore.util;

import org.apache.commons.lang.StringUtils;
import org.springframework.integration.Message;
import org.springframework.integration.annotation.ServiceActivator;
import org.springframework.stereotype.Component;

import java.util.Collection;

@Component
public class MessageGroupStoreActivator {
    @ServiceActivator
    public void handleMessages(Message<Collection<Object>> msg) throws Throwable {
        Collection<Object> payloads = msg.getPayload();

        System.out.println("-----------------------------------------");
        System.out.println(StringUtils.join(payloads, ", "));

    }
}
```

The heart of the JDBC message group store is contained in the Java configuration class JdbcMessageStoreConfiguration, as shown in Listing 16–21. This class configures the aggregator strategies and message group store.

Listing 16–21. *Java Configuration Class JdbcMessageStoreConfiguration*

```
package com.apress.prospringintegration.messagestore.jdbc;

import org.springframework.beans.factory.annotation.Value;
import org.springframework.context.annotation.Bean;
import org.springframework.context.annotation.Configuration;
import org.springframework.integration.aggregator.CorrelationStrategy;
import org.springframework.integration.aggregator.HeaderAttributeCorrelationStrategy;
import org.springframework.integration.aggregator.ReleaseStrategy;
import org.springframework.integration.aggregator.SequenceSizeReleaseStrategy;
import org.springframework.integration.jdbc.JdbcMessageStore;

import javax.sql.DataSource;

@Configuration
public class JdbcMessageStoreConfiguration {

    @Value("${correlation-header}")
    private String correlationHeader;

    @Bean
    public DataSource dataSource(){
        // ...  any database javax.sql.DataSource implementation you like
```

```
    }

    @Bean
    public ReleaseStrategy releaseStrategy() {
        return new SequenceSizeReleaseStrategy(false);
    }

    @Bean
    public CorrelationStrategy correlationStrategy() {
        return new HeaderAttributeCorrelationStrategy(this.correlationHeader);
    }

    @Bean
    public JdbcMessageStore jdbcMessageGroupStore() {
        JdbcMessageStore jdbcMessageGroupStore = new JdbcMessageStore(dataSource);
        return jdbcMessageGroupStore;
    }
}
```

The value annotation and Spring Expression Language (SpEL) are used to pass in the correlation-header property form the jdbc.properties file and the dataSource from the spring-content.xml Spring configuration file. The release strategy uses the SequenceSizeReleaseStrategy class, in which the messages are released as soon as the total number of messages that are correlated reach a value specified by the sequence number header value. The correlation strategy uses the HeaderAttributeCorrelationStrategy class, in which any messages with the specified correlation header are consider part of the same group. Finally, the Spring Integration support for a JDBC message group store is used with the data source specified in the configuration file to use the embedded HSQLDB database, as discussed previously.

To test this example, a utility class is used to generate a series of messages with the correct header values for the sequence size and correlation value. Leveraging the Spring Integration utility class MessageBuilder, the MessageProducer class sends a series of Spring payloads with a specified correlation ID. The class determines the collection size and sends the message with the correct sequence size and correlation header values. The MessageProducer class is shown in Listing 16–22. Again, annotation support is used to pass the input message channel and correlation value.

Listing 16–22. *Utilty Class for Sending a Group of Messages*

```
package com.apress.prospringintegration.messagestore.util;

import org.springframework.beans.factory.annotation.Value;
import org.springframework.integration.Message;
import org.springframework.integration.MessageChannel;
import org.springframework.integration.core.MessagingTemplate;
import org.springframework.integration.support.MessageBuilder;
import org.springframework.stereotype.Component;

import javax.annotation.PostConstruct;
import java.util.Collection;

@Component
public class MessageProducer {
    private MessagingTemplate messagingTemplate = new MessagingTemplate();

    @Value("#{input}")
```

```
    private MessageChannel messageChannel;

    @Value("${correlation-header}")
    private String correlationHeader;

    @PostConstruct
    public void start() throws Throwable {
        this.messagingTemplate.setDefaultChannel(this.messageChannel);
    }

    public void sendMessages(int correlationValue, Collection<String> payloadValues)
            throws Throwable {

        int sequenceNumber = 0;
        int size = payloadValues.size();

        for (String payloadValue : payloadValues) {
            Message<?> message = MessageBuilder.withPayload(payloadValue)
                    .setCorrelationId(this.correlationHeader)
                    .setHeader(this.correlationHeader, correlationValue)
                    .setSequenceNumber(++sequenceNumber)
                    .setSequenceSize(size)
                    .build();
            this.messagingTemplate.send(message);
        }
    }

}
```

To run this example, a main class is used to load the Spring context file and send a series of messages with string payloads. Running the example will demonstrate that the series of messages must be received before it's sent to the output message channel and logged by the service activator. The JdbcTest class to run the example is shown in Listing 16–23.

Listing 16–23. *Test Class JdbcTest to Run the JDBC Messgage Group Store Example*

```
package com.apress.prospringintegration.messagestore.jdbc;

import com.apress.prospringintegration.messagestore.util.MessageProducer;
import org.springframework.context.support.ClassPathXmlApplicationContext;

import java.util.Arrays;

public class JdbcTest {
    public static void main(String[] args) throws Throwable {

        ClassPathXmlApplicationContext classPathXmlApplicationContext =
                new ClassPathXmlApplicationContext(
                        "classpath:spring/jdbc/spring-context.xml");

        MessageProducer messageProducer =
                classPathXmlApplicationContext.getBean(MessageProducer.class);

        for (int i = 0; i < 10; i++)
```

```
            messageProducer.sendMessages(i,
                    Arrays.asList(
                            new String[]{"apple", "banana", "carrot", "date", "egg"}));

        Thread.sleep(1000 * 10);
    }
}
```

Gemfire Message Group Store

Gemfire is a distributed cache product providing elastic scalability. Nodes can be added or removed at will without taking the systems down or losing any data. The message group store example will be implemented using Gemfire to demonstrate a fully scalable example of Spring Integration where state must be maintained.

Spring Integration Gemfire support is still in development, and this example uses the snapshot version of the adapter. This may require that the adapter code be cloned from the Git repository and built for this example to run. You can do this by running the series of commands shown in Listing 16–24.

Listing 16–24. *Commands to Build the Gemfire Adapter*

```
git clone git://git.springsource.org/spring-integration/sandbox.git
cd spring-integration-gemfire
mvn clean install
```

This example is similar to the preceding JDBC example in that it allows reuse of the utility classes for sending the series of messages and logging the output of the aggregator component. The Spring configuration file is shown in Listing 16–25.

Listing 16–25. *Spring Configuration for the Gemfire Message Group Store Example spring-context.xml*

```
<?xml version="1.0" encoding="UTF-8"?>
<beans xmlns="http://www.springframework.org/schema/beans"
       xmlns:xsi="http://www.w3.org/2001/XMLSchema-instance"
       xmlns:util="http://www.springframework.org/schema/util"
       xmlns:int="http://www.springframework.org/schema/integration"
       xmlns:gfe="http://www.springframework.org/schema/gemfire"
       xmlns:context="http://www.springframework.org/schema/context"
       xsi:schemaLocation="http://www.springframework.org/schema/integration
    http://www.springframework.org/schema/integration/spring-integration-2.0.xsd
    http://www.springframework.org/schema/beans
    http://www.springframework.org/schema/beans/spring-beans-3.0.xsd
    http://www.springframework.org/schema/util
    http://www.springframework.org/schema/util/spring-util-3.0.xsd
    http://www.springframework.org/schema/gemfire
    http://www.springframework.org/schema/gemfire/spring-gemfire.xsd
    http://www.springframework.org/schema/context
    http://www.springframework.org/schema/context/spring-context-3.0.xsd">

  <context:property-placeholder location="spring/gemfire/gemfire.properties"/>

  <context:component-scan base-package="com.apress.prospringintegration.messagestore">
    <context:exclude-filter type="regex"
```

```
            expression="com\.apress\.prospringintegration\.messagestore\.jdbc.*"/>
    </context:component-scan>

    <int:channel id="input"/>

    <int:channel id="output"/>

    <int:aggregator release-strategy="releaseStrategy"
                    correlation-strategy="correlationStrategy"
                    message-store="gemfireMessageGroupStore"
                    input-channel="input"
                    output-channel="output"/>

    <int:service-activator input-channel="output" ref="messageGroupStoreActivator"/>

    <util:properties id="props" location="spring/gemfire/gemfire-cache.properties"/>

    <gfe:cache properties-ref="props" id="cache"/>
    <gfe:transaction-manager cache-ref="cache"/>

    <gfe:replicated-region id="unmarkedRegion" cache-ref="cache"/>
    <gfe:replicated-region id="markedRegion" cache-ref="cache"/>
    <gfe:replicated-region id="messageGroupRegion" cache-ref="cache"/>

</beans>
```

This example also uses the Spring `context` namespace to read-in the properties file `gemfire.properties` and to support the annotated classes. The aggregator configuration is the same as the JDBC example, except that it uses the Gemfire group message store. Spring has built-in support for configuring and kicking off a Gemfire instance. Gemfire is essentially a map key/value store that can be distributed over multiple hosts, allowing for scaling out. The basic Gemfire configuration is brought in using the familiar Spring `util` namespace. Each key/value store or map is defined as a region. Three regions or maps are required to support the Spring Integration message group store: unmarked, marked, and message group. These properties are configured in the Java class `GemfireMessageStoreConfiguration`, as shown in Listing 16–26.

Listing 16–26. *Java Configuration for Gemfire Message Group Store Example*

```
package com.apress.prospringintegration.messagestore.gemfire;

import org.springframework.beans.factory.annotation.Value;
import org.springframework.context.annotation.Bean;
import org.springframework.context.annotation.Configuration;
import org.springframework.integration.Message;
import org.springframework.integration.aggregator.CorrelationStrategy;
import org.springframework.integration.aggregator.HeaderAttributeCorrelationStrategy;
import org.springframework.integration.aggregator.ReleaseStrategy;
import org.springframework.integration.aggregator.SequenceSizeReleaseStrategy;
import org.springframework.integration.gemfire.store.KeyValueMessageGroup;
import org.springframework.integration.gemfire.store.KeyValueMessageGroupStore;

import java.util.Map;

@Configuration
```

```
public class GemfireMessageStoreConfiguration {

    @Value("${correlation-header}")
    private String correlationHeader;

    @Value("#{unmarkedRegion}")
    private Map<String, Message<?>> unmarked; // the Gemfire 'Region' interface
                                              // is aMap<?,?> impl

    @Value("#{markedRegion}")
    private Map<String, Message<?>> marked;

    @Value("#{messageGroupRegion}")
    private Map<Object, KeyValueMessageGroup> messageGroupRegion;

    @Bean
    public ReleaseStrategy releaseStrategy() {
        return new SequenceSizeReleaseStrategy(false);
    }

    @Bean
    public CorrelationStrategy correlationStrategy() {
        return new HeaderAttributeCorrelationStrategy(this.correlationHeader);
    }

    @Bean
    public KeyValueMessageGroupStore gemfireMessageGroupStore() {
        return new KeyValueMessageGroupStore(
                this.messageGroupRegion, this.marked, this.unmarked);
    }
}
```

The release and correlation strategies are the same as used for the JDBC example. What is unique about this configuration class is the way the Gemfire message group store is created. The three Gemfire regions are referenced using SpEL to support the message group store. Note that the message group store simply needs three key/value `Map` objects. The type of the objects that are injected are Gemfire's `Region` class, which is the class that represents a region inside the Gemfire cache. Using Gemfire allows the message group store to be distributed across the Gemfire instances. The elastic nature of Gemfire allows the message group store to be scaled dynamically.

To test this example, the same utility class is used to publish the series of messages. The test class is shown in Listing 16–27. The aggregator will maintain the state in Gemfire to determine when all the messages have been sent and when it is time to release the messages to the service activator.

Listing 16–27. *Gemfire Message Group Store Example main Class*

```
package com.apress.prospringintegration.messagestore.gemfire;

import com.apress.prospringintegration.messagestore.util.MessageProducer;
import org.springframework.context.support.ClassPathXmlApplicationContext;

import java.util.Arrays;

public class GemfireTest {
    public static void main(String[] args) throws Throwable {
```

```
        ClassPathXmlApplicationContext classPathXmlApplicationContext =
                new ClassPathXmlApplicationContext(
                        "classpath:spring/gemfire/spring-context.xml");

        MessageProducer messageProducer =
                classPathXmlApplicationContext.getBean(MessageProducer.class);

        for (int i = 0; i < 10; i++)
            messageProducer.sendMessages(i,
                    Arrays.asList(
                            new String[]{"apple", "banana", "carrot", "date", "egg"}));

        Thread.sleep(1000 * 10);
    }
}
```

Summary

This chapter explored some of the approaches to scaling an enterprise integration using Spring Integration. We looked to how to leverage multicore CPUs through concurrency, how to scale the transport layer by using the clustering support for some of the messaging systems, and how to scale the endpoints for web services and databases. Finally, we looked at how to scale Spring Integration when it must maintain state through the claim check pattern and group message store using a database or a distributed cache solution such as Gemfire.

CHAPTER 17

Spring Integration and Spring Batch

Today's applications can be described in terms of the frameworks they use—web applications use web frameworks, service tiers use remoting and persistence frameworks (such as ORMs and Spring's remoting hierarchy), messaging applications use messaging frameworks, and so on. Often, however, there is another type of application that sits in all these layers and handles bulk operations—operations that deal with large amounts of data, such as data loading, exporting, synchronizing. Bulk processing, or batch processing, is a common requirement for most applications, both in the initial setup and the ongoing maintenance. The only thing most batch processing applications have in common, however, is the manipulation of large amounts of data; how they get the data, where it's written, and what must be done to adapt it all tend to be unique. Spring Batch provides a very flexible, expressive way to deal with large amounts of data.

This chapter will review the Spring Batch project and how it can be used with Spring Integration. Spring Integration has the ability to launch Spring Batch jobs via messaging, allowing for event-driven batch processes. In addition, Spring Integration can be used to scale out Spring Batch using partitioning. This provides the ability to partition big batch jobs over many nodes using message channels as the coordination fabric. Finally, this chapter will discuss Spring Batch Admin, which provides a web-based user interface for Spring Batch leveraging Spring Integration.

What Is Spring Batch?

Batch processing has been around for decades. The earliest widespread technology for managing information was batch processing. The environments at this time did not have interactive sessions, and usually did not have the capability to load multiple applications in memory. Computers were expensive and bore no resemblance to today's servers. Typically, machines were multiuser and in use during the day (time-shared). During the evenings however, the machines would sit idle, which was a tremendous waste. Businesses invested in ways to utilize the offline time to do work aggregated through the course of the day. Out of this practice emerged batch processing.

Batch processing solutions typically run offline, indifferent to events in the system. In the past, batch processes ran offline out of necessity. Today, however, some batch processes are run offline because having work done at a predictable time, and having large chunks of work done at once are requirements for a number of architectures. A batch processing solution does not usually respond to requests, although there is no reason it could not be started as a consequence of messages or requests. Batch processing solutions tend to be used on large datasets where the duration of the processing is a critical factor for their architecture and implementation. A process might run for minutes, hours, or days. Jobs may have unbounded durations (i.e., they run until all work is finished, even if this means running for a few days), or they may be strictly bounded (jobs must proceed in time, with each row taking the same amount of time regardless of bounds, which lets you predict that a given job will finish in a certain time frame.)

Mainframe applications used batch processing, and one of the largest modern-day environments for batch processing, Customer Information Control System (CICS) on z/OS, is still fundamentally a mainframe operating system. CICS is very well suited to a particular type of task: taking input, processing it, and writing it to output. CICS is a transaction server (used most in financial institutions and government) that runs programs in a number of languages (COBOL, C, PLI, etc.). It can easily support thousands of transactions per second. Having debuted in 1969, CICS was one of the first containers, which is a concept still familiar to Spring Framework and Java EE users. A CICS installation is very expensive, and IBM still sells and installs CICS.

Many other solutions have come along since then, of course. These solutions are usually specific to a particular environment: COBOL/CICS on mainframes, C on Unix, and, today, Java on any number of environments. The problem is that there is very little standardized infrastructure for dealing with these types of batch processing solutions. Very few people are even aware of what they are missing, because there is very little native support on the Java platform for batch processing. Businesses that need a solution typically end up writing it in-house, resulting in fragile, domain-specific code.

The pieces are there, however: transaction support, fast I/O, schedulers such as Quartz, Spring 3.0's scheduling abstraction and solid threading support, and the powerful concept of an application container in Java EE and Spring. It was only natural that Dave Syer and his team would come along and build Spring Batch, a batch processing solution for the Spring platform, to fill in the gaps left by these many pieces to provide a comprehensive, consistent batch processing framework.

A typical Spring Batch application typically reads in a large amount of data and then writes it back out in a modified form. Decisions about transactional barriers, input size, concurrency, and the order of steps in processing are all dimensions of a typical integration. Spring Batch is a flexible but not all-encompassing solution. Just as Spring does not reinvent the wheel when it can be avoided, Spring Batch leaves a few important pieces to the discretion of the implementer. Case in point: Spring Batch provides a generic mechanism by which to launch a job, be it by the command line, a Unix `cron`, an operating system service, Quartz, or in response to an event on a messaging bus. Another example is the way Spring Batch manages the state of batch processes. Spring Batch requires a durable store. The only useful implementation of an `org.springframework.batch.core.repository.JobRepository` (an interface provided by Spring Batch for storing runtime data) requires a database because a database is transactional and there is no need to reinvent it. The database required, however, is largely unspecified, although there are useful defaults provided.

A common pattern is loading data from a comma-separated value (CSV) file, perhaps as a business-to-business (B2B) transaction, or as an integration with an older legacy application. Another common application is nontrivial processing on records in a database. Perhaps the output is an update of the database record itself. An example might be resizing of images on the file system whose metadata is stored in a database, or needing to trigger another process based on some condition.

Fixed-width data, which is often used with legacy or embedded systems, is a fine candidate for batch processing. Processing that deals with a resource that's fundamentally nontransactional (e.g., a web service or a file) begs for batch processing, because batch processing provides retry/skip/fail functionality, and most web services don't.

Spring Batch provides the same POJO-based and dependency injection approach as the core Spring Framework. Spring Batch also provides a reusable infrastructure to help build batch jobs to deal with large volumes of data. In general, a Spring Batch job can be separated into three components: Application, Spring Batch Core, and Spring Batch Infrastructure, as illustrated in Figure 17–1.

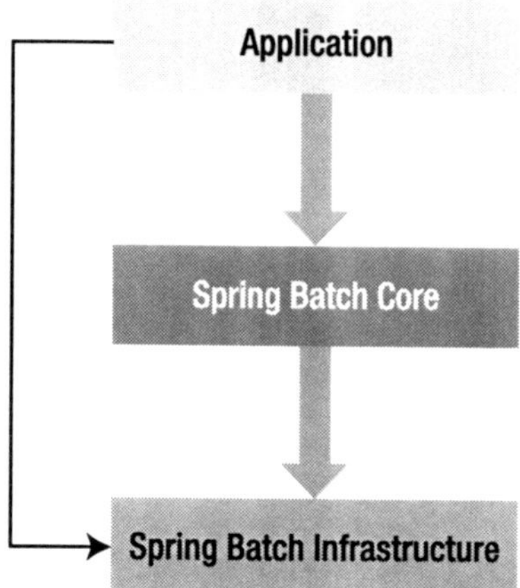

Figure 17–1. Spring Batch architecture

Spring Batch works with a `JobRepository`, which is the keeper of all the knowledge and metadata for each job (including component parts such as `org.springframework.batch.core.JobInstance`, `org.springframework.batch.core.JobExecution`, and `org.springframework.batch.core.StepExecution`). Each job is composed of one or more steps, one after another. With Spring Batch 2.0, a step can *conditionally* follow another step, allowing for primitive workflows. These steps can also be concurrent: two steps can run at the same time.

When a job is run, it is often coupled with `org.springframework.batch.core.JobParameter` to parameterize the behavior of the job. For example, a job might take a date parameter to determine which records to process. This coupling is called a `JobInstance`. A `JobInstance` is unique because of the `JobParameter` associated with it. Each time the `JobInstance` (i.e., the same job and `JobParameter`) is run, it is called a `JobExecution`. This is a runtime context for a version of the job. Ideally, for every `JobInstance` there would be only one `JobExecution`: the `JobExecution` that was created the first time the `JobInstance` ran. However, if there are any errors, the `JobInstance` should be restarted; the subsequent run would create another `JobExecution`. For every step in the job, there is a `StepExecution` in the `JobExecution`.

```
<batch:job id="importData">
  <batch:step id="step1"/>
</batch:job>
```

Thus, Spring Batch has a mirrored object graph, with one graph reflecting the design/build-time view of a job, and another reflecting the runtime view of a job. This split between the prototype and the instance is very similar to the way many workflow engines—including Activiti—work.

For example, suppose that a daily report is generated at 2 a.m. The parameter to the job would be the date (most likely the previous day's date). The job, in this case, would model a loading step, a summary step, and an output step. Each day the job is run, a new `JobInstance` and `JobExecution` would be created. If there are any retries of the same `JobInstance`, conceivably many `JobExecutions` would be created.

Setting Up Spring Batch

Spring Batch provides a lot of flexibility and guarantees to the application, but it cannot work in a vacuum—it needs to store data and job state somewhere to keep its guarantees. Add the following dependencies in Listing 17–1 to the Maven configuration file to support Spring Batch and the PostgreSQL database connection.

Listing 17–1. *Spring Batch Maven Dependency*

```
<dependency>
  <groupId>org.springframework.batch</groupId>
  <artifactId>spring-batch-core</artifactId>
  <version>2.1.6.RELEASE</version>
</dependency>
<dependency>
  <groupId>postgresql</groupId>
  <artifactId>postgresql</artifactId>
  <version>9.0-801.jdbc4</version>
</dependency>
```

To do its work, the `JobRepository` requires a database. For all the examples, PostgreSQL will be used as the database. PostgreSQL is easy to install and available for most operating systems at `http://www.postgresql.org/download`. Spring Batch requires a schema to be set up to properly maintain state. The simplest way to get that schema is to simply download the `spring-batch-2.1.6.RELEASE-no-dependencies.zip` and look in the directory at `spring-batch-2.1.6.RELEASE/dist/org/springframework/batch/core`. Within the directory, there are a number of `.sql` files, each containing the data definition language (DDL) for the required schema for the different kind of databases. PostgreSQL uses the DDL `schema-postgresql.sql`. The Java configuration required to support connecting to the PostgreSQL database is shown in Listing 17–2.

Listing 17–2. *Java Configuration for the PostgreSQL Database*

```
package com.apress.prospringintegration.springbatch.integration;

import org.apache.commons.dbcp.BasicDataSource;
import org.springframework.beans.factory.annotation.Value;
import org.springframework.context.annotation.Bean;
import org.springframework.context.annotation.Configuration;

@Configuration
public class JdbcConfiguration {

    @Value("${dataSource.driverClassName}")
    private String driverClassName;

    @Value("${dataSource.url}")
    private String url;

    @Value("${dataSource.username}")
    private String username;

    @Value("${dataSource.password}")
```

```
    private String password;

    @Bean(destroyMethod = "close")
    public BasicDataSource dataSource() {
        BasicDataSource dataSource = new BasicDataSource();
        dataSource.setDriverClassName(driverClassName);
        dataSource.setUrl(url);
        dataSource.setUsername(username);
        dataSource.setPassword(password);
        return dataSource;
    }
}
```

Additionally, there are several collaborators required for Spring Batch to do its work. This configuration is mostly boilerplate. The `JobRepository` interface is the first thing that the application has to deal with when setting up a Spring Batch process. Again, there is only one really useful implementation of the `JobRepository` interface: `org.springframework.batch.core.repository.support.SimpleJobRepository`. This stores information about the state of the batch processes in a database. Creation is done through an `org.springframework.batch.core.repository.support.JobRepositoryFactoryBean`. Another standard factory, `org.springframework.batch.core.repository.support.MapJobRepositoryFactoryBean`, is useful mainly for testing because its state is not durable—it is an in-memory implementation. Both factories create an instance of `SimpleJobRepository`. The Java configuration for the basic Spring Batch configuration is shown in Listing 17–3.

Listing 17–3. *Java Configuration with Spring Batch*

```
package com.apress.prospringintegration.springbatch.integration;

import org.apache.commons.dbcp.BasicDataSource;
import org.springframework.batch.core.configuration.support.JobRegistryBeanPostProcessor;
import org.springframework.batch.core.configuration.support.MapJobRegistry;
import org.springframework.batch.core.launch.support.SimpleJobLauncher;
import org.springframework.batch.core.repository.support.JobRepositoryFactoryBean;
import org.springframework.beans.factory.annotation.Autowired;
import org.springframework.beans.factory.annotation.Value;
import org.springframework.context.annotation.Bean;
import org.springframework.context.annotation.Configuration;
import org.springframework.jdbc.datasource.DataSourceTransactionManager;

import javax.sql.DataSource;

@Configuration
public class BatchConfiguration {

    @Value("#{dataSource}")
    private DataSource dataSource;

    @Bean
    public DataSourceTransactionManager transactionManager(){
        DataSourceTransactionManager transactionManager = new DataSourceTransactionManager();
        transactionManager.setDataSource(dataSource);
        return transactionManager;
    }
```

```
    @Bean
    public MapJobRegistry jobRegistry() {
        MapJobRegistry jobRegistry = new MapJobRegistry();
        return jobRegistry;
    }

    @Bean
    public SimpleJobLauncher jobLauncher() throws Exception {
        SimpleJobLauncher jobLauncher = new SimpleJobLauncher();
        jobLauncher.setJobRepository(jobRepository().getJobRepository());
        return jobLauncher;
    }

    @Bean
    public JobRegistryBeanPostProcessor jobRegistryBeanPostProcessor() {
        JobRegistryBeanPostProcessor jobRegistryBeanPostProcessor =
                new JobRegistryBeanPostProcessor();
        jobRegistryBeanPostProcessor.setJobRegistry(jobRegistry());
        return jobRegistryBeanPostProcessor;
    }

    @Bean
    public JobRepositoryFactoryBean jobRepository() {
        JobRepositoryFactoryBean jobRepository = new JobRepositoryFactoryBean();
        jobRepository.setDataSource(dataSource);
        jobRepository.setTransactionManager(transactionManager());
        return jobRepository;
    }

}
```

Because the implementation uses a database to persist the metadata, take care to configure a `javax.sql.DataSource`, as well as the `org.springframework.transaction.PlatformTransactionManager` implementation `org.springframework.jdbc.datasource.DataSourceTransactionManager`. In this example, the `property-placeholder` element, which will be included in the following Spring configuration file, loads the contents of a properties file (`batch.properties`), whose values are used to configure the data source. The values need to be in place to match the choice of database in this file. The properties file is shown in Listing 17–4.

Listing 17–4. *batch.properties DataSource Configuration*

```
dataSource.password=password
dataSource.username=postgres
dataSource.databaseName=postgres
dataSource.driverClassName=org.postgresql.Driver
dataSource.serverName=localhost:5432
dataSource.url=jdbc:postgresql://${dataSource.serverName}/${dataSource.databaseName}
```

The first few beans are related strictly to configuration—nothing particularly novel or peculiar to Spring Batch: a data source and a transaction manager. Eventually, we get to the declaration of an `org.springframework.batch.core.configuration.support.MapJobRegistry` instance. This is critical—it is the central store for information regarding a given job, and it controls the big picture about all jobs in the system. Everything else works with this instance.

The org.springframework.batch.core.launch.support.SimpleJobLauncher provides a mechanism to launch batch jobs, where a job in this case is the batch solution. The jobLauncher is used to specify the name of the batch solution to run as well as any parameters required. Next, an org.springframework.batch.core.configuration.support.JobRegistryBeanPostProcessor instance needs to be defined. This bean scans the Spring context file and associates any configured jobs with the MapJobRegistry.

Finally, the SimpleJobRepository (which is factoried by the org.springframework.batch.core.repository.support.JobRepositoryFactoryBean) implements the interface org.springframework.batch.core.repository.JobRepository. It handles persistence and retrieval for the domain models involving steps, jobs, and so on.

Reading and Writing

The org.springframework.batch.item.ItemReader<T> reads a chunk of data from the source, which could be a CSV file, a database result, or TCP connection. The data is processed by the org.springframework.batch.item.ItemProcessor<I, O>. Finally, the org.springframework.batch.item.ItemWriter<T> writes data to the destination, which could be anything. This process is shown in Figure 17–2.

Figure 17–2. *Basic Spring Batch process*

Listing 17–5 contains an example of a Spring Batch job. As described earlier in this chapter, a job consists of steps, which are the real workhorses of a given job. The steps can be complex or very simple. Indeed, a step can be considered the smallest unit of work for a job. Input (what is read) is passed to the step and potentially processed; then output (what is written) is created from the step. This processing is spelled out using an instance of the org.springframework.batch.core.step.tasklet.Tasklet interface. Developers can provide their own Tasklet implementation or simply use some of the preconfigured configurations for different processing scenarios. These implementations are made available in terms of subelements of the Tasklet element. One of the most important aspects of batch processing is chunk-oriented processing, which is employed here using the chunk element.

Listing 17–5. *A Spring Batch Job integration.xml*

```
<?xml version="1.0" encoding="UTF-8"?>
<beans xmlns="http://www.springframework.org/schema/beans"
       xmlns:batch="http://www.springframework.org/schema/batch"
       xmlns:xsi="http://www.w3.org/2001/XMLSchema-instance"
       xmlns:context="http://www.springframework.org/schema/context"
       xmlns:int="http://www.springframework.org/schema/integration"
       xsi:schemaLocation="http://www.springframework.org/schema/beans
    http://www.springframework.org/schema/beans/spring-beans-3.0.xsd
    http://www.springframework.org/schema/batch
    http://www.springframework.org/schema/batch/spring-batch-2.1.xsd
    http://www.springframework.org/schema/context
    http://www.springframework.org/schema/context/spring-context-3.0.xsd
    http://www.springframework.org/schema/integration
    http://www.springframework.org/schema/integration/spring-integration-2.0.xsd">
```

```
    <context:property-placeholder location="batch.properties"/>
    <context:component-scan
        base-package="com.apress.prospringintegration.springbatch.integration"/>

    <batch:job id="importData" job-repository="jobRepository">
      <batch:step id="step1">
        <batch:tasklet>
          <batch:chunk reader="dataReader"
                       processor="userRegistrationValidationProcessor"
                       writer="dataWriter"
                       commit-interval="10"/>
        </batch:tasklet>
      </batch:step>
    </batch:job>

</beans>
```

In chunk-oriented processing, input is read from a reader, optionally processed (in this example through the userRegistrationValidationProcessor bean), and then aggregated. Finally, at a configurable interval as specified by the commit-interval attribute to configure how many items will be processed before the transaction is committed all the input is sent to the writer. If there is a transaction manager in play, the transaction is also committed. Right before a commit, the metadata in the database is updated to mark the progress of the job.

There are some nuances surrounding the aggregation of the input (read) values when a transaction-aware writer (or processor) is rolled back. Spring Batch caches the values it reads and writes them to the writer. If the writer component is transactional, like a database, and the reader is not, there's nothing inherently wrong with caching the read values and perhaps retrying or taking some alternative approach. If the reader itself is also transactional, then the values read from the resource will be rolled back and could conceivably change, rendering the in-memory cached values stale. If this happens, you can configure the chunk to not cache the values by using read is-reader-transactional-queue="true" on the chunk element.

The first responsibility of the Spring Batch job is reading a file from the file system by using a provided implementation for the example . Reading CSV files is a very common scenario, and Spring Batch's support does not disappoint. The org.springframework.batch.item.file.FlatFileItemReader<T> class delegates the task of delimiting fields and records within a file to an org.springframework.batch.item.file.LineMapper<T>, which in turn delegates the task of identifying the fields within that record to an org.springframework.batch.item.file.transform.LineTokenizer. An org.springframework.batch.item.file.transform.DelimitedLineTokenizer can be used to delineate fields separated by a , (comma) character.

The FlatFileItemReader also declares a fieldSetMapper attribute, which requires an implementation of FieldSetMapper. This bean is responsible for taking the input name/value pairs and producing a type that will be given to the writer component.

The Java configurations for the writer and reader are shown in Listing 17–6. In this case, BeanWrapperFieldSetMapper will create a POJO of type UserRegistration. The fields are named so that they can be referenced later in the configuration. These names don't have to be the values of some header row in the input file; they just have to correspond to the order in which the fields are found in the input file. These names are also used by the FieldSetMapper to match properties on a POJO. As each record is read, the values are applied to an instance of a POJO, and that POJO is returned.

Listing 17–6. Spring Batch Reader and Writer

```
package com.apress.prospringintegration.springbatch.integration;

import com.apress.prospringintegration.springbatch.UserRegistration;
import org.springframework.batch.item.database.BeanPropertyItemSqlParameterSourceProvider;
import org.springframework.batch.item.database.JdbcBatchItemWriter;
import org.springframework.batch.item.file.FlatFileItemReader;
import org.springframework.batch.item.file.mapping.BeanWrapperFieldSetMapper;
import org.springframework.batch.item.file.mapping.DefaultLineMapper;
import org.springframework.batch.item.file.transform.DelimitedLineTokenizer;
import org.springframework.beans.factory.annotation.Autowired;
import org.springframework.beans.factory.annotation.Value;
import org.springframework.context.annotation.Bean;
import org.springframework.context.annotation.Configuration;
import org.springframework.context.annotation.Scope;
import org.springframework.core.io.Resource;

import javax.sql.DataSource;

@Configuration
public class JobConfiguration {

    @Autowired
    private DataSource dataSource;

    @Bean
    @Scope("step")
    public FlatFileItemReader dataReader(
            @Value("file:src/main/resources/sample/#{jobParameters['input.file']}.csv")
            Resource resource) {
        FlatFileItemReader csvFileReader = new FlatFileItemReader();
        csvFileReader.setResource(resource);

        DelimitedLineTokenizer delimitedLineTokenizer =
                new DelimitedLineTokenizer(DelimitedLineTokenizer.DELIMITER_COMMA);
        delimitedLineTokenizer.setNames(
                new String[]{"firstName", "lastName", "company", "address", "city",
                        "state", "zip", "county", "url", "phoneNumber", "fax"});

        BeanWrapperFieldSetMapper beanWrapperFieldSetMapper = new BeanWrapperFieldSetMapper();
        beanWrapperFieldSetMapper.setTargetType(UserRegistration.class);

        DefaultLineMapper defaultLineMapper = new DefaultLineMapper();
        defaultLineMapper.setLineTokenizer(delimitedLineTokenizer);
        defaultLineMapper.setFieldSetMapper(beanWrapperFieldSetMapper);

        csvFileReader.setLineMapper(defaultLineMapper);

        return csvFileReader;
    }

    @Bean
```

```
    public JdbcBatchItemWriter dataWriter() {
        JdbcBatchItemWriter jdbcBatchItemWriter = new JdbcBatchItemWriter();
        jdbcBatchItemWriter.setAssertUpdates(true);
        jdbcBatchItemWriter.setDataSource(dataSource);
        jdbcBatchItemWriter
                .setSql("insert into USER_REGISTRATION(FIRST_NAME, LAST_NAME, COMPANY," +
                        "ADDRESS, CITY, STATE, ZIP, COUNTY, URL, PHONE_NUMBER, FAX )" +
                        "values (:firstName, :lastName, :company, :address, :city ," +
                        ":state, :zip, :county, :url, :phoneNumber, :fax )");

        jdbcBatchItemWriter.setItemSqlParameterSourceProvider(
                new BeanPropertyItemSqlParameterSourceProvider());

        return jdbcBatchItemWriter;
    }

}
```

The object UserRegistration in Listing 17–7 is just a POJO.

Listing 17–7. *UserRegistration Domain Object*

```
package com.apress.prospringintegration.springbatch;

import org.apache.commons.lang.builder.EqualsBuilder;
import org.apache.commons.lang.builder.HashCodeBuilder;
import org.apache.commons.lang.builder.ToStringBuilder;

import java.io.Serializable;

public class UserRegistration implements Serializable {
    private static final long serialVersionUID = 1L;

    public UserRegistration() {
    }

    public UserRegistration(String firstName, String lastName, String company,
                            String address, String city, String state, String zip,
                            String county, String url, String phoneNumber, String fax) {
        super();
        this.firstName = firstName;
        this.lastName = lastName;
        this.company = company;
        this.address = address;
        this.city = city;
        this.state = state;
        this.zip = zip;
        this.county = county;
        this.url = url;
        this.phoneNumber = phoneNumber;
        this.fax = fax;
    }

    private String firstName;
```

```
    private String lastName;
    private String company;
    private String address;
    private String city;
    private String state;
    private String zip;
    private String county;
    private String url;
    private String phoneNumber;
    private String fax;

   // accessor / mutators omitted for brevity

}
```

The next component to do work is the writer, which is responsible for taking the aggregated collection of items read from the reader. A new collection (`java.util.List<UserRegistration>`) is created, written, and finally reset each time the collection exceeds the `commit-interval` attribute on the `chunk` element. Spring Batch's `org.springframework.batch.item.database.JdbcBatchItemWriter` attempts to write the items into a database. This class contains support for taking input and writing it to a database. It is up to the developer to provide the input and to specify what SQL should be run for the input. It will run the SQL specified by the `sql` property—in essence writing to the database—as many times as specified by the `chunk` element's `commit-interval`, and then commit the whole transaction. By doing a simple insert using the names and values for the named parameters created by the bean configured for the `itemSqlParameterSourceProvider` property, an instance of the class `BeanPropertyItemSqlParameterSourceProvider`, whose sole job it is to take POJO properties and make them available as named parameters corresponding to the property name on the POJO

While transferring data directly from a spreadsheet or CSV dump might be useful, one can imagine having to do some sort of processing on the data before it's written. Data in a CSV file, and more generally from any source, is not usually exactly the way you expect it to be or immediately suitable for writing. Just because Spring Batch can coerce it into a POJO on your behalf does not mean the state of the data will be correct. Additional data may need to be inferred or filled in from other services before the data is suitable for writing. Spring Batch allows developers to do processing on reader output by using beans that implement `ItemProcessor<I, O>`. This processing can do virtually anything to the output before it gets passed to the writer, including changing the type of the data. In this example a validation processor is added, as shown in Listing 17–8. This processor checks for a valid state, zip code, and phone number.

Listing 17–8. *Processor Class That Validates the Address*

```
package com.apress.prospringintegration.springbatch.integration;

import com.apress.prospringintegration.springbatch.UserRegistration;
import org.apache.commons.lang.StringUtils;
import org.springframework.batch.item.ItemProcessor;
import org.springframework.stereotype.Component;

import java.util.Arrays;
import java.util.Collection;

@Component("userRegistrationValidationProcessor")
public class UserRegistrationValidationItemProcessor
        implements ItemProcessor<UserRegistration, UserRegistration> {
    private Collection<String> states;
```

```
    public UserRegistrationValidationItemProcessor() {
        this.states = Arrays.asList(
                ("AL AK AS AZ AR CA CO CT DE DC FM " +
                        "FL GA GU HI ID IL IN IA KS KY LA ME MH MD " +
                        "MA MI MN MS MO MT NE NV NH NJ NM NY NC ND " +
                        "MP OH OK OR PW PA PR RI SC SD TN TX UT " +
                        "VT VI VA WA WV WI WY").split(" "));
    }

    private String stripNonNumbers(String input) {
        String output = StringUtils.defaultString(input);
        StringBuffer numbersOnly = new StringBuffer();
        for (char potentialDigit : output.toCharArray()) {
            if (Character.isDigit(potentialDigit)) {
                numbersOnly.append(potentialDigit);
            }
        }
        return numbersOnly.toString();
    }

    private boolean isTelephoneValid(String telephone) {
        return !StringUtils.isEmpty(telephone) && telephone.length() == 10;
    }

    private boolean isZipCodeValid(String zip) {
        return !StringUtils.isEmpty(zip) && ((zip.length() == 5) || (zip.length() == 9));
    }

    private boolean isValidState(String state) {
        return states.contains(StringUtils.defaultString(state).trim());
    }

    public UserRegistration process(UserRegistration input)
            throws Exception {
        String zipCode = stripNonNumbers(input.getZip());
        String telephone = stripNonNumbers(input.getPhoneNumber());
        String state = StringUtils.defaultString(input.getState());

        if (isTelephoneValid(telephone) && isZipCodeValid(zipCode) && isValidState(state)) {
            input.setZip(zipCode);
            input.setPhoneNumber(telephone);
            System.out.println("input is valid, returning");
            return input;
        }

        System.out.println("Returning null");
        return null;
    }
}
```

In this example, with very little configuration or custom code, Spring Batch allows developers to build a solution for taking large CSV files and reading them into a database.

Retry

Batch jobs deal with resources that can fail, such as networking or file access. Retrying read and write is an important requirement when implementing jobs. Spring Batch provides retry capabilities to systematically retry the read or write, as shown in Listing 17–9. This example allows Spring Batch to retry when a DeadlockLoserDataAccessException is thrown.

***Listing 17–9.** Spring Batch Job Definition with Retry*

```
<batch:job id="importData" job-repository="jobRepository">
  <batch:step id="step1" next="step2">
    <batch:tasklet transaction-manager="transactionManager">
      <batch:chunk reader="dataReader"
                   writer="dataWriter"
                   processor="userRegistrationValidationProcessor"
                   commit-interval="10"
                   retry-limit="3">
        <batch:retryable-exception-classes>
          <batch:include class="org.springframework.dao.DeadlockLoserDataAccessException"/>
        </batch:retryable-exception-classes>
      </batch:chunk>
    </batch:tasklet>
  </batch:step>
</batch:job>
```

Transaction and Rollback

Since Spring Batch is based on the Spring Framework, transaction capabilities are already built in. Spring Batch surfaces the configuration so that developers can control it. Similar to a common Spring Framework application, Spring Batch step element accepts TransactionManager by setting the transaction-manager attribute for the tasklet element, as shown in Listing 17–10.

***Listing 17–10.** Spring Batch Job Definition with Transaction and Rollback*

```
<batch:job id="importData" job-repository="jobRepository">
  <batch:step id="step1" next="step2">
    <batch:tasklet transaction-manager="transactionManager">
      <batch:chunk reader="dataReader"
                   writer="dataWriter"
                   processor="userRegistrationValidationProcessor"
                   commit-interval="10"/>
    </batch:tasklet>
  </batch:step>
</batch:job>
```

If the source of the reader is a transactional message queue and the writer is failing, the rollback may need to include the source of the reader, as follows:

```
<batch:chunk reader="dataReader"
       writer="dataWriter"
       processor="userRegistrationValidationProcessor"
       commit-interval="10"
       reader-transactional-queue="true"/>
```

If a write fails on an ItemWriter, or some other exception occurs in processing, Spring Batch will roll back the transaction. This is valid handling for a majority of cases. There may be scenarios in which the developers want to control which exceptional cases cause the transaction to roll back. Listing 17–11 shows how to specify an exception that is ignored and allow processing to continue.

Listing 17–11. *Spring Batch Job Definition with Exception Classes*

```
<batch:step id = "step2">
  <batch:tasklet>
    <batch:chunk reader="reader" writer="writer" commit-interval="10" />
      <batch:skippable-exception-classes>
        <batch:include class="com.yourdomain.exceptions.YourBusinessException"/>
      </batch:skippable-exception-classes>
    </batch:tasklet>
</batch:step>
```

Concurrency

The first version of Spring Batch was oriented toward batch processing inside the same thread—concurrency, however, was not as well integrated. There were workarounds, of course, but the situation was less than ideal. Fortunately, this shortcoming has been rectified in version 2.0.

Consider the example job shown in Listing 17–12: the first step has to come before the second two because the second two are dependent on the first. The second two, however, do not share any such dependencies. There is no reason why the audit log could not be written at the same time the JMS messages are delivered. Spring Batch provides the capability to fork processing to enable just this sort of arrangement.

Listing 17–12. *Spring Batch Job Definition with Concurrency*

```
<batch:job job-repository="jobRepository" id="insertIntoDbFromCsvJob">
  <batch:step id="loadRegistrations" next="finalizeRegistrations">
    <!--
      ...
    -->
  </batch:step>
  <batch:split id="finalizeRegistrations" >
    <batch:flow>
      <batch:step id="reportStatistics" ><!--  ...  --></step>
    </batch:flow>
    <batch:flow>
       <batch:step id="sendJmsNotifications" > <!--  ...  --></step>
    </batch:flow>
  </batch:split>
</batch:job>
```

In this example, there's nothing preventing you from having many steps within the flow elements, nor is there anything preventing you from having more steps after the split element. The split element, like the step elements, takes a next attribute as well.

Spring Batch provides a mechanism to offload processing to another process. This feature, called *remote chunking*, is new in Spring Batch 2.x. This distribution requires some sort of durable, reliable connection. This is a perfect use of JMS because it's rock-solid, transactional, fast, and reliable. Spring Batch support is modeled at a slightly higher level, on top of the Spring Integration abstractions for Spring Integration channels. This support is not in the main Spring Batch code, though.

Remote chunking lets individual steps read and aggregate items as usual in the main thread. The main job flow step is called the *master*. Items read are sent to an ItemProcessor<I,O>/ItemWriter<T> running in another process (this is called the *slave*). If the slave is an aggressive consumer, there is a simple, generic mechanism to scale: work is instantly farmed out over as many JMS clients as you can throw at it. The aggressive-consumer pattern refers to the arrangement of multiple JMS clients all consuming the same queue's messages. If one client consumes a message and is busy processing, other idle queues will get the message instead. As long as there's a client that's idle, the message will be processed instantly.

Additionally, Spring Batch supports implicitly scaling out using a feature called *partitioning*. This feature is interesting because it is built in and generally very flexible. By replacing the instance of a step with a subclass, org.springframework.batch.core.partition.support.PartitionStep, the need for a durable medium of communication is eliminated. The PartitionStep, as in the remote chunking technology, knows how to coordinate distributed executors and maintains the metadata for the execution of the step.

The functionality here is also very generic. It could conceivably be used with any sort of grid fabric technology (e.g., GridGain or Hadoop). Spring Batch ships with only an org.springframework.batch.core.partition.support.TaskExecutorPartitionHandler, which executes steps in multiple threads using a TaskExecutor strategy. This simple improvement might be enough of a justification for this feature. Another partition handler is available through the Spring Batch Integration project using Spring Integration. The org.springframework.batch.integration.partition.MessageChannelPartitionHandler allows partitioning to use a message channel as the fabric. This approach will be discussed in more detail following.

Launching a Job

Spring Batch works very well in all environments that support Spring. Some use cases are uniquely challenging. For example, it is rarely practical to run Spring Batch in the same thread as an HTTP response in a servlet container, because it might end up stalling execution. Fortunately, Spring Batch supports asynchronous execution for this particular scenario. Spring Batch also provides a convenience class that can be readily used with cron or autosys to support launching jobs. Additionally, Spring 3.0's excellent scheduler namespace provides a great mechanism to schedule jobs.

Launching a Spring Batch job, requires a job and a JobLauncher, as shown in Listing 17–13. The job is configured in the Spring XML application context while the JobLauncher is created inside the application code.

Listing 17–13. *Launching a Spring Batch Job*

```
package com.apress.prospringintegration.springbatch.integration;

import org.springframework.batch.core.*;
import org.springframework.batch.core.launch.JobLauncher;
import org.springframework.context.support.ClassPathXmlApplicationContext;

import java.util.Date;

public class Main {
    public static void main(String[] args) throws Throwable {
        ClassPathXmlApplicationContext classPathXmlApplicationContext =
                new ClassPathXmlApplicationContext("integration.xml");
        classPathXmlApplicationContext.start();
```

```
        JobLauncher jobLauncher =
                (JobLauncher) classPathXmlApplicationContext.getBean("jobLauncher");
        Job job = (Job) classPathXmlApplicationContext.getBean("importData");

        JobParametersBuilder jobParametersBuilder = new JobParametersBuilder();
        jobParametersBuilder.addDate("date", new Date());
        jobParametersBuilder.addString("input.file", "registrations");
        JobParameters jobParameters = jobParametersBuilder.toJobParameters();

        JobExecution jobExecution = jobLauncher.run(job, jobParameters);

        BatchStatus batchStatus = jobExecution.getStatus();
        while (batchStatus.isRunning()) {
            System.out.println("Still running...");
            Thread.sleep(1000);
        }

        System.out.println("Exit status: " + jobExecution.getExitStatus().getExitCode());
        JobInstance jobInstance = jobExecution.getJobInstance();
        System.out.println("job instance Id: " + jobInstance.getId());
    }
}
```

The `JobLauncher` references the `Job importData` instance, which was configured earlier in this chapter. The result is a `JobExecution` object, which contains the state of the job. The `JobExecution` object contains exit status, runtime status, and a lot of very useful information, such as creation time and starting time.

Besides being launched from a command-line Java application, Spring Batch jobs can be launched from web applications as well. This takes a slightly different approach, however. Since the client thread, for example an HTTP request, cannot usually wait for a batch job to finish, the ideal solution is to have the job execute asynchronously when launched from the controller or action in the web tier. Spring Batch supports this scenario by using the Spring `TaskExecutor`. Using it requires a small change to the `JobLauncher` in the `BatchConfiguration` Java configuration, as shown in Listing 17–14.

***Listing 17–14.** Launching a Spring Batch Job from a Web Application*

```
import org.springframework.core.task.SimpleAsyncTaskExecutor;

    @Bean
    public SimpleJobLauncher jobLauncher() throws Exception {
        SimpleJobLauncher jobLauncher = new SimpleJobLauncher();
        jobLauncher.setJobRepository(jobRepository().getJobRepository());
        jobLauncher.setTaskExecutor(new SimpleAsyncTaskExecutor());
        return jobLauncher;
    }
```

Another approach for managing a Spring Batch job is by using Spring Batch Admin, which will be discussed in detail later in the chapter. Spring Batch Admin provides a web-based user interface for launching and managing Spring Batch jobs.

Event-Driven Batch Processing

Spring Integration and Spring Batch both deal with input- and output-centric processing. While both systems will work with files and message queues, Spring Integration does not do well with large payloads, because it is hard to deal with something as large as a file with a million rows that might require hours of work as an event. That is simply too big a burden for a messaging system. For that amount of data, the term *event* has no meaning anymore. A million records in a CSV file isn't an event on a bus, it is still a file with a million records; this is a subtle distinction.

Spring Integration and Spring Batch can be used together in a complementary fashion. Spring Integration can be used to detect and react to events in a system. Spring Batch can be used to penetrate large datasets and decompose them into events, which of course Spring Integration can deal with. Similarly, Spring Integration can be used to distribute processing across multiple VMs or machines on Spring Batch's behalf. So, for a file with a million rows, you might use Spring Batch to break the file into smaller parts, and then use Spring Integration to process the parts, or chunks.

Staged event-driven architecture (SEDA) is an architecture style that deals with this sort of processing. In SEDA, the load on components of the architecture is lessened by staging it in queues, and letting advance only what the components downstream can handle. For example, if a system were running a web site with a million users uploading video that in turn needed to be transcoded, and there were only ten servers, the system would fail if it attempted to process each video as soon as it received it. Transcoding can take hours, and pegs a CPU (or multiple CPUs) while it works. The most sensible thing to do is to store the file, and then, as capacity permits, process each one. In this way, the load on the nodes that handle transcoding is managed. There's always only enough work to keep the machine humming, but not to overrun.

Similarly, no messaging system (including Spring Integration) can deal with a million records at once efficiently. Strive to decompose bigger events and messages into smaller ones. Let's imagine a hypothetical solution designed to accommodate a drop of batch files representing hourly sales destined for fulfillment. The batch files are dropped onto a mount that Spring Integration is monitoring. Spring Integration kicks off processing as soon as it sees a new file. Spring Integration tells Spring Batch about the file and launches a Spring Batch job asynchronously.

Spring Batch reads the file, transforms the records into objects, and writes the output to a JMS topic with a key correlating the original batch to the JMS message. Naturally, this takes half a day to get done, but it does get done. Spring Integration, completely unaware that the job it started half a day ago is now finished, begins popping messages off the topic, one by one. Processing to fulfill the records begins. Simple processing involving multiple components might begin using a messaging system.

If fulfillment is a long-lived process with a long-lived, conversational state involving many actors, the fulfillment for each record could be farmed to a BPM engine such as Activiti (discussed in Chapter 8). The BPM engine would thread together the different actors and work lists, allowing work to continue over the course of days instead of the millisecond time frames that Spring Integration is more geared to.

Launching Jobs with Spring Integration

By combining Spring Integration and Spring Batch, batch job automation based on events is possible. For example, by using event-driven architecture (EDA), an event could trigger a batch job to be executed, and the job could send a message indicating whether it succeeded or failed.

Libraries that support the integration of Spring Batch and Spring Integration are available from the Spring Batch Integration project. This project has now become a part of the Spring Batch Admin project, which will be discussed in more detail later in the chapter. For now, these supporting Spring Batch Integration library can be added through Maven, as shown in Listing 17–15.

Listing 17–15. Maven Dependency for Spring Batch Integration

```
<dependency>
  <groupId>org.springframework.batch</groupId>
  <artifactId>spring-batch-integration</artifactId>
  <version>1.2.0.RELEASE</version>
</dependency>
```

Spring Batch Integration includes a number of components, including a service activator that will launch a Spring Batch job. This service activator takes an input message with the payload `org.springframework.batch.integration.launch.Job.LaunchRequest` and returns a message with the payload `JobExecution`. This service activator is configured using the Java configuration shown in Listing 17–16.

Listing 17–16. Java Configuration for Lauching Spring Batch Jobs

```
package com.apress.prospringintegration.springbatch.integration;

import org.springframework.batch.core.launch.JobLauncher;
import org.springframework.batch.integration.launch.JobLaunchingMessageHandler;
import org.springframework.beans.factory.annotation.Autowired;
import org.springframework.beans.factory.annotation.Value;
import org.springframework.context.annotation.Bean;
import org.springframework.context.annotation.Configuration;

@Configuration
public class IntegrationConfiguration {

    @Autowired
    private JobLauncher jobLauncher;

    @Bean
    public JobLaunchingMessageHandler jobMessageHandler() {
        JobLaunchingMessageHandler messageHandler =
                new JobLaunchingMessageHandler(jobLauncher);
        return messageHandler;
    }
}
```

The configuration for Spring Integration is straightforward. The service activator `jobMessageHandler` is configured for the input message channel `launchChannel` and the output message channel `statusChannel`. The rest of the configuration file is identical to the previous examples as shown in Listing 17–17.

Listing 17–17. Spring Configuration File for Lauching Spring Batch Jobs integration.xml

```
<?xml version="1.0" encoding="UTF-8"?>
<beans xmlns="http://www.springframework.org/schema/beans"
       xmlns:batch="http://www.springframework.org/schema/batch"
       xmlns:xsi="http://www.w3.org/2001/XMLSchema-instance"
       xmlns:context="http://www.springframework.org/schema/context"
       xmlns:int="http://www.springframework.org/schema/integration"
       xsi:schemaLocation="http://www.springframework.org/schema/beans
    http://www.springframework.org/schema/beans/spring-beans-3.0.xsd
    http://www.springframework.org/schema/batch
```

```
    http://www.springframework.org/schema/batch/spring-batch-2.1.xsd
    http://www.springframework.org/schema/context
    http://www.springframework.org/schema/context/spring-context-3.0.xsd
    http://www.springframework.org/schema/integration
    http://www.springframework.org/schema/integration/spring-integration-2.0.xsd">

  <context:property-placeholder location="batch.properties"/>
  <context:component-scan
      base-package="com.apress.prospringintegration.springbatch.integration"/>

  <batch:job id="importData" job-repository="jobRepository">
    <batch:step id="step1">
      <batch:tasklet>
        <batch:chunk reader="dataReader"
                     processor="userRegistrationValidationProcessor"
                     writer="dataWriter"
                     commit-interval="10"/>
      </batch:tasklet>
    </batch:step>
  </batch:job>


  <int:channel id="launchChannel"/>

  <int:channel id="statusChannel">
    <int:queue capacity="10"/>
  </int:channel>

  <int:service-activator input-channel="launchChannel"
                         output-channel="statusChannel"
                         ref="jobMessageHandler"/>

</beans>
```

The main class for launching the Spring Batch job using Spring Integration is shown in Listing 17–18. The JobLaunchRequest instance is created with a reference to the Job and JobParameters objects. The JobLaunchRequest object is sent as a message payload to the launchChannel message channel. The main class then waits for the response message on the statusChannel message channel. When the job completes, the status information is logged to the console.

Listing 17–18. *Main Class for Launching Spring Batch Jobs*

```
package com.apress.prospringintegration.springbatch.integration;

import org.springframework.batch.core.*;
import org.springframework.batch.core.launch.JobLauncher;
import org.springframework.batch.integration.launch.JobLaunchRequest;
import org.springframework.context.support.ClassPathXmlApplicationContext;
import org.springframework.integration.Message;
import org.springframework.integration.MessageChannel;
import org.springframework.integration.channel.QueueChannel;
import org.springframework.integration.support.MessageBuilder;

import java.util.Date;
```

```
public class IntegrationMain {
    public static void main(String[] args) throws Throwable {
        ClassPathXmlApplicationContext context = new ClassPathXmlApplicationContext(
                "integration.xml");
        context.start();

        MessageChannel launchChannel = context.getBean("launchChannel", MessageChannel.class);
        QueueChannel statusChannel = context.getBean("statusChannel", QueueChannel.class);

        Job job = (Job) context.getBean("importData");

        JobParametersBuilder jobParametersBuilder = new JobParametersBuilder();
        jobParametersBuilder.addDate("date", new Date());
        jobParametersBuilder.addString("input.file", "registrations");
        JobParameters jobParameters = jobParametersBuilder.toJobParameters();

        JobLaunchRequest jobLaunchRequest = new JobLaunchRequest(job, jobParameters);
        launchChannel.send(MessageBuilder.withPayload(jobLaunchRequest).build());

        Message<JobExecution> statusMessage =
                (Message<JobExecution>) statusChannel.receive();
        JobExecution jobExecution = statusMessage.getPayload();

        System.out.println(jobExecution);

        System.out.println("Exit status: " + jobExecution.getExitStatus().getExitCode());
        JobInstance jobInstance = jobExecution.getJobInstance();
        System.out.println("job instance Id: " + jobInstance.getId());
    }
}
```

Partitioning

One of the most interesting techniques available to Spring Batch and Spring Integration is the ability to partition big batch jobs over many nodes using a Spring Integration message channel as the coordination fabric. Spring Batch has a general API for partitioning a step execution and executing it remotely. The messages sent to each of the step instance do not need to be durable, since they have access to the Spring Batch metadata through the JobRepository database. The Java configuration for partitioning is shown in Listing 17–19.

Listing 17–19. *Java Configuration for Partitioning*

```
package com.apress.prospringintegration.springbatch.partition;

import org.springframework.batch.core.explore.JobExplorer;
import org.springframework.batch.core.explore.support.JobExplorerFactoryBean;
import org.springframework.batch.core.partition.support.SimplePartitioner;
import org.springframework.batch.integration.partition.BeanFactoryStepLocator;
import org.springframework.batch.integration.partition.MessageChannelPartitionHandler;
import org.springframework.batch.integration.partition.StepExecutionRequestHandler;
import org.springframework.beans.factory.annotation.Autowired;
```

```
import org.springframework.beans.factory.annotation.Qualifier;
import org.springframework.context.annotation.Bean;
import org.springframework.context.annotation.Configuration;
import org.springframework.integration.MessageChannel;
import org.springframework.integration.core.MessagingTemplate;
import org.springframework.integration.core.PollableChannel;

import javax.sql.DataSource;

@Configuration
public class PartitionConfiguration {

    @Autowired
    @Qualifier("requestChannel")
    private MessageChannel messageChannel;

    @Autowired
    @Qualifier("replyChannel")
    private PollableChannel pollableChannel;

    @Autowired
    private DataSource dataSource;

    @Bean
    public MessageChannelPartitionHandler partitionHandler() {
        MessageChannelPartitionHandler partitionHandler =
                new MessageChannelPartitionHandler();
        partitionHandler.setMessagingOperations(messagingTemplate());
        partitionHandler.setReplyChannel(pollableChannel);
        partitionHandler.setStepName("step1");
        partitionHandler.setGridSize(10);
        return partitionHandler;
    }

    @Bean
    public MessagingTemplate messagingTemplate() {
        MessagingTemplate messagingTemplate = new MessagingTemplate();
        messagingTemplate.setDefaultChannel(messageChannel);
        return messagingTemplate;
    }

    @Bean
    public SimplePartitioner partitioner() {
        SimplePartitioner simplePartitioner = new SimplePartitioner();
        return simplePartitioner;
    }

    @Bean
    public BeanFactoryStepLocator stepLocator() {
        BeanFactoryStepLocator stepLocator = new BeanFactoryStepLocator();
        return stepLocator;
    }

    @Bean
```

```
    public JobExplorerFactoryBean jobExplorer() {
        JobExplorerFactoryBean jobExplorerFactoryBean = new JobExplorerFactoryBean();
        jobExplorerFactoryBean.setDataSource(dataSource);
        return jobExplorerFactoryBean;
    }

    @Bean
    public StepExecutionRequestHandler stepExecutionRequestHandler() throws Exception {
        StepExecutionRequestHandler stepExecutionRequestHandler =
                new StepExecutionRequestHandler();
        stepExecutionRequestHandler.setJobExplorer((JobExplorer) jobExplorer().getObject());
        stepExecutionRequestHandler.setStepLocator(stepLocator());
        return stepExecutionRequestHandler;
    }
}
```

The `org.springframework.batch.integration.partition.MessageChannelPartitionHandler` is the component that knows about the Spring Integration fabric controlling the remote step execution. The `MessageChannelPartitionHandler` is configured to send a message to the `requestChannel` Spring Integration channel using a `MessagingTemplate`. The reply message is returned through the `replyChannel` message channel. The remote step is `step1` and the number of instances or grid size is set to 10.

The step execution is handled by the `org.springframework.batch.integration.partition.StepExecutionRequestHandler`. The `StepExecutionRequestHandler` can access the Spring Batch metadata through the `org.springframework.batch.core.explore.JobExplorer` instances. The step can be executed on a remote system since the state is maintained through the database. However, for simplicity, the step execution will take place locally.

The Spring configuration for the remote step execution is shown in Listing 17–20. The `stepExecutionRequestHandler` instance is a service activator that responds to the `requestChannel` input channel. The results the step execution sends a message to a message aggregator using the message channel `staging`. After all steps have been completed, a reply message is sent to the `replyChannel` message channel.

Listing 17–20. *Spring Configuration for Partitioning message-partition.xml*

```
<?xml version="1.0" encoding="UTF-8"?>
<beans xmlns="http://www.springframework.org/schema/beans"
       xmlns:batch="http://www.springframework.org/schema/batch"
       xmlns:xsi="http://www.w3.org/2001/XMLSchema-instance"
       xmlns:context="http://www.springframework.org/schema/context"
       xmlns:int="http://www.springframework.org/schema/integration"
       xsi:schemaLocation="http://www.springframework.org/schema/beans
    http://www.springframework.org/schema/beans/spring-beans-3.0.xsd
    http://www.springframework.org/schema/batch
    http://www.springframework.org/schema/batch/spring-batch-2.1.xsd
    http://www.springframework.org/schema/context
    http://www.springframework.org/schema/context/spring-context-3.0.xsd
    http://www.springframework.org/schema/integration
    http://www.springframework.org/schema/integration/spring-integration-2.0.xsd">

  <context:property-placeholder location="batch.properties"/>
  <context:component-scan
     base-package="com.apress.prospringintegration.springbatch.partition"/>
```

```
  <batch:job id="importData" job-repository="jobRepository">
    <batch:step id="step1-master">
      <batch:partition step="step1" handler="partitionHandler" partitioner="partitioner"/>
    </batch:step>
  </batch:job>

  <batch:step id="step1">
    <batch:tasklet>
      <batch:chunk reader="dataReader"
                   processor="userRegistrationValidationProcessor"
                   writer="dataWriter"
                   commit-interval="5"/>
    </batch:tasklet>
  </batch:step>

  <int:channel id="launchChannel"/>

  <int:channel id="statusChannel">
    <int:queue capacity="10"/>
  </int:channel>

  <int:service-activator input-channel="launchChannel"
                         output-channel="statusChannel"
                         ref="jobMessageHandler"/>

  <int:channel id="requestChannel">
    <int:queue capacity="10"/>
  </int:channel>

  <int:channel id="staging">
    <int:queue capacity="10"/>
  </int:channel>

  <int:channel id="replyChannel">
    <int:queue capacity="10"/>
  </int:channel>

  <int:service-activator ref="stepExecutionRequestHandler"
                         input-channel="requestChannel"
                         output-channel="staging">
    <int:poller>
      <int:interval-trigger interval="10"/>
    </int:poller>
  </int:service-activator>

  <int:aggregator ref="partitionHandler"
                  input-channel="staging"
                  output-channel="replyChannel">
    <int:poller>
      <int:interval-trigger interval="10"/>
    </int:poller>
  </int:aggregator>

</beans>
```

The main class to run the partitioning example, as shown in Listing 17–21, is identical to that from the previous example of launching a job using Spring Integration. Running the main class will result in ten step instances processing and moving the registration data into the database. This could easily represent ten remote step instances running on various hosts, all connected through the Spring Integration message channel.

***Listing 17–21.** Main Class for Partitioning*

```
package com.apress.prospringintegration.springbatch.partition;

import org.springframework.batch.core.*;
import org.springframework.batch.integration.launch.JobLaunchRequest;
import org.springframework.context.support.ClassPathXmlApplicationContext;
import org.springframework.integration.Message;
import org.springframework.integration.MessageChannel;
import org.springframework.integration.channel.QueueChannel;
import org.springframework.integration.support.MessageBuilder;

import java.util.Date;

public class IntegrationPartitionMain {

    public static void main(String[] args) throws Throwable {
        ClassPathXmlApplicationContext context = new ClassPathXmlApplicationContext(
                "message-partition.xml");
        context.start();

        MessageChannel launchChannel = context.getBean("launchChannel", MessageChannel.class);
        QueueChannel statusChannel = context.getBean("statusChannel", QueueChannel.class);

        Job job = (Job) context.getBean("importData");
        JobParametersBuilder jobParametersBuilder = new JobParametersBuilder();
        jobParametersBuilder.addDate("date", new Date());
        jobParametersBuilder.addString("input.file", "registrations");
        JobParameters jobParameters = jobParametersBuilder.toJobParameters();

        JobLaunchRequest jobLaunchRequest = new JobLaunchRequest(job, jobParameters);

        launchChannel.send(MessageBuilder.withPayload(jobLaunchRequest).build());

        Message<JobExecution> statusMessage = (Message<JobExecution>) statusChannel.receive();
        JobExecution jobExecution = statusMessage.getPayload();

        System.out.println(jobExecution);
        System.out.println("Exit status: " + jobExecution.getExitStatus().getExitCode());

        JobInstance jobInstance = jobExecution.getJobInstance();
        System.out.println("job instance Id: " + jobInstance.getId());
    }
}
```

Spring Batch Admin

Spring Batch Admin (`http://static.springsource.org/spring-batch-admin`) is an open source project from SpringSource. It provides a web-based user interface as an administrative console for Spring Batch applications and systems. The user interface allows job inspection, job launching, job execution inspection, and job execution life cycle management. Spring Batch Admin also provides an API for developers to build custom web applications adding a web interface with the ability to manage Spring Batch job execution from external applications.

You can download the latest version of Spring Batch Admin, 1.2.0.RELEASE, from the SpringSource Community Download page (`www.springsource.com/products/spring-community-download`). Download and unzip the `spring-batch-admin-1.2.0.RELEASE-dist.zip` file. A complete Spring Batch Admin project will be located in the `sample/spring-batch-admin-sample` directory. An additional project in the `sample/spring-batch-admin-parent` directory is also required. This sample project will be used as the basis for the next example.

We will be adding the previous Spring Batch example to Spring Batch Admin. The basic Spring Batch component will be made available by Spring Batch Admin, so the `BatchConfiguration` Java configuration class will not be needed. All that is required is to add the Spring configuration for the job to the `src/resources/META-INF/spring/batch/jobs` directory, and all the supporting classes to the package `com.apress.prospringintegration.batch`. The required supporting classes are `JdbcConfiguration`, `JobConfiguration`, `UserRegistration`, and `UserRegistrationValidationItemProcessor`. After modifying these classes for the new Java package, add these classes to the `src/main/java/com/apress/prospringintegration/batch` directory.

The Spring configuration file for the new `myjob` job is shown in Listing 17–22. The configuration is simple; it contains only the Java configuration, the job description, and the `component-scan` element to support component scanning. This is basically all that is needed to add a job to Spring Batch Admin.

Listing 17–22. *myjob-context.xml: Spring Configuration File for Spring Batch Admin*

```
<?xml version="1.0" encoding="UTF-8"?>
<beans xmlns="http://www.springframework.org/schema/beans"
       xmlns:batch="http://www.springframework.org/schema/batch"
       xmlns:xsi="http://www.w3.org/2001/XMLSchema-instance"
       xmlns:context="http://www.springframework.org/schema/context"
       xsi:schemaLocation="http://www.springframework.org/schema/beans
    http://www.springframework.org/schema/beans/spring-beans-3.0.xsd
    http://www.springframework.org/schema/batch
    http://www.springframework.org/schema/batch/spring-batch-2.1.xsd
    http://www.springframework.org/schema/context
    http://www.springframework.org/schema/context/spring-context-3.0.xsd">

  <context:component-scan base-package="com.apress.prospringintegration.batch"/>

  <batch:job id="myjob">
    <batch:step id="step1">
      <batch:tasklet>
        <batch:chunk reader="dataReader"
                     processor="userRegistrationValidationProcessor"
                     writer="dataWriter"
                     commit-interval="5"/>
      </batch:tasklet>
    </batch:step>
  </batch:job>
```

```
</beans>
```

Add the PostgreSQL connection properties to the batch-default.properties file, located in the src/main/resources directory, to make the properties available within the Spring Batch Admin application. The modifications to the properties file are shown in Listing 17–23.

***Listing 17–23.** Adding PostgreSQL Properties to batch-default.properties*

```
# Default placeholders for database platform independent features
batch.remote.base.url=http://localhost:8080/spring-batch-admin-sample

dataSource.password=emilyk
dataSource.username=postgres
dataSource.databaseName=postgres
dataSource.driverClassName=org.postgresql.Driver
dataSource.serverName=localhost:5432
dataSource.url=jdbc:postgresql://${dataSource.serverName}/${dataSource.databaseName}

# Non-platform dependent settings that you might like to change
# batch.job.configuration.file.dir=target/config
```

To simplify running the job from the Spring Batch Admin web page, the input parameter for the file location will be changed to take the absolute path. The required change to the Java configuration file is shown in Listing 17–24.

***Listing 17–24.** Java Configuration Modification for Spring Batch Admin*

```
package com.apress.prospringintegration.batch;

import org.springframework.batch.item.database.BeanPropertyItemSqlParameterSourceProvider;
import org.springframework.batch.item.database.JdbcBatchItemWriter;
import org.springframework.batch.item.file.FlatFileItemReader;
import org.springframework.batch.item.file.mapping.BeanWrapperFieldSetMapper;
import org.springframework.batch.item.file.mapping.DefaultLineMapper;
import org.springframework.batch.item.file.transform.DelimitedLineTokenizer;
import org.springframework.beans.factory.annotation.Autowired;
import org.springframework.beans.factory.annotation.Value;
import org.springframework.context.annotation.Bean;
import org.springframework.context.annotation.Configuration;
import org.springframework.context.annotation.Scope;
import org.springframework.core.io.Resource;

import javax.sql.DataSource;

@Configuration
public class JobConfiguration {
    @Autowired
    private DataSource dataSource;

    @Bean
    @Scope("step")
    public FlatFileItemReader csvFileReader(
            @Value("file:#{jobParameters['input.file']}") Resource resource) {
        FlatFileItemReader csvFileReader = new FlatFileItemReader();
        csvFileReader.setResource(resource);
```

```
        DelimitedLineTokenizer delimitedLineTokenizer =
                new DelimitedLineTokenizer(DelimitedLineTokenizer.DELIMITER_COMMA);
        delimitedLineTokenizer.setNames(
                new String[]{"firstName", "lastName", "company", "address", "city",
                        "state", "zip", "county", "url", "phoneNumber", "fax"});

        BeanWrapperFieldSetMapper beanWrapperFieldSetMapper = new BeanWrapperFieldSetMapper();
        beanWrapperFieldSetMapper.setTargetType(UserRegistration.class);

        DefaultLineMapper defaultLineMapper = new DefaultLineMapper();
        defaultLineMapper.setLineTokenizer(delimitedLineTokenizer);
        defaultLineMapper.setFieldSetMapper(beanWrapperFieldSetMapper);

        csvFileReader.setLineMapper(defaultLineMapper);

        return csvFileReader;
    }

    @Bean
    public JdbcBatchItemWriter jdbcItemWriter() {
        JdbcBatchItemWriter jdbcBatchItemWriter = new JdbcBatchItemWriter();
        jdbcBatchItemWriter.setAssertUpdates(true);
        jdbcBatchItemWriter.setDataSource(dataSource);
        jdbcBatchItemWriter
                .setSql("insert into USER_REGISTRATION(FIRST_NAME, LAST_NAME, COMPANY," +
                        "ADDRESS, CITY, STATE, ZIP, COUNTY, URL, PHONE_NUMBER, FAX )" +
                        "values (:firstName, :lastName, :company, :address, :city ," +
                        ":state, :zip, :county, :url, :phoneNumber, :fax )");

        jdbcBatchItemWriter.setItemSqlParameterSourceProvider(
                new BeanPropertyItemSqlParameterSourceProvider());

        return jdbcBatchItemWriter;
    }
}
```

Make the change to the JobIntegrationTests class, as shown in Listing 17–25, so the project will build without errors. Essentially we are adding our new job to the unit test.

Listing 17–25. *Modifying the Unit Test for Spring Batch Admin*

```
package org.springframework.batch.admin.sample;

import static org.junit.Assert.assertEquals;
import static org.junit.Assert.assertNotNull;

import java.util.TreeSet;

import org.junit.Test;
import org.junit.runner.RunWith;
import org.springframework.batch.core.configuration.ListableJobLocator;
import org.springframework.beans.factory.annotation.Autowired;
import org.springframework.test.annotation.DirtiesContext;
```

```
import org.springframework.test.annotation.DirtiesContext.ClassMode;
import org.springframework.test.context.ContextConfiguration;
import org.springframework.test.context.junit4.SpringJUnit4ClassRunner;

@ContextConfiguration
@RunWith(SpringJUnit4ClassRunner.class)
@DirtiesContext(classMode=ClassMode.AFTER_CLASS)
public class JobIntegrationTests {

    @Autowired
    private ListableJobLocator jobLocator;

    @Test
    public void testSimpleProperties() throws Exception {
        assertNotNull(jobLocator);
        assertEquals("[infinite, job1, job2, myjob]",
        new TreeSet<String>(jobLocator.getJobNames()).toString());
    }

}
```

Build the Spring Batch Admin sample project using the usual `mvn install` command. The resultant file, `spring-batch-admin-sample-1.2.0.RELEASE.war`, will be found in the target directory. Deploy the `war` file to a servlet container such as Tomcat or Jetty by copying to the `webapps` directory. Using a browser, go to the URL `http://localhost:8080/spring-batch-admin-sample-1.2.0.RELEASE`. Click the `Jobs` tab, and then click the `myjob` link, which should bring up the page shown in Figure 17–3. In the Job Parameters text box, enter **input.file=<path to registration.cvs>**, using the path to the `registration.cvs` file used in the previous examples. Click the `Launch` button, and the Spring Batch job should run.

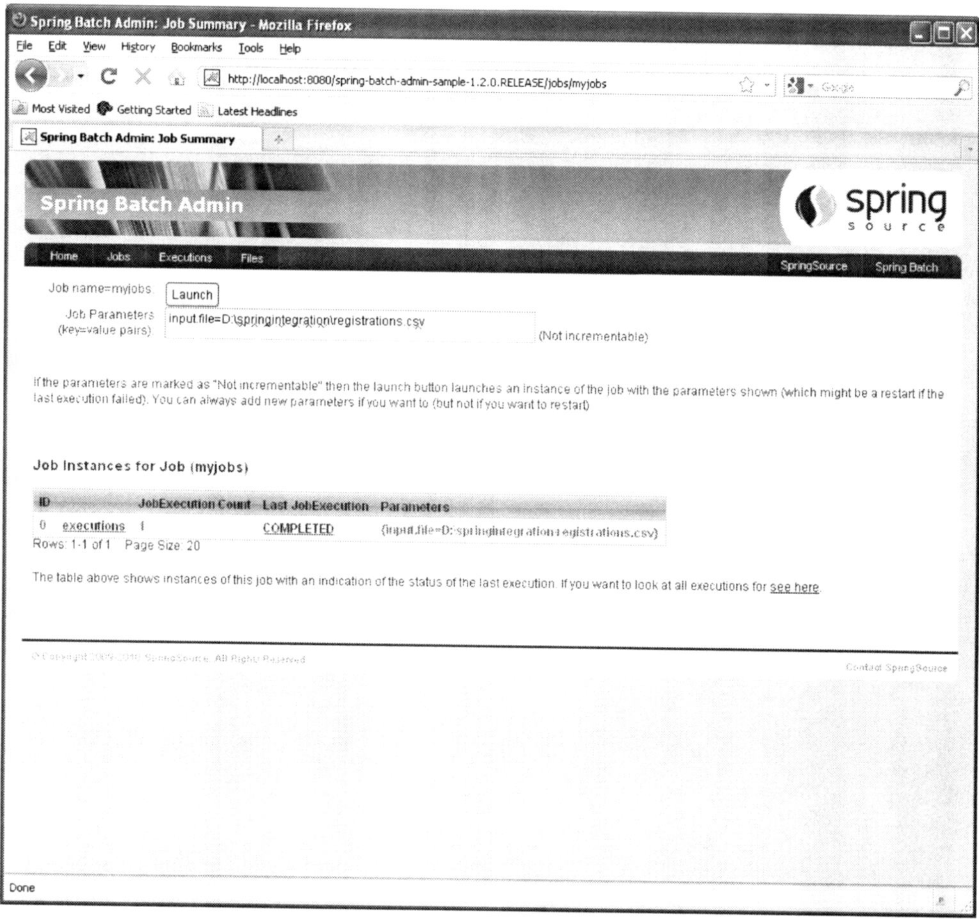

Figure 17–3. Spring Batch Admin

Summary

This chapter introduced the concept of batch processing, including some of its history and why it fits in modern-day architectures. Batch processing is used to process billions of transactions every day within mission critical enterprise applications. Spring Batch is designed to provide a runtime environment and reusable utilities for batch processing. It enables batch applications to have the same clean architecture and lightweight programming model as any other Spring Framework project.

In addition, this chapter introduced how Spring Batch can be use with Spring Integration. It demonstrated how Spring Integration can launch Spring Batch jobs via messaging to allow event-driven batch processes. It also discussed how Spring Integration can be used to scale out Spring Batch using partitioning. It described how big batch jobs can be distributed over many nodes using message channels as the coordination fabric. Finally, it have introduced Spring Batch Admin, which provides a web-based user interface for Spring Batch using Spring Integration in its internal plumbing.

CHAPTER 18

Spring Integration and Your Web Application

This tour of Spring Integration has gone full circle, covering all the different components to support integrating application horizontally across an enterprise. As discussed in the Chapter 1, the majority of the focus of application development today is on vertical database-backed web applications. While Spring Integration can of course be used from a Spring MVC controller (and, generally, other Spring beans), we will look at how Spring Integration can be used to provide HTTP-based services. Spring Integration can be used to create a basic web interface with the HTTP inbound and outbound gateways.

Most web applications operate in request/reply mode, where the user must initiate the interaction by submitting a request via a browser, in effect asking for information. With projects such as DWR, Atmosphere, and BlazeDS, the paradigm has been turned around. In this scenario, the server pushes data to the client browsers without the client browser pulling (or requesting) it. Applications such as business dashboards providing real-time display of enterprise status, chats, and any other web application that might benefit from real-time awareness of server-side events can now be realized. Many of these technologies are still in development, but this chapter will show what is available now and where the future is heading.

HTTP Adapters and Gateways

The inbound and outbound HTTP channel adapters and gateways offer the most basic support in Spring Integration for web protocols. The HTTP adapters can be used for creating simple browser views, but more typically they are used for communication using the HTTP protocol with back-end services. The inbound HTTP adapter and gateway must be deployed within a servlet container to support receiving HTTP requests. HTTP requests must ultimately deliver a reply. The inbound HTTP gateway handles requests and allows you to provide a response with a reply message. The inbound adapter works the same way, but removes the burden of providing the reply and instead supports several default operations (like returning HTTP status code 200).

The HTTP support is another example of where Spring Integration is very different from other integration servers or solutions. To use the inbound HTTP adapters, you simply configure a servlet in the container of your choice—no need to involve a separate port or enlist administrators to set up a new application process on your servers. Additionally, you are now free to deploy your HTTP request-handling code in the same environment as your web application, on the same host and context. Additionally, the inbound HTTP adapters take advantage of the core Spring web application infrastructure. The inbound HTTP adapter is an `org.springframework.web.HttpRequestHandler`, which in the Spring web context support is the simplest unit of work that can be wired to respond to HTTP requests. At a higher level, there is also an inbound HTTP gateway that supports forwarding web requests to Spring MVC controller classes, where you can take advantage of all the Spring MVC request-handling features, including RESTful controllers and components.

The most basic inbound adapter is shown in Listing 18–1. This bean is typically configured in the Spring application context and delegated by the `org.springframework.web.context.support.HttpRequestHandlerServlet` or `org.springframework.web.servlet.DispatcherServlet` in the `web.xml` file. The servlet name and the bean ID must match. The `expectedReply` flag must be set in the constructor of `HttpRequestHandlingMessagingGateway` if a response based upon the `replyChannel` is desired; otherwise, a 200-OK response will be returned. The default request methods are `GET` and `POST`, but other methods may be set using the `supportedMethods` property. A converter may be specified to map between the incoming `HttpServletRequest` and the `Message` object by setting the `messageConverters` property. If this property is not set, the default converters will be use providing basic mappings such as converting to a `String` during a `POST` when the content type is `text`. Note that this adapter only requires the Spring web support and the HttpRequestHandlerServlet, not the full Spring MVC stack.

Listing 18–1. *HTTP Inbound Gateway HttpRequestHandlingMessagingGateway.*

```
<bean id="inboundGateway"
   class="org.springframework.integration.http.inbound.HttpRequestHandlingMessagingGateway">
  <property name="requestChannel" ref="httpRequestChannel"/>
  <property name="replyChannel" ref="httpReplyChannel"/>
</bean>
```

The `HttpRequestHandlingController` serves as a Spring MVC controller class and may be used in conjunction with Spring's core web `DispatcherServlet` class to return a `ModelAndView` object. This allows you to specify a view through the `viewName` property to be passed back to the client or browser. An example of the `HttpRequestHandlingController` is shown in Listing 18–2. If you set the constructor `expectReply` flag to `true`, the gateway will wait for a reply message before sending a response back to the browser or client. This adapter requires the full Spring MVC stack but affords you much more power.

Listing 18–2. *HTTP Inbound Gateway HttpRequestHandlingController.*

```
<bean id="httpInbound"
      class="org.springframework.integration.http.inbound.HttpRequestHandlingController">
<constructor-arg value="true"/>
  <property name="requestChannel" ref="httpRequestChannel"/>
  <property name="replyChannel" ref="httpReplyChannel"/>
  <property name="viewName" value="pageView"/>
  <property name="supportedMethodNames">
    <list>
      <value>GET</value>
      <value>POST</value>
    </list>
  </property>
</bean>
```

Spring Integration also supports the outbound HTTP gateway, as shown in Listing 18–3. This bean, leveraging the `RestTemplate`, executes an HTTP request. In the example configuration, an HTTP request is made to the URL `http://localhost:8080/test`, where the HTTP body is based on the `Message` sent to the `outputChannel`.

Listing 18–3. HTTP Outbound Gateway HttpRequestExecutingMessageHandler

```
<bean id="httpOutbound"
   class="org.springframework.integration.http.outbound.HttpRequestExecutingMessageHandler">
  <constructor-arg value="http://localhost:8080/test"/>
  <property name="outputChannel" ref="httpOutputChannel"/>
</bean>
```

The converters used in mapping the channel message to the HTTP body may be specified through the `messageConverters` property, as shown in Listing 18–4. By default the HTTP request is created using the `org.springframework.http.client.SimpleClientHttpRequestFactory`. This factory uses the JDK `HttpUrlConnection`. The factory may be overridden using the `requestFactory` property. For example, you can use the Apache Commons HTTP client instead, by providing an alternative reference for this property.

Listing 18–4. HTTP Outbound Gateway Setting Converters and HTTP Request Factory

```
<bean id="httpOutbound"
     class="org.springframework.integration.http.outbound.HttpRequestExecutingMessageHandler">
  <constructor-arg value="http://localhost:8080/test"/>
  <property name="outputChannel" ref="httpOutputChannel"/>
  <property name="messageConverters" ref="messageConverterList"/>
  <property name="requestFactory" ref="httpFactory"/>
</bean>

<bean id="httpFactory
     class=" org.springframework.http.client.CommonsClientHttpRequestFactory"/>
```

HTTP Adapter and Gateway Namespace Support

Spring Integration also provides namespace support for the HTTP adapters. The namespace support can be added to any Spring XML context by adding the following: `http://www.springframework.org/schema/integration/http`. An example of configuring an inbound HTTP adapter is shown in Listing 18–5. This is a simple configuration where the incoming HTTP request is mapped to the request channel. The supported methods GET and POST are specified through the `supported-methods` attribute.

Listing 18–5. Inbound HTTP Channel Adapter

```
<http:inbound-channel-adapter id="httpChannelAdapter"
                              channel="request"
                              supported-methods="GET, POST"/>
```

In the case where you want more than just a 200-OK reply (e.g., if you want a web page response), you can use the configuration in Listing 18–6 to configure an HTTP gateway. The input and output channel are specified using the `request-channel` and `reply-channel` attributes, respectively.

Listing 18–6. Inbound HTTP Gateway

```
<http:inbound-gateway id="inboundGateway"
                      request-channel="request"
                      reply-channel="response"/>
```

An example of configuring an outbound HTTP gateway is shown in Listing 18–7. Since this a gateway, the request and reply channel must be specified. By default the outbound gateway method is a POST, with a default response type of null. In the case of a null response type, only the response status code is included in the reply message payload if the status is successful. If an error occurs, an exception will be thrown, which may be handled through the Spring Integration error handling discussed in Chapter 10. If another type is expected in the response body (e.g., String), it must be specified through the expected-response-type attribute.

Listing 18–7. Outbound HTTP Gateway

```
<http:outbound-gateway request-channel="request"
                       reply-channel="reply"
                       url="http://localhost:8080/test"
                       http-method="POST"
                       expected-response-type="java.lang.String"/>
```

If the integration is using the outbound adapter in a unidirectional way, the HTTP outbound channel adapter may be used. The adapter creates no reply message, and any unsuccessful response will result in an exception being thrown by the adapter. An example of an HTTP outbound channel adapter is shown in Listing 18–8. The configuration is similar to the gateway, except that only one message channel is configured.

Listing 18–8. Outbound HTTP Channel Adapter

```
<http:outbound-channel-adapter url="http://localhost:8080/test"
                               http-method="GET"
                               channel="request"/>
```

One of the nice features of the outbound HTTP adapters is the ability to map to the URI variables through the uri-variable subelement. For example, if an adapter will be used to perform a GET to request information about a customer with a first name of John and a last name of Smith, the configuration would look something like Listing 18–9. Note the use of Spring Expression Language to pull the data from the message payload and populate the URI variables.

Listing 18–9. Outbound HTTP Gateway Using URI Variable Mapping

```
<http:outbound-gateway
    url="http://localhost:8080/getCustomer?firstName={firstName}&amp;lastName={lastName}"
    request-channel="request"
    reply-channel="reply"
    http-method="GET"
    expected-response-type="java.lang.String">
  <http:uri-variable name="firstName" expression="payload.getFirstName()"/>
  <http:uri-variable name="lastName" expression="payload.getLastName()"/>
</http:outbound-gateway>
```

HTTP Adapter and Gateway Example

To demonstrate the use of the Spring Integration HTTP adapters, a simple example will be created. To use the HTTP adapters, the Spring Integration HTTP library dependency must be added to the pom.xml file, as shown in Listing 18–10.

Listing 18–10. *Spring Integration HTTP Dependencies pom.xml*

```
<dependency>
  <groupId>org.springframework.integration</groupId>
  <artifactId>spring-integration-http</artifactId>
  <version>2.0.1.RELEASE</version>
</dependency>
<dependency>
  <groupId>org.springframework</groupId>
  <artifactId>spring-webmvc</artifactId>
  <version>3.0.5.RELEASE</version>
</dependency>
```

In addition, since this is a web application, the value of the package element in the pom.xml file must be set to war, as follows:

```
<packaging>war</packaging>
```

The first part of creating a servlet-based web application is creating the web.xml file. This example uses the Spring DispatcherServlet and forwards a request to the Spring Integration components configured in servlet-config.xml. The web.xml file also configures a servlet mapping for only pages with the postfix html (see Listing 18–11).

Listing 18–11. *Servlet web.xml File*

```
<?xml version="1.0" encoding="UTF-8"?>
<web-app xmlns:xsi="http://www.w3.org/2001/XMLSchema-instance"
         xmlns="http://java.sun.com/xml/ns/javaee"
         xmlns:web="http://java.sun.com/xml/ns/javaee/web-app_2_5.xsd"
         xsi:schemaLocation="http://java.sun.com/xml/ns/javaee
         http://java.sun.com/xml/ns/javaee/web-app_2_5.xsd"
         id="WebApp_ID"
         version="2.5">

  <display-name>spring-http</display-name>

  <servlet>
    <servlet-name>webapp</servlet-name>
    <servlet-class>org.springframework.web.servlet.DispatcherServlet</servlet-class>
    <init-param>
      <param-name>contextConfigLocation</param-name>
      <param-value>/WEB-INF/servlet-config.xml</param-value>
    </init-param>
    <load-on-startup>1</load-on-startup>
  </servlet>

  <servlet-mapping>
    <servlet-name>webapp</servlet-name>
    <url-pattern>*.html</url-pattern>
  </servlet-mapping>

  <welcome-file-list>
    <welcome-file>
      index.jsp
```

```
    </welcome-file>
  </welcome-file-list>

</web-app>
```

The servlet-config.xml file is of course where all the action occurs. The Spring Integration components are configured through this file. The configuration file in Listing 18–12 configures both an HTTP inbound channel adapter and inbound gateway. The inbound channel adapter returns a 200-OK response code as long as no exception is thrown. The URI is /inboundChannel.html. The request is mapped into a Message object and sent to the receiveChannel. For the inbound gateway, the URI is /inboundGateway.html, and the request is mapped into a Message object and sent to the inboundChannel. The difference between the gateway and the inbound channel is that a reply Message must be sent to the outboundChannel, which will be mapped to the HTTP reply for a gateway, whereas you can leave Spring Integration to provide a simple reply using the inbound adapter. Usually a converter is needed to ensure that a browser-compatibly message is returned, or that the client can parse the message using a format such as an HTML or XML.

Listing 18–12. *Spring Integration Configuration the servlet-config.xml*

```
<?xml version="1.0" encoding="UTF-8"?>
<beans xmlns="http://www.springframework.org/schema/beans"
       xmlns:xsi="http://www.w3.org/2001/XMLSchema-instance"
       xmlns:int="http://www.springframework.org/schema/integration"
       xmlns:http="http://www.springframework.org/schema/integration/http"
       xmlns:context="http://www.springframework.org/schema/context"
       xsi:schemaLocation="http://www.springframework.org/schema/beans
    http://www.springframework.org/schema/beans/spring-beans-3.0.xsd
    http://www.springframework.org/schema/context
    http://www.springframework.org/schema/context/spring-context-3.0.xsd
    http://www.springframework.org/schema/integration
    http://www.springframework.org/schema/integration/spring-integration-2.0.xsd
    http://www.springframework.org/schema/integration/http
    http://www.springframework.org/schema/integration/http/spring-integration-http-2.0.xsd">

  <context:component-scan base-package="com.apress.prospringintegration.web"/>

  <http:inbound-channel-adapter id="httpInboundAdapter"
                                channel="receiveChannel"
                                name="/inboundChannel.html"
                                supported-methods="GET, POST"/>

  <http:inbound-gateway request-channel="inboundChannel"
                        reply-channel="outboundChannel"
                        name="/inboundGateway.html"
                        supported-methods="GET, POST"/>

  <int:channel id="receiveChannel"/>

  <int:channel id="inboundChannel"/>

  <int:channel id="outboundChannel"/>

  <int:service-activator id="receiver" input-channel="receiveChannel" ref="httpReceiver"/>
```

```
  <int:service-activator id="gateway" input-channel="inboundChannel" ref="gatewayHandler"/>

  </beans>
```

The last part of this example is a service activator that simply logs the incoming message. The service activator class for the HTTP inbound channel adapter is shown in Listing 18–13.

Listing 18–13. *Service Activator Class HttpReceiver*

```
package com.apress.prospringintegration.web;

import org.springframework.integration.Message;
import org.springframework.integration.annotation.ServiceActivator;
import org.springframework.stereotype.Component;

@Component
public class HttpReceiver {

    @ServiceActivator
    public void receive(Message<?> message) {
        System.out.println("Http Message: " + message);
    }
}
```

The service activator class for the HTTP inbound gateway is shown in Listing 18–14.

Listing 18–14. *Service Activator for the HTTP Inbound Gateway*

```
package com.apress.prospringintegration.web;

import org.springframework.integration.Message;
import org.springframework.integration.annotation.ServiceActivator;
import org.springframework.stereotype.Component;

@Component
public class GatewayHandler {

    @ServiceActivator
    public Message handleMessage(Message<?> message) {
        System.out.println("Http Gateway Message: " + message);
        return message;
    }
}
```

Build the web application by issuing the command `mvn install`, and deploy the resultant WAR file `http-adapter-1.0.0.war` to a servlet container such as Tomcat or Jetty by copying it to the `webapps` directory. If you are using the SpringSource Tool Suite, you will already have a developer edition of SpringSource tc Server configured in your Servers panel. Drag the web application to the STS Servers panel and simply click the Deploy button. The URL for the HTTP inbound adapter is `http://localhost:8080/http-adapter-1.0.0/inboundChannel.html`, and the URL for the HTTP gateway is `http://localhost:8080/http-adapter-1.0.0/inboundGateway.html`. Hitting each of the endpoints will result in a log message from the respective message handler classes.

Multipart Support

Spring Integration 2.0 now supports multipart HTTP requests. In order to support the multipart requests, additional dependencies are required, as shown in Listing 18–15.

Listing 18–15. *Maven Dependencies to Support the Multipart HTTP Request*

```
<dependency>
  <groupId>commons-fileupload</groupId>
  <artifactId>commons-fileupload</artifactId>
  <version>1.2</version>
</dependency>
<dependency>
  <groupId>org.apache.commons</groupId>
  <artifactId>commons-io</artifactId>
  <version>1.3.2</version>
</dependency>
```

The client can simply use the Spring core `RestTemplate` class to send the request. A `MultiValueMap` is created, populated with the multipart data, and sent as an HTTP request. A code example is shown in Listing 18–16. The class attaches an image file to a `MultiValueMap` for sending to the HTTP endpoint.

Listing 18–16. *Multipart HTTP Request Client*

```
package com.apress.prospringintegration.web;

import org.springframework.core.io.ClassPathResource;
import org.springframework.core.io.Resource;
import org.springframework.http.*;
import org.springframework.util.LinkedMultiValueMap;
import org.springframework.util.MultiValueMap;
import org.springframework.web.client.RestTemplate;

public class MultipartHttpClient {

    public static void main(String[] args) {
        RestTemplate template = new RestTemplate();
        String uri =
                "http://localhost:8080/ http-adapter-1.0.0 /inboundMultipartAdapter.html";
        Resource picture =
                new ClassPathResource("com/apress/prospringintegration/web/test.png");
        MultiValueMap map = new LinkedMultiValueMap();
        map.add("name", "John Smith");
        map.add("picture", picture);
        HttpHeaders headers = new HttpHeaders();
        headers.setContentType(new MediaType("multipart", "form-data"));
        HttpEntity request = new HttpEntity(map, headers);
        ResponseEntity<?> httpResponse =
            template.exchange(uri, HttpMethod.POST, request, null);
        System.out.println("Status: " + httpResponse.getStatusCode().name());
    }
}
```

Configuring the HTTP inbound channel adapter for receiving the multipart HTTP request is simply a matter of adding a service activator that knows how to parse the multipart message. The configuration for the inbound channel adapter is identical to the preceding example for a standard request. A service activator reference has been added to support reading the multipart message. The pertinent parts of the configuration are shown in Listing 18–17.

Listing 18–17. *Spring Configuration for Receiving the Multipart HTTP Request servlet-config.xml*

```
<?xml version="1.0" encoding="UTF-8"?>
<beans xmlns="http://www.springframework.org/schema/beans"
       xmlns:xsi="http://www.w3.org/2001/XMLSchema-instance"
       xmlns:int="http://www.springframework.org/schema/integration"
       xmlns:http="http://www.springframework.org/schema/integration/http"
       xmlns:context="http://www.springframework.org/schema/context"
       xsi:schemaLocation="http://www.springframework.org/schema/beans
    http://www.springframework.org/schema/beans/spring-beans-3.0.xsd
    http://www.springframework.org/schema/context
    http://www.springframework.org/schema/context/spring-context-3.0.xsd
    http://www.springframework.org/schema/integration
    http://www.springframework.org/schema/integration/spring-integration-2.0.xsd
    http://www.springframework.org/schema/integration/http
    http://www.springframework.org/schema/integration/http/spring-integration-http-2.0.xsd">

  <context:component-scan base-package="com.apress.prospringintegration.web"/>

  <http:inbound-channel-adapter id="httpInboundAdapter"
                                channel="receiveChannel"
                                name="/inboundChannel.html"
                                supported-methods="GET, POST"/>

  <http:inbound-gateway request-channel="inboundChannel"
                        reply-channel="outboundChannel"
                        name="/inboundGateway.html"
                        supported-methods="GET, POST"/>

  <int:channel id="receiveChannel"/>

  <int:channel id="inboundChannel"/>

  <int:channel id="outboundChannel"/>

  <int:service-activator id="receiver" input-channel="receiveChannel" ref="httpReceiver"/>

  <int:service-activator id="gateway" input-channel="inboundChannel" ref="gatewayHandler"/>

  <int:channel id="inboundMultipartChannel"/>

  <http:inbound-channel-adapter channel="inboundMultipartChannel"
                                name="/inboundMultipartAdapter.html"
                                supported-methods="GET, POST"/>

  <int:service-activator input-channel="inboundMultipartChannel"
```

```
                    ref="multipartReceiver"/>

</beans>
```

In addition, a `MultipartResolver` will need to be defined in the context to resolve the incoming multipart request. For this example, it is done using the JavaConfiguration, as shown in Listing 18–18. The HTTP adapter looks for the bean name `multipartResolver` by default. The `CommonsMultipartResolver` class is used for this example.

Listing 18–18. *JavaConfiguration of the Multipart Resolver*

```
package com.apress.prospringintegration.web;

import org.springframework.context.annotation.Bean;
import org.springframework.stereotype.Component;
import org.springframework.web.multipart.MultipartResolver;
import org.springframework.web.multipart.commons.CommonsMultipartResolver;

@Component
public class MultipartResolverConfiguration {

    @Bean
    public MultipartResolver multipartResolver() {
        return new CommonsMultipartResolver();
    }
}
```

The service activator is configured using Spring component scanning. The service activator class is shown in Listing 18–19. The class uses the Spring support to parse the multipart request.

Listing 18–19. *MultipartReceiver Service Activator to Support Reading the Multipart Request*

```
package com.apress.prospringintegration.web;

import org.springframework.integration.annotation.ServiceActivator;
import org.springframework.integration.http.multipart.UploadedMultipartFile;
import org.springframework.stereotype.Component;
import org.springframework.util.LinkedMultiValueMap;

import java.util.LinkedList;

@Component
public class MultipartReceiver {

    @ServiceActivator
    public void handleMultipartRequest(
            LinkedMultiValueMap<String, Object> multipartRequest) {
        System.out.println("Received multipart request: " + multipartRequest);
        for (String elementName : multipartRequest.keySet()) {
            if (elementName.equals("name")) {
                LinkedList value = (LinkedList) multipartRequest.get("name");
                String[] multiValues = (String[]) value.get(0);
                for (String name : multiValues) {
```

```
                System.out.println("Name: " + name);
            }
        } else if (elementName.equals("picture")) {
            System.out.println("Picture as UploadedMultipartFile: "
                    + ((UploadedMultipartFile) multipartRequest.getFirst("picture"))
                    .getOriginalFilename());
        }
    }
  }
}
```

Again, build the web application with the command `mvn install` and deploy the WAR file `http-adapter-1.0.0.war` to a servlet container. Running the multipart HTTP request client in Listing 18–16 will upload the multipart file `test.png`, as can be seen in the servlet log file:

```
Received multipart request: {name=[[Ljava.lang.String;@4b12d9],➥
picture=[org.springframework.integration.http.multipart.UploadedMultipartFile@c28cb7]}
Name: John Smith
Picture as UploadedMultipartFile: test.png
```

Spring Integration, Comet, and the Asynchronous Web

The previous examples all required the interaction with the web server to originate from the user. However, web applications can also be event driven. One of the issues with an event-driven web application is maintaining state so that the web server knows how to send the data to the client. The other issue is how to maintain an open socket connection to the client.

With the introduction and mainstream adoption of Ajax-style applications in 2005, developers have had an easy way for performing RPC-style interactions with web servers without refreshing the page. Additionally, the illusion of server-side push-based applications could be maintained by having the client poll the server side, or by the server keeping a single request open for an extended period of time and only flushing responses when an interesting event has occurred on the server side. This technique works—clients perceive that server-side events are visible instantly on the client, but this approach has a serious drawback because most server implementations block when they handle inbound HTTP requests. Typically, this is because HTTP requests are mapped one to one with threads—each request gets a full thread to itself. Thus, such applications are limited by how many threads the server can keep open—any more threads and they run the risk of exceeding memory. Over time, web application vendors have introduced asynchronous request-processing mechanisms. In them, a request may be made and acknowledged by the server, which then may make the responding thread passive until some other interesting event requires the responding thread to wake up and resume writing output. This has made it far more efficient to support such Comet-style interactions. However, each implementation solves this problem in its own unique way Tomcat, Jetty, JBoss, GlassFish, and others all have proprietary mechanisms that enable asynchronous responses. Recently, the Servlet specification version 3.0 was released. This latest iteration is already supported by Tomcat 7, as well as Jetty 7 and all Java EE6 implementations. Servlet 3.0 specifies support for asynchronous HTTP request handling.

The Comet style of applications is an umbrella term for all the different techniques for allowing the web server to push the data to the client or web browser. All of the approaches rely on JavaScript to support the client interaction. There is currently a Comet adapter in the Spring Integration sandbox based on the Atmosphere project (`http://atmosphere.java.net`). The Atmosphere project is a unified Comet framework. It is a hodgepodge servlet that implements all the proprietary asynchronous HTTP request-processing classes, and surfaces one unified API to work with all the different servers. In addition, it supports Servlet 3.0. The Atmosphere adapter is still in active development and will no doubt see changes before it is finished, even for the example that will be shown. However, Atmosphere—and this adapter—demonstrates the potential of an event-driven web application using Spring Integration and Comet. The Comet adapter may be downloaded and built using the set of commands shown in Listing 18–20.

Listing 18–20. Command to Download and Build the Comet Adapter

```
git clone git://git.springsource.org/spring-integration/sandbox.git
cd sandbox/spring-integration-comet
mvn clean install
```

The basic premise of this example will be to use Spring Integration to push data to the web browser by using the Comet adapter and Atmosphere JQuery library. Atmosphere provides the ability to use JQuery to subscribe to a message notification originating from the web server. Thus, real-time updates can occur on a web page based on messages published from the web server.

The current Spring Integration Comet adapter is still in development and only supports JSON messages. The adapter source code will be modified to also support string messages, which will simplify this example. Make the modification shown in Listing 18–21 to the `org.springframework.integration.comet.HttpMessageBroadcaster` class. This will allow concatenating multiple messages into a single string value so that it can be displayed on the HTML page. The code loops over the list of `org.springframework.integration.comet.HttpBroadcastMessages` and appends each message value with a ; delimiter. After making the changes, rebuild using the Maven command `mvn clean install`.

Listing 18–21. Modification to the Comet Adapter Code

```
private Message<?> mergeMessagesForBroadcast(List<HttpBroadcastMessage> messages) {

    if (!messages.isEmpty() &&
            messages.get(0).getMessage().getPayload() instanceof String) {
        StringBuffer stringPayload = new StringBuffer();
        boolean isFirstValue = true;
        for (HttpBroadcastMessage message : messages) {
            if (!isFirstValue) {
                stringPayload.append(";");
            } else {
                isFirstValue = false;
            }
            stringPayload.append(message.getMessage().getPayload());
        }
        return MessageBuilder.withPayload(stringPayload.toString()).build();
    }

    List<Object> payloads = new ArrayList<Object>();
    for (HttpBroadcastMessage message : messages) {
        payloads.add(message.getMessage().getPayload());
    }
    return MessageBuilder.withPayload(payloads).build();
}
```

This example will require the Maven dependencies shown in Listing 18–22. Note that the Comet adapter is the snapshot version previously built.

Listing 18–22. *Maven Dependencies for the Comet Adapter Example*

```
<dependency>
      <groupId>org.springframework.integration</groupId>
      <artifactId>spring-integration-http</artifactId>
      <version>2.0.1.RELEASE</version>
    </dependency>
    <dependency>
      <groupId>org.springframework</groupId>
      <artifactId>spring-webmvc</artifactId>
      <version>2.0.1.RELEASE</version>
    </dependency>
    <dependency>
      <groupId>org.springframework.integration</groupId>
      <artifactId>spring-integration-comet</artifactId>
      <version>2.1.BUILD-SNAPSHOT</version>
    </dependency>
```

To use Atmosphere, the Comet request must be handled. This is done by configuring the Atmosphere servlet class `org.atmosphere.cpr.MeteorServlet`. The configuration is shown in Listing 18–23. The important part to note is the reference to the Spring `DispatcherServlet` and the Comet adapter: the `org.springframework.integration.comet.HttpMessageBroadcaster` class. This enables the interface to the Spring Integration Comet adapter. The housekeeping task will be handled by the Atmosphere servlet, and the Spring Integration specifics will be handled by Spring MVC, which will forward the request to the Comet adapter specified by the `servlet-config.xml` file.

Listing 18–23. *Servlet Configuration web.xml*

```
<?xml version="1.0" encoding="UTF-8"?>
<web-app xmlns:xsi="http://www.w3.org/2001/XMLSchema-instance"
         xmlns="http://java.sun.com/xml/ns/javaee"
         xmlns:web="http://java.sun.com/xml/ns/javaee/web-app_2_5.xsd"
         xsi:schemaLocation="http://java.sun.com/xml/ns/javaee
         http://java.sun.com/xml/ns/javaee/web-app_2_5.xsd"
         id="WebApp_ID"
         version="2.5">

  <display-name>comet-adapter-example</display-name>

  <welcome-file-list>
    <welcome-file>
      index.html
    </welcome-file>
  </welcome-file-list>

  <!-- Handles Comet requests -->
  <servlet>
    <servlet-name>cometServlet</servlet-name>
    <servlet-class>org.atmosphere.cpr.MeteorServlet</servlet-class>
    <init-param>
      <param-name>org.atmosphere.servlet</param-name>
      <param-value>org.springframework.web.servlet.DispatcherServlet</param-value>
    </init-param>
```

```
    <init-param>
      <param-name>org.atmosphere.cpr.broadcasterClass</param-name>
      <param-value>
        org.springframework.integration.comet.HttpMessageBroadcaster
      </param-value>
    </init-param>
    <init-param>
      <param-name>org.atmosphere.useStream</param-name>
      <param-value>true</param-value>
    </init-param>
    <init-param>
      <param-name>org.atmosphere.cpr.broadcasterCacheClass</param-name>
      <param-value>org.atmosphere.cache.HeaderBroadcasterCache</param-value>
    </init-param>
    <init-param>
      <param-name>contextConfigLocation</param-name>
      <param-value>/WEB-INF/servlet-config.xml</param-value>
    </init-param>
    <load-on-startup>1</load-on-startup>
  </servlet>

  <servlet-mapping>
    <servlet-name>cometServlet</servlet-name>
    <url-pattern>/pubsub/*</url-pattern>
  </servlet-mapping>

</web-app>
```

The Spring Integration configuration file servlet-config.xml is where all the action takes place. Namespace support is not yet available, so we configure the adapter directly. The adapter class is org.springframework.integration.comet.AsyncHttpRequestHandlingMessageAdapter, as shown in Listing 18–24. The bean name maps to the message topic. The messageChannel property specifies the input channel, and the messageThreshold property specifies how many messages will be cached before being broadcasted, using server-side push or Comet, to the browser. For demonstration purposes, a simple inbound channel adapter will be configured with a poll rate of 5,000 ms (5 seconds). The adapter will call the invokeService method on the InboundService class, which is configured through component scanning, each time it is polled.

Listing 18–24. *Spring Integration Configuration servlet-config.xml*

```
<?xml version="1.0" encoding="UTF-8"?>
<beans xmlns="http://www.springframework.org/schema/beans"
       xmlns:xsi="http://www.w3.org/2001/XMLSchema-instance"
       xmlns:int="http://www.springframework.org/schema/integration"
       xmlns:http="http://www.springframework.org/schema/integration/http"
       xmlns:context="http://www.springframework.org/schema/context"
       xsi:schemaLocation="http://www.springframework.org/schema/beans
    http://www.springframework.org/schema/beans/spring-beans-3.0.xsd
    http://www.springframework.org/schema/context
    http://www.springframework.org/schema/context/spring-context-3.0.xsd
    http://www.springframework.org/schema/integration
    http://www.springframework.org/schema/integration/spring-integration-2.0.xsd
    http://www.springframework.org/schema/integration/http
    http://www.springframework.org/schema/integration/http/spring-integration-http-2.0.xsd">
```

```
  <context:component-scan base-package="com.apress.prospringintegration.comet.example"/>

  <int:channel id="recentActivity"/>

  <bean name="/recent/notifications"
      class="org.springframework.integration.comet.AsyncHttpRequestHandlingMessageAdapter">
    <property name="messageChannel" ref="recentActivity"/>
    <property name="messageThreshold" value="1"/>
  </bean>

  <int:inbound-channel-adapter channel="recentActivity"
                               ref="inboundService"
                               method="invokeService">
    <int:poller fixed-rate="5000"/>
  </int:inbound-channel-adapter>

</beans>
```

As shown in Listing 18–25, the inbound channel adapter will send a message payload string with an incrementing index. This message will be pushed to the Comet adapter and broadcasted to the browser.

Listing 18–25. *Inbound Channel Adapter Class InboundService*

```
package com.apress.prospringintegration.comet.example;

import org.springframework.stereotype.Component;

@Component
public class InboundService {

    private int i = 0;

    public String invokeService() {
        String message = "Invoking service " + i;
        i++;
        System.out.println(message);
        return message;
    }
}
```

The JQuery JavaScript makes it quite easy to subscribe to the broadcast messages and add them to the web page (see Listing 18–26). Using the Atmosphere JQuery library, the web page subscribes to the broadcast destination (having the servlet filter `pubsub`) followed by the broadcast topic `/recent/notifications`. The callback function `activityNotificationHandler` is defined, which will add each of the messages to the HTML tag `ul`. After the page has loaded, the web page will subscribe to the broadcast destination and display each message in real time as it is received. There are two major categories of methods for implementing Comet: streaming and long polling. Long polling is used for this example.

Listing 18–26. JavaScript for the Comet Adapter Example

```
$(document).ready(function() {
    var basePath = document.location.toString();

    $.atmosphere.subscribe(
            basePath + 'pubsub/recent/notifications',
            activityNotificationHandler,
            $.atmosphere.request = { transport: "long-polling" });

    function activityNotificationHandler(response) {
        if (response.status == 200) {
            var data = response.responseBody;
            if (data.length > 0) {
                $('ul').prepend($('<li></li>').text(" Message Received: " + data));
            }
        }
    }

});
```

The HTML page imports the JQuery and Atmosphere JavaScript libraries. As each of the messages is received, it will be added to the web page (see Listing 18–27). This demonstrates the ability to use Spring Integration and Comet to asynchronously publish data to a web client.

Listing 18–27. HTML Page Receiving broadcast Message from the Comet Adapter index.html

```
<html>
<head>
    <script type="text/javascript" src="jquery/jquery-1.4.2.js"></script>
    <script type="text/javascript" src="jquery/jquery.atmosphere.js"></script>
    <script type="text/javascript" src="jquery/jquery-comet-example.js"></script>
</head>
<body>
<h2>Real Time PubSub Update</h2>
<ul></ul>
</body>
</html>
```

The current example only works on Jetty 7 or later, and version 8 is recommended (see `http://download.eclipse.org/jetty`). There still seems to be some issues with older versions of the Tomcat web server and Atmosphere. Deploying Comet example application is as simple as building and copying the WAR file to the `webapps` directory of the Jetty installation. Sample output is shown in Listing 18–28, and can be seen at `http://localhost:8080/comet-adapter-example-1.0`.

Listing 18–28. Spring Integration Comet Adapter Example Output

```
Real Time PubSub Update
Message Received: Invoking service 6
Message Received: Invoking service 5
Message Received: Invoking service 4
Message Received: Invoking service 3
Message Received: Invoking service 0;Invoking service 1;Invoking service 2
```

Spring Integration, Flex, and BlazeDS

Macromedia initially released Flash to bring the animation finesse of Macromedia Shockwave to the Internet. As time went on, the animation facilities grew to include a sophisticated programming environment. The only thing missing was support for data-intensive applications, a niche formerly occupied by Visual Basic. It came as no surprise that in 2004 Macromedia announced Flex, an environment with a generous complement of data-bound controls and full support for RPC. There were early adopters, even if the interest was muted. The problem was that the platform was closed source and expensive. The tooling, SDK, and integration middleware were all costly, and Flex was an unproven architecture, which meant that few took the risk, as the barrier to entry was too high.

Adobe, which bought Macromedia in 2005, eventually started opening up the framework. The Flex platform's SDK was made available so that Flex code and scripts could be compiled from the command line. Flash offers a binary protocol called Action Message Format (AMF), which allows the Flash VMs to talk to servers. This protocol is quick and compact, especially compared to JSON and SOAP. While many open source projects had reverse-engineered the protocol and exposed similar, alternative integrations for their favorite platform (PHP, Python, and in the Java world, Granite DS), the ideal solution was a proper implementation that exposed Adobe's expensive Lifecycle Data Services (LDS) middle project. Key parts of LDS were released under an open source license and renamed BlazeDS.

The development tool, an Eclipse derivative called Adobe Flash Builder, is still a pay-for-use product; however, this does not impede others from creating their own tooling. Particularly, IntelliJ's IDEA product, versions 9 and 10, support Flex and AIR development with aplomb. Additionally, it is entirely possible to build entire Flex and AIR applications using only the command line, or with third-party tools, such as the Maven 2 FlexMojos project, which supports building Flex applications using Maven. If you are using Flash Builder, you can take the important non-Eclipse plug-ins and simply add them to the SpringSource Tool Suite's plug-in folder to get a combined STS/Flash Builder environment so you don't need to run two Eclipse derivatives.

As the platform has become more open, so too has the number of open source projects supporting the Flex environment. For BlazeDS to connect to Spring services, there is specialized support built in cooperation between SpringSource and Adobe, called Spring BlazeDS Integration. In addition, there is now support for directly connecting Spring Integration to BlazeDS. On the client side, the Spring ActionScript project provides a familiar environment for Java developers in the same vein as provided by the Spring platform. An example will be presented on how to use Spring Integration to push data to the Flex web client.

Whereas Flash provides an animation-centric environment with support for creating timelines and importing graphics, Flex is a code-centric platform. The two source artifacts of a Flex application are the ActionScript files (ending in `.as`) and the MXML files.

ActionScript files can contain classes, public functions and variables, and annotations. Indeed, ActionScript files may house any number of public classes. The look and feel of the language will feel familiar to anyone who's used to Java, C#, or Scala.

MXML files are an XML variant that describe the UI components and provide a DOM. In addition, scripts may be inline. Each tag in MXML describes a component or object that is registered with its container. In the case of Flex applications, the outermost tag is the `<mx:Application/>` tag; in AIR, it's `<mx:WindowedApplication/>`. These tags describe containers that themselves handle all the minutiae of creating components on the Flash `Stage` object.

MXML may be used to instantiate regular ActionScript objects similar to Spring's beans. However some uses will better suited to code and some to MXML. An entire Flex application may be created using only ActionScript with no MXML. When the MXML files are compiled, they are converted to ActionScript expressions as an intermediary format, and *that* is what is ultimately compiled. MXML files support a limited form of expression language binding. Flex components are wired together using the expression binding support and the powerful event mechanism underlying most of Flex.

For the purposes of demonstrating the ability to use Spring Integration with Flex and BlazeDS in the same way as we did with the Comet example, we will develop a push-based application starting with a simple MXML file. The code will subscribe to the to the BlazeDS messaging system to create an event-driven asynchronous web application where the Flex web client will display messages sent from Spring Integration through BlazeDS. The MXML file is shown in Listing 18–29.

***Listing 18–29.** Flex Client MXML client.mxml*

```
<?xml version="1.0" encoding="utf-8"?>

<s:Application xmlns:fx="http://ns.adobe.com/mxml/2009"
               xmlns:s="library://ns.adobe.com/flex/spark"
               xmlns:mx="library://ns.adobe.com/flex/mx">
  <fx:Script>
    import mx.messaging.messages.AsyncMessage;
  </fx:Script>

  <fx:Declarations>

    <s:ChannelSet id="channelSet">
      <s:AMFChannel uri="http://localhost:8080/spring-flex-1.0/mb/amf"/>
    </s:ChannelSet>

    <s:Consumer id="c" destination="client" channelSet="{channelSet}"
                message="ta.text += event.message.body + '\n'"/>

  </fx:Declarations>

  <s:applicationComplete>c.subscribe();</s:applicationComplete>

  <s:layout>
    <s:VerticalLayout/>
  </s:layout>

  <s:TextArea id="ta" width="300" height="400"/>

</s:Application>
```

The MXML is an XML file using the different Flex namespaces. The asynchronous messaging class is imported, and a listening channel is configured to subscribe to the BlazeDS message broker, which will be discussed in more detail below. The message consumer will simply append the incoming message to a Flex text window. In order to compile the MXML file, you must download the Flex SDK from Adobe, at `www.adobe.com/cfusion/entitlement/index.cfm?e=flex4sdk`. At the time of this writing, the most current version of the SDK is 4.1.

To use the SDK, download it and extract the archive. Put the `bin` folder inside the SDK on your system's `PATH` variable (as you might when setting up Ant, Maven, and the Java SDK). The Flex SDK offers two compilers: one for components and one for Flex applications. For compiling components, use `compc`. For compiling an application such as the MXML file shown previously, use `mxmlc` (e.g., `mxmlc client.mxml`). This will create a `client.swf` file that will be added to the web application root in the `webapp` directory.

The Spring Integration 2.0 support for the Spring BlazeDS integration project is currently in the Spring BlazeDS trunk, and must be downloaded and built manually for this example. Check the code out from the SVN repository using the command in Listing 18–30.

Listing 18–30. SVN Command for Checking Out the Spring BlazeDS Integration Project

```
svn co https://src.springsource.org/svn/spring-flex/trunk spring-flex
```

The BlazeDS code required to build this code is not in the public Maven repositories as of this writing. The following Maven dependency must be added to the parent `pom.xml` file, as shown in Listing 18–31, in order for the code to build.

Listing 18–31. Adobe BlazeDS Maven Repositiory

```
  <repositories>
    <repository>
      <id>repository.springframework.maven.external</id>
      <name>Spring Framework External Repository</name>
      <url>http://maven.springframework.org/external</url>
    </repository>
  </repositories>
```

The Spring BlazeDS integration requires setting up the `DispatchServlet`—the same infrastructure used for Spring Faces, Spring Web Flow, Spring MVC, and so on. Listing 18–32 shows the root Maven `pom.xml` file, which is needed to support Spring Integration, Flex, and BlazeDS.

Listing 18–32. Maven pom.xml for Spring Integration, Flex, and BlazeDS

```
<?xml version="1.0" encoding="UTF-8"?>
<project xmlns="http://maven.apache.org/POM/4.0.0"
         xmlns:xsi="http://www.w3.org/2001/XMLSchema-instance"
         xsi:schemaLocation="http://maven.apache.org/POM/4.0.0
         http://maven.apache.org/xsd/maven-4.0.0.xsd">
  <modelVersion>4.0.0</modelVersion>

  <groupId>spring-flex</groupId>
  <artifactId>spring-flex</artifactId>
  <packaging>war</packaging>
  <version>1.0</version>

  <dependencies>
    <dependency>
      <groupId>org.springframework.integration</groupId>
      <artifactId>spring-integration-core</artifactId>
      <version>2.0.1.RELEASE</version>
    </dependency>
    <dependency>
      <groupId>org.springframework</groupId>
      <artifactId>spring-webmvc</artifactId>
      <version>3.0.5.RELEASE</version>
    </dependency>
    <dependency>
      <groupId>org.springframework.flex</groupId>
      <artifactId>spring-flex-core</artifactId>
      <version>1.5.0.BUILD-SNAPSHOT</version>
    </dependency>
  </dependencies>
```

```
  <build>
    <plugins>
      <plugin>
        <groupId>org.apache.maven.plugins</groupId>
        <artifactId>maven-compiler-plugin</artifactId>
        <configuration>
          <source>1.6</source>
          <target>1.6</target>
          <compilerArgument>-Xlint:all</compilerArgument>
          <showWarnings>true</showWarnings>
          <showDeprecation>false</showDeprecation>
        </configuration>
      </plugin>
    </plugins>
  </build>

  <repositories>
    <repository>
      <id>repository.springframework.maven.release</id>
      <name>Spring Framework Maven Release Repository</name>
      <url>http://maven.springframework.org/release</url>
    </repository>
    <repository>
      <id>repository.springframework.maven.milestone</id>
      <name>Spring Framework Maven Milestone Repository</name>
      <url>http://maven.springframework.org/milestone</url>
    </repository>
    <repository>
      <id>repository.springframework.maven.snapshot</id>
      <name>Spring Framework Maven Snapshot Repository</name>
      <url>http://maven.springframework.org/snapshot</url>
    </repository>
    <repository>
      <id>repository.springframework.maven.external</id>
      <name>Spring Framework External Repository</name>
      <url>http://maven.springframework.org/external</url>
    </repository>
  </repositories>
</project>
```

There is no need for any custom BlazeDS servlet or `web.xml` configuration. The configuration lives in the `web.xml` file, and a mapping will be provided to send Flex requests. Note that the following configuration *could* be used in setting up Spring MVC or Spring Web Flow also. There is nothing specific to BlazeDS or the Spring BlazeDS integration in the code shown in Listing 18–33.

Listing 18–33. *Servlet web.xml for Spring Support*

```
<web-app version="2.4"
xmlns="http://java.sun.com/xml/ns/j2ee"
xmlns:xsi="http://www.w3.org/2001/XMLSchema-instance"
xsi:schemaLocation="http://java.sun.com/xml/ns/j2ee
     http://java.sun.com/xml/ns/j2ee/web-app_2_4.xsd">

   <display-name>Spring Flex BlazeDS integration example</display-name>
```

```
  <servlet>
    <servlet-name>spring-flex</servlet-name>
    <servlet-class>
      org.springframework.web.servlet.DispatcherServlet
    </servlet-class>
    <init-param>
      <param-name>contextConfigLocation</param-name>
      <param-value>/WEB-INF/flex-context.xml</param-value>
    </init-param>
    <load-on-startup>1</load-on-startup>
  </servlet>

  <servlet-mapping>
     <servlet-name>spring-flex</servlet-name>
     <url-pattern>/mb/*</url-pattern>
  </servlet-mapping>
</web-app>
```

This configuration is the simplest configuration possible, but it is enough to install support for Spring in the example web application. The Flex message broker will need to be set up using a Spring context file. The file `/WEB-INF/flex-context.xml` is referenced to set up the message broker.

The Spring configuration file is shown in Listing 18–34. This context file imports a number of namespaces that will be used later to support Spring Integration and messaging channels. Here, the context element is used to enable component scanning and to tell the Spring framework the package in which it should scan for and automatically register components (beans). Again, component scanning is Spring support, which will be used later in this example. So, the only thing that has been configured of any interest here is the BlazeDS message broker. The message broker, in turn, creates channels, which are like named ports from which messages may be sent or received—these are not the same as Spring Integration channels. The specifics of the channel (polling frequency, timeout settings, the specific sub-URL, streaming, etc.) are specified in the services configuration file. The message broker will, by default, look for the `services-config.xml` file in `/WEB-INF/flex/services-config.xml`. The explicit declaration may be removed, as it is redundant. It is shown here to demonstrate how to vary that location, though the default (`WEB-INF/flex`) is a very broad de facto standard.

Listing 18–34. *Spring Configuration flex-context.xml*

```
<?xml version="1.0" encoding="UTF-8"?>
<beans xmlns="http://www.springframework.org/schema/beans"
       xmlns:flex="http://www.springframework.org/schema/flex"
       xmlns:xsi="http://www.w3.org/2001/XMLSchema-instance"
       xmlns:int="http://www.springframework.org/schema/integration"
       xmlns:context="http://www.springframework.org/schema/context"
       xsi:schemaLocation="http://www.springframework.org/schema/beans
           http://www.springframework.org/schema/beans/spring-beans-3.0.xsd
           http://www.springframework.org/schema/flex
           http://www.springframework.org/schema/flex/spring-flex-1.0.xsd
           http://www.springframework.org/schema/integration
           http://www.springframework.org/schema/integration/spring-integration-2.0.xsd
           http://www.springframework.org/schema/context
           http://www.springframework.org/schema/context/spring-context-3.0.xsd">

  <context:component-scan base-package="com.apress.prospringintegration.flex"/>
```

```
  <flex:message-broker services-config-path="/WEB-INF/flex/services-config.xml">
    <flex:message-service default-channels="my-amf"/>
  </flex:message-broker>

</beans>
```

The BlazeDS message broker configuration specifies the services-config.xml configuration file, whose contents are presented in Listing 18–35.

Listing 18–35. *BlazeDS Messge Broker Configuration services-config.xml*

```
<?xml version="1.0" encoding="UTF-8"?>
<services-config>
  <channels>
    <channel-definition id="my-amf" class="mx.messaging.channels.AMFChannel">
      <endpoint url="http://{server.name}:{server.port}/{context.root}/mb/amf"
                class="flex.messaging.endpoints.AMFEndpoint"/>
    </channel-definition>
  </channels>
</services-config>
```

The endpoint's url attribute defines where this service is expected to be mounted. Any service that is exposed using the my-amf channel will be available via that URL. This value will be needed in the client Flex application. For the sample application, the service application will be deployed at the root web context. The URL http://127.0.0.1:8080/mb/amf will be used in Flex client code.

The next step is to use Spring Integration to push messages to the Flex client. The complete flex-context.xml file is shown in Listing 18–36. To simulate an inbound channel adapter, a simple MessageProducer class is created to simply publish an incrementing message to the channel clientPubSubChannel. A poller is added to trigger a new message every 5,000 ms (5 seconds). The Spring BlazeDS Integration project provides support for consuming messages from a Spring Integration message channel and publishing them to the BlazeDS message broker. A topic channel is used to allow multiple clients to subscribe to the messages.

Listing 18–36. *Spring Configuration File flex-context.xml Including Spring Integration*

```
<?xml version="1.0" encoding="UTF-8"?>
<beans xmlns="http://www.springframework.org/schema/beans"
       xmlns:flex="http://www.springframework.org/schema/flex"
       xmlns:xsi="http://www.w3.org/2001/XMLSchema-instance"
       xmlns:int="http://www.springframework.org/schema/integration"
       xmlns:context="http://www.springframework.org/schema/context"
       xsi:schemaLocation="http://www.springframework.org/schema/beans
           http://www.springframework.org/schema/beans/spring-beans-3.0.xsd
           http://www.springframework.org/schema/flex
           http://www.springframework.org/schema/flex/spring-flex-1.0.xsd
           http://www.springframework.org/schema/integration
           http://www.springframework.org/schema/integration/spring-integration-2.0.xsd
           http://www.springframework.org/schema/context
           http://www.springframework.org/schema/context/spring-context-3.0.xsd">

  <context:component-scan base-package="com.apress.prospringintegration.flex"/>

  <flex:message-broker services-config-path="/WEB-INF/flex/services-config.xml">
    <flex:message-service default-channels="my-amf"/>
```

```
  </flex:message-broker>

  <int:publish-subscribe-channel id="clientPubSubChannel"/>

  <flex:integration-message-destination id="client"
                                         channels="my-amf"
                                         message-channel="clientPubSubChannel"/>

  <int:inbound-channel-adapter channel="clientPubSubChannel"
                               ref="messageProducer"
                               method="publish">
    <int:poller fixed-rate="5000"/>
  </int:inbound-channel-adapter>

</beans>
```

The message-publishing class `MessageProducer` is shown in Listing 18–37. This class simply produces a Spring message that is pushed to the `clientPubSubChannel` message channel and eventually makes it to the Flex client.

Listing 18–37. *Message Publishing Class MessageProducer*

```
package com.apress.prospringintegration.flex;

import org.springframework.stereotype.Component;

@Component
public class MessageProducer {
    private int i;

    public String publish() {
        String message = "Pushing message: " + i;
        i++;
        System.out.println(message);
        return message;
    }
}
```

Now you can build the example project using the Maven command `mvn install`, which will produce the WAR file `spring-flex-1.0.war`. This WAR file may be deployed in any servlet container. Using a browser, go to the URL `http://localhost:8080/spring-flex-1.0/client.swf`. More than one browser may be used to demonstrate that there can be multiple subscribers. The output should look something like that shown in Figure 18–1. Note that an exception will be thrown until at lease one client hooks up, since if no client is hooked up there is no place for the message to go. This may be handled more gracefully with the addition of some error-handling code.

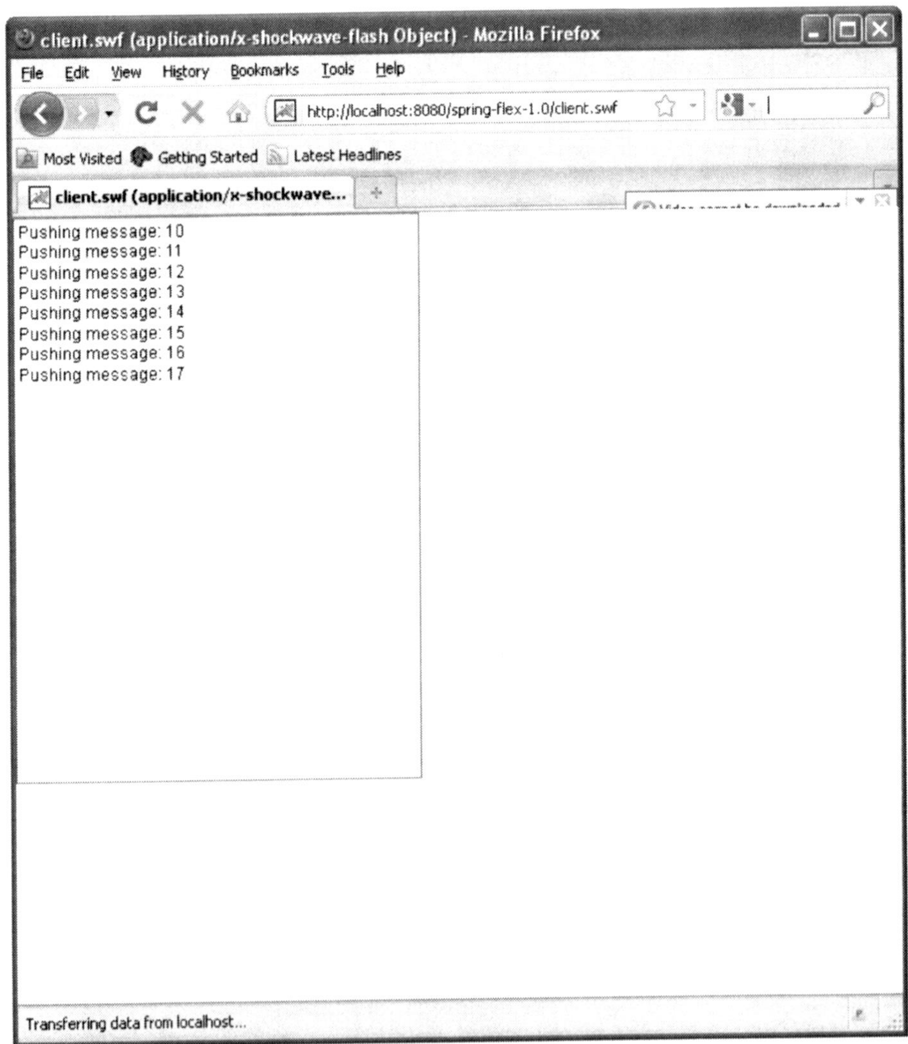

***Figure 18–1.** Flex Client Receiving Spring Integration Messages*

Summary

This has been a quick tour of how Spring Integration can be used with your web application. First, we discussed the basic HTTP gateways and adapters, which provide a simple way to create web applications. In addition, these HTTP components can be used to interact with multipart requests. Finally, the various push architectures were discussed. Moving beyond the standard request/reply interaction using a web browser, we explored technologies such as Comet and BlazeDS.

Index

Special Characters

A

B

C

D

H

I

J

N

O

P

Q

R

S

T

U

V

W

X, Y, Z

CPSIA information can be obtained at www.ICGtesting.com
224314LV00003B/40/P

9 781430 2334